THE STAKES *of* EXPOSURE

THE STAKES *of* EXPOSURE

Anxious Bodies in Postwar Japanese Art

NAMIKO KUNIMOTO

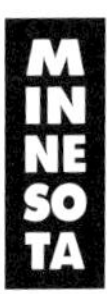

University of Minnesota Press

Minneapolis • London

Every effort was made to obtain permission to reproduce material in this book. If any proper acknowledgment has not been included here, we encourage copyright holders to notify the publisher.

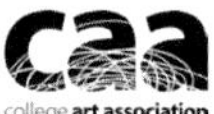 Illustrations in this book were funded in part by a grant from the Meiss/Mellon Author's Book Award of the College Art Association.

Chapter 3 is an adaptation of "Tanaka Atsuko's *Electric Dress* and the Circuits of Subjectivity," *The Art Bulletin* 95, no. 3 (September 2013): 465–83, reprinted by permission of the College Art Association, www.collegeart.org. Chapter 4 appeared in earlier versions as "Shiraga Kazuo: The Hero and Concrete Violence," *Art History* 36, no. 1 (February 2013): 154–79, reprinted by permission of John Wiley & Sons; and in "Shiraga Kazuo: The Buddhist Hero," in *Shiraga/Motonaga: Between Action and the Unknown*, Dallas Museum of Art (Dallas and New Haven: Dallas Museum of Art and Yale University Press, 2015), 74–79, copyright Dallas Museum of Art; first published in *Between Action and the Unknown: The Art of Kazuo Shiraga and Sadamasa Motonaga*, Dallas Museum of Art, 2015.

Published by the University of Minnesota Press
111 Third Avenue South, Suite 290
Minneapolis, MN 55401–2520
http://www.upress.umn.edu

Printed in the United States of America on acid-free paper

The University of Minnesota is an equal-opportunity educator and employer.

22 21 20 19 18 17   10 9 8 7 6 5 4 3 2 1

Library of Congress Cataloging-in-Publication Data
Names: Kunimoto, Namiko, 1974– author.
Title: The stakes of exposure : anxious bodies in postwar Japanese art / Namiko Kunimoto.
Description: Minneapolis : University of Minnesota Press, 2017. |
Includes bibliographical references and index.
Identifiers: LCCN 2016046647 (print) | ISBN 978-1-5179-0095-3 (hc)
| ISBN 978-1-5179-0096-0 (pb)
Subjects: LCSH: Art and society—Japan—History—20th century. | Art—Political aspects—Japan—History—20th century. | Human beings in art. | Sex role in art. | Katsura, Yuki, 1913–1991—Criticism and interpretation. | Nakamura, Hiroshi, 1932—Criticism and interpretation. | Tanaka, Atsuko, 1932–2005—Criticism and interpretation. | Shiraga, Kazuo, 1924–2008—Criticism and interpretation.
Classification: LCC N72.S6 K843 2017 (print) | DDC 701/.03—dc23
LC record available at https://lccn.loc.gov/2016046647

To Max and Kazuo Jasper

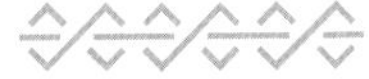

Contents

List of Illustrations ⇔ ix

Note on Translations and Names ⇔ xv

Introduction: Gendered Bodies and the Minamata Disaster ⇔ 1

1 Katsura Yuki's Bodies of Resistance ⇔ 21

2 Nakamura Hiroshi and the Politics of Embodiment ⇔ 67

3 Tanaka Atsuko and the Circuits of Subjectivity ⇔ 113

4 Heroic Violence in the Art of Shiraga Kazuo ⇔ 147

Conclusion: Thresholds of Exposure ⇔ 183

Acknowledgments ⇔ 197

Notes ⇔ 201

Bibliography ⇔ 239

Index ⇔ 257

List of Illustrations

FIGURE I.1. Kuwabara Shisei, *Ikeru ningyō (A Living Doll)*, circa 1962 ⋙ 1

FIGURE I.2. Kuwabara Shisei, *Ikeru ningyō (A Living Doll)*, circa 1962 ⋙ 1

FIGURE I.3. W. Eugene Smith, *Takako Isayama, a Congenital Minamata Disease Patient*, from the series *Minamata: Life—Sacred and Profane*, 1972 ⋙ 3

FIGURE I.4. "Eiyō shōgai mo wazawai: Machijū ga noirōze gimi" (Minamata strange disease: Is manganese the cause?), *Kumamoto Nichinichi Shinbun*, February 14, 1957 ⋙ 6

FIGURE I.5. "'Ikeru ningyō' shōjo—yonenkan kaeranu ishiki" (Girl is a living doll: Unconscious for four years), *Asahi Shinbun*, April 22, 1960 ⋙ 8

FIGURE I.6. Sugiura Yukio, *Beiei tōhō tsuihō (Purging One's Head of Anglo-Americanism)*, from *Manga*, 1942 ⋙ 9

FIGURE I.7. Sugiura Yukio, *Keshō (Makeup)*, from *Manga*, 1943 ⋙ 10

FIGURE I.8. "Akarui seihakuji Minamata" (Bright, mentally disabled in Minamata), *Asahi Shinbun* (Kumamoto edition), June 9, 1958 ⋙ 11

FIGURE 1.1. Katsura Yuki, *Ningen I (Human I)*, 1938 ⋙ 25

FIGURE 1.2. Katsura Yuki, *Ningen II (Human II)*, 1938 ⋙ 26

FIGURE 1.3. Hasegawa Haruko, Nakada Kikuyo (Yoshie), Katsura Yukiko, and others, *Daitōasen kōkoku fujo kaidō no zu (The Painting of All Laboring Women in the Empire during the Great East Asian War, Fall)*, 1944 ⋙ 28

FIGURE 1.4. Hasegawa Haruko, Nakada Kikuyo (Yoshie), Katsura Yukiko, and others, *Daitōasen kōkoku fujo kaidō no zu (The Painting of All Laboring Women in the Empire during the Great East Asian War, Spring and Winter)*, 1944 ⋙ 28

FIGURE 1.5. Katsura Yuki, *Enshū o oete (After Maneuvers)*, postcard, 1943 ⋙ 30

FIGURE 1.6. Ai-Mitsu, *Jigazō (Self-Portrait)*, 1944 ⇒ 31

FIGURE 1.7. Natori Yōnosuke, *Untitled*, from *Nippon*, 1938 ⇒ 32

FIGURE 1.8. Japanese government, *Dōbutsu tonarigumi* (Animal Neighborhood Association), still from animated film, 1941 ⇒ 37

FIGURE 1.9. Katsura Yuki, *Fujin no hi*—sukecchi (study for *Women's Day*), 1953 ⇒ 41

FIGURE 1.10. *Daigo Fukuryū Maru (The Lucky Dragon)*, fishing trawler ⇒ 46

FIGURE 1.11. Ikeda Tatsuo, *Hangenbaku series, 10,000 kaunto (Anti–Atomic Bomb Series, 10,000 Count)*, 1954 ⇒ 47

FIGURE 1.12. Cover for *Another Country*, 1962 ⇒ 50

FIGURE 1.13. Katsura Yuki, illustration for *Another Country*, from *Asahi Journal*, December 29, 1963 ⇒ 51

FIGURE 1.14. Katsura Yuki, illustration for *Another Country*, from *Asahi Journal*, November 17, 1963 ⇒ 52

FIGURE 1.15. Katsura Yuki, illustration for *Another Country*, from *Asahi Journal*, November 24, 1963 ⇒ 53

FIGURE 1.16. Katsura Yuki, illustration for *Another Country*, from *Asahi Journal*, February 24, 1964 ⇒ 55

FIGURE 1.17. Katsura Yuki, *Ihōjin (The Stranger)*, 1961 ⇒ 56

FIGURE 1.18. Katsura Yuki, photograph of unnamed hunter with elephant foot in Central Africa, 1958 ⇒ 59

FIGURE 2.1. Nakamura Hiroshi, sketches of U.S. military base at Tachikawa, 1955 ⇒ 68

FIGURE 2.2. Jasper Johns, *Flag*, 1954–55 ⇒ 69

FIGURE 2.3. Photograph of Nakamura Hiroshi, 1960 ⇒ 73

FIGURE 2.4. Yamashita Kikuji, *Akebono-mura monogatari (The Tale of Akebono Village)*, 1953 ⇒ 76

FIGURE 2.5. Katō Etsurō, *Dōmei nyūsu mangaban* (Federation News cartoon edition), July 20, 1948 ⇒ 83

FIGURE 2.6. Nakamura Hiroshi, *Te (Hand)* (two drawings), 1954 ⇒ 85

FIGURE 2.7. Nakamura Hiroshi, *Sekitan okiba (Coal Storage)*, 1955 ⇒ 87

FIGURE 2.8. Nakamura Hiroshi, *Kokutetsu shinagawa (JNR Shinagawa)*, 1955 ⇒ 88

FIGURE 2.9. Nakamura Hiroshi, *Jigazō A (Self-Portrait A)*, 1953 ⇒ 88

FIGURE 2.10. Saul Bass, poster for *The Man with the Golden Arm*, 1955 ⇒ 92

FIGURE 2.11. Nakamura Hiroshi, *Kaidan nite (On the Stairs)*, 1960 ⇒ 96

FIGURE 2.12. Nakamura Hiroshi, *Seika senrikō (Sacred Torch Relay)*, 1964 ⇒ 99

FIGURE 2.13. Maeda Jōsaku, *Hinomaru (XVIII Olympic Games)*, 1964 ⋙ 100

FIGURE 2.14. Hi Red Center, *Shutoken seisō seiri sokushin undō (Campaign for the Promotion of Sanitation and Order in the Capital,* aka *Ultra-Cleaning Event),* 1964 ⋙ 101

FIGURE 2.15. Nakamura Hiroshi, *Hōki seyo shōjo (Rise Up, Girl)*, 1959 ⋙ 103

FIGURE 2.16. Nakamura Hiroshi's scrapbooks ⋙ 105

FIGURE 2.17. Nakamura Hiroshi, *Hikōki to shōjo (Airplane and Girl)*, 1965 ⋙ 107

FIGURE 2.18. Sir Eduardo Paolozzi, *I Was a Rich Man's Plaything*, 1947 ⋙ 108

FIGURE 3.1. Tanaka Atsuko, *Denki fuku (Electric Dress), Second Gutai Art Exhibition,* Ohara Kaikan Hall, Tokyo, October 1956 ⋙ 114

FIGURE 3.2. Tanaka Atsuko, *Denki fuku (Electric Dress), Second Gutai Art Exhibition,* Ohara Kaikan Hall, Tokyo, October 1956 ⋙ 116

FIGURE 3.3. Kanayama Akira, *Alarm*, 1956 ⋙ 123

FIGURE 3.4. Tanaka Atsuko, *Butai fuku (Stage Clothes)*, 1956 ⋙ 124

FIGURE 3.5. Tanaka Atsuko installing *Sakuhin (Beru) (Work [Bell]), First Gutai Art Exhibition,* Ohara Kaikan Hall, Tokyo, October 1955 ⋙ 126

FIGURE 3.6. Tanaka Atsuko, *Work (Yellow Cloth), First Gutai Art Exhibition,* 1955 ⋙ 128

FIGURE 3.7. *Yomiuri Shinbun,* September 2, 1956 ⋙ 130

FIGURE 3.8. *Asahi Shinbun,* movie section, March 10, 1954 ⋙ 131

FIGURE 3.9. DVD cover for Kurosawa Akira's *Kumo no su-jō (Spider's Web Castle* or *Throne of Blood),* 1957 ⋙ 133

FIGURE 3.10. Tanaka Atsuko performing *Butai fuku (Stage Clothes), Gutai Art on the Stage,* Sankei Kaikan Hall, Osaka, May 29, 1957 ⋙ 136

FIGURE 3.11. Tanaka Atsuko, study for *Butai fuku (Stage Clothes)*, 1956 ⋙ 138

FIGURE 4.1. Shiraga Kazuo painting *Fan* in his studio, 1965 ⋙ 148

FIGURE 4.2. Shiraga Kazuo performing *Chō gendai sanban sō (Ultramodern Sanbasō), Gutai Art on the Stage,* Sankei Kaikan Hall, Osaka, May 29, 1957 ⋙ 152

FIGURE 4.3. Shiraga Kazuo creating *Dōzo ohairi kudasai (Please Come In),* in performance, 1955 ⋙ 153

FIGURE 4.4. Shiraga Kazuo, *Dōzo ohairi kudasai (Please Come In),* 1955 (interior view) ⋙ 154

FIGURE 4.5. Shiraga Kazuo, *Doro ni idomu (Challenging Mud)*, 1955 ⋙ 156

FIGURE 4.6. Shiraga Kazuo, *Shinchū gun (Occupation Forces)*, 1947 ⋙ 157

FIGURE 4.7. Katsushika Hokusai, *Suikoden yūshi no ezukushi (The Illustrated Water Margin),* 1829 ⋙ 161

FIGURE 4.8. Katsushika Hokusai, *Suikoden yūshi no ezukushi (The Illustrated Water Margin)*, 1829 ✹✹ 162

FIGURE 4.9. Photograph of Shiraga Kazuo and Yoshida Minoru, circa 1957 ✹✹ 165

FIGURE 4.10. Photograph of Shiraga Kazuo, circa 1957 ✹✹ 166

FIGURE 4.11. Photograph of Shiraga Fujiko and Shiraga Kazuo, circa 1957 ✹✹ 167

FIGURE 4.12. Shiraga Kazuo, *Kurenai eki (Red Liquid)*, 1956 (reconstruction 2001) ✹✹ 174

FIGURE 4.13. Shiraga Kazuo at Enryaku-ji, 1979 ✹✹ 176

FIGURE 4.14. Shiraga Kazuo, *Akai ōgi no obuje (Red Fan)*, 1965 ✹✹ 179

FIGURE 4.15. Shiraga Kazuo, *Daiitokuson*, 1973 ✹✹ 180

FIGURE C.1. Hirai Fusando, *Omoitsuki fujin*, 1950 ✹✹ 185

FIGURE C.2. "What effect did the war have on our children's bodies?" *Kyōdō News*, June 1, 1946 ✹✹ 186

FIGURE C.3. Hirai Fusando, *Omoitsuki fujin*, 1950 ✹✹ 188

FIGURE C.4. Chic Young, *Burondi* (volume 2), 1947 ✹✹ 189

FIGURE C.5. Chic Young, *Burondi* (volume 2), 1947 ✹✹ 190

FIGURE C.6. Hasegawa Machiko, reprint of first-edition book cover, *Hasegawa Machiko zenshū, 1946–50*, 1997 ✹✹ 192

PLATE 1. Katsura Yuki, *Saru kani gassen (The Battle of the Monkey and the Crab)*, 1948

PLATE 2. Katsura Yuki, *Fujin no hi (Women's Day)*, 1953

PLATE 3. Katsura Yuki, *Hito to sakana (Human and Fish)*, 1954

PLATE 4. Test bomb on Enewetak Atoll, 1952, from *Life*, May 3, 1954

PLATE 5. Okamoto Tarō, *Moeru hito (People Aflame)*, 1954

PLATE 6. Katsura Yuki, *Senbon ashi (Millipede)*, 1962

PLATE 7. Katsura Yuki, *Senbon ashi (II) (Millipede [II])*, 1962

PLATE 8. Katsura Yuki, *Hana (Trunk)*, 1967

PLATE 9. Katsura Yuki, *Hana (Trunk)*, 1967 (detail)

PLATE 10. Katsura Yuki, *Gonbe to karasu (Gonbe and Crow)*, 1966

PLATE 11. Katsura Yuki, *Yokubari bāsan (Greedy Old Woman)*, 1966

PLATE 12. Nakamura Hiroshi, *Sunagawa goban (Sunagawa No. 5)*, 1955

PLATE 13. Nakamura Hiroshi, *Jigazō B (Self-Portrait B)*, 1953

PLATE 14. Nakamura Hiroshi, *Kichi (The Base)*, 1957

PLATE 15. Nakamura Hiroshi, *Shasatsu (Gunned Down)*, 1957

PLATE 16. Nakamura Hiroshi, *Basho no kizashi (Omens of a Place 1)*, 1961

PLATE 17. Nakamura Hiroshi, *Kankō teikoku (Sightseeing Empire)*, 1964

PLATE 18. Nakamura Hiroshi, *Enkan-ressha: B—Hikō suru jōkikikansha (Circle Line B—Flying Steam Locomotive)*, 1969

PLATE 19. Nakamura Hiroshi, *Enkan-ressha: A—Bōenkyō ressha (Circle Line A—Telescope Train)*, 1968

PLATE 20. Tanaka Atsuko, *Untitled*, 1958

PLATE 21. Tanaka Atsuko, *Denki fuku (Electric Dress)*, 1956 (reconstruction 1986)

PLATE 22. Tanaka Atsuko, *Work (Pink Rayon)*, 1955 (reconstruction 2007)

PLATE 23. Tanaka Atsuko, study for *Butai fuku (Stage Clothes)*, circa 1956

PLATE 24. Tanaka Atsuko, *Drawing after Electric Dress*, 1956

PLATE 25. Tanaka Atsuko, *Jigoku mon (Gate of Hell)*, 1965–69

PLATE 26. Tanaka Atsuko, untitled notebook, circa 1956

PLATE 27. Tanaka Atsuko, *'87H*, 1987

PLATE 28. Shiraga Kazuo, *Ten'isei Sekihatsuki (Red-Haired Devil)*, 1959

PLATE 29. Shiraga Kazuo, *Inoshishi gari II (Wild Boar Hunting II)*, 1963

PLATE 30. Shiraga Kazuo, *Tenkūsei Kyūsenpō (Impatient Vanguard)*, 1962

PLATE 31. Shiraga Kazuo, *Abiraunken*, 1975

PLATE 32. Shiraga Kazuo, *Fudō Myō-ō*, 1975

PLATE 33. Shiraga Kazuo, *Kannon Fudara Jōdo*, 1972

PLATE 34. Shiraga Kazuo, *Akai ōgi (Red Fan)*, 1965

Note on Translations and Names

Following East Asian practice, Japanese surnames precede given names, except for those Japanese whose English-language works have been cited. Macrons in Japanese words have been omitted in well-known Japanese words and place names such as Tokyo, Osaka, and Kyoto. All translations are mine unless otherwise indicated.

Gendered Bodies and the Minamata Disaster

If I go mad, like Grandma, I too
May be kicked out of the house
Bodily
—Ishimure Michiko

The Minamata Disease Municipal Museum in Kumamoto Prefecture, Japan, sets the tragic tone for its permanent exhibition with an oversized portrait by photographer Kuwabara Shisei (born 1936) of a young girl named Matsunaga Kumiko, who contracted mercury poisoning disease at age six (Figure I.1). The museum organizers have positioned the enlarged portrait opposite the entrance, forcefully demanding the viewer's pathos.[2] Matsunaga's hands are deformed, clawlike, and unable to touch others in a normal manner (Figure I.2). Her head is turned to one side, her uneven gaze focused outward beyond the frame. The photograph is titled *A Living Doll*, directly citing a foreboding headline about Matsunaga that appeared in the newspaper *Asahi Shinbun* in 1960: "Girl Is a Living Doll: Unconscious for Four Years."[3] Both the photograph and the news headline emphasize her liminal state between life and death and, perhaps unintentionally, make reference to her new role as an object for the visitor's gaze. Kuwabara's close-up portrait highlights the virtuous, vulnerable, feminine beauty of the young girl through the details of her smooth skin, long eyelashes, and soft, dark eyes.

Images such as this one played an influential political role in stirring local and global concern about Minamata disease and encouraging survivors to try to seek compensation. Other artists responded, such as Tabe Mitsuko (born 1933), one of the principal members of Kyūshū-ha (Kyūshū School), an avant-garde artist collective active in the nearby city of Fukuoka in Kyūshū from 1957 to 1970. Tabe's 1957 work *Gyozoku no ikari (Anger of Fish Tribes)* is a distortion of asphalt and bamboo rings that expresses the imbalance between industry and nature. Tabe's abstract, mixed-media piece never achieved the acclaim of

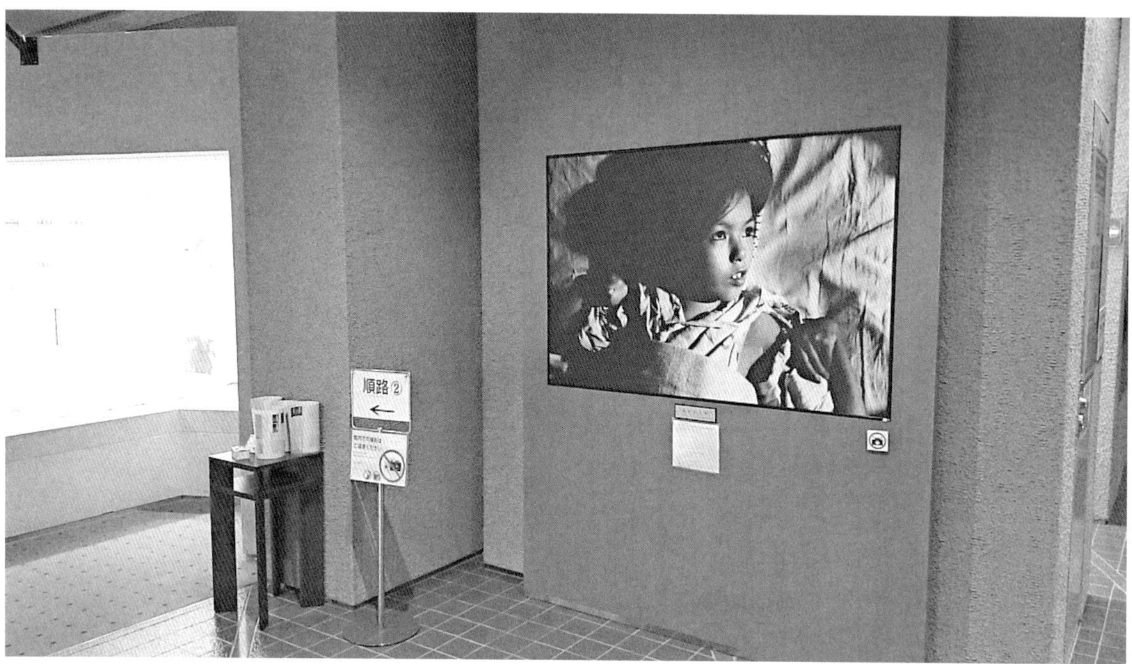

FIGURE I.1. Kuwabara Shisei, *Ikeru ningyō (A Living Doll)*, circa 1962, as exhibited at the Minamata Disease Municipal Museum in 2014. Copyright Kuwabara Shisei. Courtesy of the Minamata Disease Municipal Museum. Photograph by the author.

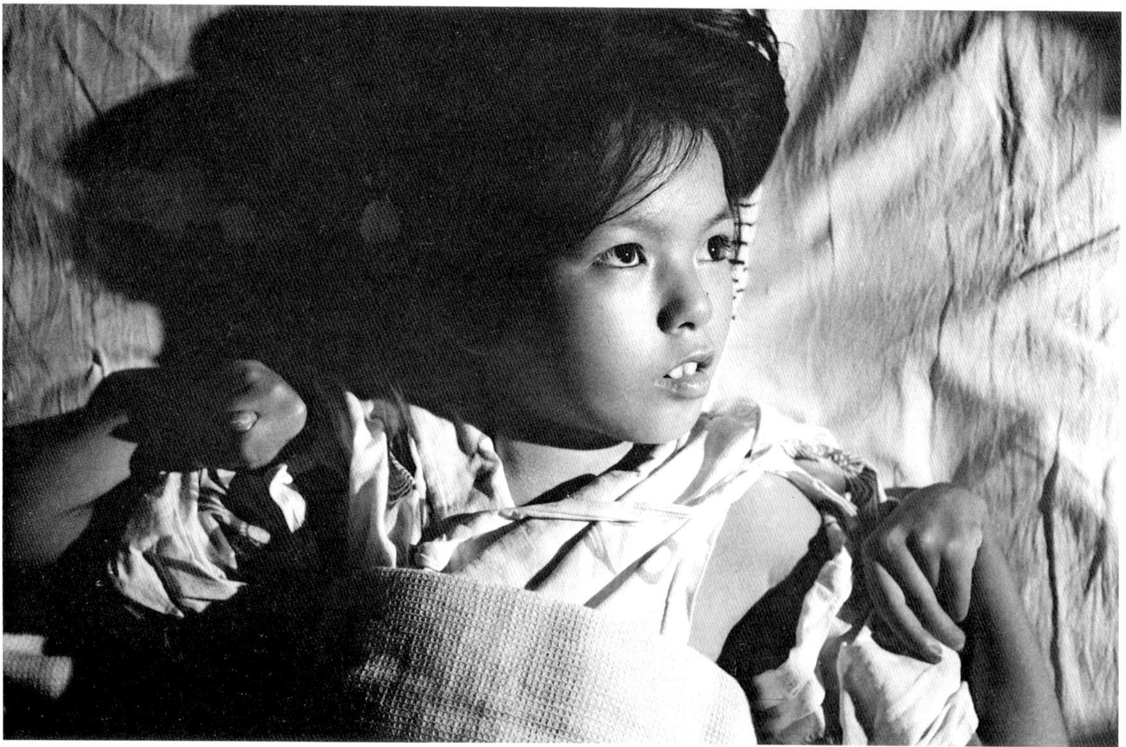

FIGURE I.2. Kuwabara Shisei, *Ikeru ningyō (A Living Doll),* circa 1962. Copyright Kuwabara Shisei.

photographer W. Eugene Smith's famous series *Minamata: Life—Sacred and Profane* (1971–72), which relies on photographs of bodies to foreground the corporate and governmental failure to protect Japan's citizens from industrial pollution (Figure I.3).[4]

In Smith's *Takako Isayama, a Congenital Minamata Disease Patient* (1972), a mother holds her daughter's stiff and angled body in front of Minamata Bay, where empty fishing boats line the shore. The sea is both their source of livelihood and their source of suffering. Smith's photograph demands empathy not only for the deformed child but also for the anonymous mother, who is hopelessly burdened with grief. One of the most infamous images in the series is *Tomoko in Her Bath,* which also depicts a mother cradling her severely deformed daughter. Smith constructed a pietà-like scene: a moment of maternal tenderness and loss that highlights, through contrasts of light and shadow, the child's exposed, disease-ravaged body. However, as Gennifer Weisenfeld notes, "the photograph's mournful serenity belies a story of extreme violence against the environment, humanity, and decades of sometimes violent physical and political struggle by the fishing communities and victims' families in their efforts to receive recognition and compensation for unimaginable suffering and loss."[5] The photograph was first published in June 1972, appearing as

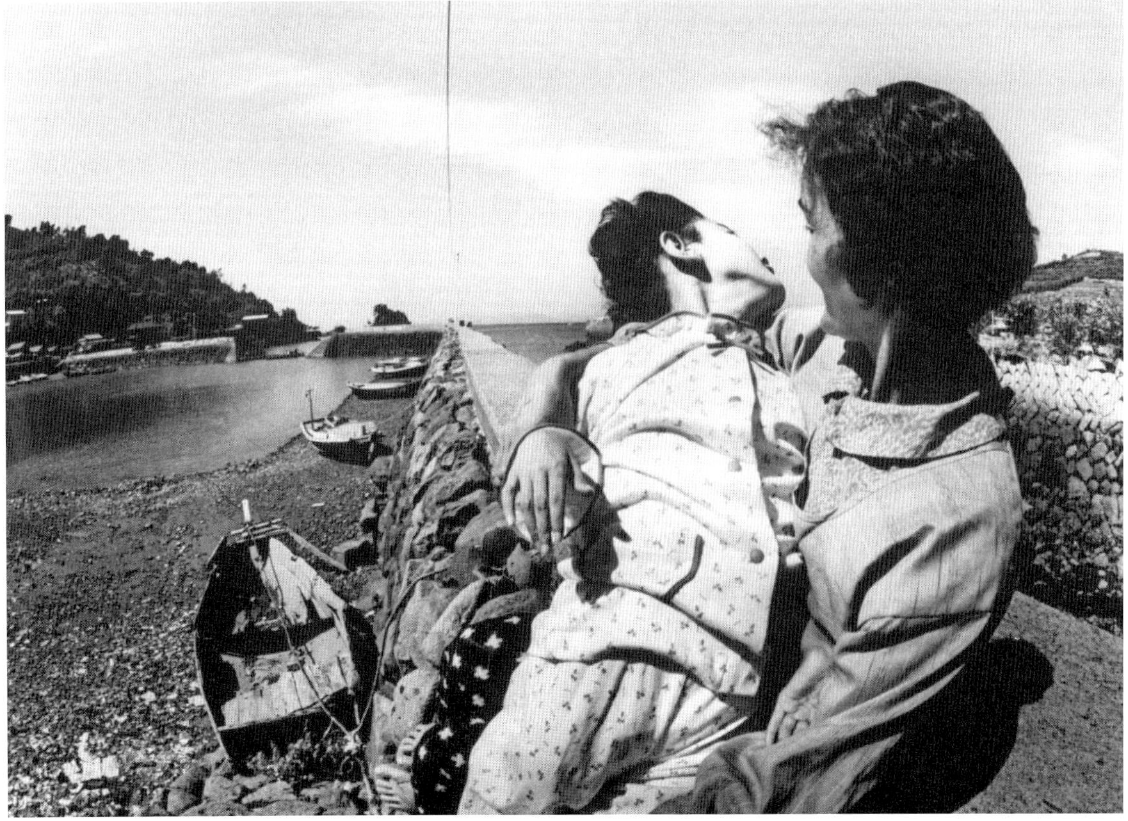

FIGURE I.3. W. Eugene Smith, *Takako Isayama, a Congenital Minamata Disease Patient,* from the series *Minamata: Life—Sacred and Profane,* 1972. Copyright Aileen M. Smith.

a two-page spread in *Life* magazine. Smith's powerful image concluded his photo-essay on the Minamata disaster, titled "Death-Flow from a Pipe," which helped significantly to expand the scope of concern over the disease (the series *Minamata: Life—Sacred and Profane* was published in book form in Japan in 1973 and in the United States in 1975).[6] Some have called *Tomoko in Her Bath* the prolific photojournalist's most significant work.[7]

Not only did Tomoko's image represent the disaster, but her living body did as well. During the court case that stemmed from the disaster, Tomoko was taken to the Central Pollution Board to be witnessed. Activist patients demanded that the board members "look, touch, hold this child, and remember the experience as they evaluated human beings in dollars and cents."[8] Yet the Kamimura family, who initially agreed to participate in these events and allowed their daughter to be photographed, later requested that the image be withdrawn from circulation after she passed away so they could let her spirit rest *(yasumasete agetai)*.[9] Their change of heart bespeaks their awareness of the easy slippage of such portraiture from a vehicle for social change to an intimate family memorial to an objectifying image displayed largely for shock value.

Historical events such as the Minamata disaster were not simply the "context" for postwar art making in Japan. Rather, visual culture was closely related to art and aesthetics and often shared similar political references about gender and nation, as I will demonstrate through attention to the visual aspects of political history. Although varied in their intentions and profit margins, art and visual culture coalesced around common themes and often were capable of shifting aesthetic sensibilities and political meanings. Indeed, events such as the Minamata disaster reveal that hard-and-fast distinctions between "art" and "visual culture" are unsustainable given the recurrence of Matsunaga Kumiko's image in contexts as seemingly disparate as newspapers, exhibitions, and books about Kuwabara's photography, and at the entrance of a municipal museum, where it stands as an ideologically loaded memorial to the disease's victims. Moreover, the Minamata disaster unfolded across different media in a manner that heightened anxieties about bodily exposure in postwar Japan.

The details of these events reveal the ways gender, representation, and the body were deeply entwined in the 1950s and 1960s. In April 1956, in Minamata City, Kumamoto Prefecture, a five-year-old girl named Tanaka Shizuko began trembling while trying to eat dinner. By morning she had lost the ability to speak or walk, and soon thereafter she lost her sight. Shizuko's younger sister, Jitsuko, developed similar symptoms just ten days later. Her mother first sought help at local clinics, where doctors were baffled by the symptoms, before taking Shizuko to the general hospital owned by the Chisso Corporation (the Shin Nippon Chisso Fertilizer Company, Minamata). On May 1, 1956, Dr. Hosokawa Hajime submitted a report to the public health office describing a strange disease *(kibyō)* that he was unable to treat.[10] Soon after, as new cases emerged, the phrase "strange disease" began to circulate widely in the region and in the press.[11]

The cause of the illness was unknown, but its localization raised fears of a contagion. The Tanakas' home was sprayed with disinfectant and the family faced extreme ostracization.

As others in the area fell ill, they were quarantined in ramshackle quarters on the outskirts of town, living like outcasts. Victims of the mysterious sickness lost their ability to speak and were recorded "howling like dogs."[12] No one wanted to risk contracting a disease that made one suffer seizures, debilitating sensory impairment, insanity, and often death. The media did their part to spread alarm. On May 8, 1956, the *Nishinippon Shinbun* ran the headline "Casualties and Insanity: A Strange Infectious Disease in Minamata."[13] The human body seemed extraordinarily vulnerable to unseen contaminants that could be neither identified nor contained. With no known cause and no known treatment, the disease stirred profound anxieties and contributed to a growing sense that even a decade after the Pacific War had ended, no one in Japan felt safe.[14]

Although Hosokawa officially announced the disease shortly after Tanaka Shizuko's diagnosis in 1956, its causes and effects had begun much earlier. As with many political and cultural events in the 1950s, the origins of the disaster began in the 1930s, in this case with the establishment of the Chisso Corporation's chemical manufacturing plant in Minamata. The company produced acetaldehyde, which is used in the production of perfumes, polyester resins, and basic dyes. It is also used as an intermediate in the synthesis of other chemicals and relies on mercury sulfate as a catalyst.[15] In 1931, Minamata's booming industrial port had pleased Emperor Hirohito, who visited and commended the town for its modern progress. The factory continued to be an important manufacturer of munitions as well as chemicals throughout World War II.[16] Near the end of the Pacific War the company closed down its operations, but in 1951 the Chisso Corporation reopened following the end of the Allied Occupation. During this period it vastly increased production, discharging into local waters large amounts of waste containing methylmercury compounds. Fish and other ocean life in Minamata Bay began to die soon after. In 1953, villagers were alarmed when cats began acting crazed, convulsing and throwing themselves into the ocean.[17] Following Hosokawa's announcement of the disease in 1956, fifty-four patients who were already hospitalized for other conditions were recognized to have "Minamata sickness," and seventeen deaths were retroactively attributed to it. In 1962, the first baby was born with congenital defects known to be related to mercury poisoning, and many others soon followed.

Despite the fact that the "strange disease" emerged in 1956 and the Kumamoto Medical team pointed to pollution from the Chisso plant as the likely cause of the disease as early as 1957, the source of the illness remained unconfirmed until well into the 1960s. Throughout this period, the Chisso Corporation continued to discharge mercury-laden factory waste into local waters, poisoning even greater numbers of people.[18] Hosokawa and his colleagues at the Chisso General Hospital conducted experiments on cats in 1959 that confirmed that bioaccumulated factory drainage was the source of the disease. The results were not disclosed, however—in fact, Hosokawa was silenced—and the corporation simply rerouted its waste, discharging it upstream into the Minamata River rather than directly into Hyakken Harbor and Minamata Bay, where tests were being conducted by the prefectural hospital. Minamata disease spread inland.

In 1959, the Kumamoto University Study Group announced publicly that Minamata disease was an illness that attacked the central nervous system and that it was likely caused by the ingestion of fish and shellfish contaminated with mercury. The Chisso Corporation vehemently denied its role in the spread of the disease and contended that residues linked to explosives used in the war were the cause of the sickness. The corporation and the government volleyed responsibility for the disaster back and forth from that time onward, and court battles went on for decades. Legal loopholes and a failure on the part of local and national governments to take action allowed the disease to spread and those already affected to suffer without proper medical and social support.

The story of the Minamata disaster (for to call it simply Minamata disease—the direct translation of *Minamatabyō*—circumvents the terribly consequential choices made by the government and the Chisso corporation) unfolded in highly gendered terms.[19] Minamata sickness affected more men than women, since many fishermen worked directly with (and subsisted on) contaminated fish. It was young girls, however, who triggered community attention. Tanaka Shizuko's entrance into the hospital seemed to propel Hosokawa's announcement. Subsequently, and perhaps not surprisingly, sickened young girls were most often featured in the media.[20] For example, in one image from a Kumamoto newspaper, a naked two-year-old girl is displayed, her eyes blocked out in a gesture to hide her identity (Figure I.4). In the previously mentioned article on Matsunaga Kumiko in the *Asahi Shinbun* (a statewide publication), the child is identified rather informally in the

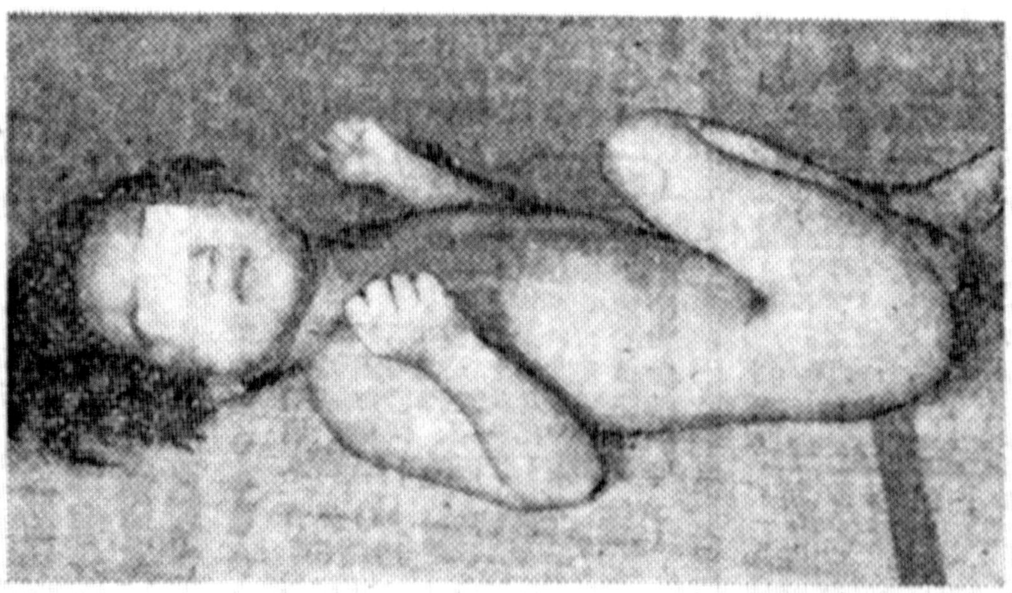

FIGURE I.4. "Eiyō shōgai mo wazawai: Machijū ga noirōze gimi" (Minamata strange disease: Is manganese the cause?), *Kumamoto Nichinichi Shinbun,* February 14, 1957. Courtesy of *Kumamoto Nichinichi Shinbun.*

caption as "Kumiko-chan," *chan* being a term of affection for children or those younger than oneself (Figure I.5). Young girls were perceived as those most vulnerable and exposed to the unknown, threatening disease. Media coverage, one might argue, only extended the ways in which their bodies and identities were exposed.

Woman as a metaphor for the nation—as well as a metaphor for the threats to the nation—existed long before the postwar period. The trope of the female body as a symbol of the purity of the nation has a long history and gained greater popularity in the 1930s, when wartime propaganda began featuring women's bodies (Figures I.6 and I.7). Through subtle connections to images that represented woman as nation in the past, the gendered representation of Minamata victimhood in the 1950s cast this episode as more than a local tragedy—it represented a national crisis. As Weisenfeld notes: "Minamata is a palimpsest of Japanese modernity. Its history of exploitation reveals the conflicted status of Japan's periphery in the face of the nation's rapid industrialization when national interests were often privileged at the expense of individuals and local communities."[21]

In 1958, the Kumamoto edition of the *Asahi Shinbun* ran the headline "Bright, Mentally Disabled in Minamata" alongside a photograph showing a little girl standing shirtless before a nurse, who has her hand against the girl's stomach as though to feel for signs of illness (Figure I.8).[22] Beside them, a bespectacled male doctor in a white jacket takes notes. The headline chillingly recalls the government's promotion of a "bright life" *(akarui sei-katsu)*, a concept related to rationalization and modernization in the 1950s. As historian Simon Partner points out, this rhetoric was employed by companies that sold electrical goods, which relied heavily on women's cheap labor for their success.[23] Other accounts in the popular press that focused on the municipal and national governments' efforts to rehabilitate victims likewise featured young girls.[24] These images, and the narratives connected to them, suggested both the vulnerability of the child and the somewhat misleading assurance that municipal forces were at the ready to provide treatment.

In fact, the disease spread for many more years and appeared in other prefectures. During the 1960s, a series of severe diseases were discovered in Japan, including *itai-itai* (literally "it hurts it hurts") disease (caused by cadmium poisoning), Yokkaichi asthma (caused by exposure to burning petroleum and crude oil), and Minamata disease, which was later found beyond Minamata City.[25] In 1965, officials in Niigata Prefecture linked cases of mercury poisoning to the Shōwa Denkō Corporation and initiated litigation against the company. That the disease was no longer geographically contained caused sweeping alarm.[26]

On September 26, 1968, twelve years after the first cases were discovered in Minamata, the Japanese federal government officially recognized Minamata sickness as a pollution-related disease caused by the Chisso Corporation's release of methylmercury directly into Minamata Bay. One wonders if the timing of this late capitulation was related to events taking place far from the shores of Minamata, such as demonstrations in Tokyo demanding a true democracy and the global struggles for change that peaked in May 1968.[27] The

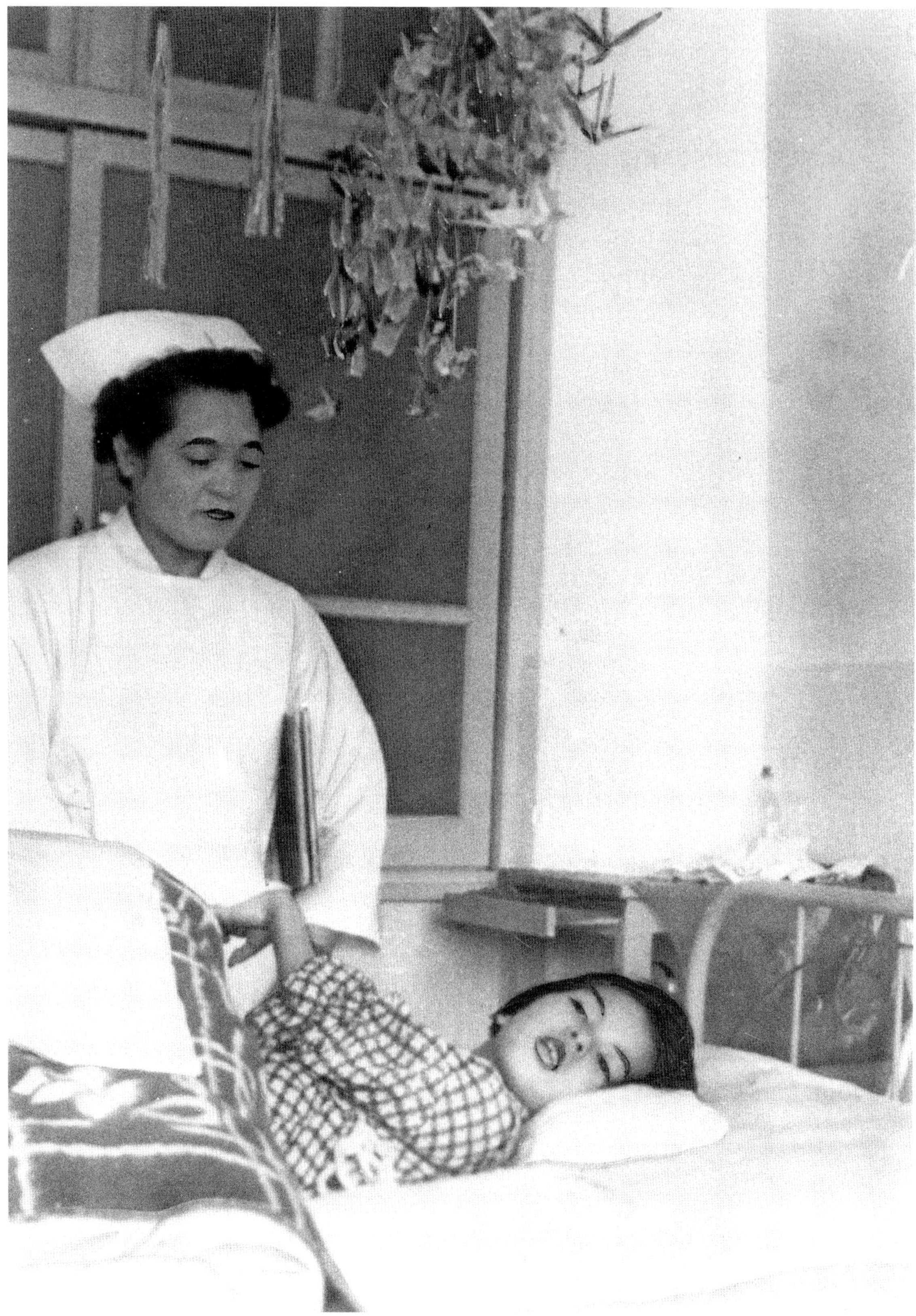

FIGURE I.5. "'Ikeru ningyō' shōjo—yonenkan kaeranu ishiki" (Girl is a living doll: Unconscious for four years), *Asahi Shinbun*, April 22, 1960. Courtesy of the *Asahi Shinbun*, via Getty Images.

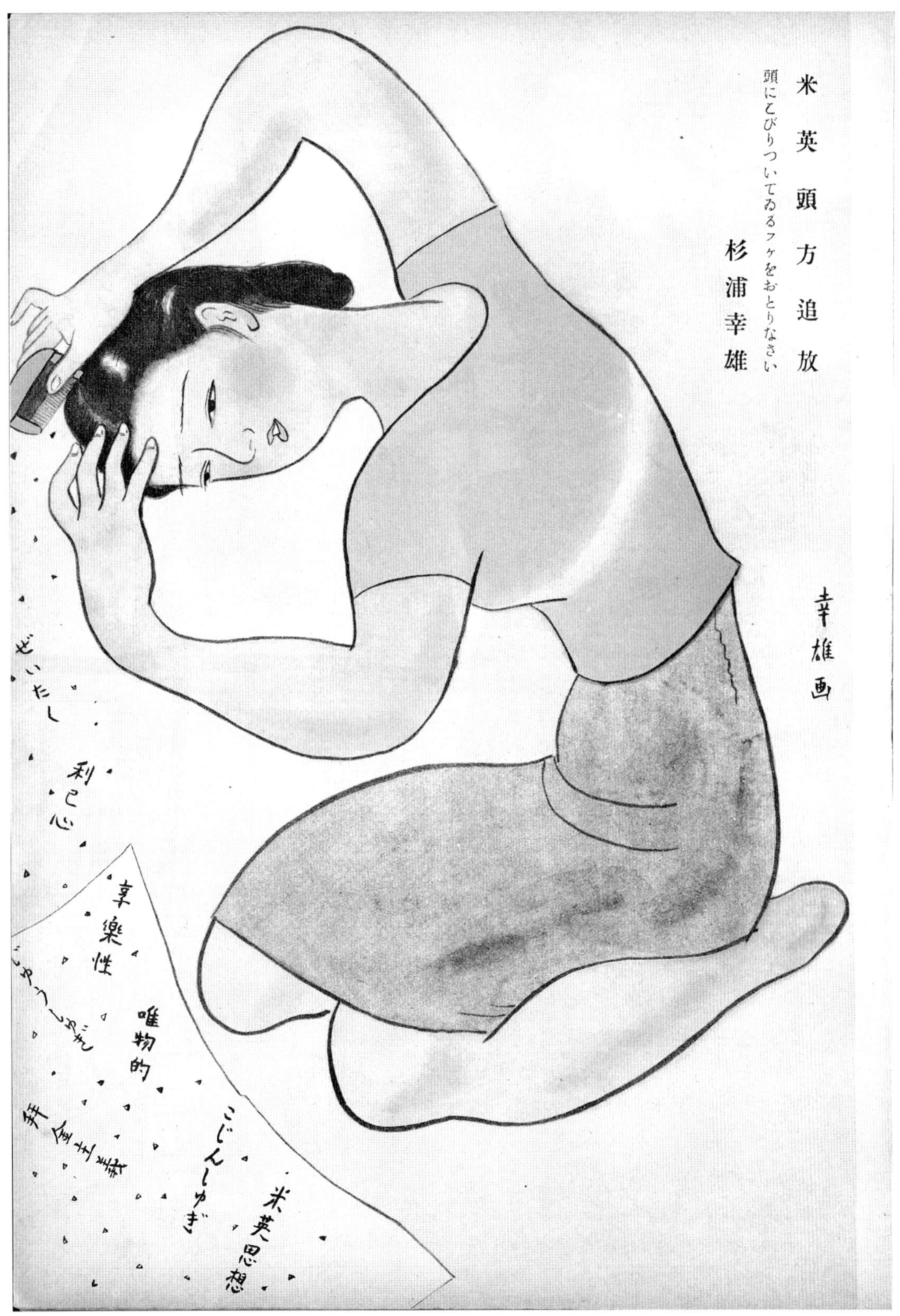

FIGURE I.6. Sugiura Yukio, *Beiei tōhō tsuihō (Purging One's Head of Anglo-Americanism), Manga* 10, no. 5 (1942): 17. 29 × 20.3 cm. Copyright Sugiura Jun. Photograph from Manga Collection, The Ohio State University Billy Ireland Cartoon Library and Museum.

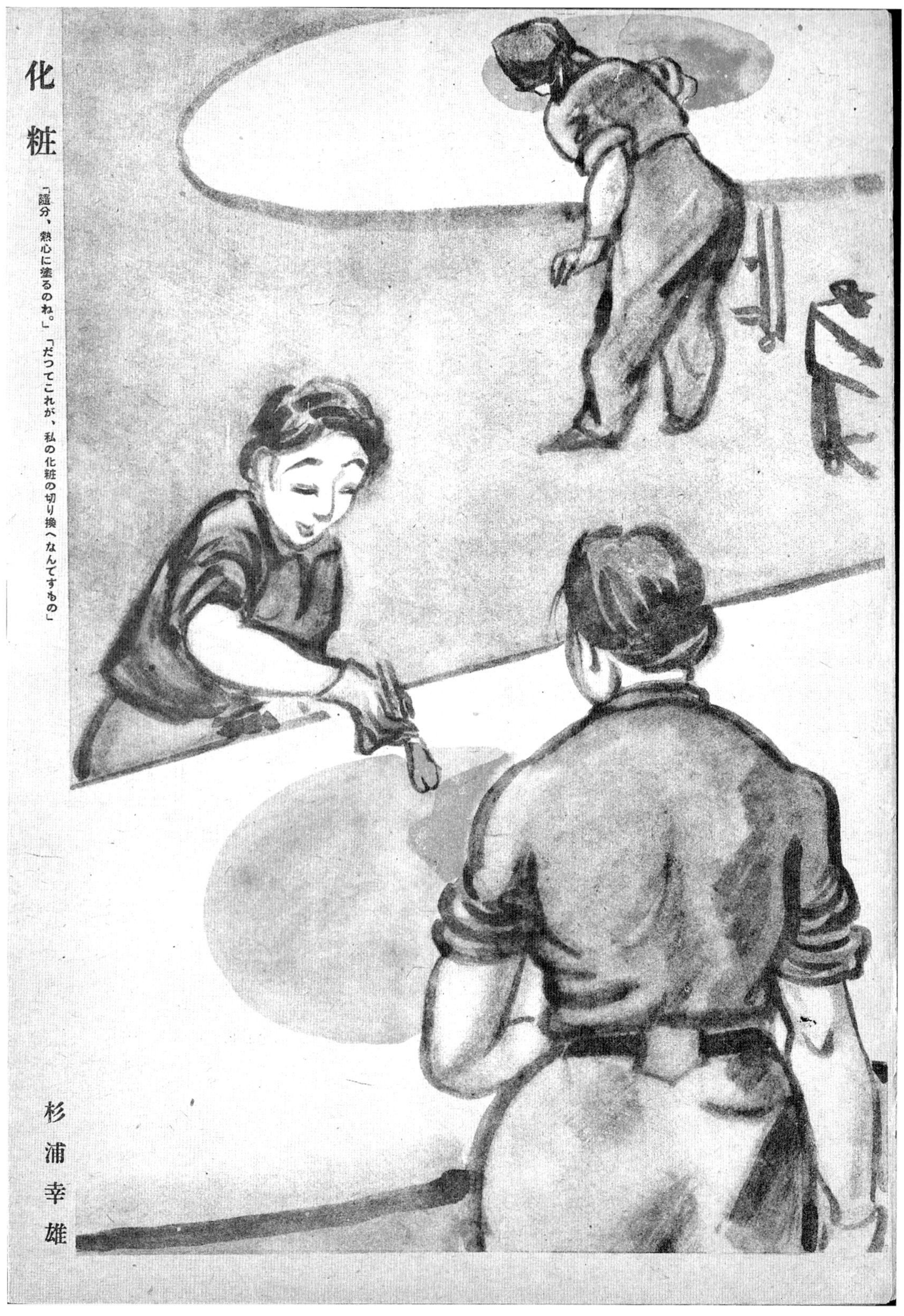

FIGURE I.7. Sugiura Yukio, *Keshō (Makeup), Manga* 11, no. 12 (1943): 18. The text reads: Person A: "You are painting very neatly." Person B: "That's because I'm busy painting the flag rather than my face." 29 × 20.3 cm. Copyright Sugiura Jun. Photograph from Manga Collection, The Ohio State University Billy Ireland Cartoon Library and Museum.

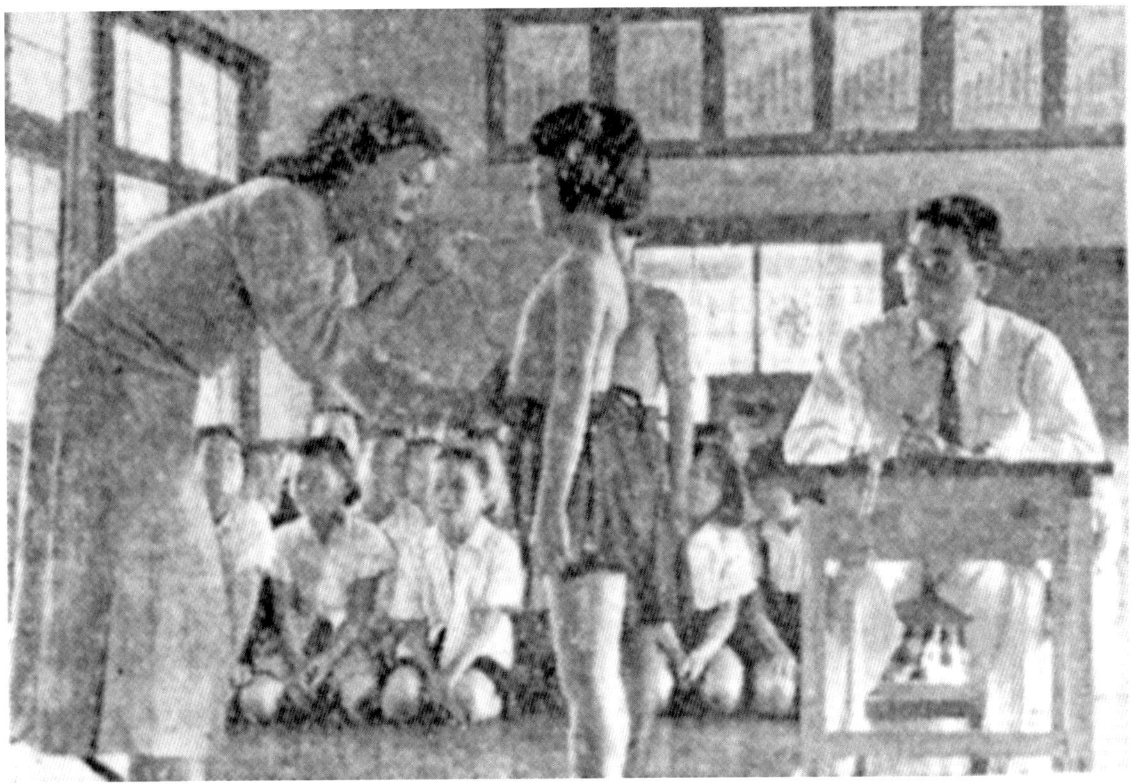

FIGURE I.8. "Akarui seihakuji Minamata" (Bright, mentally disabled in Minamata), *Asahi Shinbun* (Kumamoto edition), June 9, 1958, 10. Courtesy of the Kumamoto Kenritsu Toshokan. Author's photograph.

illnesses, negligence, and trials that followed were a microcosm of Japan's struggle to designate responsibility for its citizens in a time when national economic growth was the primary concern. From the time of its official recognition as a disease caused by pollution, Minamata sickness revealed the drive toward industrialization as ruthless and reckless, with the poor and disenfranchised bearing the greatest risks.[28] As we have seen, the stakes of these events were frequently—and perhaps most powerfully—communicated through art and visual culture.

Bodily Exposure in Postwar Japan

I begin with the tragic events in Minamata because they exemplify the intersection of gender, the body, nationhood, and representation examined in this book. The disaster fed into other anxieties circulating in Japan in the postwar period—namely, that the physical body could not withstand exposure to the ravages of modern times, be they unknown contaminants in the air and water, the nuclear weapons wielded by the United States, or rapid changes to the urban environment. Fears about bodily contamination were also linked to the arrival of the Allied Occupation forces (made up primarily of American troops).[29] Japanese historian Harry Harootunian writes:

> The Americans resorted to massive detoxification of the Japanese with DDT—a legacy from colonial rule in the Philippines—in order to subject the population to "a new regulatory regime that aspired to produce clean, democratic bodies." Japanese were made to submit not only to forms of detoxification and immunization but also to programs to increase calorie intake. Despite exemplifying the democratic principle of valuing each individual, the immunological programs reinforced the Japanese conviction that the American military was carrying out multiple invasions, and now in the most private and intimate domain—the body.[30]

The body's centrality and vulnerability were not lost on artists and illustrators working at the time, who were as wary about the Japanese government's complicity with commercial neoliberalism as a means to control the Japanese body as they were about the political role of the United States in Japan.

As in the case of the events in Minamata, photography, painting, and visual culture became critical means of discourse about events that posed a threat to Japanese bodies, such as the atomic bombings of Hiroshima and Nagasaki, the nuclear bomb testing at Bikini Atoll, and the expansion of U.S. military bases. Art communicated and repressed fears, publicized personal tragedies, and demanded that the state take responsibility for its citizens. Moreover, this discourse was often deeply gendered in a multiplicity of ways that obfuscated the hegemonic order it sought to buttress.

Beginning this book with a description of the Minamata disaster disrupts the common narrative that art and visual culture in Japan began from "ground zero" following the atomic bombings in 1945.[31] Art historians in Japan have frequently referred to the tabula rasa of postwar Japanese art, and this perception of a theoretical blank slate is punctuated by the war and its "leveling" of Japan. Similarly, English-speaking art historians have tended to equate the whole of Japanese postwar art production with traumatic outpourings stemming from the atomic bombings.[32] Allowing the destruction of Hiroshima and Nagasaki to continue to dominate art historical practice repeatedly reinvents particular national frameworks of power—namely, the militaristic, economic, and cultural hegemony of the United States. As cultural theorist Rey Chow writes, "Above all, the unleashing of the bombs was perhaps the crowning event of the ascendance of the United States to the position of supreme world power."[33] Thus, it is troubling to consider how often that violent ascendancy is visually reinforced in the ubiquitous image of the fist-like mushroom cloud over Nagasaki—notably, the photograph of the mushroom cloud produced by the bomb over Hiroshima was less "picturesque" and appears far less frequently, attesting to the powerful politics of vision. While the bombings clearly conditioned much postwar artistic production, they were but one of many issues confronting Japanese artists in the aftermath of World War II, and not the single point of departure for all cultural expression thereafter. Moreover, the context of the Cold War and the participation of the Japanese people tends to be overlooked in this line of inquiry. The Japanese themselves were equally implicated in the social, political, and environmental conditions of the postwar period, and in the drive to measure up to the United States and other global powers. The ongoing relationship and series of asymmetrical exchanges between the United States and Japan is what is critical, not a simplistic idea of American ascendancy (and its victims) symbolized by the atomic bomb.

Japan's modern history has been shaped by periods of contact with the United States since 1853, beginning with the arrival of Commodore Perry's ships and his course of gunboat diplomacy and continuing well past the Allied Occupation of Japan (1945–52).[34] These fraught moments of contact have meant that when political and cultural exchanges have taken place, it has often been on uneven terms. Relations with the United States had an immense impact on Japan in the postwar period, and this influence informs several chapters of this book. Events such as Japan's militarization (or "total war"), the atomic bombings, the Allied Occupation, and the Bikini Atoll nuclear tests all contributed to tensions between the two countries. This troubled geopolitical relationship caused Japan to define itself vis-à-vis an economically, culturally, and militarily dominant Other (which in turn relied on Japan as a base from which to expand its Cold War agenda).[35] Ann Sherif notes that "the Cold War was, among other things, an ideological clash between liberal capitalism and state socialism, manifested as a battle of propaganda in which superpowers vied to expand their spheres of influence. Images and words became their primary weapons."[36] Following the dramatic end of the Pacific War, Japan underwent a period of contentious redefinition that circulated not only around questions of national identity and responsibility for its citizens versus economic growth and ties to the United States but also around such critical issues as gender subjectivity and its interrelationship with nationhood and the use of culture (particularly Zen Buddhism and avant-garde art) rather than military prowess to resituate Japan on the global stage.[37]

Issues like the Minamata disaster demonstrate that the road to economic prosperity was filled with risks and perilous decisions about corporate versus state accountability, the advantages and hazards of rapid industrialization, and the repression or support of political activism. Japan's postwar desperation to rise from defeat to become an advanced, economically powerful country meant that companies like Chisso were heralded rather than monitored. In the early 1950s, such events and their consequences formed a new and composite identity for the nation. The ongoing political and cultural presence of the United States in Japan demonstrates that the "transnational," the notion of the heightened interconnectivity between nations, is discursively and inextricably related to the national—something that must be kept in mind as we turn to representations created during this time.

The Integral Nature of Gender and Nationhood

Theorists of the nation, notably Eric Hobsbawm and Benedict Anderson, have demonstrated that the nation is a constructed and contingent category, but they have paid less attention to the ways in which gender identities and national identities are mutually imbricated. Gender studies scholar Nira Yuval-Davis has written that it is ironic that women are "usually 'hidden' in the various theorizations of the nationalist phenomena" even though it is they who (along with men) "reproduce nations, biologically, culturally and symbolically."[38] In *Gender, Nation and State in Modern Japan,* Andrea Germer, Vera Mackie, and Ulrike Wöhr draw attention to this lacuna: "All modern nation-states are gendered, and they operate according to the principles of inclusion and exclusion. Governments are interested in regulating gender relations and in the management of sexuality. Indeed, we can add that nation-states manage the physical bodies of their citizens and subjects."[39] These authors also acknowledge that while all nation-states are gendered, the processes of gendering manifest differently, both temporally and geographically. As historian Igarashi Yoshikuni has argued, Japan's memories were "discursively constructed through bodily tropes, where bodies became sites for national rehabilitation."[40] Yet Igarashi at times overlooks that Japanese bodies were not "rehabilitated" equally. In her study of postwar France, *Fast Cars, Clean Bodies,* Kristin Ross shows how men and women surged forward in the postwar democracy of consumption in different ways.[41] Through attention to both female and male artists, this book will demonstrate the diverse responses to the nation and their contingency on gender subjectivity.

The indivisibility of gender and nation in Japan was further cemented with the rewriting of the national charter by the Allied Occupation forces in 1946. Immediately following the Allied victory over Japan the previous year, the U.S. General Headquarters rapidly drafted a constitution for Japan under the orders of General Douglas MacArthur. He selected twenty-four members of the drafting committee, four of whom were women. Although a women's suffrage movement was active in the 1920s and 1930s, women were unable to vote until a change in the election law in late 1945 (women both voted and stood for office in the April 1946 elections). The revised constitution also mandated freedom from gender discrimination—a sweeping change that held out much promise for a new society free of gender inequity. That promise was never fulfilled. As Vera Mackie has pointed out, "The barriers to [Japanese women's] political participation lie not in political structures and the legal system, but in the familial structures and employment practices which shape their activities in the public sphere."[42] Thus, the charter set up new opportunities as well as challenges. The burdens of social reproduction, especially child care and domestic labor, remained the domain of women (as they do today); furthermore, the new constitution did not overturn societal expectations of "proper" feminine behavior. Traditionally feminine roles were idealized, and being a housewife was the most readily available occupation for women, primarily because men who had returned from the war began to reclaim jobs that women had undertaken in their absence.

In the postwar period, citizens felt the burden not only of accepting the constitution and its ideals for rebuilding a modern, progressive nation but also of embodying those ideals.[43] Yet the ideals were far from clear. Democracy in Japan was contentious, as initial growth in labor union activity was suppressed by American collusion with those Japanese who sought to reestablish a conservative power monopoly, an effort supported by the American policy known as Reverse Course.[44] In William Marotti's words:

> The gap between artists' investigations, and dreams of revolution, and the state's policing of art and thought, reveals the politics of culture as confrontation. Such conflicts provide the opportunity to understand commonly separated phenomena, institutions, and experiences at a different level of analysis, viewing them through their complex interrelations as revealed in events, without reducing them to this dimension alone or to anticipations of events to come.[45]

Following Marotti, I focus in this book on the shifts in gender subjectivity and embodiment and their relation to the state as constructed, reflected, and transformed by art practices. I also consider how dialectical tensions between the transnational and the national surfaced in, shaped, and were suppressed in the Japanese visual field from the 1940s to the 1970s. While the setting of this book is postwar Japan—a period that lacks a clearly defined end point—I incorporate discourse about Japan's militarized past in the 1930s and 1940s. I examine how political contention over Japan's new democracy (including tension between Japan and the United States) was expressed, disavowed, and reimagined through representations of the gendered body. How could the body be represented in postwar Japan? Why did artists often represent the body as under duress, fragmented, covered, or disaggregated?[46] How did artists critically engage in the discourses of gender and nationhood?

To examine these issues, each chapter of this book focuses on a key artist active in the postwar period: Katsura Yuki (1913–91), Nakamura Hiroshi (born 1932), Tanaka Atsuko (1932–2005), and Shiraga Kazuo (1924–2008).[47] I feature these artists because of their innovative artistic contributions, certainly, but also because of their synchronous engagement with gender, national, and artistic identity, as well as for their regional representation.[48] (Katsura and Nakamura were based in the Kantō or Tokyo area, while Tanaka and Shiraga were involved in the Gutai Art Association, which was based in the Kansai area, near Kyoto and Osaka.) This selection of artists also highlights the diverse aesthetic approaches that were practiced in postwar Japan, including performance art, abstract art, socialist realism, and figural painting, and the divergent ways these media engaged politics. This project moves away from the privileging of Japanese avant-garde artists by English-speaking scholars in favor of an approach that includes artists who exhibited in state-sanctioned spaces as well as those who displayed art in experimental spaces. Ideally, this approach reveals a lack of consensus about politics and aesthetics, about radical art and normativity, and about the role of the gendered body.

Paying attention to individual artists goes against the grain of current scholarship, which tends to focus on art groups in postwar Japan and at times glosses the rich and distinctive aesthetics and political choices made by individuals. All of the artists discussed here had different, and often shifting, relations to politics. For example, Nakamura was at one point closely involved with the left-wing activist groups, while Katsura's political ideals usually surfaced through her illustrations and collages; by contrast, Shiraga and Tanaka disavowed direct involvement in politics despite the fevered social context in which they worked and the political relevance of their art. Through a close examination of these artists' paintings, illustrations, assemblages, and performance art, this book reveals that even with dissimilar artistic priorities and divergent political interests, artists in the postwar period were invested in the entangled issues of gender and nationhood that at the time were redefining Japan and its role in the world. For all of these artists, I argue, art making was the primary ground for political intervention.

The Stakes of Exposure: Anxious Bodies in Postwar Japanese Art is not a comprehensive survey of the artists active in the postwar Japanese art world (nor does it address a full range of gender identities). Instead, it advances interpretations of some of the most visually compelling, politically surprising, and often overlooked artworks of the period while focusing on three themes: (1) the mutually constitutive nature of gender and nation and its relevance to art, (2) the political stakes of art, and (3) the anxieties that characterized postwar art and politics in Japan and how artists actively investigated these anxieties and their political causes through the representation of bodies, both exposed and concealed. For all four artists, the body was a key zone for presenting and disputing the fraught nature of selfhood in postwar Japan.

Anxiety and the Body

Events like the atomic bombings of Hiroshima and Nagasaki, the radioactive fallout from nuclear testing, massive urban change, and the Minamata disaster sharpened anxiety over bodily exposure, permanence, and presence. The represented body was a site where state rhetoric, commercial desire, and subjectivity converged. Under these charged social and psychological circumstances, artists relied on the performative or represented body as they examined the ways gender and nation had been represented in the past and what they could stand for in the future. Art also functioned as a way for artists to express, consider, and release the anxiety and uncertainty of the times. As Sigmund Freud writes in "Beyond the Pleasure Principle": "'Fright,' 'fear,' and 'anxiety' are improperly used as synonymous expressions; they are in fact capable of clear distinction in their relation to danger. 'Anxiety' describes a particular state of expecting the danger or preparing for it, even though it may be an unknown one."[49] The postwar period was not simply about recovering from the trauma of war; it was also about braving the expansive uncertainties (economic, environmental, gendered, and national) of present and future Japan.

I use the term *anxiety* to refer to this state of unease, apprehension, or solicitude, as well as to its secondary meaning: "strained or solicitous desire (for, or to effect, some purpose)."[50] The latter definition applies because the desire for—and uncertainty over—an established position in the larger art world dominated by the West was often an underlying cause for unease among artists in postwar Japan. Katsura, Nakamura, Tanaka, and Shiraga stood on the periphery of the global art world, well aware of the centers to which they did not belong. How could they respond to the conflicting demands to make art that would be in dialogue with dominant Western art practices without seeming derivative? In this moment of intense change and possibility, there was considerable pressure to create art that would have currency as cultural capital. I suggest that these artists self-consciously turned the tables on this pressure and used their art to question the limits of representation and self.

Scholars have overwhelmingly assumed that Japanese postwar art is about celebrating and engaging with a nascent democracy through expressions of individualism.[51] However, conceptions of democracy in the early 1950s were divergent and fluid. How would artistic practice contribute to political change? Furthermore, how could artists negotiate the imbalanced global dynamics in the art world while still maintaining a sense of aesthetic and political authenticity? Unlike those who were, as John Dower describes, "embracing defeat," many artists were openly critical of the trajectory of Japanese politics and did not see liberal democracy as a desirable goal.[52]

The purported philosophy of "individualism" among postwar Japanese artists—in contrast to an earlier, more normative tendency to work in groups—has typically been seen as consonant with the ideals of liberal, American-style democracy. But the simplicity of that opposition is predicated on the notion that earlier Japanese artist groups were cohesive. Individualism as an artistic philosophy had strong roots in the prewar period, as Gennifer Weisenfeld and Alicia Volk have shown.[53] The misconception that individualism is a uniquely American characteristic is reinforced by the fact that American artists are often exhibited and written about as individual creators, whereas Japanese artists are almost always treated as members of collectives in North America. Although many Japanese artists employed the cultural and economic strategy of working in groups to network and share materials, their "groups" rarely committed to specific shared artistic goals.[54] Art groups were less cohesive than scholars have imagined, and art movements in Japan (as elsewhere) often fostered heated debate and individual artistic invention.[55]

By closely examining specific artworks by individual Japanese artists, this book challenges the subtle but powerful binary categories that have all too often shaped our understanding of art practices, such as individualism versus collaboration, original versus derivative, and East versus West. At times, these dualisms reinforce one another—for example, Western culture is aligned with individualism and Eastern culture with collaboration; Western art is associated with original creativity and Eastern art with derivation. By focusing on individual artists and artworks, I attempt to move away from these simplistic divisions and engage in readings of artworks in all of their complicated detail. Bringing together Katsura's humorous assemblage works, Nakamura's political reportage paintings, Tanaka's elaborate performance art, and Shiraga's earnest displays of masculine heroics complicates the assumption (prevalent in much English-language scholarship) that postwar Japanese art constituted a broad but stylistically homogeneous movement that ushered in American-style democracy. My aim in this study is to reveal the disorienting diversity of aesthetic strategies, examining rather than obscuring the contradictions at play in this moment of heightened creative production.

Dimensions of the Study

Chapters 1 and 2 examine the political engagement of two leading artists working in Tokyo in the postwar era and how they took a stand against American liberal democracy through somatic representation. Nakamura Hiroshi and Katsura Yuki aimed to mobilize social action, relying heavily on themes of embodiment and disembodiment, exposure and concealment. For them, art making was a discursive process that negotiated local and global tensions through paintings of anxious and gendered bodies.

Chapter 1, "Katsura Yuki's Bodies of Resistance," illuminates the work of the award-winning painter in relation to political change. Unlike Tanaka, Shiraga, and Nakamura, Katsura exhibited her work in juried exhibitions (such as those presented by the Nika Association) and was not affiliated with any painting movement. My inclusion of Katsura in the book serves to broaden the picture of the art scene in postwar Japan, which was discursively influenced by painters and their involvement with juried exhibitions. Current English-language scholarship on postwar art has tended to privilege radical, avant-garde groups such as Hi Red Center, the Gutai Art Association, and Jikken Kōbō. Although Katsura might not have been considered an experimental artist, her art was groundbreaking, both in content and in style. For example, she used newspapers and other everyday materials for her collage paintings, and she drew illustrations for a serialized translation of the James Baldwin novel *Another Country* that opened up space for a wider discourse on gender, sexuality, and race in Japan. Chapter 1 addresses these mass-culture illustrations as well how Katsura's assemblage paintings, such as *Gonbe to karasu (Gonbe and Crow)* (1966) and *Saru kani gassen (The Battle of the Monkey and the Crab)* (1948), draw on themes from Japanese folklore but recast each role to upend the conservative values usually embedded in the tales. These satirical allegories evaded the overdetermined masculine heroics of abstract expressionism and action art that had taken Japan by storm in the postwar period, forging an innovative mode of expression that was whimsical and strange in its tone but nonetheless had a potent political thrust.

Chapter 2, "Nakamura Hiroshi and the Politics of Embodiment," explores Nakamura's representations of gender as a site of political contention and dynamic action. Recent footage of the artist in the documentary film *ANPO: Art X War* (2010) and his inclusion in

Tokyo: A New Avant-Garde, a 2013 exhibition at New York's Museum of Modern Art, have attracted greater interest in his production but have also flattened understanding of his political motivations by highlighting only his paintings from the 1950s and his involvement with the reportage movement. Through a visual analysis of his early and late-career paintings, as well as his multivolume collection of magazine and newspaper advertisements, this chapter examines how Nakamura's political trajectory shifted while the artist remaining steadfastly focused on the intertwined issues of nation and gender.

In the early 1950s, the workingman was an idealized symbol for those who sought to legitimate a new democratic consumer society in Japan, as well as for those who fought to establish a socialist form of government. In this context, the representation of the male body became an implicit battleground in art and visual culture. An examination of Nakamura's oeuvre shows how he negotiated the shifting political spectrum through a gendered lens that constructed the male body as a site of labor, struggle, and active movement. But his canvases also reveal a deep-seated anxiety about Japanese masculinity. In the late 1950s, Nakamura exiled the male body from his paintings in favor of masculinized machinery. From the 1960s onward, he painted images of schoolgirls that critiqued (and perhaps perpetuated) sexist consumption, relying on movement to engage viewers and maintain a masculine presence on the canvas.

The third and fourth chapters of this book focus on two artists, Tanaka and Shiraga, who were among the most successful members of the Gutai Art Association. Gutai, which means "concreteness" or "embodiment," sought to create a new avant-garde in the 1950s, one that rejected figuration and often relied on bodily action.[56] Recent studies frame Gutai work as an apolitical celebration of new art forms. Yet to declare Gutai work apolitical misses much of what was at stake in its practice.[57] These artists instead raised questions about the status of Japanese art and their position within that sphere through some of the most experimental painting and performance art of the 1950s and 1960s. At times their work directly engaged visual vocabularies that resonated with Japan's nationalist symbols. At other moments, their creations pitted the body against the elements in a manner suggesting the risks of war and urbanization. Their work questions the role of representation in relation to the nation through gendered posturing and subtle manipulations of nationalist motifs.

Chapter 3, "Tanaka Atsuko and the Circuits of Subjectivity," considers Tanaka's personal and artistic negotiations with the overwhelming industrial transformation of Osaka, the shifting social status of women, and Tanaka's ambivalent relationship to female subjectivity. Specifically, the chapter examines her pivotal 1956 performance pieces *Denki fuku (Electric Dress)* and *Butai fuku (Stage Clothes)* as interrogations of surface and selfhood in 1950s Japan. Comparing Tanaka's performance works with advertisements and promotional images for contemporary films exposes the penchant for self-fashioning that was circulating at the time, as well as the gendered consumer economy behind it. The double-edged nature of *Electric Dress* is evident in the frivolity of costume and neon spectacle juxtaposed with the production of heat and looming physical threat to the body. *Electric Dress* can be interpreted as a vivid cloak that shrouds the artist-subject while simultaneously testing the limits of the self through elements of risk. Tanaka's art explored subjectivity as a process reliant on visual signifiers, bodily performance, and the context of industrialization, urbanization, and the encroachment of technology into all aspects of everyday life. The stakes of exposure, for Tanaka and her peers, were a matter of life and death.

Chapter 4, "Heroic Violence in the Art of Shiraga Kazuo," explores how Shiraga referenced archetypal models of the hero while deftly taking up the formal language of modernism. The artist's reworkings took many forms, appearing, for instance, in his overt literary references to the heroes of the Chinese epic *The Water Margin* in his paintings' titles, in the spectacular self-heroization of his overtly physical performance art, and in the heroic challenges he undertook in his daily life. These multiple configurations of the masculine body in Shiraga's art reveal the stakes of gendered subjectivity and their ramifications for art and the nation.

This book examines the relationship between gender and nation in Japan from the 1950s until 1970 through an analysis of individual artists and their provocative works. Katsura, Nakamura, Tanaka, and Shiraga played important roles in a growing realm of art production following the end of the Allied Occupation that drew inspiration from a wealth of visual culture in magazines, television, and film. Their interests in engaging critical questions about national identity were articulated through representations of the gendered body. Rather than a celebration of the times, I argue, art production was a key means through which these artists articulated fresh understandings of the self and thought through their relations to gender, art, and nation. Their seemingly outlandish performance art and paintings were part of personal and public evaluations of gender and nation and reveal the transformative potential of art for political subjectivity. Katsura's allegorical assemblages, Nakamura's vibrant paintings of trains and schoolgirls, Tanaka's electric mappings of circuits and circles, and Shiraga's violent spectacles all charted new artistic territory, raising questions about selfhood and its contingent relation to gender, artistic status, and the unstable and uncertain postwar nation.

1

Katsura Yuki's Bodies of Resistance

When Katsura Yuki (Yukiko) (1913–1991) began her career in the 1930s, she was one among a handful of women exhibiting in the prestigious Nika Association exhibitions alongside figures such as Gutai Art Association leader Yoshihara Jirō.[1] The arc of her career across the prewar, war, and postwar periods upsets popular periodizations in Japan's art history that assert the postwar as a time of rupture and renewal. In Carol Gluck's words, "This long postwar was one consequence of the original *sengo* [postwar] consciousness that wished and hoped for—although not necessarily believed in or lived—a history that could begin again at noon, August 15, 1945."[2] Writing in 1993, Gluck expressed a notion that remains popular in art historical scholarship to this day—namely, that art (and much else) in Japan began anew following the explosion of the atomic bombs, reinforced by exhibitions and scholarship that privilege artists born in the 1930s and came of age in the postwar period.[3] This limited view of Japanese postwar art is especially prominent in North America, where, through the body of research and large-scale exhibitions, many people have become knowledgeable about art groups such as the Gutai Art Association (two prominent members of which are discussed in chapters 3 and 4) but have never heard of Katsura Yuki, who had far more solo shows than the other artists addressed in this book and who participated in numerous international exhibitions from the 1930s onward.[4] This omission of Katsura is all the more remarkable in light of her near-celebrity status. She appeared as a guest on television shows, was featured in newspaper columns, was invited to represent Japan on an international friendship-building boat trip to Russia, and published a best-selling memoir in 1962.[5]

My focus on Katsura is meant to challenge this "postwar paradigm" while elucidating Katsura's negotiation of ethics and plurality during drastically different political eras. In the course of her long and productive career, Katsura experienced fascism under the militaristic government and censorship and national "renewal" under the Allied Occupation, and she was sensitive to (and at times complicit with) the state's self-serving manipulations of gendered identities in each of these periods. Alicia Volk writes that Katsura relied on "empowering folkloric iconography" to confront the "problems with being a female artist" in a male-dominated society. Insightfully concluding that a fierce autonomy ran through the diversity of Katsura's art production, Volk shows how Katsura was "a rare Japanese counterpart to those European and American women who sought to realize fully modernism's promise of social and aesthetic freedom."[6] Extending Volk's analysis, in this chapter I consider how Katsura negotiated the implications of total war and fascism, followed by the contradictory changes to gender status and censorship under the Allied Occupation, in her work. Specifically, I explore her use of allegory and representation of the body in key works from thirty years of her career. I argue that Katsura was invested in shifting the discursive possibilities of folkloric virtue and investigating new modes of aesthetics, often by focusing on exposure and concealment of the body in a manner that influenced the political subjectivity of both artist and viewer.

The Body under Total War

Katsura's work was a mode of politics according to Jacques Rancière's notion of "dissensus," which he defines as "a dispute over what is given and about the frame within which we see something as given."[7] Consensus, in Rancière's model, is the opposite pole: the reduction of politics to the police state. In *Dissensus: On Politics and Aesthetics,* Rancière states that aesthetics are an intrinsic part of politics:

> Art and politics each define a form of dissensus, a dissensual re-configuration of the common experience of the sensible. If there is such a thing as an "aesthetic of politics," it lies in the re-configuration of the distribution of the common through political processes of subjectivation. Correspondingly, if there is a politics of aesthetics, it lies in the practices and modes of visibility of art that re-configure the fabric of sensory experience. . . . Within any given framework, artists are those whose strategies aim to change the frames, speeds and scales according to which we perceive the visible, and combine it with a specific invisible element and a specific meaning. Such strategies are intended to make the invisible visible or to question the self-evidence of the visible; to rupture given relations between things and meanings and, inversely, to invent novel relationships between things and meanings that were previously unrelated.[8]

Rancière sees genuine art and politics as capable of creating new relations between the visible and the invisible, potentially liberating bodies from their assigned places and breaking with the "natural" order of the sensible. Yet Rancière's lack of attention to the constituents of the community leaves aside important questions about race, nationhood, and gender. Katsura, on the other hand, seemed to open up dialogue about these political stakes. In this chapter, I argue that by experimenting with the exposure and concealment of the body through allegory and material layering, Katsura reoriented aesthetic-political sensibility and disrupted forms of belonging, thereby fostering wider discourse on gender and nationhood in Japan.

Katsura's early production was rapidly circumscribed by the demands of the nation. In 1931, at age eighteen, she graduated from an all-girls high school and began private lessons in oil painting just as the state began to intensify its military operations.[9] The year 1931 and the Manchurian Incident marked the beginning of the Fifteen-Year War: a period of "total war," when all citizens were expected to mobilize on behalf of the empire. Artists were not excluded from this national mobilization and, indeed, played important roles in visually shifting a narrative of Japan's aggression into acts of glory, triumph, and self-defense.[10] By 1937, wartime action and rhetoric had moved into high gear. Japan embarked on an undeclared war with China, opening its first "comfort stations" in Nanjing and enacting the Kokumin Kokka Sōdōinhō, or National Mobilization Law, which expanded the power of the military.[11]

Ueno Chizuko points out that the government was "fully aware that the cooperation of women on the 'home front' was indispensable, and pushed ahead with the organisation of the female population. In the year following the Manchurian Incident (1931), the Greater Japan Women's Association for National Defence *(Dainippon Kokubō Fujinkai)* was hastily formed."[12] The National Mobilization Law directly affected women, even though they were not conscripted. While the rhetoric of "total war" clarified and strengthened the demand for unity with the nation, as Ryūichi Narita has pointed out, the "call for active identification with nation" was extant even in the latter half of the 1920s: "It was merely clarified under the wartime system as changing circumstances brought the national dimension to the fore."[13]

Even as early as the late 1800s, issues of gender and nationhood were intertwined in government policies. Jennifer Robertson has cogently argued that eugenics and "the concept of 'pure blood' as a criterion of authentic Japaneseness began circulating in public discourse by the 1880s in many venues and media. 'Purity' referred metaphorically to a body—including the national body—free from symbolic pollution and disease-bearing pathogens, as well as to genealogical orthodoxy."[14] In the 1940s, eugenic counseling centers opened in department stores "in order to make available to consumers information about social and race hygiene, as well as associated behaviors and practices. Women especially were targeted, as 'female citizenship' was defined not in terms of legal rights but in terms of procreation and consumption."[15] By the beginning of the twentieth century, women's role in the nation was under pressure as the Ministry of Education introduced the slogan, *Ryōsai kenbo* (Good wife, wise mother).[16] Later, the Kokumin Yūsei Hō (National Eugenics Law; 1941), which advocated sterilizing women with hereditary diseases, and *Jinkō seisaku kakuritsu yōkō* (Outline for establishing population growth policy; 1942), which aimed to prevent healthy women's access to birth control, emphasized women's role as producers of healthy, "pure," national subjects. How did Katsura interpret and respond to these dramatic changes?

In 1938, just after the National Mobilization Law went into effect and Japan began its official war with China, Katsura created *Ningen I (Human I)* and *Ningen II (Human II)* (Figures 1.1 and 1.2), two paintings that she described as products of her period of hopeless "black humor."[17] Both works, which were shown at the exhibition of the Kyū-shitsu Kai (Ninth Room Association) in 1940, seem to be responses to the eruption of declared war. The entire background of each composition is black, the latter painting detailed with thin scratches in the paint. In *Human I* five loosely formed bodies stand in line as a larger creature looks on, its gaze suggesting a Foucauldian disciplinary force. Along the bottom of *Human II,* Katsura positions a dagger-shaped body, a sword on its chest, with a small blot of red paint marking a wound. The corpse-like image, in its content and mode of representation, gives the lie to government-sponsored war paintings that glorify the unified body politic, even in death. The teeming energy and unity of war paintings is transformed into a comment on the urge to conform and its sad consequences.

In *Human I,* bodies are reduced to amorphous blobs, lined up with thoughtless obedience, each set of eyes cast in a different direction. More like slugs than like soldiers, these indistinct forms appear ready to be manipulated into any shape, just as the complacent sidelong expressions on the figures' faces and their soft bodies suggest they are more than willing to follow the leader, whoever that might be.[18] In the background, a triangular formation is a reduced version of Mount Fuji, a national symbol of strength and grace repeatedly represented by fervently patriotic and successful artists such as Yokoyama Taikan. While Yokoyama's *Mount Fuji* works as a blunt metaphor for the rising power of Japan, Katsura's rendition refutes majesty. Instead, the mountain is comically linear, foreshortened, and stumpy. It seems to foreshadow Katsura's statement in 1985:

> I used to think Mount Fuji had shape particular to itself, but I once happened to see it from right above while on an airplane, and it looked like a flat object with a big, messy *[darashinai]* hole, not at all like my image of Mount Fuji. But that was certainly the substance of Mount Fuji too. Perhaps my findings are not only about visuality but mainly about the state of my own heart.[19]

Katsura's depiction of the oft-celebrated mountain accordingly reduces its magnificence: like the bodies below, the peak is colorless and vague in shape, rather than a striking natural metaphor for the virtue and strength of the nation.

In *Human II,* the queue of formless bodies is depicted in a realm of negative space. The figures gaze at one another as though seeking direction, tiny lines of apprehension visible around their eyes, much as in *Human I.* In the center of the painting, one creature with the darkest pupils glances furtively downward to the dead or injured figure lowest in the frame. Through these anxious bodies, Katsura's representation denies the heroic greatness

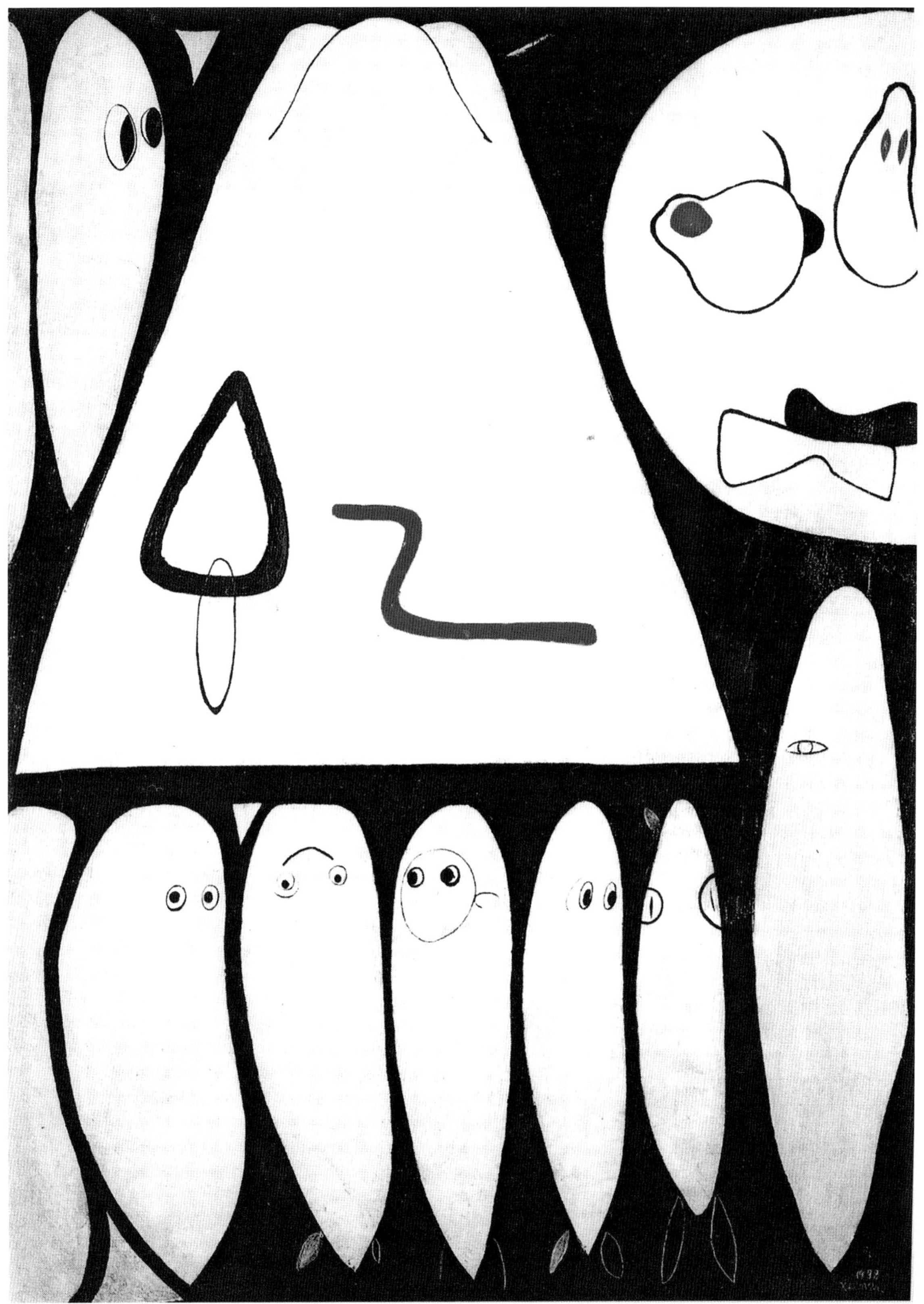

FIGURE 1.1. Katsura Yuki, *Ningen I (Human I)*, 1938. Oil on canvas, 90.9 × 64.8 cm. Copyright Katsura Akinari. Previously published in Yuki Katsura, Kazuko Sotodate, and Museum of Modern Art, Ibaraki, *Katsura Yuki no sekai* (Katsura Yuki's world) (Mito: The Museum of Modern Art, Ibaraki, 1998), 20.

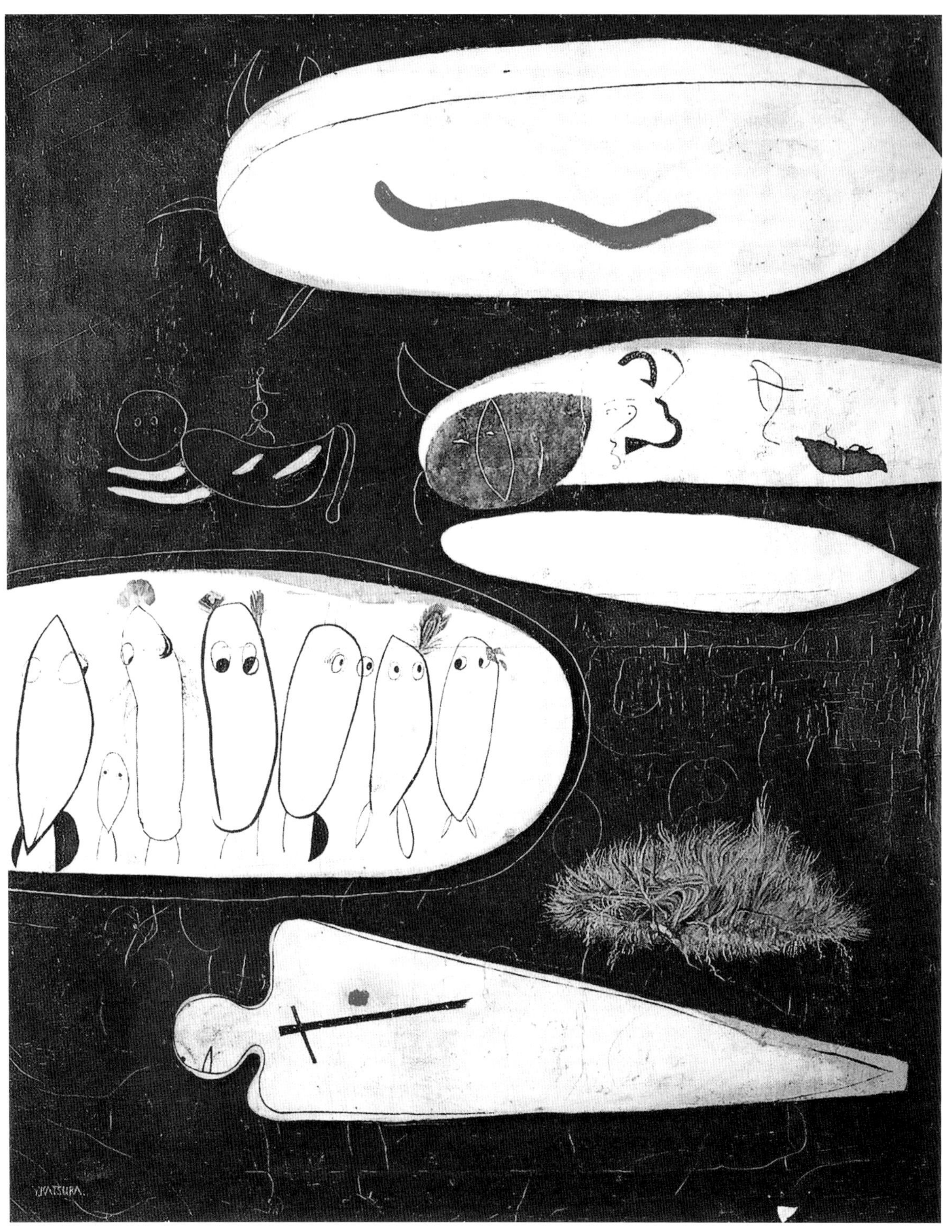

FIGURE 1.2. Katsura Yuki, *Ningen II (Human II)*, 1938. Oil on canvas, 90.8 × 72.4 cm. Copyright Katsura Akinari. Previously published in Yuki Katsura, Kazuko Sotodate, and Museum of Modern Art, Ibaraki, *Katsura Yuki no sekai* (Katsura Yuki's world) (Mito: The Museum of Modern Art, Ibaraki, 1998), 20.

of war. Painting at a time when giving one's life in the name of the country was mandated legally and through cultural hegemony, simply depicting anxiety over death was dangerous ground.[20]

Given the prevailing social conditions, Hamamoto Satoshi has noted, Katsura was rebellious.[21] To this we might add that Katsura engaged the often unspoken aesthetic debates of embodiment to articulate and refute the rising tides of nationalistic aggression.[22] In *Human I* and *Human II* she uses the formless bodies against the grain of the heroic *sensō-ga* (war paintings) that augment physical might and victory. War paintings and propaganda rely on the exposure of bodies to manifest their message of glorified unity.[23] Katsura here conceals represented bodies, averting the possibility of the figures being implicated in symbolic purity and notions of embodied physicality that were once allied with patriotism. As Rancière might say, her reworking is a form of "dissensus," an emancipation that opens up the closed effect of hegemonic ideology. Further, it shows that any aesthetic form that colludes with predicated forms of consensus can be similarly reimagined.[24] *Human I* and *Human II* enact dissent, shifting the aesthetic mode of a recognizable nationalist icon and disrupting our sense of the body politic and the politics of the body.

Yet not all of Katsura's art rebelled against the state. As Japan became increasingly militarized, citizens felt pressure to support the nation by whatever means were available to them. Artists fell in line with slogans like *Saikan hōkoku* (Serving the nation through art), with very few openly rejecting that mission.[25] In January 1940, the English-language newspaper the *Japan Times* made the connection between the nation and art overtly clear, with the headline "Japan's Art World Active in '39 Despite China Affair—Many Good Exhibitions Held Downtown, National Art Movement Gains Strength." The review went on to mention Katsura and Yoshihara Jirō, leader of the Gutai Art Association, as standout painters of abstract art.[26] Katsura was soon asked to participate more directly in the war effort. In the early 1940s, she was invited by fellow artist Hasegawa Haruko to help organize a women's wing of the Rikugun Bijutsu Kyōkai (Army Art Association). Katsura demurred, saying that she was *namakemono* (lazy).[27] Hasegawa and others nevertheless formed the Joryū Bijutsu Kyōkai (Women's Art Organization) to support the war effort and, according to Katsura, later reprimanded her for not supporting her country.[28]

Eventually, Katsura agreed to participate in the creation of a large-scale artwork in collaboration with other women in the group (Figures 1.3 and 1.4).[29] Katsura drew the draft, with others contributing sections.[30] Unlike in *Human I* and *Human II,* naturalistic representations of bodies became the foundation of the image. The artists' drawings were reconstructions based on clippings from newspapers and magazines, including images of female firefighters, female farmers, and female students.[31] The work, grandly titled *Daitōasen kōkoku fujo kaidō no zu (The Painting of All Laboring Women in the Empire during the Great East Asian War)* and hereafter referred to as *Kaidō no zu,* consists of two parts: one with the scenery of spring and summer and one with the scenery of fall and winter. Displayed at the

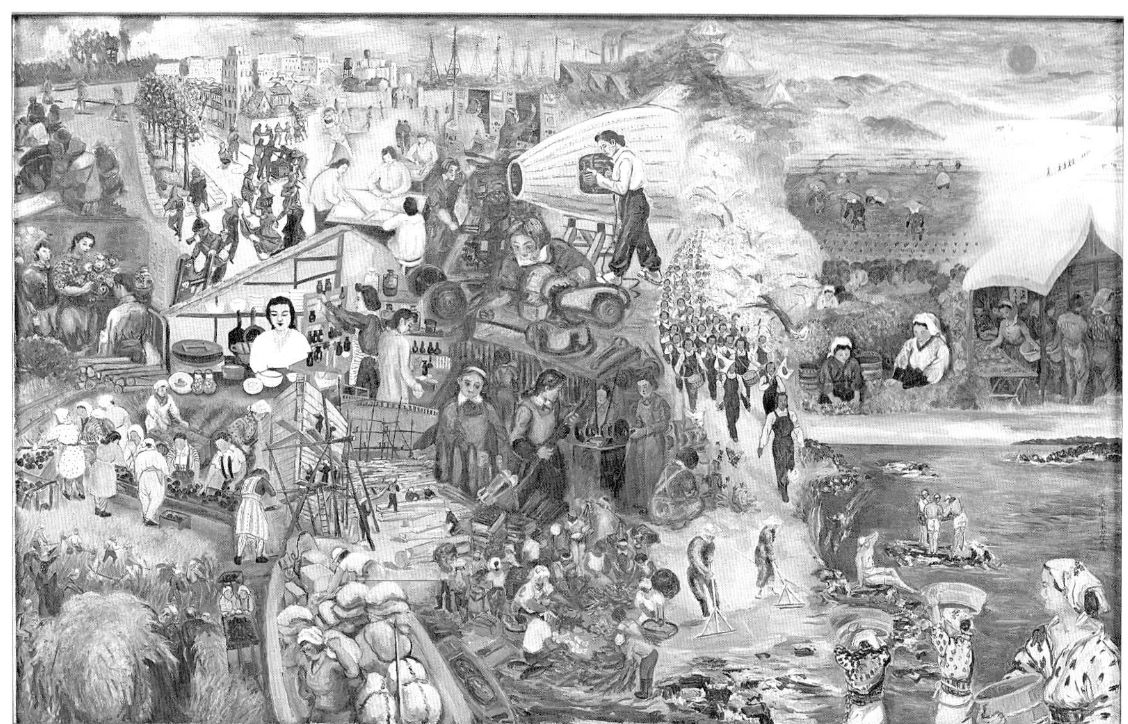

FIGURE 1.3. Hasegawa Haruko, Nakada Kikuyo (Yoshie), Katsura Yukiko, and others, *Daitōasen kōkoku fujo kaidō no zu (The Painting of All Laboring Women in the Empire during the Great East Asian War, Fall)*, 1944. 186 × 300 cm. Courtesy of Yasukuni Shrine. Copyright Katsura Akinari and Hasegawa Masaru.

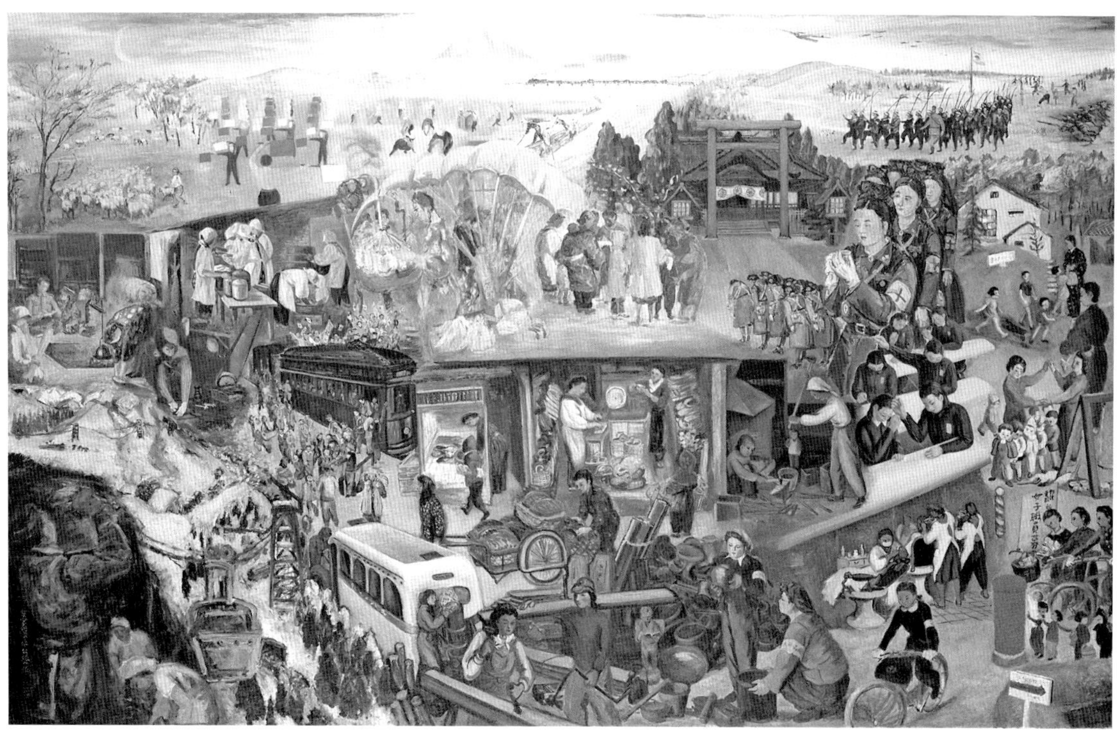

FIGURE 1.4. Hasegawa Haruko, Nakada Kikuyo (Yoshie), Katsura Yukiko, and others, *Daitōasen kōkoku fujo kaidō no zu (The Painting of All Laboring Women in the Empire during the Great East Asian War, Spring and Winter)*, 1944. 186 × 300 cm. Copyright Katsura Akinari and Hasegawa Masaru. Courtesy of Hakozaki Shrine.

Military Art Exhibition in Tokyo in March 1944, it emphasized the role of the female body in relation to the nation. On the back of the canvases are the signatures of Hasegawa Haruko, Nakada Kikuyo (Yoshie), and Katsura Yukiko (who used her full given name, although she most often signed her works as Yuki), indicating their central role in the project.[32] The collage-like piece foregrounds the multiplicity of women's abilities through the representation of their bodies and therefore could be read as a feminist piece of war propaganda. Another interpretation might be that it is a cynical statement about the manipulation of women's bodies by the state. Hariu Ichirō concurs with this sentiment. In his discussion on Katsura, he notes that this collaborative experience "gave her the opportunity to satirize women supporting everyday life, and to sharpen one's ironic viewpoint."[33]

Yet this conclusion is weakened by the fact that many of these women also participated in the highly controversial (if not morally questionable) exhibition *Tatakau shōnenhei (Fighting Child Soldiers)* from September to December 1943, which featured 120 works, all depicting children as soldiers. Katsura and others (including Maruki Toshi, who would later go on to create the *Hiroshima Panels,* which condemn war in general and nuclear war specifically) contributed art pieces and texts to *Fighting Child Soldiers,* which attempted to motivate parents to send their underage sons to war because of troop shortages.[34] Katsura's contribution was a postcard, *Enshū o oete (After Maneuvers)* (Figure 1.5), featuring young soldiers driving tanks in a line under a beautiful sky. Katsura even included text describing the soldiers as "baby eagles" training in "Japan, the greatest country in the world."[35] The exhibit, which was not mandated by the government, was so controversial that a backlash against it was evident in several newspaper articles.[36]

Yet the theme had made its way into popular culture. Kimonos were even designed that featured images of children as soldiers.[37] Thus, Katsura and others who participated in the exhibit were part of a strong and growing majority. During the 1930s and 1940s, as art historian Bert Winther-Tamaki has shown, painting the individual body of the Japanese citizen as one fully dedicated to the state, physically and psychically, became prevalent. In *Maximum Embodiment,* Winther-Tamaki describes the richly dense paintings of Ai-Mitsu, Fujita Tsuguharu, and others who endeavored to convey the strength of the Japanese body in their paintings (Figure 1.6).[38] *Kaidō no zu* suggests the strength and versatility of the female Japanese body rather than the male, while the flatness and vernacular nature of the work's repainted clippings denies the embodied materialism that other painters sought. Although in keeping with government expectations for wartime art (indeed, the piece is currently in the collection of Yasukuni Shrine, a site that glorifies the Pacific War), *Kaidō no zu* is unusual in its focus on women as strong, versatile, and skillful workers.[39] Images from the period in the state-sponsored, internationally distributed publication *Nippon* showcase modern women as capable factory workers but emphasize that historically women have taken part in more domestic pursuits. In a two-page spread from 1938, the cutting-edge publication depicts women as cultural repositories: beautiful, gentle, homogeneous, and engaged in traditional crafts (Figure 1.7).[40] One cannot deny that the

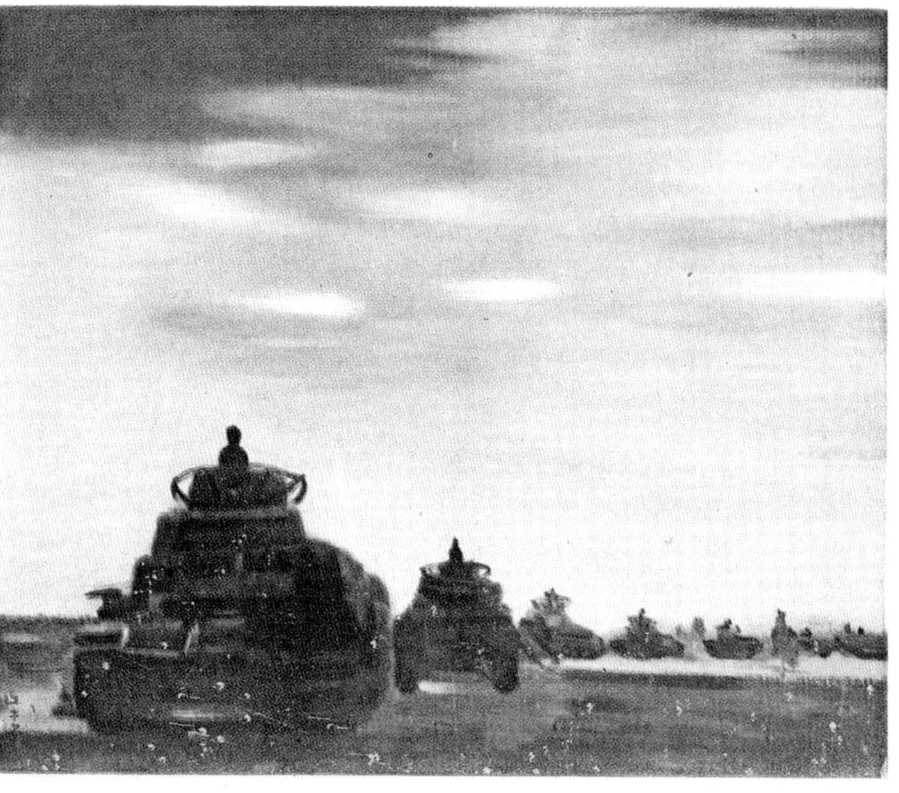

FIGURE 1.5. Katsura Yuki, *Enshū o oete (After Maneuvers)*, postcard, 1943. Approximately 10 × 14.8 cm. Copyright Katsura Akinari. Private collection.

suggested harmonious union of the hardworking figures in *Kaidō no zu* was premised on imperial desire in a manner akin to the *Nippon* piece.

How did Katsura come to feel about her participation in the exhibition and the collaborative painting, both of which relied heavily on marshaling the representation of the human body as a committed and steadfast pillar of the nation? In later interviews, she suggested, perhaps defensively, that it was at Hasegawa's urging that she eventually agreed to participate. Importantly, *Kaidō no zu* also marked a gradual turning point in Katsura's oeuvre: whereas in the collaborative work the multiplicity of bodies is the primary content, in her work after the war, naturalistic human bodies rarely appear.[41] Perhaps her complicity with the militaristic state troubled Katsura, making her aware of the dangers of consensus, of allowing the body—both the represented body and the artist's own body—to conform to the demands of the state. She refrained from making an outright war painting, or any other image that might be perceived to be in collusion with the government, again. Significantly, in her works thereafter Katsura went so far as to eschew bodily presence by wrapping it, zoomorphizing it, or obfuscating it, thereby going against the grain of *sensō-ga* and even making tacit critiques of the state.

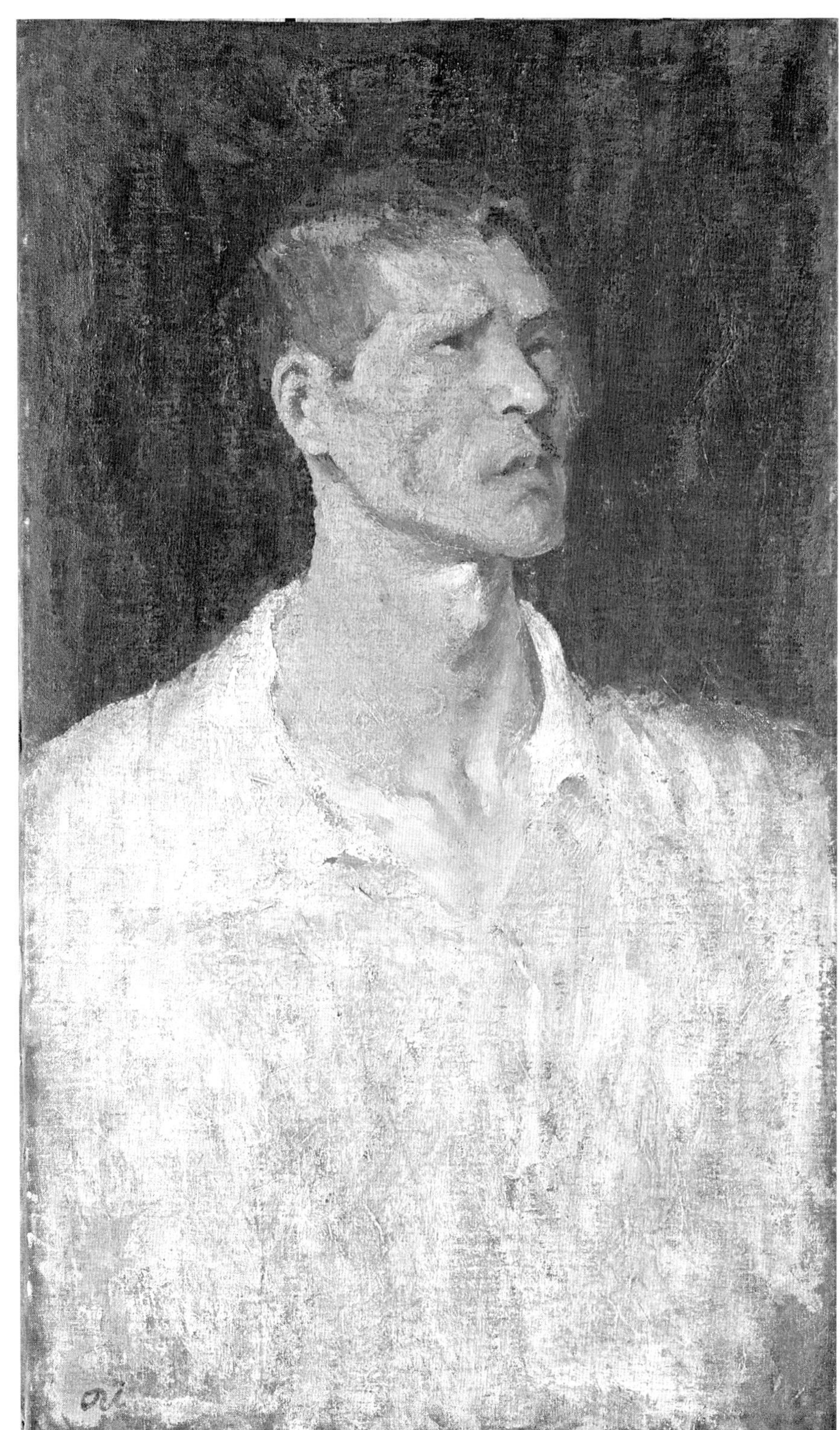

FIGURE 1.6.
Ai-Mitsu, *Jigazō
(Self-Portrait)*,
1944. Oil on
canvas, 79 × 47
cm. National
Museum of
Modern Art Tokyo
and DNP Art and
Communications.

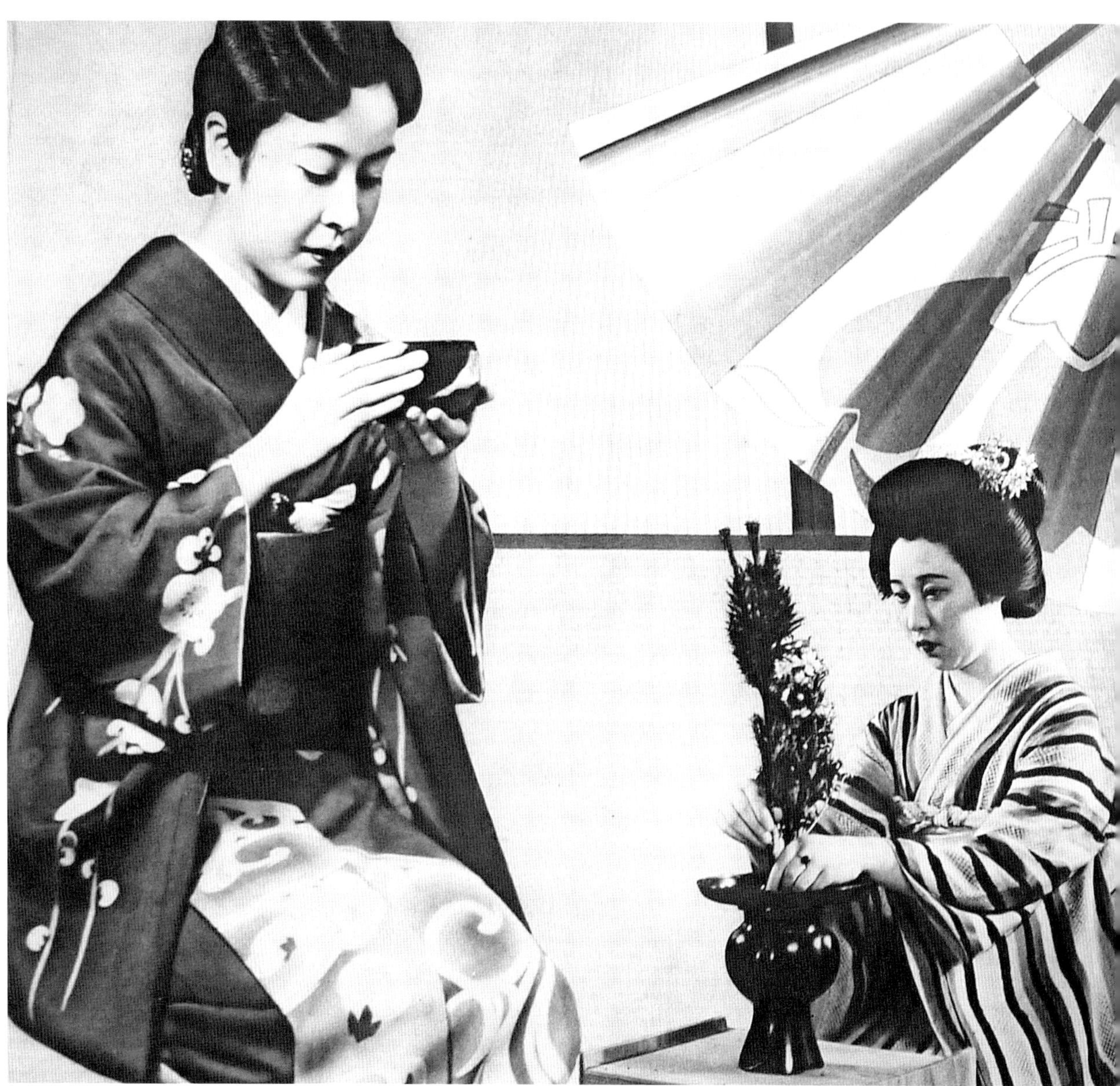

FIGURE 1.7. Natori Yōnosuke, *Untitled,* from *Nippon* (1938), 21–22. Courtesy of the Japan Foundation Library Collection.

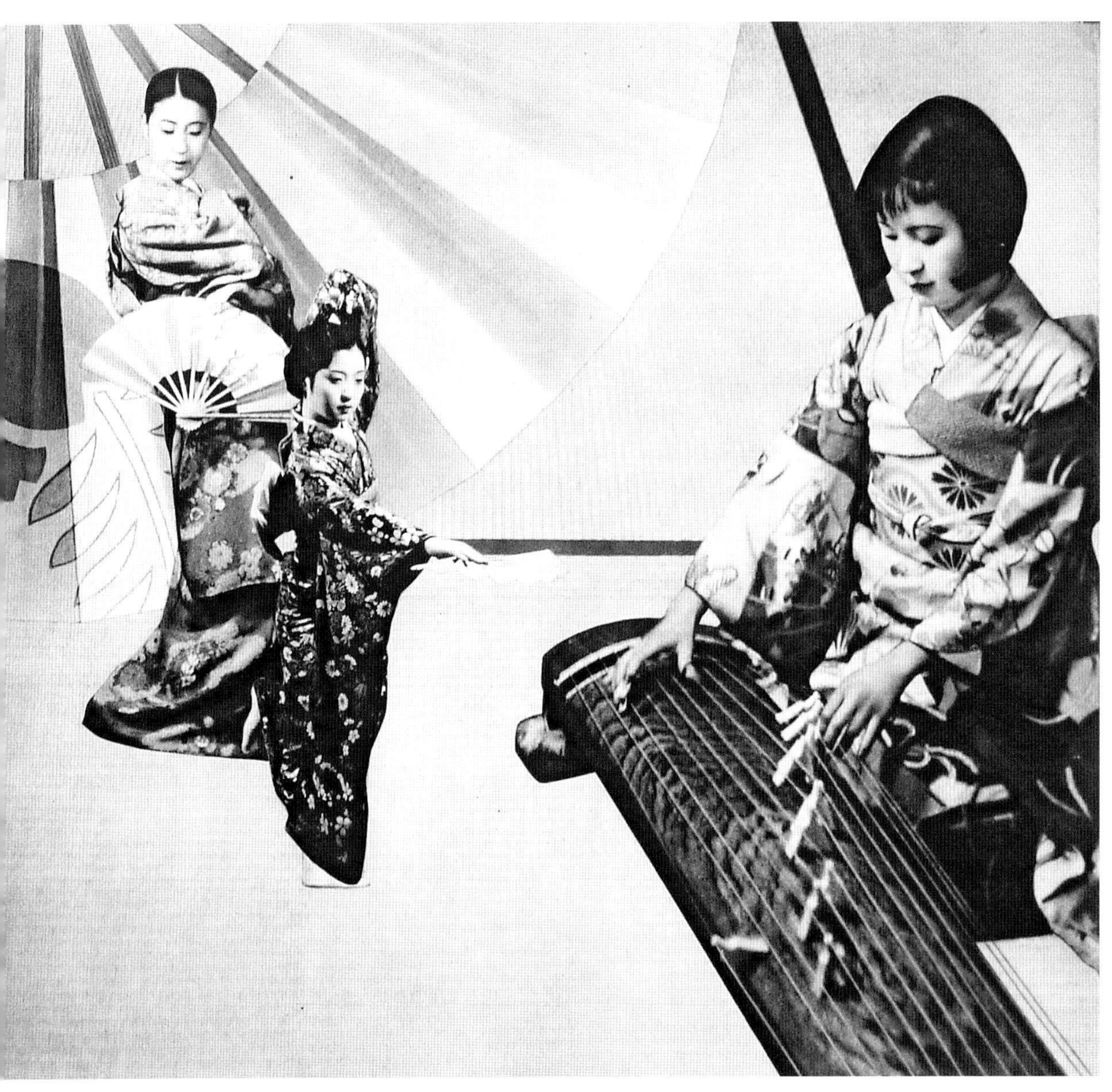

Shifting Folkloric Virtue

In 1945, as the Allied Occupation troops arrived, censorship shifted rather than disappeared. While General MacArthur and his staff were busy rewriting the Japanese constitution, keen attention was also paid to art and representation. The occupation leadership drafted detailed and wide-ranging rules, including strict regulations against the raising of the military flag but extending also to such things as showing images of American GIs in film or in print, lest these remind the citizens of the war or, worse, the ongoing occupation itself.[42] Sharalyn Orbaugh has pointed out that the first official directive of the supreme commander of the Allied Powers after Japan's surrender was to establish the right to perform censorship. Quoting an official memorandum, Orbaugh notes: "'Destructive criticism of the Allied Forces of Occupation [or anything] which might invite mistrust or resentment of those troops' was outlawed."[43] Visual or textual references to the atomic bomb and the devastation of Hiroshima and Nagasaki were not permitted, nor were allusions to the firebombing of Tokyo.[44] The Allies had a keen appreciation for the politics of vision. These laws were relaxed in 1948 and discontinued by 1949; however, the effects of censorship remained. As Jay Rubin observes: "The flood of atomic bomb related materials that emerged in 1952 also illustrated that the mere presence of the Allied occupiers had been enough to discourage publishers and filmmakers from revealing the full extent of the nuclear horror."[45] Although much has been written about Japan's eager embrace of democracy, the United States offered a very particular brand of liberal democracy, one that imposed a disciplinary visual regime on art and the citizens who might view it.[46] Censorship by the Japanese state also continued long after the end of the Allied Occupation.[47]

Katsura's critical attitude toward the political climate revealed itself well before the occupation was over (as *Human I* and *Human II* suggest), and zoomorphic allegory increasingly became her principal tool in her provocative work. As early as 1948, she staged painterly satires such as *Saru kani gassen (The Battle of the Monkey and the Crab)* (Plate 1), in which she recast a popular Japanese fable. The original tale tells of a crab that is outwitted by a monkey and, in darker versions, is killed by the monkey. The crab's offspring then rely on a host of allies to seek revenge and thereby fulfill their filial obligations. Decades before Katsura, in 1923, Japanese novelist Akutagawa Ryūnosuke (1892–1927) also reworked the fable as satire. In his short story, after avenging his mother's death by attacking the monkey, the crab receives the death penalty and his accomplices are sentenced to life imprisonment. In a scathing, humorous tone, Akutagawa recounts the responses to the judgment from various members of society, including Marxists, Buddhists, and politicians.[48] Restaging such traditional fables offered artists and writers a way to reenvision the past toward a new future. Folktales are forms of oral tradition that prescribe the moral logic of a culture or, in this case, of a nation, promoting a consensual notion of "commonsense."[49] The Japanese government cleverly augmented the visual power of these moral orders through film, illustrated books, and state-sanctioned art. Katsura broke with this consensual model and raised the underlying ethical questions: For whom do these rules apply? Who has dictated them, and for what purpose?

While these folkloric themes are familiar to many Japanese, they are indecipherable to someone without knowledge of East Asian folklore. This puts Katsura at odds with what Gennifer Weisenfeld has described as a tendency among contemporary Japanese artists, such as Murakami Takashi and Araki Nobuyoshi, toward "reinscribing tradition."[50] Simultaneously counterculture and hybrid, as well as generalizing and culturally nationalist, these artists rely on received essentialized notions of Japanese tradition that authenticate their production in the eyes of the globalized marketplace. Ultimately their artworks, although contemporary in content and medium, tend to appeal to the notion of tradition as fixed. This approach was echoed in earlier art genres such as *Nihonga* (Japanese-style painting), popular in the 1930s and 1940s. Katsura's composition diverges from this direction. While some artists were ambitiously committed to creating art that would be well received in the international community, Katsura took up themes that would likely be impenetrable for anyone without knowledge of their subtle folkloric references.[51] In this sense, Katsura, one of the most well-read and well-traveled artists of her time, was very much focused on the conditions of politics and painting in Japan. Her visual tactics were echoed in her essay "Duralumin Wall" from 1952, in which she argued that those who thought Japanese art was better than French art and those who thought it worse were both falling into the same trap. Instead, she suggested,

> we should turn our eyes far and wide to the world and, needless to say, I think it would be worthless if [our art] looks like our neighbors. . . . If the head of a household is an elegant and brilliant person, then they would not imitate their neighbor. . . . They would think that their neighbors and themselves are both human beings, but they had grown up differently and under different circumstances so it's natural that they should create different things.[52]

Following her own advice, Katsura's painting *The Battle of the Monkey and the Crab* is layered in ambiguity and humor, distancing itself from the clear-cut didactic mode of the folktale. Rather than a Confucian lesson in filial piety, Katsura produces an ambivalent and theatrical version of the story. In the top right corner, the rotund crab humorously relishes its victim status, nursing its wounds with an ice bag on its head and wrapped in an excessive amount of bandages. Its self-absorption is further indicated by spatial distinctions: the crab is on the right side of the painting, housed in a small, square area with its own distinct roof. A second roof frames another character in the story, the *usu* (mortar), which has sprouted arms and legs and dances with revelry on the pitiable monkey, wearing a *hachimaki* (headband) and the summer outfit of a traditional Japanese villager. Standing on top of the monkey, a small bee joins in the vengeful revelry, dressed as a Japanese military commander wielding a sword. Katsura casts a diagonal line of shadow across the work, emphasizing the dark elements within the lighthearted parody. Through its ambivalent but playful tone, this version of the tale suggests that revenge is a childish and aggressive impulse that can easily transform into a mob mentality.

Katsura's representation seeks to destabilize the meanings associated with the fable on multiple levels. Filial piety is questioned rather than revered, and violent retribution is no longer upheld as a moral ideal. In *The Battle of the Monkey and the Crab,* Katsura leaves the viewer to engage with the image and at the same time decipher his or her own moral position in relation to it. Like many artists and thinkers in the postwar period, she sought to expose representation as misleading and rhetoric as untrustworthy. Her refiguring of allegorical fables invites comparison with Paul de Man's conception of allegory as having a metalinguistic function that can heighten the ambiguity of meaning and demand an investment on the part of the viewer.[53] This is precisely why allegory is Katsura's most pivotal tool.[54] For de Man, modes of discourse often rely on binary oppositions, which metaphor can disrupt, revealing the tensions between representations and reading. As de Man reveals the limits of "textual authority," Katsura similarly reveals the potential misreadings of representational authority and illustrates allegory as a "failure to read."[55] Katsura playfully asks her contemporary viewers to reconsider the ways the folktale makes meaning as well as the stakes of aggression and retaliation embedded in the original tale.

Katsura's refiguring of the fable takes on greater meaning when considered in relation to wartime propaganda. The wartime state relied not only on *sensō-ga* to direct the sentiments of the nation toward unification for battle but also on films and visual culture that were intended to shape the outlook of Japanese children.[56] For example, the animated film *Dōbutsu tonarigumi* (Animal Neighborhood Association), produced in 1941, shows a host of cute and humorous anthropomorphized animals who, brought together as a community, work to keep each other safe in troubled times (Figure 1.8).[57] In one scene in this ten-minute short, a fire breaks out in the neighborhood. Following the alarmed cry of one of the villagers, the animals rapidly form an organized team of water carriers to douse the flames. Once the danger has been removed, the villagers, composed of a rabbit, monkeys, an old goat, a bear family, and other creatures, raise their hands in a unanimous and euphoric cry of "Banzai!" The film's theme centers on collectivity in a manner that discreetly underscores consensus in allegiance to the nation. Thomas Lamarre has aptly characterized this type of anthropomorphism as "speciesism," which "entails the displacement of problems associated with race relations onto species relations, and vice versa."[58] Lamarre shows how Japanese animation often relied on speciesism to characterize the imperialist Greater East Asia Co-prosperity Sphere as a harmonious, desirable union: "In effect, speciesism in Japanese wartime animation constituted a powerful attempt to move beyond (Western) racism, a concerted effort to imagine the multinational or multiethnic world proposed in pan-Asianist thinking."[59] He writes:

> With reference to Japan's national empire, I see not only a process of excluding, "inferiorizing," and dominating others through the generation of a sense of Japanese solidarity and

superiority but also simultaneously a process of including and celebrating others—the realm of pan-Asianism, the Greater East Asian Co-Prosperity Sphere, and multicultural ideals. Too much emphasis has been placed on how so-called common people are passively duped or tricked into backing the nation and too little on how people come to desire empire, actively enough.[60]

Lamarre is careful to emphasize that this form of speciesism, common in wartime propaganda, became even more prevalent in the postwar period. Pointing to Tezuka Osamu's animated series *Janguru taitei* (Jungle emperor, 1951–54—later adapted for North American syndication as *Kimba the White Lion*) and other examples, Lamarre states: "Postwar manga and animation refine, intensify, and redouble the wartime aspiration of 'overcoming racism' by summoning and implementing (often in the context of war) a multispecies ideal, which often takes the form of a peaceable kingdom in which different populations (species) coexist productively and prosperously."[61]

Katsura's interest in speciesism should be considered in its discursive relation to the visual culture ubiquitous at the time. Her own painted references to fables that foreground

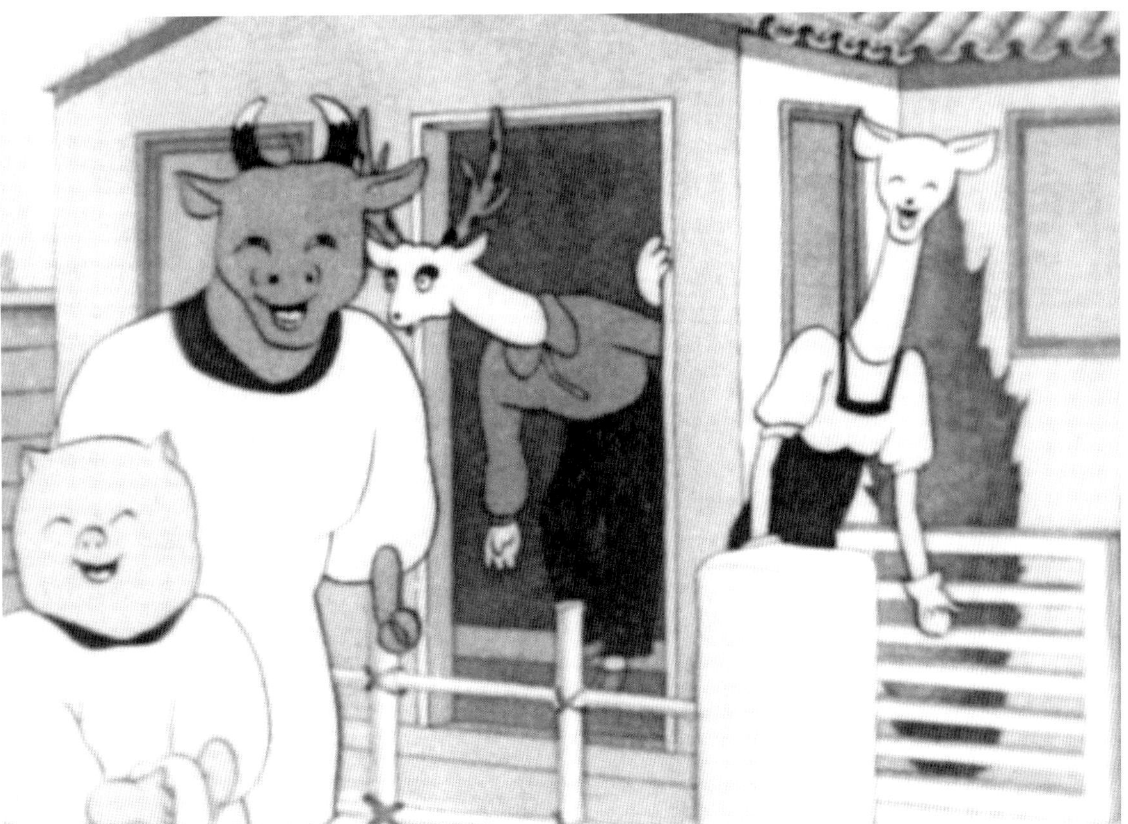

FIGURE 1.8. Japanese government, *Dōbutsu tonarigumi* (Animal Neighborhood Association), still from animated film, 1941. Courtesy of the Japan Cultural Foundation for Animation.

representations of animals, such as *The Battle of the Monkey and the Crab* and her award-winning painting *Gonbe and Crow* (see Plate 10), draw on propaganda that sought to naturalize unity and support for the state at the same time they destabilize, pluralize, and question the moral messages that were previously contained within such fables.[62] These works stop short of the cuteness displayed by Tezuka's figures, but they draw on the desires that speciesism piques. Katsura casts her figures with a distinctive darker edge. The monkey's buckteeth and scrawny and out-of-focus limbs mark him as a much more ambivalent figure than the animals in *Dōbutsu tonarigumi* or *Janguru taitei*. Unlike anime and manga animals, which demonstrate what Lamarre dubs "plasmaticity," or the sense of their invulnerability and resilience to injury, the monkey seems uncertain of bodily safety. His arm has been bent at such a jagged angle it appears to have been lopped off, and his body and face are compressed to the floor as the other characters dance on him. Katsura pushes up against the edge of plasmaticity, and up against the limits of the viewer's empathy, disturbing the subsurface notions of national unity at work in speciesism.

Gender and Nation in Postwar Japan

As John Dower notes regarding postwar Japan, "No modern nation ever has rested on a more alien constitution—or a more unique wedding of monarchism, democratic idealism, and pacifism; and few, if any, alien documents have ever been as thoroughly internalized and vigorously defended as this national charter would come to be."[63] The General Headquarters (GHQ) rapidly put together the constitution after General MacArthur concluded that domestic forces would be unable to write a charter that would not contravene the Potsdam Declaration. MacArthur selected twenty-four members of the drafting committee, four of whom were women.[64] One of those four women was Beate Sirota, who has only recently been celebrated for her role in the process.[65] Sirota, who, according to Dower, was the only member of the committee with any "genuine knowledge" of the country, helped to make advances for women a key part of the new constitution.[66] At the time, she was twenty-two years old. She had attended elementary school in Tokyo as a child and had graduated from Mills College in California with a degree in modern languages; she was fluent in Japanese as well as other languages. She had returned to Japan after the surrender to look for her parents, with whom she had lost contact, supporting herself by working in the Tokyo government section doing research on women and minor political parties.[67] In her *New York Times* obituary, Sirota is described as "almost single-handedly" writing women's rights into the constitution: "Her work—drafting language that gave women a set of legal rights pertaining to marriage, divorce, property and inheritance that they had long been without in Japan's feudal society—had an effect on their status that endures to this day."[68]

How would Japan enact these new demands of the constitution? Most Japanese felt a mixture of hope, cynicism, and plain confusion about the new charter. The fact that it was written by the GHQ and other foreigners such as Sirota heightened the perception of it as an alien document. The *Asahi* newspaper, for example, described the government draft of the charter as "somewhat ill fitted, like a borrowed suit of clothes."[69] Nonetheless, the constitution went into effect on May 3, 1947, with much pomp and circumstance, including a large ceremony at the emperor's palace. Almost immediately, Japan's inability to live up to the new standards of gender equality came under fire. Following the imperial celebration (a strange irony in and of itself), the emperor's youngest brother, Prince Takahito of Mikasa, wrote a letter to a newspaper lambasting the emperor for not including the prince's wife's name on the invitation and for not including the empress's name in the announcement of the event. The prince concluded it was no surprise that Japanese women elected to the Diet (Japan's bicameral legislature) for the first time were faced with great challenges.[70]

Challenges for women were not limited to those in the Diet. Women artists, then as now, had difficulty receiving the same level of attention as male artists. Maki Kaneko has insightfully shown how the National Museum of Modern Art in Tokyo has consistently set up a binarized, masculinized view of the war and the postwar period in the section of its permanent exhibition space titled "Art during and after the War." She notes that between 2002 and 2012 the museum displayed campaign-record paintings,

> with almost no exceptions, on the right wall of the room, facing works by such artists as Matsumoto Shunsuke [1912–48], Ai-Mitsu (1907–1946), and Kazuki Yasuo (1911–1974) hung on the left wall. The artists featured on the left wall are generally regarded as victims of war or those artists who, according to the text panel, "created works that aim to leave evidence of humanity." . . .
>
> . . . While female figures were not entirely absent from the display, the domination of males both as subjects and creators was palpable, as if war, resistance, defeat, and art-making were the territory of Japanese men. . . . This significant homogeneity in terms of gender, ethnicity/race, and nationality, and the unequivocal distinction made between military collaborators and humanists, inform us of the lasting power of the foundational narrative, which aggregated the multifaceted constituencies and dimensions of the Japanese imperialist enterprise, colonialism, and wars into the homosocial melodrama of Japanese struggle, conversion, rescue, performed exclusively by two male protagonists: Emperor Hirohito and General MacArthur.[71]

Katsura has been notably absent from these retrospective wartime narratives, despite the fact that she inserted herself strategically in the discourse of gender and nation in the 1950s. Her oeuvre demonstrates that she was well aware of the struggles of feminism, often illustrating how women, on the verge of liberation, were not yet perceived as fully embodied citizens. For example, Katsura's 1953 painting *Fujin no hi (Women's Day)* (Plate 2) is an ambivalent celebration of advances for women brought about by the new constitution, illustrated through themes of exposure and concealment. The painting conveys the double registers of hope and confusion predominant in the postwar period. In the composition, a woman stands central, wearing a peasant's dress, one hand raised in a gesture of victory, her fingers grazing the top of the canvas, the other hand wrapped around the bamboo handle of a broom. With the bristles pointing upward, the broom is changed from a house-cleaning implement to a symbol of domestic duties overturned. Katsura's woman is represented in a manner unlike the feminized, well-groomed women featured in the ubiquitous cosmetics advertisements circulating at the time. The housewife's wide-legged stance is grounded and ready for labor. Despite the triumphant nature of the work's title, it is difficult to read the image as altogether emancipatory. Instead, Katsura paints the ambivalence of politics: "the confrontation between the power and the impotence of a body, between a life and its possibilities," as Rancière writes.[72]

A comparison of the final composition with a pencil, pastel, and watercolor study done for *Women's Day* reveals how Katsura consciously emphasizes a sense of uncertainty in the image (Figure 1.9). For example, in the study, the figure wears a simple brown dress, but in the painting, Katsura has added a white apron—a reminder that freedom from domestic duty has not been reached. The apron may also reference the white *kappōgi,* which, in the 1930s and 1940s, was the uniform for the National Defense Women's Organization (established in 1932 to provide aid to soldiers and their families), suggesting the dual demands of home and state on women's bodies. In Katsura's study, a belt-like rope around the woman's middle is tied in an elongated bow, fitted against the dress. In contrast, in the final version the rope has become another entity. It now hovers loosely around the woman's waist, forming an uneven, knotty hole at the center of her body. Rather than the smooth texture that appeared in the study, the rope is now thick, with visible coils coarsened from apparent overuse. Positioned at the front of the woman's body, the rope mitigates the viewer's sense of bodily access and suggests the limitations of newfound freedom.[73]

The rope reappears in later works from the mid-1950s, such as *Hito to sakana (Human and Fish)* and *Tora no i o karita kitsune (Donkey in a Lion's Skin),* as a sign of conflict and contention. Nakamura Hiroshi has pointed out that viewers might mistakenly assume Katsura's rope to be a commonly used material at the time, but it appeared outdated and traditional even in the 1950s.[74] In this light, we might understand how Katsura purposefully conflates an image of tradition with a motif of tension and restriction, implicitly demanding greater change.

Modifications to the color scheme of *Women's Day* further alter the tone of the final composition. The woman's dress has become a vibrant purple, setting the figure off against the complex white vortex of space behind her. Unlike the simple background in the sketch, the painting's brightly lit, whirling atmosphere contrasts with the woman's steady stance, and consequently the figure appears to be tilting forward, off balance. Such an uneven background suggests ephemerality and the temporal limits of women's "day," where an ever-changing political landscape can upend any social progress.[75] This turbulent white

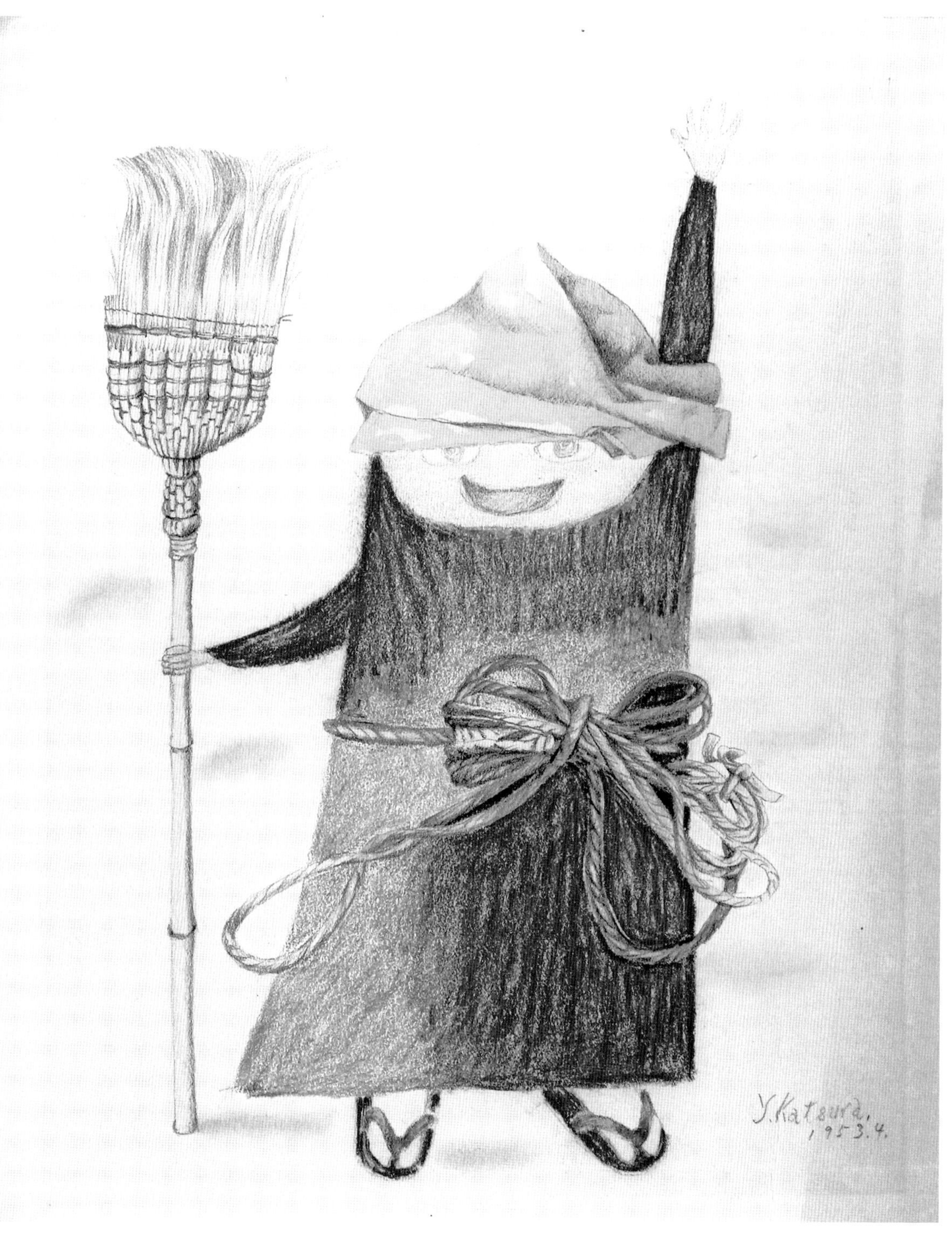

FIGURE 1.9. Katsura Yuki, *Fujin no hi*—sukecchi (study for *Women's Day*), 1953. Pencil, pastel, and watercolor on paper, 35 × 28 cm. Copyright Katsura Akinari. Courtesy of the Museum of Art, Tokyo.

background would reemerge, with more sinister effects, in her painting about the *Lucky Dragon* incident of 1954.

Representing the *Lucky Dragon* Incident

Katsura's most overtly political work is *Human and Fish,* created in 1954 (Plate 3). This is an abstract figural, yet at the time instantly recognizable, reference to the *Daigo Fukuryū Maru (Lucky Dragon 5)* incident, in which a Japanese tuna trawler was exposed to and contaminated by nuclear fallout on March 1, 1954, as the result of U.S. testing of a thermonuclear device on Bikini Atoll. This tragedy triggered political action, incited civil disobedience, and increased tensions between Japan and the United States. The incident was a frightening demonstration of the willingness of the United States to exercise power and hegemony over Asia less than a decade after hundreds of thousands had been killed in the atomic bombings of Hiroshima and Nagasaki. Moreover, the immense spread of radiation generated by the thermonuclear test suggested that the American government did not have a firm sense of, much less control over, its own destructive capabilities. Scientists at the time reported that the blast far exceeded expectations: "Military teams making the measurements at the coral reef were told to expect a blast of 7 megatons (7 million tons of TNT), the biggest explosion ever (the bomb on Hiroshima measured 0.02 megatons). The Bikini device detonated with an actual force of 15 megatons, more than double the yield predicted."[76] The new nuclear "super" weapons dwarfed the capacity of the atomic bombs used in 1945. Hundreds of residents of Rongelap were covered with radioactive ash following the Bikini Atoll test, as were numerous U.S. military personnel (the latter were rapidly removed from the exposed areas and treated).

The trawler *Lucky Dragon* had been circulating forty miles outside the fallout zone designated by the U.S. military when the twenty-three crew members began to show symptoms of radiation exposure.[77] The men reported nausea and skin inflammation (their skin blackened two days following the explosion), but the problem was not diagnosed as radiation sickness until after the ship had returned home. Tragically, *Lucky Dragon* radio operator Kuboyama Aikichi died from exposure on September 23 at the age of forty. The United States refused to acknowledge that his death was linked to exposure to the "death ash," despite an autopsy proving otherwise.[78] Some four hundred thousand mourners attended his funeral. Fear and panic spread when news broke that the ship had delivered nine tons of irradiated tuna to the Tsukiji market, the largest wholesale fish market in Tokyo, as well as to other (distant) markets.[79] It seemed to many that the United States had the power to corrupt the Japanese national body without consequence.[80]

Antinuclear activism coalesced around the event, and the *Lucky Dragon* incident became a starting point for a large-scale international antinuclear movement—a movement that was gendered from the outset. Immediately after the news of the irradiated fish spread, housewives of the Suginami Ward in Tokyo began circulating a petition against nuclear warfare; they also helped bring together local movements across the nation.[81] Members of this movement convened at the first international Mothers' Congress in 1955 in Japan under the (rather cumbersome) slogan "It is the earnest desire of all mothers that the life they have created be nurtured and protected." The language and social roles cultivated by the group intimated the mutually constitutive discourses of gender and national politics that persisted in the postwar period. It was powerful rhetoric: by August 1955, more than thirty million signatures had been gathered on petitions protesting atomic bombs.[82]

Initially, the antinuclear movement united members of the Communist and Social Democratic Parties in Japan against nuclear activity and, by extension, against allowing continued unchecked American influence over national politics. But as the Cold War raged on, the issue divided along party lines, with some supporting the Soviet Union's nuclear tests and others critical of that stance.[83] The U.S. interest in nuclear warfare was directly related to the Cold War. President Eisenhower, in 1954, had described the urgent need to ensure that Japan's industrial rise (and potential for supporting industrial warfare) did not fall under Soviet control. Losing Japan, he warned, would mean the United States would lose control of the Pacific; the area would become a Communist stronghold.[84] Nuclear tests were perceived as important to technological advancement in Cold War defense weaponry, but it also seems likely that this spectacular display of power in the Pacific was a bold assertion of American influence over the region.

The visual display of the power of the atomic bomb in the United States makes for striking comparisons to the visual treatment of the bomb in Japan, where art and photography focused explicitly on the effects on Japanese bodies. The Bikini Atoll test was not the first of its kind. Another test bomb, called "Mike," had been dropped on Enewetak Atoll on October 31, 1952. In 1954, images of that explosion recirculated after the Federal Civil Defense Administration released a photograph to the public. Art historian John O'Brian has described how a photograph of the ferocious orange bomb was featured in *Life* magazine on May 3, 1954 (just two months after the Bikini Atoll incident), with only the simple caption "Fireball Boils Brightly" (Plate 4).[85] The image, like the frequently reproduced image of the atomic bombing of Nagasaki, showcases the mushroom cloud as scientific spectacle—even an achievement. Repercussions of the explosion, such as the damage to biological life, are not, literally or metaphorically, part of the picture.[86]

Significantly, this image was prominently displayed as the final photograph in the highly attended exhibition *The Family of Man,* held at New York's Museum of Modern Art in 1955.[87] It was the only photograph to be displayed in color. In Rey Chow's words, "Following Heidegger's suggestion that in modernity the world has come to be grasped and conceived as 'a picture,' we may say that in the wake of the atomic bombs the world has come to be grasped and conceived as a target—to be destroyed as soon as it can be made visible."[88] Indeed, the visibility of the bomb and its targeted effects seemed to gather more attention than the lives of those it affected. O'Brian describes this problematic emphasis on the visual effects of the bomb as "atomicity," meaning "the structural force and the visual effects produced by processes of nuclear fission and fusion. . . . Atomicity places a premium on scientific nuclear discourse as opposed to discussion of the bomb's realpolitik instrumentality as a weapon, its power to obliterate whole populations, to contaminate the natural world and to awe enemies."[89] From Japan's perspective as a country situated as a base to launch the Korean War and as a bulwark against feared Communist influence, the Cold War felt incredibly hot.

In *Human and Fish* (Plate 3), Katsura's rendition of these events from 1954, three fish painted with thick white outlines appear on a gray surface (perhaps referencing the fishing trawler), while the fish that remain in the water are nothing more than shadows. Strong black lines circulate around the humanlike face, suggesting the dissolution of form, radiating outward into the watery background. The overlay of strong, dark circles against light beige and white circular strokes gives the figure a hypnotic look, encouraging a feeling of vertigo in the viewer. In the painting the interdependence and fragility of marine life and human life are brought to the fore by the lack of spatial definition, the use of circles and interconnected lines, and the conscious placement of naturalistic and nonnaturalistic elements, bringing them into dialogue with each other. In the painting, the human body is exposed to the same watery, white negative space as the fish. Through this threatening dissolution of form, the composition emanates fear for the body in jeopardy.

Katsura's "human" is barely identifiable as humanoid: we are given vague reference to facial features in the strange blue ovals of the eyes, the slight shading to indicate the nose and nostrils, and the series of loose circles to suggest a gaping mouth, marked with a bright red tongue at the center of the composition. Characteristic of Katsura's penchant for contrasting verism with abstraction, at top right she retains a highly naturalistic rendition of a straw rope *(shimenawa)*—a rope not so different from the one in *Women's Day.* Significantly, the *shimenawa,* literally meaning "closing rope," is used in the Japanese religion of Shinto to designate pure, sacred space. Thus positioned at the top right of the painting, it marks the canvas itself as a key ritual space; in other words, a space where transformation can occur. Katsura knots the rope in an unconventional form, suggesting the difficulties of spatial, cultural, environmental, and aesthetic boundaries as well as the impossibilities of purity. The thick texture of the rope appears heavy against the flat linearity of the figure, making the rope more realistic than the fisherman himself. Moreover, the contrast suggests the easy slippage from life to still life, from mammal to mutation, and from life to death.[90]

Katsura's *Human and Fish* tests the limits between figuration and abstraction, and it is precisely this ambiguity that elicits a feeling of discomfort: the fish bodies and the human body are overlapping in what viewers may perceive as an impure biological state—directly referencing the discomforting reality that many humans had eaten radioactive tuna (fears of contamination that reemerged following the Fukushima nuclear disaster in March 2011). Moreover, the biological impurity suggests miscegenation, breaking the covenant of speciesism, in which separate species coexist but never intermix. One fish is positioned as though it were the person's neck. Visible distinctions—markers of subjectivity—begin to disappear for both the fish and the human. The twin thresholds of exposure and invisibility are revealed to be equally dangerous. Katsura described wanting to express "not something social or ideological, not something like that, but something physical/bodily *[nikutaiteki]* or instinctive *[honnōteki]* that any Japanese would feel."[91] She sought to put the body, and our experience of it, on the precipice.

Katsura stages our worst fears: the distortion of bodily self and the loss of physical presence. The black lines of the face splice the fish's body, while the back half of the fish's body and its tail lack any details: the body is reduced to a watery gray shadow, as though dissolving. Invisibility is the total disappearance of selfhood, an ultimate destructive power that nuclear bombs achieve instantaneously, most infamously marked by the shadows of human bodies that were burnt into buildings in Hiroshima and Nagasaki. Katsura sought to manifest the stakes of the national body in the painting: she toyed with the idea of calling it *Nihonjin (The Japanese),* to make her message as direct as possible.[92]

Human and Fish was displayed at the thirty-ninth Nika exhibition in Tokyo in November 1954, along with two other provocative pieces by Katsura: *Hito ga ōsugiru (Too Many People)* (a common phrase about the state of Tokyo in the postwar period) and *Minna rakujanai (No One Has It Easy).* One reviewer panned *Human and Fish,* complaining that it was busy and overly ornamental. But the respected critic Hariu Ichirō applauded Katsura's ambiguity and "consciousness of life" *(seikatsu ishiki).*[93] What makes Katsura's "consciousness of life" present on the canvas, it seems, is the representation of the *dissolution* of life, the threatening dissolve of individual physical presence into an amalgam of indistinct form. The figure's darkly colored eyes set against his inchoate, white face are suggestive of the uncontrollable ephemerality of life.[94]

Human and Fish was discussed in reviews of the time, even appearing in the *Asahi* newspaper before it was shown at the Nika exhibition in part because the painting was part of a larger effort to draw attention to the issue of nuclear disarmament.[95] The *Lucky Dragon* trawler became a site in the antinuclear movement as a large-scale indexical symbol of nuclear terror. In 1970, an organization was formed to preserve the vessel; it took ownership of the *Lucky Dragon* and created a memorial site (Figure 1.10). In March 1954 the Young Artist Association began a petition against hydrogen bombs, and artists and filmmakers rallied around the cause. For example, the 1954 film *Gojira (Godzilla),* which includes a long monologue against the dangers of nuclear power, was made following the *Lucky Dragon* incident, as was Tanaka Atsuko's *Electric Dress* (a key work examined in chapter 3).[96] Reportage artists like Ikeda Tatsuo (born 1928) created numerous works around the theme of the *Lucky Dragon,* and Tezuka Osamu's *Atom Boy* was intended to be critical of the power of advanced technological weaponry. In 1954–55, Nakano Hideto made *Uoichiba (Fish Market),* Tsuruoka Masao made *Shi to kumo to hito (Death, Cloud, and People),* Yonekura Hisahito painted *Kuroi taiyō (Black Sun),* Ikeda Tatsuo made *10,000 kaunto (10,000 Count)* and *Umerareta sakana (Buried Fish),* and Okamoto Tarō created *Moeru hito (People Aflame)* (Plate 5).[97] Later, Maruki Toshi and Iri painted the large-scale *Yaizu,* the title of which refers to the village from which the *Lucky Dragon* set sail.[98] The Lithuanian-born American social realist Ben Shahn (1898–1969) also completed a series of drawings from 1960 to 1962 called *Lucky Dragon.*[99] The ink-on-paper drawings document the worried, upturned faces of the exposed men, their gear, and their port of departure. In 1959, director Shindō Kaneto released *Dai-5 Fukuryū Maru,* a feature film based on the events. In these varied artworks, gruesome images of dead fish simultaneously broadcast the deathly effects of the incident and forecast the hazards of allowing U.S. power to continue unchecked.

Art, then, became a forum where dissension and contention enabled resistance to the imposition of institutional and national ideology. It was a key site where this dialectical practice could take place, enabling expression, visualization, and discourse about the anxieties, anger, and conflict circulating at the time. These visual and artistic discourses are part of what Rancière refers to as "new forms of collective enunciation" that "re-frames the given by inventing new ways of making sense of the sensible, new configurations between the visible and the invisible, and between the audible and the inaudible, new distributions of space and time—in short, new bodily capacities."[100] Artists and activists enacted dissensus, shifting the ground of "sensibility."

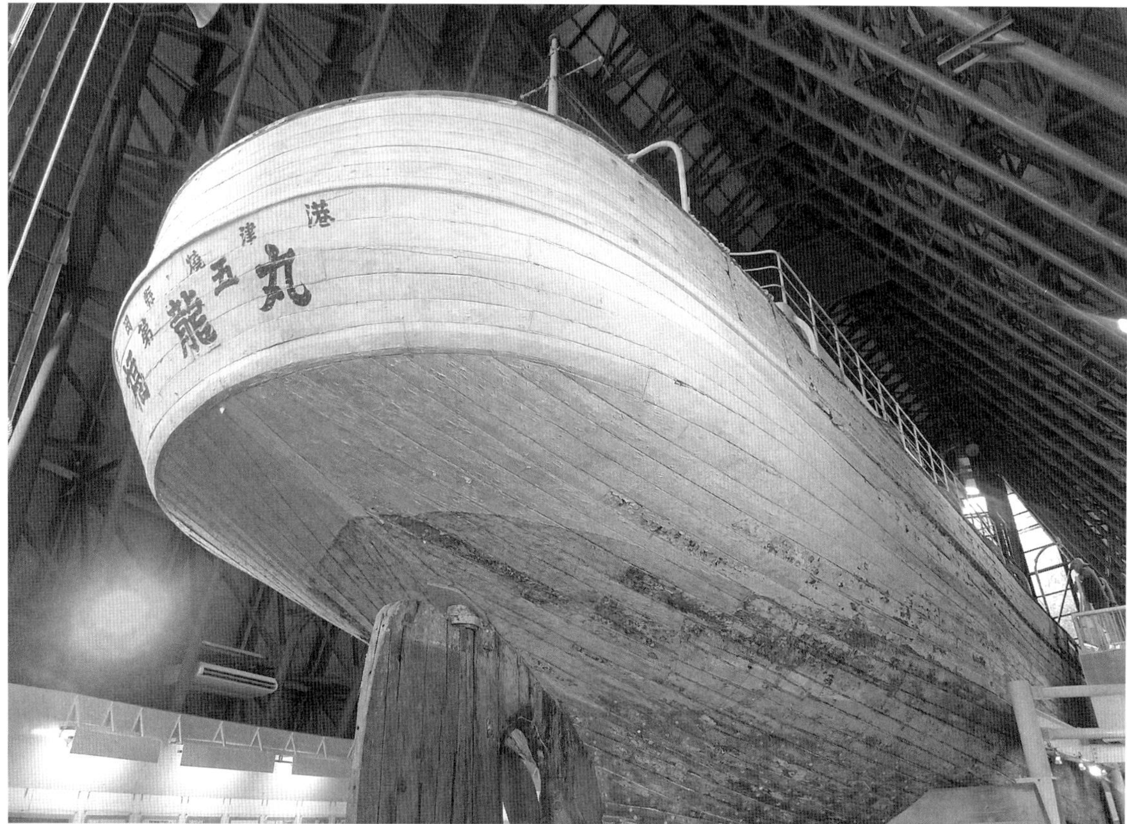

FIGURE 1.10. *Daigo Fukuryū Maru (The Lucky Dragon),* fishing trawler. Courtesy of the Public Interest Incorporated Foundation Daigo Fukuryū Maru Peace Society. Author's photograph, 2014.

The most famous of the Japanese artists involved in depicting the *Lucky Dragon* incident was Okamoto Tarō (1911–96). He and Katsura were of the same generation and seemed to share a friendly rivalry.[101] His large-scale painting *People Aflame* (Plate 5) is awash in his characteristic colors of bright yellow, blue, and red. Eyes peer out from the corners of the frame, as if transfixed by the brilliant flames. The breakdown of bodies in Okamoto's work takes a backseat to the flame-like colors that occupy the central space of the canvas, and consequently the artist's signature style seems to take precedence over the politics of the event. *People Aflame* seems reminiscent of the aesthetic "atomicity" present in the U.S. government's photograph of the Enewetak Atoll hydrogen bombing, the coloring remarkably similar. Katsura's work, in contrast, demonstrates a preference for negative space, ambiguity, and the centrality of the human face. While Okamoto depicts the spectacle of disaster, *Human and Fish* draws attention to the loss of visibility of the subject.[102]

The pernicious effects of American imperialism on fishermen was a theme deployed by reportage artist Ikeda Tatsuo even before the *Lucky Dragon* incident in his series titled *Hangenbaku* (1954) (Figure 1.11). Ikeda, who had been drafted as a kamikaze pilot (the

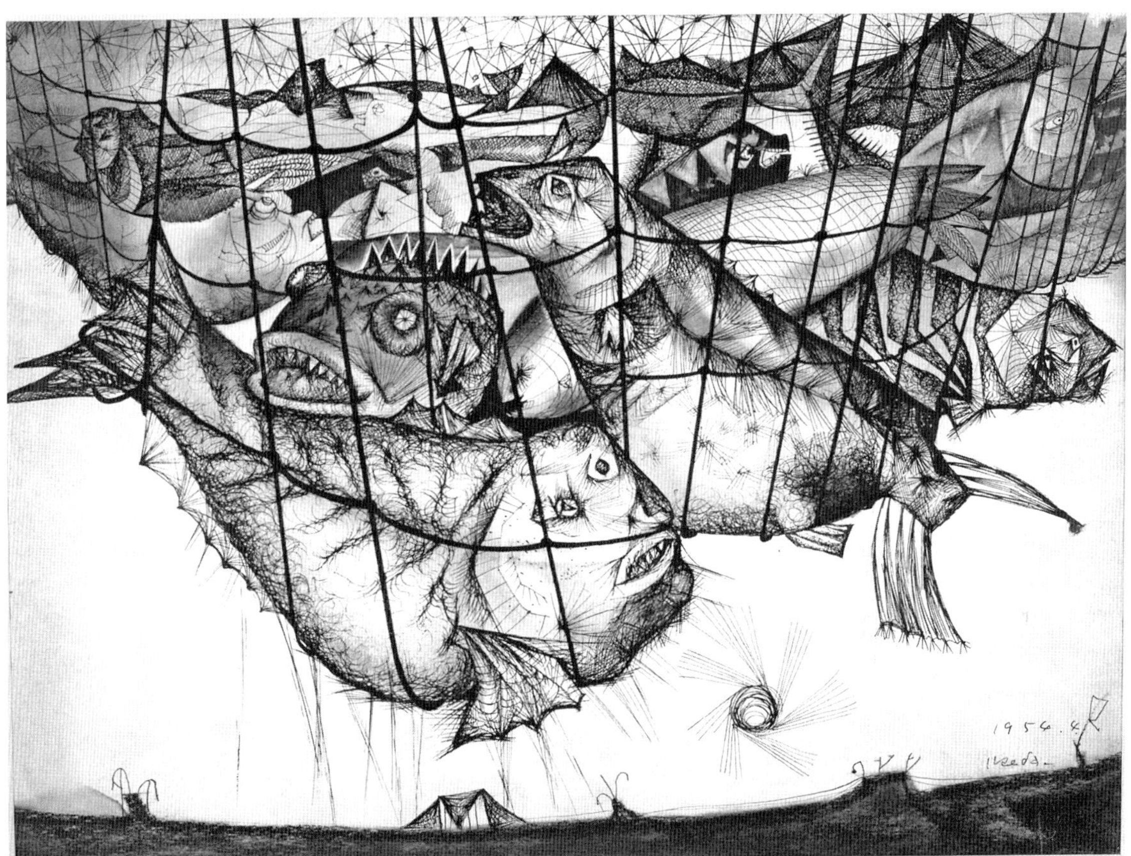

FIGURE 1.11. Ikeda Tatsuo, *Hangenbaku series, 10,000 kaunto (Anti–Atomic Bomb Series, 10,000 Count)*, 1954. 27.8 × 37.3 cm. Copyright Ikeda Tatsuo. Courtesy of the Museum of Contemporary Art, Tokyo.

war ended before he was forced to take a suicide mission), joined the Avant-Garde Art Association soon after 1945. He traveled to the town of Uchinada in Ishikawa Prefecture, along the Sea of Japan, to witness and protest the growing presence of the U.S. military bases. As discussed in the following chapter, for reportage artists, the *genba,* or site, of actual events is an important part of the artistic process. Ikeda found that the U.S. military had taken over the beaches in an effort to advance the Korean War. This turn of events meant that those who owned fishing boats were able to profit from leasing them to the United States, but the fishermen (the laborers) immediately lost their jobs.

Katsura's and Ikeda's works represent in contrasting ways the threat of the radical transformation of the Japanese body brought about by the presence of the United States. While Katsura's *Human and Fish* emphasizes disappearance and invisibility, in Ikeda's *Hangenbaku* series, as well as in his depictions of the *Lucky Dragon* incident, fish become grotesquely oversized. In another ink drawing, *Shūkaku (The Haul),* in the *Uchinada* series (1954), a deformed man carries the corpse of an immense fish with a smaller, gasping fish still caught in its mouth. These sinister images implicitly suggest how the encroachment of the United States shifted relations among the Japanese themselves, not least by amplifying divisions of class.

While Ikeda makes overt reference to the site by depicting the beach, fishing nets, and the bodies of the fisherman, in *Human and Fish* Katsura places her figures in an undefined area of white. The current-like white brushstrokes suggest the movement of the water and its ability to transport fish, people, and, more menacingly, radiation beyond any limited space. Her composition gestures toward the larger terror: that the world as a whole may fall victim to death by nuclear warfare. The exposure of the body, under these circumstances, often illuminates the stakes of life and death. Katsura would continue to pursue these themes throughout the 1950s and into the 1960s, while exposing herself to new experiences across the globe.

Illustrating *Another Country*

As it did for the other artists discussed in this book, the mid-1950s marked a period of new directions for Katsura. From 1956, she traveled to Paris, the Central African Republic, Egypt, and the United States, returning to Japan in April 1961, a few months after her father, Katsura Benzō (1874–1961) had passed away. Upon her return, she began to receive offers to create art for book covers and illustrations, and she completed several such projects, including drawings for a Japanese translation of James Baldwin's best-selling novel *Another Country.* The book, originally published in the United States in 1962, was serialized in the *Asahi Journal* in Japan from November 3, 1963, to February 23, 1964. Baldwin's story examines the challenges of personal and artistic integrity, the depths of loss, and taboo topics such as the deep-seated passions and hostilities of biracial and gay couples in New York City. These topics were unusual even for a radical press in Japan, where deep prejudice toward interracial couples and homophobia were (and remain) commonplace.[103] Baldwin and Katsura both sought social change, yet within different geographic arenas and political climates.[104] Despite these differences, Katsura and Baldwin both believed that art could reveal social problems and help overcome them.

Baldwin thoughtfully describes the problem of the author in terms that may have been provocative to Katsura: "The writer's task is to imagine a renewed world that can bridge divisions of class and color. . . . [The] problem the writer has . . . is to somehow unite these things, to find the terms of our connection, without which we will perish."[105] For Baldwin, friendship is defined and shared through corporeal intimacy. He "imagines sex as a powerful vehicle to achieve new ties of affiliation."[106] In *Another Country,* Baldwin is at his most expressive, describing a discreet relationship between a black man, Rufus, and his male Caucasian friend, Eric:

> Rufus had watched him, smiling. He felt a flood of affection for Eric. And he felt his own power.
>
> He walked over to Eric and put his hands on Eric's shoulders. He did not know what he was going to say or do. But with his hands on Eric's shoulders, affection, power, and curiosity all knotted together in him—with a hidden, unforeseen violence which frightened him a little; the hands that were meant to hold Eric at arm's length seemed to draw Eric to him; the current that had begun flowing he did not know how to stop.[107]

On the cover for the 1962 American edition of *Another Country,* Dell Publishing took full advantage of the controversial sexual nature of the novel, featuring an interracial couple (notably, a heterosexual couple—perhaps featuring a gay couple would have been too financially risky), eyes closed in passion, arms around each other in a naked embrace (Figure 1.12). Katsura seems less willing to broker in skin. In nearly all of her thirty illustrations, the bodies that feature so prominently in the story are clothed, wrapped, or otherwise distanced from the viewer or each other (Figure 1.13).

In a catalog essay for Katsura's 2013 retrospective at the Museum of Contemporary Art, Tokyo, curator Seki Naoko mentions how Katsura often depicted covers, wrappings, and other apatetic devices following her work on *Another Country,* suggesting how the artist used layers to address the visibility of social issues.[108] What social issues were of concern to Katsura? How did these issues manifest? Expanding on Seki's observations, I argue that Katsura particularly engaged allegory as a mode of dissensus, examining gender and nation through modes of exposure and concealment, often electing to compose an inaccessible figure, a covered figure, or a figure composed of fragments.

Admittedly, any graphic illustration of sexuality may have been too much even for the radical *Asahi Journal*'s editors; yet Katsura does not even make oblique visual reference to the novel's homoerotic story line. Katsura reinterprets Baldwin's story through her illustrations, which nonetheless reference specific events of the narrative, distilling the heated

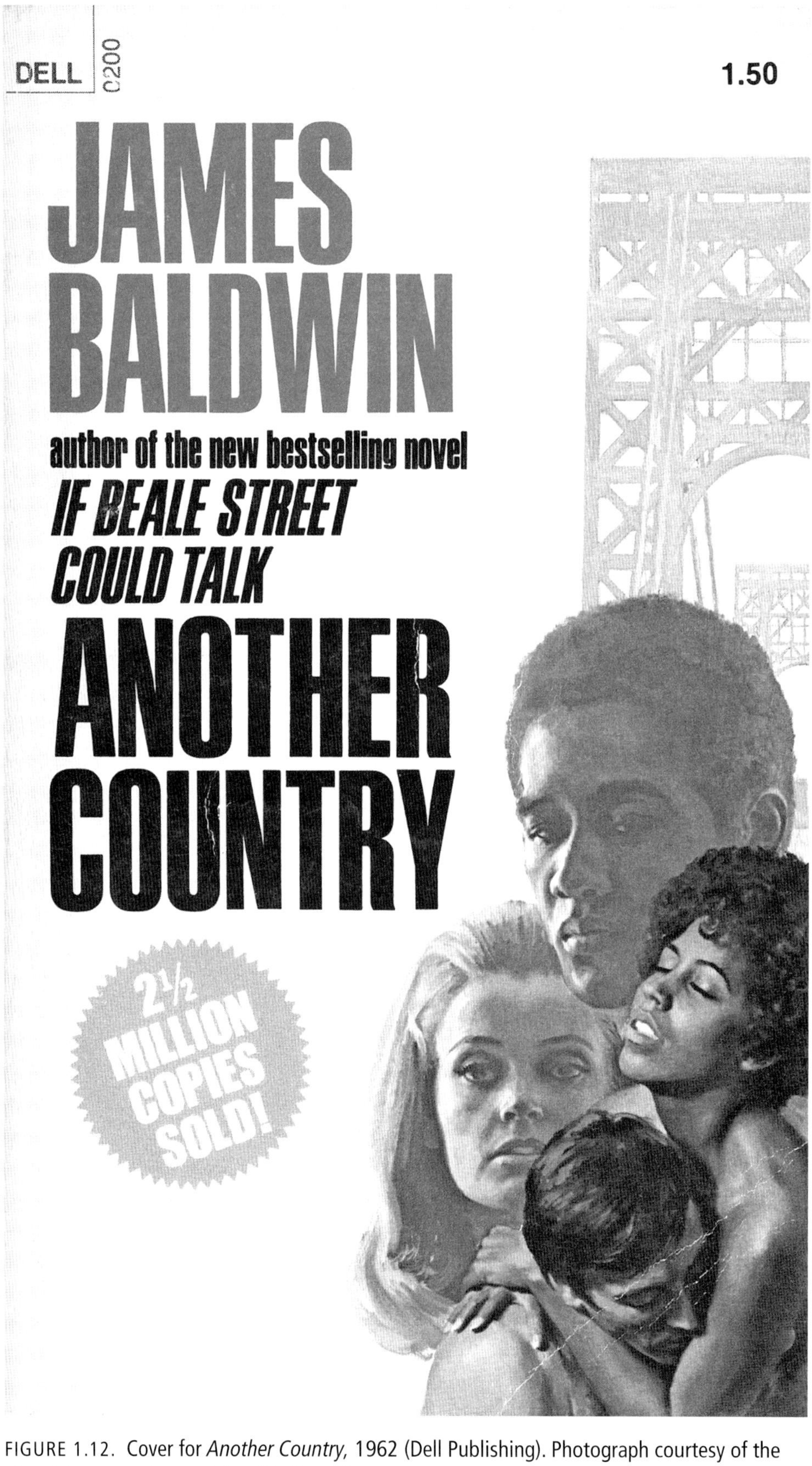

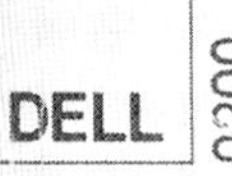

FIGURE 1.12. Cover for *Another Country*, 1962 (Dell Publishing). Photograph courtesy of the Visual Resources Library, The Ohio State University.

passion of sex and lust into depictions of intimate but platonic friendships or, at other times, marking the moments of rupture between bodies. For example, in the second serialized episode of *Another Country,* a group of racists in a bar have beaten up Vivaldo (a white man) and the protagonist, Rufus (a black man). Rufus and Vivaldo's friendship is beset by unconsummated gay love, antagonistic racism, and internalized racist feelings, which Baldwin describes through the tension and intimacy of their bodies.[109] In Katsura's illustration of the event, corporeality is suppressed: Vivaldo is depicted as wrapped from head to toe in bandages, his body completely covered, despite the lesser injuries he sustains in the story. The thick, mummy-like wrappings seem overdetermined in their efforts to cover the body (Figure 1.14). They mark his past exposure, rendering him closer to invisibility. Race becomes unreadable as the two men are depicted with similar features and the same skin tone.

In Katsura's illustrations of *Another Country,* intimacy is conveyed through the shared space of the frame and the composition of the bodies in relation to each other, not through physical contact. Rancière describes this very tactic in his discussion of dissensus: "The efficacy of art resides not in the model (or counter-model) of behavior that it provides, but first and foremost in the partition of space and time that it produces to define ways of

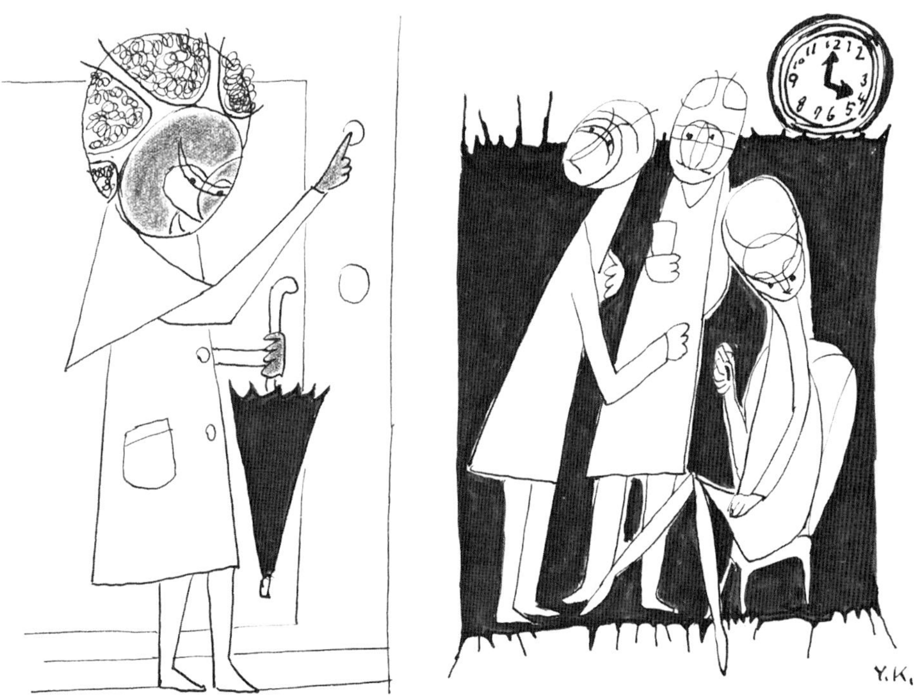

FIGURE 1.13. Katsura Yuki, illustration for James Baldwin's novel *Another Country, Asahi Journal,* December 29, 1963. Ink and pencil on paper, 15.3 × 20.3 cm. Copyright Katsura Akinari. Courtesy of the Museum of Contemporary Art, Tokyo.

being together or separate, being in front or in the middle of, being inside or outside, etc."[110] Katsura draws attention to the covering of bodies in a manner that conversely suggests the possibility of the body's exposed nakedness and simultaneously reveals the tensions of touch and the meaning behind contact or withdrawal in terms of forging or rupturing community.

In the illustration released with the third installment of *Another Country* in the November 24, 1963, issue of the *Asahi Journal,* three figures stand at a bar drinking, with forlorn expressions on their faces. The tallest man leans toward a seated man, their bodies close (Figure 1.15). The closeness of their bodies forges a temporary haven from the outside world but does not suggest the sexual desires that mediate their relationship in the story. Katsura's drawings emphasize both distance and togetherness, suggesting mitigated contact and the fractured distances between bodies rather than an idealized notion of community. Katsura shows us how emotional and physical tensions, life-threatening fears, and the passion of and against racism and sexism are in fact the very constituents of community. She positions a black throw rug behind the figures to suggest their shared space—a sign that recurs throughout the series of illustrations. The small rug, with its frayed edges,

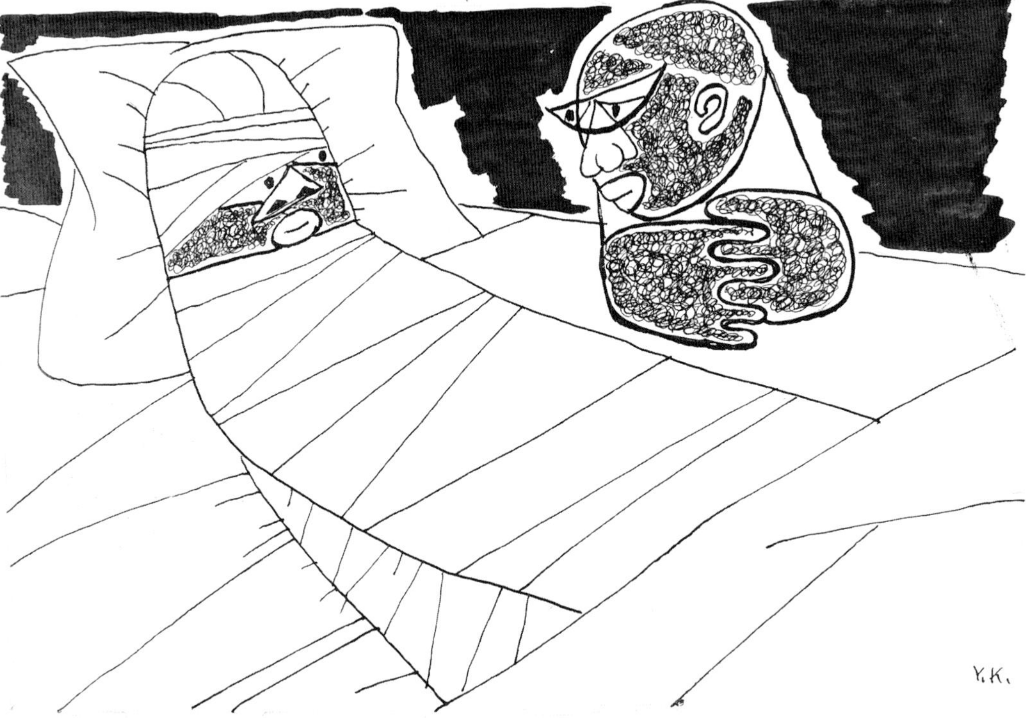

FIGURE 1.14. Katsura Yuki, illustration for James Baldwin's novel *Another Country, Asahi Journal,* November 17, 1963. Ink on paper, 21 × 27 cm. Copyright Katsura Akinari. Courtesy of the Museum of Contemporary Art, Tokyo.

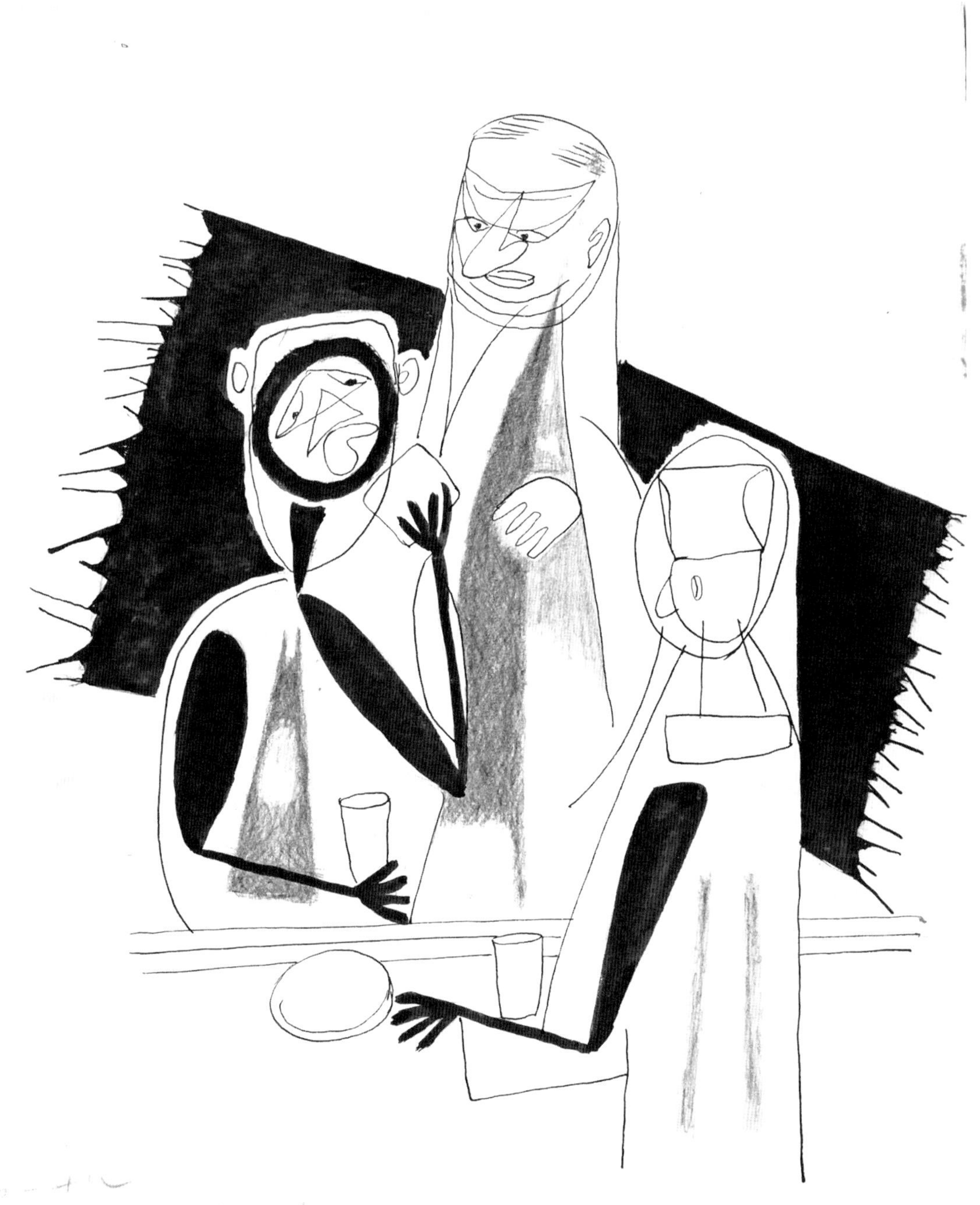

FIGURE 1.15. Katsura Yuki, illustration for James Baldwin's novel *Another Country, Asahi Journal,* November 24, 1963. Ink and pencil on paper, 27.4 × 23.5 cm. Copyright Katsura Akinari. Courtesy of the Museum of Contemporary Art, Tokyo.

appears four other times, visually linking the characters who are in different psychological states and who appear, through the pages of the *Asahi Journal,* at different moments in time. The rug bears a strong visual relation to two works Katsura painted the previous year: *Senbon ashi (Millipede)* and *Senbon ashi (II) (Millipede [II])* (1962), which I will show to be indicative of personal and political mutability. Like Baldwin, Katsura stages fragile moments of intimate exposure, or self-offering, that remain fraught, never concluding in stable unification.

Katsura's interpretation of *Another Country* shows her commitment to social progress and her willingness to take on transgressive topics. Her work shares terrain with the work of the Japanese author Oda Makoto (1932–2007), who documented his travels in the best-selling novel *Nan demo mite yarō* (I'll take a look at anything), published in 1961. Oda mingles with the gay community in Greenwich Village and African Americans in the Jim Crow South, his text displaying "his willingness to emphasize and encourage affinities between himself and these marginalized figures."[111] Similarly, Katsura's illustrations exhibit emotional expressivity and sensitivity to the broad themes of the novel while redirecting the sensual physicality described in the story. Her commitment to concealing the body can even be read as a protective maneuver. As Anne McKnight points out, Oda's *"I'll Take a Look at Anything* uses the conceit of looking at 'anything' to display the seeming openness of the traveler. . . . But the easy detachment and attachment to foreign places came under critique by contemporary readers who questioned the consumerist role that even bohemian tourism appeared to advocate. When Japanese journalists began reporting on Vietnam in the late 1960s, the Teflon gaze of the Japanese traveler sparked a critical commentary in the form of the bystander novel."[112] Katsura, it seems, was aware of the stakes of exposure and used the wrapping of bodies as well as ambiguous racial representations to work against the Teflon gaze.

In the final illustration in the series, Katsura focuses closely on the face of Ida (Figure 1.16), an African American female character whose brother has committed suicide and who struggles to find a life outside the ghetto. Katsura foregrounds the features of the African American face in a manner that draws attention to its exotic otherness, strategically positioned to engage the viewer with the character directly. Katsura depicts only a simple bust against a frame of carpet. Ida's body, which in the text is demeaned and filled with expressive power, has been left out of the image. The erasure of Ida's body, which is her conduit for her relations to others in the novel, effectively heightens the character's isolation and sadness. The tragic face, her hypnotic eyes filled with tears, emblematic of female compromise, is the final illustration in the series.

Allegorical Bodies in the 1960s

In the remainder of this chapter, I focus on Katsura's use of insect and animal bodies in her paintings to examine more fully how she posed questions about Japanese social change in

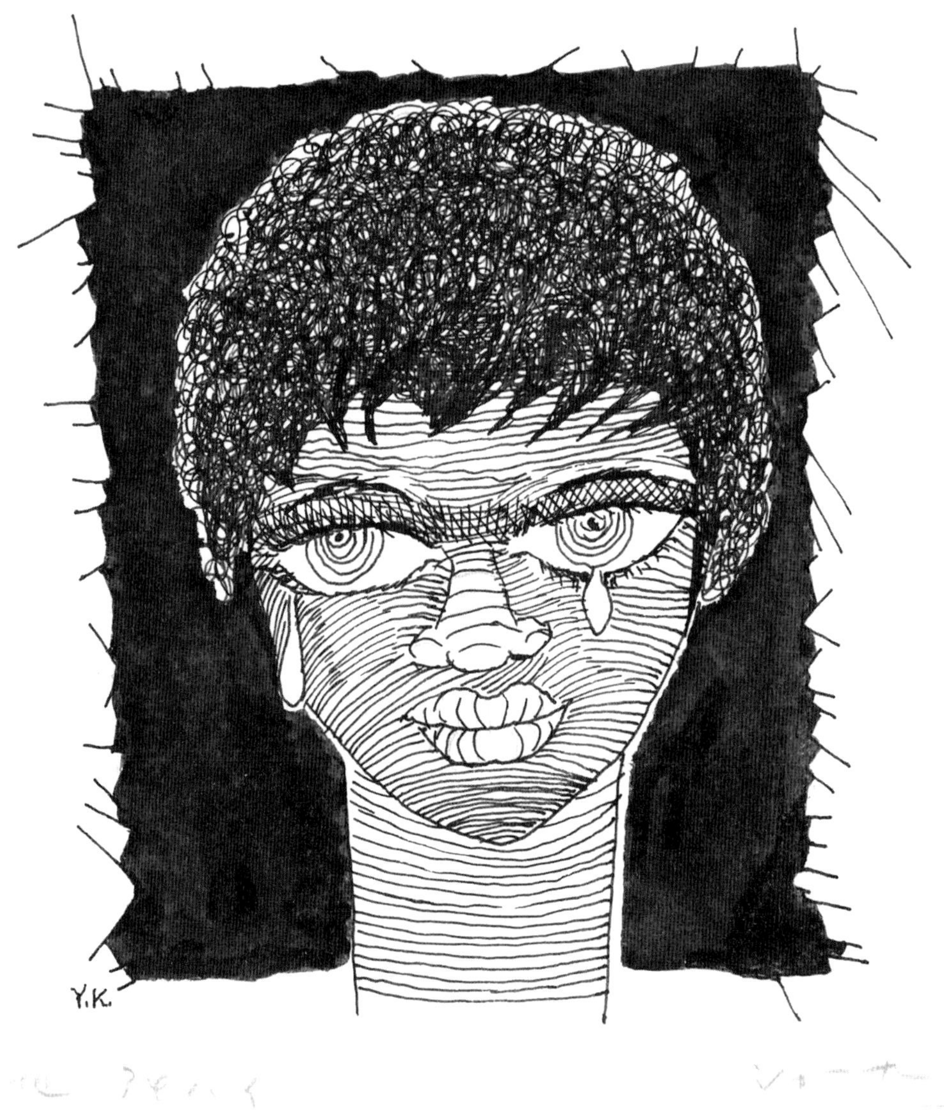

FIGURE 1.16. Katsura Yuki, illustration for James Baldwin's novel *Another Country, Asahi Journal,* February 24, 1964. Ink on paper, 16 × 14.5 cm. Copyright Katsura Akinari. Courtesy of the Museum of Contemporary Art, Tokyo.

relation to the self. In the 1940s and early 1950s, the artist relied on the representation of animals for many of her allegorical works, including *The Battle of the Monkey and the Crab,* discussed earlier. In 1959 she began painting abstract color-field paintings (Figure 1.17), but after a few years, the abstract forms began to transform again. *Millipede* (1962) (Plate 6), an assemblage of oil and paper on canvas, marked her return to organic themes and her departure from abstract color-field works. Indeed, Katsura commented that the painting arose from a feeling that she had a millipede inside her body, and once dreamed

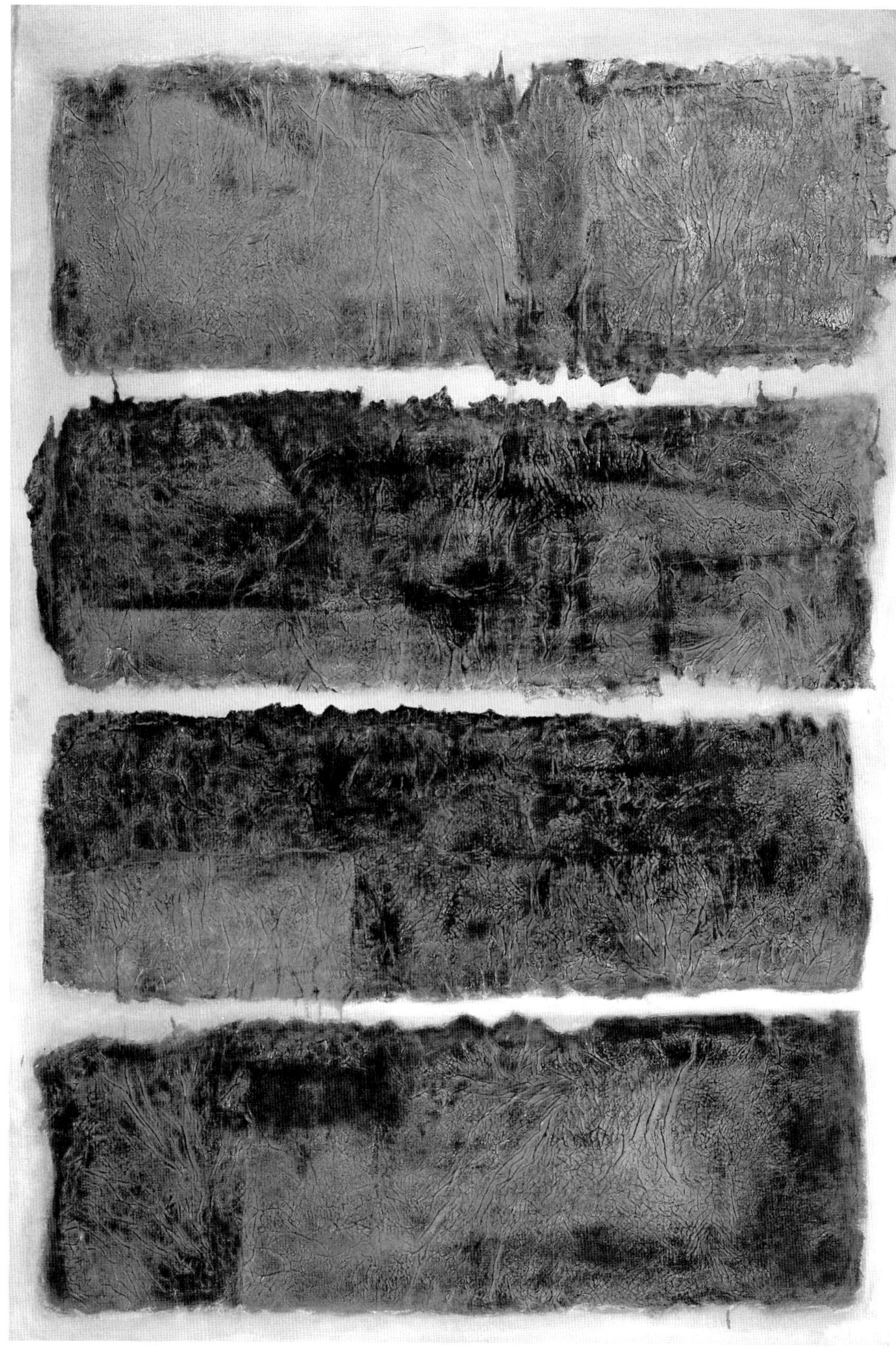

FIGURE 1.17. Katsura Yuki, *Ihōjin (The Stranger),* 1961. Oil and paper on canvas, 255 × 173.9 cm. Copyright Katsura Akinari. Courtesy of the Yamaguchi Prefectural Art Museum.

she had turned into a millipede.[113] Considering Katsura's interest in existentialism, it is perhaps not surprising that her dream is remarkably similar to the story line of Franz Kafka's novel *The Metamorphosis,* first published in 1915 but translated into Japanese twice in 1952, by two publishers using two different translators.[114]

Katsura created a second version of the work the same year. *Millipede (II)* (Plate 7) features an amorphous green creature surrounded on all sides with cilia-like lines. Here the cilia have sprouted into legs, covering the top and bottom of the insect. Taken together, the works strongly suggest themes of mutability—a concept that would reappear the following year in Katsura's illustrations for *Another Country.* Two blotches of paint, one black, one yellow, suggest eyes—a key marker of consciousness and transformation for Katsura. She once commented that, after all, anything you put eyes on becomes a living thing.[115] The birth of the millipede paintings also marked an artistic mutation for Katsura: a return to the figural or, more accurately, the zoomorphic. That same year, 1962, she completed an untitled painting of a tortoise and a wild boar, never returning to pure painted abstraction.[116]

In postwar Japan, figuration came under fire. As Winther-Tamaki has shown, in the early postwar period,

> one of the primary means of achieving the strengthening of subjectivity would be submitting the body to painterly assault. Kikuhata Mokuma would later point out an irony that was no doubt lost on the postwar painters of harmed bodies, namely the fact that their "painting of the flesh" was oddly similar to some of the more gruesome late-war *sensōga* battle scenes. From 1943 through 1945, Tokyo exhibition visitors viewed officially sanctioned painting of gory patriotic sacrifices made by fellow Japanese subjects on the front lines in order to protect the purity of the body politic *(kokutai)* represented by the emperor. After the war, other painters, including many who had experienced the war as combatants, seemed to continue this focus on bodies in duress.[117]

But this irony was not lost on postwar painters for long, as the so-called realism debate increasingly became critical of figuration and its links to wartime modes of representation.[118] Painters rapidly turned away from the depiction of bodies and toward greater abstraction. But casting aside the body could also be construed as casting aside any further interest in the politics of the body. For Katsura, the representation of animals allowed her to continue to pursue this line of inquiry while avoiding the traps of the realism debate.

In discussing their theory of "becoming-animal," Gilles Deleuze and Félix Guattari argue that in Kafka's writings, it is the role of the animal to find an escape from political circumstance: "To the inhumanness of the 'diabolical powers,' there is the answer of a becoming-animal: to become a beetle, to become a dog, to become an ape, 'head over heels and away,' rather than lowering one's head and remaining a bureaucrat, inspector, judge, or judged."[119] Becoming-animal allows a politics that exists outside the currents of political normativity, potentially shielding one from the anxieties that "the powers that be" can exert. In effect, becoming-animal limits one's exposure to the dangers of consensus. For Katsura, painting animals may have offered an escape from the pressures to convert *(tenkō)* to fascism in the 1930s and 1940s, yet her works engaged and challenged the speciesism that was co-opted by propaganda in wartime and by latent imperial desires in the postwar period. This tactic allowed her to avoid "a certain impasse in contemporary radical politics that seeks to counter such normativity."[120] For Katsura, becoming-animal also permitted artistic freedoms, as she remained outside the polarized and heated art historical debates over abstraction and figuration, realism and surrealism, Western modernism and East Asian contemporaneity that circulated in Japan in the 1950s and 1960s.[121] Katsura's animals, like Kafka's, "never refer to a mythology or to archetypes but correspond solely to new levels, zones of liberated intensities where contents free themselves from their forms as well as from their expressions, from the signifier that formalized them."[122] Katsura, when asked about her shifts in style before and after the work, tellingly remarked that in wartime, "humans become inhuman."[123] Steve Baker sees Deleuze and Guattari's theory of becoming-animal as tied to artistic selfhood: "There is at the very least an implicit parallel between the animal's line of flight, or metamorphosis, and the artist's creative production."[124]

Throughout her oeuvre, Katsura's strange tone is jarring, and it is only upon a second look that one begins to understand her ability to transform bodies into meaningful allegorical modes of dissensus. In *Hana (Trunk)* (Plate 8), from 1967, for example, Katsura depicts only the appendages of an elephant: four wide feet and an elongated trunk reaching out for two small, perfect peanuts that are just beyond its grasp. Katsura has built up the painted layers, first painting small faces above text. These images appear like pasted-on scraps of newspaper obituaries (Plate 9).[125] She has also painted a Japanese mortuary tablet and then covered these images over in a wash of gray paint. It seems a simple, humorous composition, but below the surface, her jests take shape from fragments of loss, faint echoes of somatic experience, and hints of exposure to violence.

One of Katsura's photographs from her trip to the Central African Republic provides a reference point for the subject of the painting (Figure 1.18). It shows an expressionless man using two hands to hold up an elephant's foot that has been severed from the animal's body.[126] The foot is as wide as the man's torso, and the flap of skin where it was cut off hangs loosely. For most viewers in the developed world, Katsura's photograph is a gruesome image that documents the killing of a once-majestic beast. Katsura, who was privileged to be the only female to join Bambari male villagers on a hunt (because of her status as a foreigner and affiliation with a local doctor), vividly recalled the men killing and cutting up wild animals, eating their organs on the spot. She was so overcome by the sight that she fainted.[127] In her memoir about her adventures, *Kitsune no dairyokō* (The travels of a fox),[128] she recalls:

> However, what I remember the most about animals is the scene where the natives were gathering around the elephants and bison that they had just hunted. They were cutting off heads, torsos, and limbs, and they cut the stomachs and took the internal organs out.

The natives had tattoos all over their bodies, and were working on the animals using their knives like crazy, as if they were taken over by something. Surprisingly they started heartily eating the raw internal organs with their bloody hands.

I saw fresh blood and a pile of green feces taken from the bison's stomach on the field, and I felt overcome. As I was watching this, I was so tired and thirsty. It was all so shocking that I passed out. After all, we had started walking before dawn and chased after wild animals for sixty kilometers.

One of the natives found water somewhere far away and carried it back for me. It had a lot of mosquito larvae, but I drank it, and recovered. And, I came home alive.[129]

Considering her text and the photograph of the elephant's foot, we see that *Trunk* flatly denies the resilient plasmaticity of cute anime and manga, and the text and photo also inform our reading of the mortuary tablets in the work. *Trunk* hints at the transformative power of death, the risks of "becoming-animal," and the boundaries of belonging and estrangement that the acts of hunting, dying, killing, and eating construct. Akira Lippit has described the disturbing paradox of the mediatized animalscape: in the age of mass extinction, nonhuman animals are on the verge of disappearance, yet they proliferate in

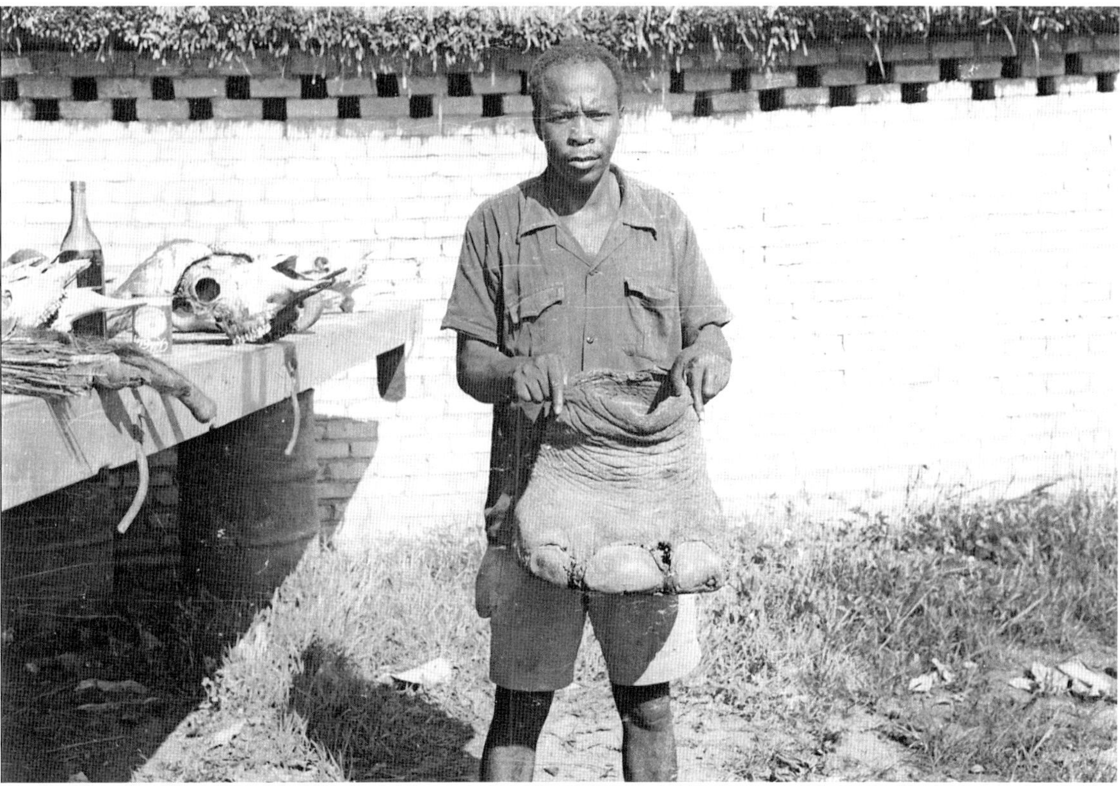

FIGURE 1.18. Katsura Yuki, photograph of unnamed hunter with elephant foot in Central Africa, 1958. Copyright Katsura Akinari. Courtesy of the Museum of Contemporary Art, Tokyo.

spectral forms, on screens, in books, and, in this case, in paintings.[130] Katsura's painting brings a conflict between our initial sense of delight and the undercurrent of death that is built into the assemblage piece through the references to obituaries and mortuary tablets and the experience of seeing an elephant killed in Africa. "Animals enter a new economy of being during the modern period, one that is no longer sacrificial in the traditional sense of the term but, considering modern technological media generally and the cinema more specifically, *spectral*."[131] If, as Lippit suggests, "modernity can be defined by the disappearance of wildlife from humanity's habitat and by the reappearance of the same in humanity's reflections on itself: in philosophy, psychoanalysis, and technological media such as the telephone, film, and radio," then *Trunk* can be understood as an assertion of political modernity.[132] Katsura partially attempts to recuperate the dead elephant, breaking with the natural order of hunting, killing, and eating, reframing and animating her experience into "a new form . . . of *dissensual* 'commonsense.'"[133]

Katsura achieved this mode of zoomorphic dissensus in other works, and it seemed to appeal to her in general—even her musical taste showed an interest in the politically disruptive potential of animals. In 1962, the *Asahi Shinbun* ran a column about famous people and their favorite records featuring Katsura as well as opera singer Satō Yoshiko, poet Kondō Yoshimi, and graphic designer Yamashiro Ryūichi.[134] While the others predominantly chose classical music and jazz, Katsura chose Georges Brassens's recording of his song "Gorilla" (1952), a bawdy tune that was critical of the death penalty and was banned from airplay until 1955 (capital punishment was banned in France in 1981 but remains legal in Japan today).[135]

Katsura's zoomorphic paintings continued in the 1960s, winning her acclaim. In 1966, Katsura painted *Gonbe to karasu (Gonbe and Crow)* (Plate 10), an image that received the highest award at the 1966 Contemporary Japanese Art Exhibition in Tokyo. At first glance, this and other examples of Katsura's works seem simple, playful (even childish), and funny—perhaps this is the reason English-language scholars have largely neglected to take her work seriously. But a second glance reveals the artist's capacity to manipulate human and animal bodies into potentially politically transformative allegories. *Gonbe and Crow* is a large-scale assemblage work that features a large black crow, his triangular body merging into his oversized black beak, his bright-yellow eyes peering upward at the compressed, upside-down body of Gonbe, the farmer. Consistent with Katsura's post-1950s disavowal of the human body, the farmer has no visible torso and instead is wrapped in a *tenugui* (hand-wiping cloth) that covers all of his features save his eyes. Along the left side of the image, seven smaller crow-like shapes cast their own bright-yellow eyes upward. *Gonbe and Crow* draws on a traditional Japanese folktale and does not venture into abstract expressionism, surrealism, or other artistic trends perceived to come from the West and circulating in Japan at the time. Yet it was made during a time of intensely competitive artistic international exchange. What was at stake for Katsura in refiguring a fable like *Gonbe and Crow* and focusing on such a regional theme?

In the fable, Gonbe, the son of a samurai *(bushi),* becomes a farmer to pursue his dead father's dream. Gonbe, then, is a model of filial piety, honor, and humility. At first his efforts at cultivation are futile, since the mischievous and lazy Crow eats all of his seeds. But through sheer industriousness he becomes the most successful farmer in the village (in some versions he hunts and kills Crow). Gonbe goes on to kill a snake that has been attacking other villagers, and in the process he is poisoned and dies. Hence the fable also valorizes self-sacrifice, a key value of imperialism.

In Katsura's version, much as in her previous reworking of *The Battle of the Monkey and the Crab,* the conservative morality tale is circumvented. Katsura makes Crow the protagonist by positioning him (or perhaps her) as the central figure of the composition and giving him (or her) a comical, worried expression. Crow is refigured as a sympathetic, parental character who does what he (or she) must to feed the seven baby crows lingering at his (or her) side. Katsura depicts Gonbe on the border of the canvas, his stumpy figure looking altogether unheroic. Viewers familiar with the tale would have trouble reconciling its original moral didacticism with Katsura's new depiction, which opens up questions of relationality between the two. Adhering to patriarchal convention is no longer tenable, Katsura asserts, and becoming-animal is presented as a new avenue for circumventing the system.

In the 1960s, when *Gonbe and Crow* was completed, Japanese artists and activists were deeply engaged in protesting the re-signing of the Treaty of Mutual Cooperation and Security between the United States and Japan (*Nippon-koku to Amerika-gasshūkoku to no Aida no Sōgo Kyōryoku oyobi Anzen Hoshō Jōyaku,* 1960 and 1970), known as the ANPO treaty, and the Tokyo Olympics (1964). The Olympics marked Japan's entrance onto the global stage, welcoming masses of international tourists into the country. As the Olympics were taking place, the spaces for contemporary art practice were shifting. The *Yomiuri Indépendant* exhibitions, which had supported avant-garde art since 1960, were closed down by the Olympics organizers, and controversy arose in the media over the value and nature of traditional painting and exhibition spaces.[136] Many avant-garde artists turned away from oil on canvas during this time and brought their art and performance to the streets. Katsura, however, continued to produce paintings that remain surprising in the strangeness of their tone and their adherence to figuration.[137] What form of politics did she seek through these aesthetic choices, and why did her work stray from the trend toward action-based art?

In contrast to Katsura, in the 1960s the avant-garde group Hi Red Center was challenging expectations in the streets and in the courts with its radical events and found art.[138] Historian William Marotti has cogently shown how activist artists like Akasegawa Genpei enacted Rancière's concept of political dissensus through their interventionist art practices. Akasegawa had participated in performance works such as *Shutoken seisō seiri sokushin undō (Campaign for the Promotion of Sanitation and Order in the Capital,* also known as *Ultra-Cleaning Event),* wherein he and other members of Hi Red Center donned lab coats and scrubbed the streets of Tokyo in 1964 to satirize the state's push to sterilize the city for the Olympics (see Figure 2.14). One year earlier, Akasegawa had notoriously printed an exhibition announcement on paper that appeared to have a 1,000-yen note on the opposite side (with the same serial number as a known counterfeit bill whose maker the police had repeatedly failed to track). The police then charged Akasegawa with counterfeiting money, and a long trial ensued. He was indicted in 1965. Describing an essay titled "The Intent of the Act Based on the Intent of the Act—Before Passing through the Courtroom," which Akasegawa penned in response to the 1000-yen note trial, Marotti writes:

> Akasegawa thematizes this "moment" [the moment wherein the counterfeit is discovered as a fake] as not just an interruption but as a point of possibility, one which contains the hope of difference, of transformation of the everyday world of action and consciousness. Translated to Rancière's terms, it is the moment of politics: a break in the usual apportionments of daily life, affording new perceptions and claims. It is a politics made possible by Akasegawa's practice.[139]

Considering the radical nature of Akasegawa's practice, perhaps it is unreasonable to describe Katsura's paintings, which hung quietly in spatially and socially normative galleries in Tokyo and addressed a more socially conservative group of people, as also enacting dissensus (Katsura's work was not shown in major museum institutions until 1980, with several large retrospectives following after her death in 1991).[140] Yet, if Marotti's text examines how the avant-garde "yielded a critique of an everyday world and a practice designed to alter it," then Katsura's interventions in aesthetic conventions and her drive to upset the moral standards of traditional fables, were, I would suggest, a comparable mode of politics, though perhaps more subtle.[141]

Given Katsura's age (she would have been fifty-three in 1966), her gender, and her upper-class upbringing, not to mention her penchant for covering, wrapping, and distancing bodies, it is not surprising that she did not involve herself with activist radicals such as the members of Hi Red Center, who, for example, photographed themselves nude in their performance piece *Shelter Plan*.[142] Hi Red Center and artists associated with neo-Dadaism were understood to be a part of the Anti-Art movement, which grew out of the *Yomiuri Indépendant* exhibitions and sought to transgress the limits of the institutional setting of the museum. Katsura, on the other hand, after leaving the Nika Association, systematically avoided participating in any movement even though the vast majority of artists at the time belonged to collectives or other art organizations. Perhaps she sided with art critic Miyakawa Atsushi, who argued that the logic of Anti-Art "is still the same old dualism of abstraction and figuration, which, moreover, makes Anti-Art nothing more than an exercise in art hygiene."[143] Katsura's mode of politics, in contrast, sought to step outside such dualisms and find a means to reconsider the future's reliance on the past and the stakes of bodily exposure. It is possible that she was aware of just how easily the mainstream could reject or, worse, ignore radical art. Her own priorities, I propose, involved seeking painterly change by walking the line between established art modes and avant-garde art.

Katsura completed a second large-scale piece in 1966 titled *Yokubari bāsan (Greedy Old Woman)* (Plate 11). The "woman" of the title is simultaneously singular, referring to a woman—perhaps Katsura herself—and plural, referring to women at large.[144] Katsura's painting can be seen as an expressive self-portrait and a comment on the times. The woman hoards her treasures in her overloaded arms, including items such as Japanese money, hiking shoes, whiskey, imported cars, plastic clothespins, a rice paddle, a memorial tablet, and a postcard bearing the artist's name. In the left rear ground of the composition, cars, an airplane, high-rise apartment buildings, and a factory pumping out a plume of gray smoke hint at recently industrialized Tokyo. Amid the woman's thick, mummy-like layers of wrappings, more yen notes are buried. Yet it seems that the figure's voracious appetite is not for financial gain alone, since she also hoards worthless items from everyday life: old clothespins, postcards, and shoes.

With her inclusion of these items, Katsura reveals concerns parallel to those of Hi Red Center, which, as Marotti has demonstrated, had a consistent interest in the fragmentation of everyday life, gendered and structured by a politicized mass culture and money.[145] Clothespins, for example, had been a key marker of this interrogation for Nakanishi Natsu-yuki at the fifteenth and last *Yomiuri Indépendant* exhibition in 1963.[146] As Marotti points out, Nakanishi's piece, provocatively titled *Sentaku basami wa kakuhan kōi o shuchō suru (Clothespins Assert Agitating Action),* "was a pun conflating 'political agitation' and the 'agitation' *(kakuhan)* of washing machines, a fine example of the humorous yet nonetheless serious concern these artists had with the relation between political action and the transformations of daily life brought about by the new boom in mass consumption."[147] Nakanishi himself became an extension of the work, as Takamatsu Jirō pinned the clothespins all over his body, in a manner somewhat reminiscent of Tanaka's *Electric Dress* (discussed in chapter 3). Tanaka's and Katsura's work seemed more engaged with women's work in relation to consumption and everyday life.

The "greedy old woman" in Katsura's work hangs on to other everyday items with nonetheless loaded significance. The rice paddle, placed below a bottle of "special reserve, imported liqueur" and an image of two sporty cars, for example, was a symbol used by the Housewives' Federation *(Shufuren),* established in 1948. Shufuren chose the cooking implement because it "(a) indicated the status of housewives' rights; (b) represented the 'skills needed for communal activities' since it is used to keep stirring food on the stove to prevent it from burning; (c) evoked the 'housewife's dream' of bountiful food; and (d) suggested the meaning of 'winning' through a pun on the word for food *(meshi)* and the word for the 'spirit to hold on' *(meshitoru).*"[148] The organization, led by Oku Mumeo, carried over the conservative values pursued and established in the 1920s and 1930s and sought to clarify women's role in the home and curb consumption through rationalization.[149]

When *Greedy Old Woman* is hung on the gallery wall, the large (180.3 × 120 cm) oil and paper on board composition looms over viewers, yet its comical nature gives the work a lighthearted, inviting air. The figure's isolation and densely covered body resonate with Katsura's illustrations for *Another Country* and Tanaka's invisible body in *Electric Dress*. Although the artwork clearly casts womanhood as its theme, the physical presence of femininity or even femaleness is suppressed. We know the figure's gender only by the title. Unlike a long lineage of modernist artworks, "woman" here is shown to have neither breasts nor flowing hair nor shapely legs. The mummified figure is also without feet or hands, and even her eyes—Katsura's characteristic googly eyes—appear pasted on, giving no sense of a "real" person below the surface. Her body is a palimpsestic mummy, built up from old newspapers, money, and wads of white paper. No natural body exists; the physical self is a fiction held together by consumption and rhetoric. Even this collage is a mirage, as Katsura has again painted, rather than pasted, the built-up layers.

Katsura was concerned, it seems, with the risks of bodily exposure and interested in the political and aesthetic consequences of concealing, wrapping, and separating bodies from one another. Her works, in their complex representations of gender, nation, and the fraught nature of community, sought political change through shifts in aesthetics and notions of what constitutes "common sense." The contradictory nature of Katsura's work (for example, the juxtaposition of the explicit recognition of Gonbe and Crow as characters from a fable with the implicit impossibility of meshing Katsura's representation with the same didactic lesson), in Rancière's words, "undoes, and then re-articulates, connections between signs and images, images and times, and signs and spaces, framing a given sense of reality, a given 'commonsense.' It is a practice that invents new trajectories between what can be seen, what can be said and what can be done."[150] In other words, aesthetic shifts may offer an alternative strategy for altering political ideology, one that differs from the radical fracture of Hi Red Center's events of the 1960s or, as we shall see in the following chapter, the direct actions of the Sunagawa protesters, including Nakamura Hiroshi.

Katsura rejected traditional moral rectitude in *Gonbe and Crow* and other works, and, at the same time, she rejected aesthetic consensus, abstaining from the turn to abstraction that was then dominating Japanese modern art. Many of her contemporaries seemed to associate figuration with traditionalism and saw abstraction as the only model of modernity. Many of these artists were also accused of being heavily influenced by the West. Katsura's answer was to bring abstraction and figuration together in visually humorous but conceptually sophisticated assemblage works that relied heavily on reinterpretations of Japanese culture. Katsura's persistent representation of collage and assemblage suggests fragmentation and transformations of everyday life, a critical investigation of the unsettling assumptions that lie behind representations of unity and harmony.

Katsura was interested in the ways that the building up of material, of attention to the separations and slippages between bodies, animals, and things, could mediate and alter relationships. This was evident in her fascination with collage, her repeated depictions of layers, and her illustrations of bodies. Like Tanaka Atsuko, Katsura was invested in the ways that the surfaces of the body could prevent or abet communal contact and was intimately aware of the risks of bodily exposure. Painted collage also allowed Katsura to push the body below the immediate surface of the canvas—working against the legibility and didacticism that had, since she first began painting, too often been co-opted by the state and the restrictions of gender.

Unlike the overly direct representation of the nude—the conscious exposure of the female form—that defined an embodied modernity in the Taishō period, Katsura followed her own allegorical impulse that revealed the limitations of past modern painterly modes. Her work operates as allegory in its "explicit challenge to formalist aesthetics," thereby asserting Katsura's avant-garde status and practice through concealment and wrapping of the body.[151] This pioneering artist's work was a tool to lay out the stakes for a Japanese art at a time when questions of violence and responsibility, as well as questions of gender and artistic status, loomed large.

2

Nakamura Hiroshi and the Politics of Embodiment

What is the individual's ongoing relation—how does she belong—to the national culture she may serve or criticize, but which has helped shape her life and thought?

—ANNE WAGNER, *A House Divided*

Anne Wagner poses the question above in an essay on the American contemporary artist Jasper Johns (born 1930), but it applies with equal weight to many postwar Japanese artists. The question is concerned with hegemony, which, as Wagner reminds us, "is a dualism—it requires both force and consent."[1] In the 1950s, the stakes of political hegemony (including gender, cultural, and national identity and the stakes of the individual within the party system) were paramount in both Japan and the United States. Japanese artist Nakamura Hiroshi (born 1932) made sketches for what would become his most exhibited and most iconic work, *Sunagawa goban (Sunagawa No. 5)* (Figure 2.1), during the same period when Jasper Johns created his best-known work, *Flag* (Figure 2.2). Following the end of World War II, artists in the 1950s were rethinking the role of representation in relation to the nation and the role of the nation in relation to the international stage. *Sunagawa No. 5* (Plate 12) is a painting of a pivotal political event through which Nakamura expressed and analyzed his own anxieties about masculinity and political selfhood.

In Nakamura's painting, Japanese policemen stream in from the left to face off against Japanese peasants, farmers, and students, who stoically join forces to protest the expansion of the American military base at Sunagawa. One protester is already being carted away by a large, grim-faced policeman while the dark, cloud-filled sky above threatens to burst. The composition depicts an anti-American protest and reveals the fraught national dimensions of the conflict by setting Japanese body against Japanese body.

Johns's *Flag,* made of encaustic, oil, and collage, bears little resemblance to *Sunagawa No. 5.* The former is a collaged symbol of the United States, the latter a figural representation

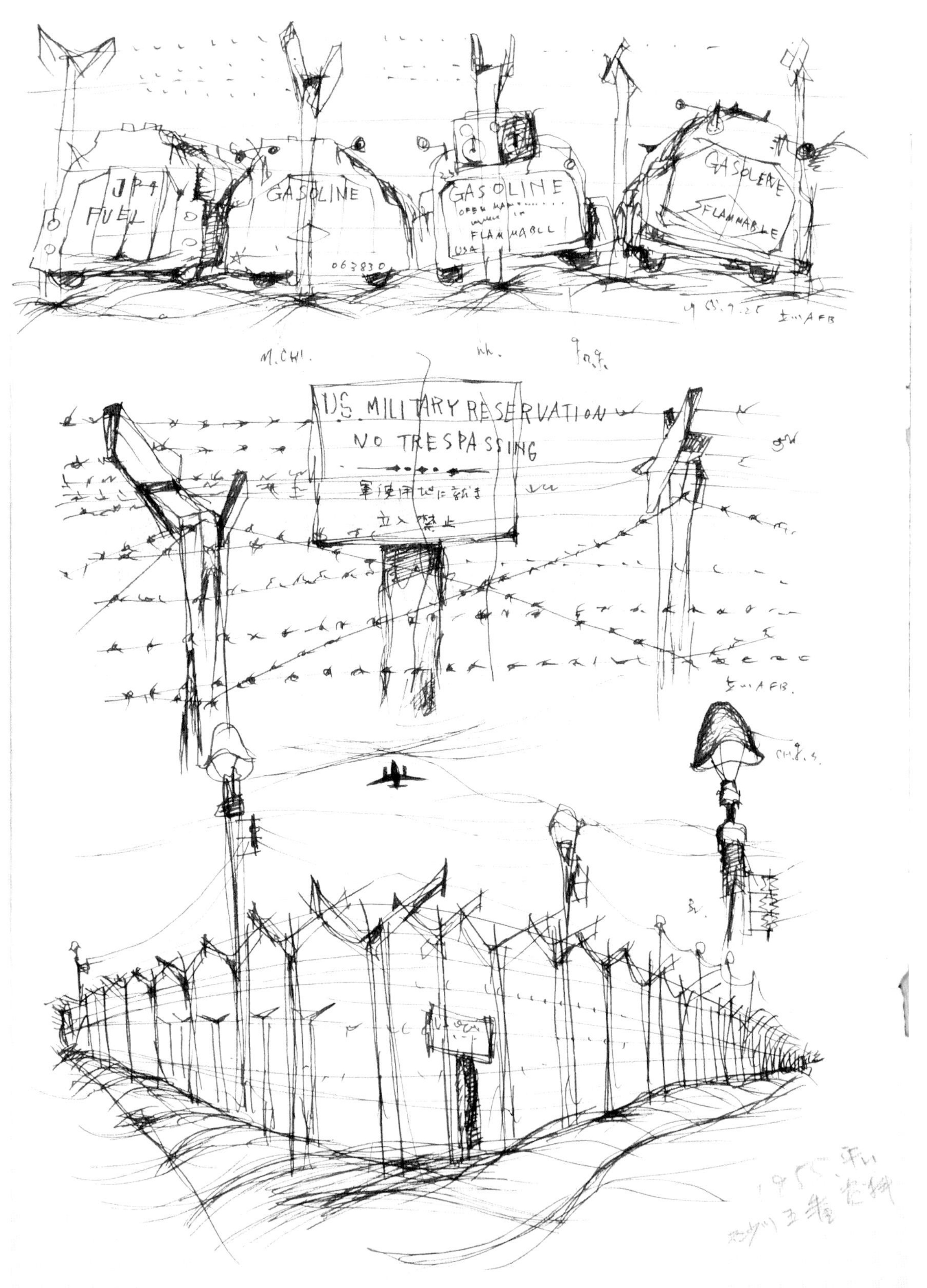

FIGURE 2.1. Nakamura Hiroshi, sketches of U.S. military base at Tachikawa, 1955. Ink on paper, 35.9 × 25.2 cm. Copyright Nakamura Hiroshi. Courtesy of the Museum of Contemporary Art, Tokyo.

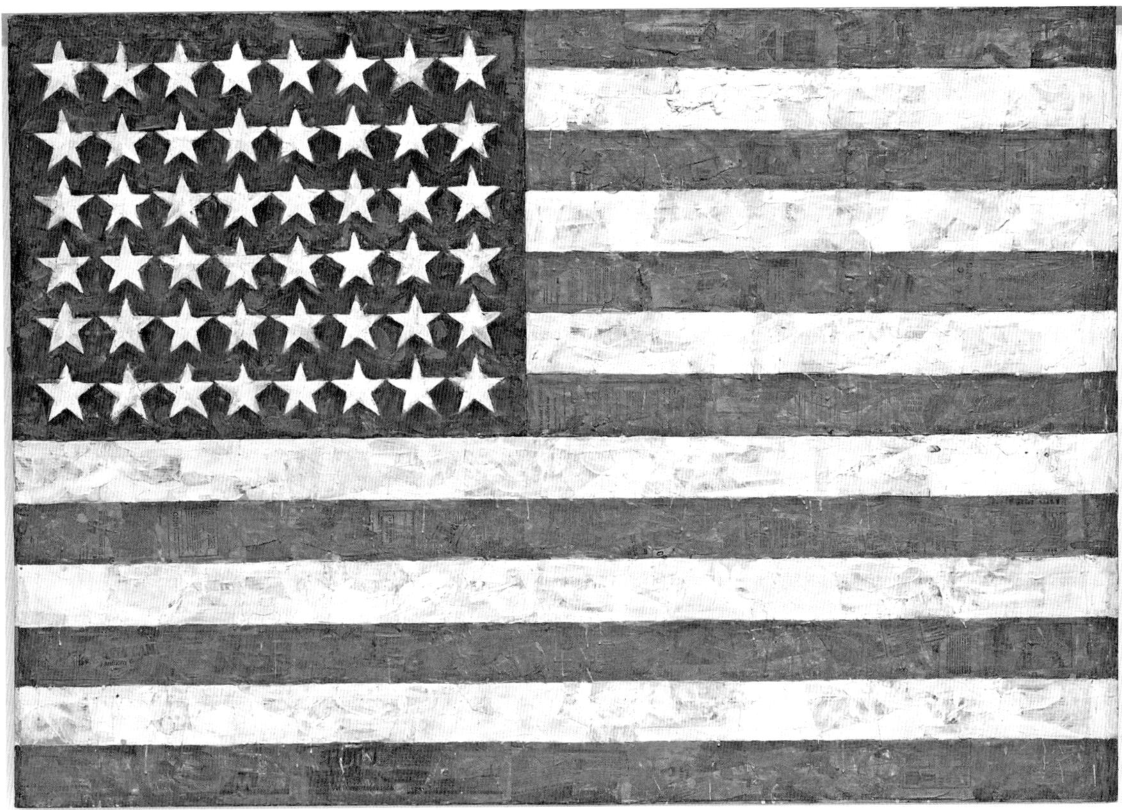

FIGURE 2.2. Jasper Johns, *Flag*, 1954–55. Encaustic, oil, and collage on fabric mounted on plywood, three panels, 42¼ × 60⅝ inches. Copyright VAGA, NY. Digital image courtesy of the Museum of Modern Art; licensed by SCALA / Art Resource NY.

of an event in a remote part of Japan. One implies the national body yet openly reveals no corporeal forms (although an initial layer of drawing suggested a female face), while the other shows oppression and oppressor in masculine, muscular tension.[2] Nakamura's work foregrounds gender as an essential site of tension, while Johns's canvas sublimates gender. Yet both give visual form to destabilizing national tensions characteristic of the Cold War, from the perspective of the United States in the case of Johns and from the position of Japan in the case of Nakamura.

Nakamura and Johns were born only two years apart and were at the height of their youth during the dynamic postwar period. It makes sense that both artists stood before canvases in the mid-1950s and attempted to picture the state of the nation. It was the dawn of American postwar global ascendency, a new era ushered in with the defeat of Japan's imperialist aims, occupation of the country, and establishment of a democratic capitalist government. Johns was well aware of these changing global dynamics and particularly the relationship between Japan and the United States. He had been stationed in Sendai, Japan, during the Korean War in 1952–53. During that time, Nakamura was actively protesting the presence of the American military in Japan. Both were "reflecting . . . on the nation, its citizens, [and] its signs."[3] The political tensions that these two very different canvases depict were in fact intimately intertwined. The ascendancy of the United States as a global power was bound up with the nation's postwar military expansion underwritten by the Cold War.

Wagner's reflections on Johns set the stage for this chapter's consideration of the political and artistic tensions between Japan and the United States that dialectically heightened tensions within the Japanese state. These tensions played a defining role in Nakamura's art and notions of masculinity in the 1950s and continued to shape his work into the 1960s and 1970s.

"Civil War"

According to Nakamura, "Japan in the 1950s was a civil war."[4] Indeed, during this period left-wing student groups and communist movements were forming an organized resistance against American imperialism and the United States' increasing investment in the Cold War. Yet the term *civil war* glosses over the complexities of the conflict in Japan.[5] The battle between those domestic forces upholding the will of the United States through proxy imperialism and those militantly against that presence was central, but behind this conflict were a number of other issues related to political subjectivity and democratic revolution. How would one's political subjectivity emerge in the postwar period, and how would it be contingent on the limitations and expectations of gender? What did it mean to be a male avant-garde artist in Tokyo? I argue that for Nakamura, these issues were worked out on the canvas: art was a way of negotiating and discovering new political selfhoods, not just representing them. In other words, art making was where politics happened.

In wartime propaganda, Japan was often represented as a heroic soldier, a strong and protective leader of other nations in the so-called Greater East Asia Co-prosperity Sphere. At other times the nation was represented as a woman whose purity must be preserved by the noble and brave deeds of her male citizens (such representations were commonplace in the journal *Nippon*) (see Figure 1.7). By the 1950s, the image of American masculine heroism loomed large throughout the world, and especially over Japan. The cowboy-style freedom embodied in the work of artists like Jackson Pollock was backed by U.S. postwar hegemony cemented through a host of political, military, and economic institutions.[6] How did Japanese artists respond to these new geopolitical and cultural currents? This chapter will discuss the depiction of the gendered body in Japan's left-wing anti-imperialist movement in the 1950s and in the increasingly globalized, mediatized 1960s, with a primary focus on the work of Nakamura Hiroshi, an artist closely associated with the reportage movement.

Reportage was an artistic movement that emerged in the 1950s and was affiliated with the Japanese Communist Party. Inspired by the postwar realism movement and led by writer Abe Kobō (1924–93), filmmaker Teshigahara Hiroshi (1927–2001), and painter Yamashita Kikuji (1919–86), the reportage movement was part of a larger resistance against the heavy-handedness of the Allied Occupation, the remaining occupying military forces, and the rise of Cold War ideology.[7] The Japan Art Alliance trained Nakamura and many other postwar artists in reportage-style painting. Other artists, such as Ikeda Tatsuo and Ishii Shigeo, also participated in the movement. In Justin Jesty's words, "Reportage became more than a style: it was a social practice which aimed to realize alternative communities through research and art."[8] Jesty's study helps us understand the mutually constitutive nature of art and politics at the time. Unlike many other art groups who were, in John Dower's terms, "embracing defeat" after the war, reportage artists were openly critical of the trajectory of Japanese politics and rejected liberal democracy as the ultimate goal.[9]

While some artists believed they could disavow the past and start with a clean slate following the end of the Pacific War, reportage artists were wary of the ways representation had been manipulated in Japan's militaristic past. In its initial form, the movement aimed to represent "reality" through depictions of relevant political events. Yet the movement was plagued by doubts about the reliance on naturalistic realism and its claims to faithful depictions of the truth. Artists such as Kawara On (1933–2014) pointed to the fact that this was the same visual language deployed in fascist Japan.[10] Reportage, then, sought to negotiate the vexing relationship between politics and representation. It pursued questions such as, Could the public be educated—or converted to communism—through art? How could artists explore artistic freedom and individualism while also supporting the mandates of a party?

By the end of 1960, with the re-signing of the ANPO treaty, the reportage group was dismantled and enthusiasm for the protest movement waned. For some artists, the dual demand to explore individual expression while furthering the left-wing political movement became untenable. Nakamura's aesthetic and political conversion away from reportage was already well under way. William Marotti, describing the growth of these tensions, writes:

> The 1955 reappearance of the Japan Communist Party (JCP) from its years of underground armed struggle led, within art, to a constriction of modes of socialist realist expression and a retreat from earlier art-popularizing efforts, as the resurgent party sought to impose greater central control over its cultural strategies. And while some fell into line with the party's cultural politics, artists such as Nakamura Hiroshi, who had been pursuing a broader strategy of experimentally representational reportage, pushed back against such formal and political narrowness.[11]

Moreover, Nakamura's resistance to political constraint was negotiated in gendered terms. As early as 1957 Nakamura turned his focus away from the male body, instead filling his canvases with surrealist landscapes and provocative adolescent female bodies. Choosing to leave party politics behind, the young artist explored the politics of media, gender, and violence. To better understand his works from the 1950s, we shall first examine the political backdrop of the reportage movement: the anti-ANPO movement.

The ANPO treaty was created in 1951 as part of the peace settlement between Japan and the United States. Signed at the close of the Allied Occupation, the treaty was intended to help Japan maintain its newly established democracy. The treaty was also part of U.S. efforts to curb the perceived threat of Communism following Mao Zedong's victory in 1949 and the recent Communist offensive in Korea in 1950. As the Cold War mounted, the United States increasingly came to rely on bases in Japan to stage its advances into East Asia. In the treaty the United States claimed the right to station 100,000 U.S. troops on Japanese soil, as well as the right to intervene in Japan's domestic affairs. Although controversial within Japan at the time, the treaty was passed. The first renewal of the treaty was in 1960, by which point public outcry had reached new levels. In Tokyo, the slogan "Never again" could frequently be heard—however, approximately 31,000 U.S. troops remain in Japan today.

The anti-ANPO movement, of course, was not only about the Japanese postwar constitution and the disproportionate power that the United States continued to hold over Japan long after the end of the Allied Occupation. It was also about the profound role of American imperialism (defined here as the ways the United States sought to exert its economic, military, and cultural influence) in shaping the Japanese state. Anti-ANPO, at its heart, was a movement that was about the desire for change, about enacting resistance, and about empowering peripheral members of society in response to the perception of increasing American imperialism. In Marotti's words:

> Examining the path to these moments of conflict reveals a wider politics of culture in Japan after the Second World War, embedded in a larger set of social practices and political confrontations. Such complexities were recognized by the participants in the events, who—in the paradigmatic activist experience during the global moment of the 1960s—found their daily lives bound up with issues of political protest and violence, law and the Constitution, state authority and legitimacy, the cold war, American hegemony, neoimperialism, and Fordist capitalism.[12]

It was a time of interdisciplinarity, experimentation, and activism.[13] In Nakamura's words, "You couldn't be a student without being a leftist then, it was part of the times."[14]

In the early 1950s Nakamura's political and artistic selves coevolved. At age nineteen, eager to move away from home, he left Hamamatsu and moved to Tabata, Tokyo, to attend the Asagaya School of Art and Design. A few months later he transferred to Nihon University's Art Department, where fellow students introduced him to the ideas of Karl Marx and the history of the Russian Revolution. Nakamura was compelled by the literature to join Zengakuren (the All-Japan Federation of Students' Self-Governing Associations), and he quickly became involved in protests, along with many other young artists and activists. (See Figure 2.3 for a photograph of Nakamura engaging in civil disobedience in 1960 along with Yoshimoto Takaaki, also known as Yoshimoto Ryūmei. He later said he was attempting to hide his face in this photo for fear the police would be able to track him down and charge him with protesting in an illegal area.)[15] Nakamura also organized a student art group, recruiting members from numerous art departments.[16] These artists joined forces with the Young Artist Association (Seinen Bijutsuka Rengō). Looking back on these events, Nakamura has reported feeling simultaneously shocked and inspired by the members' radical actions and motivations.[17]

In the 1950s, art groups and activist groups were collaborating closely, to the point that Nakamura has retrospectively suggested that the viewership for his art was mostly composed of left-wing activists.[18] Nakamura was involved in the June Action Committee,

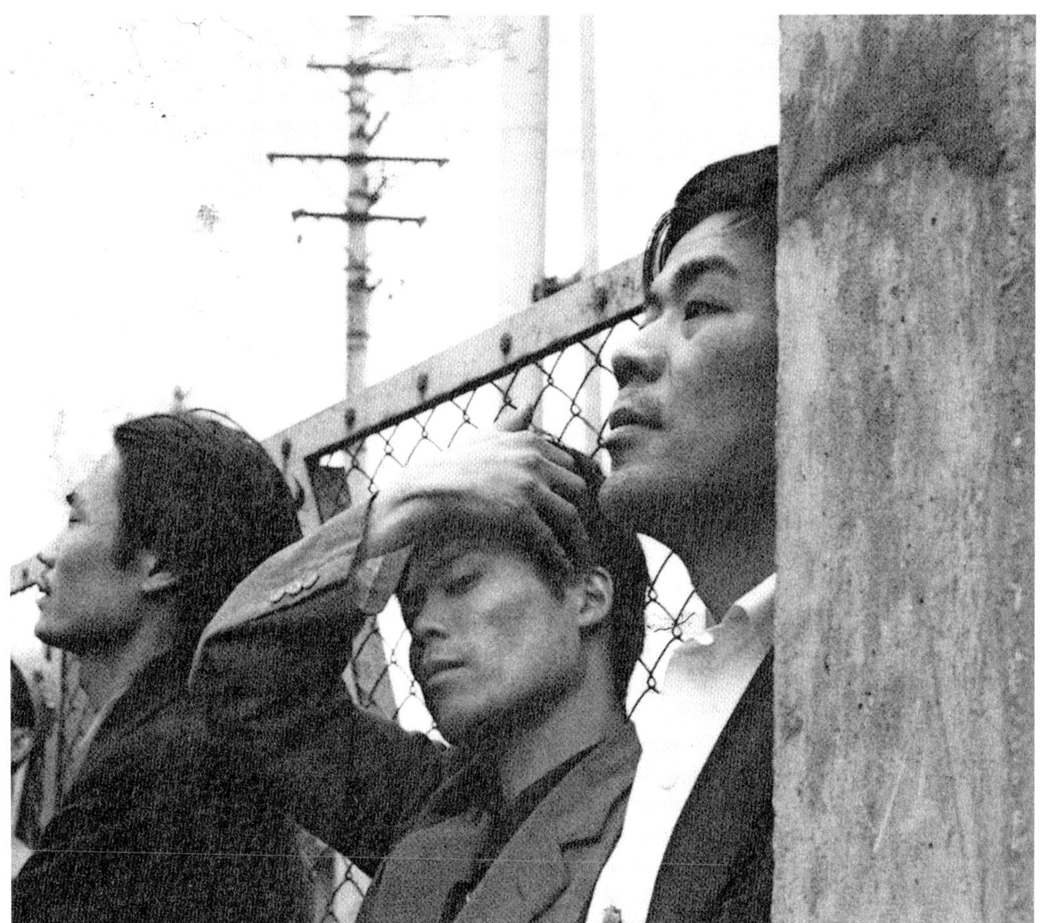

FIGURE 2.3. Photograph of Nakamura Hiroshi, age twenty-eight, at a protest rally in Tokyo near Tabata Station, 1960. From right: Yoshimoto Takaaki, Nakamura Hiroshi, and Oda Tatsurō. Copyright Nakamura Hiroshi. Originally printed in *Taburoo kikai: Nakamura Hiroshi gashū* (Tableau machine: Nakamura Hiroshi art exhibit catalog) (Tokyo: Bijutsu Shuppansha, 1995), 96.

which was part of the anti-ANPO movement. The group held demonstrations at places such as the Japanese National Railways rail yard in Tabata, Tokyo, and the houses of the National Diet.[19] On April 30, 1952, Nakamura attended a festival on the eve of May Day, but he was frightened by the violent tactics of the left-wing activists and decided against attending the demonstrations the following day. Anxiety seemed to shadow his desire to actualize political action.[20] Nakamura found himself out of step with many of his peers: just three short days after the end of the Allied Occupation, hundreds of thousands of protesters flooded the streets.[21]

The *Yomiuri Shinbun* reported that between 200,000 and 500,000 people gathered in front of Jingū Gaien pictorial arts museum in Tokyo to begin the May Day march.[22] As the level of violence from both sides mounted, the protesters moved into the public plaza in front of the Imperial Palace (a zone where protest had recently been prohibited). These were the first demonstrations since the San Francisco Peace Treaty had been signed in 1951. The May Day Declaration stated:

> Now we face a critical moment for the peace, freedom, democracy and destiny of the nation. Despite our will to establish friendly relations with every nation in the world, an unjustified administrative agreement has been thrust upon us. As a result, even though we desire independence, there is nothing left for us but indignity and subordination. . . . Oppose rearmament! Fight for national independence!
>
> Our unified struggle will end low wages!
>
> With these words, we will keep fighting until victorious![23]

Police used tear gas and fired pistols at unarmed civilians who were exercising their newly established constitutional right to demonstrate. All told, four hundred people were injured, and two protesters and a policeman were killed. It was an alarming new face of recently democratized Japan. Nakamura's fears, it seems, were justified: protest demonstrations had grown chaotic and violent. Following this tragic event, police were forbidden to carry guns during demonstrations, and they did not use tear gas again until the protests of the 1960s.[24]

Such an unprecedented level of violence shocked the nation, and the incident soon became known as Bloody May Day. For some, Japan's new democracy was irrevocably tarnished. Yet many activists were buoyed by the vast numbers of people willing to risk their lives in the name of democracy and against the so-called Security Treaty. At this intense moral crossroads, everyone was asked to take a position, to consider Japan's militaristic past, and to commit to its future. Young artists and students were at the forefront of these issues.

The Japanese Communist Party formed ties with other Marxist-oriented opposition groups such as the Socialist Party (with union ties) and the *kakushin interi* (progressive intellectuals), a conglomerate of artists, writers, and others tied to a theater group invested in political action. These groups also worked with Zengakuren. The reportage movement grew from its connections to the JCP, which regularly sent willing artists to military bases and other sites of struggle to record and express injustice.

Fractured Bodies and Reportage

While Nakamura was too young to have been conscripted during World War II, some artists involved with reportage, like Yamashita Kikuji (1890–1973), had completed military service with the imperial army and, after the war, were eager to reorient their identities away from the state. Yamashita was drafted in 1939 to fight in China. Although he did not discuss his experiences openly with his family, in 1970 he published an article titled "A Glimpse into Discrimination," in which he describes horrifying aspects of his tour of duty, including following orders to bury a Chinese prisoner alive.[25] Viewed in light of Yamashita's experiences, the abject, fragmented bodies in his artwork suggest that his art became a way for him to understand and represent his complicity in these traumatic events. Following the war, Yamashita became active in the anti-ANPO protests and the Japanese Communist Party.

In 1952, the JCP requested that Yamashita travel to the village of Akebono in Yamanashi Prefecture to create a painting based on the mysterious death of an activist who had been killed there, seemingly over land rights, earlier that year.[26] *Akebono-mura monogatari (The Tale of Akebono Village)* (Figure 2.4), completed in 1953, is a dark rendition of those events.[27] In the painting, Yamashita connects events from the prewar and postwar periods rather than offering any clear-cut explanation of the Akebono incident. In the far left, he depicts events leading up to the incident, such as initial prewar protests against a landowner. The section on the far right also addresses the prewar context, depicting an older woman who hanged herself after losing everything. She was a victim of a financial scheme that was rigged by landowners in the chaos of prewar Japan.[28] The slain activist, Ishimaru Kaname, appears in the middle section twice, drowned in the river and in a straw bag. Time is collapsed in the panels and the viewer is invited, as Justin Jesty has noted, to make his or her own connections among the past, present, and future.[29]

For many, *The Tale of Akebono Village* exemplifies reportage painting: it is based on a site of injustice and the artist conducted research with the aim of exposing that injustice. Yet the bold presence of decaying bodies in Yamashita's painting pushes uncomfortably against the edges of social realism, suggesting the porousness of labels like "realism" and "surrealism." *The Tale of Akebono Village* emphasizes the abject condition of the human body and expresses excessive raw emotion and anxiety, going beyond a political call to action. In the immediate foreground, for example, the rotten corpse of the hanged woman dangles above a bloody river and a dog is clinging to the side of the body, licking up the putrid waste.

Members of the reportage movement often shared political goals, but artists brought their own individual psychological mapping to their work and varied in their willingness

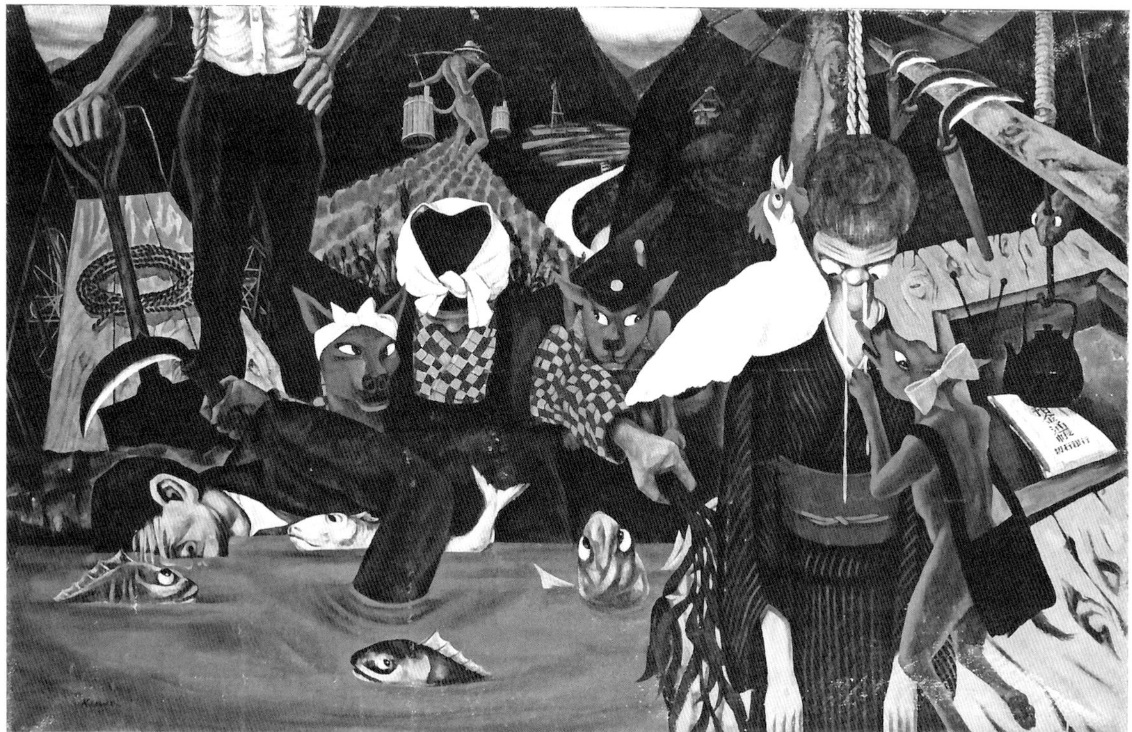

FIGURE 2.4. Yamashita Kikuji, *Akebono-mura monogatari (The Tale of Akebono Village)*, 1953. Oil on jute, 123 × 214 cm. Courtesy of Nippon Gallery, Tokyo.

to toe the Communist Party line, both formally and aesthetically.[30] Despite their differences, Ishii, Yamashita, and Nakamura all relied on representations of the body to register destructive loss and the potential for transformation. This was not a new phenomenon, however. Winther-Tamaki notes how *yōga* (Western-style painting) in the Meiji period aimed to achieve "maximum embodiment" through four components: the materiality of oil paint pigments on the picture surface, the illustration of the human body, the imagined somatic presence of the artist in the painting, and rhetorical metaphors of social incorporation.[31] He further suggests that from the mid-1930s to the mid-1950s artists displayed a tendency toward "maximum disembodiment." He writes: "These problems of life and art in postsurrender Japan stimulated a linkage between disembodiment in figurative painting and the reconstruction of subjectivity."[32] As Winther-Tamaki shows, Shiraga Kazuo's work is typical of this form of disembodiment.[33]

Nakamura followed this trajectory, if belatedly, continuing to work on embodied representation as late as the mid-1950s. Embodiment is indeed heightened in his best-known painting, *Sunagawa No. 5* (Plate 12), through scale and the accentuation of physicality in the depiction of markers of class and gender difference. The painting, a pivotal work in his career, exemplifies this tendency in the context of the explosive social movements around anti-U.S. imperialism. But by the late 1950s, he began to paint disembodiment, gradually shifting away from figuration to perspective. I will address his engagement with disembodiment (that is, the breakdown and abstraction of the represented body) later in the chapter, but first I present a discussion of the context of the Sunagawa incident to fully illuminate the stakes of Nakamura's most lauded painting and to illustrate the complex dynamics of political subjectivity in postwar Japan.

Sunagawa: Site and Struggle

The Sunagawa struggle was a movement that began in 1955 against the expansion of the Tachikawa military base in Sunagawa-chō, on the outskirts of Tokyo. Popular anger and protest were so vociferous that the plans for the expansion of the base were eventually abandoned, although the governments of the United States and Japan had formally agreed to the development. This was a pivotal time, and protests were ongoing from 1955 to 1959. Student activists, residents, and Labor Party members joined forces as never before and clashed with the state police.

The tensions between Sunagawa village and the nearby Tachikawa Airfield were of long duration and complex, although the events are often misleadingly referred to as the "Sunagawa incident."[34] Between May 1955 and March 1959, farmers staged frequent protests, ranging from circulating petitions to hurling dirt clods at surveyors; students and left-wing groups rallied, riot police were increasingly present, and legal battles over the boundaries of the base played out in the courts.[35] The dispute was over a rather small area of land, but the ramifications for the town were large—without farmland, the village would collapse.

The expansion of the Tachikawa base would also have direct consequences for the perceived international political position of Japan as the United States pushed its agenda into East Asia; additionally, the loss of the Pacific War to the United States had placed territory in a heightened symbolic role. The conflict over territory was seen as part of a larger struggle to define Japan's status as an independent and self-determining nation-state. Prime Minister Hatoyama Ichirō, elected one year before the Sunagawa struggle began, was attempting to negotiate a peace treaty with the Soviet Union, with the long-term aim of securing membership in the United Nations. Within the country, various political groups, such as the JCP and the Japanese Socialist Party, were attempting to organize. Zengakuren was recovering from a loss of leadership due to arrests under the Allied Occupation.[36] In this light, we can easily see how Sunagawa became a meaningful site in terms of exploring the limits and possibilities of political selfhood in relation to larger issues of political hegemony.

The region has a contentious history—during the Pacific War it was a base for kamikaze training actions. Tachikawa was consequently a prime target for the U.S. military, and it was heavily bombed in June 1945.[37] Although the *shintentai,* an anti–aerial attack group, defended the site, the grounds and surrounding city were in ruins. The U.S. armed forces moved into the area on September 4, 1945, and began to use it as a transport base.[38] Since the 1930s, Sunagawa village had been infringed upon six times by expansions of the base, and the threat of further loss to the United States was especially troublesome.[39]

On March 15, 1954, the United States submitted a formal request to extend the base by approximately fifty acres, an expansion that would occupy parts of the civilian town of Sunagawa. Although Hatoyama had acquiesced to expansion in principle, he may have been willing to adopt a formal position of agreement because he did not believe that the expansion would ever actually materialize. The agreement required that all of the farmers would sell the requisite land. In fact, only a fraction did so. The long history of land loss to the Japanese military base had embittered most of the farmers, who had been anticipating regaining land, rather than losing more, at the war's end.[40] Protests against this development grew rapidly. On May 8, 1955, Aoki Ichigorō and other townspeople formed the Anti–Base Expansion Struggle Committee and asked Mayor Miyazaki Denzaemon to prevent any land surveys.[41] A story about the formation of the committee appeared on the front page of the national newspaper two days later.[42] Sunagawa was suddenly nationally, even internationally, recognized, and oppositionists hoped to take advantage of this attention. In August 1955, approximately seven hundred farmers rallied and successfully turned back the surveyors again.[43] On September 13, the government stepped up security, bringing in a thousand Japanese policemen to control the protesters. The *Asahi Shinbun* reported that five hundred farmers and twelve hundred labor union members resisted the police, resulting in thirty-eight injuries, sustained mostly by police officers.[44] The following day, the number of protesters increased and police arrested twenty-six people. In the daylong protest on September 14, more than three thousand protesters clashed with approximately two thousand police. Again, union activists and students joined farmers in the area to attempt to prevent a survey for expansion of the base. Seventy-four people were injured in that clash even though no weapons were used, indicating a marked level of hand-to-hand violence. The incidents involved a remarkable number of bodies in violent confrontation—an element that Nakamura attempted to capture in his work.

The slant of reporting in the American press diverged from that in Japan. The numbers of protesters reported in the *New York Times* tended to downplay the scale of the opposition, while Japanese newspapers reported turnouts thousands higher. In every *New York Times* article, even from the early days of the protests, blame was cast on "communist agitators" or "left-wing forces" that were "taking advantage" of the opposition. Interestingly, however, the JCP's daily broadsheet, *Akahata,* did not cover events at Sunagawa until 1956. Similarly, Zengakuren did not announce that it would support the movement until September 13, 1956. The leaders of the movement arose from within the ranks of local farmers in the area, who worked together with other supporting groups. The Japanese newspapers' documentation of the court cases and protests led by Aoki and Sunagawa's mayor reveals the degree of commitment and the scope of the alliances that fueled these events.

By August 1956, twenty-two union members were fired from the base for "security reasons," and thousands of Japanese employed there went on strike. Not only was the

United States losing control over its expansion plans, but it also could no longer rely on the teams of Japanese workers necessary to make the base operate.[45] On October 12, 1956, an hour-long "fistfight" between Japanese police and Japanese protesters led to 120 injuries (nine protesters and four police officers were seriously injured).[46] Clashes continued for two more days, and 300 people were injured. The ferocity of these events underscores the physical, bodily level of action at the forefront of the political struggle. As we shall see, representing this embodied physicality was vitally important to Nakamura.

In October 1956, activists published "The National Declaration for the Sunagawa Struggle against the Base":

> Victory for the Sunagawa struggle is close at hand. The labor movement, students, and peasants, and many people from all different social classes from all over Japan are strongly unified for independence and the protection of peace for our motherland. We never stepped back from 2,000 rampaging armed policemen. This struggle has caused the government, which has trampled our lives and rights solely for the profit of the United States, to give up the land survey. This indicates our glorious victory in the Sunagawa base struggle.[47]

On January 8, 1959, the *Mainichi* newspaper reported that the United States had conceded to the protesters and, in a rare victory for the left-wing movement, indefinitely postponed plans to expand the base. More than six thousand people were reported to have participated actively in the movement, including local farmers, organizers from the Japanese Communist Party, women's groups, union workers, and student activists. Such a victory at this moment was pivotal. It opened up possibilities for civic freedom in a new Japanese-led democracy, fueled hope for support of the JCP, and ultimately rekindled a fading belief that American dominance would not last forever. The outpouring of support for the protesters following the Sunagawa struggle helped push public perception further to the left, encouraging even greater numbers of people to take to the streets during the anti-ANPO protests that followed.[48]After the expansion plans had been scrapped, the limited capacity of Tachikawa could not keep up with the growing needs of the military during the Cold War. By 1964, the United States had begun to rely more heavily on the nearby Tama Airfield (now Yokota Air Base). The grounds at Sunagawa were formally returned to Japanese control on November 30, 1977.[49]

Significantly, no U.S. military personnel were present during these violent episodes. It was the Japanese police forces that were set against the Japanese opposition in a desperate fight to determine not only the future of Sunagawa but also the shape of politics to come. Although in many ways the Sunagawa struggle was about the continuing territorial expansion of power by the United States, it also symbolized a foundational issue for the Japanese: the urgent need to come to terms with a new sense of national identity.

The Sunagawa struggle magnified the concessions and schisms that Japanese citizens faced at the end of the Allied Occupation in the early 1950s. At a time when the country was still emerging from the disasters of the war, the future appeared fluid and uncertain. It was not a simple matter of a unified Japanese mass against the hegemony of the United States; rather, each person was part of an evolving, sometimes devolving, form of political democracy—and the shape of Japan's future political landscape in 1955 was far from clear. As Victor Koschmann writes:

> Why did this analysis of the situation [in postwar Japan] provide the occasion for a debate on subjectivity? Because, put crudely, the accepted Marxian framework prescribed that each stage of historical development would be led by the social subject appropriate to it. . . . That is, the success of the postwar Japanese democratic revolution involved an intrinsic connection to a suitable revolutionary social subject, and "subjectivity," or *shutaisei,* was understood to be that subject's normative criterion.[50]

In terms of political selfhood, the choice between supporting the Security Treaty, with its compromised sovereignty and the international protection it claimed to offer, or joining forces with a precarious, sometimes fractious, grassroots movement was a complicated matter. Individual actions could be contradictory, and within union groups opinions were hotly contested. Such a state of "civil war" was often deeply internalized by those involved. A tragic example is the suicide of Ido Hiroshi, a member of the Metropolitan Police Board Reserve Corps who was troubled by his feelings of complicity with the state while involved with the Sunagawa struggle.[51] Similarly, many artists were critical of themselves for their own perceived hypocrisies. Some artists who were active in the Communist anti-American movement, such as Ikeda Tatsuo, found themselves taking commissions from U.S. army members in order to make ends meet.[52]

The Sunagawa struggle, then, became a defining moment of victory in the ongoing anti-ANPO battle and a site where individuals could carve out their own senses of political selfhood, building a solidarity that, unlike the wartime state rhetoric, allowed for dissensus. Protesters proved their grit and commitment, maintaining a presence on the base over years despite numerous arrests, the firing of union workers, and the ongoing threat of violence. This internal conflict demanded a reexamination of moral and political direction, and often art was a key means for that exploration.[53] Nakamura's depiction of the Sunagawa struggle contributed to the emotional and societal impact of the events, just as depicting the struggle drew attention to the artist.

Painting *Sunagawa No. 5*

Sunagawa No. 5 is a polemical indictment of the pivotal events of the Sunagawa struggle and also marks the zenith of Nakamura's personal investment in grassroots activism (many critics have also assumed that it represents the zenith of his artistic development). The painting depicts an ideal—and idealized—moment of unity in the movement, a time when farmers, union activists, students, regional government officials, women's organizations, and Buddhist temple members came together to fight the base's expansion. Nakamura reports that he had been notified about participating in the Sunagawa struggle through Nihon Bijutsu Kyōkai (the Japan Art Association), a group of about two hundred members, including Nakamura, mobilized by the large Sōhyō labor union. Initially, his primary objective in traveling to Tachikawa was to participate in the rallies. To his surprise, he found there were already hundreds of protesters along the route (via Itsukaichi Way), including a large number of children.[54] Absorbing the energy of the crisis, he decided to base an artwork on the clash. The oil-on-plywood work marshals the energy of political action through its composition and depiction of bodies.

The painting depicts a moment when the policemen are removing random people from a group of sitting protesters for detention and arrest. Nakamura himself was nearly plucked from the crowd.[55] Although he recalls that it was mainly student groups and Communist Party members that surrounded him, he elected to focus more on the peasants in his painting, perhaps to heighten the David and Goliath effect of the work, and thus inspire others to action. He has described being propelled by a great sense of urgency to complete the paintings and have them be seen.[56] Indeed, Nakamura completed the work in only a few short months after visiting the site, perhaps hoping to optimize its currency and political impact.

Socialist realists in Japan at the time claimed an investment in the geographical site of an actual political event. The site was understood as the place of politics, even after the event had ended. *Genba,* a word derived from the combination of the characters for "actual" and "place," conveys the notion of authenticity and suggests that locale is bound up with that authenticity. "Place," Yi-Fu Tuan tells us, "is a center of meaning constructed by experience."[57] This might be seen in opposition to location—an arena of space that holds reduced experiential, subjective, and potentially gendered meaning. The binding of meaning to place is central to reportage's visual strategies. The title *Sunagawa No. 5,* for example, rather than referring to a series, ties the work closer to the site of action: "no. 5" makes reference to *5-chome,* the fifth block in the district where that protest was taking place. This is where Nakamura himself participated in the demonstrations.[58]

Illustrating the concept of *genba,* Nakamura negotiates the tension between location and place by situating a map, detailed and sinuous, prominently in the left foreground of the picture. Maps epitomize Cartesian space—space that is rendered abstract and geometric, the better to monitor and control it. Here we note that the artist depicts police officers standing atop a map highlighting the state's classic ocular relation to knowledge and power over territory (a motif that has its own colonial art historical tradition). In this fashion, Nakamura points to the state's use of the village of Sunagawa as a minor location in a larger battle to consolidate power and capital set against the backdrop of U.S. imperialism. Moreover, the painting's multiple vanishing points and differing logics of space do not cohere pictorially, reinforcing the sense of tension in the work.

Farmers, suggests Nakamura, do not need a map to find their way. The village is the place of the farmer. Despite the fact that farmers also aim to directly control, plot, and plant the land, in this heavily ideologized canvas they are *of* the land, as reinforced by the neutral tones of their clothing, their physical proximity to the earth, and their work-worn hands. Like Shiraga, whose struggle in *Challenging Mud,* discussed in chapter 4, recalls the GI's proximity to the ground, Nakamura represents the on-site struggle over place—for place to be occupied, embodied, and visually surveyed by the people. Site and body are in a dialectical relationship that authenticates and binds the two into political action.

Scale augments the dominance of the state's forces in *Sunagawa No. 5.* The large black boot of the police officer is lowest in the picture plane, the inflated size lending weight to the perceived strength of the enemy. The policeman's hunched body overpowers the slight figures of the peasants, their faces turned upward to emphasize the height differential between them. Ominously, the police officers' caps cover their eyes, and they are without much character save for their overwhelming physicality. We know them as those who carry out the law of the land: their oversized shoulders and monotonous blue-black uniforms leave no room for emotionality or intelligence (in fact this was not at all true, as the afore-mentioned policeman's suicide suggests). Nakamura contrasts the police, represented as ox-like figures, with the peering faces of the protesters, who are depicted as wide-eyed, their lined faces expressive of their sensitivities and vulnerabilities. Although the details of their clothes suggest a broad range of identities, their anxious faces share similar expressions and their bodies lean forward collectively.

A diminutive monk (representing the militant Red Monks of Myōhōji) is in the fore-ground, his expression stoic as he squares off against men many times his size. (The spiritual warrior is reminiscent of Shiraga Kazuo's encounters with Tendai Buddhism at Mount Hiei, which will be described in chapter 4.) Relying on the exaggerated binaries of good and evil that surface in heroic narratives of mass culture, Nakamura brings the codes of lowbrow, mass-culture illustration—a medium flourishing at the time—to the highbrow practice of oil painting.[59] Significantly, Nakamura had taken work illustrating book jackets, magazine covers, and posters to supplement his income throughout his career.

A historian of the Nikkyōso Fujinbu (Women's Section of the Teachers' Association) reports that teachers and mothers were heavily involved in organizing at Sunagawa, picket-ing the site regularly. These women understood that participating in the events at Tachikawa could lead to a larger role for women in the left-wing movement.[60] The women who par-ticipated dressed in specific clothing for these events: they often wore *monpe* (women's work pants), which indicated their commitment to hard work, or donned *kappōgi* (body-length aprons used by women for cooking and cleaning, and also worn by women doing war sup-port work in the 1930s and 1940s). Thus, women sought to foreground their gender in a manner that emphasized the body as part of a community. Nakamura depicts several women at the heart of the conflict, their positions and comportment not so different from those of their male counterparts.

This progressive representation of women differs sharply from the depiction of women by the labor movement. Historian Christopher Gerteis has shown that while the Allied Occupation forces endeavored to have women join labor unions, ultimately the dominant labor organizations like Sōhyō (the largest union in Japan at the time) fell back on corporate and conservative gender models. For example, in one union poster, political cartoonist Katō Etsurō draws a bare-chested man leaning in with an insecticide spray pump to exterminate a swarm of naked and half-dressed men and women fleeing a container labeled: "erotic grotesque culture" (Figure 2.5). According to the transparent visual code of the union propaganda posters, men were charged with making choices about their responsibility for the nation: one could become a union member (embodied in the caricature of the shirtless, virile, laboring man) or be equated to the hapless, miniaturized, effeminate men. Even these limited choices were unavailable to women. Katō's images make clear that any assertion of masculinity is dependent on operations of othering for its efficacy.

Although both men and women seem to participate in the conflict ostensibly as equals in *Sunagawa No. 5,* close analysis reveals that Nakamura renders the corporeal presence of the male farmers in somewhat greater detail. For example, the hands of the men, in

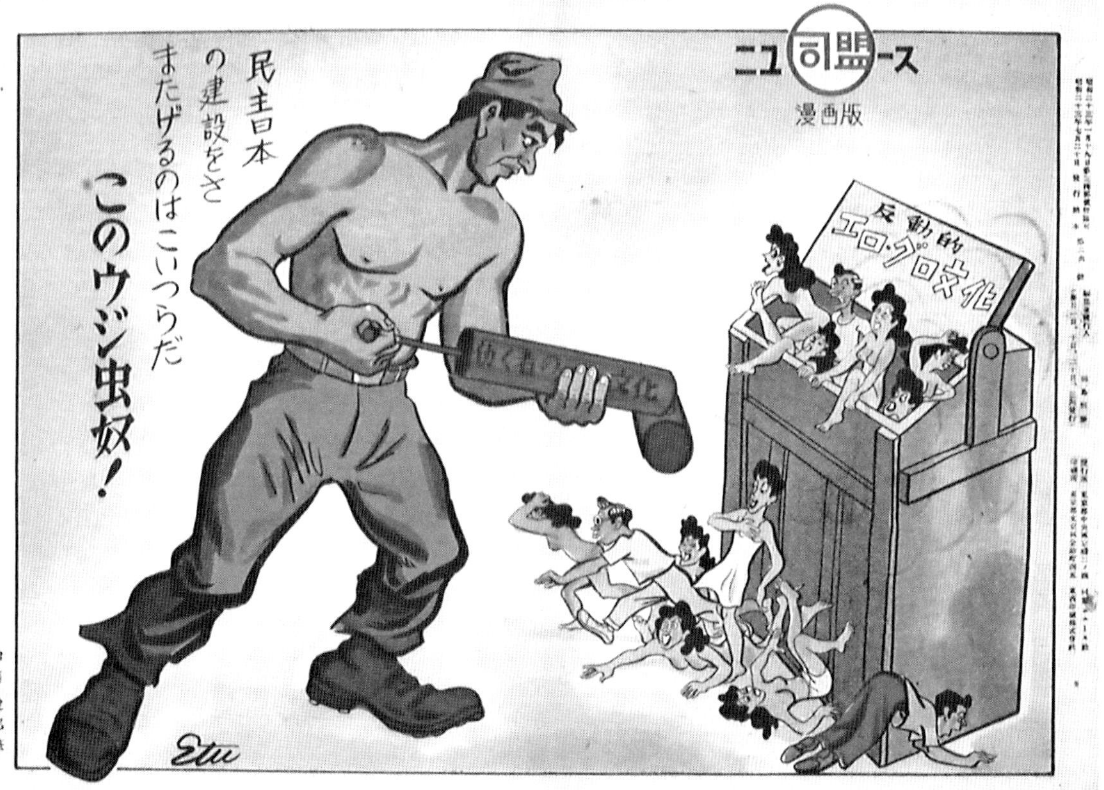

FIGURE 2.5. Katō Etsurō, *Dōmei nyūsu mangaban* (Federation News cartoon edition), July 20, 1948. Courtesy of the Ohara Institute for Social Research, Hōsei University. Copyright Katō Hitoshi.

contrast to those of the women, are depicted in an exaggerated manner: oversized, veined, and curved. The male farmers' hands are exposed, unlike those of the policemen, which are nowhere to be found. Hands are a humanizing feature, signifying work, touch, and community.

Nakamura's oeuvre, particularly his early work, illustrates an investment in hands as a marker of masculinized labor and life. Just one year before painting *Sunagawa No. 5,* he completed two drawings on October 17, 1954, both called simply *Te (Hand)* (Figure 2.6). The first ink-on-paper study shows one hand facing upward, its fingers curled as if about to form a clenched fist, or perhaps as if something had just slipped from its grasp. Nakamura shows us experience through his deep linear emphasis on the lifeline across the palm and through the darkened fingernails. It is a metonymic portrait.

The second drawing turns the palm directly up, fingers open and uncurled. The steep vertical orientation of the hand gives the drawing an architectural quality. Arching to the left below the upturned hand, a dark shadow further reinforces the structure of the composition. The top of the palm is darkened, its texture heightened and contrasting with the pale heel. Palm and heel are distinctively separated where the markings of accrued contact run deep. Each finger reveals the swirling marks of fingerprints, hypnotically overarticulated, suggesting the ways the hand must have once touched, worked, and pressed on innumerable elements in the exteriorized world. Nakamura exposes both the vulnerabilities of the palm and the weight of past encounters. For him, hands are the embodiment of labor.

Images of hands are often invoked as a sign of artistic authorship, as Murillo, Rembrandt, and others have shown us.[61] While other great artists draw attention to their hands as part of whole self-portraits, Nakamura fragments the hand from the body, drawing the hand only from the wrist. This fracture between artist's body and the tool of its expression is suggestive of Nakamura's unwillingness to portray himself as a fully embodied, confident artist akin to Murillo or Yokoyama Matsusaburō, a nineteenth-century photographer and painter who also employed the motif of the hand to attest to his mastery of his medium. Nakamura's early drawings may have influenced his later role as an art instructor. As a teacher at the experimental, uncertified art school Bigakkō (School of Beauty), Nakamura emphasized the importance of the artistic hand.[62] In 1969, Bigakkō started a pilot program with workshops by Nakamura and Nakanishi Natsuyuki. The school's brochure stated:

a. We position Bigakkō as the best device to fully intervene in contemporary aesthetics and ethics.
b. *The Bigakkō curriculum is primarily concerned with *tewaza* [manual skills or, literally, hand skills] and training through close relationships between teachers and students. Students are to acquire the teachers' aesthetic ideas.[63]

Hence, Nakamura saw the hand—both as a representation and as a tool for creative labor—as a key means to mobilize artistic and political thought and action.

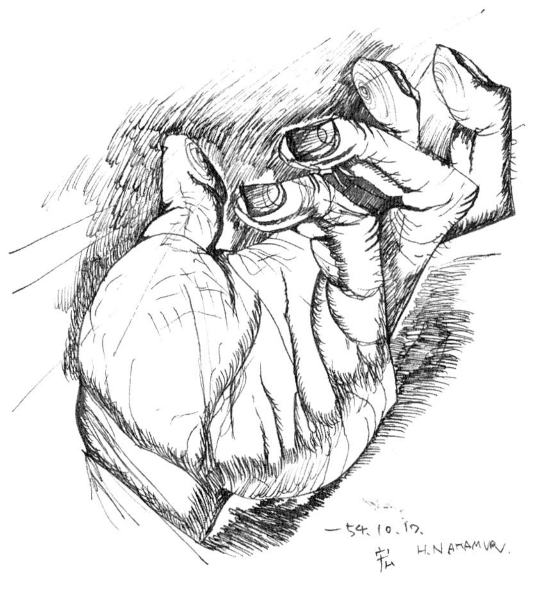

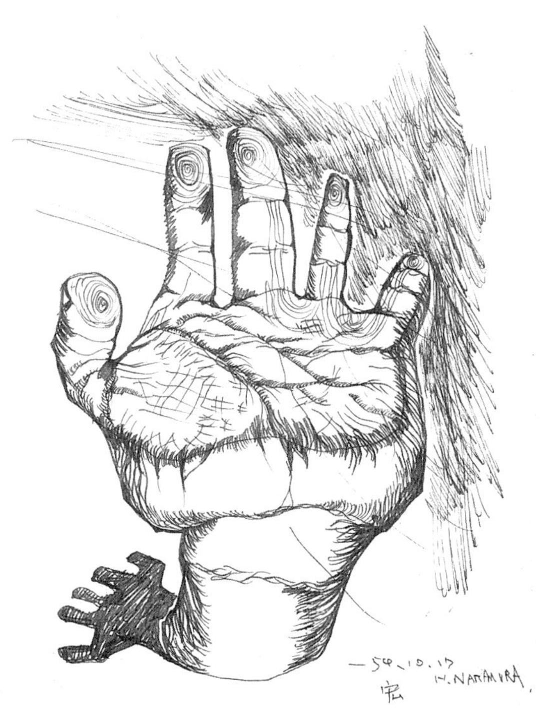

FIGURE 2.6. Nakamura Hiroshi, *Te (Hand),* 1954. Ink on paper, 25.8 × 17.8 cm (each). Copyright Nakamura Hiroshi. Courtesy of Nerima Art Museum.

The hand motif appears in other works he created in the early 1950s. Large men's hands heighten the value of the working male body in *Sekitan okiba (Coal Storage)* (1955) (Figure 2.7), and Nakamura analogizes their strength to trains in *Kokutetsu shinagawa (JNR Shinagawa)* (1955) (Figure 2.8), suggesting that for him, labor is bound up with gender. Nakamura's use of the train as a metaphor for the male body would be expanded in his work in the late 1950s, as we will see in the final section of this chapter.

Nakamura was not alone in his interest in the vitality of the body at this time, even as this interest reached its peak in Japan. Citing reviews in the journal *Bijutsu hihyō*, Winther-Tamaki points out how in the mid-1950s "Mexican embodiment was envied as 'muscular optimism,' heralded as the 'peak attainment of figurative art,' fantasized as 'vital racial power,' and admired for distinguishing Mexican art from that of 'the West.'"[64] Nakamura indeed saw the exhibitions of Mexican painting at the Tokyo National Museum in 1955 and became an admirer of Diego Rivera.[65] As in Rivera's work, Nakamura's investment in the male body, his composition, and his content all conveyed a clear political direction. Yet Nakamura's male bodies never reached the levels of vitality and optimism seen in Rivera's paintings. *Sunagawa No. 5* represents the height of Nakamura's interest in masculine embodiment, but even for these farmers and students, victory seems out of reach. It is the state-backed police forces, with corresponding military and physical power, that appear to have victory in hand. Thus, *Sunagawa No. 5* is as much about the anxiety of losing the battle as it is about recording the event itself. This fissure of fear runs through much of Nakamura's early work.

Many of Nakamura's drawings and paintings of male bodies created in the years leading up to *Sunagawa No. 5* feature gaunt and hollow-chested men rather than muscular figures. For example, in *Jigazō A (Self-Portrait A),* from 1953 (Figure 2.9), the subject leans a sharply angled jaw on an oversized left hand. The hand is not the weathered hand of labor; instead, we witness the softly curved palm cupping a tense jaw, the subject's face marked by dark, heavily lined creases under the eyes.

Jigazō B (Self-Portrait B) (Plate 13), created the same year, is an unusually cadaverous self-portrait. The skinny torso and sunken chest all too easily meld into the discolored background. Jutting straight down toward the ground, the blunt fingers and penis are depicted in a similarly straight and simplistic manner, yet we sense a greater tension emanating from the taut hands than from the flaccid penis. The subject's heavy jaw is turned sharply aside as though he cannot bear to face our gaze. For Nakamura, representing the self was a troubling enterprise.

It seems Nakamura's desire to represent the male body as the site of labor and experience in *Sunagawa No. 5* was at odds with the gendered anxieties that surfaced in his early works. *Sunagawa No. 5* operated in numerous ways: as a report of the event, as a celebrated example of reportage painting, and as an avenue through which the artist could explore his own position vis-à-vis the changing political landscape in postwar Japan. It was an authenticating revolutionary painting through which his personal political selfhood in

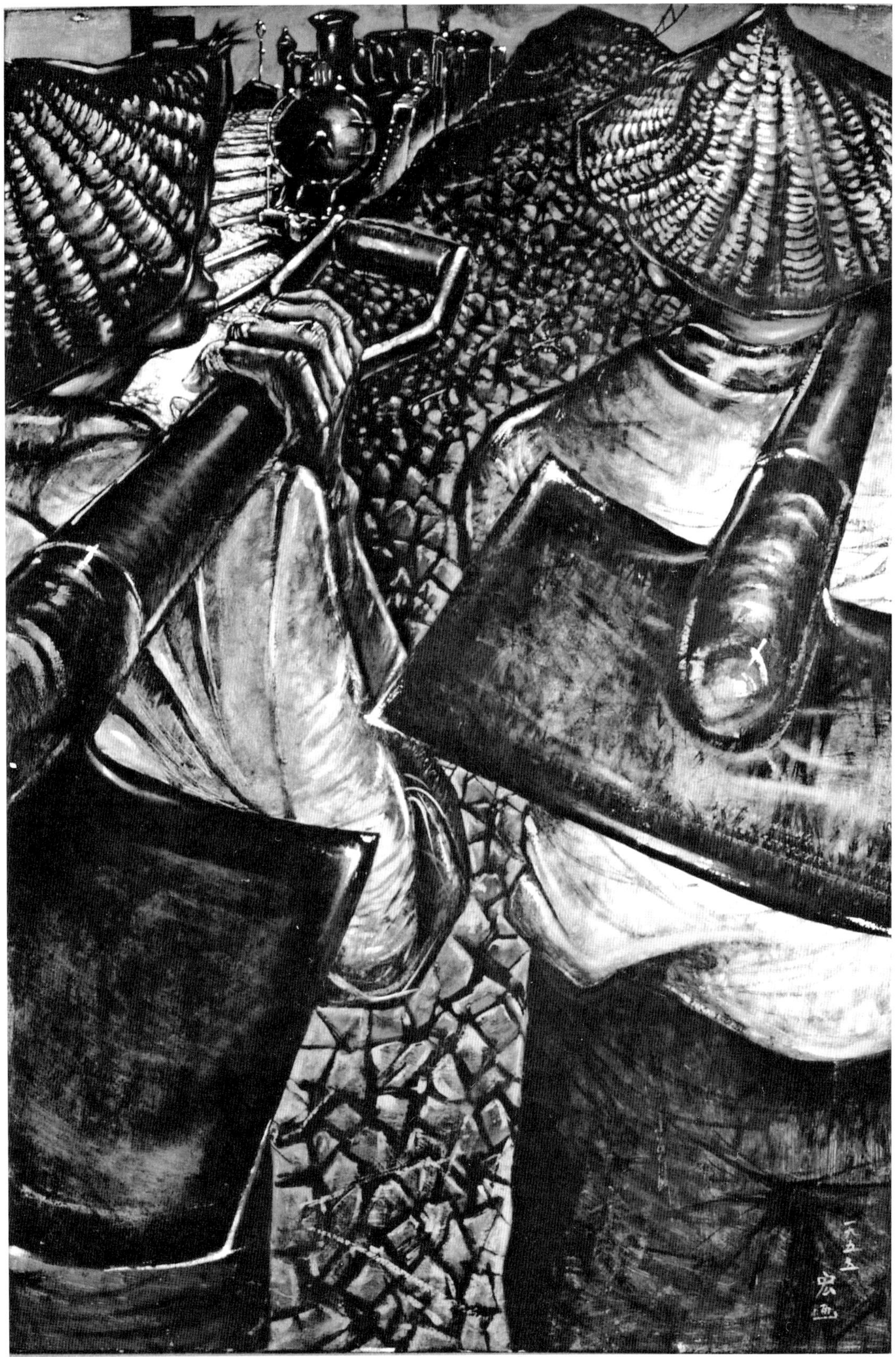

FIGURE 2.7. Nakamura Hiroshi, *Sekitan okiba (Coal Storage)*, 1955. Oil on canvas, 72.8 × 49.8 cm. Copyright Nakamura Hiroshi. Courtesy of the Kariya City Art Museum.

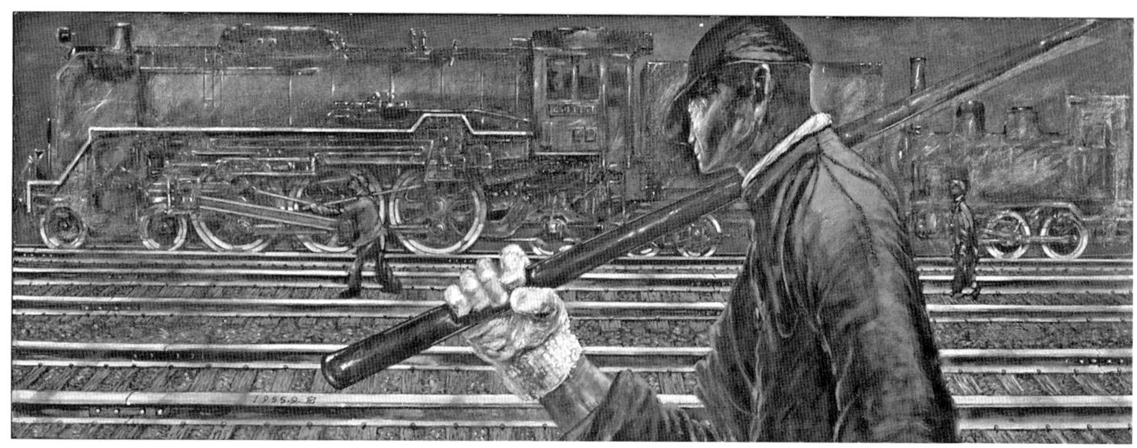

FIGURE 2.8. Nakamura Hiroshi, *Kokutetsu shinagawa (JNR Shinagawa),* 1955. Oil on canvas, 37.5 × 101.5 cm. Copyright Nakamura Hiroshi. Courtesy of the Hamamatsu Municipal Museum of Art.

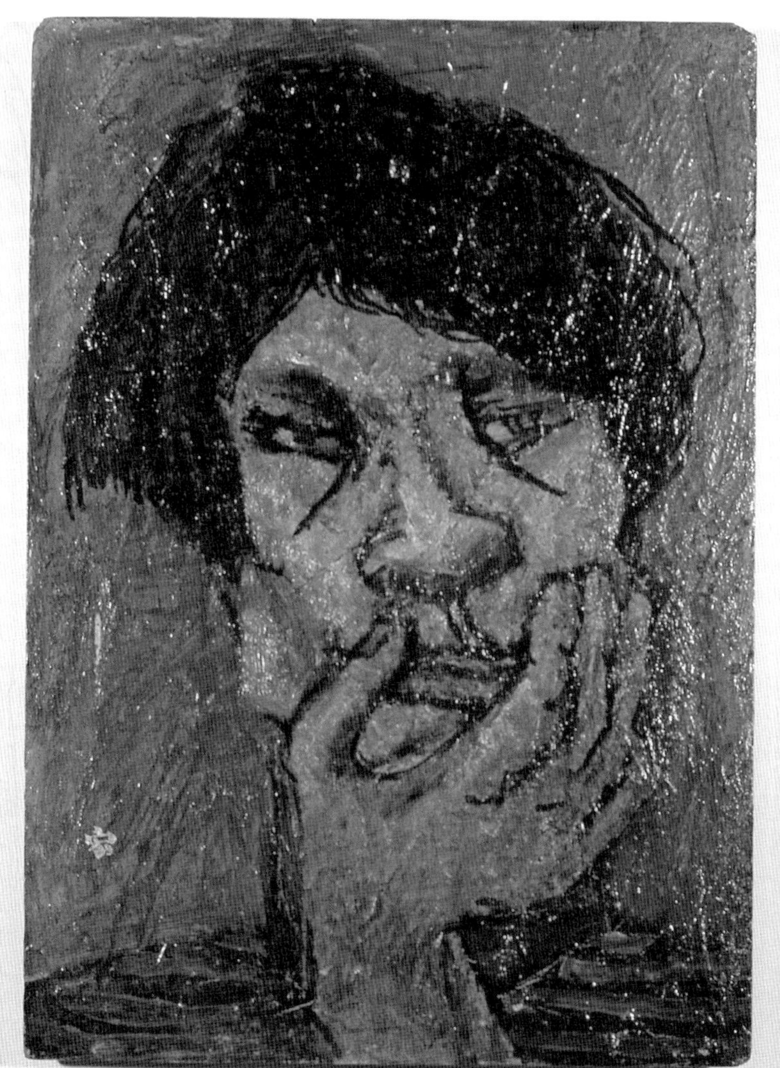

FIGURE 2.9. Nakamura Hiroshi, *Jigazō A (Self-Portrait A),* 1953. Oil on wood, 33 × 24 cm. Copyright Nakamura Hiroshi. Courtesy of the Hamamatsu Municipal Museum of Art.

relation to leftist activism emerged. Yet this relation seems to have failed for him, as he broke away from his generation's embrace of the bodily tactics of protest, a tension that is already visible in this pivotal work. *Sunagawa No. 5* would be the apex of Nakamura's overtly political work and the closest he would come to "muscular optimism." Within two short years, he redirected his political compass. By 1957, the power of the male hero was sublimated into ambivalent metaphor in his paintings, and his participation in direct political action seemed to wither. An analysis of his final reportage works will shed light on that transformation.

Gunned Down

Nakamura created his last socialist realist works in 1957, painting two versions of the event known as the Girard incident—the tragic shooting of an unarmed Japanese mother of six by an American soldier. Between these two depictions of the incident a significant shift occurs in Nakamura's work. He moves from emphasizing site *(genba)* to removing any sense of place, from depicting the masculine body to representing the feminine body under the masculine gaze, which in turn effects a definitive break with the representation of embodiment and ushers in a new interest in disembodied perspective.

The first version, titled *Kichi (The Base)* (1957) and painted on plywood (Plate 14), has come to epitomize the mounting political opposition to the Allied Occupation and the Japanese state police in the 1950s.[66] Yet we might also consider the way that it allowed Nakamura to reconsider his own artistic direction. In the painting, the stark foregrounding of the skull beneath the armored helmet, its eye sockets black and vacuous but for a cold, blue glint, equates war and death in no uncertain terms. The living flesh of man has already been reduced to its postmortem state. We stare into a world that is represented as unknowable and dark. With its play of geometric forms (such as the repeated orbs of the rifle target, the eye sockets, and the circular basin encircling the tank in the background), the withering surreal landscape invites us to look further, to explore the linear quality of movement that encompasses the hills in the furthest reaches of the picture plane. This landscape threatens the socialist realist agenda, yet describing this space as "landscape" is tenuous. Fractured moments of time and space rupture the stability of the image, a technique that Nakamura would develop more fully in his later work.

The oversized skull and helmet (marked as that of the U.S. military) dominate the space of the painted plywood, but it is the small detail right of center that is vital both to the painting's content and to Nakamura's new directions. One of three rectangular framed portals ruptures the space of the canvas, disrupting the craggy landscape in the background. In the middle frame is a woman collapsed forward, only her bare feet and large rump visible to the viewer. The undignified image is a sharp reminder of the brutality of the Allied Occupation forces. On January 30, 1957, a soldier guarding a base in Sōmagahara, Gunma Prefecture, shot and killed a forty-six-year-old mother of six. The woman, Sakai

Naka, was retreating from collecting empty shell casings to sell (presumably as a means to feed her family) when she was shot in the back.[67] Sakai had wandered into an area that was off-limits when being used by the military but was otherwise available to Japanese citizens. A soldier who had been accompanying Girard testified that shell casings had been thrown out to entice Japanese civilians to approach.[68] Girard admitted that he had not given Sakai and the other Japanese who were present a warning but had fired the shot as a "joke" on the "brasspickers."[69]

The tragic case became an issue of international law. The United States argued that Girard had acted while on duty and was thus under the jurisdiction of U.S. military courts, while the Japanese government held that Girard's actions had taken place during a period of rest, making him subject to Japanese law. After much legal dispute, the U.S. military determined that Girard's actions were "unauthorized," and he was turned over to the Japanese courts. The *New York Daily News* reported that Girard had been "sold to the wolves" to appease the Japanese.[70] However, the Japanese courts deemed Sakai's shooting a death by wounding—the least serious homicide charge for which Girard could have been convicted. The incident aggravated ill feelings among those Japanese who were against the Security Treaty, further fanning the flames of anti-Americanism.

By the late 1950s, Nakamura, like the other artists discussed in this book, withdrew from the project of representing the gendered body's relationship to the state. For Nakamura, negotiating the representation of Sakai's death was a point of artistic and political no return. As Marotti notes: "Nakamura's evolving and idiosyncratic representational style had originated in a long engagement with, and the critique of, the narrowing field of Socialist Realism and reportage in the face of a repositioned cultural policy by the Japanese Communist Party. Nakamura disputed this formal and ideological narrowness in both his canvases and critical writing, championing a flexible and independent role for a nonetheless committed art."[71] Adding to this, we might consider just *how* this artistic political resituating took place in his canvases and how it was informed by gender politics.

By comparing *The Base* to his second painting dealing with the Girard incident, *Shasatsu (Gunned Down)*, we can trace Nakamura's gradual shift away from reportage painting to explorations of fetish and movement. His first version of the events retains its reportage roots: in *The Base,* the body remains relatively naturalistic, if somewhat exaggerated in its position and rounded form. The painting retains a sense of *placeness* because of the continuous hilly landscape in the background, even if it is disrupted by the rectangular frame surrounding the woman's body. Although the vulnerable woman is a small element of the painting compared with the large skull and oversized rifle, the viewer's gaze is drawn to her, set just off center. She is in a demeaning position, perhaps intended as a representation of Girard's view. To him, her life and death were nothing more than a joke. With her face turned away, she is unidentifiable and shows no sign of life; yet the roundness of her matronly rump and the contours of her heels and toes suggest her physical presence.

Working on *The Base* in August 1957, Nakamura still sought to depict embodiment—a key value for *yōga* in the prewar period as well as for *sensō-ga.*

On September 15, 1957, just a month after finishing *The Base,* Nakamura completed *Gunned Down* (Plate 15). Abandoning direct references to the military such as the tank and the dead-eyed soldier, in this work he focuses instead on the woman's body in the moments between life and death. Here, her rear end is shifted so that it lines up directly with our point of view. Her feet are splayed further apart, the left foot outsized, the smooth contours now hardened into thick lines. It is no longer a depiction of someone's foot; rather, it is a marker of "foot."

Nakamura pushes the disaggregation of Sakai's body, illustrating the obscene nature of her death. Her oversized hands are splayed awkwardly to one side, angular and tormented. Jagged and roughly indicated, the hands differ markedly from the experienced hands of the male laborers that appear in Nakamura's earlier works. Sakai's hands are like cutout puppets shoddily attached to the canvas, their jet-black coloring only further divorcing them from the white rounded feet. Three hands are represented, indicating the body's shift away from a recognizable life-form. The flat, illustrative quality of the representation recalls images imported from mass culture, such as promotional materials for the American film *The Man with the Golden Arm,* which was released in 1955 (Figure 2.10).[72] In depicting the woman with her backside indecorously pointed upward and her exaggerated bare foot jutting out, the artist embraces vulgarity as a self-conscious visual code.

The sinewy terrain of the base is eclipsed by negative space, punctuated only by a few hypnotizing disks on the ground. A clear sense of place is absent—the site or *genba* is no longer fundamental—and the distorted body lies dormant, surrounded by the barrels of eight smoking guns. No subject wields the guns; they jut into the frame of the canvas without reference to ownership, responsibility, or bodily presence.

Nakamura's stylistic shift in *Gunned Down* was a way to come to terms with his own changing political identity, but it was also part of a broader trend. Surrealism had renewed currency for other Japanese artists, writers, and thinkers at the time. As Sas has argued, the writer Takiguchi Shūzō, the dancers Ohno Kazuo and Hijikata Tatsumi, and others aimed "to reach a space of (sur)reality or 'actuality'" beyond socially defined boundaries of understanding.[73] With *Gunned Down* Nakamura transitioned from representing a frightening political incident to representing the psychological exploration of individual terror, focusing increasingly on montage over veristic figuration.

By 1960, the art world as understood in Japan had shifted dramatically. In the previous decade, key exhibitions such as *Art of the World Today* and shows by groups like the Salon de Mai had been held in Tokyo, featuring artists such as Jean Fautrier, Jean Dubuffet, Mark Tobey, Willem de Kooning, Jackson Pollock, and Francis Bacon. Soon after, Japanese artists began rapidly abandoning figurative painting for abstract expressionism. Gutai Art Association members, including Tanaka Atsuko and Shiraga Kazuo, were encouraged by

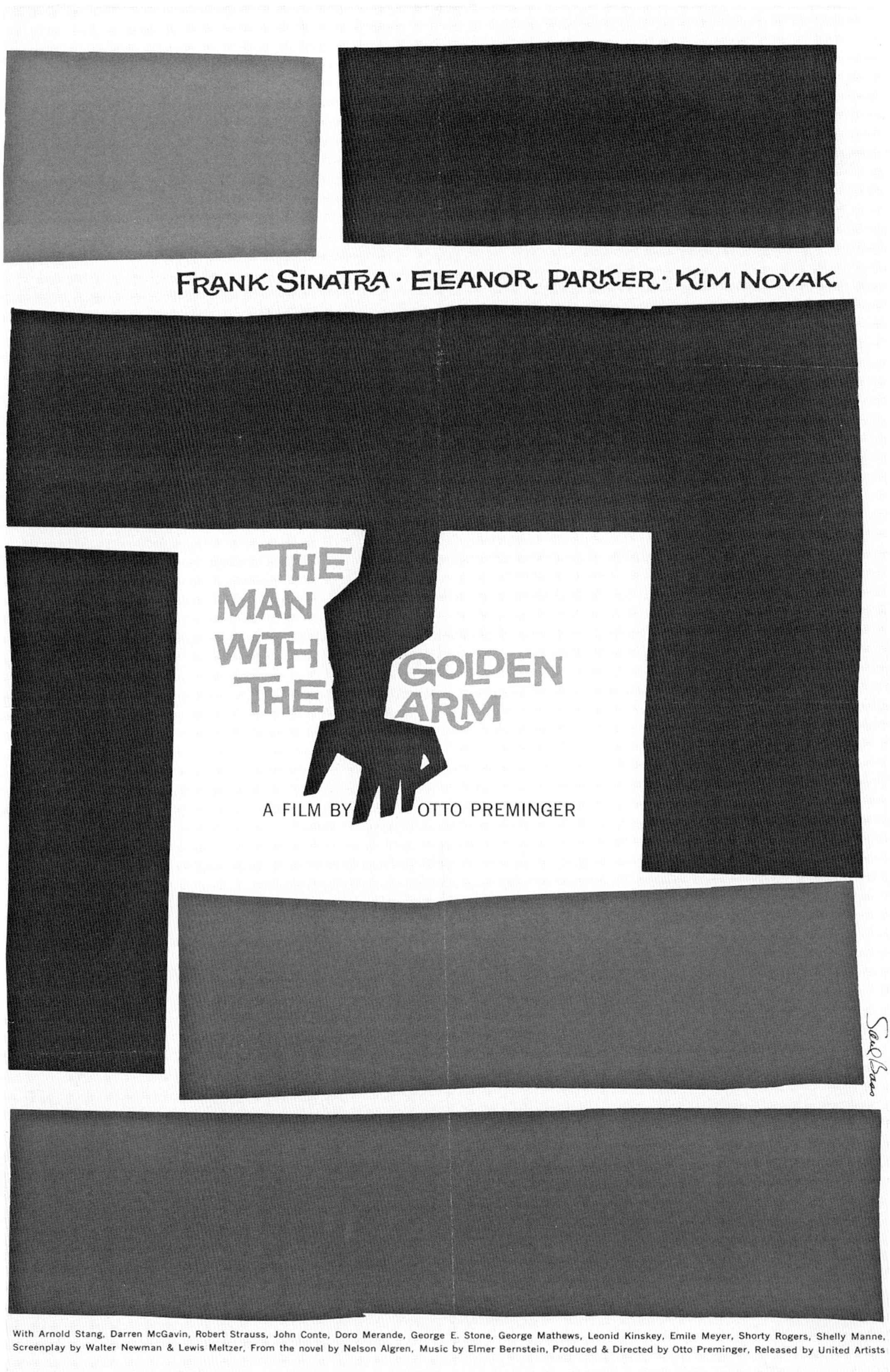

FIGURE 2.10. Saul Bass, poster for the film *The Man with the Golden Arm,* 1955. Copyright Jennifer Bass. Digital image courtesy of the Museum of Modern Art; licensed by SCALA / Art Resource, NY.

their group's leader, Yoshihara Jirō, to do something altogether new and were discouraged from giving their paintings titles or indulging in what Yoshihara felt were passé figural modes of expression. By the 1960s, compared to the antics of groups like Hi Red Center, painting seemed out of sync.

Other critics and artists had expressed strong feelings about the direction of art and politics as early as 1956. Art critic Hariu Ichirō, writing in *Nihon Bijutsu News* and *Bijutsu hihyō,* called for greater self-criticism in art.[74] Nakamura responded directly to these critiques, writing, "In Hariu's logic, [postwar] socialist realism shares the same fate with the [prewar] proletariat art, and it is as if the methodological consciousness *[hōhō ishiki]* of socialist realism has been completely denied." "The Tableau," he concluded, "cannot critique itself."[75] Many were concerned that the documentary quality of socialist realism was tainted by the style's link to wartime propaganda that shared the impulse to sway the public through representation. Significantly, this argument turned on notions of subjectivity and politics. Hariu argued that an artist must react to the exterior world by means of his or her interiority *(naimensei),* or subjectivity *(shutaisei),* and by means of forms *(keishiki),* rather than treating external politics as mere exterior phenomena. But Nakamura took issue with this presumption: "In fact, the creativity of the tableau is born out of the sensitivity that belongs to the process of appreciation, and this is precisely the point at which the artist acquires his or her subjectivity."[76] Rather than a disjointed two-part process whereby the artist is the source of production and the viewer the site of received meaning, he understood the generation of meaning to take place through the painting. In this way, art offered a transformative experience for both the artist's and the viewer's sense of political selfhood.

Yet, for Nakamura, the consequences of transformation were ambiguous, and his personal political aspirations in relation to *Sunagawa No. 5* gave way to a deep-seated ambivalence about masculinity, the state, and the overdetermined relation between the two. Personal events also ushered in this change. In 1958, Nakamura's father passed away suddenly (at the age of fifty-eight), and the artist became keenly aware of the lost opportunity to connect with him.[77] For Nakamura, the tides had turned politically, psychically, and aesthetically; he left party politics and abandoned the pursuit of masculine embodiment. After 1958, his paintings never again pictured a male body directly. To Nakamura. the ideal of male heroism (also discussed in chapter 4 with regard to Shiraga Kazuo's work) seemed increasingly doomed to repetition and failure.

Many union members, students, and artists shared Nakamura's political cynicism. The peak of the anti-ANPO protest movement was in 1960. Despite the gathering of ten million signatures on a petition against it, Prime Minister Kishi Nobusuke signed the Security Treaty. As historian Wesley Sasaki-Uemura describes this time: "Political activity reached a crescendo in May and June 1960 after Kishi mobilized the police on May 19 to expel opposition party members from the parliament and forcibly ratify the treaty, turning a limited diplomatic controversy into a general crisis of democracy."[78] The signing of the treaty was bitterly crushing for the movement. Students, laborers, and everyday citizens would not join forces to the same degree again.

Hundreds of thousands of protesters filled the streets in Tokyo on June 15, 1960, and student activist Kanba Michiko was killed. The police claimed she was trampled by protesters, but an autopsy "concluded that Kanba had been strangled to death, which implicated the riot police, who were using their billy clubs to put choke holds on those they were arresting."[79] Sasaki-Uemura points out that her death was shocking not only because the protesters were exercising their right to petition the government but also because Kanba was a female student at the prestigious University of Tokyo, where women accounted for only 15 percent of the total student population.

> Going to demonstrations was considered improper or dangerous for educated, middle-class women, and parents often tried to prevent their daughters from participating. It was even more unusual for Kanba to have been an officer in Zengakuren. The student movement leadership was virtually all male, and even when women were represented at student rallies, they were usually relegated to giving the greetings and leading songs. Kanba's death was also unexpected because women students were generally placed at the rear of demonstrations and surrounded by male students. . . . One of Kanba's female friends who saw her shortly before her death urged her to pull back from the front, but Kanba insisted that as a student leader she had to remain where she was.[80]

Her death amid the riotous environment forced President Eisenhower to cancel a planned visit to Japan. On June 18, a memorial service for Kanba was held, and an estimated 330,000 participated in a peaceful protest. The treaty went into effect the following day. These were the final days of rage and grief.[81]

For many, this was a time of failure, not only of the anti-ANPO movement but also of the Japanese state, which had failed to demonstrate its commitment to the fledgling democracy. Ikeda Tatsuo summed up this bitter turn: "As far as I am concerned, I believe it was the failure of the movement to overturn the revision of the Treaty of Mutual Cooperation and Security in 1960 that finally brought about the end of avant-garde art, although its decline started during the latter part of the fifties."[82] By this time Nakamura's focus turned to dark surrealist tales filled with one-eyed schoolgirls in sailor uniforms, crimson skylines, and steam locomotives bursting with anachronistic power. Critics such as Mita Haruhiko have written that in the late 1950s Nakamura rejected politics outright, but this is overstating the case.[83] The young artist continued to engage with social issues of the time, responding to the television age and society's mediatized, gendered engagement with vision and movement.

Movement and Masculinity

In this final section, I examine how Nakamura employed the representation of movement and gender to resolve personal artistic tensions and to explore the vast changes within the social body during the consumerist economic boom of the 1960s and 1970s. This was a moment when television sets were entering new middle-class homes, advertising was expanding its influence on television and print media, and cinema was reaching new heights of popularity. Historian Simon Partner notes: "In the early 1950s, consumption had more to do with putting rice on the table than with the pursuit of pleasure. By any comparative statistic, the Japanese people still lacked many of the bare essentials."[84] Yet, as a result of rigorous marketing efforts—involving education, cajoling, and demonstration—people often purchased televisions before other goods, sometimes even ahead of housing.[85] Thus, the desire for visual pleasure and its related consumer desires ran high. Nakamura's work suggests the disembodying effects of consumption amid perpetual technological advancement and the urgency to put images to action. His art asks: How does our new visuality alter our sense of the political? Our sense of our belonging in the world?

Cultural theorist Paul Virilio has pointed out how the mechanisms of war, particularly speed and vision, have altered the very nature of human existence. Virilio shows how dromology, or time–space compression, is actualized in part through the cinematic phenomenon of creating movement through still images.[86] Both Virilio and Nakamura share a fascination and concern with how war, technology, and speed form a new visuality, and how that visuality is indicative of the changing nature of selfhood as it is wrought through an increasingly mediatized world. Nakamura created a form of painted montage, using still images to suggest the movement and time–space compression of cinema.

Movement is represented in Nakamura's work in at least five different ways: through content that depicts moving objects, through grids and screens that suggest movement visually, through figures that are repeated to indicate their movement through space and time, through exaggerated forms and coloring that provide a three-dimensional effect, and through montage. Painted montage enabled Nakamura to transition from the public representation of politics to an individual response to the political stakes of the 1960s. This shift marks his break away from a concern with representation of gendered bodies toward a new concern with (disembodied) gendered perspective. By representing action at several points of narrative time, his *eigateki kōzu* (film-like compositions) build action within a single frame. Rupturing and reassembling the visual field, these paintings illustrate the fracturing of self while simultaneously asserting their own contemporaneity.

Nakamura's art of the 1960s moves away from an interest in socialist realism to embrace modernist Soviet montage.[87] It begins with representational clarity and heightens fragmentation of space and time, rupturing linear visual narrative. By contrasting images, Nakamura asks viewers to make conceptual, aesthetic, and political connections (in this way, the contingency of the singular moment is also revealed). His painting *Kaidan nite (On the Stairs)* (Figure 2.11) provides an example of his use of montage and movement. This work, finished in February 1960, exemplifies the crosscutting used by Sergei Eisenstein in the film *Battleship Potemkin* (1925) to heighten horror and spectacle. Although *Battleship Potemkin* was censored under the Allied Occupation in Japan, the Sōhyō labor union

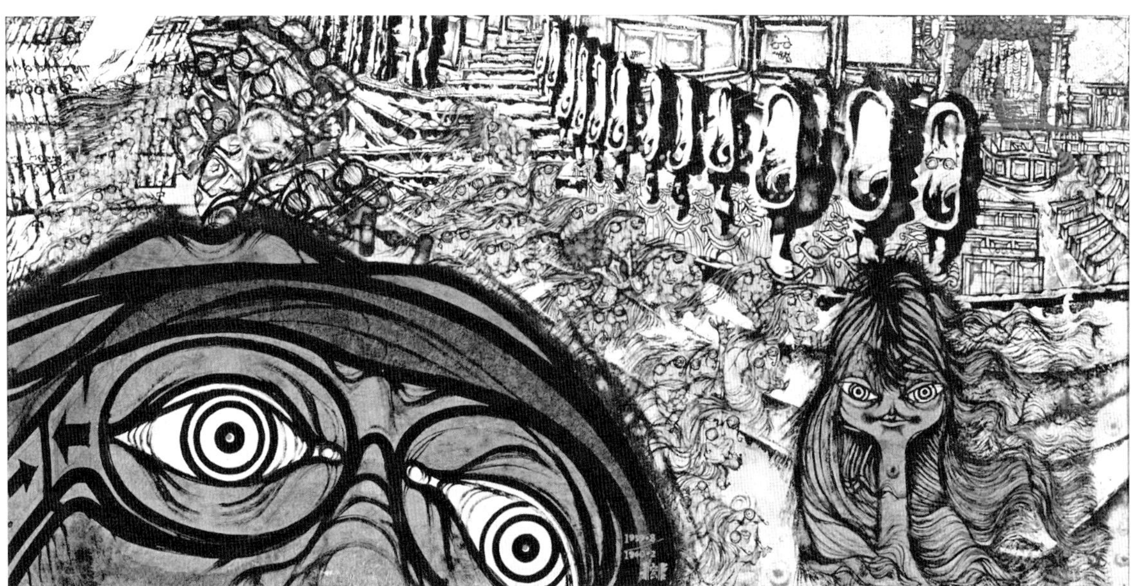

FIGURE 2.11. Nakamura Hiroshi, *Kaidan nite (On the Stairs)*, 1960. Oil on plywood, 90.5 × 181.5 cm. Copyright Nakamura Hiroshi. Courtesy of the Miyagi Museum of Art.

screened it for members, including Nakamura. The film made a deep impression on the young artist, and he later recalled thinking to himself, *"This* is montage."[88] Yet it was not until August 1959, just prior to the climactic defeat of the anti-ANPO protests, that Nakamura decided to base a painting on the 1905 failed democratic uprising in Russia.[89]

Battleship Potemkin is well known for its reliance on montage to create ideological impact. For Eisenstein's fictional re-creation of the first Russian Revolution, the Odessa Steps provided the perfect space to set a reenactment of an attack on the most vulnerable members of society. Creating an oppositional dialectic where upward motion is set against downward action, haphazardly falling bodies are cut against the arrhythmic marching of the soldiers, and long views of the masses are juxtaposed with large-scale shots of discrete figures, Eisenstein uses montage to intensify dramatic effect. It is not at all surprising that Nakamura turned to the director who had eschewed narrative convention for multiperspectival action. Rather than clearly mapping a moral and narrative path for the viewer (as both propaganda films and reportage seek to do), montage juxtaposes distinct shots and allows the mind of the viewer to bring forth its own conclusions. Consequently, we might see how Nakamura's shift did not leave politics behind, but rather reoriented his political project toward gendered disembodiment and the play of perception in the mind of the viewer.

A famous scene from *Battleship Potemkin* resonates with the story of Sakai Naka, and Nakamura's painting gathers its force from this connection. Nakamura turns to a tragic and vulnerable female character, isolating on his canvas the wild stare of the old woman with pince-nez from the 1925 film (a character also said to be inspirational to Francis

Bacon). Nakamura, it seems, identified with Eisenstein's ill-fated figure of idealism, who attempted to persuade the soldiers not to fire. Perhaps he understood her role and her death to be symptomatic of the state of the left-wing movement in Japan. In the painting, he flattens the utopian figure into a caricature. Suggesting complete disembodiment, the older woman's face appears over and over again, reduced to a monochromatic outline of the glasses and vague reference to her other features. Yet while in the 1950s Nakamura painted Sakai Naka as helplessly facing downward, unable to see, here the woman, who is likewise powerless against the forces of violence that threaten her, is granted agency through her ability to see. The woman's wild eyes are multiply emphasized: the eyeglasses encircle the hypnotic shapes, each dotted with a single point of red in the center. Nakamura makes clear that vision is what matters: vision witnesses political subjugation, reducing the political actor to spectator or, alternatively, transforming the spectator into political actor.

Nakamura's examination of the relationships among vision, movement, and subjectivity came at a time when technologies of vision were developing at a faster pace than ever before. From 1957 through 1960, more than one billion people went to the movies in Japan.[90] By 1962, the city of Tokyo itself was at a turning point: the population passed ten million, and urban sprawl stretched up and outward into the rural areas. One might argue that the city was becoming increasingly stratified, socially designated, and poised for consumption.[91]

Reimagining the place of the subject in a world that disrupts the perceptual experiences that affirm subjecthood became increasingly important with the vast changes taking place in the city and the country, as Tanaka Atsuko's *Electric Dress* (discussed in the following chapter) also demonstrates. Television transformed the media ecology of the period. As cultural historian Thomas Doherty observes: "The greatest leap forward in the graphic revolution, television radiated through the life of the present and the memory of the past with a force that dwarfed the impact of the other media. Soon print itself came to seem the hieroglyphics of a lost civilization."[92] Television both enabled consumption and indicated social mobility. Although the technology was invented in the 1920s, it was not until after World War II that television sets were widely manufactured and distributed. Japan became one of the first nations in the world to see widespread use of television after it was introduced broadly in 1950. The United States was the leading consumer of television—in 1949, one in ten American homes had a television set; by 1959, nine of ten homes did.[93] Black-and-white television viewing peaked in Japan in 1968, but the fastest rise in viewership came in 1964, corresponding to the Tokyo Olympic Games.[94] Japanese housewives went from watching an hour and a half of television per day in 1960 to four hours per day by 1965 (in subsequent years the rate would increase by only one hour).[95] The era of television not only heightened the primacy of vision and spectacle but also reinforced the role of the consumer and drew greater attention to the cultural hegemony of the West.

A pivotal moment came in 1963, when a broadcast was transmitted successfully by a satellite television linkup between the United States and Japan. Some of the first images ever to be shared through this link were images of American violence. The televised coverage of President Kennedy's assassination played out across the world, immediately marking a moment of global uncertainty. Yet these startling images also reinforced the sense that the United States was center stage in the global theater of spectacle.

Japan's opportunity to participate in the production of global spectacle came with the 1964 Olympic Games. Tokyo underwent vast architectural and infrastructural development in preparation for tourists and worldwide viewing audiences, and trains became a highly visible symbol of Japan's economic status. New industrial parks and construction of more transportation lines caused changes so convulsive that some felt the profound growth made the city unrecognizable. As will be discussed in relation to Tanaka's art in chapter 3, the speed and iconic power of trains were harnessed to serve as a national symbol, representing a force that defined modernity; however, this force also altered familial and bodily relations. For Tanaka Atsuko, the introduction of the Tōkaidō Line in the 1950s had consequences for her hometown of Osaka as well as for her sense of self. For Nakamura, the inauguration of the bullet train on the Tōkaidō Line in 1964 brought with it a sense of a new modernity that marked the death of an old world. The train as a metaphor for both the past and the future became a tool for Nakamura, enabling him to engage critically with the unsteady promises of Japan's statehood and to bring to light the reemergence of the drive to modern industrialization that characterized prewar Japan.

The *shinkansen,* or bullet train, an icon of Japanese design and modernity, was unveiled in time for the Olympics, but intense anticipation had been building long before. In 1957, the Railway Technology Center described a "Super Express of Dreams" that would cut the travel time between Tokyo and Osaka down to three hours.[96] A few years later, the World Bank provided an $80 million (28.8 billion yen) loan for construction of the Tōkaidō *shinkansen.*[97] Historian Christopher Hood notes: "By the 1950s, Japan's infrastructural problems were more domestic. Capacity had been reached on the Tōkaidō line linking Tokyo and Osaka with serious implications for safety."[98] Thus the new bullet trains were at once a salve for the overcrowded train lines and a means and symbol of economic expansion. Opening just nine days before the Olympic ceremonies began, the trains were a powerful expression of new Japan's position on the global stage under Prime Minister Ikeda's "income-doubling" *(shotoku baizō)* program.

Significantly, the introduction of the new *shinkansen* was a highly mediatized event: the first test run of the *hikari* line between Tokyo and Osaka was broadcast live for four hours on NHK (Nippon Hōsō Kyōkai), Japan's national public broadcasting station. Millions watched as one train left Tokyo for Shin-Osaka station and another departed Shin-Osaka for Tokyo. Some Olympic competitions were held in Osaka, despite the 500-kilometer distance, simply because the new transportation breakthroughs allowed for it. On October 1, 1964, the Tōkaidō Line opened with much fanfare, carrying 36,128 people. Every single seat was reserved. The public was eager to participate in showcasing Japan's latest technological advances on the global stage. The Olympic Organizing Committee took pains to demonstrate Japan's rise from the ashes, choosing Sakai Yoshinori, a boy born on August 6, 1945 (the day the United States dropped an atom bomb on Hiroshima), to be the final carrier of the Olympic torch. According to Yoshikuni Igarashi, the media heightened this sense of recovery by making reference to Sakai's aesthetically pleasing body and running style.[99]

In the years before the Olympics, bright crimsons filled Nakamura's canvases, evoking the firebombing of the Nakatajima coast, the seaside area near his hometown in Hamamatsu, as in *Basho no kizashi (Omens of a Place 1)* (1961) (Plate 16). To this day he recalls watching from the woods with his family while the beaches of his youth were engulfed in flames.[100] These paintings reflected on his past as it had been shaped by relations between Japan and the United States. But in 1964, Nakamura addressed the Tokyo Olympic Games and Japan's spectacular reemergence on the world stage with a turn toward a striking new style. *Seika senrikō (Sacred Torch Relay)* (Figure 2.12), made especially for the Olympics, exemplifies the bright-red coloring and strong sense of movement that became increasingly

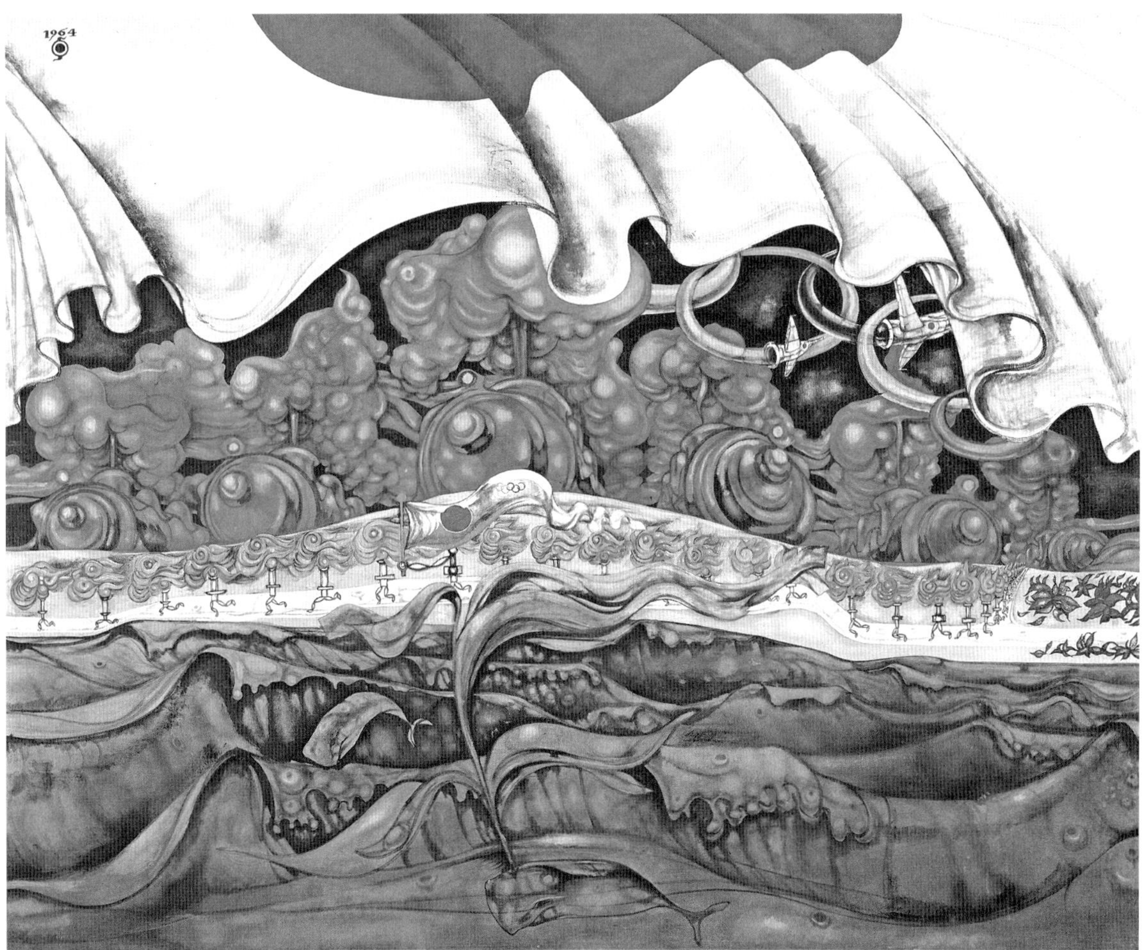

FIGURE 2.12. Nakamura Hiroshi, *Seika senrikō (Sacred Torch Relay)*, 1964. Oil on canvas, 130 × 162 cm. Copyright Nakamura Hiroshi. Courtesy of the Takamatsu City Museum of Art.

present in his oeuvre. Although hallmarks of celebratory patriotism such as the *hinomaru* flag, the Olympic rings, and the Olympic torch are clearly visible in the work, the image stops short of pure triumphalism. The flag is cut from the frame, billowing up and revealing a teeming group of abstract mechanical red forms, lending the painting a menacing edge. In comparison, Maeda Jōsaku's *Hinomaru (XVIII Olympic Games)* (1964) (Figure 2.13) seems much more celebratory of Japan's growth and internationalism, with the *hinomaru* so much larger than the other flags, in a manner reminiscent of the Greater East Asia Co-prosperity Sphere propaganda produced in the 1930s. Both of these paintings were exhibited as part of a group of works on the theme of the Olympics in the *Sixth Contemporary Art Exhibition of Japan,* an independent exhibition sponsored by the *Mainichi Shinbun.* The exhibition's catalog bemoaned the lack of originality in the works, asserting that priority was given to concept over form. An exception was made for Nakamura's work, however, which was heralded for its own artistic merit.[101]

Yet *Sacred Torch Relay* is by no means a radical artwork. Compare it with Hi Red Center's *Ultra-Cleaning Event* (Figure 2.14), which took place six days after the end of the Tokyo Olympics as a response to the government's campaign to clean up the city. During the event, which was held in the Nishi-Ginza district of Tokyo, members of the group (including Takamatsu Jirō, Akasegawa Genpei, and Nakanishi Natsuyuki) donned white lab coats and proceeded to scrub the street with minuscule implements like toothbrushes.

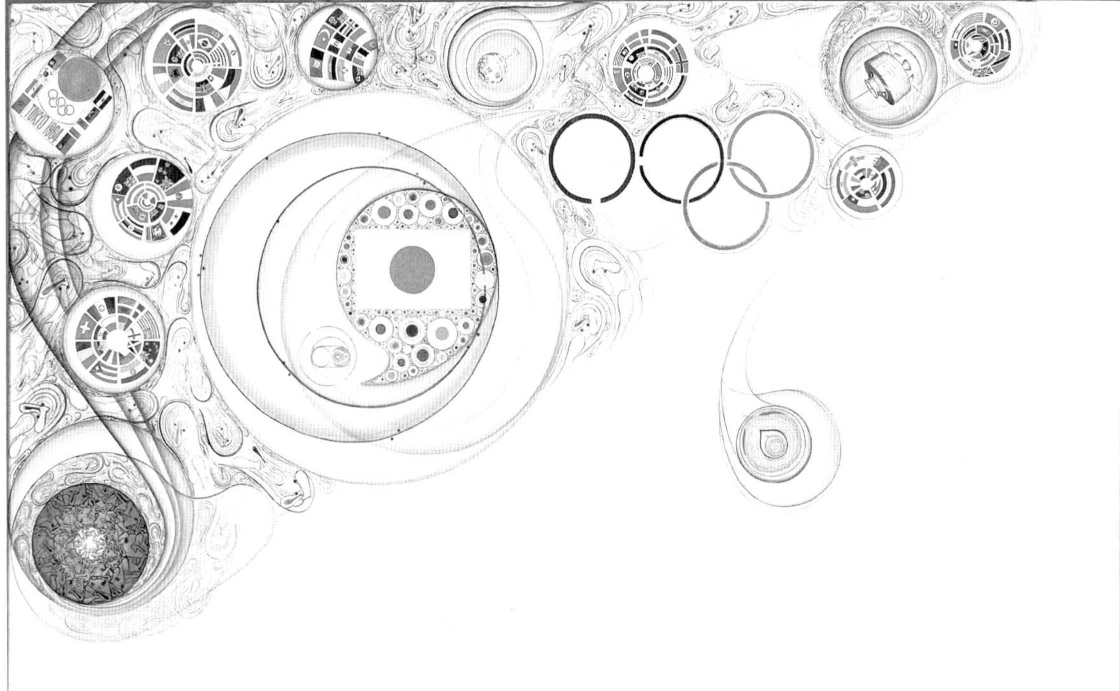

FIGURE 2.13. Maeda Jōsaku, *Hinomaru (XVIII Olympic Games)*, 1964. Oil on canvas, 182 × 290 cm. Copyright Maeda Momoyo. Courtesy of Niigata City Art Museum.

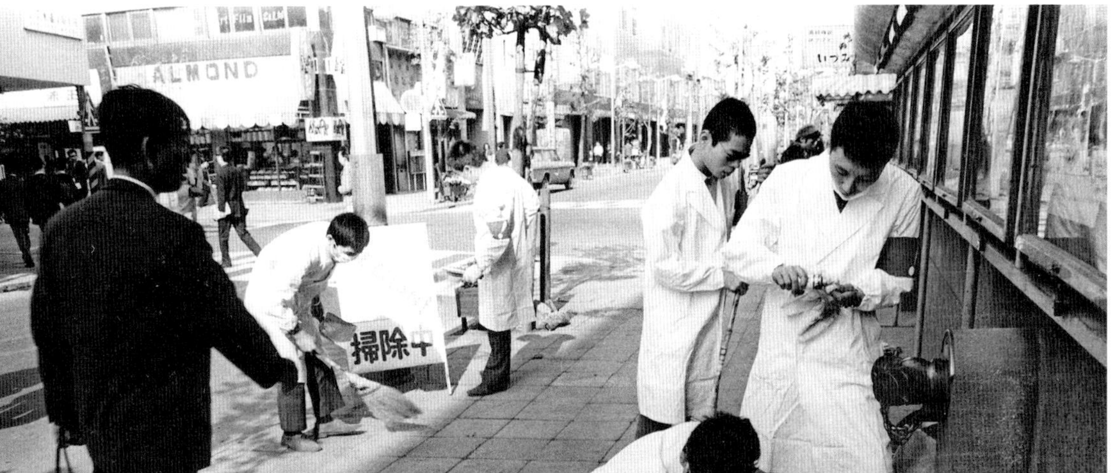

FIGURE 2.14. Hi Red Center, *Shutoken seisō seiri sokushin undō (Campaign for the Promotion of Sanitation and Order in the Capital,* aka *Ultra-Cleaning Event),* Tokyo, October 16, 1964. Photograph by Hirata Minoru. Copyright Hirata Minoru.

Many passersby thought that they were official government street cleaners. Their creative endeavor aimed to reveal the state's penchant for sterility, the overreach of government control, and the use of athletic bodies for state development. Nakamura, in contrast, was willing to produce works that supported the citywide celebrations even if they bore traces of cynicism and ambivalence.

These double registers of doubt and complicity with the state were obdurately present in other compositions he painted that year. For instance, *Kankō teikoku (Sightseeing Empire)* (1964) (Plate 17) attempts to defy the two-dimensionality of the canvas, its doubled vision lurching toward the viewer across red ruins. Rather than depict the *shinkansen,* Nakamura opts for the steam locomotive, an emblem of the mechanized past, rich with nostalgia. The image situates masculinized machinery as a national emblem of power and disaster. Nakamura's trains are a vibrant crimson, the hue of the *hinomaru* flag and his color of choice for many works in this period. The engines in *Sightseeing Empire,* exuding excessive amounts of red steam, are so powerful they have literally gone off the rails. As Virilio reminds us, with the invention of the train came the invention of derailment.[102] Nakamura fills his canvas with the machines and their disasters, knowing that both possess the power to captivate. By linking an icon of the past to the contemporary moment, Nakamura's vibrant exaggeration connects the disastrous consequences of imperial Japan's ambitions to the rhetoric of new state power embodied by the postwar emphasis on infrastructure and economic growth.

Art critic Nakahara Yūsuke has argued that Nakamura's frequent depiction of steam trains was a means to examine the problem of painting. Steam engines, Nakahara points out, appear in many nineteenth-century modernist works by artists such as Turner and Monet; certainly there is a long-standing relationship between modernity and the image of the train. Because of Nakamura's reliance on the image of the steam locomotive, Nakahara argues that the artist is unwilling to let go of past forms of mechanization and medium, choosing instead to commit to a "machine art" that remains stubbornly on the canvas.[103] But what was at stake for Nakamura in this new mode of art making? More than the painter of anachronism (as art critic and writer Shibusawa Tatsuhiko has dubbed him),[104] Nakamura sought to expose the risks of Japan's new industrialized future, its dependence on the United States, and its impact on the gendered body. His works reveal the fragmentation of vision and disaggregation of the body that came with the Cold War and the collapse of the anti-ANPO movement. As Virilio argues:

> One could go on for ever listing the technological weapons, the panoply of light-war, the aesthetic of the electronic battlefield, the military use of space whose conquest was ultimately the conquest of the image—the electronic image of remote detection; the artificial image produced by satellites as they endlessly sweep over the surface of continents drawing automatic maps; life-size cinema in which the day and the light of film-speed succeed the day and the light of astronomical time. It is subliminal light of incomparable transparency, where technology finally exposes the whole world.[105]

Nakamura's works thus employ movement to reveal how technologized vision, acutely important during the Cold War, threatened the integrity of selfhood at both the individual and the national level.

Nakamura's trains emphasize perception in a manner that recalls Kristin Ross's formulation of cars and film: "In production, cars had paved the way for film; now, film would help create the conditions of the motorization of Europe: the two technologies reinforced each other. Their shared qualities—movement, image, mechanization, standardization—made movies and cars the key commodity-vehicles of a complete transformation in European consumption patterns and cultural habits. Much of that transformation involved a change in perception, a change in the way things were *seen*."[106] Nakamura's paintings, with their emphasis on perception, examine how gender played a profound role in these new visual modes. In the bottom corner of *Sightseeing Empire* lurks a female clad in a sailor suit. Her ghostly, erotic presence is a foil to the train's phallic eminence. This sexualized female would emerge in various incarnations in Nakamura's canvases for fifty years to follow: she first appears as a small figure in the painting *Hōki seyo shōjo (Rise Up, Girl)* in 1959 (Figure 2.15) and reappears in *On the Stairs* in the following year. Feminist artist and scholar Shimada Yoshiko has argued that Nakamura's images of young girls have been largely overlooked because scholars have neglected to understand how eros, or eroticism, functioned in the 1960s.[107] Rather than reproduce images of pretty girls as symbols of love and peace, Nakamura resituated the schoolgirl as antiauthoritarian and oppositional.[108] For him, the sailor's uniform represented standardization and dehumanization and was linked to his fear, admiration, and hatred of uniforms as he witnessed them during the war and at the school for girls that his family operated in Hamamatsu City while he was growing up.[109]

In *On the Stairs,* an adolescent girl appears as a long-necked figure who stares blankly back at the viewer as though transfixed. The young woman's billowing hair and dark complexion call up the mother character in *Battleship Potemkin* who watches as her son is trampled on the steps in dramatic slow motion. In the painting, the girl's vulnerability is

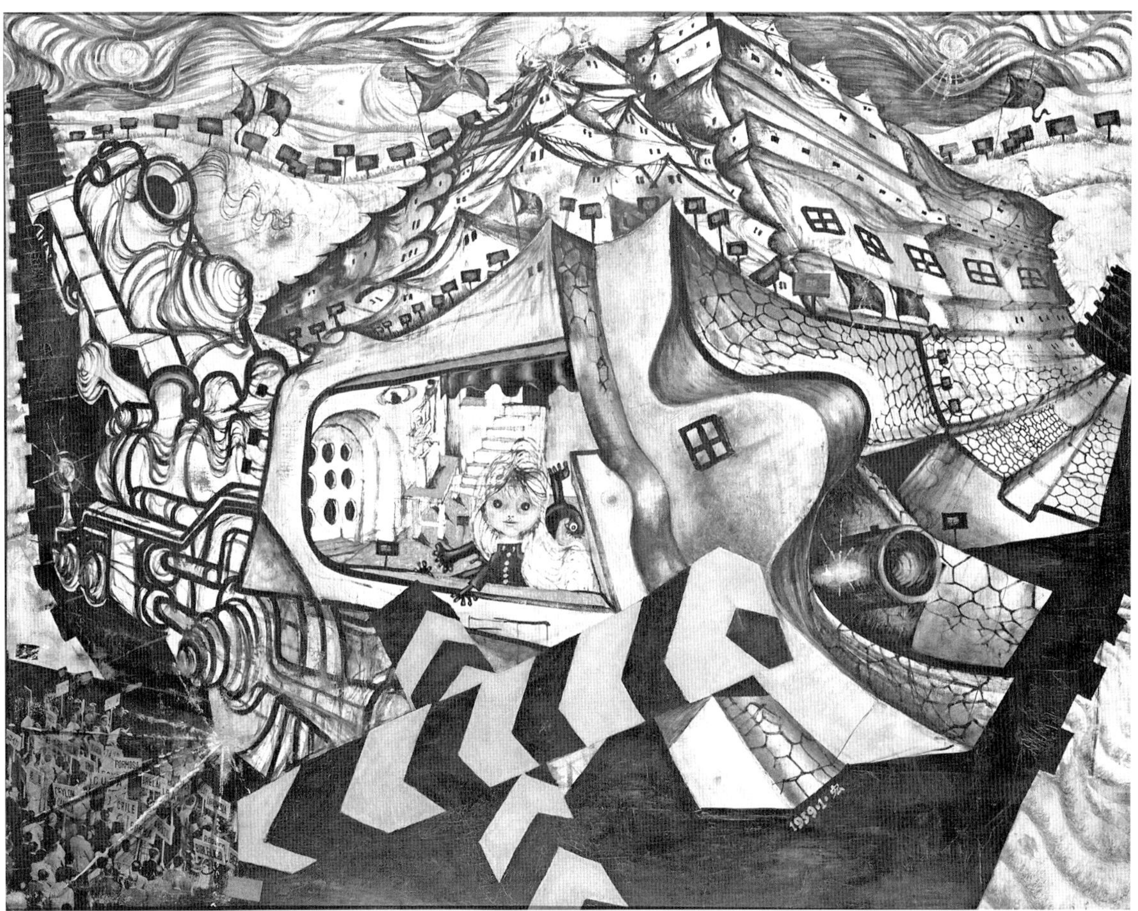

FIGURE 2.15. Nakamura Hiroshi, *Hōki seyo shōjo (Rise Up, Girl)*, 1959. Oil, gravure on plywood, 91 × 117 cm. Copyright Nakamura Hiroshi. Courtesy of Nerima Art Museum.

heightened by her bodiless figure and sinewy neck. As in *The Base* and *Gunned Down*, Nakamura turns to the woman's body as a site of violence and rupture and as a symbol of the failure of political action against the state. Yet, unlike these previous paintings, *Sightseeing Empire* elicits a sexually charged response with the female figure's short skirt and youthful body. The girl in this painting, like the equally troubling figures in *Ensoku (Hiking)* (1964), *Ese kikai (Pseudo Machine)* (1971), and many of Nakamura's illustrations and paintings, is cheaply complicit with mainstream advertising and photographs in men's magazines. Yet it is precisely Nakamura's blurring and confusion of the codes of mass media and figure painting that gives these works a certain disturbing critical potency.

The image of the uniformed adolescent girl was ubiquitous on television and in all manner of advertising, for products from pens and bicycles to automated toilets. Nakamura was conscious of the commercial overreliance on the image and collected eye-catching advertisements from magazines and newspapers that successfully marshaled the youthful female form into an object of consumer desire (Figure 2.16).

With her kneesocks and jet-black hair, the Japanese schoolgirl was a recognizable archetype of Japan nationally and transnationally. In an essay titled "Art of Non-resistance," Aida Yuen Wong notes that "the image of the *jogakusei* (schoolgirl) had antecedents in early Shōwa-period (late 1920s–early 1930s) *nihonga*."[110] Wong describes how these images "encapsulated Japan's attainments in social progress and leisure since the Meiji period. Education had not always been widely available to Japanese girls. Although compulsory elementary schooling was implemented in the late nineteenth century, it was not until the 1920s that middle schools for girls became widespread. . . . The *jogakusei* thus embodied the improvement of literacy and culture among the populace, as well as the economic elevation of the middle class."[111] In the postwar period, the *jogakusei* remained an attractive and alluring symbol, presumably educated and economically mobile, evidencing Japan's modernity. Yet the image of the schoolgirl was also troubling. In 1955, when prostitution was more visible on the street than ever before and increasing numbers of middle-class women were participating in the comparatively lucrative but risky occupation, a particular case hit the front pages of the Tokyo newspapers. A teahouse had been transformed into a brothel that was frequented by powerful local men, including politicians, newspaper editors, and construction company executives, and, as Sarah Kovner notes, "nine of the twenty-four workers in the establishment were under eighteen—and they wore their [school] uniforms to work."[112] Thus, the schoolgirl was a highly charged figure: an icon of consumption, freighted with perceived sexual victimhood as well as perceived sexual threat. However, she was rarely perceived as having agency.

Sightseeing Empire resituates this paradigmatic figure: she glances aside mischievously as she squats and appears to urinate. The act disrupts our voyeurism, making her body too biological, too vulgar. She is an anxious figure, transgressing moral orders through the suggestion of her exposed body, nonetheless cautious of retribution, toying with the power of lust while disarming it. The fetish emerges from men's fear of castration (or, put another

a
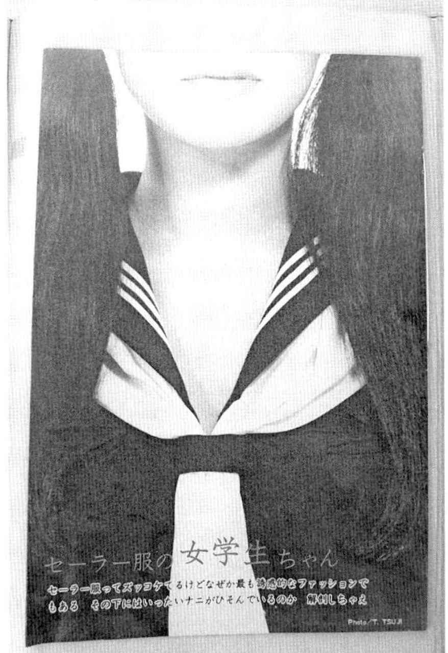

c
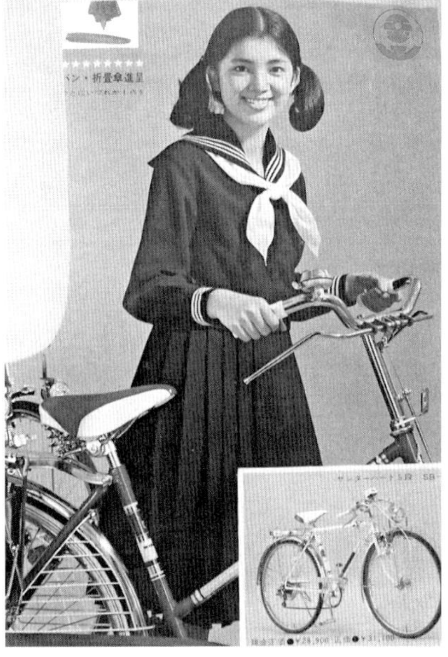

b
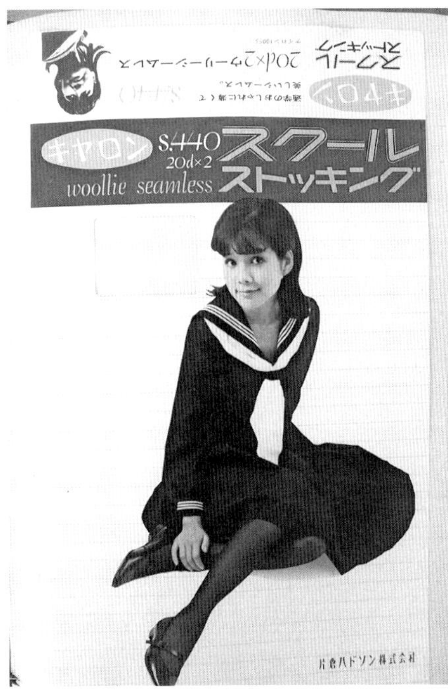

d
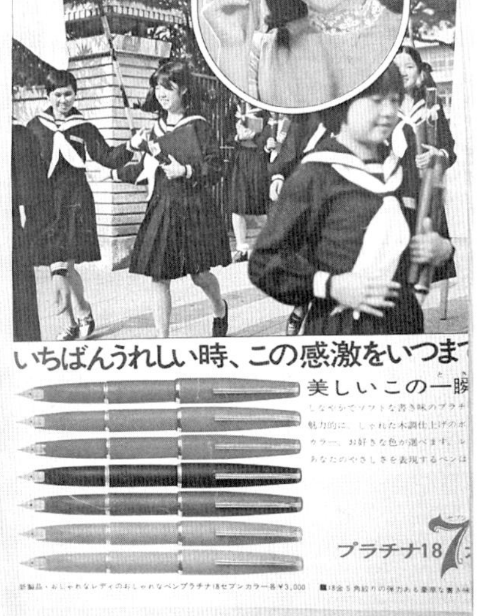

FIGURE 2.16. Nakamura Hiroshi's scrapbooks. (a) *Jogakusei* (schoolgirls) scrapbook 2, page 29. (b) *Jogakusei* scrapbook 1, page 38, repeated page 39. (c) *Jogakusei* scrapbook 2, page 1, repeated page 15. (d) *Jogakusei* scrapbook 2, page 26. (e) *Jogakusei* scrapbook 3, page 53. Copyright Nakamura Hiroshi. Photographs by the author. Courtesy of the Museum of Contemporary Art, Tokyo.

e
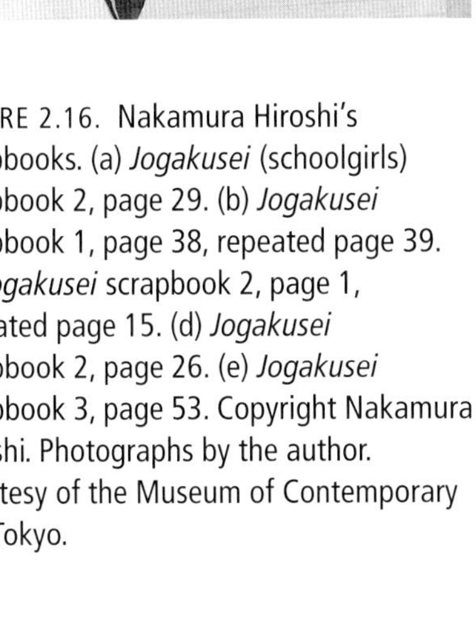
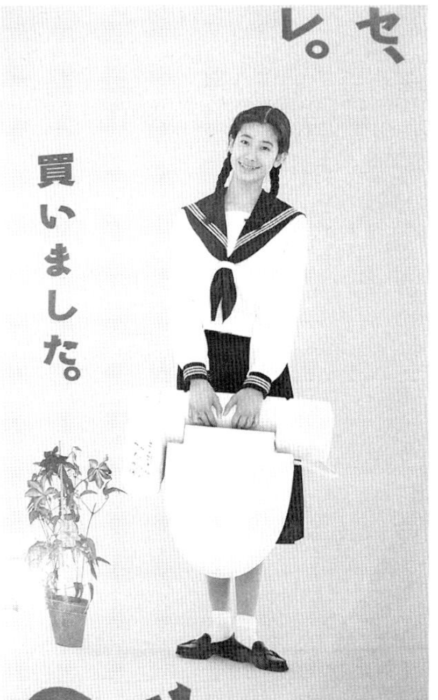

way, man's fear of emasculation); thus, Nakamura's self-conscious representation of the fetish is a move that redirects sexual energy and renders it unproductive. Like his use of montage, it effects a fracturing of vision that invites introspection on the part of the viewer, even as it plays on the viewer's base desires.[113]

Nakamura's fetishistic schoolgirl can be read as an apposite critique of the burgeoning consumer culture that draws on images of women and manipulates their desires and self-identity. But the painting is also a strong source of visual pleasure that is in a symbiotic relationship with the fetish. Literary scholar Marjorie Garber writes that "fetishism is a kind of theater of display—and, indeed, that theater represents an enactment of the fetishistic scenario. Thus Freud's 'penis,' the anatomical object, though understood through Jacques Lacan's 'phallus,' the structuring mark of desire, becomes reliteralized as a stage prop, a detachable object. No one has the phallus."[114] Similarly, active, embodied sexuality is not represented in *Sightseeing Empire*. The active ground of the canvas suggests sexuality, with its red trains pulsing forward toward the girl, but physical engagement of any kind is repressed in favor of fantasy. Instead, male bodies are reorganized into the "stage prop" phallus of the train, and female bodies are painted as fetish object.

In *Hikōki to shōjo (Airplane and Girl)* (1965) (Figure 2.17), the schoolgirl has moved away from the bushes; she sits coquettishly, glancing sideways. Above her, the brightly flushed red nose of the plane rises up, masculine energies at full throttle. Nakamura's talent for representing texture is evident in the glossy shadows on the plane's side, the steaming mists of red clouds, and the gray blur of the front wheel. Yet the schoolgirl is depicted only in black and white, in a comparatively flattened style. It is as though the painter aims to contain her capacity for deviance, destruction, and sexual power but meets with only limited success.

Nakamura's vision of seductive speed and disaster was culled directly from his immediate visual context. The artist has carefully documented advertisements from magazines and newspapers in more than thirty-eight personal scrapbooks, each labeled by content, including "schoolgirls," "railways," and "accidents." The collection betrays how alluring the dangerous denaturing effects of the high-velocity, mediatized world were to Nakamura himself. His postreportage work examined his own desires and fears and how they were constructed. Where could one find footing, find a clear-cut political direction, in this compelling, fast-paced aesthetic world?

Within the broader transnational context, other postwar artists were also collaging machines and female bodies together in what art historian Julian Myers refers to as a "fetishistic hum" that rewrote "the tense political situation [of the Cold War] as a dirty joke, an innuendo."[115] For example, Sir Eduardo Paolozzi's *I Was a Rich Man's Plaything* (1947) (Figure 2.18) features a burlesque girl, an American military plane, and an advertisement for Coca-Cola, all cut from magazines and brought together to suggest how the body becomes a commodity and how propaganda becomes pornography. Both Paolozzi and Nakamura were illustrators who collected images from mass media and used them to create

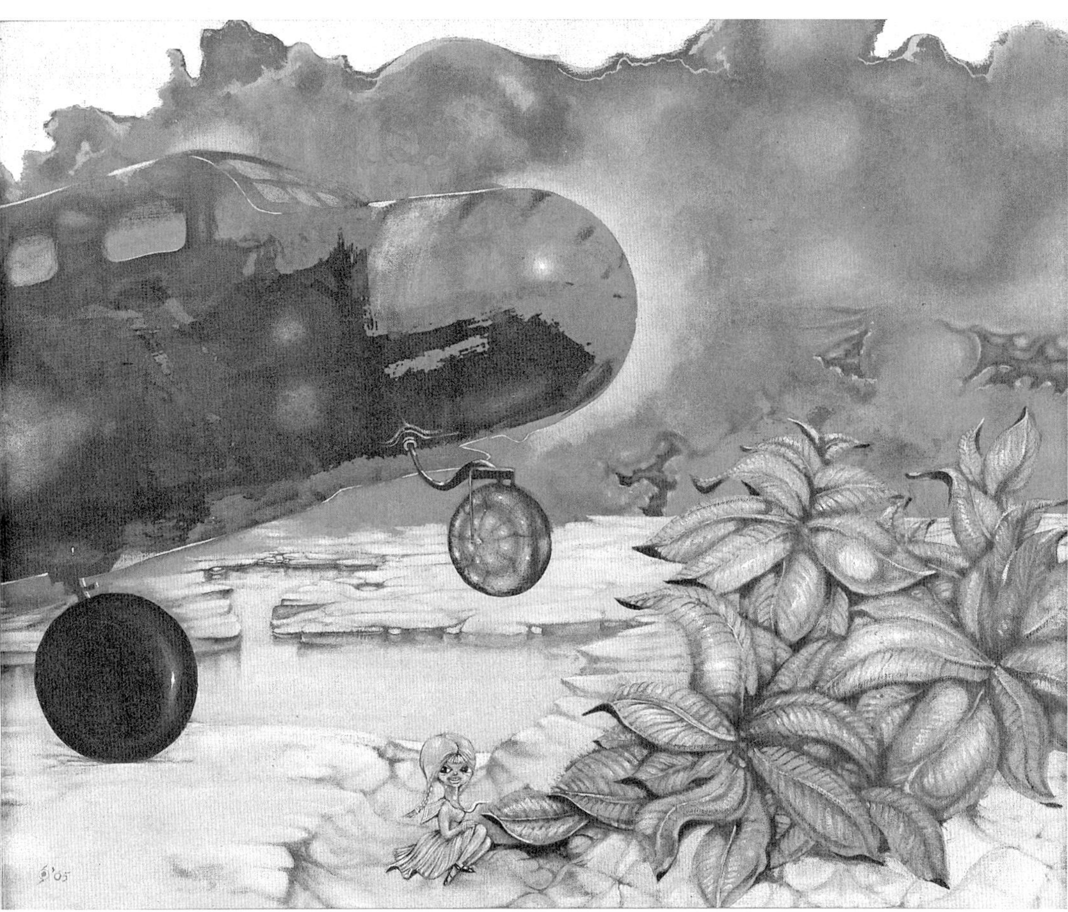

FIGURE 2.17. Nakamura Hiroshi, *Hikōki to shōjo (Airplane and Girl),* 1965. Oil on canvas, 53 × 65.2 cm. Copyright Nakamura Hiroshi. Private collection.

private iconographies that nonetheless reverberated with contemporary visual culture that struck out at state politics.

Like Paolozzi's *I Was a Rich Man's Plaything,* Nakamura's *Sightseeing Empire* teems with nationalistic energy reworked as sexual energy. The steam trains, once loaded with supplies and bound for military bases, are refigured as phallic surplus, facing derailment and disaster down the tracks. As in Paolozzi's work, the sharp contrast in *Sightseeing Empire* "rewrites militarism and nationalism as sexual bravado, patriotism as libido, and both as pulp cliché."[116] In *Airplane and Girl,* the confusion between the body politic and the fetishized body is similar: the obsolescent fighter plane raises its fiery head above the small schoolgirl who sits innocently unaware, bare legs tucked to the side. In Myers's words: "The fighter-phallus, for all its fantastic techno-masculinity, cannot consummate this relationship: its collision is, so to speak, a premature ejaculation."[117] Thus the schoolgirls and trains overtook, even compensated for, Nakamura's hollow-chested self-portraits and depictions of crises related to the American domination of Japan.

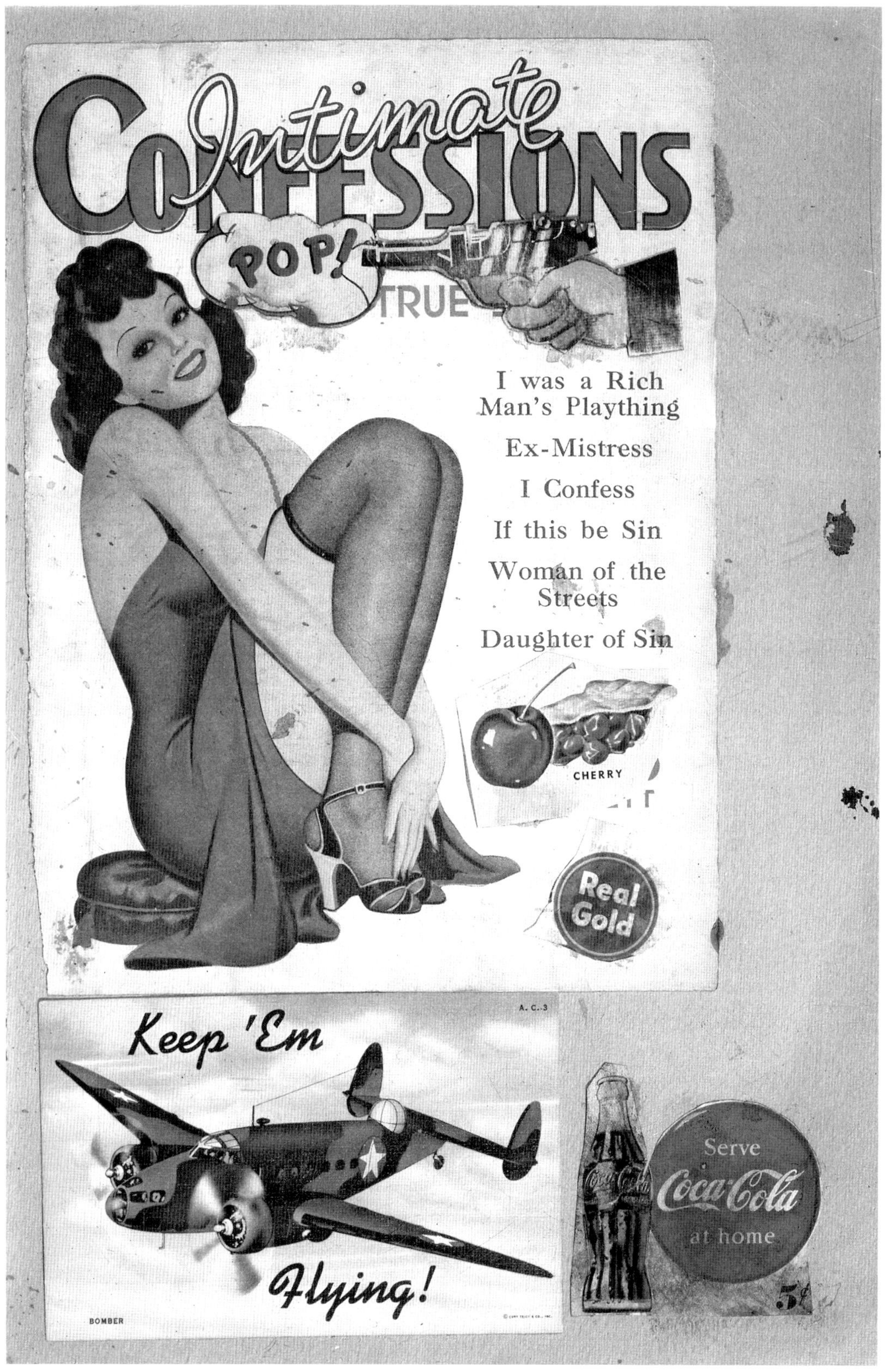

FIGURE 2.18. Sir Eduardo Paolozzi, *I Was a Rich Man's Plaything,* 1947. Collage mounted on card, 359 × 238 inches. Courtesy of the Tate Gallery. Copyright 2016 Trustees of the Paolozzi Foundation. Licensed by DACS / Artists Rights Society (ARS), New York.

In his compositions from the mid-1960s, trains and planes serve as Nakamura's overt metaphor for empowered masculinity. Rather than depict the male body as fully embodied or physically present, an effort that Nakamura found unsustainable, he refigures masculinity as machinery or as movement itself. Replacing male bodies with the muscular armature of machinery resolved Nakamura's long-standing problem of depicting the masculine figure, freeing him from the vexingly anxious self-portraits that characterized his early work. Masculinity, in the past, had largely manifested in his oeuvre as an anxious body, thus the imagery of the train offered a stabilizing alternative. Machines and movement—symbols more reliably masculine and powerful than a representation of the artist's own body—thus became the phallus.

In 1968, the anti-ANPO movement geared up again to fight the 1970 re-signing of the Security Treaty. Nakamura did not take part, however. Instead, he examined his ambivalence toward state politics through the canvas. In his 1969 work *Enkan-ressha: B—Hikō suru jōkikikansha (Circle Line B—Flying Steam Locomotive)* (Plate 18), Nakamura shows us that the iconic train—charged with national symbolism, ever powerful—goes backward as much as forward. Whether chugging along as a steam locomotive in imperial times or breaking new records as a bullet train, it is a vehicle of state power constructed from state rhetoric. It is racing forward to a time when political selfhood is constructed by the dynamics of vision, the body reduced to a spectacle of sexist conspicuous consumption. The experienced illustrator also knows how to draw the eye to eros and disaster, to convey the cheap pleasures of speeding headlong into a future that only circles back to an ominous past. State rhetoric, as he shows us, was forward moving but ever cycling back—a point brought home in his rendition of the Tokyo circle line, *Enkan-ressha: A—Bōenkyō ressha (Circle Line A—Telescope Train)* (1968) (Plate 19).

In *Circle Line A,* Nakamura depicts the singular vision of a telescope awash in a water-filled bubble of deep blue, yet cleaves this singularity into an unfolding binocular view of a train. The angle suggests that the train has been folded, allowing the viewer an unusual vantage point from which both lengths are visible. Nakamura's signature schoolgirl has multiplied into a team of adolescent cyborg cyclops, gazing outward toward oblivion. The artist has explained that the single eye was inspired by Yanagita Kunio's "one-eyed goblin" theory, and he has emphasized that the girls are not passively being seen; rather, they are staring back, aggressively.[118] As Shimada argues in her review of Nakamura's work, we can understand the single eye as that of the author, as the eye of the erotic schoolgirl of the 1960s, or as the eye of revolt that refuses a passive gaze.[119] The monstrousness of the girls, in contrast to the laboring man of the 1950s, is further emphasized by the erasure of their hands. Although roughly fifty-eight schoolgirls are depicted aboard the train, only two nondescript hands are visible. Other hands are mysteriously tucked deep into the folds of the skirts of the girls' uniforms.

Through the panels of glass on the passenger train, we glimpse a calm stretch of scenic ocean, but the telescope obscures a full panoramic view. For all the visibility that ocular technologies provide, they do not ultimately disclose the quiet landscape. Virilio writes:

> Thus, alongside the "war machine," there has always existed an ocular (and later optical and electro-optical) "watching machine" capable of providing soldiers, and particularly commanders, with a visual perspective on the military action under way. . . . Seeing and foreseeing therefore tend to merge so closely that the actual can no longer be distinguished from the potential. Military actions take place "out of view," with radio-electrical images substituting in real time for a now failing optical vision.[120]

Following Virilio, Nakamura shows us that sight and aim can be both interconnected and blinding. The telescope focuses on an eddy of waves just above the surface, as though preparing to submerge. The windows of the train suggest the optics of selfhood—they are like frames of a film reel, or like television screens. Rather than windows that give one access to a wider world, they work to emphasize our passive role as viewers.

As Virilio has suggested, the mechanisms of war construct a direct interest in speed that has brought about a complete remeasurement of selfhood. Nakamura similarly raises these issues by re-creating the shooter's viewpoint in *Gunned Down* and by painting a blinding telescope encircled by a train in *Circle Line A.* The artist draws attention to the connections between war and vision and extends his analysis to the impact of technology on our vision and experience of Tokyo's urban environment. Through painting, he examines the anxieties of the machine age and their privileging of optic experience.

Nakamura's later works disavow male embodiment and instead offer a masculinized gaze (which is to say, not a male gaze but a masculine gaze that could be provocative for both women and men).[121] These paintings, created at a time when women were increasingly visible as objects in the marketplace, as subjects in universities and the workplace, and as participants on picket lines, are tinged with aggression toward women. Nakamura negotiates the disembodying effects of perpetual technological advancement and the vast changes to the social body during Japan's rise on the economic world stage during the consumerist boom of the 1960s and 1970s.

Whereas in Nakamura's reportage works the Other was dangerously—though transparently—embodied in the uniform-clad police forces, this duality of good and evil began to come undone for him in the 1960s. In the years that followed, he exposed and flirted with national symbols and their alluring dangers yet remained ever ambivalent, illustrating how his own sense of self was contingent on the state of the nation, and the state of the nation was contingent on the mediatized optics of global power.

Like the art of Shiraga, Tanaka, and Katsura, Nakamura's paintings were not simply a mode of personal expression; they were also the artist's means of performing, critiquing, or disavowing gendered identity and his own sense of political identity. Nakamura's investigations of embodiment and disembodiment charted profound changes in the political landscape as he attempted to locate his own relational position within that space. As his career grew, his work circulated abroad.[122] Despite his international acclaim, to this day the artist has never boarded a plane, preferring to visualize movement and experience the disembodied masculine gaze through his artwork alone.

Nakamura has persistently explored the relationship of the gendered body to the structures of power: in the 1950s he represented the struggles between farmers and the state, and between Japan and the United States, but by late 1958 he turned his focus toward tensions between gendered human agency and machines, delving into themes of movement and visuality. From the 1960s onward he simultaneously critiqued and participated in the visual culture of the schoolgirl fetish that perpetuated sexist consumption, employing visual signs of movement both to provoke the viewer and to secure a masculine viewing position within the picture. The stakes of exposure captivate in Nakamura's work, drawing us to his visible, profound ambivalence toward the state and the men and women who must serve, criticize, represent, and sell the body politic.

3

Tanaka Atsuko and the Circuits of Subjectivity

With the unprecedented changes occurring in Japanese cities in the 1950s and the reevaluation of gender roles taking place at the same time, for some individuals it seemed that their very sense of self was being destabilized and reimagined. For Tanaka Atsuko (1932–2005), attempting to become an important avant-garde artist from Osaka in the early 1950s meant that she had to chart a challenging course: to restructure her own sense of place in the world, through art and for art. Tanaka used her creative drive to interrogate the interrelationships among gender subjectivity, artistic status, and representation.

From Tanaka's first days as a member of the short-lived Zero-kai (Zero Group), followed by her ten-year involvement with the Gutai Art Association, her work has stood apart.[1] She garnered acclaim for her performance works, particularly for *Denki fuku (Electric Dress),* a piece involving a garment made of electric lightbulbs that Tanaka first made and wore in 1956 (Figure 3.1). Reviewers, as well as the Gutai group's leader, Yoshihara Jirō, lauded her paintings.[2] Over the past decade, international recognition of her vivid acrylic paintings and groundbreaking 1950s performance art has skyrocketed. Tanaka's first solo exhibition in North America, *Electrifying Art (1954–1968),* was held in 2004–5, and since that time her work has been featured in the *Elles* exhibition in Paris (2010) and Seattle (2012) and in *Documenta 12* in Kassel, Germany (2007). The first large-scale retrospective exhibition of her work, *Tanaka Atsuko: The Art of Connecting,* was held at Birmingham's Ikon Gallery (2011), Espai d'Art Contemporani de Castello (2011), and the Museum of Contemporary Art, Tokyo (2012). In February 2013 the Guggenheim included her work in the first North American retrospective on the Gutai Art Association. International demand for Tanaka's work has never been higher. Yet a deeper understanding of her oeuvre requires a fuller consideration of its connections to the social context of 1950s Japan than it has thus far received.

Tanaka was a twenty-year-old artist in Osaka in 1952 when the Allied Occupation of Japan came to a close. Within a few short years, destabilizing changes took place in the

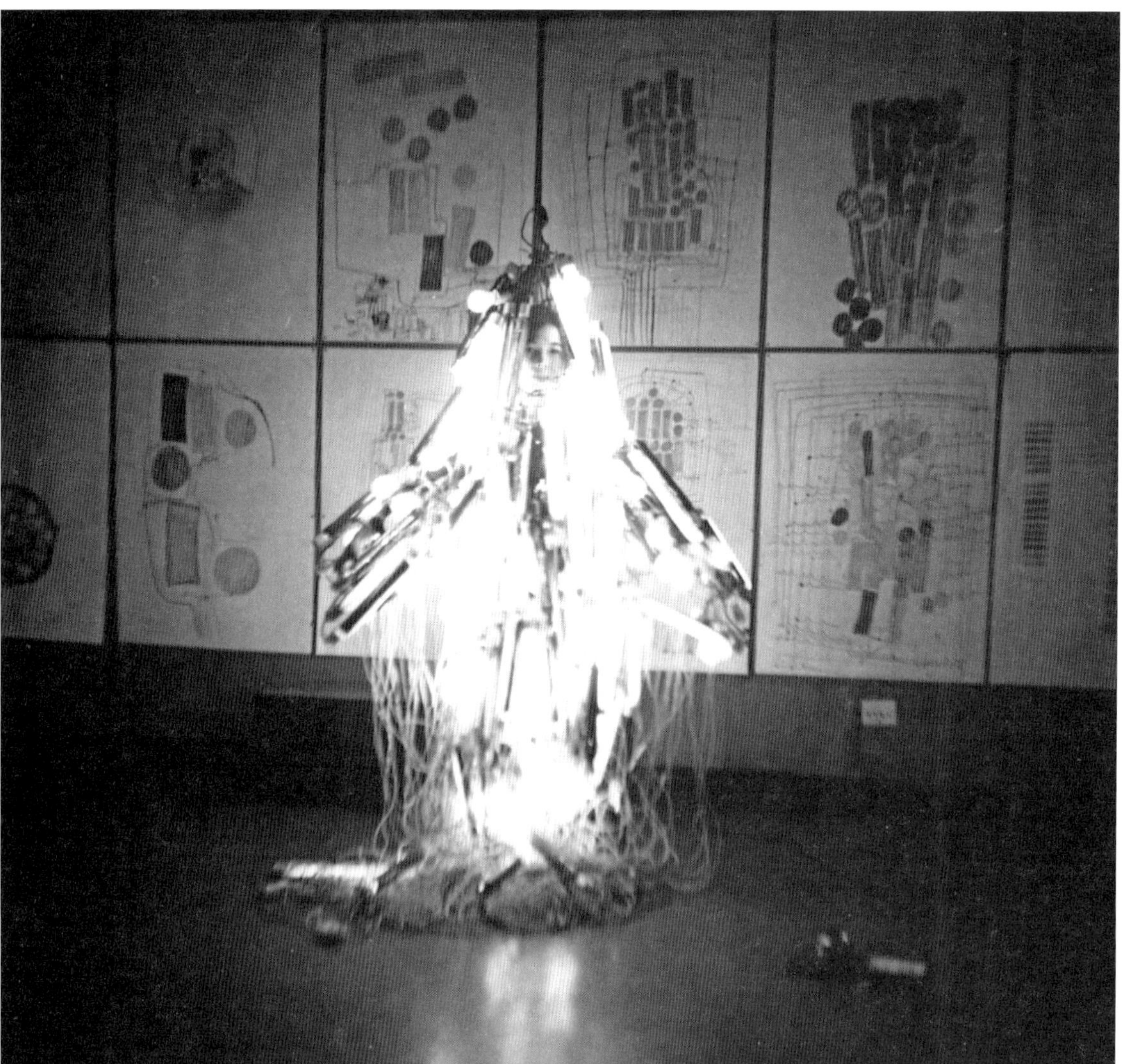

FIGURE 3.1. Tanaka Atsuko, *Denki fuku (Electric Dress), Second Gutai Art Exhibition,* Ohara Kaikan Hall, Tokyo, October 1956. Vinyl paint on lightbulbs, electric cords, and control console, approximately 165 × 80 × 80 cm. Tanaka wears the dress in this photograph and stands in front of drawings of Electric Dress. Courtesy of Osaka City Museum of Modern Art. Copyright Kanayama Akira and Tanaka Atsuko Association.

artist's hometown: a marked growth in population density due to transportation upgrades, a sudden increase in the commercialization of women's bodies in the media, unprecedented industrial development, and a surge of productivity in the arts. The average amount of private living space per person in the city dramatically decreased.[3] Osaka's built environment, replete with the cache of modernism and uneven social geography, was a paradigm of what Henri Lefebvre has described as the paradoxes of postwar life.[4] What effects would this unsettled environment have on an individual's sense of self, and how would that bear on art?

Tanaka painted with vibrant vinyl colors and produced mesmerizing entanglements of circles and wiry lines that are distinct from the action-based gestural works of other Gutai members like Shiraga Kazuo, Shimamoto Shōzō, and Murakami Saburō. Curator Katō Mizuho has played a major role in drawing attention to Tanaka's solo career. Katō curated Tanaka's first retrospective show, *Atsuko Tanaka: Search for an Unknown Aesthetic, 1954–2000,* in 2001 and also cocurated *Electrifying Art (1954–1968)* with Gutai scholar Ming Tiampo in 2004–5. In the catalog for the 2001 exhibition, Katō argues convincingly that Tanaka searches for boundaries in her work. The artist's interest in boundaries and the body, according to Katō, "was of an entirely different nature from *Challenging Mud* by Shiraga, or *Breaking through Many Screens of Paper* by Murakami, as she sublimated the materiality of the work instead of bringing it to the fore."[5] Katō concludes that physicality has a role to play in Tanaka's art, "yet rather than being elucidated directly by spontaneous and dramatic gestures, the relation to the body emerges symbolically from the animated surface with its appeal to the sense of touch and visible surface of the body."[6] Still, it remains unclear what may have motivated Tanaka's unique interest in boundaries and surface materiality.

English-speaking scholars have widely interpreted the work of the Gutai Art Association (and postwar Japanese art in general) as an embrace of American-style democracy and individualism.[7] While it is indeed true that some artists were invested in expressions of individualism, assuming that all artists shared political ideals and a common sense of selfhood leads us to overlook important divergences in artistic identities and the social anxieties of the time. Later in this chapter, I will examine the problematic nature of the recourse to individualism as an explanation of artistic practice. Rather than an articulation of individualism emerging from a fixed sense of self, Tanaka's work expressed the frailty of subjectivity. This inconstancy of self is revealed when performance pieces like *Electric Dress* and *Butai fuku (Stage Clothes)* (1956) are considered in relation to her extensive painted mappings of circles and lines. In this chapter I will argue that Tanaka's art investigates the instability of female subjectivity in light of urbanization in Japan through the materiality of surface.

Electric Dress

Without question, Tanaka's 1956 performance piece *Electric Dress* has become the most celebrated of her works.[8] The captivating quality of this early performance piece was due in no small measure to the tension it created between the sphere of cyborg spectacle and the vulnerable female body. *Electric Dress* is roughly the height of the average human body and covers the wearer from head to toe. The few available photographs of the piece, which have been widely circulated, show Tanaka's barely visible but recognizable visage peering out from behind a veil of tubular lightbulbs.[9] Photographs provide impressions of the mass of the piece, its fullness covering the artist's head and the sides of her face (Figure 3.2). As is evident from a full-length photograph, her legs were completely covered by spiraling wires resembling an overgrown vine. Only her impassive expression and portions of her hands were visible. The work's nearly two hundred bulbs, many hand-painted with synthetic resin enamel paints, resulted in an exceptionally heavy contraption, especially given the density of 1950s industrial materials; some have estimated that it weighed more than 50 kilograms (approximately 110 pounds).[10] To help offset the weight, the piece was suspended from the ceiling while Tanaka wore it.

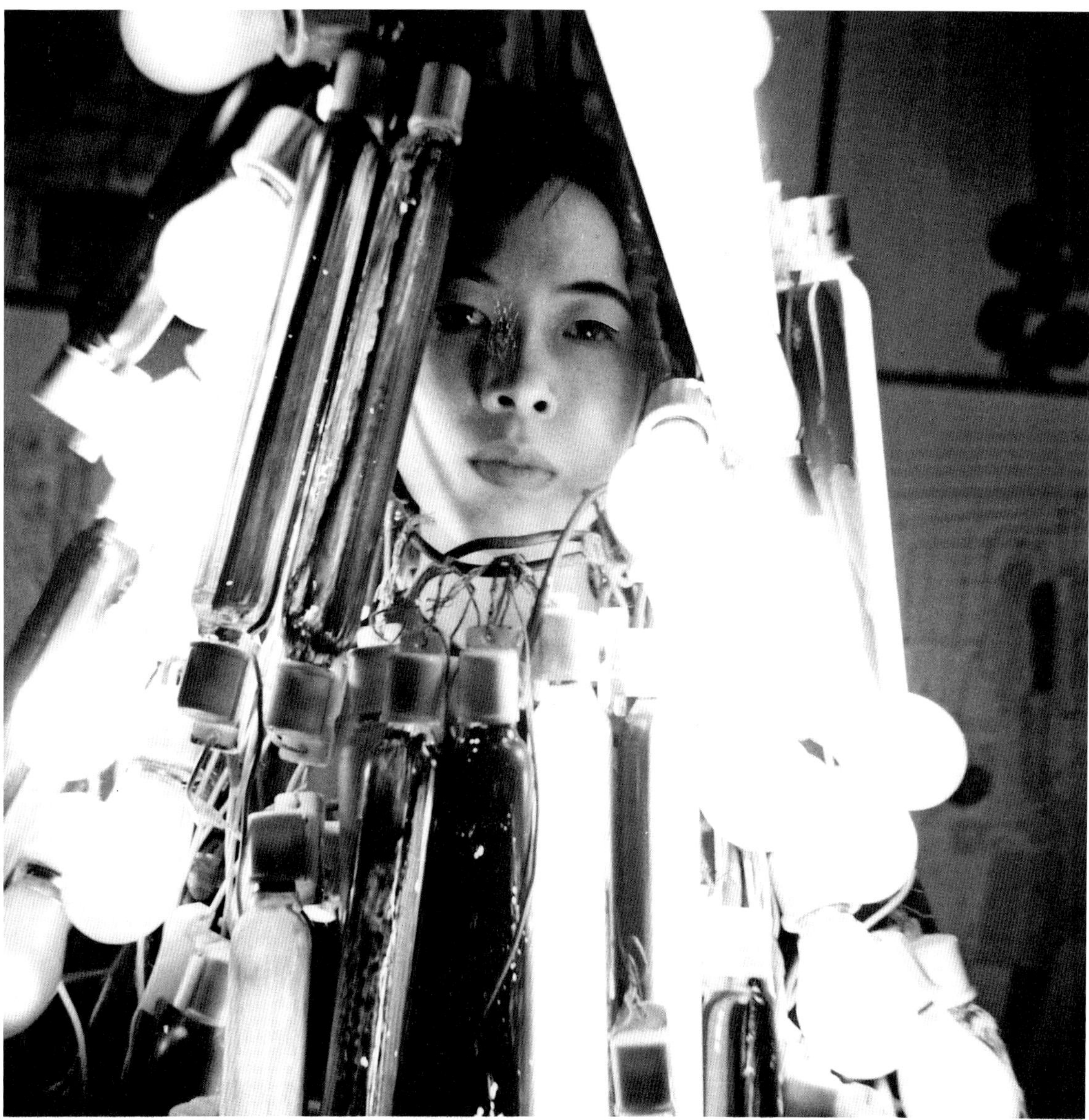

FIGURE 3.2. Tanaka Atsuko, *Denki fuku (Electric Dress), Second Gutai Art Exhibition,* Ohara Kaikan Hall, Tokyo, October 1956. Courtesy of Osaka City Museum of Modern Art. Copyright Kanayama Akira and Tanaka Atsuko Association.

Tanaka first wore the dress at the Gutai Art Association's 1956 Tokyo debut at Ohara Kaikan Hall, in the *Second Gutai Art Exhibition* (see Figure 3.1). She positioned herself strategically before a wall of her own paintings and drawings that were plans for *Electric Dress*—a testament to her interest in the relational development between three-dimensional and two-dimensional art forms. For the *Gutai Art on the Stage* show in 1957 at Sankei Kaikan Hall in Osaka, she performed *Stage Clothes.* In this performance, fellow Gutai members Shiraga Kazuo, Satō Seiichi, and Toyoshima Takashi wore costumes made of colored flashing bulbs. Unlike the version worn by Tanaka, these were not suspended from the ceiling and were not given titles; instead, they acted as a theatrical segue from Tanaka's *Stage Clothes.*[11] For the *Third Gutai Art Exhibition* at the Kyoto Municipal Museum of Art in 1957, the piece was displayed and not worn. In 1958, for the *Second Gutai Art on the Stage* exhibition at Asahi Kaikan Hall, Osaka, Tanaka directed and performed an untitled piece featuring an electric dress and illuminated disks.[12]

The multiple iterations of *Electric Dress*—as a performance piece worn by the artist, as a piece worn by male performers, as an unworn installation, as a reconstruction, and, as it is most widely seen, as a photographic record of her performance—make defining and assessing the piece challenging. Because Tanaka prefigured the work in drawings and later reused the bulbs to create tableau art that hung on the wall akin to a painting, even pinning down the start or end point of the work is problematic. *Electric Dress* thus lacks a stable reference point, which leads to confusion, a result that Tanaka likely courted.

The often overlooked fact that men, too, wore versions of the piece raises complicated questions for analysis. If men and women both wore it, is gender irrelevant to the piece? While the work may have resonated differently with male and female actors, it was conceived and created in a particular time and place. Here I will consider how Tanaka's gendered experiences in postwar Japan, and specifically Osaka, may have informed her creative motivations. Tanaka, by her own definition, was no feminist. She balked at the term, as perhaps most artists of her generation would.[13] Determining if Tanaka was a participant in the women's liberation movement is beyond the scope or interest of this chapter. Feminism is a different issue than simply stating that gender played a formative role in her political, personal, and creative experiences.

Electric Dress emphasized the ability of industrial force to overwhelm the senses. Powered by an electrical circuit codeveloped by Tanaka and an electrician she befriended, the bulbs in the piece flashed sequentially, and the velocity of the signals increased until they reached levels that Tanaka called "incessant and chaotic."[14] The adornment of the physical form bombarded the senses of the wearer—the incandescent brightness of *Electric Dress* hazing or blinding vision, its mass limiting mobility, its sound impeding hearing, its heat impairing touch, its immensity overwhelming. Viewers were also vulnerable to the work's effects, although to a lesser extent; it was a noisy and heat-producing contraption that could not go unnoticed.[15]

The piece drew attention not least because it appeared at some of the first performance art shows seen inside or outside Japan. In performance art, the gaze of the viewer activates the encounter, and *Electric Dress* was no exception. The apparatus drew the eye, yet at the same time its enclosure effectively blocked access to the performer. The contraption both illuminated and concealed the subject, with flashing lights that heightened the tension between access and denial. Unlike other Gutai members who boldly claimed their individualism through destructive spectacle, Tanaka's spectral subject was partially exposed, partially hidden.

A composite of machine and body, *Electric Dress* suggested an unfamiliar, incomplete subject. This merging of electrics and the body prefigured later conflations of the body in evidence at the *Yomiuri Indépendant* exhibitions, such as Akasegawa Genpei's *Aimai no umi (Ambivalent Ocean)* series (1961), which collaged body parts and technologies of vision. These artworks negotiated the arrival of mass consumer society—which in Japan was built largely on electronic goods—and the related changes to everyday life. As William Marotti notes:

> Everyday life in urban Japan by the late 1950s was changing at all levels, and yet apart from an explosion of enthusiastic advertising, television, and light journalism, the *effects* of this transformation constituted the great unaddressed political phenomenon of the period. This was in spite of the fact that many of its *causes* were directly related to the security arrangement with America, including Korean War procurements, a transistor and television industry arising from technology transfers, and continuing beneficial trade arrangements— directly related, in other words, to the cold and hot wars in Asia.[16]

These larger global political issues put pressure on Japan's national identity and, in turn, on the individual's sense of self within the nation.

Subjectivity and the Postwar Period

Following Japan's defeat in World War II, imperialist rhetoric that fostered commitment to the nation over the individual was roundly rejected, and a reevaluation of subjectivity *(shutaisei)* held great philosophical currency.[17] The notion of shared experience, perception, and interpretation among members of a common nation was brought into question. New theories of subjectivity were often divergent, contradictory, and ambiguous, yet academics and art critics have consistently employed the concept of "individualism" as having critical purchase on postwar artists such as those in the Gutai Art Association.

Arguments promoting Japan's postwar embrace of individualism also falsely frame intellectual development in Japan. How can we be sure that the nationalist messages of prioritizing community over the individual were thoroughly internalized before 1945? How can we determine that a clear notion of individualism emerged only after the war? The abrupt shift from imperialism to constitutional democracy, authored largely by the Allied Occupation forces, no doubt altered the relation between the individual and the state. But we cannot assume that subjectivity was underdeveloped or entirely group-based before the postwar period. This misconception may be fueled by deeper assumptions that individualism is an American trait helpfully introduced to Japan by the occupation forces.[18] James A. Fujii discusses Japan since the Meiji period, underscoring how notions of the self are often problematically assigned by nationality:

> In Japan, a nation persistently and misleadingly characterized by foreigners and Japanese alike as a society where "group" (family) displaces "self," Western (particularly Romantic) conceptions of the individual continue to be embraced with considerable fanfare. Naturalized by over a century of sustained rumination, individualism has been adopted as a powerfully attractive ideal, whether it finds popular expression as an insistent and revealing emphasis on *kosei* (individuality) or when it appears repeatedly as the subject of scholarly discourse.[19]

The conclusion that Gutai art speaks to a newborn sense of individualism overlooks the fact that this notion has largely been constructed by scholars and curators. In reality, struggles to express a sense of artistic self certainly predate the 1950s.[20] Furthermore, the argument for individuality obscures the complex struggles in which Tanaka engaged. It neglects the resistance to and complicity with gender roles that framed her production.

Tanaka's ambivalent relationship to individualism further distinguishes her from Gutai colleagues such as Shiraga Kazuo, whose quest for individualism was made explicit in his writings and art.[21] Although Tanaka discussed her own work, talent, and search for originality, her comments veered away from notions of the individual. In fact, she expressed a sense of distance from her art and a yearning for fixity that seemed to be difficult for her to achieve. In 1963, Tanaka wrote:

> It feels strange to look at a work that is well done. If the work in question is mine, I wonder how on earth I could have made it. Then, I want to make something like this again. However, if I am too absorbed with its surface and fail to understand the underlying idea, what I create is no good. If I am hesitant, it disappears, like a liquefying lump of sugar.[22]

Rather than mounting a campaign for the new and modern individual, Tanaka revealed in her work as well as in her words a lack of fixity of the work of art and the subject, and a sense of uncertainty about the strength and physical presence of self. For Tanaka, selfhood was not a consummate form, with art as its vehicle for expression, but rather a set of chance circumstances. Subjective identification was circuitous, experienced through connection, disconnection, and repetition.

Throughout her career, Tanaka was based in the Kansai region, first in Osaka and then in the remote area of Asuka, Nara. Rarely traveling, she chose to remain in Japan even while many of her pieces were shipped abroad. Thus, Tanaka's connections to the outside world were negotiated through paintings and performance art. For Tanaka, art was a means to examine agency and apprehensions about contact with the outside world. Her status as an underrepresented avant-garde woman artist was not declarative, but tentative and cautious. While Yoshihara persistently demanded originality to declare Gutai's artistic autonomy to the international world, Tanaka used surface to negotiate and question her sense of self far from the center of the art world. Although Tanaka's art was exhibited widely abroad, she did not venture outside Japan until the late 1990s.

Transportation and Urban Change

Although Tanaka resisted international travel, movement was a source of thrill and anxiety for her and her husband, Kanayama Akira (1924–2006). Curator Jinno Kimio reports that Kanayama and Tanaka often enjoyed taking drives in their speedy cars. Considering that Kanayama drove and Tanaka did not have a license, it is possible that Kanayama was the one more taken with the thrill of speed.[23] Kinetic energy in general attracted the artist, however; she described the train as her muse, reporting that most of her ideas came to her while she was on the train or near Osaka station.[24] Significantly, trains were a marker of the intense changes in Tanaka's hometown.

Following the Allied Occupation, rapid transformations occurred in Japan at a number of different levels, including changes to urban geography, population, and transportation. In Osaka, a major industrial hub, these changes were magnified. This period was as crucial for Tanaka's artistic development as it was for the development of the city as a whole. Despite its high population, Osaka often received less cultural and governmental attention than other cities, a reality that posed challenges to an artist from the area in terms of grants, venues, and publicity. The changes to the municipality brought a growing awareness that resources and attention were routinely accorded to Tokyo and Kyoto. Critics were attuned to the notion that industry dominated Osaka at the expense of cultural production. Writing in 1965, art critic Jules Langsner noted:

> On first acquaintance, Osaka appears to be a most unlikely city for the emergence of a creatively vital, exuberantly non-conformist development in the twentieth century art. The business of Osaka is business. . . . With a population of over 3,000,000, Osaka is without a single gallery of significances *[sic]* other than the Gutai Pinacotheca. Under the circumstances, it is not surprising that there is not one art critic of national stature in the town, leaving Gutai on the fringe of attention in the art press of the country.[25]

From the outset, Tanaka's art took up a modernity that was tethered to its roots in Osaka and the Kansai region. Art in Osaka was outside Tokyo's sway over Japan's contemporary art scene. The second most populous city in Japan, Osaka experienced rapid industrialization and immigration in the 1950s. The city developed faster during this period than even Tokyo and cemented its position as a major industrial center. Migrant laborers and *Zainichi* Koreans (permanent ethnic residents of Japan) became the city's biggest social groups.[26] Many workers were forced to live in the city's low-income peripheral districts, and the city was ill equipped to handle the increased commuter population. In 1954, more than fifteen hundred illegally built homes were located on sites where land readjustment projects such as new roads and parks were scheduled.[27] By 1955, the housing shortage was estimated at more than sixty thousand units. Reporting on Osaka's population influx, Hasegawa Jun'ichi notes that "from 1941, the standard of 3.65 *jō* [1.08 square meters, or the size of one tatami mat] fell to 3.04 in 1948, and to 2.9 in 1953."[28] This increase in urban population density profoundly affected everyday life. Moreover, the daytime population tripled, resulting in packed trains and chaotic traffic.[29] In 1955, the year Tanaka displayed her first electrical works, Osaka saw the highest population growth to date and a cresting tide of urban transformation.

Despite being an emerging economic powerhouse, Osaka provided a sharp contrast to the Kansai region's more picturesque cities of Nara and Kyoto. The port city's garish industrialism denied it a reputation for beauty and historical grandeur, despite its also being an ancient city. People from Osaka are reputed to talk and walk faster than those in the rest of Japan and are notorious for their colloquialisms. Moving through the city can be a challenge, as it has none of the orderliness of Tokyo, the tourist-focused organization of Nara, or the cherished (and constructed) tranquility of Kyoto. As late as 1998, Tanaka's memories of Osaka were characterized by recollections of clattery train stations, which she juxtaposed with her quiet lifestyle after moving to Nara: "I really liked the nature here [Nara], but even though I've lived here a long time, Osaka is still my favorite place, I miss it. Particularly when I see Tsuruhashi . . . I get very nostalgic. When I hear the noise of the loop line, I really miss it. I always took the train at Tsuruhashi station."[30]

In 1956, Japan was poised for a period of breakneck technological and industrial development and was practically buzzing with mechanical momentum. Key to the impending series of transformations was the reestablishment of Japanese National Railways in 1949 by the U.S. General Headquarters, which set into motion circuitries of movement across the nation at unprecedented speeds.[31] Connections between Tokyo and Osaka were to form the primary transport arteries. By November 1956, the Tōkaidō express train was running on electricity, enabling a passenger to travel the distance in six hours and thirty minutes and paving the way for the next development in transportation, the *shinkansen*.[32] High-speed trains were proposed during wartime, and then again in 1957. The bullet train was heavily promoted throughout the 1950s and had its first run in 1964 on the Tōkaidō Line.[33] Like Tanaka, Nakamura Hiroshi was fascinated by the speed, risk, and visual politics of the train. As discussed in chapter 2, many of his works feature lurching steam engines and railway workers. Other artists, too, were drawn to the train as a site for artistic investigation. In 1962, Nakanishi Natsuyuki and Takamatsu Jirō (who, in the following year, would become members of Hi Red Center), along with Kawani Hiroshi, Murata Kiichi, and Kubota Noboru, organized the "Yamanote event," in which they performed art actions aboard the Yamanote train line (the main train line in central Tokyo) while dressed in everyday clothing and wearing white face paint.[34] Capable of enormous speeds and powered by the country's advancing technical specialization, Japan's train network and the *shinkansen* in particular were trenchant symbols of the nation's modernity—emblems of the country's progress that emerged in the 1870s and that continue to absorb a great deal of statewide focus today.[35]

More important, the trains actively manufactured that modernity through the rapid transport of objects and bodies. Although intended to heal the great rural/urban divide, the introduction of high-speed transport in fact may have exacerbated the problem, as commuting distances could be longer and members of families increasingly began to live in different regions. Kristin Ross's description of the car in postwar France reveals parallels to Japan's fascination with trains: "During the 1950s and 1960s in France mobility was the categorical imperative of the economic order, the mark of a rupture with the past; every individual must be free to be displaced, and displaceable in function of the exigencies of the economic order. The car performed (and continues to perform) the activity most embedded in ideologies of the free market: displacement."[36]

The flashing lights and sense of disorder in *Electric Dress* are a synecdoche of the hustle and bustle of the city, vividly evoking the transportation networks that were central to postwar urbanization and economic development. Even in the work's earliest versions, the haphazardly grouped lights had an unruly effect that negated their decorative aspect and emphasized the ability of the media to overcome the subject-wearer.

Tanaka was a child of Japan's industrial age, the youngest of nine children supported by their father who worked in a match manufacturing plant. For Tanaka, the train stations of her hometown were always a prime fixation. In 1993, reflecting on her initial interest in *Electric Dress,* she said:

> For a long time I tried to come up with an interesting idea. After half a year or so, I was seated on a bench at the Osaka station, and I saw a billboard featuring a pharmaceutical advertisement, brightly illuminated by neon lights. This was it! I would make a neon dress![37]

Like a traffic signal, the flashing colors command the viewer to stop and look. One can almost imagine the pulsating sensation that mesmerized the young artist as she witnessed the visual effects of the city's rapid commercialization. Kanayama's found art piece known as *Alarm,* exhibited in 1956 at the *Outdoor Exhibition to Challenge the Midsummer Sun,* meshes with Tanaka's preoccupations.[38] In this conceptual work, Kanayama simply placed a railway crossing signal inside Ashiya Park, juxtaposing the greenery with the bold metal form (Figure 3.3). It seems that the burgeoning transportation system was a source of inspiration and angst for both Kanayama and Tanaka. In the same exhibition Tanaka displayed

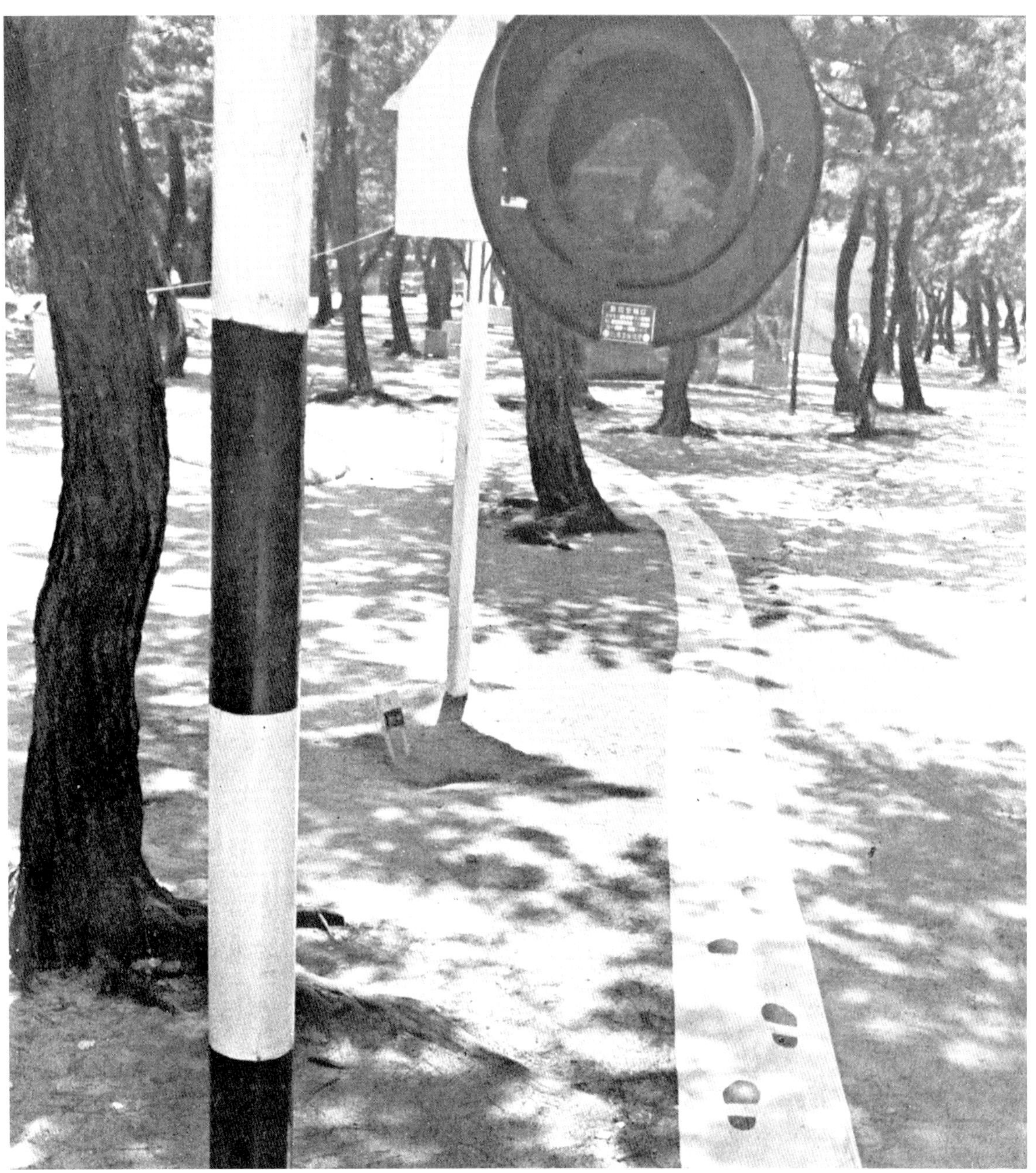

FIGURE 3.3. Kanayama Akira, *Alarm*, 1956 (no longer extant). Photograph copyright Kanayama Akira and Tanaka Atsuko Association.

an electrical piece called *Stage Clothes* (one of two of her pieces that share the same name) that consisted of a series of cutout doll-like shapes, more than fourteen feet tall, illuminated by electrical lights that lit up in succession. The rhythm of the bell on Kanayama's "borrowed" railway crossing coincided with that of the electric light in Tanaka's installation, bespeaking their mutual interest in urbanization and each other (Figure 3.4).

Fujii has shown how trains further emerged as a space for cultural production in the Kansai area with the development of the Hankyu rail after the turn of the century:

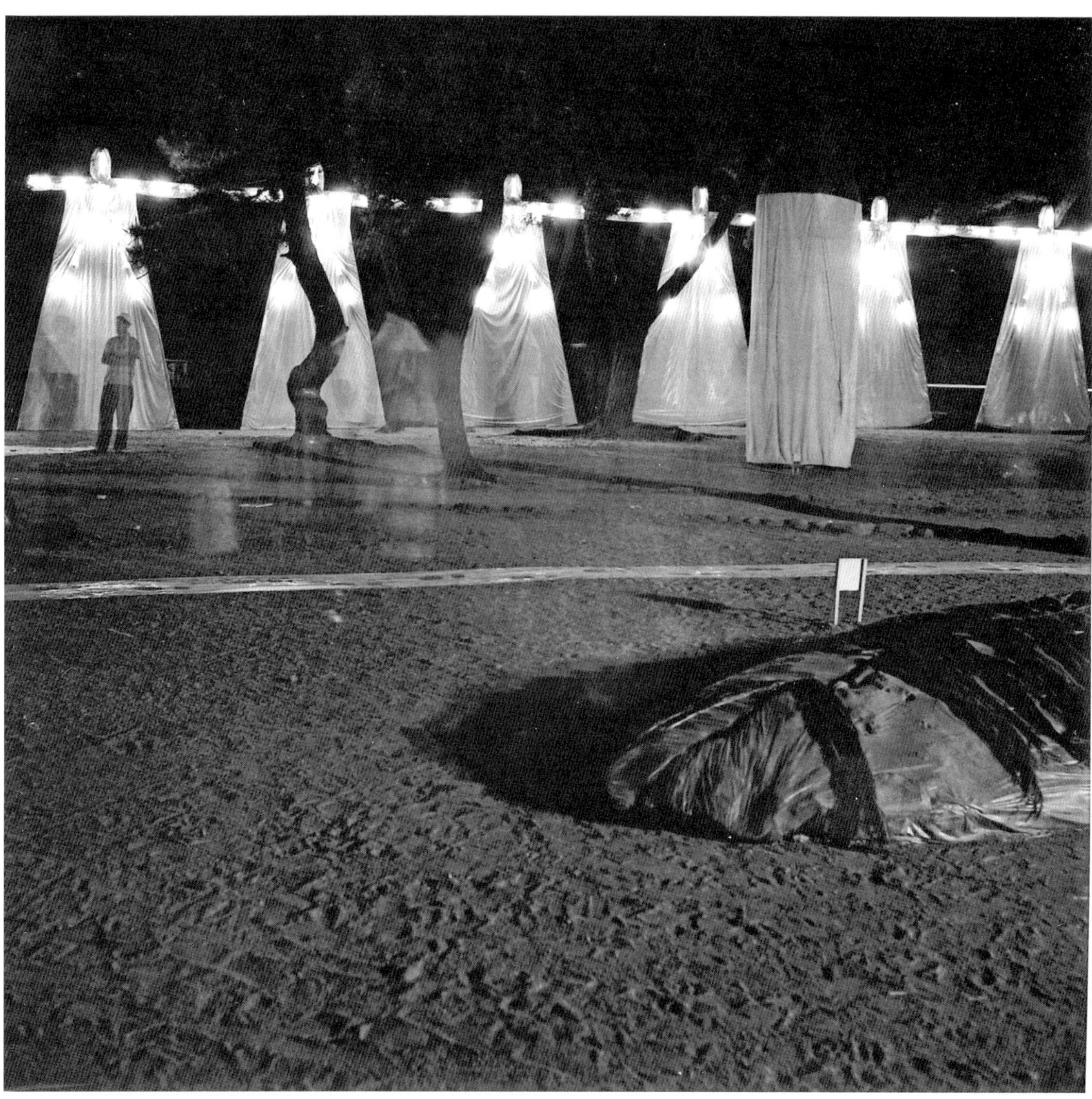

FIGURE 3.4. Tanaka Atsuko, *Butai fuku (Stage Clothes),* 1956 (not extant). Vinyl paint on lightbulbs, electric cords, plywood, vinyl sheets, motor, gears, and pulleys; seven objects, 436 × 364 × 7 cm each. Courtesy of Osaka City Museum of Modern Art. Copyright Kanayama Akira and Tanaka Atsuko Association.

If Marx was right in seeing the transfer of goods from the worker's shop to the market as a process of commodification, the commute must be seen as a form of transfer that subjects the commuter to its rigid temporal and spatial requirements—converting them into commodities in the process. . . . Technology devised for utilitarian ends also gives rise to new shapes and deformations of sensibility, pleasure, desire, and fetishism.[39]

One could presume that during the postwar population boom the train's transient space of social contradiction and "intimate alienation" of fashion, secretive gazes, and an increasing paucity of personal space would intensify to the point of subconscious and conscious disturbance. Significantly, Tanaka, in her performance pieces, covered herself with "made in Japan" exports of cloth and cheap industrial lights, drawing attention to capitalist evaluative systems that can treat bodies and products equally. Notably, textile and light industry commodity production was often women's work; hence, the production was often as gendered as the consumption.[40] Tanaka's work emerged from this "fragmentation of young women into their body parts and their fantastic recreation," which "tellingly speaks to the logic of commodity production."[41] Fujii's remarks reveal the train as a site of "disconnected encounter" crucial to subject formation in postwar Japan. It was in this heady atmosphere of speed and dislocation, when vast electrical circuits were laid across Japan, that Tanaka turned to wiring her own works.

Wires and the connections and disconnections of circuitry are perhaps the most common element of Tanaka's work. They materialize in the sequence of cords in *Sakuhin (Beru) (Work [Bell])*, one of the first sound pieces ever made (Figure 3.5).[42] Circuits were also predominant in the wires in *Electric Dress,* and even in the threaded connections that linked the costumes in the performance of *Stage Clothes.* Most evident are the series of circles and wiry lines in Tanaka's paintings that followed *Electric Dress,* such as an untitled work from 1958 made from vivid acrylic and vinyl paint (Plate 20). Here, circuits are reenvisioned as surface, a locus of entangled threads. Viewed in relation to her performance work, Tanaka's circuitries seem to enact a negotiation with the geography of the ever-changing city and state; moreover, they are symptomatic of the hazardous position of the subject within that uncertain frame. The repetitive presence of line and circle speaks to the tension between limits and limitlessness.

In its emergence in a time of elevated confusion and anxiety, *Electric Dress* is like a double-sided skin. On one hand, it shines like the alluring city, spectacularizing the utilitarian lights and Tanaka herself. On the other, it is a luminous shield that keeps the outside at bay. Inviting as the vividness of the dress may be, it refutes touch in its incandescence. The glow and reflection of the lights enact movement, but the weight of the piece restricts bodily action. Tanaka's art experiment set the subject within a specifically 1950s technology that was physical and spatial, unlike the work of later artists such as Eva Hesse, who took up similar formal interests in wiry connections. *Electric Dress* thus seems to activate surface as a means to explore subjectivity as a nexus between inside and outside, negotiating how the

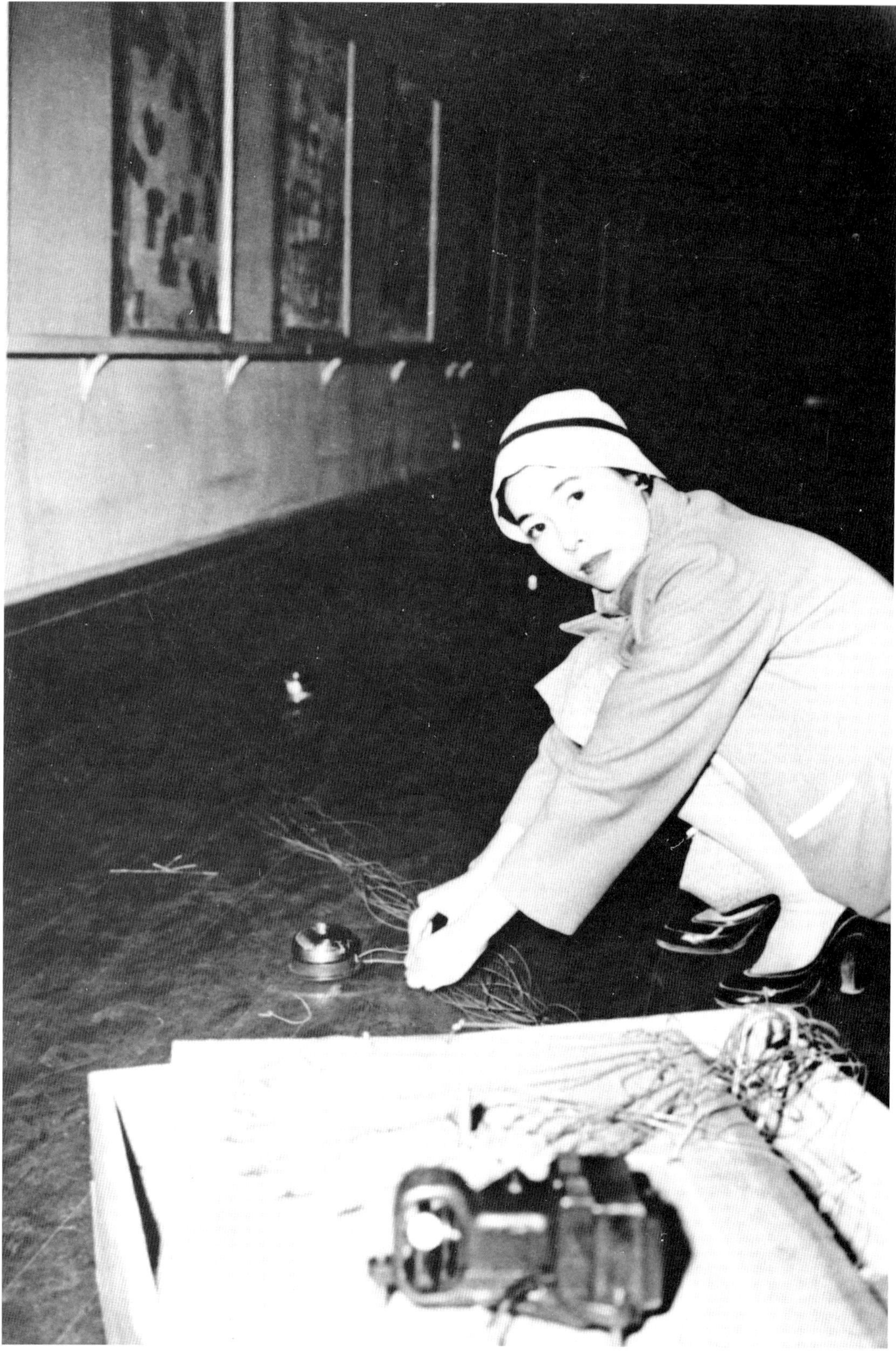

FIGURE 3.5. Tanaka Atsuko installs *Sakuhin (Beru) (Work [Bell])* at *First Gutai Art Exhibition*, Ohara Kaikan Hall, Tokyo, October 19–28, 1955. Twenty bells, electric cords, switch, and motor. Courtesy of Kanayama Akira and Tanaka Atsuko Association. Copyright Kanayama Akira and Tanaka Atsuko Association.

new technologies of postwar Osaka might be tested in the realm of performance art and representation as well as on the body.

Electric Dress is in a constant referential relationship to the body. When exhibited as an installation, the unfilled void at the center of the piece refers to its subject-creator, playing on the tension between the totality of the worn dress and the void of partiality it constructs (Plate 21).[43] Without electricity, there is a deadened sense to the work overall, as it hangs in empty stasis. Illuminated, the individualized glowing forms of the bulbs give way to a unified shape, and the shining figure is brought to the fore. Hence Tanaka's choice to have the lights blink on and off enacts the oscillation between part and whole; furthermore, it suggests that wholeness is ultimately an illusion brought about by the activation of segments.

Mapping the Senses

Tanaka's diverse oeuvre suggests a strong interest in sensory experience. *Bell,* for example, worked with sound, *Work (Yellow Cloth)* (Figure 3.6) was inviting to touch, and *Electric Dress* transfixed viewers and evoked the melding of skin and machine. *Bell,* an innovative sound installation, was originally installed in 1955 and reconstructed in 1985, 2000, and 2004.[44] It is composed of a set of approximately twenty small bells that are of similar appearance placed at roughly two-meter equidistant points around the floor of a gallery.[45] The silver, circular bells resting on their bases have a functional, nondecorative quality and are connected by a series of wires. A willing gallery visitor activates the piece through a single touch of a button. Each bell then sounds in sequence, and while all of the bells ring in an aggressive, high-pitched tone, each sound differs from the last, in a seeming endless series of discordant noises that is sustained for about two minutes. It is a work that requires bodily action to be initiated and incurs bodily responses once sounded—if not the usual embarrassed and alarmed expression, a startled jump while covering one's ears or at least an extreme vibration of the ear drum.

Key to *Bell*'s effectiveness is the visitor's integration into the sensory experience. Tiampo aptly points to the significance of the interaction but characterizes the engagement as positive: "Despite its irritating sound, interacting with the work is extremely pleasurable. First there is the thrill of transgression—creating a racket in the quiet space of contemplation that is the art exhibition, as well as breaching the sacred rule, 'do not touch.'"[46] Yet this so-called transgression is at the request of the gallery/artist, and, in fact, the ensuing prolonged, shrill din creates at best a mix of annoyance and displeasure. The piece is interesting because of this disjuncture, not despite it. Considering the prevailing behavioral tenets in the 1950s, it is likely that the gallery visitor who initiated the work would have found his or her responsibility for the noise acutely embarrassing.[47] Yoshihara commented that the work received severe criticism, adding that Tanaka's "dangerous projects often terrorized us," perhaps in part due to the fact that her art would have violated norms of female aesthetics.[48]

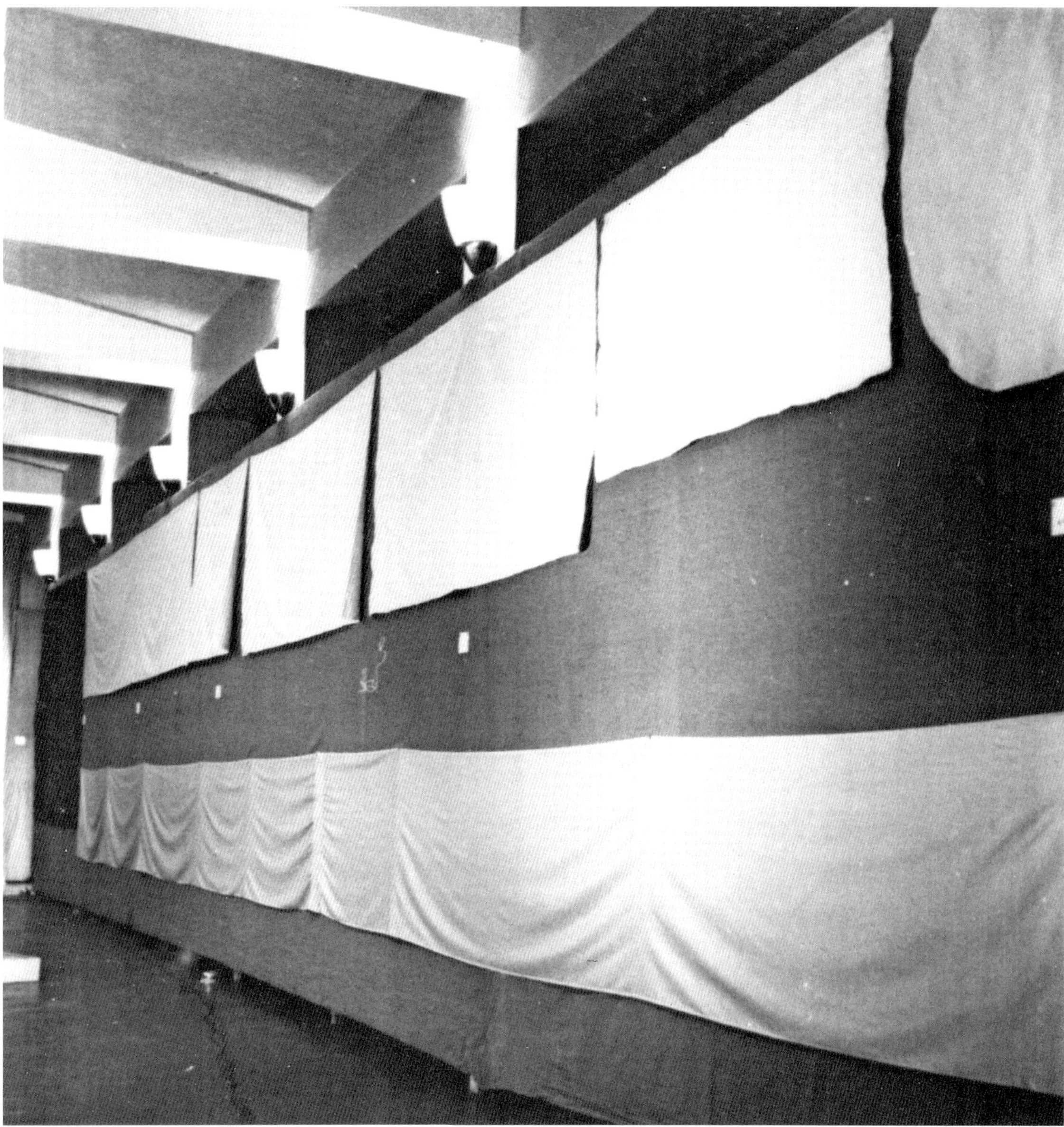

FIGURE 3.6. Tanaka Atsuko, *Work (Yellow Cloth), First Gutai Art Exhibition*, 1955. Commercially dyed cotton, 100 × 208 cm, 100 × 20 cm, 100 × 377 cm. Copyright Kanayama Akira and Tanaka Atsuko Association.

Bell's invitation to and subsequent denial of pleasure suggest the risks in exposure to new media, a theme that recurs in *Electric Dress*. Viewers I observed interacting with *Bell* at the *Electrifying Art* exhibition in 2005 denied responsibility or expressed dismay after having pressed the button: "I didn't know it would do that!" "I don't know how to make it stop . . ." These common responses suggest that rather than "breaking the boundary between art and life," as Tiampo states (thus making reference to Kaprow's text on happenings),[49] *Bell*

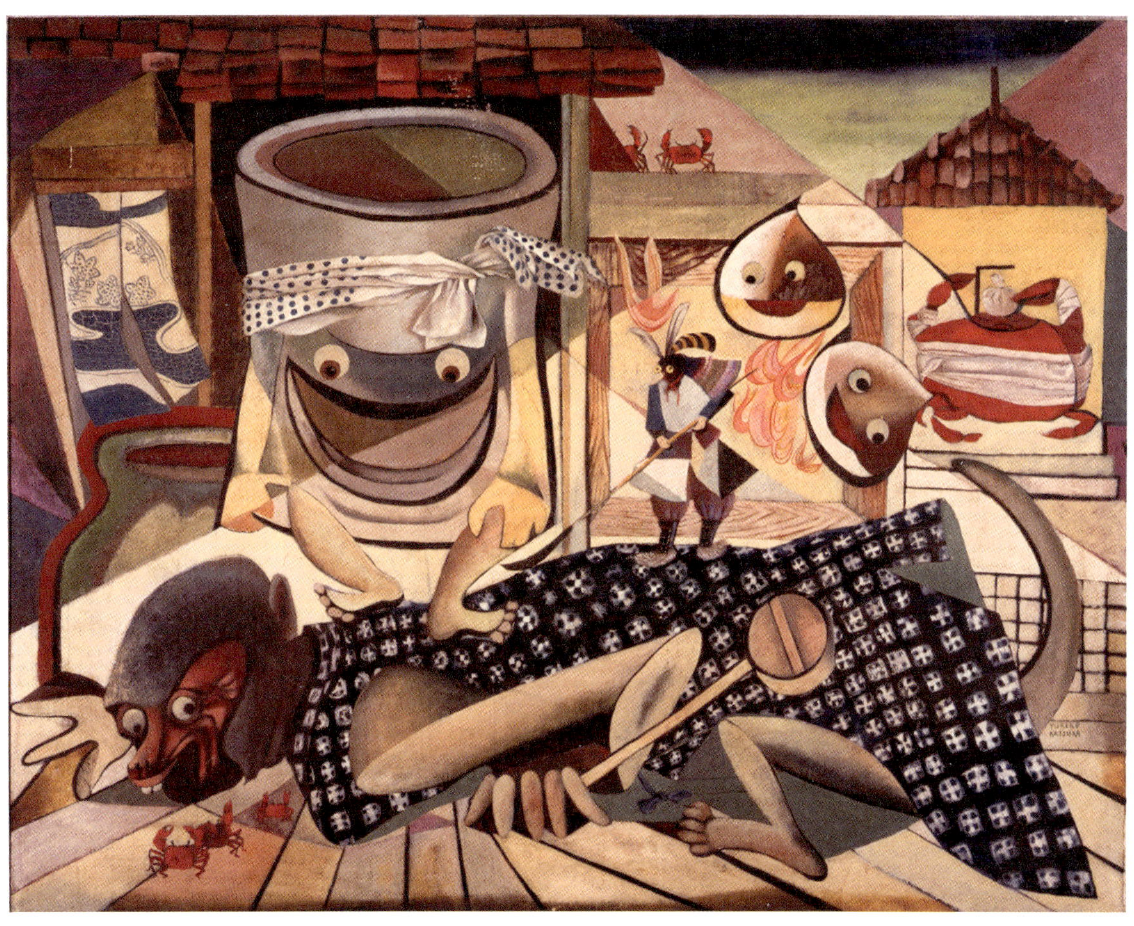

PLATE 1. Katsura Yuki, *Saru kani gassen (The Battle of the Monkey and the Crab)*, 1948. Oil on canvas, 90 × 115 cm. Copyright Katsura Akinari. Courtesy of the Tokushima Modern Art Museum.

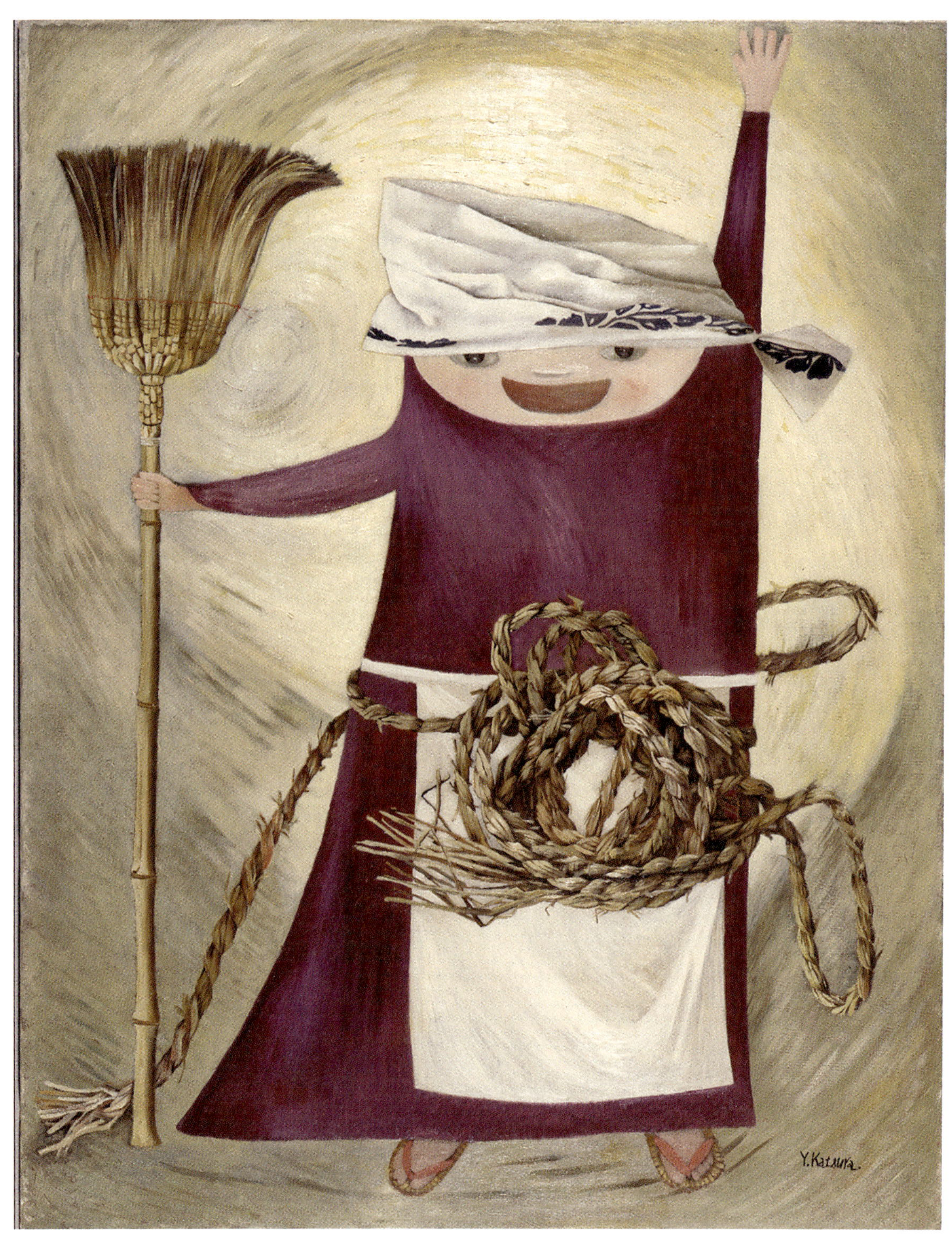

PLATE 2. Katsura Yuki, *Fujin no hi (Women's Day),* 1953. Pencil, pastel, and watercolor on paper, 35 × 28 cm. Copyright Katsura Akinari. Courtesy of the Miyagi Museum of Art.

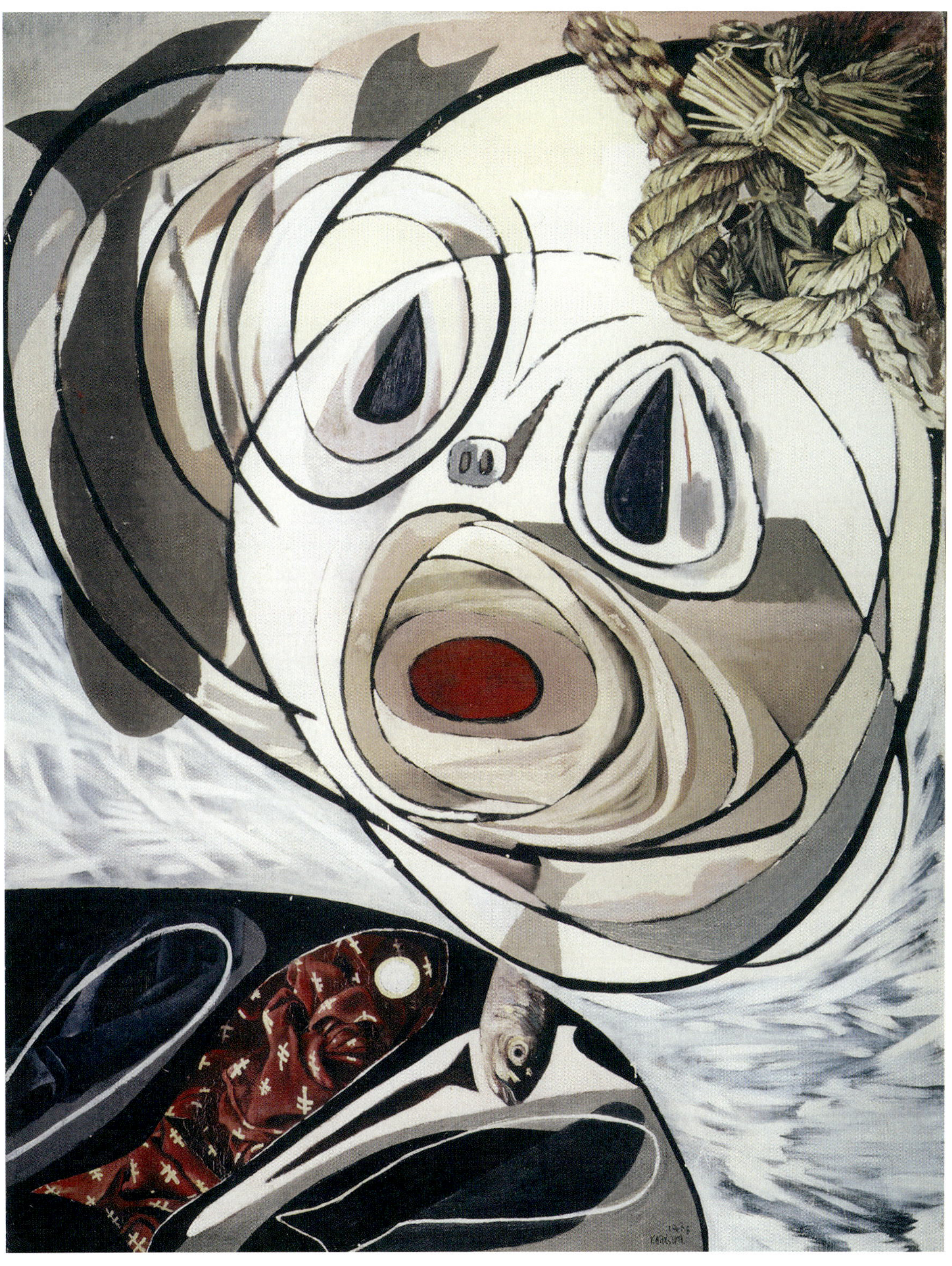

PLATE 3. Katsura Yuki, *Hito to sakana (Human and Fish),* 1954. Oil on canvas, 116 × 90.8 cm. Copyright Katsura Akinari. Courtesy of the Aichi Prefectural Museum of Art.

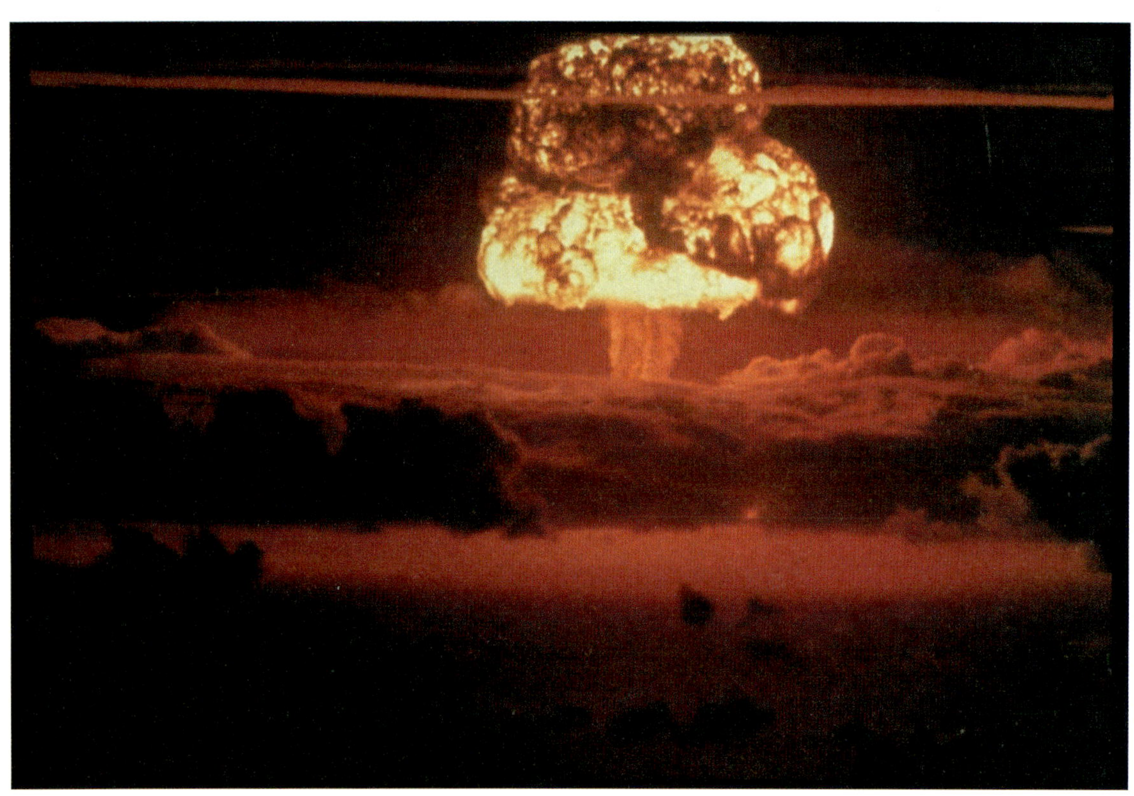

PLATE 4. Test bomb on Enewetak Atoll, 1952. Published in *Life,* May 3, 1954.

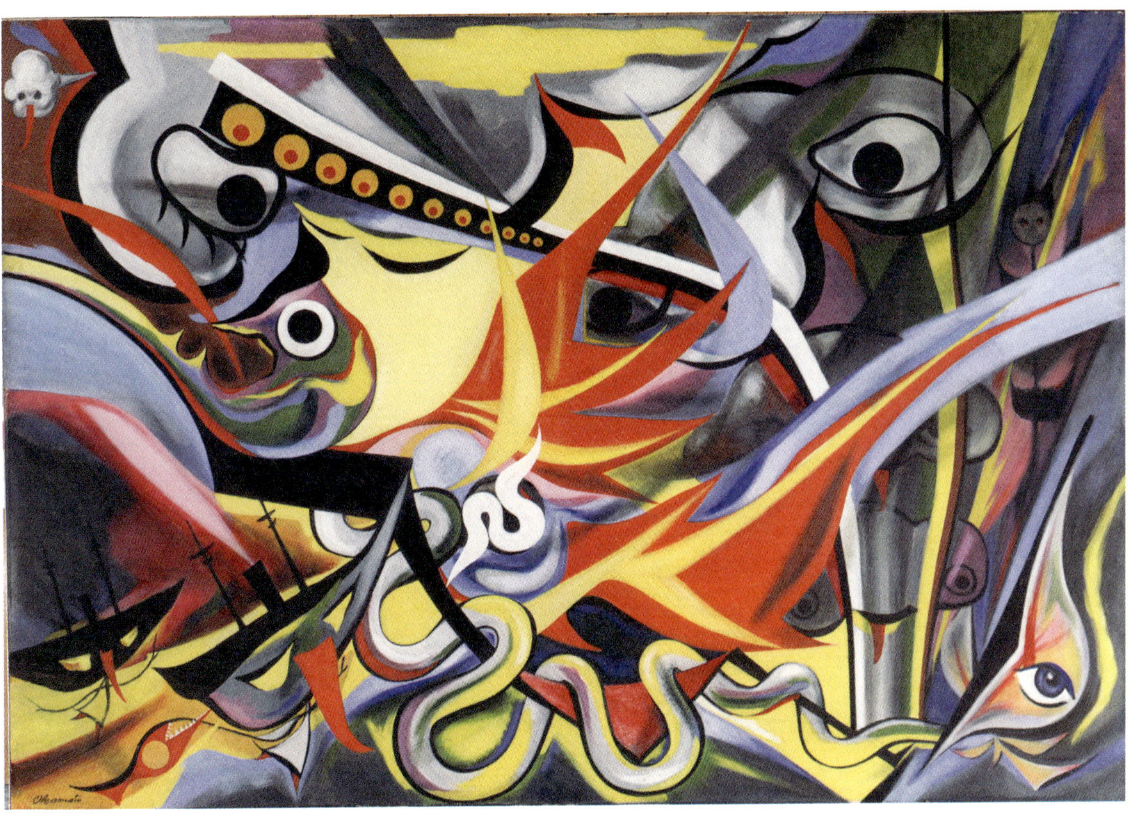

PLATE 5. Okamoto Tarō, *Moeru hito (People Aflame)*, 1954. Oil on canvas, 212.5 × 308.5 cm. Copyright Takahashi Yoshio. Courtesy of the Okamoto Tarō Memorial Museum. Photograph from National Museum of Art Tokyo and DNP Art and Communications.

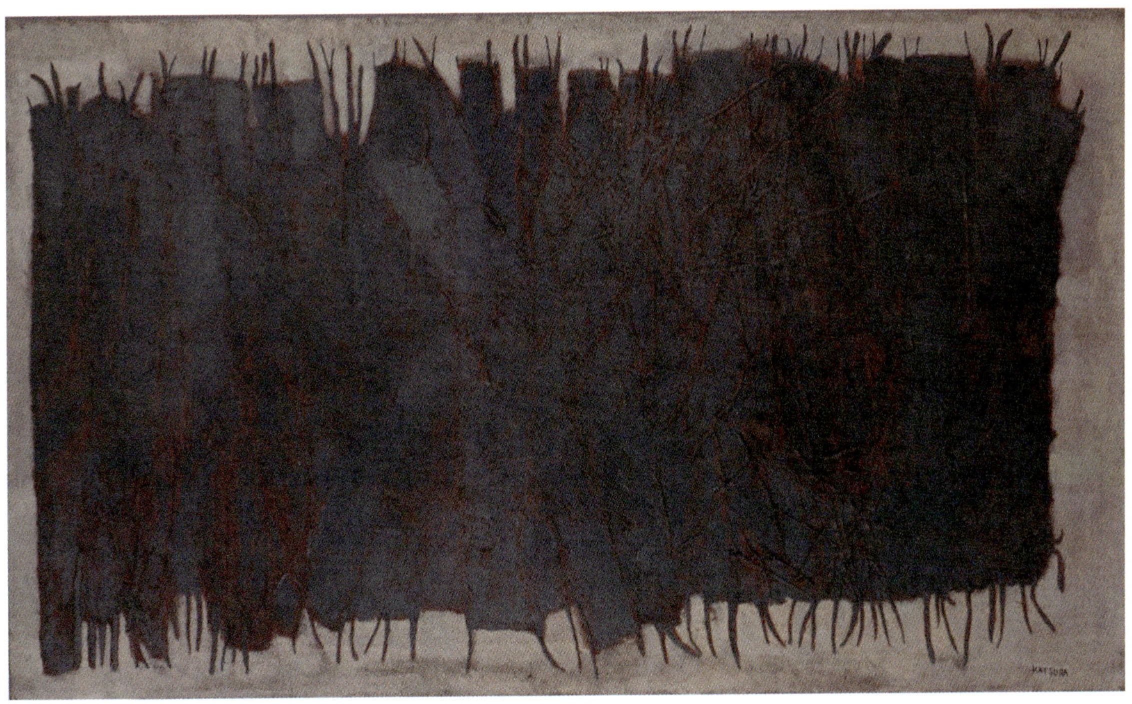

PLATE 6. Katsura Yuki, *Senbon ashi (Millipede)*, 1962. Oil and paper on canvas, 106 × 179 cm. Copyright Katsura Akinari. Courtesy of the Shimonoseki City Art Museum.

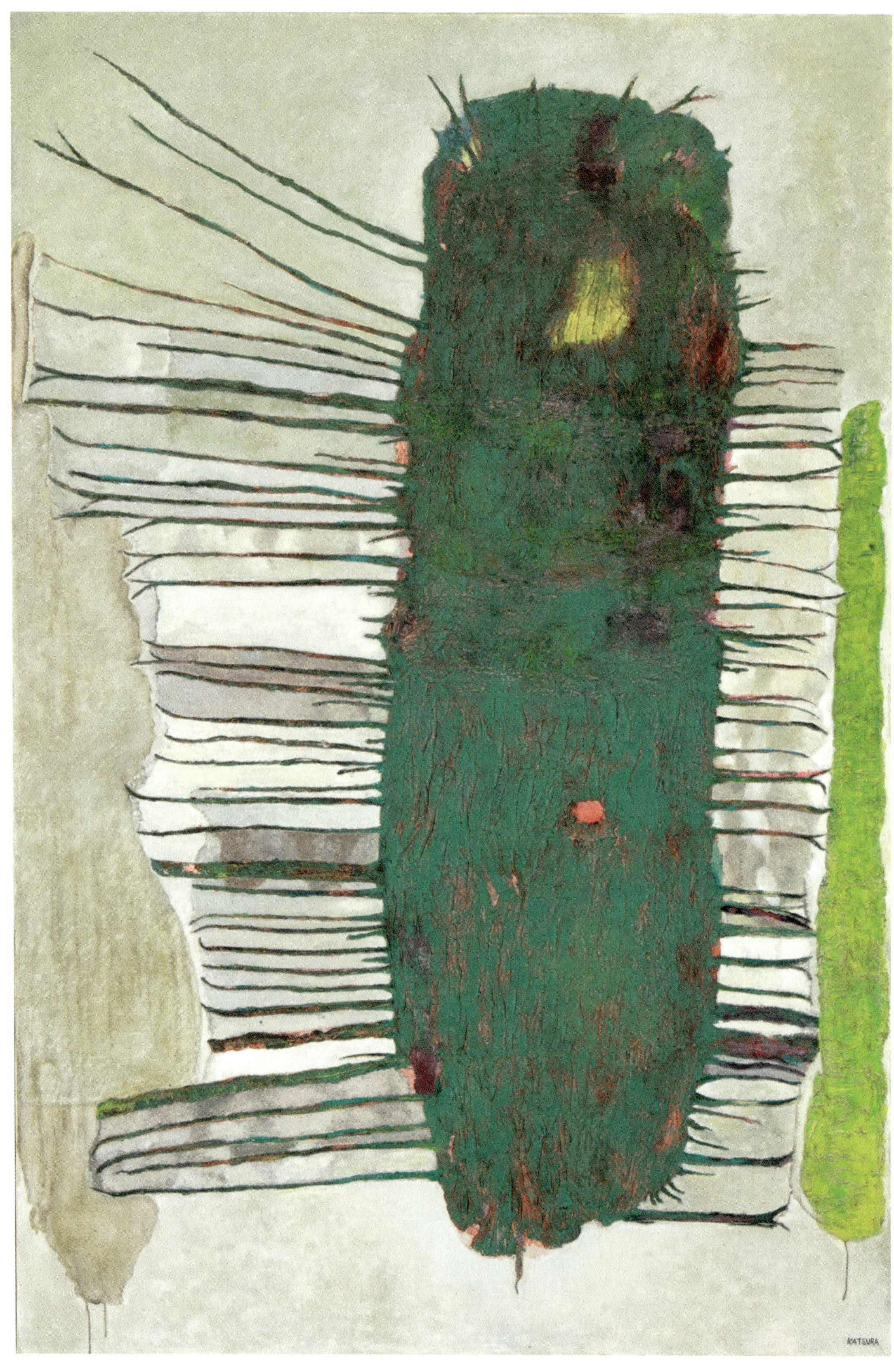

PLATE 7. Katsura Yuki, *Senbon ashi (II) (Millipede [II])*, 1962. Oil, paper, and string on canvas, 193 × 130.3. Copyright Katsura Akinari. Courtesy of the Museum of Contemporary Art, Tokyo.

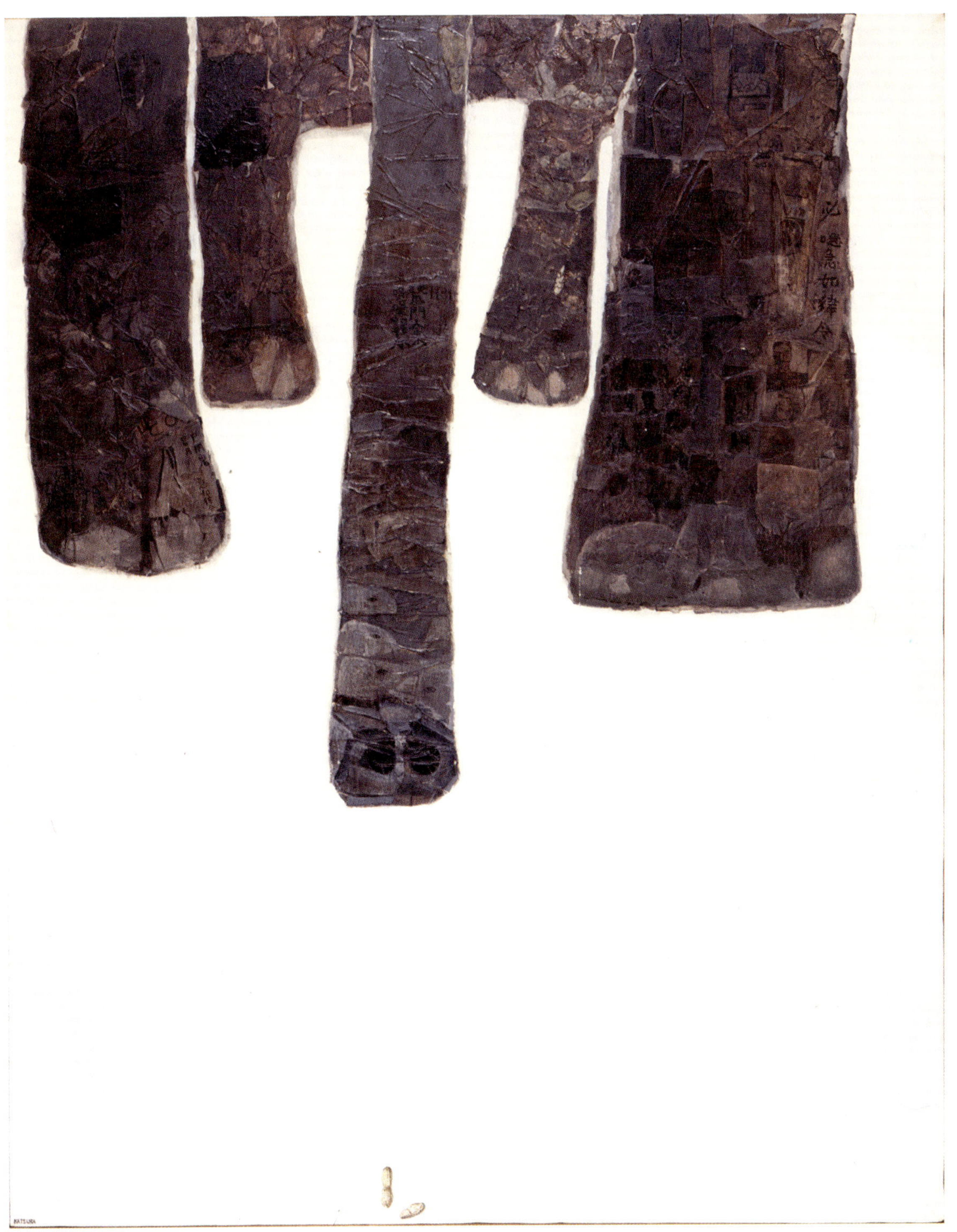

PLATE 8. Katsura Yuki, *Hana (Trunk),* 1967. Oil and paper on canvas, 226.8 × 181.5 cm. Copyright Katsura Akinari, Takamatsu City Museum of Art.

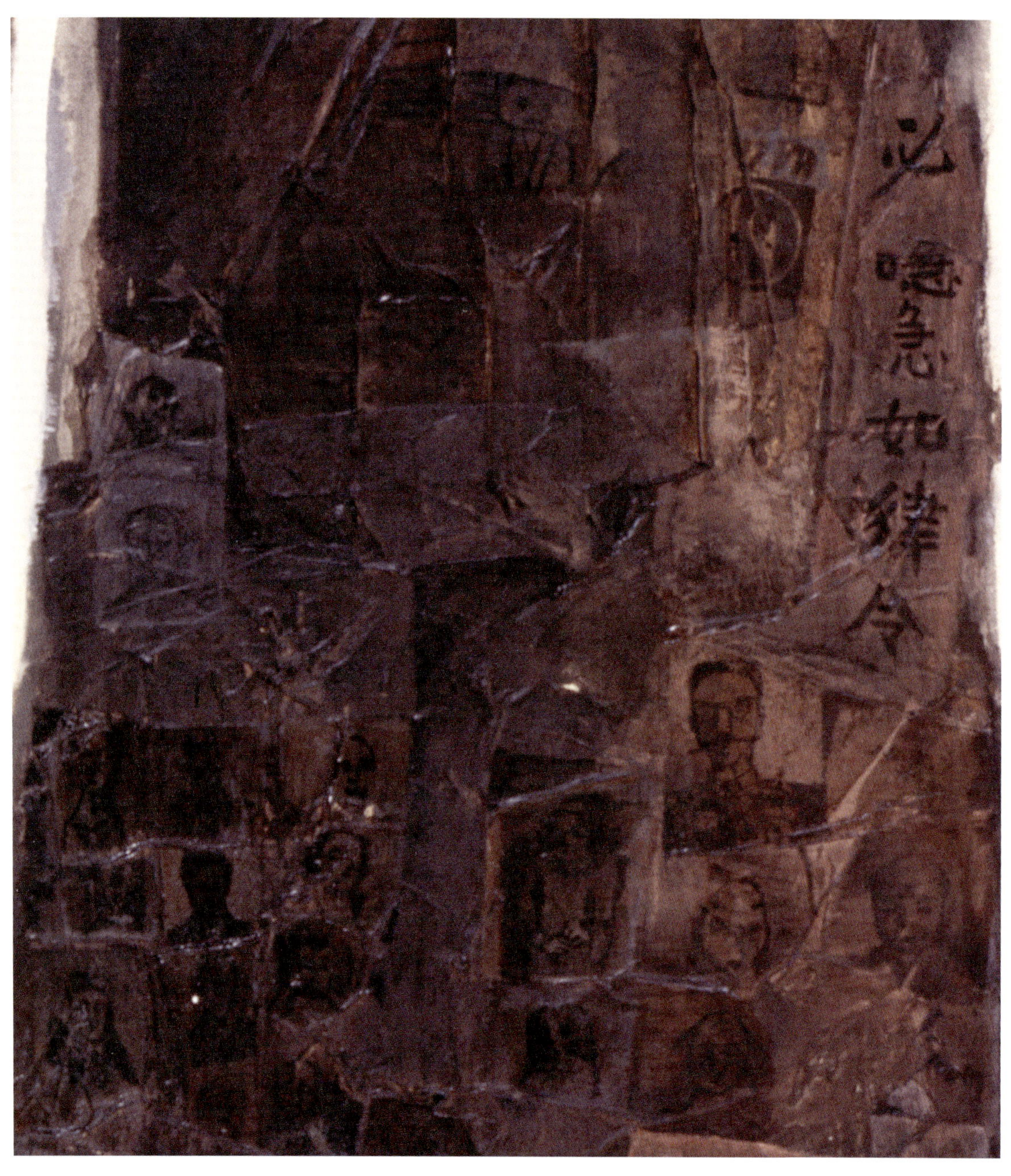

PLATE 9. Katsura Yuki, *Hana (Trunk)*, 1967 (detail). Copyright Katsura Akinari, Takamatsu City Museum of Art.

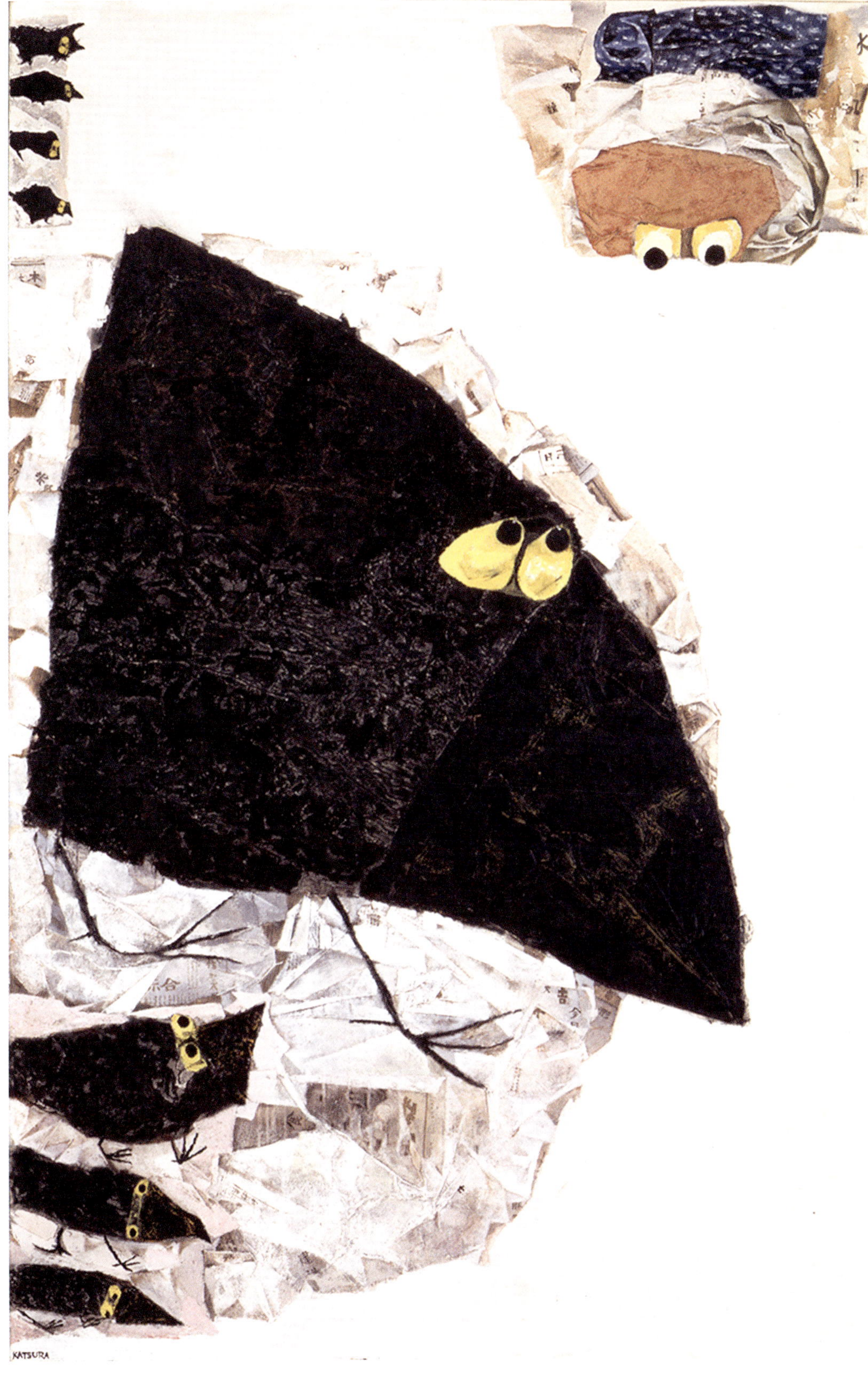

PLATE 10. Katsura Yuki, *Gonbe to karasu (Gonbe and Crow),* 1966. Oil, charcoal, paper, and string on canvas, 200 × 130.2 cm. Copyright Katsura Akinari. Courtesy of the National Museum of Modern Art, Tokyo.

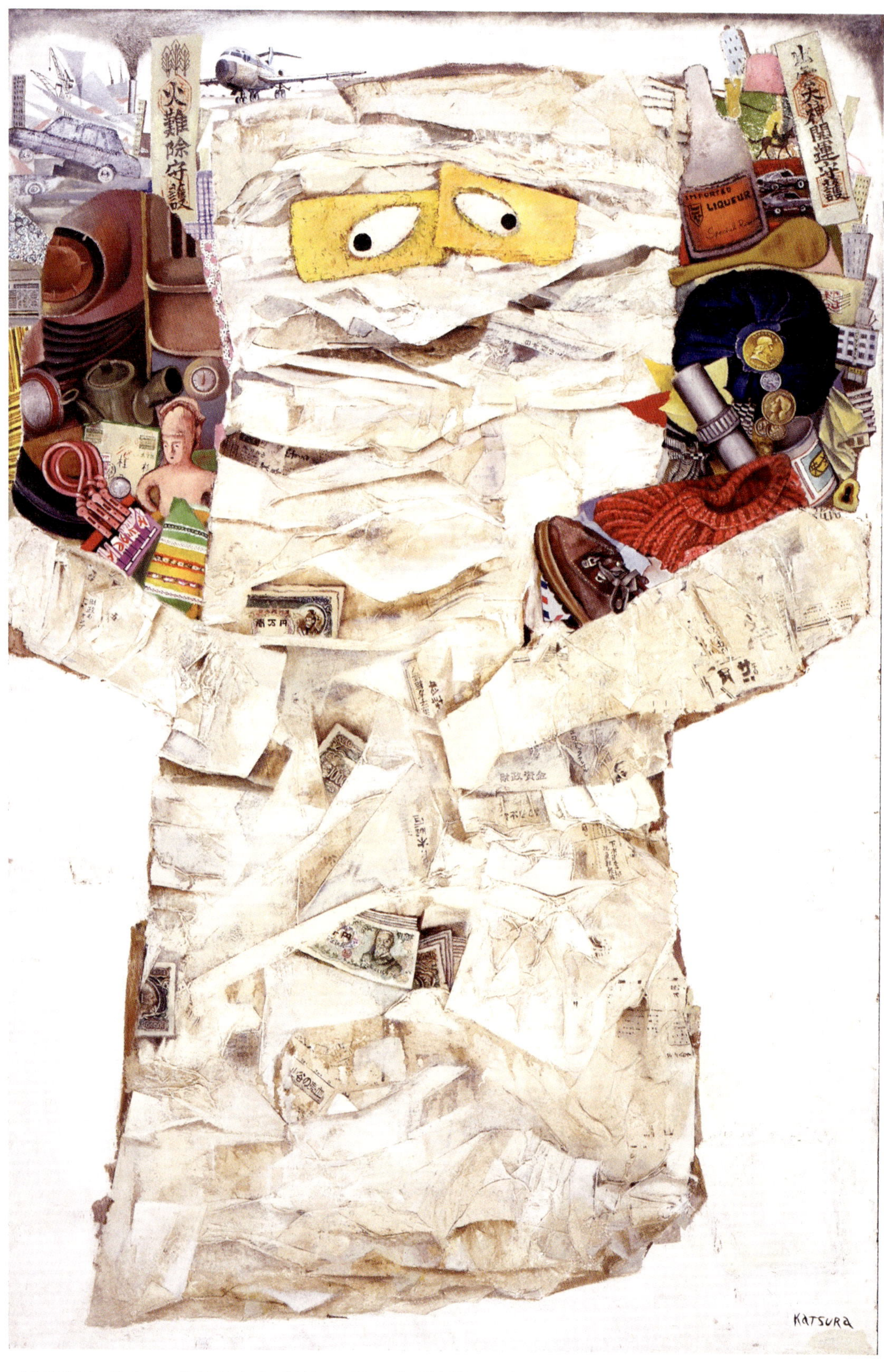

PLATE 11. Katsura Yuki, *Yokubari bāsan (Greedy Old Woman),* 1966. Oil and paper on board, 180.3 × 120 cm. Copyright Katsura Akinari. Courtesy of the Yamaguchi Prefectural Art Museum.

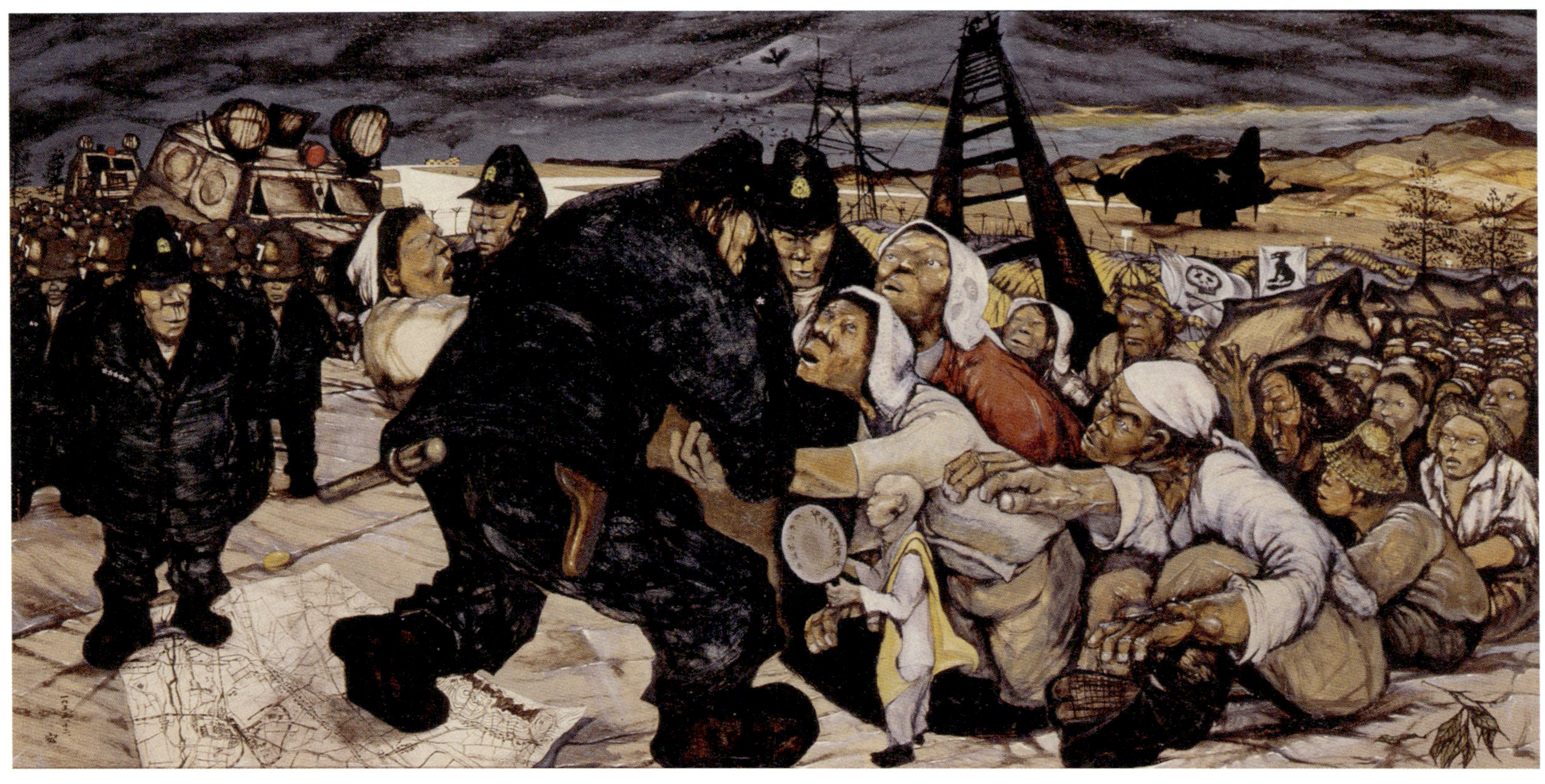

PLATE 12. Nakamura Hiroshi, *Sunagawa goban* (*Sunagawa No. 5*), 1955. Oil on board, 92.5 × 183 cm. Copyright Nakamura Hiroshi. Courtesy of the Museum of Contemporary Art, Tokyo.

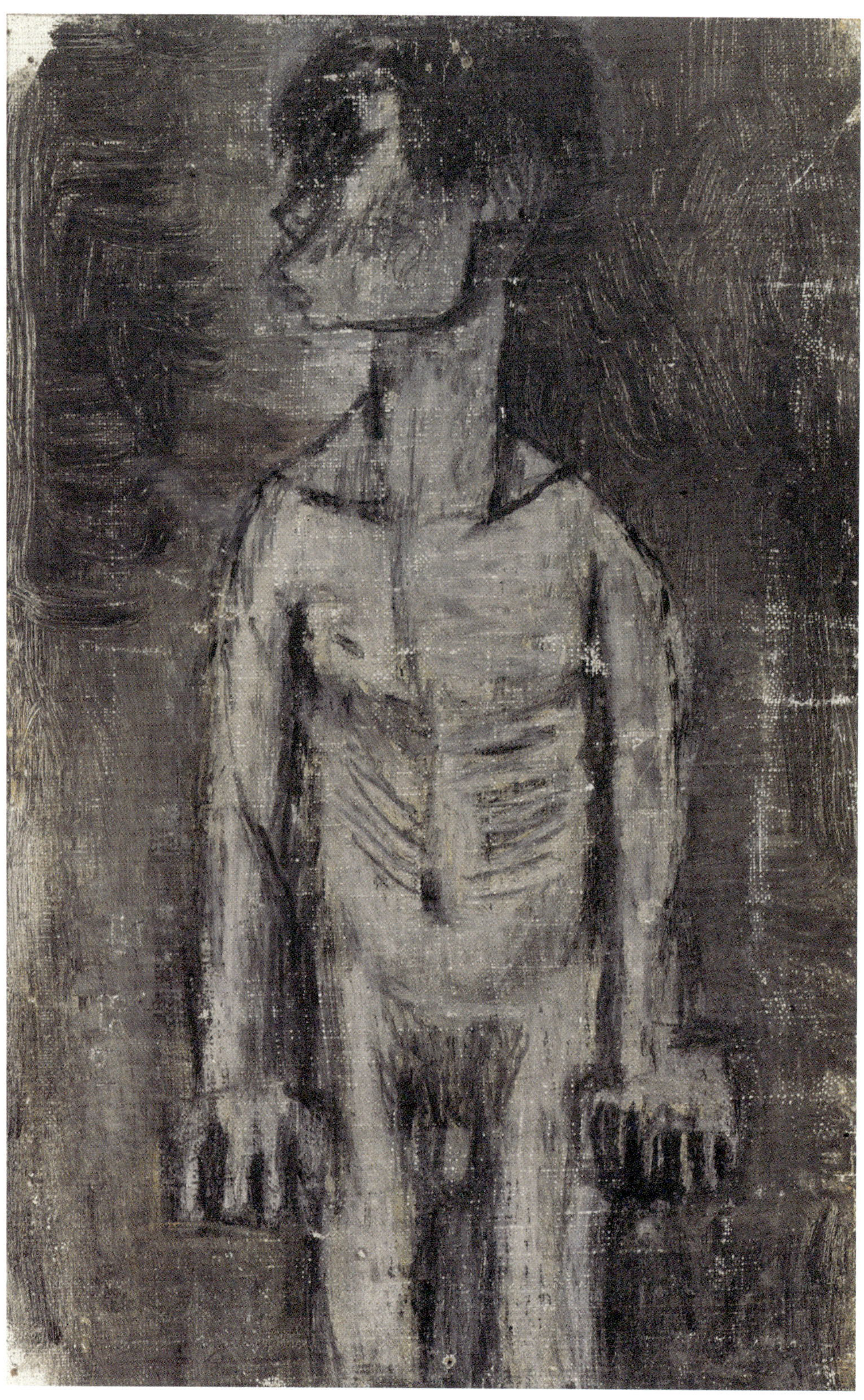

PLATE 13. Nakamura Hiroshi, *Jigazō B (Self-Portrait B),* 1953. Oil on canvas, 24.4 × 17.5 cm. Copyright Nakamura Hiroshi. Courtesy of the Nerima Art Museum.

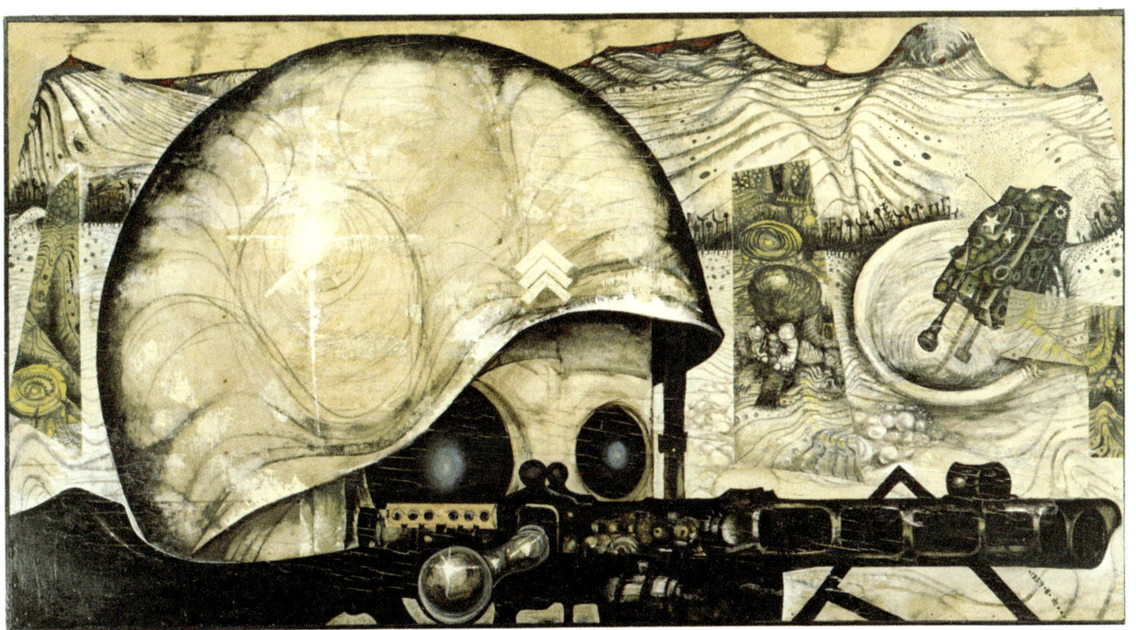

PLATE 14. Nakamura Hiroshi, *Kichi (The Base)*, 1957. Oil on canvas, 92 × 175 cm. Copyright Nakamura Hiroshi. Courtesy of the National Museum of Modern Art, Tokyo, and DNP Art and Communications.

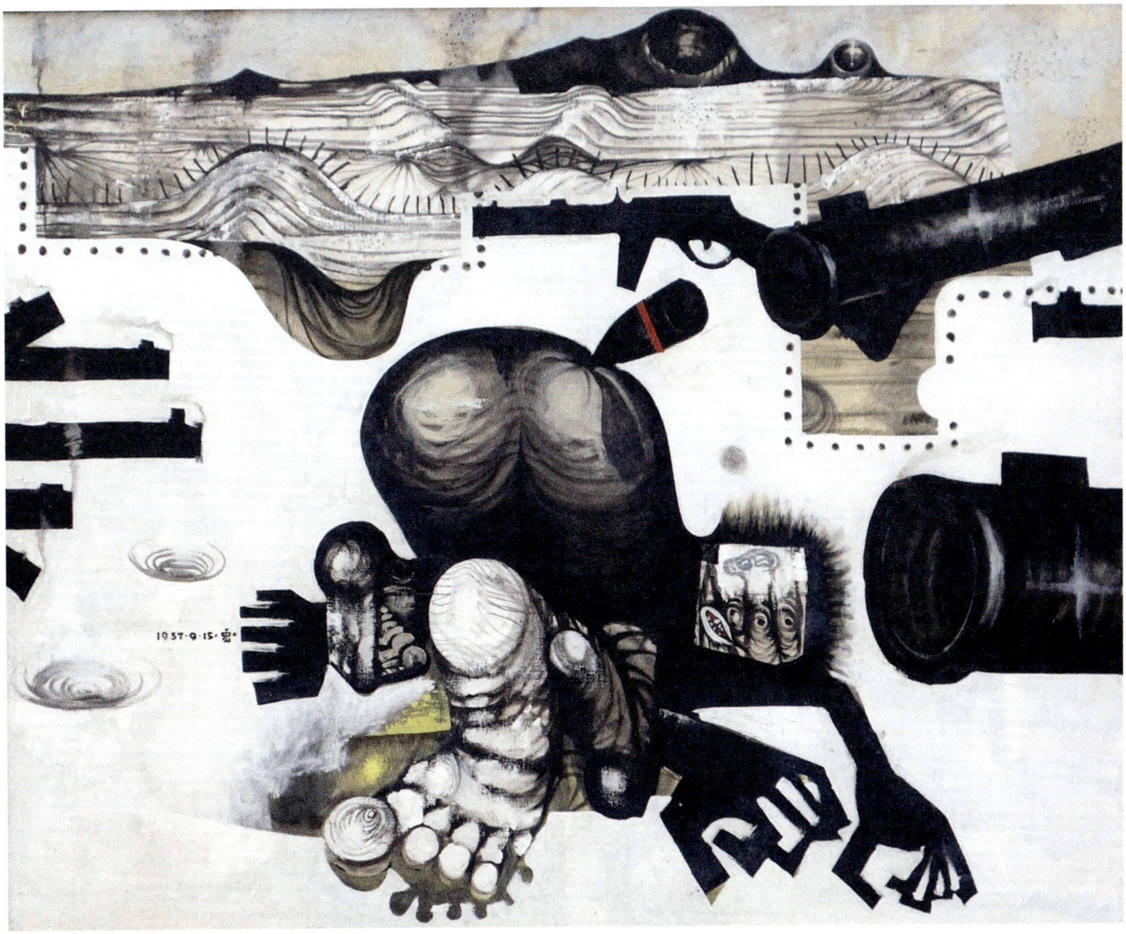

PLATE 15. Nakamura Hiroshi, *Shasatsu (Gunned Down)*, 1957. Oil on canvas, 73 × 91 cm. Copyright Nakamura Hiroshi. Courtesy of Kōriyama City Museum of Art.

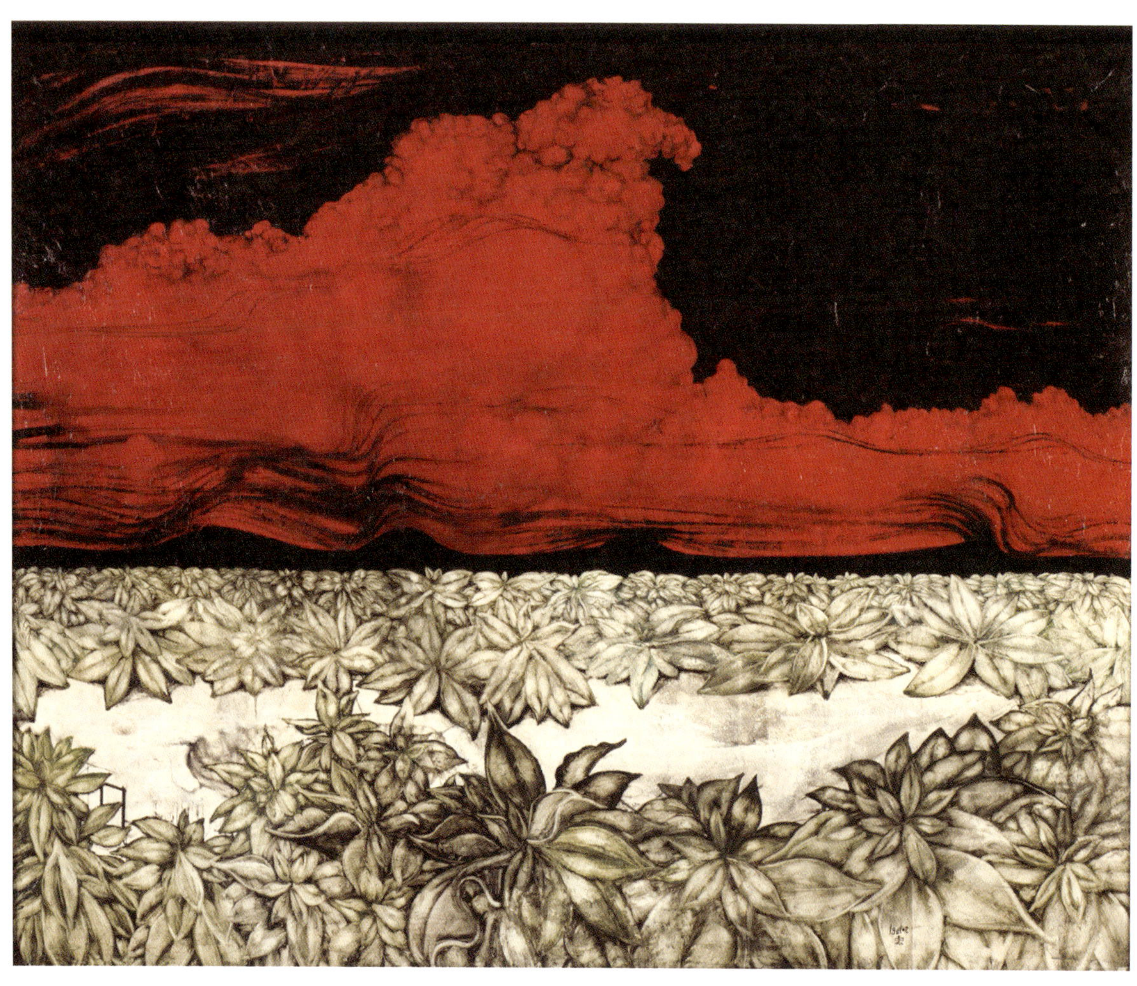

PLATE 16. Nakamura Hiroshi, *Basho no kizashi (Omens of a Place 1),* 1961. Oil on canvas,
130 × 163 cm. Copyright Nakamura Hiroshi. Courtesy of the Hamamatsu Municipal Museum of Art.

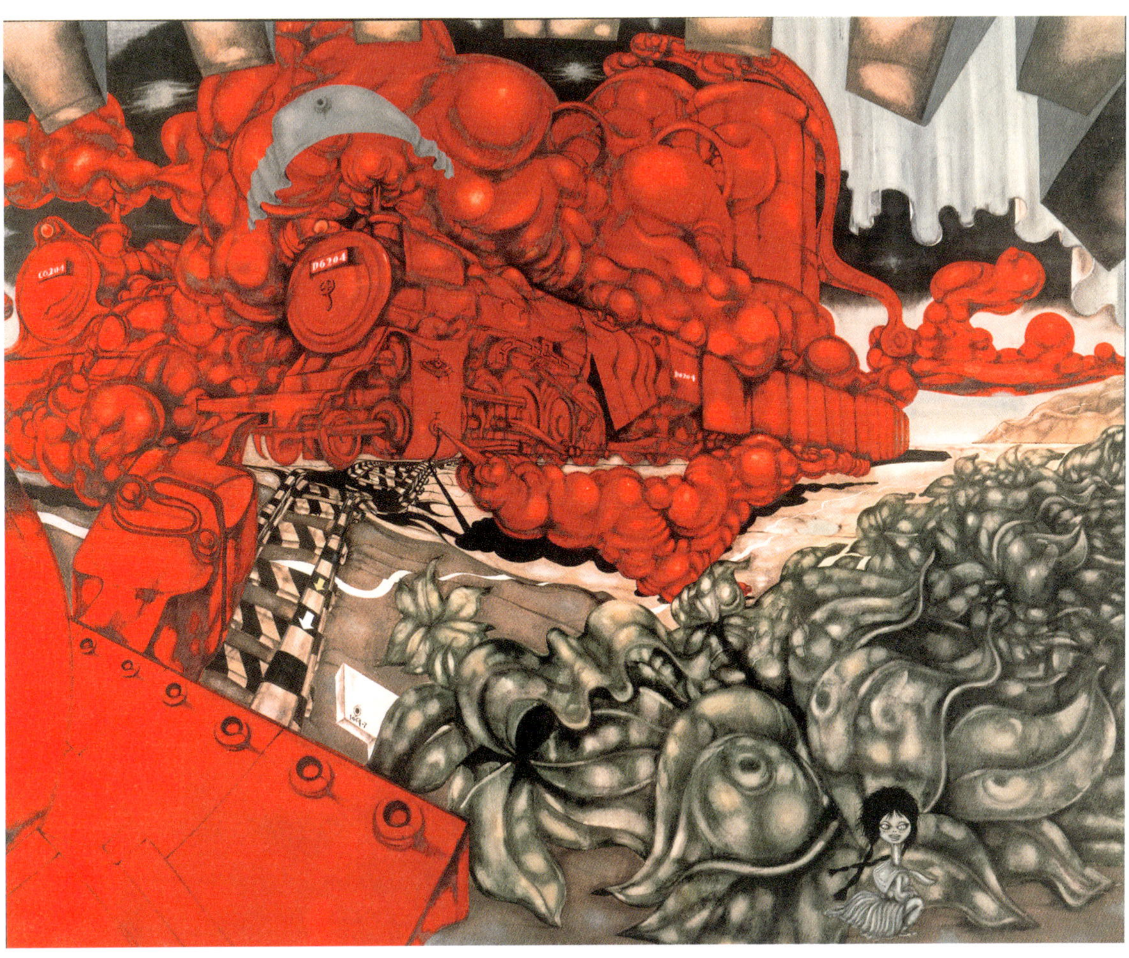

PLATE 17. Nakamura Hiroshi, *Kankō teikoku (Sightseeing Empire),* 1964. Oil on canvas, 130.3 × 162.1 cm. Copyright Nakamura Hiroshi. Courtesy of the Yokohama Museum of Art.

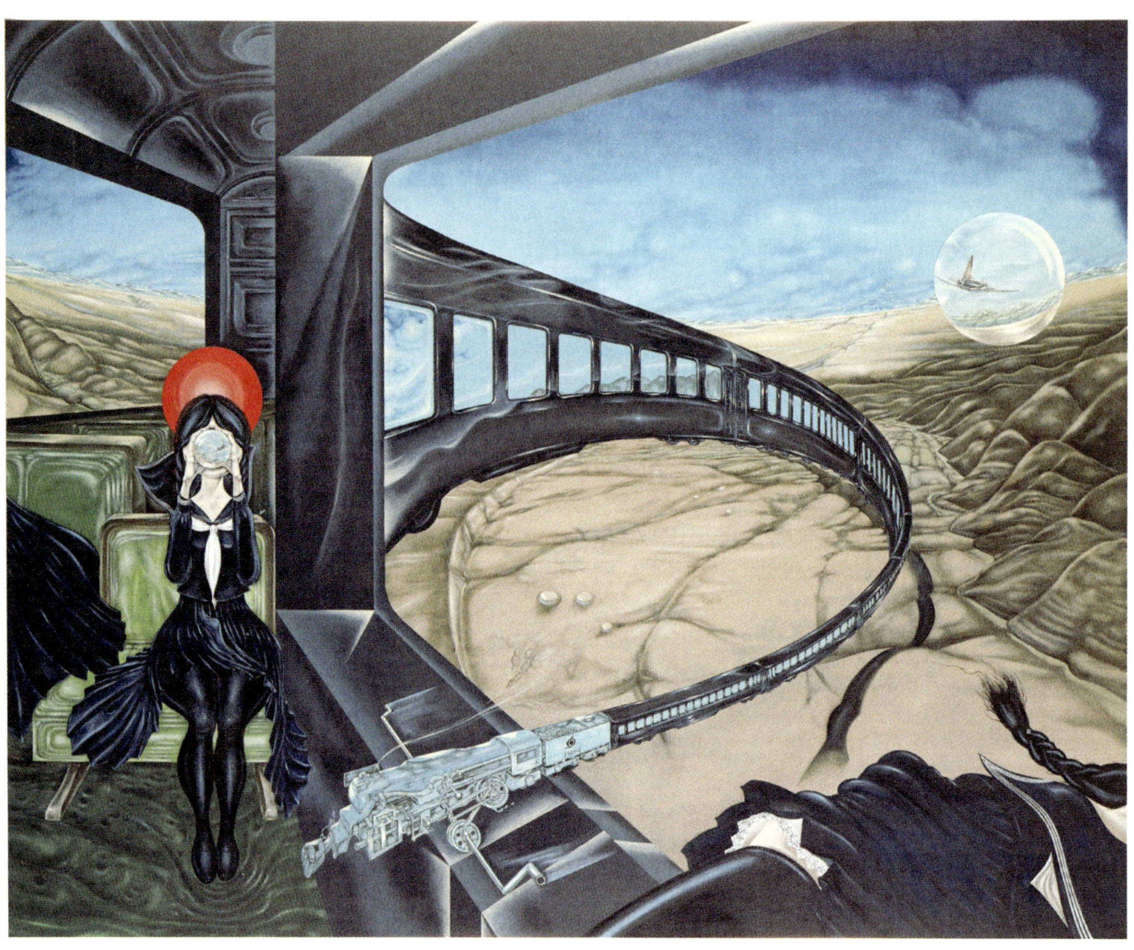

PLATE 18. Nakamura Hiroshi, *Enkan-ressha: B—Hikō suru jōkikikansha (Circle Line B—Flying Steam Locomotive),* 1969. Oil on canvas, 181 × 238 cm. Copyright Nakamura Hiroshi. Courtesy of the National Museum of Modern Art, Tokyo, and DNP Art and Communications.

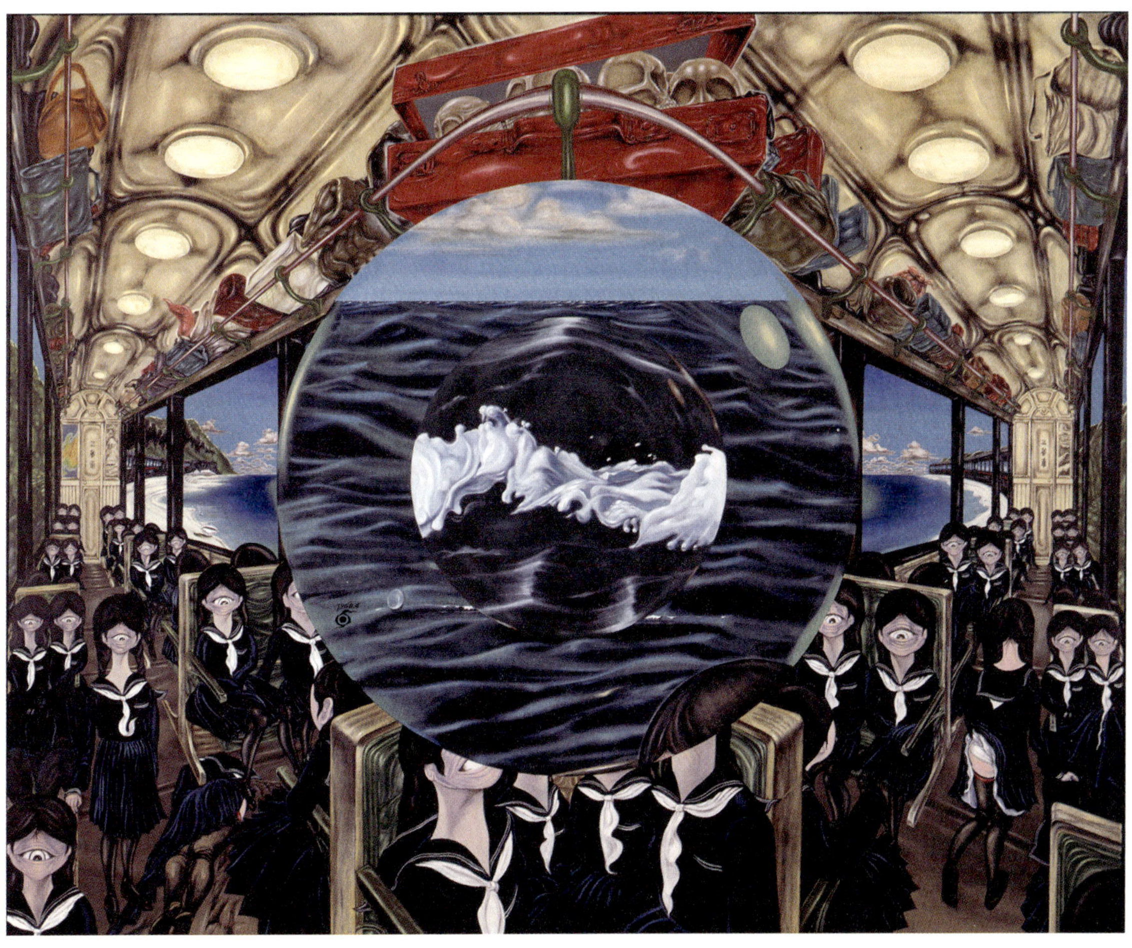

PLATE 19. Nakamura Hiroshi, *Enkan-ressha: A—Bōenkyō ressha (Circle Line A—Telescope Train)*, 1968. Oil on canvas, 182 × 227.5 cm. Copyright Nakamura Hiroshi. Courtesy of the Museum of Contemporary Art Tokyo.

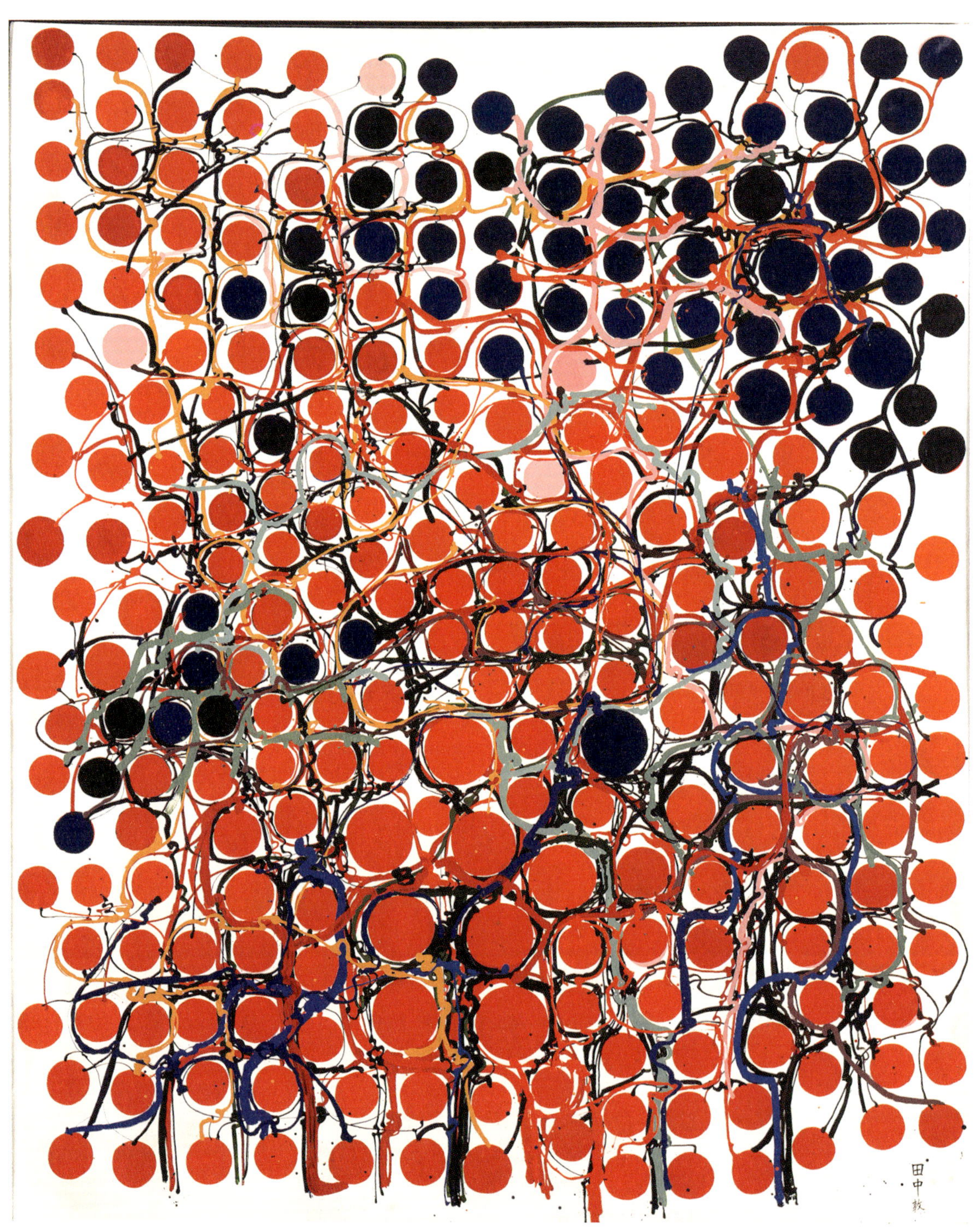

PLATE 20. Tanaka Atsuko, *Untitled*, 1958. Lacquer on canvas, 223.8 × 183.5 cm. Copyright Kanayama Akira and Tanaka Atsuko Association. Courtesy of the Hyōgo Prefectural Museum of Art.

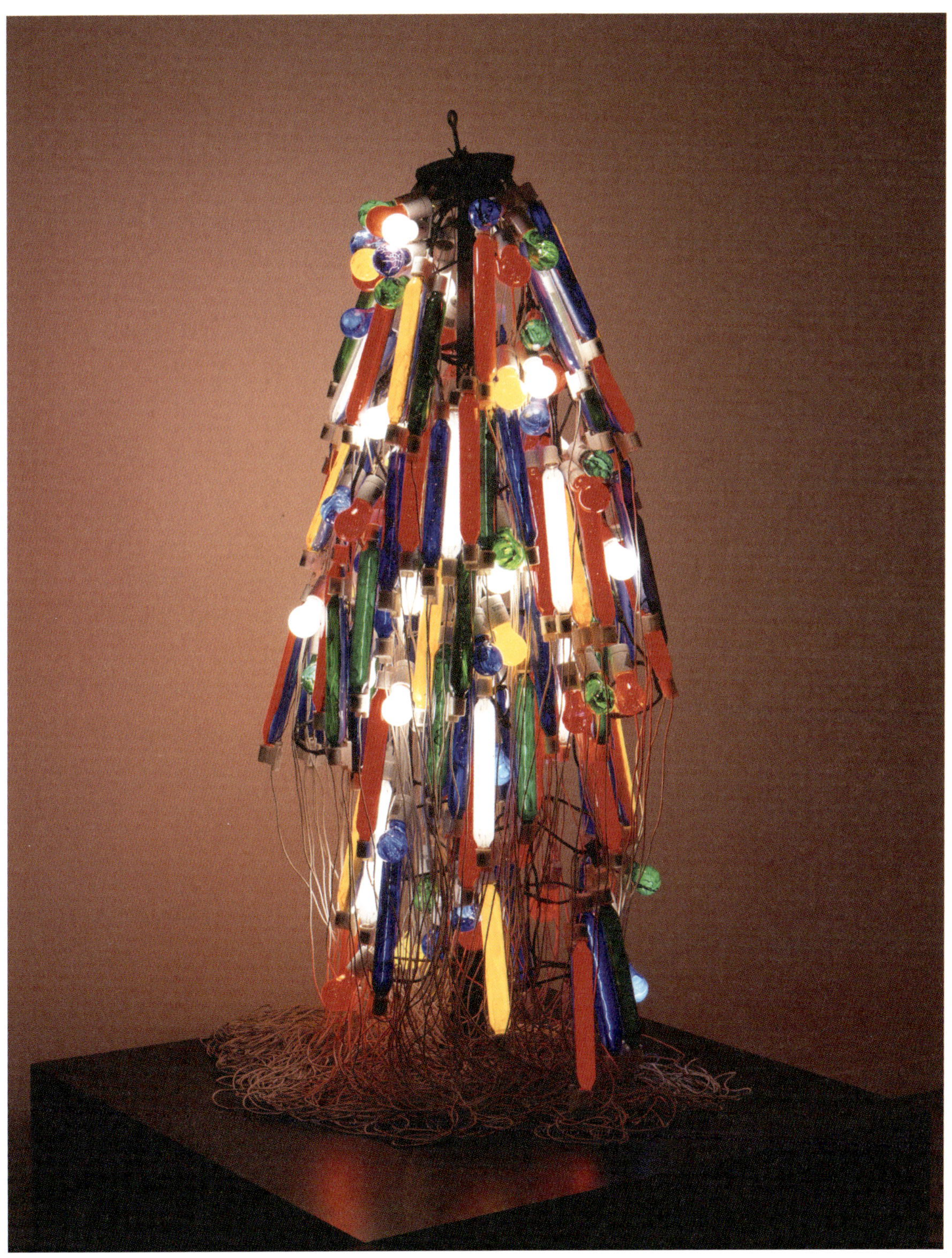

PLATE 21. Tanaka Atsuko, *Denki fuku (Electric Dress),* 1956 (reconstruction 1986). 165 × 80 × 80 cm. Copyright Kanayama Akira and Tanaka Atsuko Association. Courtesy of Takamatsu City Museum of Art.

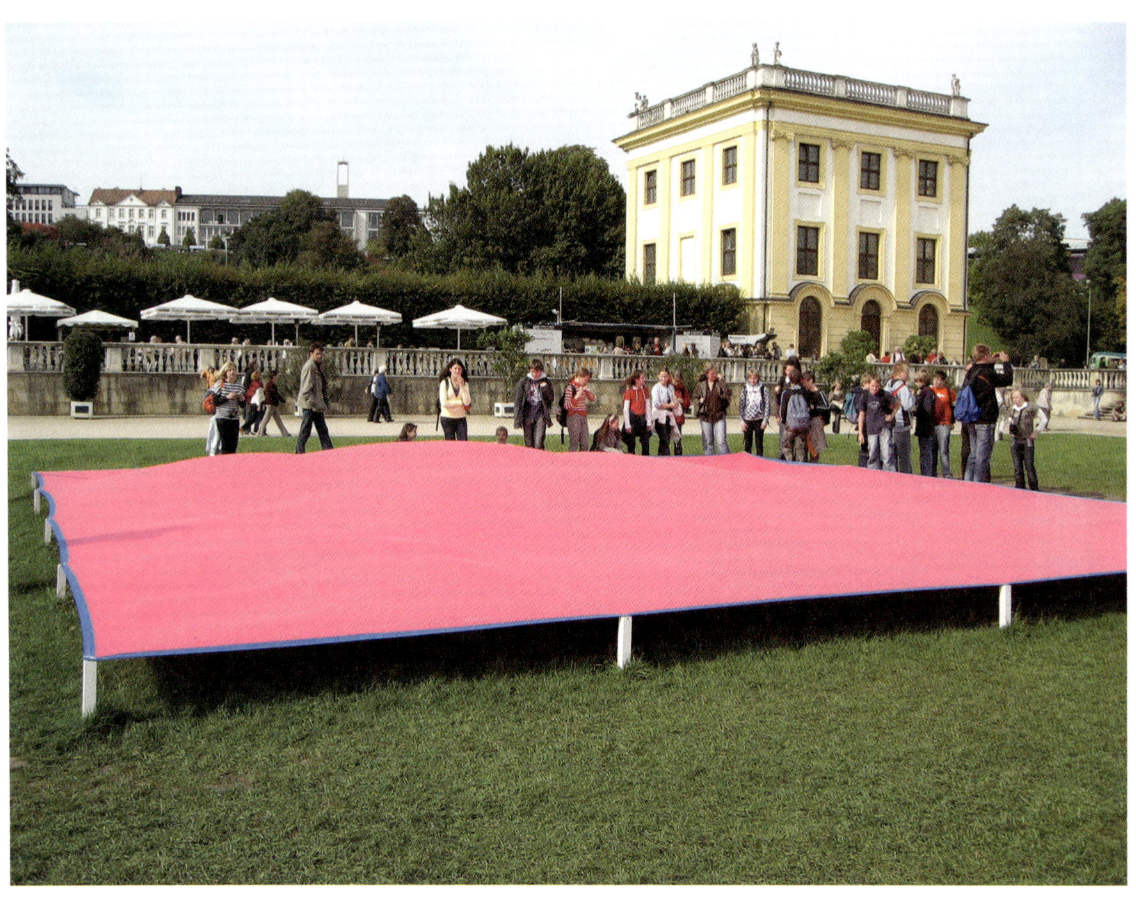

PLATE 22. Tanaka Atsuko, *Work (Pink Rayon)*, 1955 (reconstruction 2007) (not extant). Pink rayon, 1000 × 1000 cm. Copyright Kanayama Akira and Tanaka Atsuko Association. Photograph from Documenta 12, Kassel, Germany, 2007.

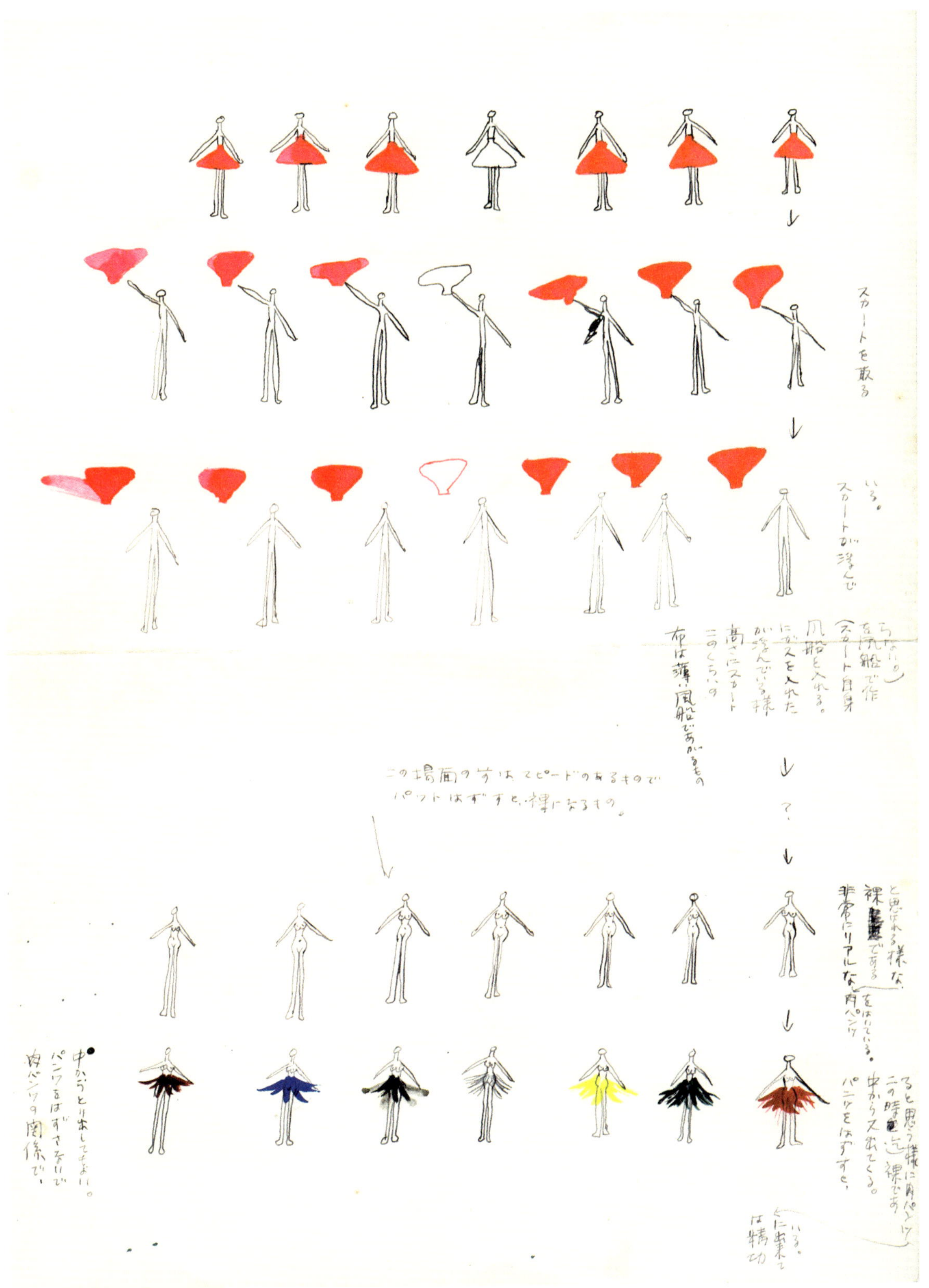

PLATE 23. Tanaka Atsuko, study for *Butai fuku (Stage Clothes)*, circa 1956. Ink, watercolor, and pencil on paper, 29.48 × 22.09 cm. Copyright Kanayama Akira and Tanaka Atsuko Association. Courtesy of Osaka City Museum of Modern Art.

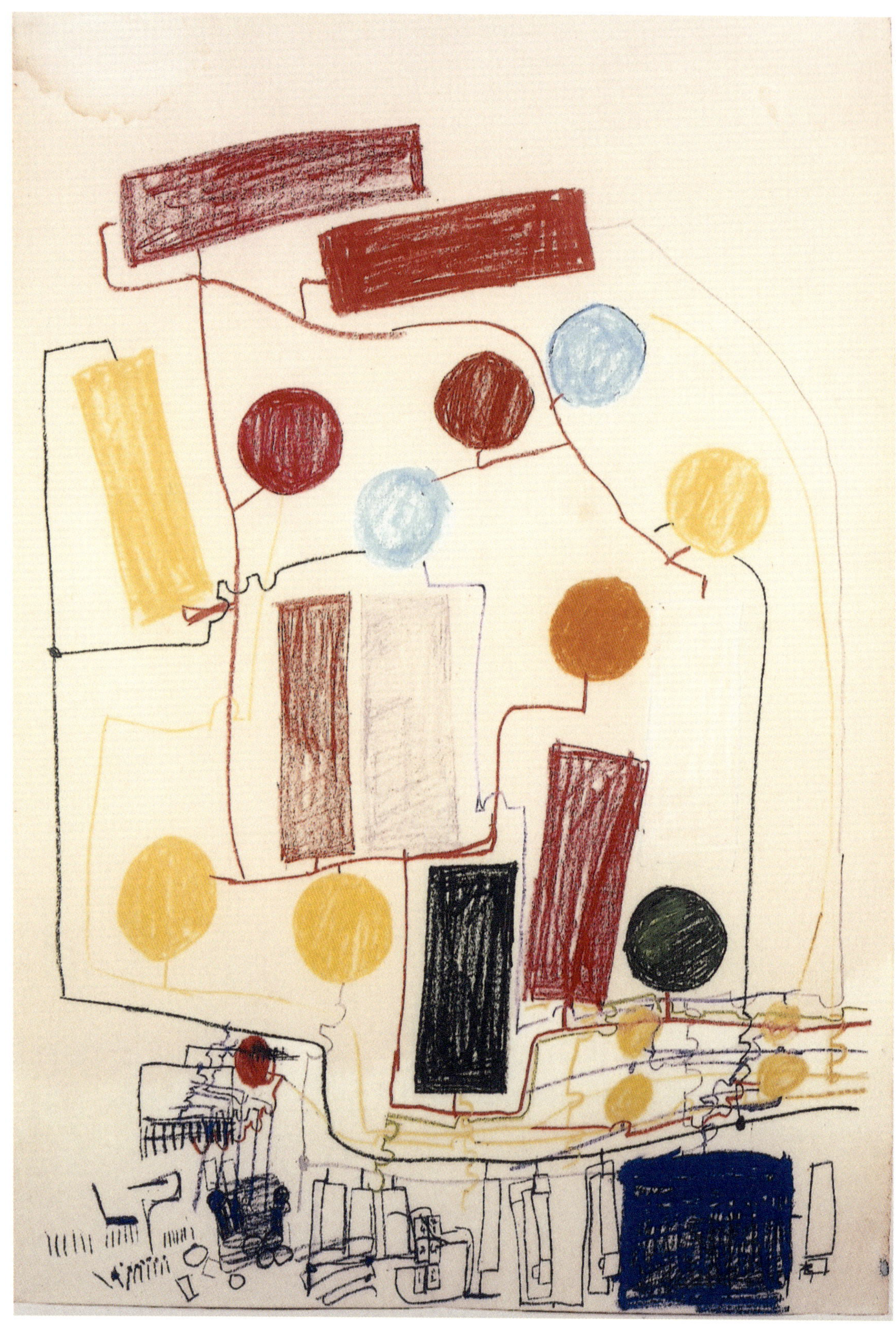

PLATE 24. Tanaka Atsuko, *Drawing after Electric Dress,* 1956. Crayon on paper, 108.6 × 76 cm. Copyright Kanayama Akira and Tanaka Atsuko Association. Private collection.

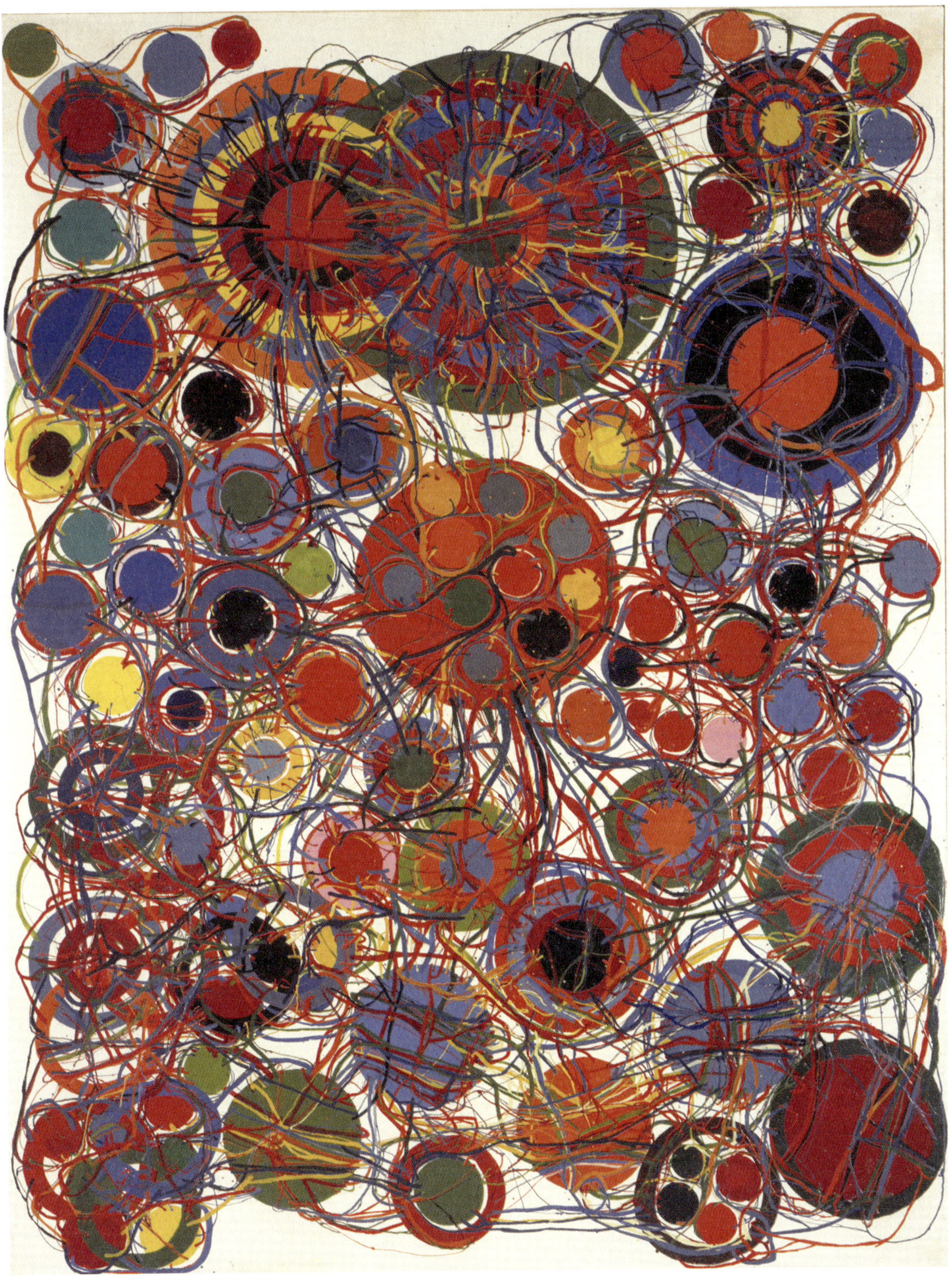

PLATE 25. Tanaka Atsuko, *Jigoku mon (Gate of Hell)*, 1965–69. Vinyl paint and acrylic on canvas, 331.5 × 245.5 cm. Copyright Kanayama Akira and Tanaka Atsuko Association. Courtesy of the National Museum of Art, Osaka.

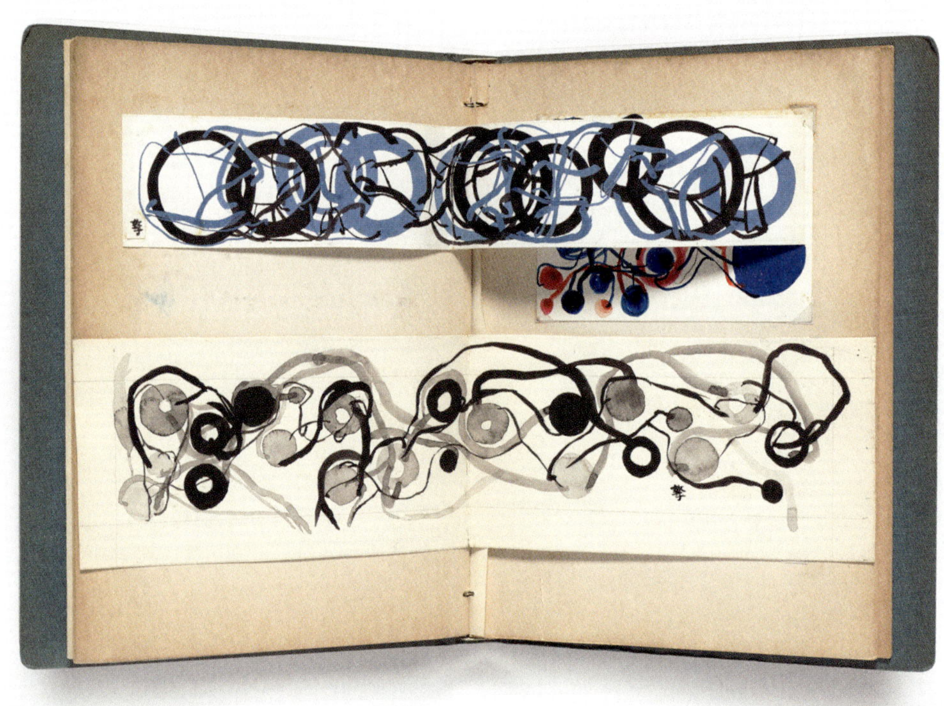

PLATE 26. Tanaka Atsuko, untitled notebook, circa 1956. Ink and pencil on paper. Copyright Kanayama Akira and Tanaka Atsuko Association. Private collection.

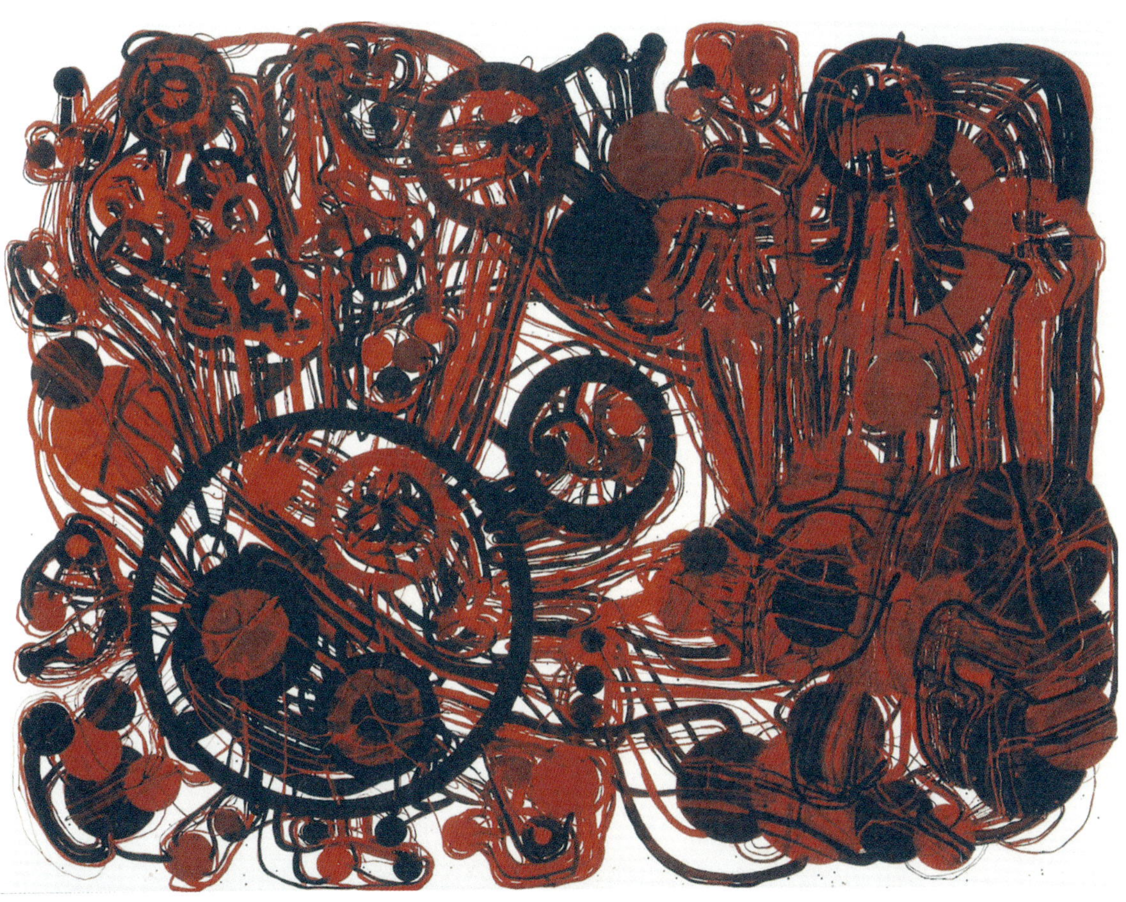

PLATE 27. Tanaka Atsuko, *'87H*, 1987. Enamel paint on canvas, 193.7 × 257.5 cm. Copyright Kanayama Akira and Tanaka Atsuko Association. Courtesy of the Ashiya City Museum of Art and History, Ashiya.

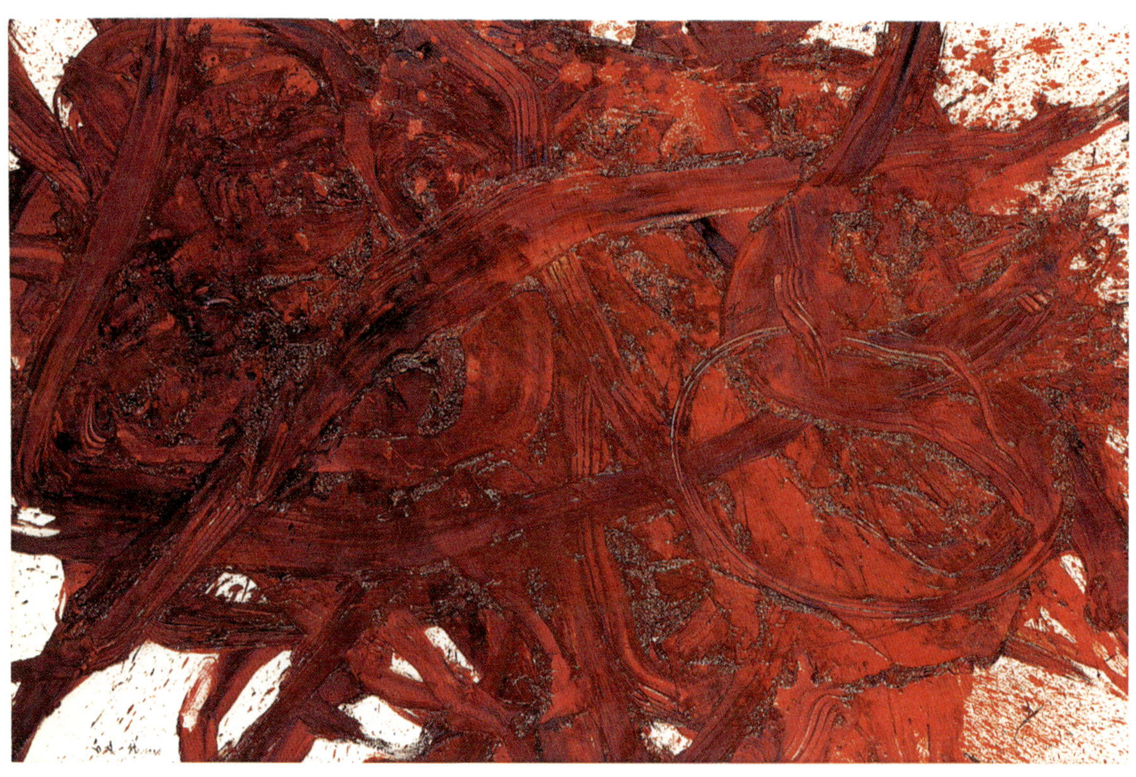

PLATE 28. Shiraga Kazuo, *Ten'isei Sekihatsuki (Red-Haired Devil)*, 1959. Oil on canvas, 182.3 × 272.6 cm. Copyright Shiraga Hisao, Kobe. Courtesy of Hyōgo Prefectural of Art, Yamamura Collection.

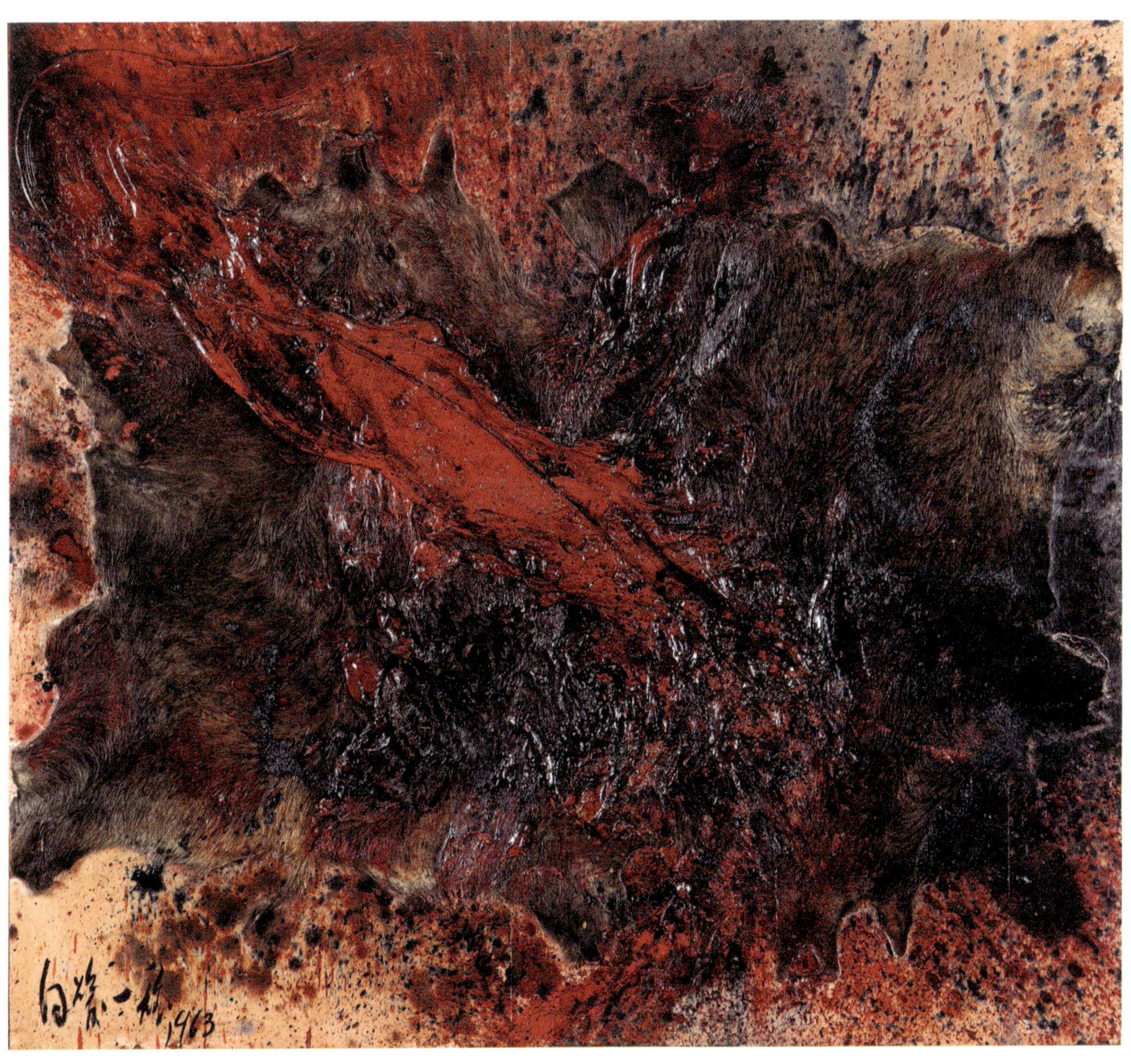

PLATE 29. Shiraga Kazuo, *Inoshishi gari II (Wild Boar Hunting II),* 1963. Oil, fur, spent bullets on board, 183 × 204.3 cm. Copyright Shiraga Hisao. Courtesy of the Hyōgo Prefectural Museum of Art.

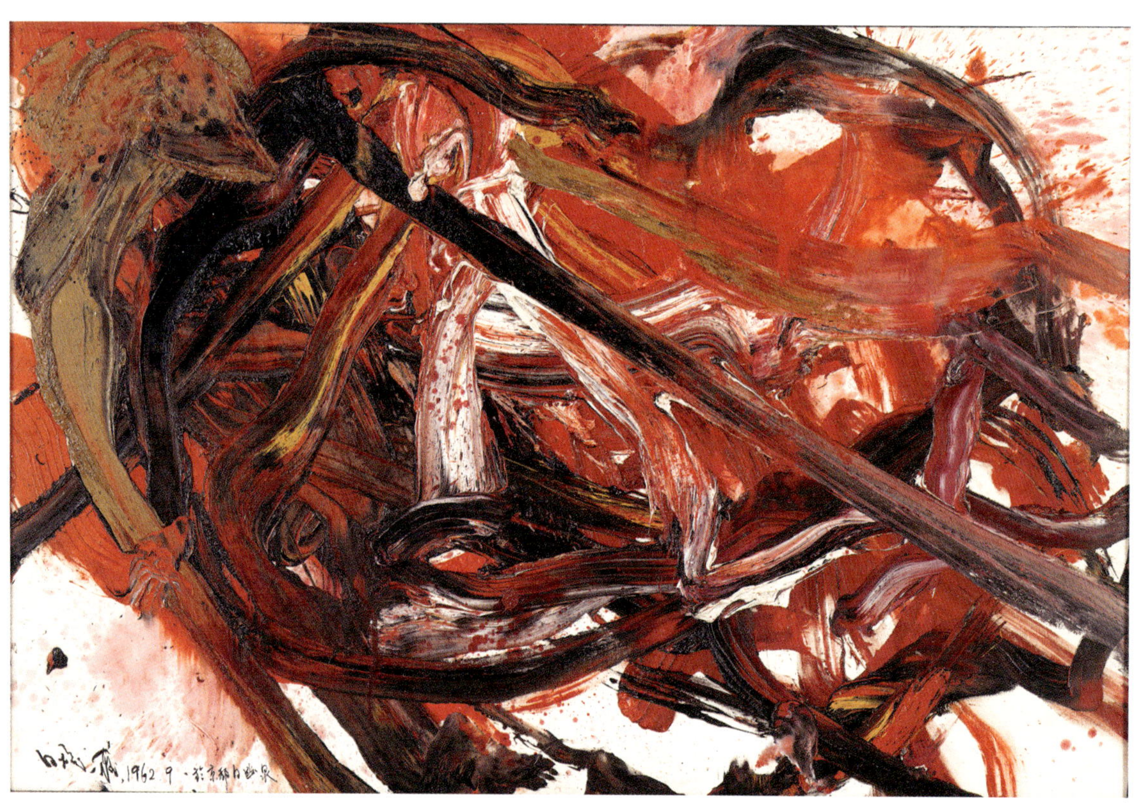

PLATE 30. Shiraga Kazuo, *Tenkūsei Kyūsenpō (Impatient Vanguard),* 1962. Oil on canvas, 182.9816 × 203.98 cm. Copyright Shiraga Hisao. Courtesy of the Hyōgo Prefectural Museum of Art.

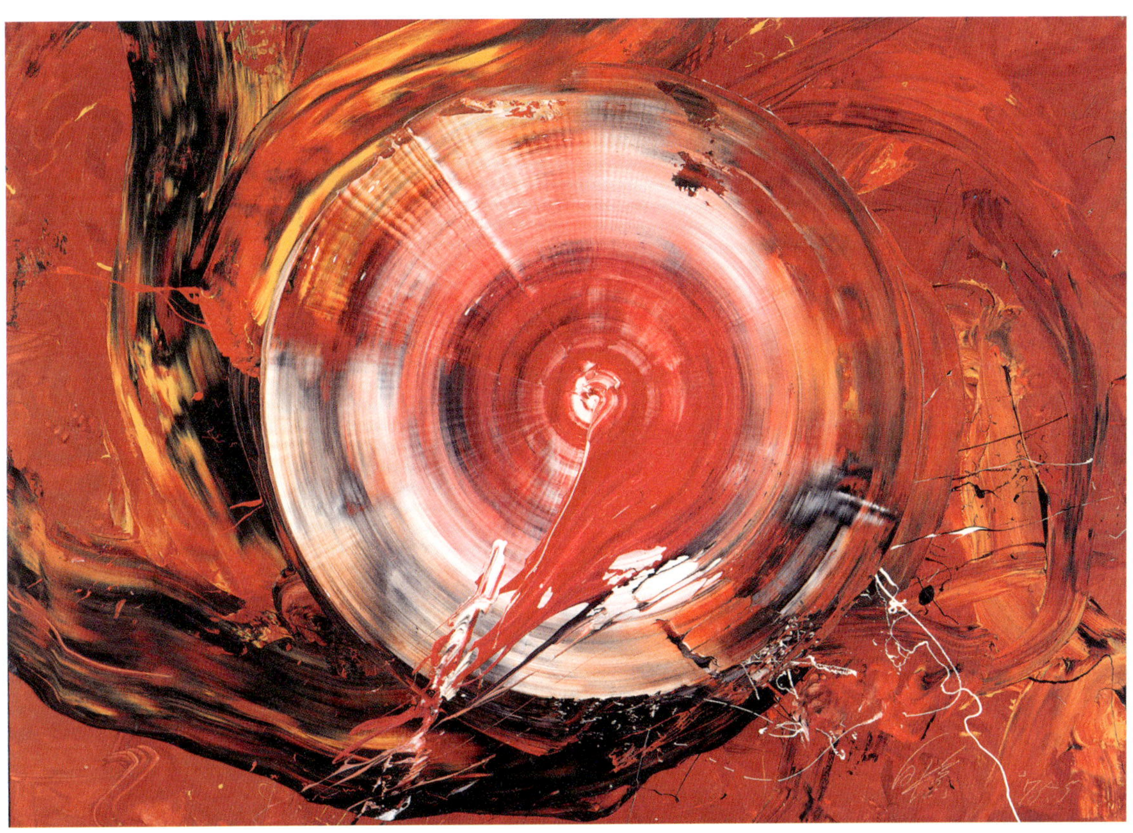

PLATE 31. Shiraga Kazuo, *Abiraunken*, 1975. Alkyd paint and cloth, 130.98 × 258.97 cm. Copyright Shiraga Hisao. Courtesy of the Hyōgo Prefectural Museum of Art.

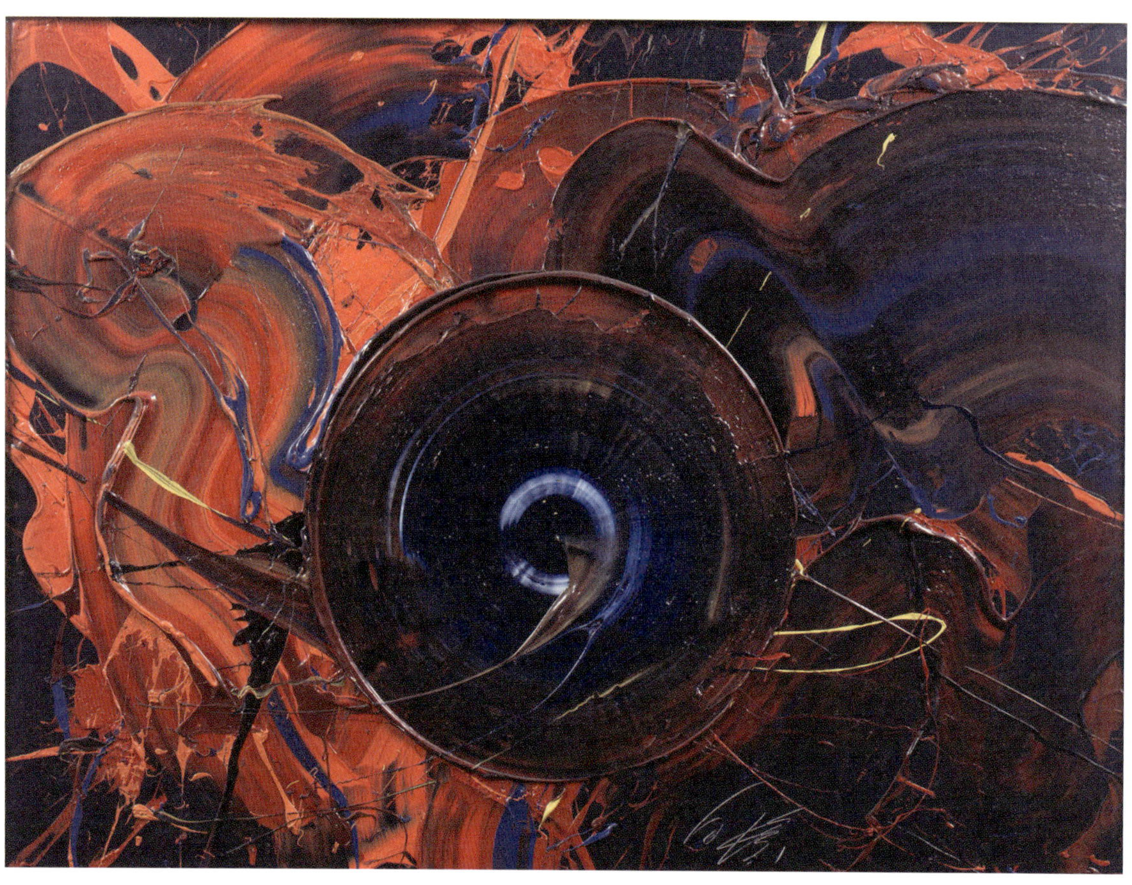

PLATE 32. Shiraga Kazuo, *Fudō Myō-ō,* 1975. Oil on canvas, 97 × 130 cm. Copyright Hisao Shiraga.
Photograph courtesy of Amagasaki Cultural Center. Private collection.

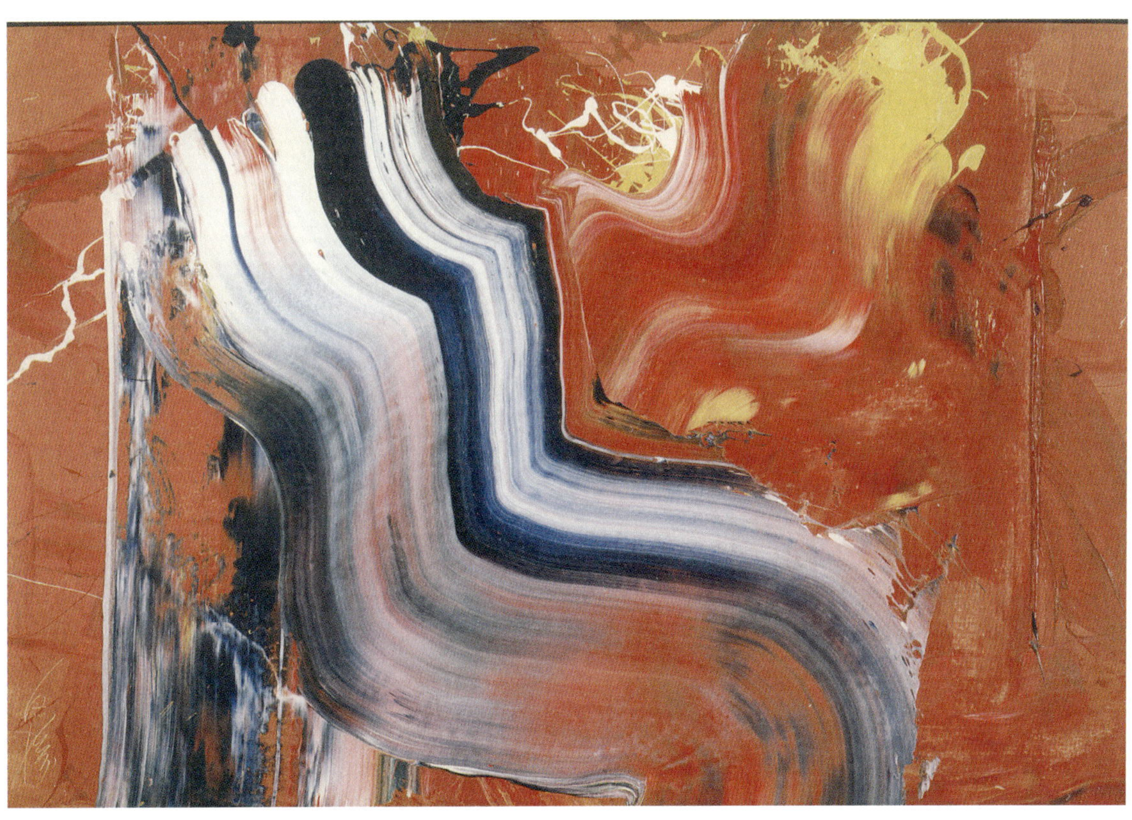

PLATE 33. Shiraga Kazuo, *Kannon Fudara Jōdo,* 1972. Alkyd paint on canvas, 130 × 194 cm. Copyright Hisao Shiraga. Bridgestone Museum of Art, Ishibashi Foundation.

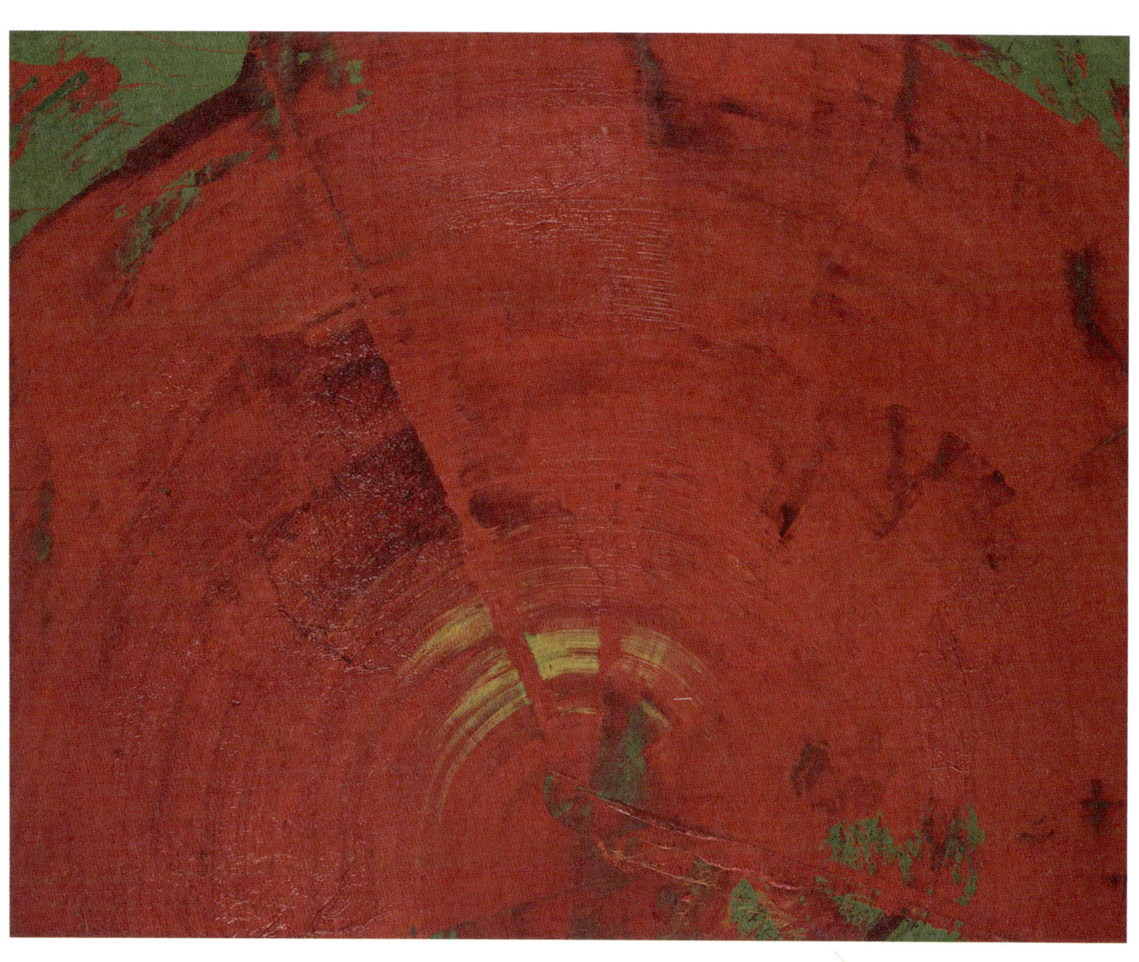

PLATE 34. Shiraga Kazuo, *Akai ōgi (Red Fan)*, 1965. Oil on canvas, 200 × 270 cm. Copyright Shiraga Hisao, Paul and Karen McCarthy. Photograph by Antonio Maniscalco. Courtesy of Hauser and Wirth.

presents the possibilities of our agency but ultimately reaffirms its limits. A gallery visitor may choose to depress the button but may be unaware of the potential noisy consequences and helpless to reverse them. In the spaces of the sound intervals, viewers are faced with their own corporeality and the performative possibilities (as the security guards and other gallery visitors look on) within that frame.[50]

In contrast, *Electric Dress* elevates the sensory experience of vision and physical contact through its context and production on stage. It is our eyes that meet the surface of the dress, confounding material and light as one. There is no tangible point of contact with the work as in the case of *Bell.* Both *Bell* and *Electric Dress,* then, invite sensory contact but deny any sense of sensory pleasure. In the latter, an envisioned, imagined physicality, one that displaces Tanaka's own presence, is the active site of contact. The repetitious flashing lights anchor the work in a system that is comforting in its reoccurrence and off-putting in its heat and light. The work urges us to imagine our own immobility as we watch the lone figure who can only make small gestures from within her luminous costume. Likewise, the electric clothes render the body hidden and sexless. Watching *Electric Dress,* we have the opportunity to realize that it is we who sex the hidden subject, overly accustomed as we are to seeing the female body on display. To be sure, following the end of the Allied Occupation, the costumed woman's body took on an overexposed visibility that is critical to our understanding of *Electric Dress.*

Gender and Visual Culture

Ross has argued that "the arrival of the new consumer durables into French life—the repetitive, daily practices and the new mediations they brought into being—helped create a break with eventfulness of the past, or better, helped situate the temporality of the event itself as a thing of the past."[51] In a section headed "Housekeeping," Ross adds, "The commodity form does not merely symbolize the social relations of modernity, it is the central source of their origin—in this case, a new arena of competition between women. But the ultimate competition for the French woman, her distant horizon of excellence, was the American woman who washed her hair every day."[52] As was the case in France, Japan relied heavily on the image of women as evidence of the nation's appealing modernization and its wary, competitive eye on American standards. Commercial visual culture and gender were tightly intertwined as Japan struggled to regain economic footing after the war. A wave of popularity for tailoring, fashion icons, and "dressing up" in the 1950s is evident in the visual culture of magazines, newspapers, and posters of the time.[53] The pages of the *Yomiuri Shinbun,* for example, reveal that advertisements for newly opened dress shops, cosmetics companies, and fashion guides (Figure 3.7) appeared frequently. New Japan, these images promised, would be modern and captivating.[54] Some observers were critical of this commercial surge. Katsura Yuki published an essay titled "Queen of Dream: Dressmaking School Art Kingdoms" that disparaged the "big three kingdoms" of Japanese design houses,

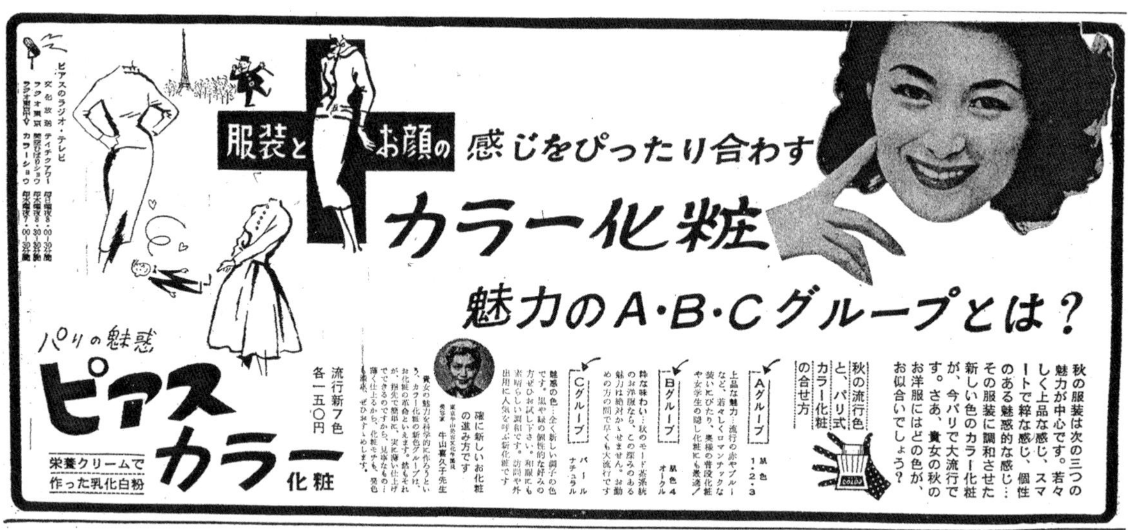

FIGURE 3.7. *Yomiuri Shinbun,* September 2, 1956.

arguing that designers in the 1950s had more skills in politics and branding than they did in drawing or design.[55]

Movie listings in the largest newspapers featured depictions of Marilyn Monroe with each film she released, usually in advertisements that were larger than all the others on the page. In one example, Monroe's legs were shown uncovered and extending over the boundaries of the illustrated marquee, as though this boldly fashioned star, an excess of size and allure, was enticing the Japanese reader to be complicit in the glamorous dream of sexualized capitalism (Figure 3.8). Monroe's figure in this ad, promoting *How to Marry a Millionaire,* stands in competition with other advertisements for handmade Western-style dress patterns and discounts on kimonos. As in France, "women's magazines played a leading role in disseminating and normalized the state-led modernization effort."[56] Magazines like *Shufu no tomo* (Housewife's companion) maintained high levels of popularity following the war and often featured articles on how to turn kimonos into dresses and new ways to apply cosmetics to make one's eyes appear larger.[57]

Tanaka was a part of this surge in self-fashioning. She also took up the highly gendered role of amateur seamstress—an activity that informed her art practices, as *Yellow Cloth* and *Stage Clothes* reveal. *Yellow Cloth* is easy to mistake for a readymade; however, a closer look reveals that Tanaka cut into each piece of fabric and then subtly glued the cut edges back together. This work further demonstrates Tanaka's interest in surface fractures (see Figure 3.6). As the visibility of women's bodies skyrocketed in advertising, *Electric Dress* offered an alternative visualization of the female body, one that neither collaborated with the commercialized female body nor affirmed it as empowered. Curator and critic Tatehata Akira has dismissed Tanaka's works as "fashion play."[58] But "fashion" for Tanaka was more than a consumerist trend, it was fashion as a verb: to fabricate, adjust, configure. She understood

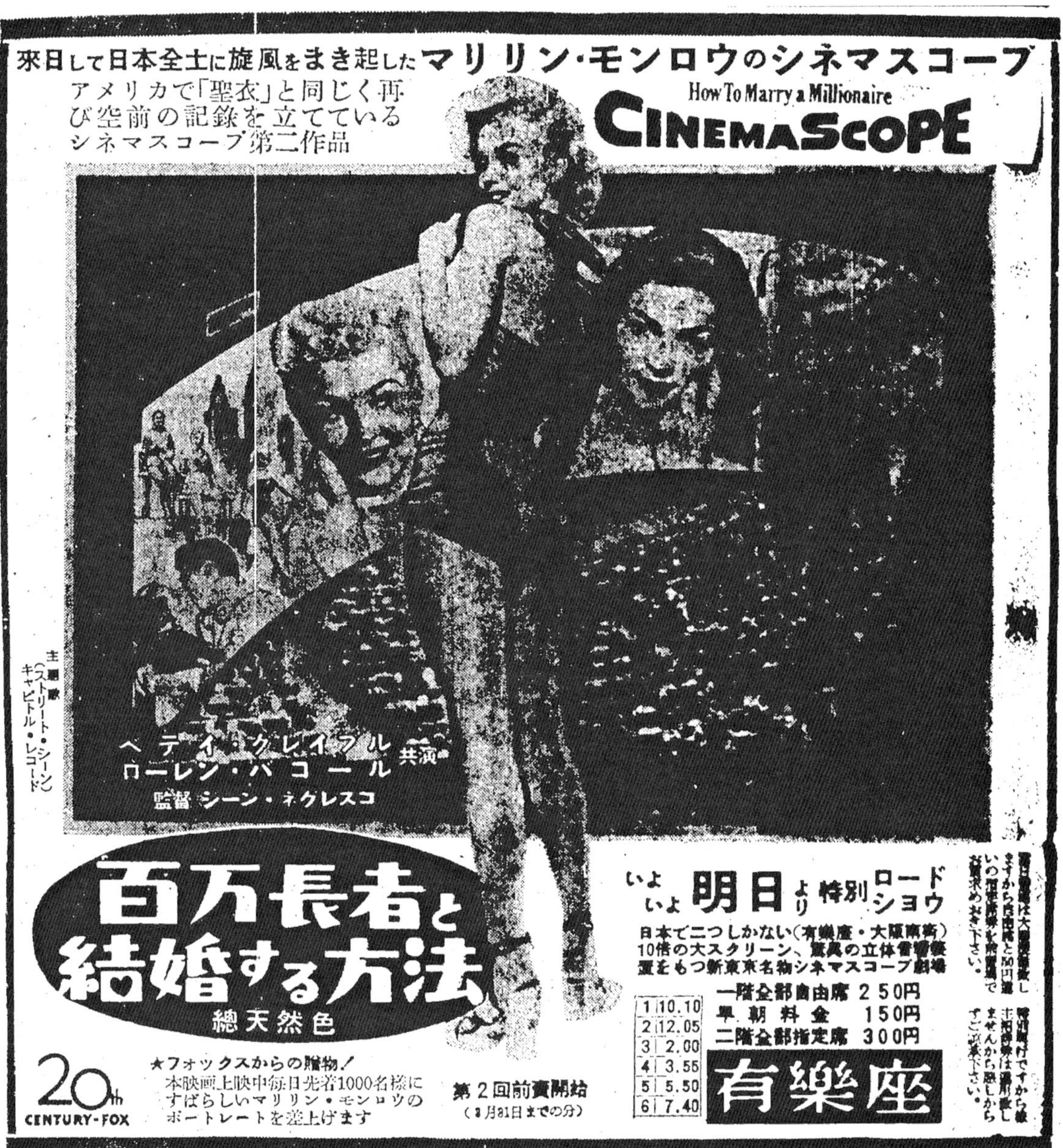

FIGURE 3.8. *Asahi Shinbun,* movie section, March 10, 1954. Courtesy of Getty Images.

that the world of fashion was producing and responding to changes in the representation of the female body, corresponding to the influx of Western and Westernized women on television, in film, and in advertisements. Rather than seeking out fashionability, Tanaka instead exposed how it had become both cage and armor for the female form and instrumental to constructing subjectivity.

We might reconsider her interest in clothing as a preoccupation with the materiality of surface: the point of contact between the body and the outside world. The body's surface as an interface was also of interest to Katsura Yuki. The surfaces of clothing, especially in the 1950s, were a site of gender differencing. Surfaces become an arena of distinction, presented in Tanaka's work as alluring and available as a potential, if elusive, site of contact. After all, surface is the external face of an object, structuring interaction. Emmanuel Levinas tells us that the face-to-face encounter is the irreducible relation that brings about our sense of subjectivity.[59] *Electric Dress,* as worn by Tanaka, was an elaborate presentation of the artist's face, though obscured, that offered the opportunity for encounter. Consequently, we might understand that surface for Tanaka is foundational yet always uncertain terrain, allowing the subject the opportunity to hide or withdraw.

Françoise Levaillant has remarked on Tanaka's use of surface in related terms, arguing that Tanaka deliberately brought into question the traditional social relation between the feminine body and its envelopment.[60] Levaillant has usefully summarized Gutai members' work involving electricity in the 1950s and has argued that Tanaka's colleagues, such as Yoshihara Michio (son of the group's leader) and Sumi Yasuo, employed electricity as a signal, in an expressive, gestural, masculinist manner, while Tanaka used the energy contained within the material to give it its full plastic richness.[61] Tanaka meant for us to see that the female body was simultaneously bound and displayed by visual media.

Television in postwar Japan found its largest audience in housewives, and viewership increased during the 1950s and early 1960s.[62] On-screen, women appeared with greater frequency than did men. Sandra Buckley has noted how commercialism and images of women were intertwined:

> Television advertising increasingly focused on a well-dressed (Western) and perfectly coiffured woman (also often Western or Japanese-American) standing in a spacious Western-style kitchen surrounded by state-of-the-art electric appliances. Women were drawn into a relationship of desire with this technologized, Westernized, domestic interior.[63]

To be sure, commercialized desire had emerged in previous decades, but it surged in the 1950s. Significantly, these representations were part of a contradictory order of gendering. Images of highly feminized models circulated in magazines and newspapers at a time when women increasingly found themselves in workplaces and in subject positions that had previously been reserved for men.[64]

Films, too, addressed the embattled terrain of gender and help shed light on the backdrop of Tanaka's budding career. Kurosawa Akira's *Kumon no su-jō* (*Spider's Web Castle*; released in the United States in 1961 as *Throne of Blood*) was released in 1957 but was made the same year as *Electric Dress.* Throughout the film, a reinterpretation of *Macbeth* set in feudal Japan, Mifune Toshirō's character, Washizu, wears bright metallic armor that contrasts with the shadows surrounding him, the armor symbolizing the failure of the powerful masculine body against the psyche and the unknown (Figure 3.9). Fear of heroic failure (a poignant metaphor in the period following the war) similarly plays out in the

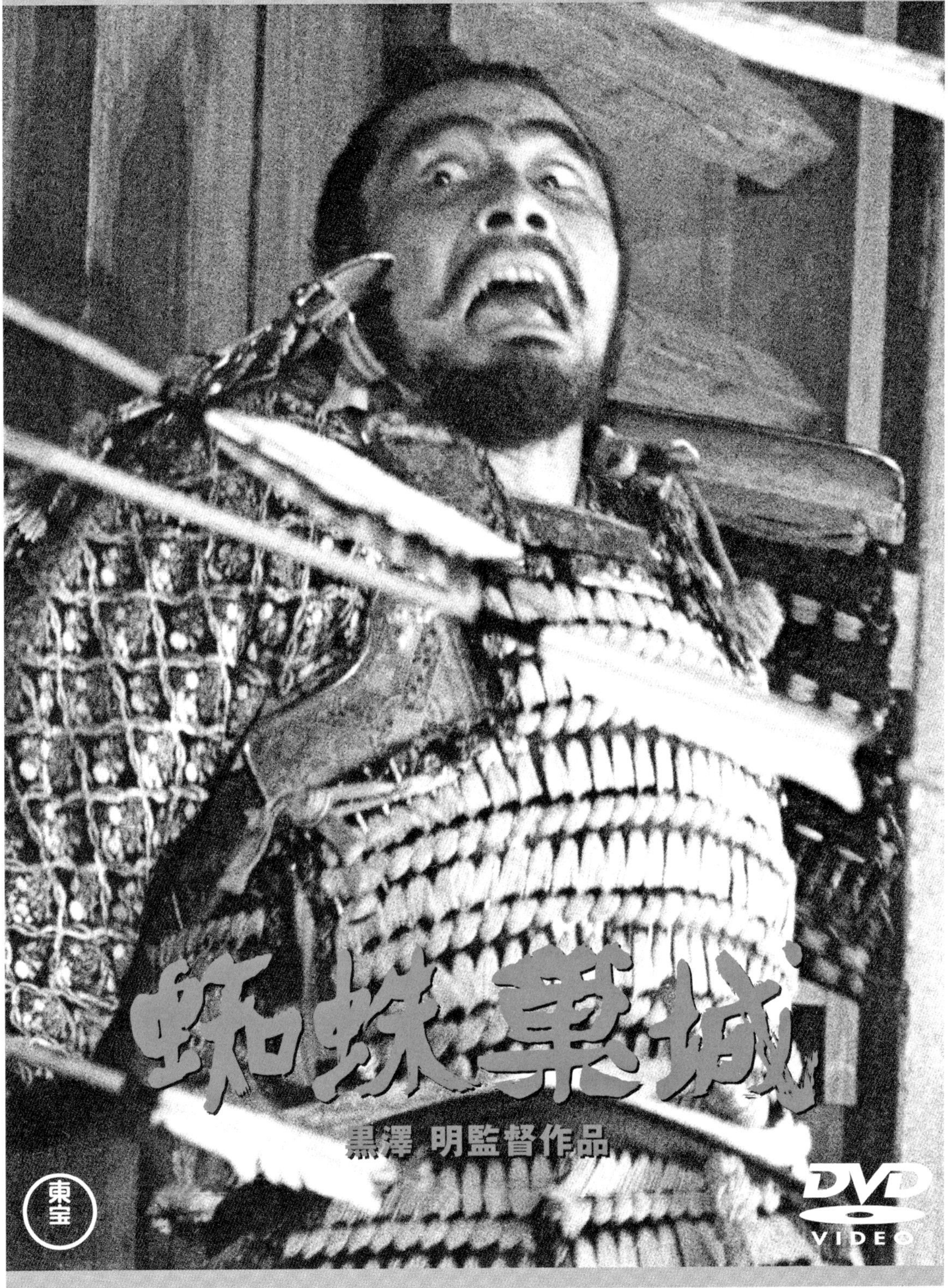

FIGURE 3.9. DVD cover for Kurosawa Akira's *Kumo no su-jō* (*Spider's Web Castle* or *Throne of Blood*), 1957. Toho Cinema. Photograph courtesy of the Visual Resources Library, The Ohio State University.

work of Shiraga Kazuo (see chapter 4) and Nakamura Hiroshi (see chapter 2). Washizu's armor provides a striking comparison to Tanaka's piece. The glittering regalia offers no defense as Washizu battles his inner demons of ambition, fear, and anxiety. This battle, too, is played out in a highly performative and theatrical manner, framed through the glittering surface of metaphoric armor.

Similarly, physical threats take a backseat to cultural anxieties in Ozu Yasujirō's 1953 film *Tokyo monogatari (Tokyo Story),* in which female characters represent the fraught position of the modern woman. In this film, the mother is a full-bodied matriarch who lumbers slowly through quiet interiors, still carrying the psychological burden of losing her son in the war. When she passes away, her large body is laid out for a private wake held in a cramped living room, her physical presence a metaphor for the motherland of Japan and the loss of tradition. The film also features the much-loved star Hara Setsuko (1920–2015) portraying the widowed wife of the dead son. Only this idealized woman, appearing prim and resolute, renounces personal goals, social connections, and material values to protect the customs of the familial unit. In this film and many others, female morality and loyalty to the family are coded, not so subtly, as the rules of the game for women. It was in this context that Tanaka, one of a small minority of female artists in Japan, began her difficult career path.

Tanaka and other female members of Gutai were given ample space in exhibitions and in the pages of *Gutai,* the group's newsletter (produced from 1955 to 1965).[65] In this sense, and in many others, Gutai was ahead of the times. Yet there is no doubt that Tanaka's artistic abilities were viewed through a gendered lens, both by critics and by those within the group. For instance, Gutai member Shimamoto Shōzō, said in 1956: "Among these few examples of avant-garde art, Tanaka's work has taught me about an aesthetic sensitivity that I did not have, especially an alternate possibility of rigorous beauty that can be created from womanly sweetness and frailty. They were a great influence on me."[66] His comments reveal that Tanaka's art forced Shimamoto to revise his preconceptions of gender, if only within a given perimeter.

Both Kanayama and Yoshihara expressed surprise that Tanaka was able to lift some of her larger installation pieces and frequently contrasted the slightness of her figure with her work. In an exhibition brochure, Yoshihara described Tanaka as "an annoying person of violence who is . . . endowed with a tiny body that can be held in one hand. When she plans her works, she expects no assistance from others. But who can just watch from the sidelines?"[67] Tanaka herself may have contributed to this image; in several photographs from the 1950s and 1960s she posed standing at a side angle, dwarfed by the artworks next to her. The power of visual scale and its complicated relationship to gender was not lost on her.

Contemporary reception of Tanaka's art was likewise highly mediated by comments about the artist's sex. At least one reviewer posed her success as uncharacteristic of her sex, stating that her work was dynamic and "unwomanly."[68] In another example, the headline of a 1955 edition of the *Asahi Newspaper* ran, "Twenty Bells Take You by Surprise: A Young Lady's Work Accepted to Genbi's Exhibition without Problem."[69] Nearly ten years later, the same patronizing tone can be detected in another headline: "Tanaka Atsuko: With Her Outlandish Ideas, She Is Bold, Despite Her Frail-Looking Physique."[70] In the English-language edition of the *Mainichi News,* Tanaka was repeatedly referred to as "Miss Tanaka"—language that may have been axiomatic at the time but nonetheless signals difference; Yoshihara and other members of Gutai were referred to simply by their surnames.[71]

This overemphasis on her supposed frailty, as well as the everyday challenges of sexism, may have elicited a degree of resentment in Tanaka, a resentment that surfaced through her art. In an untitled work, she placed neon-pink rayon material against a dirt surface, juxtaposing the saturated color with the unmanipulated ground (reconstruction, Plate 22).[72] Describing her aims in 1955, she said:

> I wanted to shatter a stable beauty with my work. In the case of the pink fabric the size of twenty tatami mats [about 32.8 × 32.8 feet], I wanted to use the most distasteful color imaginable. I walked all over the city of Osaka and finally found this rayon. I wanted to destroy the superficiality of the conventional "artist-look," using the weird sheen that resulted from sunlight reflecting from the cloth covering the ground.[73]

Note Tanaka's desire to express instability rather than wholeness in this piece, which has come to be known as *Work (Pink Rayon)*. She chose the fabric—a vivid, nearly nauseating pink, a color that was extremely difficult to find or make at the time—because, she said, it was the color she disliked the most. Nevertheless, the bald monochrome suggests more than the limits of taste. It registers how color alone can connote the gendered issues of artifice, makeup, dress-up, and made-up frivolity, things that Tanaka may have responded to with ambivalence. Surely, her work had a comedic "lightness" to it, but it was a humor directed at the most serious and dangerous matters. This approach has a long history in art, as Daumier and others have shown us. Too often, reviewers of Gutai members' works have caught on to the "fun" while missing the punch line of the joke—namely, that nothing short of women's agency was at stake.[74] Throughout her career, her works took up a timely interest in fabric and women's fashion that was charged with an undercurrent of disquieting dissent.

Stage Clothes

In the filmed version of *Stage Clothes,* performed in Osaka in 1957 (Figure 3.10), Tanaka concocted a direct response to the growing demand for commercialized beauty, inverting the sexiness of the striptease. The young artist appeared in a green organza dress and wore one yellow sock and one green sock, her face expressionless. She then proceeded to take off the sleeves and midsection of the dress, revealing a yellow frock underneath that she then

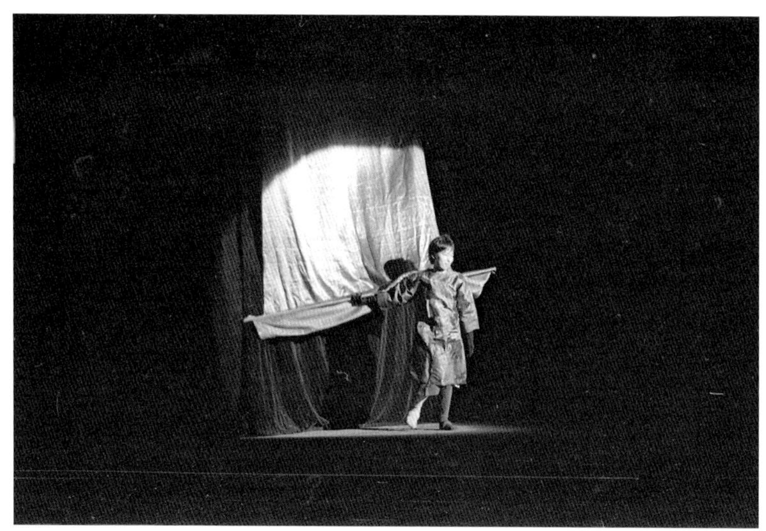

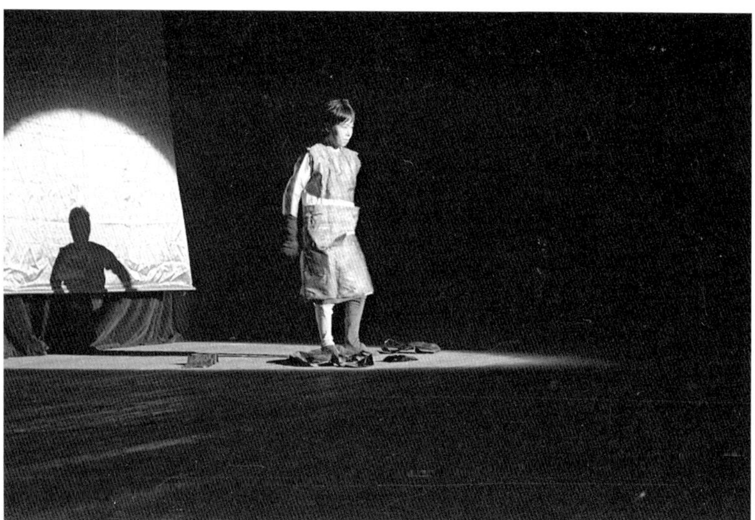

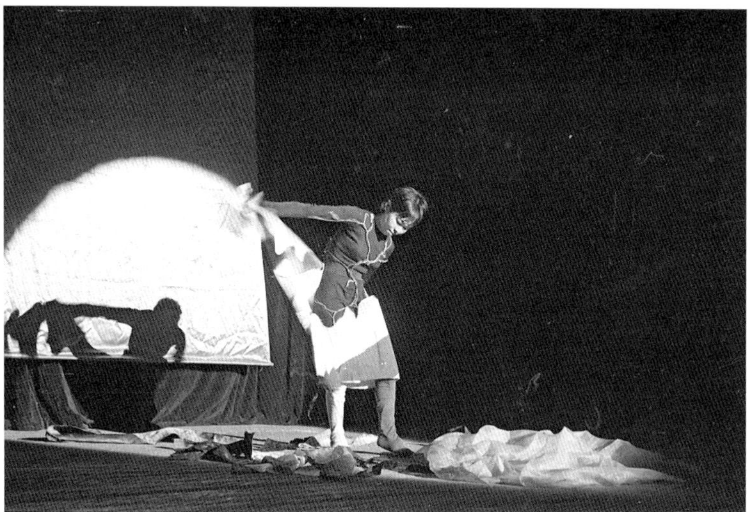

FIGURE 3.10. Tanaka Atsuko performs *Butai fuku (Stage Clothes)*, *Gutai Art on the Stage*, Sankei Kaikan Hall, Osaka, May 29, 1957. Courtesy of Osaka City Museum of Modern Art. Copyright Kanayama Akira and Tanaka Atsuko Association.

pulled off to expose a fuchsia chiffon gown. She removed the layers of costumes rapidly and matter-of-factly, each action revealing another color and style of gown beneath the one before. Although the dresses were frilly, colorful, and generally ostentatious, her clipped movements and efficient manner maintained an insistently sober atmosphere. She did not smile. Movements superfluous to the changing of clothes were kept to a strict minimum.

With the mysterious way that each dress appeared, using trick sleeves and removable panels, the performance was akin to a magic show rather than a fashion show. Tanaka offered no sexy strut down a catwalk, no embellished turns. It was no surprise, then, that the work finished without a flourish. Instead, the artist simply stopped when she was wearing only a thick black leotard that rendered her form invisible against the dark stage background. That decision was significant. This was a striptease of anticlimax, where the body was virtually obscured in a black void. *Stage Clothes* constructed tension between the viewer's desire to see and know the contours that define the individual body or character and the denial of that sexualized visibility by the artist.

Tanaka's studies for *Stage Clothes* (1956) bear out a similar interest in transformation rather than individualization (Plate 23 and Figure 3.11). In one study, the figure is drawn in a series of lines across the page (Plate 23). Tanaka delineates the ways each piece of cloth will be worn or removed by using red watercolor to indicate the placement of the cloth on the subject. In the first three rows the repeated figure is a minimally detailed shape with legs, and in the final two rows the rudimentary figure appears with vague breasts and hips. Regardless of the state of dress, the subject in the drawings and in the performances remains expressionless, sexually neutral, and vacant of personal gesture.

This refusal of the erotic stands in opposition to the ubiquitous availability of women's skin in the postwar period. As Dower observes, "The eroticization of defeated Japan in the eyes of the conquerors took place almost immediately, creating a complex interplay of assumed masculine and feminine roles that has colored U.S.–Japan relations ever since."[75] The sexual commerce between American soldiers and Japanese women was so pervasive that children frequently played a game called *panpan asobi,* in which they would pretend to be GIs and freelance prostitutes.[76] During the war and the Allied Occupation, the status of women underwent further changes. Sarah Kovner writes: "After Allied Forces landed in 1945, no figures were more notorious than the panpan. They were the source of desire, debate, and derision. . . . Ubiquitous photographs, newspaper articles, and literary descriptions proffer vivid images of heavily made-up women, standing on street corners, posing on subway platforms, or lurking under bridges. Panpan wore the latest Western fashions, it was said, where ordinary women were still clad in wartime work trousers."[77] Concerns over women's morality and self-presentation loomed large in the 1940s and continued into the 1950s. Considering the alarming intensification of traffic in women's bodies, *Stage Clothes* hits a nerve. Rather than an exultation of individual spirit, as some scholars have suggested, the performance piece bespeaks the anxiety over the status of Japanese women in the postwar era. Kovner notes: "For some Japanese males—particularly veterans, returnees from

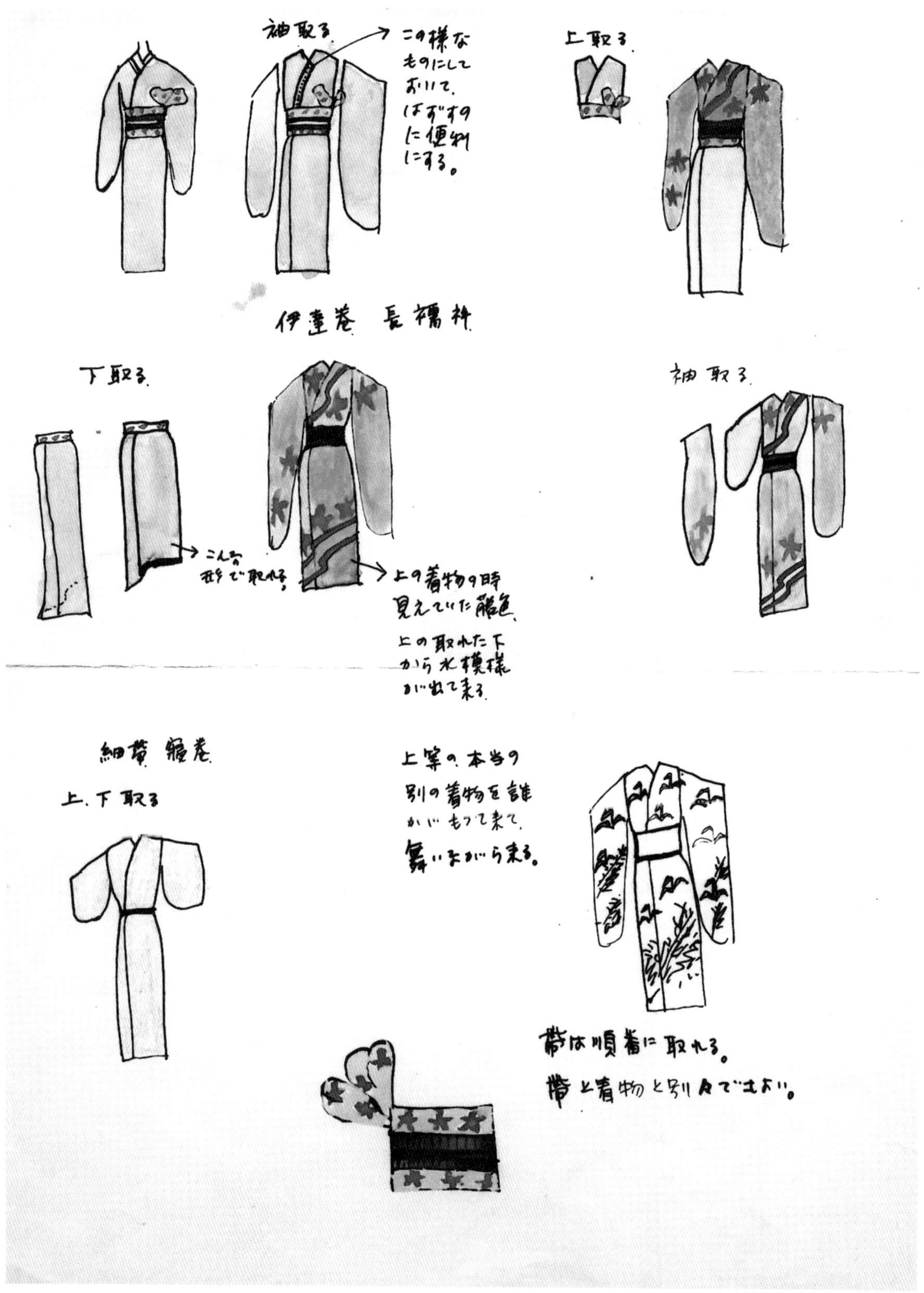

FIGURE 3.11. Tanaka Atsuko, study for *Butai fuku (Stage Clothes),* 1956. Ink, watercolor, and pencil on paper, 29.48 × 22.09 cm. Courtesy of Osaka City Museum of Modern Art. Copyright Kanayama Akira and Tanaka Atsuko Association.

Japan's colonies, or the unemployed—condemning the panpan served as an oblique and effective way of criticizing the occupiers and expressing dissatisfaction with postwar life."[78] Perhaps it is telling that Japan's first anti-prostitution law was passed by the Diet in 1956, the year *Electric Dress* and *Stage Clothes* were created. *Stage Clothes,* in its attention to fashion as well as to the relationship between body and performance, reveals the constructs of gender without reinventing the oft-seen icons of the *Moga* or the *panpan.* Like the majority of Tanaka's works, it explores the touchpoints between the physical self and the world.[79] At the same time, the viewer's obscured vision and the performer's multiple transformations suggest the impossibility of the viewer confidently securing any identification with the performer. Tanaka's reiterative transformations make it clear that she is performing— we do not come to know the artist as an individual but witness the appearance of self as a facade, in all its changing manifestations.

While Katō clarifies how Tanaka's oeuvre diverges from that of the Gutai group as a whole due to the artist's concern "not with the body in motion but with its everyday character," she stops short of relating surface to gendered subjectivity.[80] Surface in Tanaka's work is presented as alluring and available as a potential site of contact akin to the sexual capital of the postwar period. Be it the artist's small face framed within the lights or the captivating use of color and mechanics, *Electric Dress* invites speculation about who it is that would don such a dress. Yet just as the lights and colors draw us in, the heat and unwieldiness of the piece keep us at bay. As Judith Butler reminds us, surface and the boundaries of the body play a profound role in gender subjectivity: the "boundaries of the body are the lived experience of differentiation, where that differentiation is never neutral to the question of gender difference or the heterosexual matrix."[81] Butler sees agency and vulnerability as inextricably intertwined, foundational to the embodied subject, just as it seems Tanaka did.[82]

To understand fully the stakes of her work, we might consider the dominant modes of art practice that Tanaka did not pursue. A common interpretive framework posits that postwar cultural production sought to emphasize bodily carnality as an antidote to wartime propaganda that gave primacy to the union of the state rather than to the individual. Through textbooks and propaganda materials, the government officially promulgated terms such as *kokutai* (national body), which referred to the uniqueness of the Japanese as authenticated by their "divine origins." Slogans such as *Ichioku isshin* (One hundred million with one spirit) and, later, *Ichioku gyokusai* (One hundred million shattered jewels) romanticized the notion of harmony and beauty through national unity even in destruction. The heavy-handed rhetorical use of *kokutai* in state propaganda was rejected in the postwar period, and some artists instead celebrated the oppositional *nikutai* (carnal body). Terms like *nikutai bungaku* (literature of the flesh) and *nikutai-ha* (carnal movement) became common, and scholars have often described this cultural turn as a potent postwar period antidote to fascism.[83] Yet while the body was a primary arena for questioning the state of the nation, political inclinations did not neatly map onto the binary of the carnal body against the national body.

As Slaymaker points out, relying too heavily on a facile understanding of the *nikutai* versus *kokutai* approach can be reductive, as it fails to account for the gendered dynamics of national politics.[84] Slaymaker further shows how these performative models could re-create the circumstances they sought to shake off: "Anxieties concerning masculinity and attempts to forge one anew, however, led these male writers to an identity most often imagined as a sexually aggressive male: to fall back on, that is, the conceptualization they ostensibly decry." In addition, this "discourse of liberation through the body is dependent on the Other of a female body. . . . The experience of empire is never far for these writers: the body of a woman, actual or metaphorical, becomes terrain to be explored and subjugated."[85]

Thus, relying solely on the *kokutai* versus *nikutai* approach is problematic for several reasons. First, this approach suppresses continuities of imperial desire that were extant in the pre- and postwar periods—a line of inquiry that becomes increasingly important as the Japanese government has recently resorted to reincarnations of blatantly nationalistic metaphors.[86] Second, assuming that most postwar art falls into this framework elides female participants: their only recourse is to appear as subjects of sex and violence on the canvas. Women had no purchase on the art of the carnal body because of the obvious strictures against female nudity, transgressiveness, and female sexual desire.

The policing of women's sexuality became heightened as prostitution increased: in 1955, it was estimated that one out of every twenty-five women in Japan was working in the commercial sex industry.[87] As Kovner notes, "This moral panic entailed renegotiating normative boundaries not just within one society, but in terms of how Japanese men and women would relate to the rest of the world."[88] For many, Japanese prostitutes transacting business with Allied servicemen was a discomfiting reminder of the times when Japanese colonists had their own "comfort women."[89] Ironically, a female artist who participated in the *nikutai-ha* would be read as subjugating herself to Western, masculine (imperialist) forces, rather than perceived as having agency in the liberatory rejection of fascism. For a female artist, sexually transgressive art would add a troubling nuance to "embracing defeat" and likely bring negative judgment on the artist rather than raise questions about the art itself.

Art by women, instead, tended to show the body as inaccessible, like *Electric Dress,* or safely contained within layers, as was the case in Katsura Yuki's work. All of these artworks—perhaps none more than Tanaka's *Stage Clothes*—raised questions about gender, artistic status, and the body, in part by refusing the prurient gaze.

Tanaka's own life was marked by tensions between her desire to push herself toward exposure and her decision to remove herself from the pulsating arena of the city; ultimately she chose (as her doctor and husband urged) to withdraw from the pressures of urban life and reposition her artistic status. As the young woman attracted the limelight, the Gutai group as a whole was receiving less press, and this strained relations between the group's leader, Yoshihara, and Tanaka.[90] Some have suggested Yoshihara became envious of the younger artist's success.[91] In 1965, with the pressures of her solo career and the tensions within the Gutai group mounting, Tanaka became mentally ill and received psychotherapy.[92] Tanaka left Gutai, together with Kanayama, and continued to pursue her solo career. Kanayama committed to looking after her and took over the administrative responsibilities for her exhibitions. He initiated the move to a detached house that his parents owned on the grounds of the Buddhist temple Myōhō-ji in Osaka. She continued to work, both at Myōhō-ji and at her parents' house in Tennōji-ku, Osaka.[93] Both Tanaka's doctor and Kanayama felt the move to the quiet of the temple surroundings would further facilitate her recovery.[94]

Tanaka's struggles with the gender hierarchy, artistic status among her peers, the changing urban environment, and her own personal issues were all likely factors related to her institutionalization—the precise nature of her private challenges can never be known. It may be tempting to conclude that Tanaka's creativity was fueled by her unique mental instabilities (an idea that is only furthered through comparisons to Kusama Yayoi, who has relied on an autobiographical psychological narrative to attract attention to her work).[95] Yet we might also ask to what degree Tanaka's suffering was indicative of the uncertainty and anxiety that were pervasive among her peer group in the Kansai region of Japan. Her performances and paintings were a means of asking questions about the viability and vulnerability of the gendered self. Rather than representing a crazed (read: hysterical) female artist whose genius stemmed from her exceptional mental state, Tanaka's art expressed an aura of disquiet that was shared by many who faced great uncertainties about what it meant to be a young woman in postwar Japan. Statistics reveal that there was an acute rise in depression among this demographic in the mid-1950s, as well as an upswing in drug abuse, ultimately indicative of larger cracks in the system, a point to which I will return shortly.[96]

Spatial Dimensions in *Electric Dress*

Tanaka's seemingly never-ending series of lines and dots is a painterly means of finding the limits of self and other, of examining how equivalence and difference can be achieved by testing the relationship of two basic elements (circle, line) on the arena of paint and canvas. Perhaps the most relevant boundary that Tanaka pursues is the limitations of space between personhood and media. She seeks out the upper limits of heat, sound, luminosity, and size that the physical body can bear. Tanaka determines the interstices between the body and technology, revealing how our mediatized selves produce gendered selves in their expectations, juxtapositions, and dangers. Although Tanaka was a reluctant participant in direct politics, *Electric Dress* seemed uncannily in tune with the politics of consumption debated at the time. In 1955, the Hatoyama election campaign focused on the notion of "bright Japan" *(akarui Nihon)*, the goal of which was to oppose increasing materialism and Westernization.[97] Ironically (or perhaps predictably) it was the electronic goods companies that "seized in particular on the concept of the bright life *(akarui seikatsu)*, which seemed ideally suited to the products they were selling. The fluorescent light bulb was one of the new products that spread rapidly throughout Japan in the 1950s."[98] It was Matsushita's National brand that adopted the slogan "Bright National," which registered among consumers. Historian Simon Partner shows how "a women's-group diary eloquently sums up the desire evoked by the bright life to escape the grim present: 'When we look at the lights of the Occupation solider gleaming on the hilltop, and compare them with our own dim lives, we feel we must act to make our lives brighter: for if we don't, who will?'"[99] Tanaka's medium relied on the products of "Bright National," which, like the "Bright, Disabled in Minamata" headline discussed in the introduction to this volume, showed the darker side of the industry that leaned so heavily on women's labor: "Electrical goods companies competed directly with textile factories for young female labor. . . . Underneath the apparent revolution in technology development and industrial structure lay a profound continuity based on the abundance of extremely cheap, relatively docile female labor."[100]

Tanaka produced compositional plans for *Electric Dress* and also drawings after *Electric Dress* that were exhibited in the background of the 1956 exhibition at Ohara Kaikan Hall, suggesting the importance of the work to her creative trajectory (see Figure 3.1 and Plate 24). The drawings and paintings that followed the piece were based on its form, color, and patterning (see Plates 20 and 25). While some of the drawings refer to the circuitry and others map the structure of the piece, most are focused on the "pattern" of the dress—the surface composed of lines and circles. Tanaka made four hundred two-dimensional works, and all rely on this sequence. Throughout her oeuvre, circles may appear within other circles and in varying degrees of proximity to each other, but other geometrical forms are rarely represented. Circles, circles, circles repeat (Plate 26) and yet do not repeat, for each composition is observably unique. *'87H,* for example, is at once abstract, geometric, and serial (Plate 27). Vivid circular shapes (which appear consistently throughout her body of work) are connected, bounded, distorted, and layered over by meandering lines. In the top right, the bold circle is held in tension by the wave of lines that seem to suggest a leftward movement. The intensity of lines on the left begins to meld, and distinguishing each element becomes increasingly difficult. *'87H* is compact, with thick wiry lines and dark black circles that lend the work a mechanical aesthetic. Acrylic and vinyl paint, which Tanaka used throughout her career, even when their artificial tones made them unpopular, emphasize the synthetic nature of the textured, painted material in a provocative manner.[101]

Many scholars have become interested in the question of Gutai's painterliness, arguing that even the group's performance works were ultimately means to investigate the nature of painting.[102] This is likely true, but the argument suggests that Gutai performance works need to be recuperated and have relative value only in comparison with the traditional genre of painting. Beyond an interest in the nature of medium, Tanaka's performance works and paintings ask us to consider larger questions about selfhood through an interrogation of surface. Her paintings after *Electric Dress* ask if surface is whole or formed by its accumulations of fractures. Obliquely this line of visual inquiry may be bound to the confounding issue of the modern subject in Japan. Where the figure is absent, where perspective is overridden for expansiveness, where tension is palpable between chaos and order, the solidity of self is replaced with the connections and disconnections of lines and circles. Tanaka affirmed these tensions in the darkly titled *Jigoku mon (Gate of Hell)* (1965–69) as well as through the sense of confounding pressure produced by the dense repetition of acrylic circles and lines (see Plates 25 and 27). These paintings refer back to *Electric Dress* but sublate the three-dimensional quality of the work. While depressing the fullness of the dress, eliminating its mass and the noise of its cranking gears, the paintings still preserve some aspects of the original through color and the form of line and circle. *Electric Dress,* too, was disassembled and reused in a painterly arrangement of bulbs that hung on the wall on a vinyl sheet.

As the movement and transformational quality of surface in *Electric Dress* became immobilized and circumscribed, did this sense of entanglement speak to Tanaka's sense of the suppressive snare of Osaka and the pressures on a young artist who faced conflicting demands of gender hierarchy and artistic status? Tanaka's art suggests the threat posed by technological advancement, wherein the possibility of direct physical contact with the human body is removed and replaced by the interface of the televised body and the commercially represented body. Industrial development held the promise of progress and change, but often it revealed the risks of swift transformation.

The Female Subject on the Precipice

While the new high-speed trains on the Tōkaidō Line resulted in economic growth and access to jobs for a wider demographic, the headlines that celebrated the railway's unremitting increases in velocity soon shifted focus. Increasingly, alarming reports of young women committing suicide by jumping in front of trains took precedence in the newspapers, gruesomely literalizing the obliteration of bodies by industrialization.[103] Japan had the highest suicide rate in the industrialized world in this period, peaking at a yearly rate of 24 per 100,000 people in 1956—precisely the year that *Electric Dress* was made.[104] Furthermore, those most likely to commit suicide were Tanaka's peers, women between twenty and twenty-four years old.[105] This was the only historical moment to date when female suicides exceeded male suicides. Japanese women were four times more likely than their American counterparts to commit suicide in 1955.[106] Suicide was (and remains) the leading cause of death for Japanese women between the ages of fifteen and thirty-four.[107] *Tobikomijisatsu,* meaning suicide by train, was very common at the time and is still the main cause of delayed trains. When a train is delayed due to suicide (a regular occurrence in Tokyo), the railway's public announcement system broadcasts a standard euphemistic statement: "There has been a human incident *[jinshin jiko]."* In the 1950s, the urban center with the highest suicide rate was Osaka.[108] Tanaka, who had faced her own challenges with mental health and fascination with train stations, may not have been aware of the statistical realities, but she could not have missed the heightened levels of mental instability and anxiety felt by her young female peers. She reenacted and explored these apprehensions in *Electric Dress.*

Viewing the most frequently published photograph of the performance of *Electric Dress,* one can sense Tanaka's tenuous mastery of the production; she occupies a central yet unstable position (see Figure 3.2). The work is a peculiar visionary spectacle yet somehow restrained in movement and difficult to see—it is eye-catching and blinding, drawing the viewer in to try to focus on the artist-subject. Like a whisper, the low-level perceptibility of the subject-wearer marks hidden import. In the act of looking, the viewer too is complicit in the performative construction. Tanaka, in the making and wearing of her "electric clothes," risks her own body's security through exposure to heat and electrical wiring in the performance while at the same time literally illuminating her own role as artist. If, as Judith Butler asserts, the self is constituted through the reiterative performative actions of the body, *Electric Dress* reveals the performative power to obliterate the body, even when the performative is what constitutes the self that "wears" it.[109]

In *Understanding Media,* Marshall McLuhan describes art as something that helps us prepare for the coming changes in the outside world, an idea whose relevance in performance art has been further articulated by Anne Wagner.[110] In her essay "Performance, Video, and the Rhetoric of Presence," Wagner argues that video art, particularly in its formative stage, seeks to examine and expose how "art's summoning of selfhood is compromised by what we might call a 'media effect.'"[111] She sees early video art not as electronic narcissism but as a politicized engagement with media that reveals that video, as McLuhan argues, "is the medium that shapes and controls the scale and form of human association and action."[112] Wagner mentions Vito Acconci, Joan Jonas, and Peter Campus, among others, as artists who know about "narcosis and numbing, know how to induce them and know that the reality of the body and of its senses—the reality of personhood—are somehow at stake."[113] Tanaka too was absorbed in the potentially destructive aspects of urbanization in modern Japan. She described the first time she wore *Electric Dress* in 1955:

> When I was finished, I was uncomfortable with the electrical connections. Since somebody had to wear it, I covered myself with vinyl and put the electric dress on. The moment Mr. Sannomiya said, "I am turning the electricity on," I had the fleeting thought: is this how a death-row inmate would feel?[114]

Tanaka's comment compellingly suggests the central thesis of this chapter: that *Electric Dress* evokes the overwhelming aspects of technology—so ubiquitous in postwar Osaka—constructed through a visual interrogation of surface, and, in doing so, the work explores the interstices and limits of gender subjectivity. The double-edged nature of this performance piece is evident: the riotous color and spectacular language of the dress versus the explicit threat of its weight and heat—and the channeling of a current that is deadly when misused. While the early performance piece occupies a critical position in Tanaka's work, it has consequences beyond the scope of her personal artistic maturation. Her piece is revealing of self-exposure and self-destruction, issues that loomed large in the 1950s for young women in Osaka. *Electric Dress* displays gender subjectivity as unstable and uncertain rather than declaratively individualistic. It suggests how developing one's sense of self in postwar Japan was a process that was powerful and yet rife with risks, revealing subjectivity as vulnerable to the effects of surface contact, reliant on bodily performance, and exposed to industrialization, urbanization, and manufactured commercial desires.

4

Heroic Violence in the Art of Shiraga Kazuo

Shiraga Kazuo (1924–2008) has been both lauded and dismissed for his spectacular action paintings (Figure 4.1). A member of the Gutai Art Association from 1954, Shiraga developed a signature style of painting with his feet that caught the attention of critics but also allowed his notorious early performance work to be seen as a passing novelty. Images of his bare-chested body launched against a heap of mud or swinging haphazardly over a paint-smattered canvas were featured on the opening pages of the handful of catalogs and texts on his art.[1] Reviewers in the 1950s focused on Shiraga's unusual "body-centered action painting" and seemed unsure how to assess the antics of the artist, who, it was often pointed out, lived outside the epicenter of contemporary art in Tokyo.[2] The extravagantly overt nature of his production has encouraged some commentators to assume that Shiraga's oeuvre is interpretively transparent and has contributed to a facile equation of his performance artworks with the Gutai manifesto's declarations against fakery and in favor of "concreteness."[3] This equation overshadows the subtle and important differences between Gutai's ideology as declared in the commissioned manifesto and Shiraga's creative ethos.[4] Further, it leads to an underestimation of the important ways Shiraga's work intertwines with the contested politics of nation, gender, and aesthetics circulating in postwar Japan.

In 1952, Shiraga joined the informal art group Zero-kai with other notable artists from the Kansai area, including his longtime friend Kanayama Akira and Murakami Saburō. A few years later, Tanaka Atsuko joined the group, and Uemura Fujiko, who would later marry Shiraga, also participated.[5] These five members then disbanded Zero-kai in 1954 and joined the Gutai Art Association, which had been formed a few months before.

Largely interpreted as playful celebrations of democracy, Shiraga's works used violence as art: never gently daubing, Shiraga used his feet and legs as paintbrushes, hoisting himself above his canvas with the strength of his torso. His consistent exercise of physical exertion was definitively violent, causing harm to himself and his materials. In this chapter,

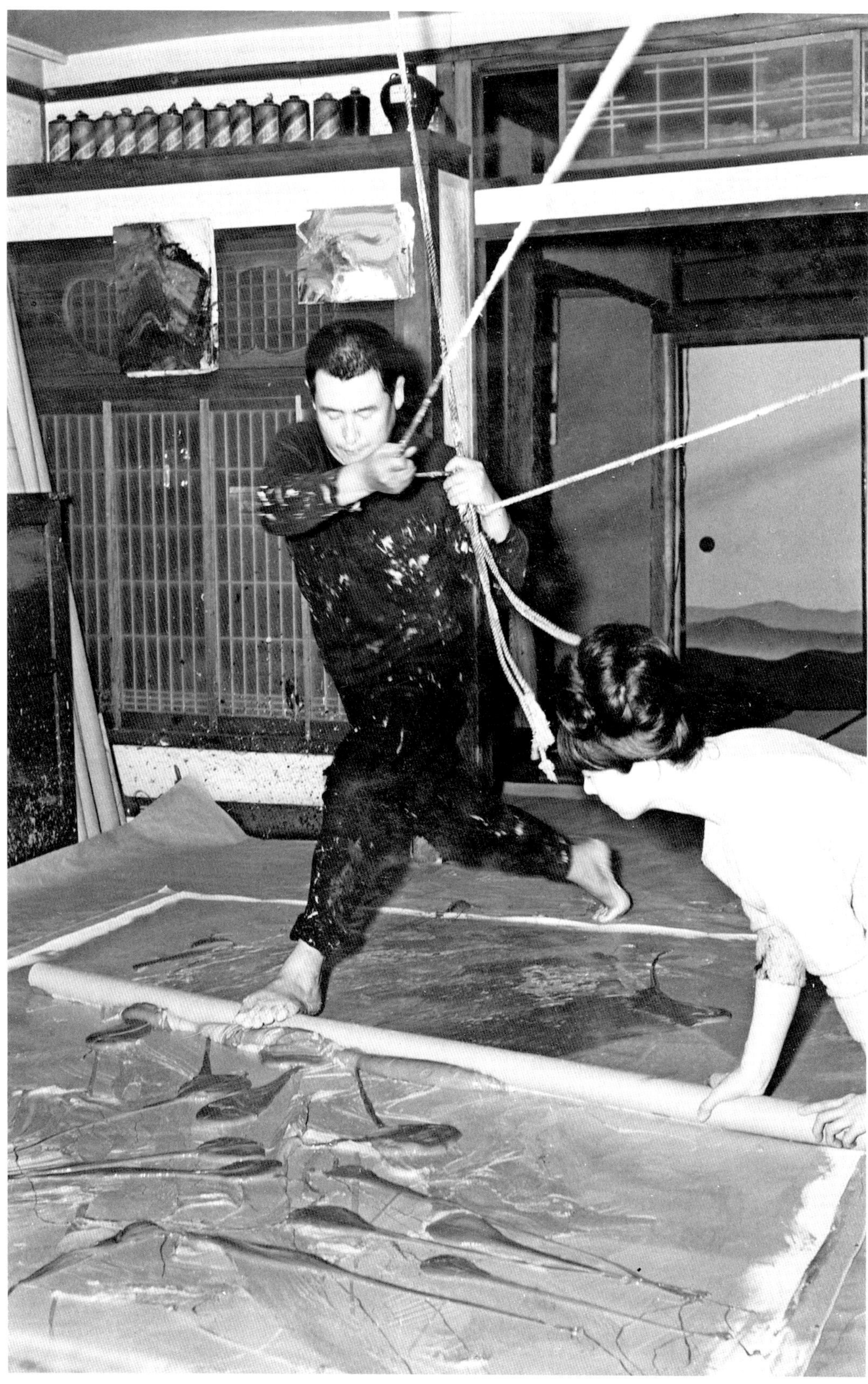

FIGURE 4.1. Shiraga Kazuo painting *Fan* in his studio in 1965. Copyright Hisao Shiraga. Courtesy of Amagasaki Cultural Center.

I examine the insistent focus on aggressive bodily action in Shiraga's methods and writings to show how he used violence as art to comment on tropes of masculinity that staged critical encounters among himself, his art, and the state.

Shiraga's references to the archetypal models of the hero took many forms, appearing in the literary allusions in the titles he gave to his paintings, the spectacular self-heroization of his performance art, and the masculine acts that were subtly interwoven into his photographic and written biography.[6] What did these multiple, relational, configurations of gender suggest about art making in Japan in the 1950s? How was the Kansai-born artist's body a site for the exploration of gender and subjectivity? Shiraga's staging of warrior-like characters was more interrogative than internalized and was fraught with anxiety over failure. As the figure of the American soldier loomed large, Shiraga's multiple enactments of the hero give the lie to the notion of a fixed masculine ideal. Yet his insistent embodiment of masculinist archetypes also calls attention to, and perhaps advances, their power.

To recognize that Shiraga's art is coded with heroic tropes is not to assert that he was innately masculine and powerful. In contemporary gender theory, the conceptualization of feminized and masculinized roles is "predicated linguistically and socially upon binary oppositions and their implied hierarchies of value."[7] If the postwar period brought about a renewed interest in the ideal of the heroic artist, how could masculinity be shaped following the defeat in war and the omnipresence of the Allied Occupation? Shiraga's actions pointed not to his own virility but to an ineffable sense of ideal, embodied masculinity. The portrayal of a desire for power that would bolster the nation was exhibited in much of his performance art; however, the converse pole of emasculation, resonating with its concomitant rhetoric of humiliation and shame, was likewise interrogated. Conceptual binaries of victory and loss were inexorably tied to the reevaluation of the male subject following the end of the Pacific War, and Shiraga was engaged artistically and corporeally in this contentious discourse.

In 1950s Japan, artists were highly aware of the dangers of militarism, just as they were mindful of the loss of the war and its consequences for global power relations, including impacts on economics, international relations, and artistic status. Both waging war and the "shameful" defeat that followed also had significant ramifications for gender relations.[8] During the war men were expected to internalize the ideal of the soldier and to replicate this unsustainable paragon of masculinity.[9] In wartime, acts of aggression performed to protect the purity of the nation were a means to reach toward this ideal, just as these acts masculinized the body that performed them. But Japan's surrender in 1945 disrupted this phenomenon. The feminization of the nation that began with the historiographical notion of Commodore Perry's "opening of Japan" was reignited during the Pacific War and the Allied Occupation. The reduction in status of the emperor from divinity to a mere human replete with shortcomings, particularly when compared to General MacArthur, and the authoritative presence of the occupation forces transformed the Japanese soldier from a symbol of power into an abject, weakened specimen.[10] During the occupation this inversion of the masculine ideal became commonplace in government rhetoric and in fiction that reiterated this characterization of the Japanese male as infantile and emasculated.[11]

Into the late 1950s, artists became increasingly aware of the burden of re-creating a strong national identity as Japan sought to reinvent itself in the postwar period. Feelings ran deep over conflicting visions of Japan's future, but a constructed sense of belatedness in the art field was widely perceived. Shiraga described attending the *Yomiuri Indépendant* exhibition in 1951 and seeing art from the United States (including a work by Jackson Pollock) and other countries that "looked very fresh" and made an impression on him.[12] Many artists under Yoshihara's instruction were aware that circumventing the labeling of Japanese abstract painting as second-rate, derivative abstract expressionism was a difficult maneuver, and imbuing works with the coveted value of "originality" was rich with potential for cultural capitalism. The works of the Gutai group were largely ignored or dismissed by critics in Japan and abroad. Dore Ashton panned the 1958 Gutai exhibition at the Martha Jackson Gallery in New York: "In spite of unorthodox techniques—tar, plastic bags or crumpled papers mashed together—the effects are orthodox. They resemble paintings in Paris, New York, Amsterdam, London and Mexico City that resemble paintings by Pollock and his followers."[13] Ray Falk, however, gave a more positive review of Gutai in 1957, calling the group members innovators and refuting any kind of derivation, stating that their art was not "cubism, surrealism, or Dadaism; it is not even Japanese."[14] In Japan, a reevaluation of Gutai did not begin until the 1980s, initiated perhaps by an article published by Hikosaka Naoyoshi in 1973, which suggested that Michel Tapié seriously affected the creative direction of Gutai (Tapié collaborated with the Gutai group from his arrival in Japan in 1957).[15] Hence, issues of authenticity and artistic originality plagued Gutai from its origins until well past its reevaluation following the group's demise. Shiraga's search for new forms of art was driven, in part, by these discourses.

Shiraga's creation of art as violence offered a model of renewed masculinity that dislodged the heroic from the battlefield—an arena now associated with shameful loss and regret—and brought it into the domain of international art. This was an achievement that could not only gain recognition for Japanese contemporary art in general but also elevate Shiraga's own marginal status as the son of a kimono merchant from the city of Amagasaki in the Kansai region, where industry and commercial products competed for space far from the artistic limelight of Tokyo. This geographic distance and cultural climate made it challenging for Kansai-area artists to garner critical acclaim. Achieving international attention could elevate both the national and the regional status of avant-garde art, but it would undoubtedly be an uphill battle that would demand a reconfiguration of artistic status.

Performing the Hero

Shiraga's compositions and his persona as an artist were fraught with concern over the role of the hero. A hero is defined by his bravery, his noble deeds, and his physical prowess as well as by his role in narrative. *Heroism* here refers to performative male posturing that expresses a sense of power through the stance and gesturing of the male body. Heroism is also tautological in nature: the status of the hero is articulated largely through the hero's role in an epic narrative that consolidates and builds on his acts of courage.[16] Certainly, to some degree, Shiraga sought admiration for his artistic ability and often positioned himself in the leading role in the story of his own work, yet he seemed simultaneously to find himself unworthy of the role. With art as his stage, he would often undertake a series of heroic tests for himself. Falk, who attended the 1957 *Gutai Art on the Stage* exhibition in Osaka, described Shiraga's work there:

> Kazuo Shiraga shoots arrows into a long white screen. Soon he is joined by four apprentices in black, all shooting arrows. Then Shiraga comes back for the kill, throwing red spears at the screen, closing in for the coup de grace. . . . Perhaps Kazuo Shiraga best illustrates what the Gutai artists are trying to achieve in creating new impressions through sight and sound. The curtain rises on a screen marked by vertical red lines. The slow beat of a temple drum is heard. With each beat one of the red lines, which turn out to be sticks, falls forward. The beat changes and sometimes two or three sticks knock each other down. Pretty soon one sees not red falling sticks but soldiers stumbling on a battlefield as the drum beat begins to sound like a cannonade.[17]

Falk did not fail to connect Shiraga's performative, explosive energies with the visual (and aural) language of the battle (Figure 4.2).

One of the most important of Shiraga's early forays into heroism and art occurred in 1955 at the *Manatsu no taiyou ni idomu yagai modan a-to jikkenten (Experimental Outdoor Exhibition of Modern Art to Challenge the Midsummer Sun,* sometimes referred to as the *First Gutai Outdoor Exhibition),* held in Ashiya, Hyōgo Prefecture, in 1955. Shiraga built a cone-like structure made of ten poles, each twenty-three feet tall and painted bright red, wedged into the sandy ground amid the shady pines. He stepped inside, bare-chested and wielding a six-pound ax (Figure 4.3).[18] Armed and exposed, Shiraga's body contrasted starkly with the quaint wooden structure and the politely worded invitation "Dōzo ohairi kudasai (please enter)," which was placed adjacent to the children's playground nearby. Shiraga stood inside his tepee-like abode and began to hack at the red columns with broad swings of his ax. With each hit, wood chipped away, leaving white scars etched into the poles, endangering both the artist and the handful of viewers nearby. Following this intervention, viewers were encouraged to enter the structure.

If the exterior of the installation was already quite unusual for a 1950s artwork, the interior of *Dōzo* (as the work came to be known) offered an entirely different experience to the viewer.[19] The carefully splayed-out wooden poles revealed a small circle of space in the center, from which the poles radiated in a manner similar to the rays of the rising sun. *Dōzo,* especially in one photograph taken by a Gutai member (Figure 4.4), can be seen to

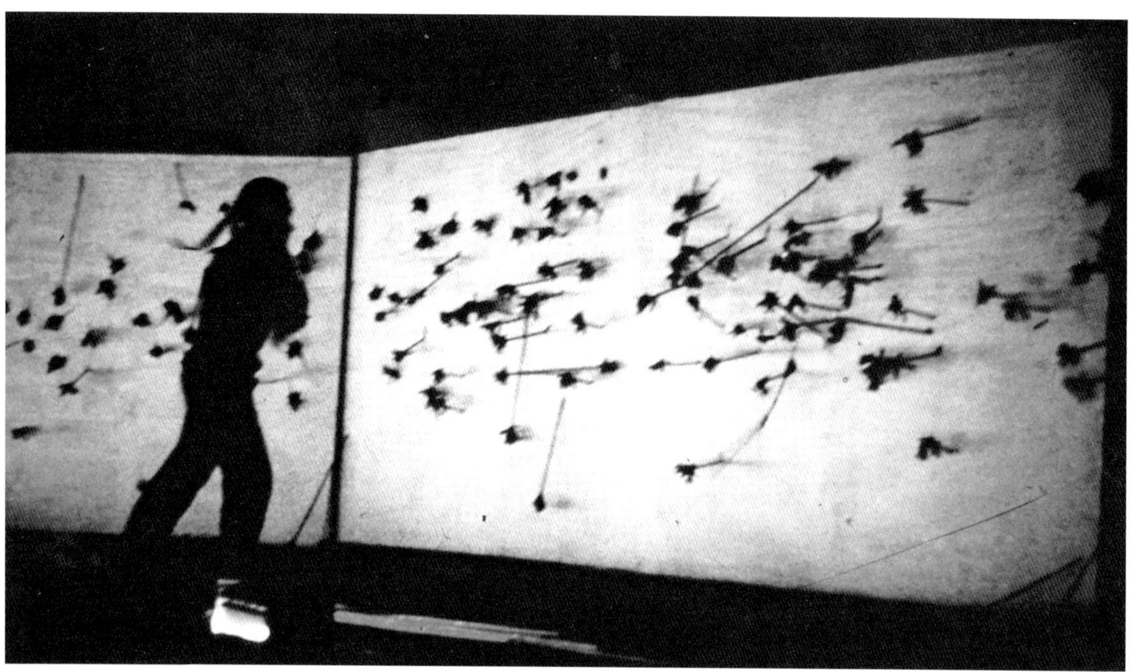

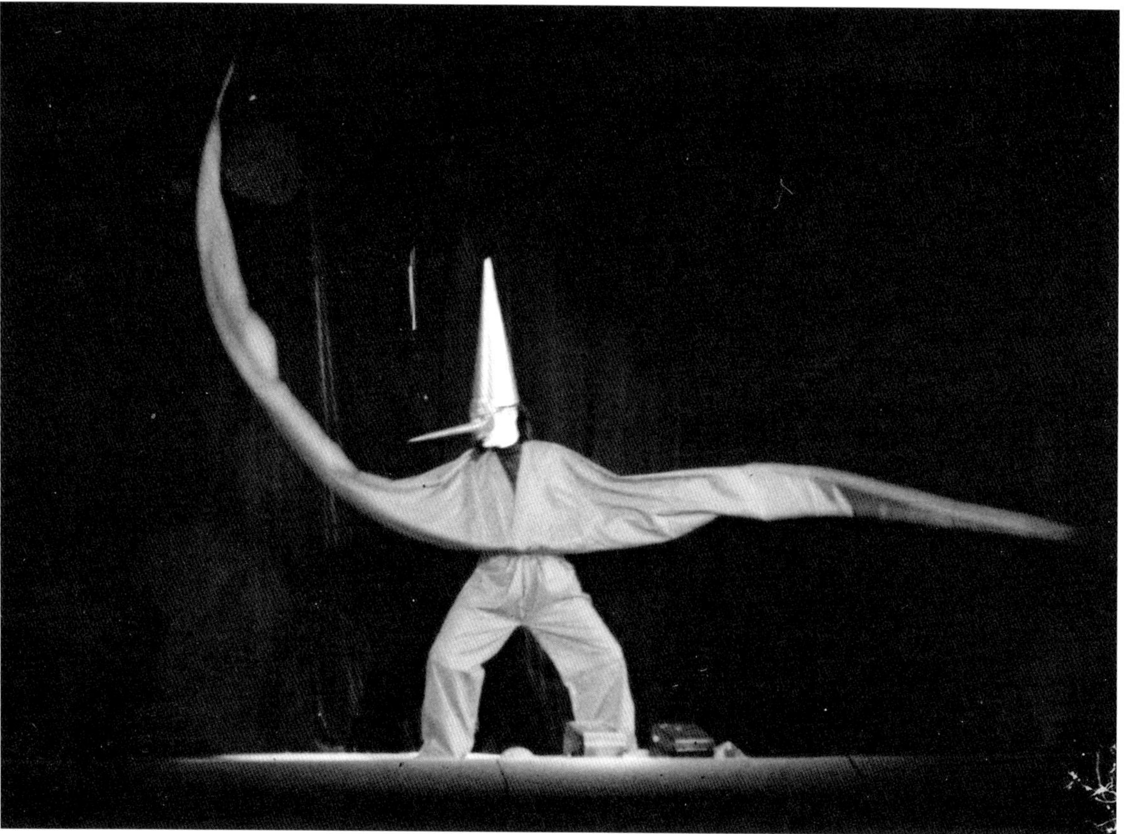

FIGURE 4.2. Shiraga Kazuo performs *Chō gendai sanban sō (Ultramodern Sanbasō)*, *Gutai Art on the Stage*, Sankei Kaikan Hall, Osaka, May 29, 1957. Copyright Shiraga Hisao. Courtesy of the Osaka City Museum of Modern Art.

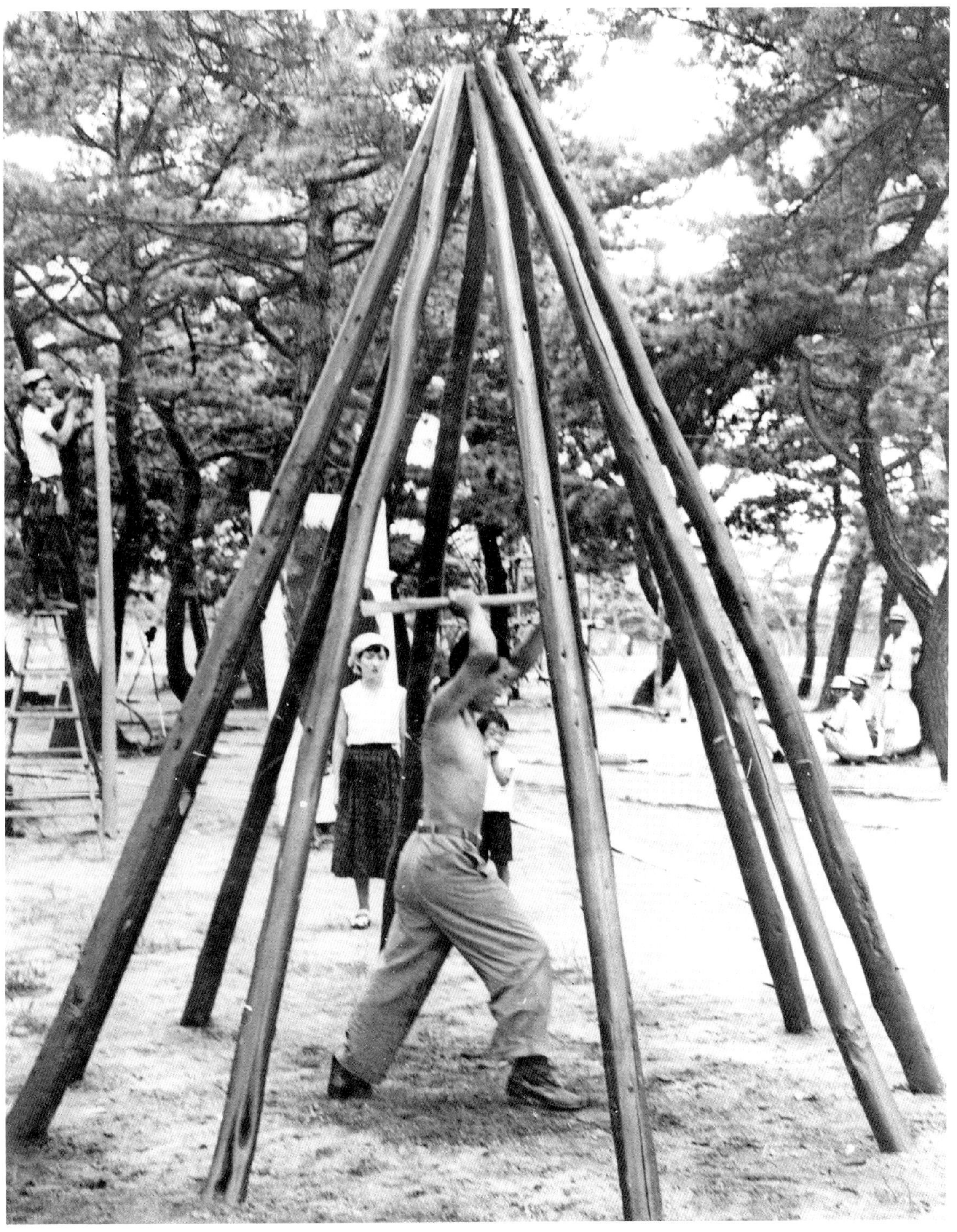

FIGURE 4.3. Shiraga Kazuo creates *Dōzo ohairi kudasai (Please Come In),* performance, 1955. Copyright Shiraga Hisao. Photograph courtesy of the Amagasaki Cultural Center.

recall the former imperial military flag of Japan, which was banned from use in 1945. The overlay of the poles with the rays of the sun created an encounter between reality and representation. From inside the piece, the bold red poles fractured the light of the sun, and in the right moment the effect may have led the viewer to feel that he or she was standing below a three-dimensional Japanese military flag. The position of the upward shot of the photograph in combination with the exhibition's provocative call to "challenge the sun" brings the relationship between the sun and the imperial flag into sharp relief.[20]

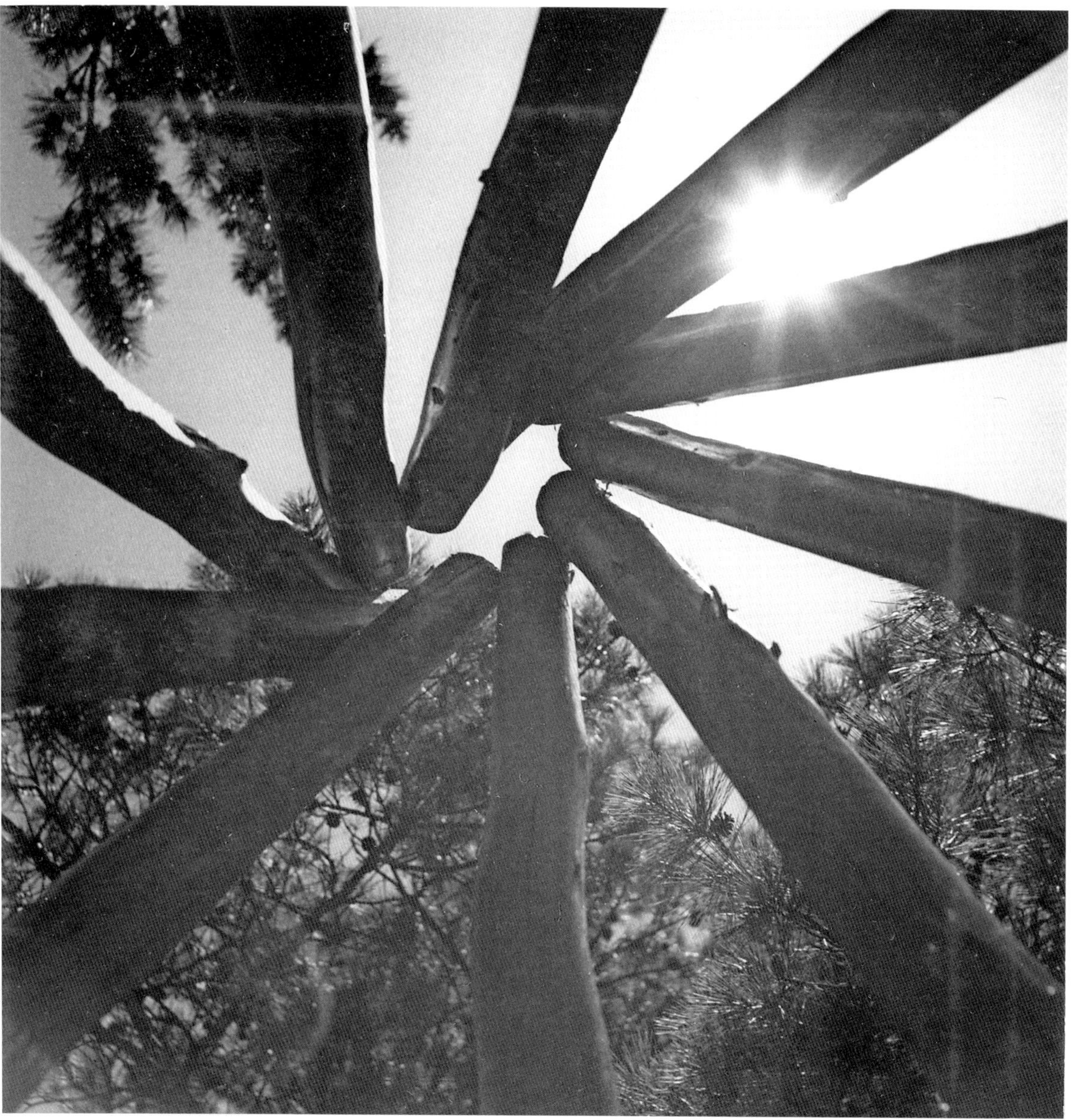

FIGURE 4.4. Shiraga Kazuo, *Dōzo ohairi kudasai (Please Come In)*, 1955 (interior view). Copyright Hisao Shiraga. Courtesy of Amagasaki Cultural Center.

Shiraga's investigations, particularly in the 1950s, seemed based on encrypted, destroyed, or reenvisioned nationalist visual motifs. Shiraga's oeuvre as well as his personal artistic development paralleled—and productively participated in—a period of intense reevaluation of the state.

Dōzo contained more than this discovered reference to the state's flag, for modernism in Japan already had deep symbolic ties to the sun. In 1910, Takamura Kōtarō wrote a manifesto titled "The Green Sun" that championed artistic freedom and the authority of the individual.[21] Alicia Volk observes, "The image of the sun was frequently invoked by a wide spectrum of late-Meiji intellectuals as a metaphor for the emancipated self and perhaps most conspicuously so in the field of art."[22] *Dōzo* brings the sun and the modern, artistic self together through the physical action of Shiraga as the manifestly male, aggressive, woodsman. Furthermore, in its examination of the imperial flag, the work accomplishes a double interrogation into the ambivalent significance of the relationship between the subject of the nation-state and male subjectivity.

Another of Shiraga's early performance works, *Doro ni idomu (Challenging Mud)*, likewise examines the nature of war, gender, and representation through its interpolation of body and material (Figure 4.5). *Challenging Mud* took place at the *First Gutai Art Exhibition* on a plaza outside Ohara Hall in Tokyo in October 1955. It was the Gutai group's debut in the nation's capital, and Shiraga chose to celebrate the occasion by depositing his messy one-ton pile (a rather literal metaphor for human waste that Shiraga was likely far from oblivious to) at the entrance of the exhibition site. *Challenging Mud* was engineered from a heaped mass of mixed, viscous gray materials—stone, cement, sand, gravel, clay, plaster, and twigs—intentionally worked into an extremely dense consistency to allow only a small degree of constrained movement. When Shiraga, dressed in a loincloth, heaved his body onto the mess, the detritus lacerated his skin. As he became dirtied by his own actions, the definition of his body against the medium was increasingly diminished. Shiraga's muck-covered torso seemed to bear a resemblance to his own memories of the mud-streaked bodies in Osaka during the war: "I just saw people covered with blood. I just saw war victims and Osaka burnt to the ground. A lot of people, totally smeared with blood, soot, and mud were coming to Osaka Castle for help."[23] By extension, the gray muck that surrounded him suggested the terrain of a battlefield or trench. Kanayama reported that Shiraga gave himself a close haircut, "just like a GI," before performing *Challenging Mud* for the first time.[24]

Challenging Mud and *Dōzo* were highly performative works that took gestural expression in new directions yet also questioned the parameters of the masculine subject in postwar Japan. During the 1950s, Japan's history as both victim and aggressor in World War II resurfaced in the struggle over the political and cultural forms the future nation might take. The small city of Ashiya, Shiraga's hometown and the site for the *Experimental Outdoor Exhibition,* had been gravely affected during World War II.[25] Half the city's residents had been injured or killed.[26] As a conscripted soldier attending to the wounded at Osaka

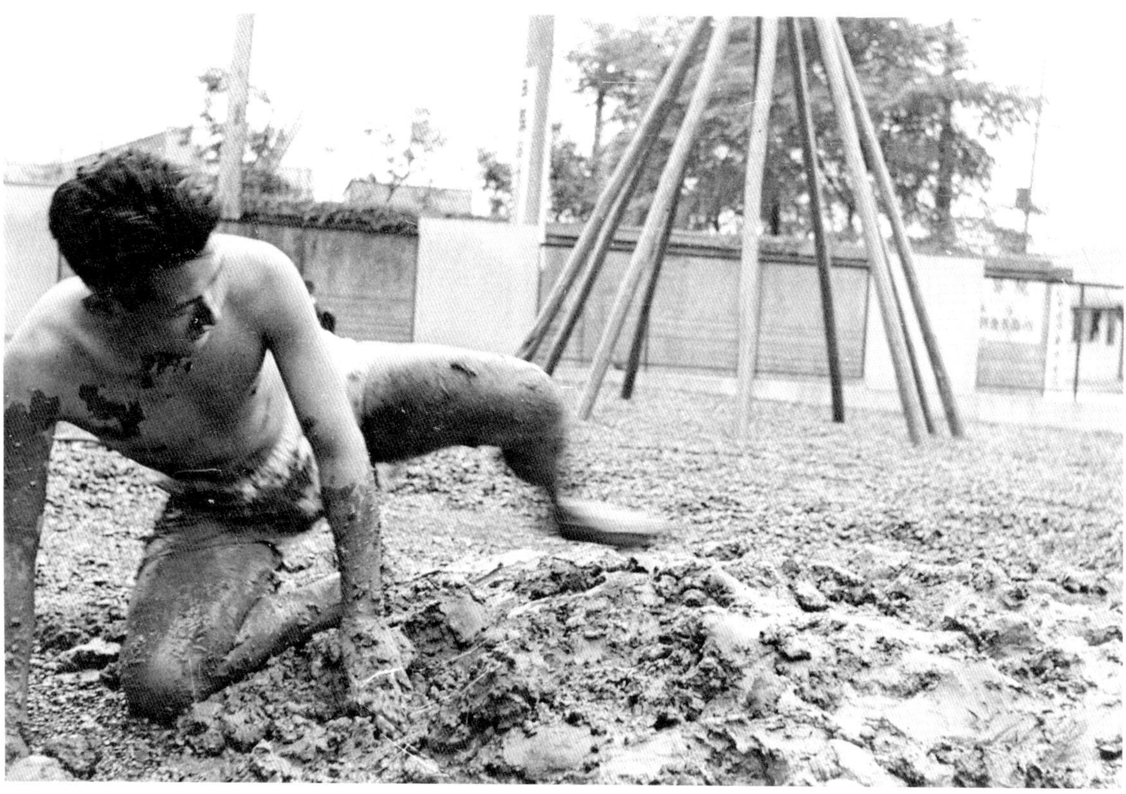

FIGURE 4.5. Shiraga Kazuo, *Doro ni idomu (Challenging Mud),* 1955. Mud, twigs, cement, rocks. Copyright Hisao Shiraga. Photograph courtesy of Amagasaki Cultural Center.

Castle, Shiraga had firsthand encounters with the aftermath of war, but he did not experience combat.[27] When Ming Tiampo first met Shiraga in 1998, he recognized her to be of Chinese descent and proceeded to open the conversation by explaining, without provocation, that he did not kill any Chinese during the war.[28] His comment indicates that the contextual backdrop of the war and the military remained prominent throughout his life. Shiraga could not have avoided the American (male) presence in Japan, as two of his early drawings, *Kōbe Sannomiya shinchūgun kyanpu (Occupation Forces Camp Sannomiya, Kobe)* (1947) and *Shinchū gun (Occupation Forces)* (1947) (Figure 4.6), reveal. In the latter, a soldier is sketched repeatedly sixteen or seventeen times, suggesting the artist's exploration of masculine posturing. The depicted solider stands erect, tall, and proud (this is most pronounced in the figure on the far right), but not without a gentlemanly elegance suggested in the delicate placement of the feet and the balance of the body. In the center of the lower row of sketches, the soldier is depicted in a jaunty, wide-legged stance, a model, in more ways than one, of American masculinity.

Kanayama and Shiraga, two childhood friends who grew to be longtime colleagues (and sometimes competitive peers) in Zero-kai and Gutai, make a productive comparison for the ways they sought to represent the opposing, mutually reliant, sides of the hero:

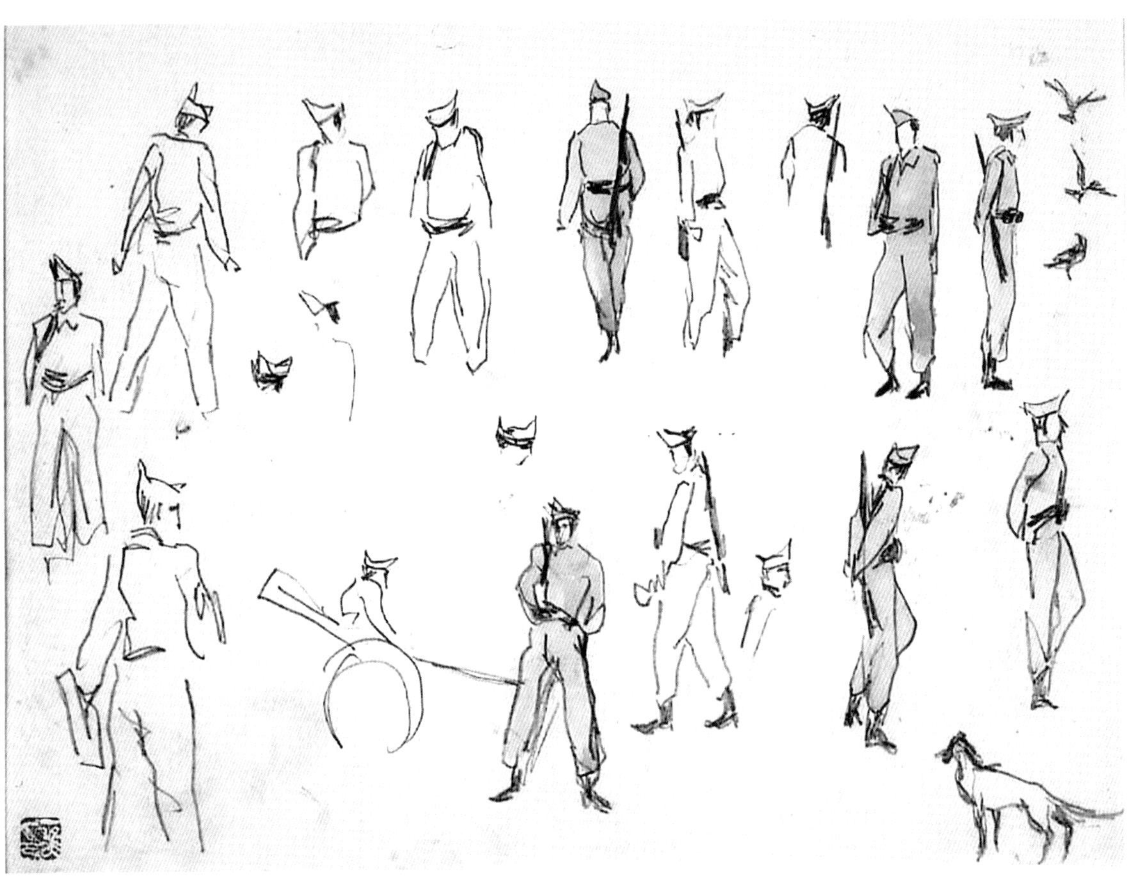

FIGURE 4.6. Shiraga Kazuo, *Shinchū gun (Occupation Forces),* 1947. Watercolor and pencil on paper, 26 × 35.5 cm. Copyright Hisao Shiraga. Courtesy of Amagasaki Cultural Center.

male bravado, dripping amid paint, versus the effete and emasculated youth who mockingly stares with disappointment at his own deflation.[29] A rarely discussed work from 1970, *Circle: Kanayama's Red Balloon* (filmed in 16 mm by Fukuzawa Hiroshi and performed by a friend of Fukuzawa) is three minutes and thirty-seven seconds of filmic impotence. The film, made in Nara at Sakurai-shi, opens with a young man in a red jumpsuit standing alone in an unidentified rural area, a sandy lot and tractor in the background. In the opening long shot, viewers might mistake the man for a child. He encourages the characterization, it seems, as he playfully fills an extremely long red balloon with air from two oxygen tanks. Once filled with air, the balloon forms a great border to the circular abandoned lot, and the young man proceeds to grab it by one end, making the two sides join together as he gleefully runs up the hill. This takes all of two seconds. Once at the top, the balloon deflates, and the jumpsuit-wearing figure pulls the wrinkly, deflated material back down the hill. *Circle* closes with a humorous still shot of the lone man, his childish head, with its bowl haircut, hanging down slightly as he stands motionless beside his deflated, pink, flaccid, material.

In 1970, as Kanayama worked on *Circle,* the Gutai Art Association (which Kanayama had left in 1965) was participating in the world's fair in Osaka, Expo '70. Taking part in Expo '70 was controversial, as many had criticized the fair for its complicity with the nationalist agenda of the Japanese government.[30] Gutai's participation caused further fractures in the group, contributing to its disbanding in 1972 following Yoshihara's death.[31] Kanayama's work, then, made in the same year as Expo '70, could be read as a critique of the pageantry of Osaka's big-budget art projects and their backing by corporate sponsors and committees intent on bolstering national status. *Circle,* an ironic, antiheroic artwork, deflates that hype.

Like Kanayama, Shiraga experimented with the trope of the masculine in works that had their own moments of hilarity and foiled machismo. For example, during one performance of *Challenging Mud* in 1955, his pants became so weighed down that they fell off.[32] Spontaneity, a value linked closely to heroic action art, also sometimes proved to be difficult to achieve. Yoshihara describes Shiraga working for several days on the consistency of the mud for *Challenging Mud,* despite the fact that the piece was meant to be evocative of his spontaneous interaction with the material.[33] Similarly, for a photo shoot for *Life* magazine in April 1956, Shiraga completed a foot painting three times over to perfect it and exhausted himself in the process.[34] By his own record, Shiraga botched his hunting adventures and eventually left his monk's training at Mount Hiei, which he began in 1971, a subject I will return to momentarily.[35] Even the painting *Inoshishi gari I (Wild Boar Hunting I)* was inexplicably unsatisfactory in the artist's eyes, and he described it as unsuccessful.[36] Thus, Shiraga's visual narratives did not always declare man triumphant. His postures of performance were multiple: fallen soldier, failed hunter, strapping woodsman, and action painter. The performances were not a simple means to enact the possession of power; rather, they were test cases that left open the opportunity for attainment or defeat, suggesting how the artist can become trapped in a repeated and "doomed effort to get it right."[37] In his writings, Shiraga often earnestly described his art in terms of achievement or failure. For example, writing in 1955 for the newsletter *Gutai,* he said:

> I didn't understand the meaning of *Dōzo* when making it at the time. But the work filled my heart. The ax represented the burning strength of my passions. Still I was not satisfied and felt that I had not achieved anything. My action was too weak.[38]

For Shiraga, individual passion was not sufficient; heroic strength was the path to artistic victory.

Reinscribing the Heroes of *The Water Margin*

Shiraga's interest in the heroic may have emerged most clearly in the 1960s with the titling of his artworks.[39] He titled 106 of his abstract paintings after some of the 108 heroes in the classic Chinese novel *The Water Margin* (Japanese translation circa 1757), using the Japanese versions of the Chinese names, such as *Ten'isei Sekihatsuki (Red-Haired Devil)* (Plate 28), titled for the character named Liu Tang in Chinese. Another character from the story, Koyasuyoshi (Li Kui in Chinese; Black Whirlwind in English), who carried an ax in each hand, inspired Shiraga to use an ax in *Dōzo*.[40] Curator and Gutai scholar Hirai Shōichi attributes Shiraga's interest in *The Water Margin* to exposure to the text at school.[41] This straightforward explanation leaves unaddressed the question of why this particular text had such a strong influence. What else might account for the enduring appeal of this legendary narrative and its significance for Shiraga?

The Water Margin is a vernacular novel dating to the fourteenth century.[42] It is remarkable for the degree of violence it depicts. Heroism has little to do with whether the characters fight for good or evil; rather, it is a trait acquired through aggressive acts. The novel was first translated into Japanese from Chinese at the beginning of the eighteenth century, and its popularity in Japan has yet to ebb.[43] Remakes of the story abound: in Japan alone, filmic versions number around fifty. A popular television series that began in 1977 was based on it, as have been numerous animated features, manga, and video games.[44] Artists have been drawn to the story repeatedly over time, many creating vivid portrayals of the characters and capitalizing on the serial structure of the narrative and the opportunity to represent the dynamism of the 108 heroes. The continual reenvisioning of *The Water Margin* attests both to the desire to tell and witness heroic tales and to the sometimes urgently transformative power of the imagination that can shift a compelling narrative from one geographic context to another (in this case, from China to Japan) or into new forms of media.

Like the heroic status of the characters in *The Water Margin,* Shiraga's art relies on violence to achieve its full salience. His abstract paintings are not allegorical, nor do they figurally represent the characters or development of the story. *Red-Haired Devil* lacks any veristic quality and is an eruption of thickly textured color. A large streak seeming to move from the bottom left corner to the top right is suggestive of forceful movement. More than a gesture, the span of the painterly line exceeds normal arm's length. Thinner pressure points with larger streaks recall the toes of a sweeping leg, pulled along by momentum. These indexical traces of Shiraga's body reinforce a sense of speed, and with it the alluring, albeit constructed, impression of spontaneity.

Red-Haired Devil was painted in Shiraga's color of choice: crimson lake. In an interview, Shiraga stated: "The reason I liked it [the color] was that it somehow seemed to reek of blood. . . . I also liked the fact that it was the most transparent paint and that it straddled both dye and pigment."[45] He used crimson lake almost exclusively throughout the 1950s, beginning with his 1953 painting *Aka no sanban (Red III),* and it was prominent in his performance works as well as his paintings. For example, when *Dōzo* was displayed as an installation, it was referred to simply as *Red Logs.* For a 1957 performance of *Chō gendai sanban sō (Ultramodern Sanbasō)* for the exhibition *Gutai Art on the Stage* (for which Shiraga received top billing), he dressed in a costume that was entirely red while other performers shot arrows at a white canvas (see Figure 4.2).[46] The elongated arms of his costume allowed him to use 'human gestures to paint a red picture" on the white background.[47] Although he later reintroduced a wider palette into his work, red persistently recurred—a characteristic Shiraga shared with the artist Nakamura Hiroshi. Despite the literary origins of the title, *Red-Haired Devil* is abstract and seems ironically beyond words; for example, figures are entirely absent from the painted field, as are linear perspective and sense of depth. Sharp variations in the crimson field create a division between the left side, where rich applications of burgundy are mottled into scabby layers, and the right side, where light strains of red give an impression of an evenly applied underlayer before the circular sweeps of color were painted over top. The explosive splashes of red in the right top and bottom corners are reminiscent of blood splattering and evocative of violence.

Bert Winther-Tamaki, describing the demise of the *yōga* movement in the 1950s, points out that Shiraga

> demonstrated how dispensing with the representation of the human figure permitted an extraordinary magnification of the *matière* to great swaths of thick, oozing oil paint. . . . Thus, Shiraga's abstraction elevated the idea of the contact between the artist's body and the paint vividly into focus as the content of the work. In effect, such works renounced one aim of Yōga embodiment, the depiction of the human body, in order to fulfill two of its other aims more dramatically, namely, articulating the oil-on-canvas *matière* and endowing it with a strong somatic sense of the artist's presence.[48]

He continues: "Even in its decrepitude and obsolescence, the Yōga painting remained a body, though now an ancestor, whose blood relation could not be denied. Yōga may have been eviscerated by the violent phase of its wartime and postwar disembodiment, but its passionate attempt to give body to Japanese people's sense of Self as well as the surging impulses of disembodiment that it fostered were surely epochal passages of Japanese modernity."[49] Thus, paintings such as *Red-Haired Devil* could be seen both to disavow and to reinforce their dependence on American abstract expressionism through a nominal allegiance with an Asian past that is simultaneously represented and occluded through the violence inherent in the bodily manifestation of the composition.[50]

Shiraga's work is in dialogue with a long line of depictions of warriors. The genre of *musha-e,* or paintings and prints of warriors, emerged around 1660. In 1805, a new Japanese translation of *The Water Margin* was released; titled *New Illustrated Edition of the Suikoden,* it featured prints by Katsushika Hokusai. Hokusai's series seems to revel in violence (Figure 4.7). Toward the end of the book, the artist collapses negative space, and the image becomes a circular amalgam of bodies and weapons (Figure 4.8). In each of Hokusai's final illustrations, a strong sense of motion is emphasized through the curvature of the heroes' limbs as they grip their weapons tightly.[51]

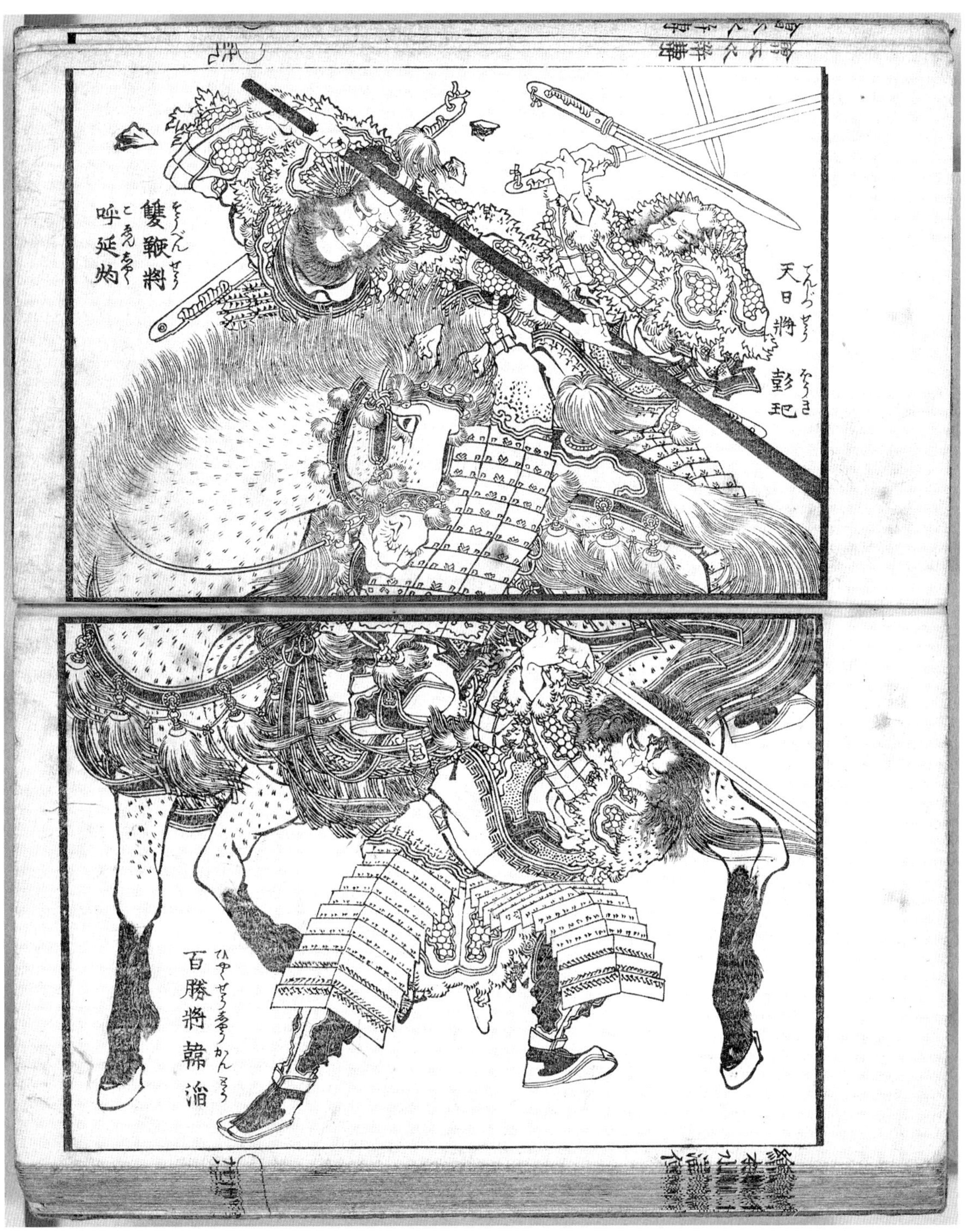

FIGURE 4.7. Katsushika Hokusai, *Suikoden yūshi no ezukushi (The Illustrated Water Margin)*, 1829, pages 28b–29a. Ink on paper. Courtesy of the C. V. Starr East Asian Library, University of California, Berkeley.

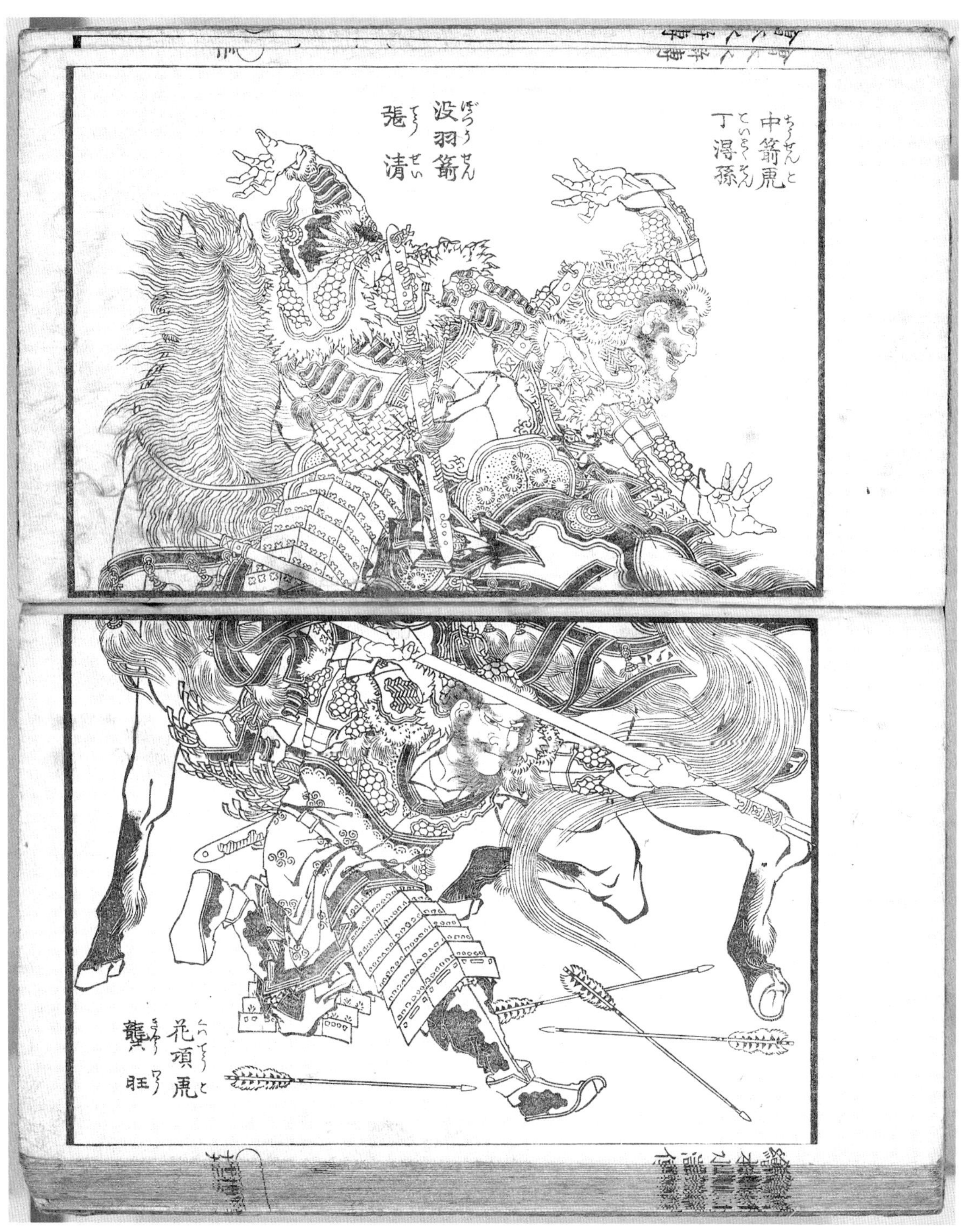

FIGURE 4.8. Katsushika Hokusai, *Suikoden yūshi no ezukushi (The Illustrated Water Margin)*, 1829, pages 29b–30a. Courtesy of the C. V. Starr East Asian Library, University of California, Berkeley.

Shiraga's foot paintings, though nonfigural, are similarly awash in the representation of circular but chaotic movement. The artist was interested in Hokusai and collected his prints along with the works of other Meiji-period print artists.[52] He also collected Japanese swords and cowboy hats, prioritizing masculine accoutrements over the "decorative" Japanese arts of lacquer, pottery, and *bijin-ga* (images of beautiful women), which gained popularity in twentieth-century histories of art.[53] It seems that Shiraga was cognizant of the parallels to be drawn between warrior-hero and artist-hero, and he took special notice of the treatment of masculine subjects in the history of Japanese art, rather than (as some critics suggested) simply seeking to mimic forms of American art.[54] Unlike the Hokusai series, Shiraga's paintings are neither illustrative nor figural. Although they refer to warriors, they do not definitively fall into the category of *musha-e,* yet they build on this tradition and its association with masculine power. Beyond the names, the paintings bear no obvious relationship to the story of *The Water Margin* at all; this is because Shiraga's aim is not to narrate a story but to situate himself within it, playing the protagonist.

The question arises as to why Shiraga did not make any overt references to Taishō-era (1912–26) or Shōwa-era (1926–89) models of heroism, embodied by *yōga* artists such as Yorozu Tetsugorō, a leading figure in the modernist movement in the late Meiji and early Taishō periods. Certainly both artists shared a preoccupation with freedom that was ultimately personal rather than directly political, both prioritized self-discovery over beauty, and both were faced with overcoming the challenge that new forms of Western art seemed to pose for them (in Yorozu's case, French paintings of the nude; for Shiraga, the works of Jackson Pollock and other abstract expressionists).[55] Ironically, these similarities between the two may explain why Yorozu would not be an ideal artist for Shiraga to emulate, as emphasizing commonalities with another artist would not support his quest for originality and newness. Further, at least in the eyes of critics, Yorozu was never able to escape the hegemony of Western painting. Volk writes: "The new artist (and in the context of Taishō Japan, the artist was nearly always a 'he') was a hero, but a tragic one."[56] For Shiraga, reinventing a past tragic artist would not do; in short, unlike Hokusai, Yorozu was on the wrong side of *Japonisme.* As Winther-Tamaki has shown, *yōga* also became increasingly associated with the "colonial status of past Japanese imitations of European culture" at best and with the fraught history of *sensō-ga* (wartime paintings) at worst; consequently, for Shiraga and most other artists at the time, turning to Taishō models of art was not viable.

Murayama Tomoyoshi of Mavo is another heroic artist whose work might have interested Shiraga, particularly given Murayama's exploration of individuality.[57] Yet Shiraga did not share Murayama's interest in revolutionary political change and anarchism, and the underground status of the Mavo movement (and the fact that its base was in Tokyo) may have meant that Shiraga was unfamiliar with Murayama's work. More important, Shiraga's engagements with the trope of the hero were not a personal commitment to political revolution. Although at times a political activist may be heroic, all heroes are not necessarily revolutionary. In fact, in narrative epics and folktales the hero more often functions to restore collective political order. The hero's exploits may be rebellious and unexpected, his abilities outside the norm, but in his actions he ultimately strives to protect the status quo rather than to awaken political change through anarchy, as Mavo sought to do. Murayama was largely responsible for the twentieth-century popularizations of the rebellious outsider figure of the ninja, emanating from his historical fiction, *Shinobi no mono,* featured in the popular late 1950s manga by Shirato Sanpei (whose father, Okamoto Toki, was a close friend of Murayama).[58] On the other hand, Shiraga's unprecedented actions ultimately sought to reaffirm a stable position for the Gutai Art Association on the international stage, as opposed to embracing anarchism or directing a comprehensive critique of the political system.

Shiraga's interest in artists from the Edo period prefigures the work of contemporary artists like Tenmyouya Hisashi (born 1966), whose depictions of samurai soccer players align with a nebulous sense of "traditional" Japan that authenticates his own position as a distinctively Japanese modern artist. For these artists, the Edo period is positioned far enough in the past that referencing its art does not run the risk of mimicry. As Marc Steinberg has suggested, the Edo period has been constructed "as the lost-but-not forgotten authentic Japan, the 'pre'-western outside modernity. It was also, conversely, the precursor and reflection of Japan's consumerist, postmodern present."[59] In producing a version of gestural abstract painting while "reinscribing" older Japanese themes, Shiraga negotiates the dual demands of the nation and the modern.[60] His work asks: What does it take for a Japanese artist to be modern, to be heroic?

Enacting Swordplay

Photographs taken around 1957 show Shiraga playing up his male bravado with fellow Gutai members Yoshida Minoru and Motonaga Sadamasa (Figure 4.9).[61] The images provide a rare glimpse into the ways that art and performance could mutually inform masculine subjectivity and gender relations. Rather than housing official documents of Gutai's activities, the Yoshida archives consist of snapshots of Yoshida Minoru's family members, picnics, and leisure time spent with friends, many of whom were members of the Gutai group.[62] According to Hirai Shōichi, Shiraga maintained a large collection of old cameras and was seemingly well aware of the ways photographs could dramatically alter the reception of a work.[63] Yoshida and Shiraga strike different poses in each shot, making stabbing gestures and ironically taking up martial stances. In each of the images, Shiraga's body is exposed: he is bare-chested, a pair of trousers buckled about his trim waist. Yoshida's vestments are similarly minimal. He stands somewhat stooped, his shallow chest shrunken in laughter, his face darkened by the shadow of Shiraga's upright sword. They stand with frozen grimaces, swords crossed, facing outward in an ironic and affected stance of brotherhood, an image that recalls the "gallant fraternity" of the outlaws of *The Water Margin*.[64] Shiraga's untitled work from 1956 creates a backdrop for the photo shoot, the interweave of color patterns set against the shadows of the photograph, reinforcing the correspondence between Shiraga's art and his social diversions.

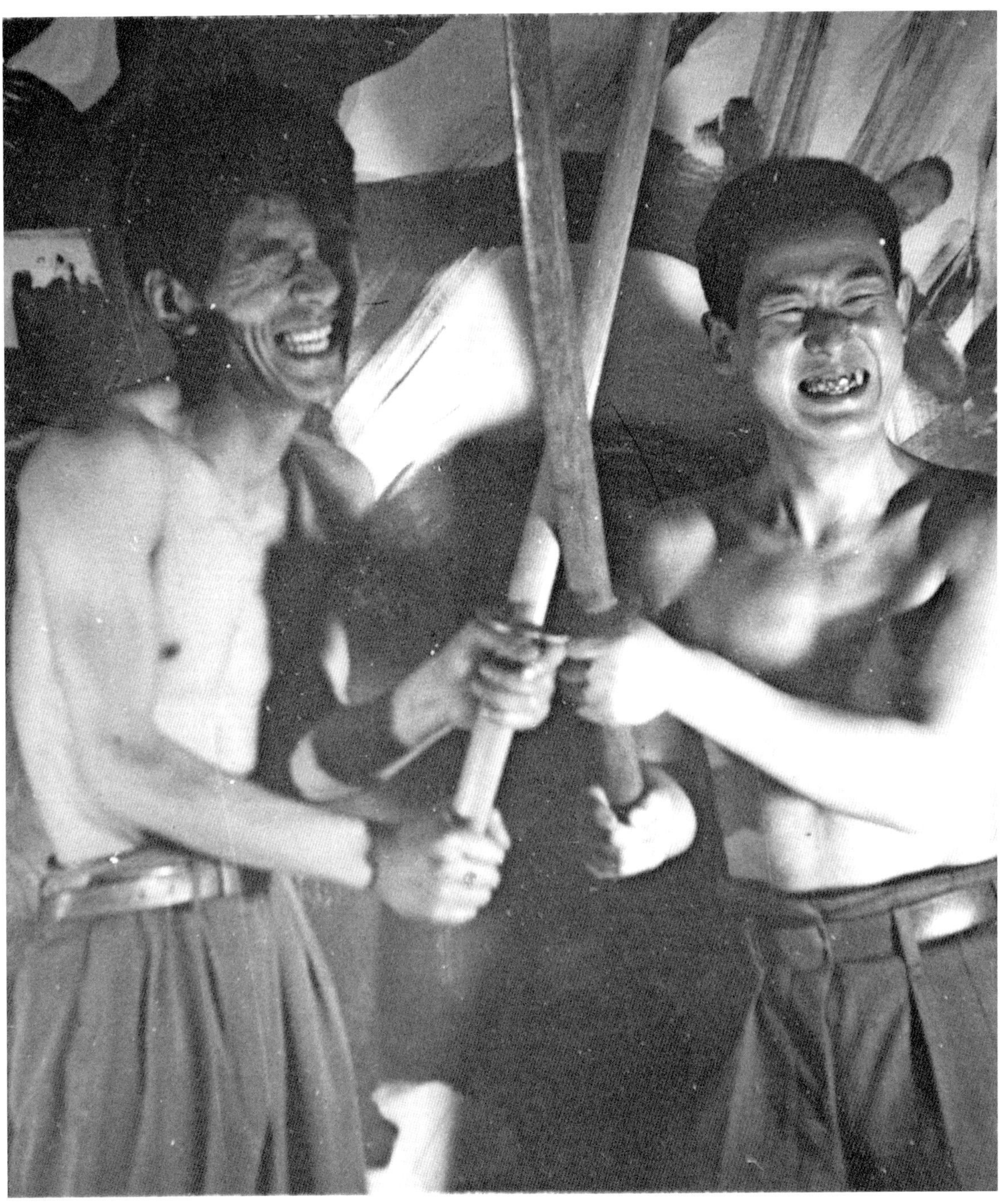

FIGURE 4.9. Shiraga Kazuo and Yoshida Minoru, circa 1957. Courtesy of the Osaka City Museum of Modern Art.

An irrefutable but also subverted masculinity is evident in the physical presence of the bare-chested figures (underwritten by the thinness of their frames) as well as in their combative, pseudosamurai poses and the phallic presence of the swords. In one photograph Shiraga holds the wooden sword directly at his groin, the long stick angled suggestively upward (Figure 4.10). Mockingly juvenile in his stance, Shiraga accentuates the ribald connotations of his phallic bodily extension. His self-conscious exercise of masculinity both on and off the stage suggests a playful testing of gender stereotypes, especially as his emphasis on heroics frequently includes their downfall. For example, the photograph of Shiraga's phallic pose is pasted in an album adjacent to an image in which his empty-handed wife, Fujiko, dressed in a skirt and buttoned cardigan, hair pulled neatly back, disarms him of his symbolic sexual power with a single swift gesture (Figure 4.11).[65] The photograph captures the sword midfall, and the scene is enhanced by Shiraga's wounded warrior expression. It seems the heroic struggle, as artifice, as performance, or as embodied truth, was never far from his daily pursuits even as he encountered and enacted failures.

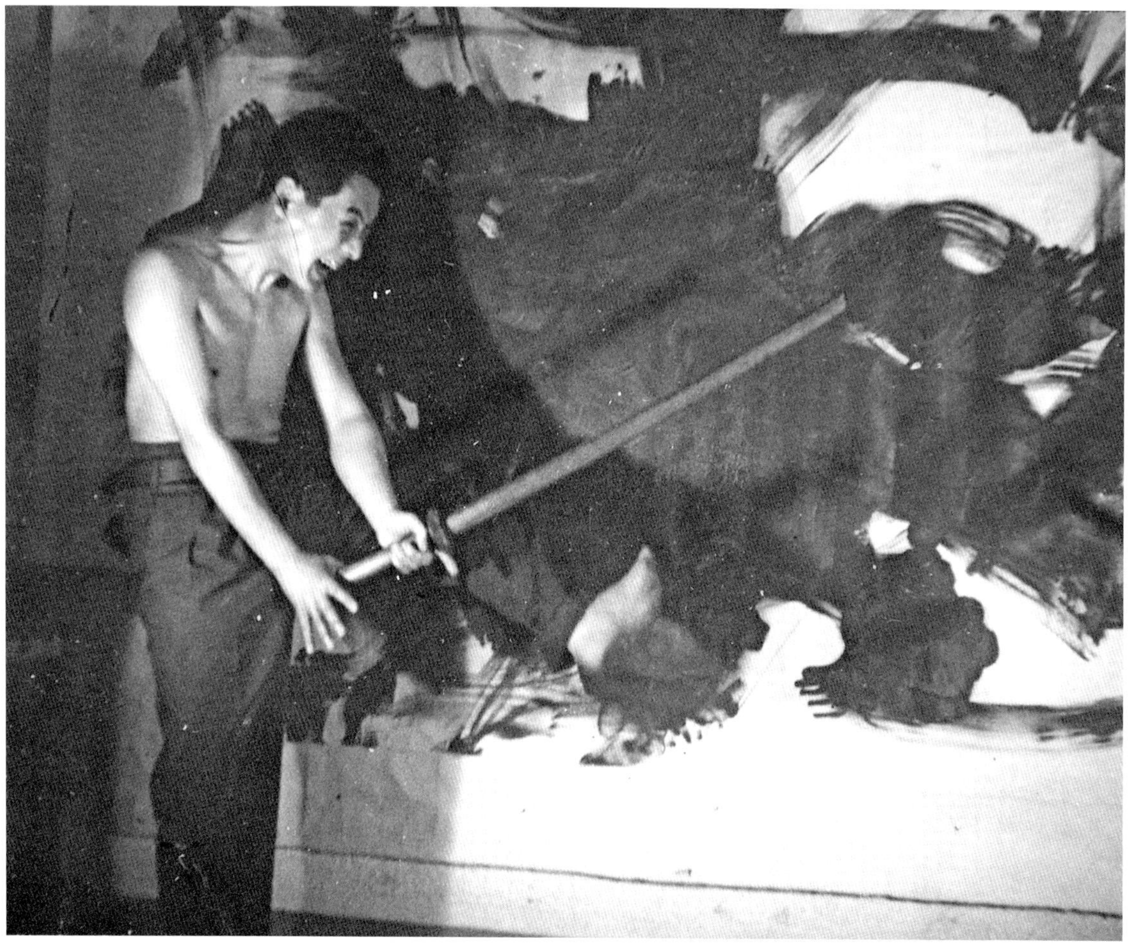

FIGURE 4.10. Shiraga Kazuo, circa 1957. Courtesy of the Osaka City Museum of Modern Art.

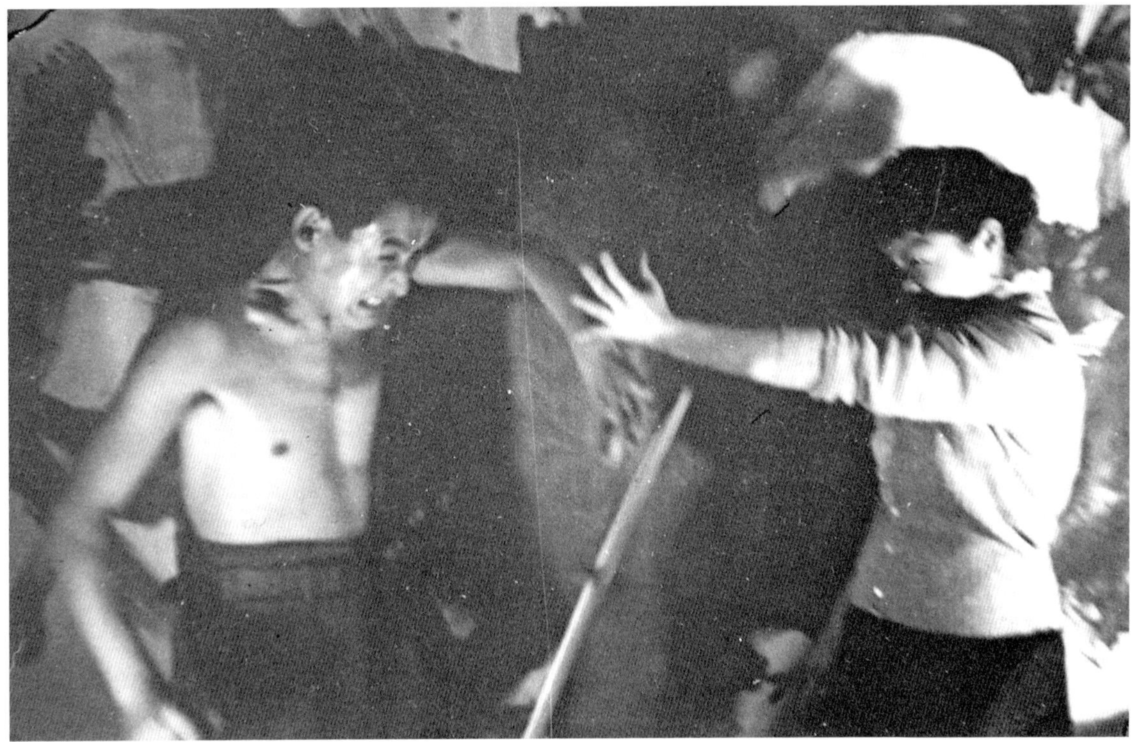

FIGURE 4.11. Shiraga Fujiko and Shiraga Kazuo, circa 1957. Courtesy of the Osaka City Museum of Modern Art.

Whereas I view Shiraga's physical engagement with his material as self-conscious and exploratory, other scholars have tended to naturalize his masculinity or suggest that it springs from a well of Japanese traditional practice.[66] Some have described his art as the expression of sheer spontaneous aggression. For example, the Gutai member Ukita Yōzō described Shiraga as motivated to "express instinctive destruction."[67] A second look at film footage and documentary photographs suggests that his movements were premeditated and graceful, despite their inherent violence.[68] In a 1955 *Mainichi Hōso* newsreel that captures less than a minute of *Challenging Mud,* Shiraga moves his limbs in a conscious, careful, but nonetheless forceful manner.[69] Complicating the temptation to understand Shiraga's works as essentialized exteriorizations of his individualized, masculine self, as a whole these works ask complex questions about the position of the modern male subject in postwar Japan and its definition through violent modes of representation.

Writings on Selfhood and Violence

In his essays "Action Itself" (1955), "Thoughts" (1955), "On Temperament" (1956), "The Importance of Sensitivity" (1956), and "Establishment of the Individual" (1956), Shiraga describes the self as composed of different and often opposing elements.[70] For example, he contrasts the rational mind with the forces of the body, privileging the physical as the source of creativity. In part, this fixation on the body is not isolated from the current of thought that fetishized "the concrete" in the 1950s. Shiraga understood the concrete—an abstract and unstable concept—to be irreducible and bound with identity. As artists began distancing themselves from the slippery rhetoric of wartime propaganda, many grew increasingly fond of the notion that higher artistic truths lay in the absolutes of materiality and corporeality.[71] Of course, this is a trend in which Gutai played no small part. After all, *gutai* means "concreteness" or "embodiment"; this was a term, according to the Gutai manifesto, that would bring the group "beyond the borders of abstract expressionism."[72]

Certainly the Gutai group members were aware of American and European gestural abstract art, and their declaration to go beyond those borders reveals their concern with international competition. The third *Yomiuri Indépendant* exhibition, held in Tokyo in 1951, showcased artists such as Jackson Pollock, Mark Rothko, and Jean Dubuffet and was highly influential for the development of abstract expressionism in Japan. It should be noted that much of the debate about the future of art circulated around Tokyo artists and critics, whereas the Gutai group was based in the Kansai region. An exhibition of French painting that traveled to Japan in 1951, presented by the Salon de Mai, was so eye-opening for Japanese artists that Japanese art historians have since come to refer to the event as the postwar "shock." Reflecting on this moment five years later, art critic Hariu Ichirō noted, "When the Salon de mai came to Japan in 1951, we were spellbound by works of the middle generation of French artists who had experienced the Second World War. After the initial shock had passed, many of us felt that the work in the salon was coloured by moralistic and eclectic attitudes and we could also see how much we had been starved of modern art by the fact that we had been so impressed by such works."[73] Japanese artists realized they would have difficulty proving their sophistication without running the risk of being labeled derivative. Shiraga's unique style of action art predated the so-called shock; his first foot paintings were done before he joined Gutai, as early as 1952, and he began his abstract work as early as 1946. This is not to suggest that he was not influenced by exposure to European and American gestural abstract art, however. As noted above, in reflecting back on the *Yomiuri Indépendant* exhibition of 1951, he commented, "I do remember that the paintings from America as a whole looked very fresh."[74] Shiraga's anxious awareness of the ever-advancing international art scene and the need for Japanese art to reinvigorate itself was already propelling him to search for answers about the future of his own artistic status immediately following the end of the Allied Occupation. But of course even this unequal transnational discourse was a two-way street. American artists in the 1950s and 1960s also seem to have found Shiraga's work to be inspirational and provocative. In 1958, Michael McClure wrote a long statement in his personal notebooks regarding his dreams about *Challenging Mud,* despite never having seen it performed (however, copies of *Gutai* with photos of the performance work were circulating at the time). He understood the work to be mythical and primitivistic, perhaps as reflective of Japan as a naive, newly born nation that needed civilizing (a concept General MacArthur did much to promote).[75] Shiraga's momentum toward new styles of art making likely motivated Yoshihara Jirō to invite the artist and several other members of Zero-kai to join the Gutai Art Association in 1954.

To underscore the unique character of Gutai art, Yoshihara outlined a position on the materiality of the body in the group's 1956 manifesto:

> Gutai art does not change the material but brings it to life. Gutai art does not falsify the material. In Gutai art the human spirit and the material reach out their hands to each other, even though they are otherwise opposed to each other. The material is not absorbed by the spirit. The spirit does not force the material into submission. If one leaves the material as it is, presenting it just as material, then it starts to tell us something and speaks with a mighty voice. Keeping the life of the material alive also means bringing the spirit alive, and lifting up the spirit means leading the material up to the height of the spirit.[76]

What exactly did "spirit" and "originality" mean to Gutai, Yoshihara, or Shiraga? The two concepts were often seen as being in a mutually constitutive relationship, with the spirit understood to be an elevated and naturalized essence key to unlocking originality. Originality, according to the manifesto as well as Shiraga, was tied to rejection of, or marked separation from, the past. With the disabuse of imperial propaganda and the feeling that Western art had surged ahead of Japan, art had to negotiate multiple demands. In an interview, Shiraga stated:

> Assuming that everything from Cezanne to the Cubists and Mondrian is an example of cool abstraction, then it must be someone's destiny to take it in an even cooler direction. To me, it seems like Van Gogh's passionate direction provided the German Expressionists with things by way of Fauvism. By that time, we had arrived at Abstract Expressionism, and I set out to move even farther beyond that. I simply came up with the theory that actions could be used to pursue a certain direction and also to give me strength.[77]

Both art makers and art viewers felt compelled to move into something new—but who could claim authorship over such untrodden territory was open to debate. Shiraga saw bodily strength as the path to originality.

Shiraga described differences of opinion with Yoshihara and intimated that he did not fit in well with the goals of the Gutai group.[78] However, it seems that Yoshihara felt that Shiraga's work was apposite, since the single-page printing of the manifesto included a photograph of Shiraga painting with his feet.[79] Shiraga's ambivalent feelings about his relationship to the manifesto may demonstrate that his own artistic status was undergoing reevaluation. Both the manifesto and Shiraga's texts disparage those who allow the theoretical ideas of other people to impinge on their creative processes of self-development. Although they never explicitly articulate it, both Yoshihara and Shiraga address an underlying anxiety about the influence of other artists and present an agenda that seeks out and then guards (at times through semantic sidestepping) a self-defined notion of authenticity. Yoshihara argues in favor of a "centrifugal approach" in the manifesto, and Shiraga emphasizes the importance of staying true to one's own aesthetic sensibilities.[80] Yoshihara pays individual attention to Shiraga's methods in the manifesto, suggesting Shiraga's cohesiveness with the group. Moreover, he uses a description of Shiraga to bolster his argument for the unique approach and production of Gutai:

> Kazuo Shiraga placed a lump of paint on a huge piece of paper, and started to spread it around violently with his feet. For about the last two years art journalists have called this unprecedented method "the Art of committing the whole self with the body." Kazuo Shiraga had no intention at all of making this strange method known to the public. He had merely found the method which enabled him to confront and unite the material he had chosen with his own spiritual dynamics. In doing so he achieved an extremely convincing result.[81]

Other Gutai members invoked a similarly belligerent attitude toward the field of painting, with Murakami Saburō (born 1925) coming closest to Shiraga's aggressive methods. The two shared a common body-centered approach, which was not surprising given that they had worked together since 1952 as members of Zero-kai.[82] In 1955, Murakami performed an untitled work that has come to be known as *Breaking through Paper,* in which he punched through six canvases as a performance piece for *Gutai Art on the Stage.* Forcing himself through the thick canvases took a toll, and later Murakami remarked, "After making the sixth hole I was overcome with exhaustion."[83] The same newsreel mentioned above includes footage of men inside Murakami's paper box, staring through the holes that his body has torn through with expressions of seeming satisfaction.[84] Yet Murakami's interest in violence was comparatively short-lived, and the remainder of his oeuvre was much more reserved in nature, such as his *objet* series of unmanipulated wooden boxes.[85]

While Yoshihara described the freedom of each group member to create and seemed to present a cavalier attitude in his description of the "spirit" in the Gutai manifesto, in fact he acted as unequivocal judge and jury of the younger Gutai members' work. Although Shiraga's art shares terrain with the art of some other members of the Gutai group, and in some sense his work does express an interest in concrete materiality as articulated in the manifesto, Shiraga went beyond "shaking hands with the material," and in some works he brought out a sense of vulgarity to which Yoshihara was opposed.[86] Tanaka's and Kanayama's art (described in chapter 3), on the other hand, was much more conceptual, revealing the limitations of the manifesto and the diversity of production in the Gutai Art Association, which included more than fifty-nine members during the eighteen years it was active.

Shiraga's discourse frequently went further than the manifesto's refusal of fakery and articulated a valuation on violence and force. In "Thoughts," the artist argued that painting is like a battlefield that he must face "as a warrior would." He went on to describe eschewing the easel because he preferred to "take an ax to his canvas" until he was sweating and his heart was racing.[87] True enough, Yoshihara affirmed that Shiraga bought a "magnificent axe" to perform *Dōzo*, which he polished daily.[88] The overwrought metaphors continued in "Action Itself," as Shiraga wrote that he hoped to digest his heart "like a monster with a big stomach."[89] Shiraga relied on linguistic turns that echo the models of heroic violence to which he laid claim in his paintings. The alignment between painting production and corporeality is furthered in his accounts of art making: he compared the strokes of his arm with patting or scratching his own body.[90]

The fourth issue of the *Gutai* newsletter included an essay by Shiraga titled "Establishment of the Individual," wherein he proposed that the making of art, particularly action-based art, is a means to differentiate oneself from a group.[91] Shiraga recoiled from an alliance with a common Gutai aesthetic in many of his interviews, insisting on his contrariness. Violence is also a means by which to establish difference: it segments and ruptures wholeness. Shiraga's aggression was the most consistent manner in which this difference was articulated, especially pronounced in his use of weapons such as the ax, the knife, the gun, and the bow and arrow, tools that were never taken up by any other members of the group.[92]

That Shiraga wrote about his thinking on the subject of violence while exploring it physically further troubles the notion that he was giving unmediated expression to his masculinity. Rather, his texts reveal an interrogation of the body and art underpinned by his belief that physical, masculine aggression could itself be art. Joan Kee offers an insightful analysis of the Gutai group's use of "whimsy and violence" that moves away from comparative models. She notes that these qualities were important to Shiraga as a member of Zero-kai.[93] But was it ever whimsy that Shiraga was after? To be performative and ironic is not necessarily to be whimsical, and although he undoubtedly approached his work with a playful attitude and embraced the performative aspects of the masculine, Shiraga was earnest and ambitious. What mattered most to him was to enact the artist-hero, personally and artistically, and his means of achieving this was through acts of violence orchestrated as artworks.

Imaging Violence

In *The Ground of the Image,* Jean-Luc Nancy defines violence as that which "always makes an image of itself."[94] His provocative (and absolutist) argument posits that the violence of the image is at once the act of violence and the confirmation of it (for example, the images of trauma that remain burned in the mind of an individual). Susan Sontag sees violence as bound to the arena of spectacle.[95] Both theorists concur that seeing violence affirms its existence, "completing itself in the image."[96] Shiraga's art, I believe, reinforces the visual dynamic of violence. Action and object are in a mutually affirming relationship in Shiraga's performance works such as *Dōzo* and *Challenging Mud.* The completed composition testifies and even authenticates the violent experience. Violence, Nancy reminds us, wants to be "demonstrative," and certainly Shiraga's work bears out its own violence, never more so than in the context of his 1963 experiment *Inoshishi gari II (Wild Boar Hunting II)* (Plate 29).

In *Wild Boar Hunting II,* Shiraga's apex of vulgar revelry, thick, glutinous paint is congealed on a matted boar hide, resulting in an object that few would find beautiful. Individual hairs of the boar are clearly visible, and the paint is so dense that it has its own form, equivalent in thickness to the hide. Holes have worn through the hide in several places, suggesting that even before it was painted on, it was imperfect and aged. A congealed oblong mass of paint resembles intestines, as though Shiraga turned the creature inside out. *Wild Boar Hunting II* is overtly primitivistic, a hybrid of the caveman's hunt and his grotto paintings. But the atavistic quality of the work is precisely why it is important. It stages a return to an imaginary moment before civilization, when the hunt was a testament to manhood. This mode of primitivism was certainly not unique to Shiraga, as it shared ground with European movements like CoBrA.[97] Yet *Wild Boar Hunting II* also stands apart. The dark tone of this and other pieces marks Shiraga's departure from the direction taken by mainstream personalities such as Okamoto Tarō, who produced brightly colored figural paintings that made reference to the primitive (see, for example, Plate 5). Unlike artists who referenced primitivism through color and titling, Shiraga attempted to *inhabit* the primitive performatively and somatically.[98]

Initially Shiraga had tried to shoot a boar himself, obtaining a license and purchasing a new lever-action gun. He once went so far as to seek out a store specializing in guns related to the occupation forces, whose omnipresence was undeniable given that by the end of 1945, more than 350,000 U.S. personnel were stationed in Japan. In an interview, Shiraga said: "I enjoyed looking at [the gun] and touching it. I soon wanted to go hunting with it, and joined a local hunting club in Amagasaki. The most heroic is wild boar hunting. . . . You wait for a boar to come out. I thought, 'This is a good rifle, I will definitely shoot a boar.' However, none appeared. They did for other hunters in the group, but not to me. No matter how many excursions I made."[99] Ceding his hunter role, he ultimately decided to purchase a hide instead. Having no background knowledge about hunting or animal processing, Shiraga purchased an untanned hide to use as a canvas. Working at home, he proceeded to paint on material that must have become increasingly rancid and foul. His neighbors and wife complained about the putrid smell, and eventually the decay caused the composition to rot.[100] Stubbornly, Shiraga bought another hide, this one tanned, and remade the work.[101] Even then, he must have felt dissatisfaction, as he created two separate versions of the work. Shiraga's hunting trips served as investigations that allowed the artist to bring himself closer to understanding the creative processes; yet, at the same time, the purchase of hunting gear was a conscious enactment of the masculine hero. Shiraga stated: "In my boar-hide works, such cruelty is expressed as painting."[102] On another occasion Shiraga attempted to make a piece of art from a dead dog, and he once covered a board with slices of lamb meat and cut them into bits using a sheet of glass. These works were not completed, but they speak to the degree to which Shiraga sought out a visceral engagement with his materials.

Today, despite the ubiquity of "shock art" (art that aims to disturb, such as Tracey Emin's stained bedsheets and Orlan's plastic surgeries), *Wild Boar Hunting II* remains decisively grotesque. The slick manner in which the paint adheres to the woolly grain of the boar's hair makes it seem as though it were completed recently, sitting moist and lurid on the whitewashed gallery walls. When I encountered the piece in 2012, more than forty years after it was created, a strange scent of leather and congealed paint still wafted up from its surface. Shiraga's most carnal work was an apex for his career in more ways than one. His production slowed after its completion in 1963, and when Shiraga reemerged in 1973, following his monk's training and a two-year hiatus from alcohol, his color palette had changed to swirling zones of black and white, with the reds of the 1950s appearing with far less frequency.

Still, the provocative and repellent quality of *Wild Boar Hunting I* and *Wild Boar Hunting II* extends into the rest of Shiraga's oeuvre. For example, another painting from the *Water Margin* series, *Tenkūsei Kyūsenpō (Impatient Vanguard)*, done the year before *Wild Boar Hunting II*, looks like it has been smeared with excrement along the left side and the upper central area (Plate 30).[103] The canvas is filled with red globs that look like blood spots, and green and yellow smears make it difficult to look at the painting for very long. None of Shiraga's pieces, except perhaps his last series of silkscreens, display harmonious coloring, a balanced sense of perspective, or a linear progression. They share none of the rhythmic evenness exemplified by Jackson Pollock's later works, which Yoshihara lauded in the manifesto. Of the 1950s postwar artists, Shiraga is distinctive in his sustained investment in violence and the performative use of the body.

A lesser-known piece that exemplifies Shiraga's investigation of the grotesque is *Kurenai eki (Red Liquid)* (1956), which showcases the distended innards of three pigs, overlapping in a small glass container, each stuffed with cement and surrounded by red-colored water (Figure 4.12). The nauseating appearance of the animal innards prefigures Shiraga's later exploits in *Wild Boar Hunting II*. The simple, gross display of the intestines demonstrates a forceful manipulation of biological matter. Stuffed with cement, the pale tissue creates a contrast of soft curved edges and jutting zeppelin-like ovoid forms. Rather than the body and the object working together, as the Gutai manifesto would have it, here the organic becomes fully objectified by its visibility in the glass container, and the connotations of *gutai* (concreteness, embodiment) take on literally solid form through the hardening of the cement lodged in the biomatter. *Red Liquid* brings us too close to deadened life, the illumination at the front of the glass permitting a clear view of the forced expansion of the guts, bringing the tissue to the brink of rupture. Violence here goes beyond thematics: it is the visualization of assault on the material, it is an insistence on violation of the body. Both Shiraga's intention and the aftermath of his works suggest an opposition to composition. He once commented that he sought to eliminate any sense of order:

I no longer felt the need to make studies, and I started creating non-objective, automatist paintings through direct action on the canvas . . . but I wanted to inject more heat and explosive energy into my expression. Therefore I decided to ignore my own previous work and the trends of art history and start over from the beginning with an empty slate, to discard all formal elements and start from zero. It proved extremely difficult, however, to reject everything from the past. Abstract painters had already rejected the attempt to depict three-dimensional space with light and shade that had been emphasized in previous representational paintings, but I was still faced with the knotty problem of eliminating composition and a sense of color.[104]

Nancy writes that violence is that which cannot be negotiated, composed, ordered, or shared, and this concept of violence as a form of nullification provided a productive avenue for Shiraga.[105] This alternative was all the more relevant in the face of growing concerns about avant-garde competitiveness and belatedness. The notion that violence negates order is similarly fulfilled by Shiraga's oeuvre, in which his hundreds of shambolic representations do not deliver any sense of development or teleological maturation.

Instead of demonstrating complicity with a specific political agenda, Shiraga's oeuvre might be understood to be actively questioning the relationship between art and the state, with violence forming the backbone of that question. Violence was an active means to negate overt relations to politics and Gutai ideology, and an attempt to forcefully rupture links with past art forms, although this attempt was often complicated and contradictory.

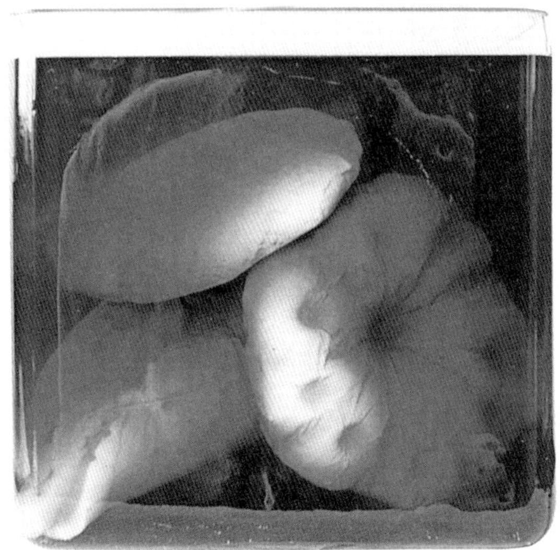
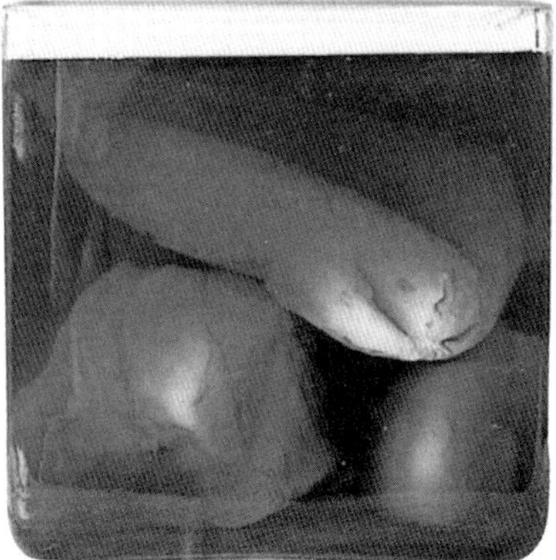

FIGURE 4.12. Shiraga Kazuo, *Kurenai eki (Red Liquid)*, 1956 (reconstruction 2001). Glass case, white cement, red liquid, 26.28 × 27.50 × 21 cm (above), 20.29 × 19.98 × 17.09 cm (below). Copyright Hisao Shiraga. Photograph courtesy of Amagasaki Cultural Center.

Moreover, violence allowed the artist to redirect his anxieties about artistic status, masculinity, and the state of the nation. Much in the same way that Shiraga swung like a pendulum above his canvases, his ideology, insofar as it can be ascertained, was fluid and shifting. Political tensions were channeled into aggressive art, rendered strategically illegible through intensity and force.

The Buddhist Hero

Shiraga's experiences with Buddhism resonate with the notion of the embodied, masculine hero. As a university student Shiraga often visited Yōgen'in, a Momoyama-era temple in Kyoto that is well known for its bloodstained ceilings.[106] The ceilings are made of wood repurposed from the floors of Fushimi Castle, which were stained by the blood of Torii Mototada and his ten remaining troops when they committed ritual suicide after losing an eleven-day siege. Given that Kyoto is home to hundreds of temples, it is interesting to consider that Shiraga was drawn to Yōgen'in and its representations of violence. Perhaps the aura of the temple acted as a kind of inspiration for Shiraga, as bloodstained footprints are still visible in the wood. Indeed, for Shiraga, Buddhism and violence were not necessarily at odds. For example, his choice to title 106 paintings for the violent heroes of *The Water Margin* was also tied to Buddhism. The specific number of heroes is related to the Buddhist conception that there are 108 worldly desires: in Japan on New Year's Eve, the temple gong is rung 108 times to chase away the worldly desires of the year. Given that Shiraga produced so many paintings in this series, why did he leave two heroes out? Both characters, Hakushō and Jisen, are low-ranking earthly warriors whose acts and reputation for thievery are the most dishonorable in the group: Hakushō names his brother for crimes while being tortured, and Jisen's foolish actions lead others into danger.[107] It seems that for Shiraga, the nexus of violence and spiritualism offered opportunities for ethical choice; his decision to include only the most heroic of the 108 heroes reinforces this notion.

Shiraga's curiosity about Buddhism was reignited sometime in the early 1960s, when on a hunting trip by the Ina River near the Sanda Mountains, he noticed votive stone Buddhist monuments forcefully inscribed with Sanskrit characters *(itabi)*.[108] This encounter later prompted him to visit Enryaku-ji, a temple of the Tendai Buddhist sect near Mount Hiei, north of Kyoto in the Kansai region (not far from his hometown of Amagasaki), in November 1970. In 1971, Shiraga abruptly ceased painting, and in April of that year he decided to undergo rigorous training at Enryaku-ji, living at the monastery for thirty-five days.[109] In May he was officially ordained as a monk and took the Buddhist name Shiraga Sodō (Simple Path). Under the tutelage of Yamada Etai, the head priest of the Tendai sect, he received his initiation rites. He continued his training until June 1974, making paintings with Buddhist-related titles after he resumed painting in 1972; he maintained a connection with Enryaku-ji long after (Figure 4.13). Shiraga reflected on his desire to create Buddhist works: "After I finished my ascetic training and came back from Mount Hiei,

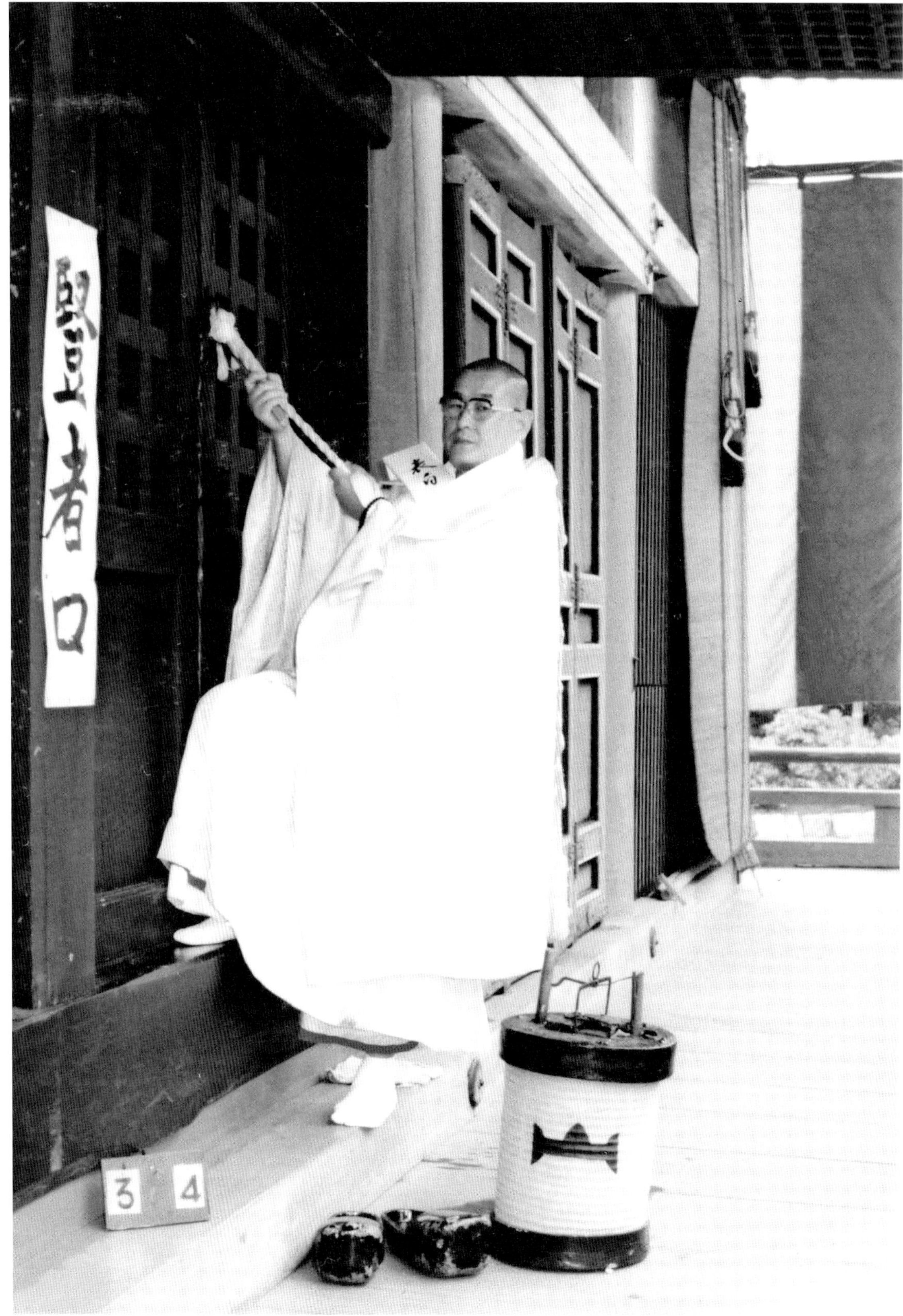

FIGURE 4.13. Shiraga Kazuo at Enryaku-ji, 1979. Copyright Hisao Shiraga. Photograph courtesy of Amagasaki Cultural Center.

I remember being very aware of trying to paint pictures of Buddhas. I thought that was part of my job as a priest. Since I can't proselytize in words, I thought having people look at my pictures would have a somewhat similar effect, so I painted Buddhas."[110]

In comparison to other avant-garde artists, Shiraga was relatively late in coming to an interest in Buddhism. American Mark Tobey, for example, spent a month studying meditation at Enryaku-ji in 1935.[111] In the postwar period, other American artists also became interested in Buddhism (particularly Zen), including John Cage and Ad Reinhardt. In France, Japanese Buddhism inspired Pierre Alechinsky, Jean Degottex, and Yves Klein. The geospiritual terrain shared by these artists and Shiraga points to the competitive, globalized milieu of abstract expressionism. Shiraga's position was perhaps most comparable to that of Japanese contemporaries like Morita Shiryū (1912–98), an acquaintance who was similarly interested in revitalizing art through Japanese religious practice.[112] Later in his career, Shiraga also experimented in works with links to Zen ink painting; for example, his wash drawings from the 1970s bear some resemblance to Morita's gestural calligraphy. Zen Buddhism had become an integral part of postwar Japan's reconstructed national identity and a new form of artistic inspiration transnationally.

Why did artists seek out spiritual guidance at Enryaku-ji in particular? Other temples, like Myōshin-ji (located in Kyoto), were conveniently situated in city centers and openly encouraged laypeople and foreigners to visit. Perhaps Enryaku-ji's inconvenience was its draw: set deep in the mountains, the temple offered a respite from the Kansai area's rapid industrialization. Tendai Buddhism is also famed for its rigorous *shugendō,* or ascetic mountain practice, and provides an ideal setting for exploring a highly physicalized spirituality. The infamous marathon monks, who are said to run a fifty-mile circuit around Mount Hiei on a regular basis, belong to this sect. Shiraga, an artist whose work often demonstrated marked corporeal, even violent, qualities, may have been drawn to the somatic demands of *shugendō.* The Tendai sect, in fact, is entirely compatible with masculine tropes of heroism and aggression. While nonviolent today, Enryaku-ji has a long martial tradition.[113] In the premodern period, the temple had its own army of warrior monks, who battled monks from other religious centers. Well before his turn to Buddhism, Shiraga had tested his physical and psychological limits through his art. His interest in Tendai Buddhism was thus a continuation of his ceaseless testing of himself as an artist and as a man.[114] The extreme nature of isolated, mountain meditation presented the opportunity for artists— men only—to venture into the wild and test themselves against the elements. Yet the need to prove one's manliness repeatedly also bespeaks an underlying anxiety about it.

Shortly after Shiraga began studying Buddhism at Enryaku-ji, he began to title his compositions in reference to Buddhist deities and sutras (Buddhist sermons), such as *Fudōsan* (1973) and *Abiraunken* (1975) (Plate 31). (*Abira Unken* is a mantra associated with Dainichi Nyorai, or Mahavairocana, the Universal Buddha.) Shiraga remarked: "Before I begin the action of painting, I invoke Fudō. When I am painting I pray so that I will myself become the god Fudō, and when the divinity enters my body, the work is done.

This belief accompanies me throughout the creative process."[115] Shiraga titled a 1975 piece for the deity as well (Plate 32). Fudō, or Fudō Myō-ō, is a fierce protector of the Buddhist faith, often depicted holding a flaming sword and noose, and typically pictured as powerfully muscular. *Shugendō* practitioners often pray to this Wisdom King. Few images associated with esoteric Buddhism are more extraordinarily fierce and physically dynamic than those of the Five Kings.[116]

As Shiraga's spiritual and perhaps even his ethical approach to his art changed, so did his physical relationship to his art, as he began using wooden poles, boards, squeegees, and other implements to work on the surface of the canvas rather than his bare feet. Judging from photographs, his wife, Fujiko, often helped him manipulate the objects with his legs as he applied paint (see Figure 4.1). *Kannon Fudara Jōdo,* from 1971, takes up Buddhist themes with new techniques of painting (Plate 33). The title refers to the island where the Water Moon Kannon, a deity (bodhisattva) in Buddhism, dwells. Shiraga made the painting, which is predominantly red, by spreading alkyd (a quick-drying medium similar in viscosity to house paint) with a handheld squeegee. Beginning in the top left corner, discernible rows of black, white, and blue paint are overlaid across the red and spread steeply downward in two sharp cascades before flattening along the bottom portion of the frame. It is a dramatic, abstract waterfall. Perhaps Shiraga intentionally referenced the natural settings where the bodhisattva is most often depicted.

Kannon Fudara Jōdo evokes a sense of fierce movement that is present in much of Shiraga's production. Consider, for example, one of his most vibrant and dramatic creations, *Akai ōgi (Red Fan),* from 1965 (Plate 34). Shiraga destabilizes the uniformity and centralized balance of the circular composition, showing the vulnerabilities of form with an uneven distribution of red oil paint that reveals splotches of green base paint below.[117] The work is the result of Shiraga's testing his body against the paint, part of his characteristic physical manner of interacting with the canvas.

In its title and materiality, *Red Fan* also reveals an ambivalent engagement with Japanese cultural symbols. The painting is in dialogue with another 1965 work titled *Akai ōgi no obuje* (also known simply as *Red Fan* in English), an *objet* (Figure 4.14) made of red lacquered tissue paper folded like a traditional Japanese fan. Shiraga's cross-medium exploration of a recognizable Japanese symbol and his resituating of the fan within an avant-garde mode of expression suggest his awareness of the fluidity of representation and how representation can potentially reshape conceptions of Japanese "essence." *Red Fan*'s self-conscious engagement with traditional Japanese symbolism prefigured Shiraga's later Buddhist-influenced pieces such as *Kannon Fudara Jōdo* and *Daiitokuson* (1973) (Figure 4.15). *Daiitokuson* also refers to one of the Five Great Wisdom Kings. Shiraga chose to depict the Wisdom King of the Western arena (whether this was a metaphor for overcoming Western dominance in the field of abstract expressionism, we shall never know), who is often associated with the color red (notably, the same color as the Japanese national flag). *Daiitokuson* is a magnificent array of crimson and black against a dark-green background.

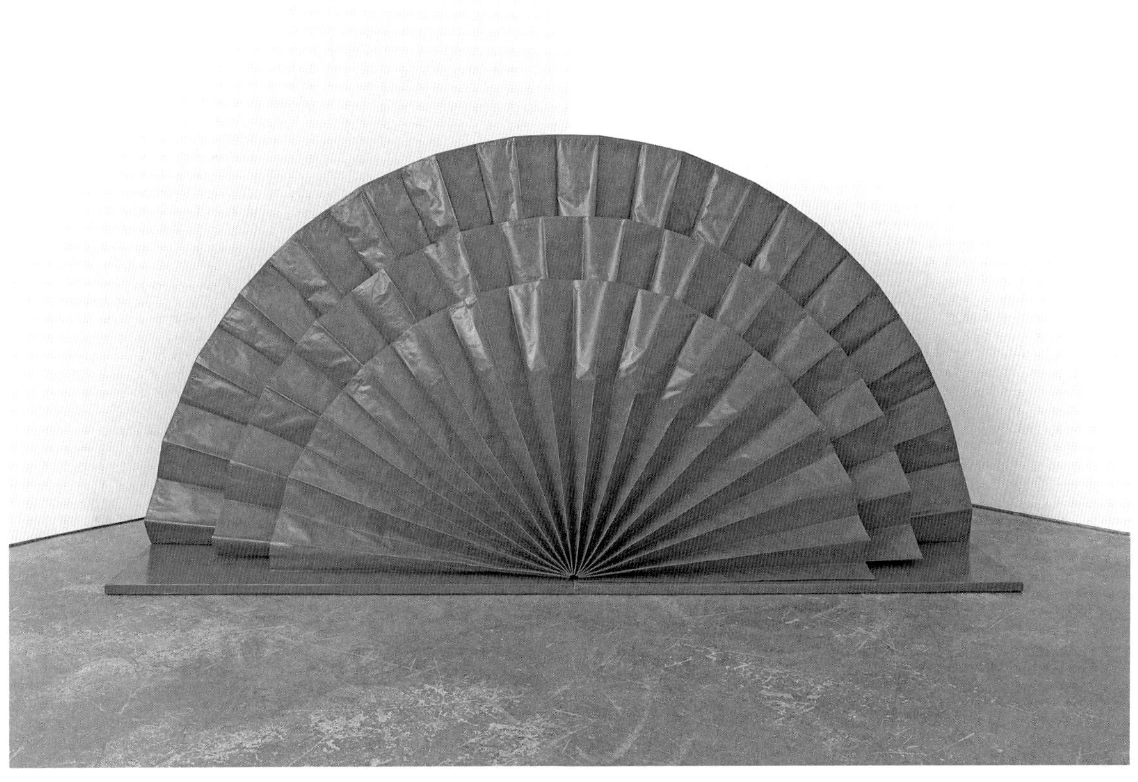

FIGURE 4.14. Shiraga Kazuo, *Akai ōgi no obuje (Red Fan),* 1965. Red lacquered tissue paper and wood, 310 × 155 × 55 cm. Copyright Shiraga Hisao. Private collection. Courtesy of Hauser and Wirth. Photograph by Todd White Photography London.

A bold flourish of white oil paint sweeps across the upper portion of the canvas, a possible reference to the deity's association with a white cow. This uniquely abstract interpretation of the Japanese Wisdom King displays Shiraga's efforts to breathe new life into identifiably Japanese cultural formations.

Was Shiraga invested in Buddhism because of its spiritual wealth, or did he opportunistically embrace it as an artistic identity that would be perceived as authentic by the West? Buddhist spiritualism, even as late as the 1970s, was a significant source of cultural capital for Japan internationally (as it continues to be today). Yet Shiraga's interest also emerged just as the Gutai Art Association was in its final phase: the group's imminent dissolution was finalized with the death of leader Yoshihara Jirō in 1972. Perhaps this moment of instability also motivated the young artist to turn to other sources of inspiration and institutional security. Shiraga was likely aware that Zen Buddhism could offer him a new source of indigenous spiritual inspiration grounded in masculine aggression while also carrying currency among the global postwar avant-garde.[118] For Shiraga, it was

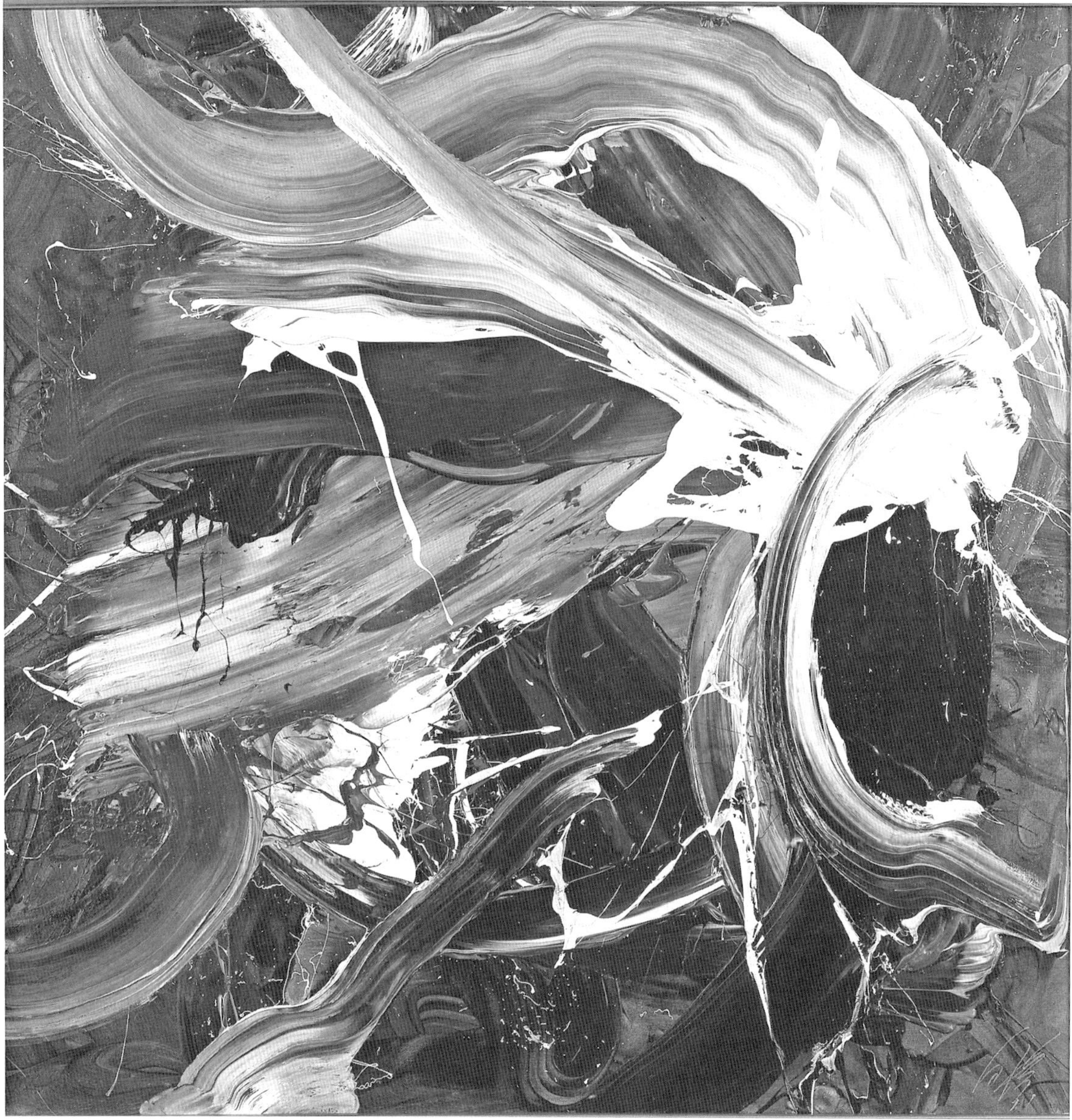

FIGURE 4.15.　Shiraga Kazuo, *Daiitokuson,* 1973. Oil on canvas, 196 × 195 cm. Copyright Hisao Shiraga. Photograph courtesy of Amagasaki Cultural Center.

only *shugendō,* rather than other common forms of Buddhist practice, that offered appropriately rigorous physical and spiritual training.[119] Shiraga's intentions remain unknown, but it seems the 1970s marked an ethical turn for him, even as he showed a continuing interest in violent heroism.

Shiraga responded to the complex artistic politics of the postwar period in a manner that sought to capture ever-elusive originality, aggressively engaging the field of painting. Bodily action, he believed, could open up opportunities for art, and he relied on templates of the masculine hero to inform his practice as well as to potentially bolster his artistic status, within Japan and beyond. When Shiraga's performance art and paintings are considered as a whole, the self-conscious positioning of the artist within a heroic narrative and his conceptual framework of violence as art becomes evident. This approach shifts perspective away from isolated moments of "inspiration" originating from a narrow culturalist influence (such as essentialized Japanese traditions like *Bushidō,* the way of the warrior, or *matsuri,* Japanese festivals) and frames Shiraga's body-based painting within the broader context of postwar Japan and the larger vectors of the asymmetrical art world.

Shiraga's was a shifting self-stylization that was highly generative and yet relied on pre-existing tropes of masculinity. Templates of the masculine hero are relational, with each narrative forming a constellation of issues to inform the next, just as Shiraga's artist-warrior configurations transformed from woodsman to soldier to outlaw to hunter. Articulated through the gendered interface of the Japanese hero, Shiraga's radicality was imbued with a deliberately overdetermined sense of masculine identification. Tying together the complex tropes of gender, representations of the nation, and notions of postwar modernity in elaborate artworks, Shiraga opened up a space for critical encounters with his performance of overtly male roles: between man and medium, state and subject, representation and envisioned nation. Aggressive action and the spectacle of masculinized bodily exposure made violence a platform for art making through the narrative of the remasculinization of the nation, a narrative filled with potential for both triumph and failure and deeply imbricated in Japan's fragile status in the international art scene. The repetition of violence enacts, facilitates, and empowers the construction of the masculine hero. Additionally, for Shiraga, art making was a process enmeshed in the discourse of self, enabling him to understand his artistic identity in relation to his fellow artists and to work through his beliefs and anxieties about both gender and nationhood. On and off the stage, Shiraga's strategic performances revealed that art might be used to question what the state could be and what role the artist-hero might have within that field, just as his violent actions molded and shaped his own body into one that enacted and idealized the trope of the masculine artist-hero.

Thresholds of Exposure

In the late 1940s and early 1950s, the relationships among representation, the body, gender, and nation played out in Japan in the art galleries and in the sites of protest; they also played out in the mass media, demonstrating the pervasiveness of the phenomenon. A boom in manga, and publishing in general, brought these images into wider consciousness and was indicative of the concerns of postwar Japanese art.[1] Several of the most popular manga, which occupied the prime visual space of national newspapers, focused on characters with circumscribed gender roles, such as the housewife.[2] While each comic presented familial narratives with characters that appeared to enact dominant, heteronormative gender roles, as a whole these serials revealed divergent levels of agency, economic consumption, and bodily exposure.[3] Certainly cultural norms are always in a state of transition, yet the degree of related but dichotomous representations emerging in the hegemonic mainstream media of the postwar period is revealing of the stakes of the times. While one might read these comics as presenting gender roles as stable, homogeneous, and defined by familial bonds and obligations, the multiple opposing narratives and the freighted representational variations between the comics implied transition and uncertainty, a tone that was often conveyed in the anxious bodies created by Katsura, Nakamura, Tanaka, and Shiraga.

Hirai Fusando's comic *Omoitsuki fujin* (Conscientious housewife), popular in the 1930s and resurrected in the early postwar period in the *Asahi Journal,* offered illustrated tips on how to run a household in an economical manner.[4] The context of economic deprivation in the 1950s was so similar to that of the 1930s that Hirai's narratives of household frugality were again in demand, and the illustrator reused the ideas in many of the earlier panels, simply redrawing them while keeping the content identical.[5] The comic featured a housewife modestly dressed in a traditional kimono covered by a *kappōgi* going about her duties as a means of demonstrating household efficiency. Comparable to the housewife portrayed in Katsura Yuki's *Women's Day,* her simple clothing effaces bodily form and she similarly holds a broom as her only accessory. But unlike Katsura's figure, who seems at once liberated and bound by the changes to gender status in the postwar period, Hirai's character is less ambivalent. She cheerfully and efficiently maximizes space in her small home by using wires to hang cooking implements and toothbrushes, and, in another scene, keeps her family's *geta* (wooden sandals) clean by banging them together, dipping them in water, and lining them up to dry (Figure C.1). *Omoitsuki fujin* was initially created to address the need for households to be thrifty when the Japanese government was relying heavily on citizens to fund the war. The values portrayed in the serial are in harmony with those of the Housewives' Federation (Shufuren), established in 1948 and led by Oku Mumeo, who had similarly called for rationalization (as described in chapter 1).[6]

Day-to-day living conditions had not improved in the early postwar period; poverty was rampant, and gruel replaced rice as a mainstay of many people's diets. In the first three months following Japan's surrender, an estimated three thousand people died in Tokyo from causes related to malnutrition.[7] Imagery helped to deepen this sense of crisis. In a 1946 state-issued poster, the height of the average elementary school child in 1937 is shown as much taller than the average child in 1945, with urban children hardest hit by malnutrition (Figure C.2).[8] The leading, enlarged text reads: "What effect did the war have on our children's bodies?" Rendered in simple outlines, four elementary school children (one urban boy, one rural boy, one urban girl, and one rural girl) stand in profile, wearing only white underwear. Each child's face is depicted with two dots for eyes and a short, horizontal line for a mouth, indicating a dejected mood. Behind the children, their former selves loom as shadows, heartier and taller. Girls and boys today, the poster suggests, are not only physically smaller but also diminished in their corporeal presence. *Omoitsuki fujin* presented the struggle with poverty and hunger as commonplace, honorable, and left to be managed by women.

Other serials took up the role of the housewife, although sometimes with drastically different forms of representation. Like Hirai, American cartoonist Chic Young emphasized the femininity of his central character, Blondie, from the 1930s onward. *Burondi* (the translation of *Blondie,* created with the *katakana* foreign-language syllabary) was translated and serialized in the newspaper *Shūkan Asahi* beginning in June 1946, not long after the start of the Allied Occupation.[9] Simple Japanese text (with a limited amount of *kanji* characters) was used for the inset dialogue, and explanations in English were printed below. The practical application of the comic as an English-language learning aid, at a time when Americans were flooding into the country, only increased readership. *Burondi* and *Omoitsuki fujin* were two of the most popular comics, their prominence speaking to a fascination with household gender roles.

The comics shared familiar settings and a focus on "typical" domestic life, but the modes in which they depicted the body differed. *Omoitsuki fujin* featured a woman whose body was obscured beneath layers of clothing: first, her full-length white petticoat, visible at the neckline, then her kimono, and finally her long apron, which draped over her arms

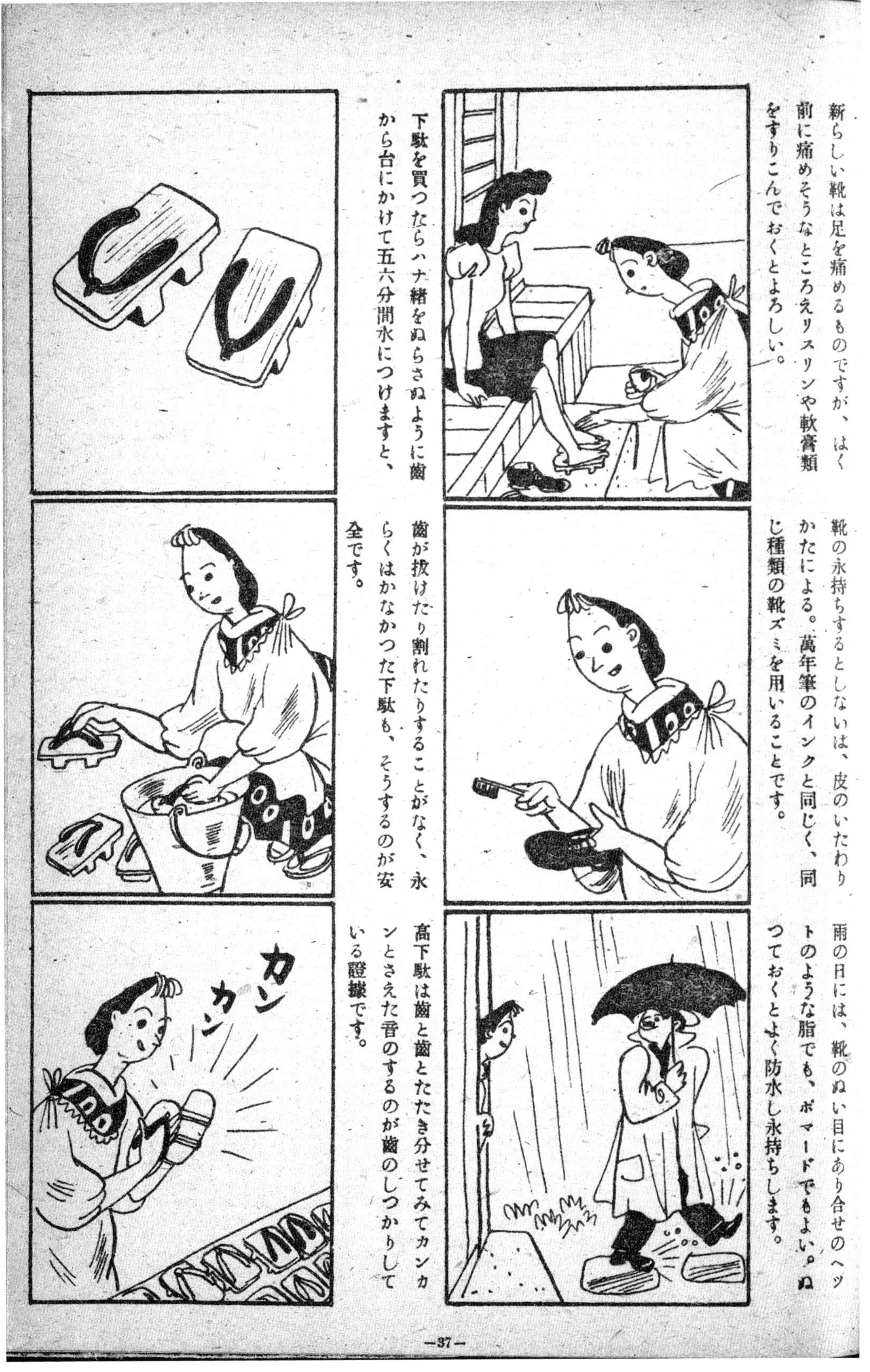

FIGURE C.1. Hirai Fusando, *Omoitsuki fujin* (Osaka: Asahi Shinbunsha, 1950), 37. Photograph from Manga Collection, The Ohio State University Billy Ireland Cartoon Library and Museum.

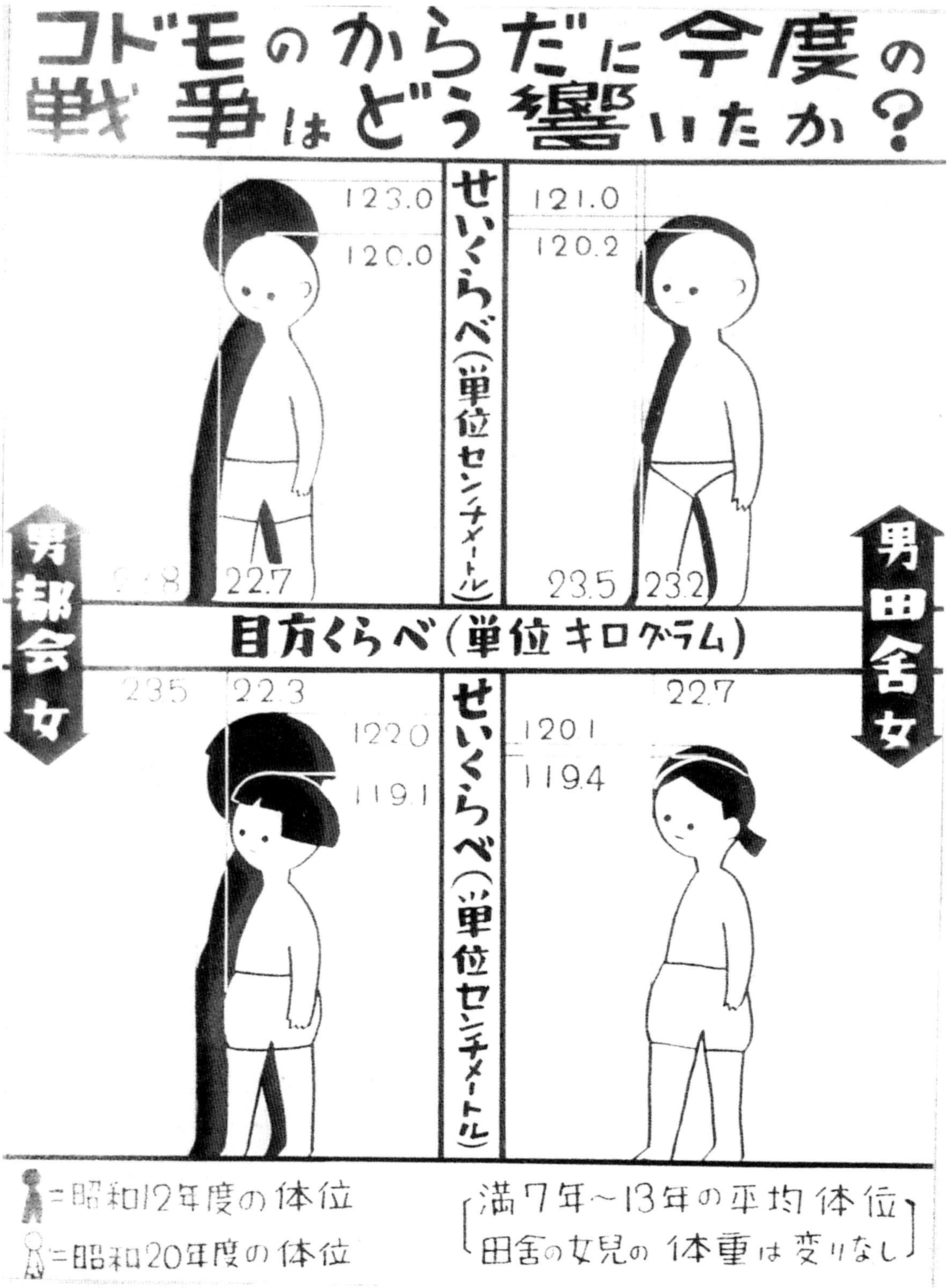

FIGURE C.2. "What effect did the war have on our children's bodies?," *Kyōdō News,* June 1, 1946.

as well as her entire torso. The body was concealed, obfuscated, and wrapped in a manner similar to Katsura's penchant for apatetic devices displayed in her paintings such as *Greedy Old Woman* (see Plate 11) and her illustrations for the Japanese serialization of James Baldwin's *Another Country* (see Figures 1.13–1.16). Hirai's drawings communicate the housewife's femininity not through the overall form of her physical body but in finer details such as her elongated eyelashes and the delicate manner in which she uses her hands to complete her domestic duties.[10] Significantly, Hirai also designated the housewife's femininity through the types of labor she performs (Figure C.3).

Like the housewife in *Omoitsuki fujin,* Blondie sports an apron; by comparison, however, hers seems as small and as decorative as a doily. Blondie goes about her daily household chores wearing black pumps, an image that would have surprised readers on several registers. Even in the United States, where the comic originated, high-heeled shoes were a luxury item that would be neither comfortable nor suitable for housework, and in Japan, shoes are not worn inside the house at all. Young completes Blondie's outfit with a short-hemmed, short-sleeved, low-cut polka-dot dress (Figure C.4). While the main character in *Omoitsuki fujin* can be read as a feminine persona largely through her labor, Blondie's femininity resides primarily in her bodily form, her clothing, and her role as a consumer. Her body, fashionably outfitted and set among new appliances, stands as a bright and attractive symbol for consumption, akin to the schoolgirl in her sailor uniform so predominant in the Japanese advertisements that Nakamura referenced in his post-1957 oeuvre (see Figure 2.16). *Blondie* was a titillating narrative of family life with jokes often turning on the ineptitude of Blondie's husband, Dagwood, the patriarch, which tacitly played into the construction of consumer desire and its conflation with the female body. Nakamura's work, while alluring and even potentially erotic, critiqued liberal democratic capitalism and its manipulation of vision and the female form. Making this association clear, Nakamura relied on a vibrant color palette and linear patterns familiar to consumers of mass culture.

Omoitsuki fujin and *Burondi* were published concurrently during a period when gender roles were exceptionally unstable and potentially open to radical reinterpretation. While both comics presented gender roles as stabilized, the strong differences between them reveals the indeterminacy of gender and the sense that even idealized, dominant narratives of domesticity remained contentious. The two cartoons showcased women of the same generation involved in the role of the appealing, efficient, and considerate housewife, ensconced in the family home. They shared readership in the most widely read periodicals. The most substantive difference between the two representations was that the Japanese female body was marked as concealed, while the American female body was represented as relatively exposed and available.[11] Moreover, Blondie's sexualized body was often conflated with the material belongings showcased in the series. In the very first volume of collected strips released in 1947, Young daringly shows Blondie suggestively bent over, her dress caught in her own electric washing machine's wringer (Figure C.5).

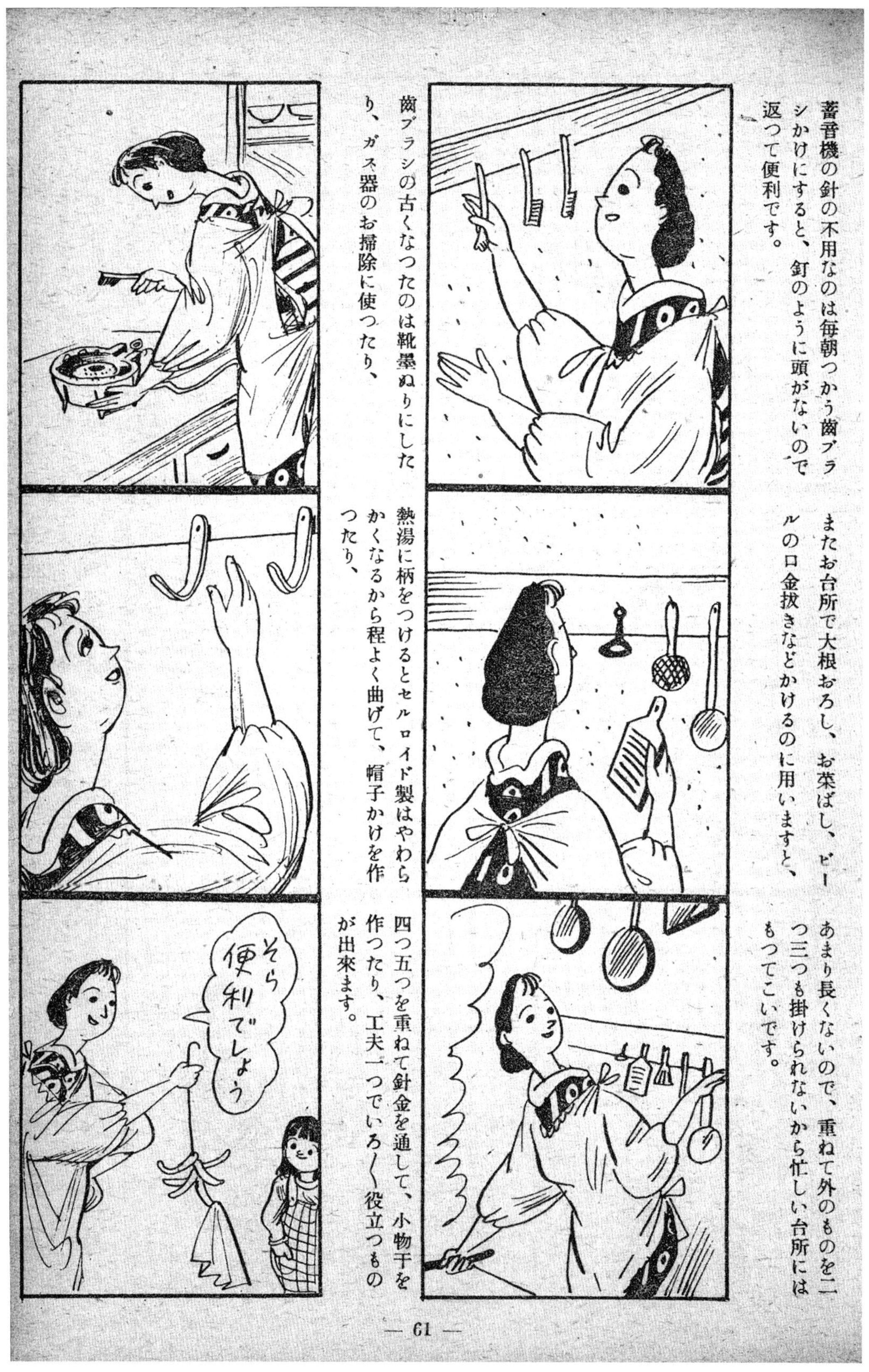

FIGURE C.3. Hirai Fusando, *Omoitsuki fujin* (Osaka: Asahi Shinbunsha, 1950), 61. Photograph from Manga Collection, The Ohio State University Billy Ireland Cartoon Library and Museum.

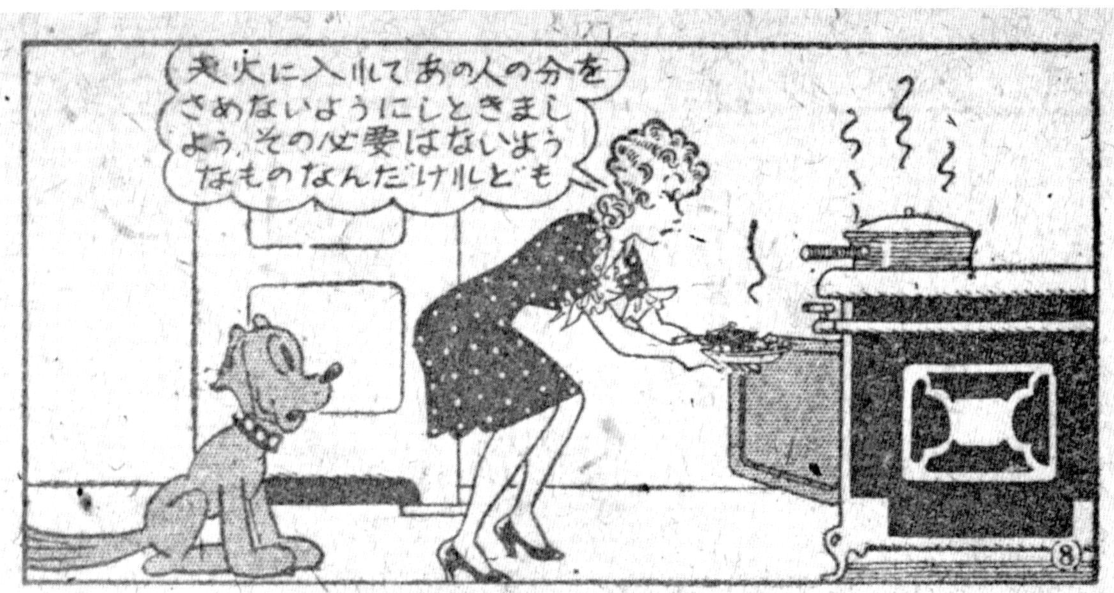

FIGURE C.4. Chic Young, *Burondi*, 1947, 2:17. Courtesy of King Features Syndicate; all rights reserved. Photograph from Manga Collection, The Ohio State University Billy Ireland Cartoon Library and Museum.

For many Japanese readers, such images of implicit sexuality and wealth were assumed to be representative of "the" American experience, with the United States depicted as a land filled with expensive luxury items like washing machines, elegant lamps, and comfortable chaise longues. The female body was both encumbered and liberated by commercial products, including the home itself. A common postwar period quip referred to the "three imperial regalia" as the refrigerator, the washing machine, and the television.[12] "The bright life," a concept promulgated by Prime Minister Hatoyama and then marketed by a savvy electronics industry, was a formative ideal that reshaped the body's relationship to technology.[13] As described in chapter 3, artists like Tanaka were aware of rapid industrialization and the stakes for female subjectivity—how the body could be both illuminated and destroyed by electronic goods and the new systems that they introduced.

Manga scholar Natsu Onoda Power notes, "Japanese citizens were shocked by the American middle-class lifestyle depicted in *Blondie,* equipped with refrigerators, cars, and telephones. At this time, most Japanese relied on candles to light their homes, due to the unreliable supply of electricity."[14] Throughout the series, Blondie regularly breaks up her day of cooking and cleaning by going shopping. She returns from her outings overloaded with parcels, many of which are exquisitely wrapped (a practice that Japanese department stores perfected in the 1950s and continue to this day). These consumer practices, like the ideal of blond hair, were out of reach for the vast majority of Japanese. Yet desire is often predicated on impossibility. The global spectacle of American consumer culture, as

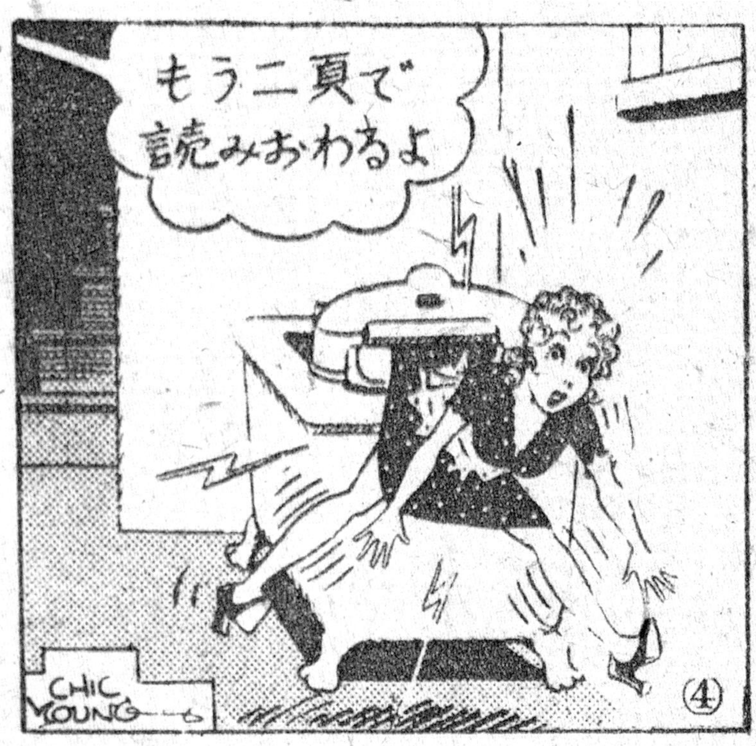

FIGURE C.5. Chic Young, *Burondi,* 1947, 2:39. Courtesy of King Features Syndicate; all rights reserved. Photograph from Manga Collection, The Ohio State University Billy Ireland Cartoon Library and Museum.

the British artist Richard Hamilton conveyed in his 1956 work *Just What Makes Today's Homes So Different, So Appealing?,* was intoxicatingly commingled with gendered mystique.

Burondi faced direct competition for newspaper space from a Japanese cartoon that also focused on the microdramas of everyday home life: *Sazae-san.* The manga, by the female cartoonist Hasegawa Machiko—who hails from Kumamoto, the same prefecture where the Minamata disaster occurred—ran from 1946 until Hasegawa retired in 1974 and featured lighthearted stories about the protagonist, Sazae, and her family. It was initially published in a Kyūshū-based local paper, *Fukunichi Shinbun,* before being serialized in the nationally circulated *Asahi Shinbun* in 1949, the same year that *Burondi* moved to the *Asahi Journal.* As in *Burondi,* the main character in *Sazae-san* is a housewife who lives with her husband and their children. Sazae, however, also shares her home with her parents and her younger siblings. Although in comparison to *Burondi* the manga might seem traditional, Sazae's family structure was unconventional. Unlike most Japanese families at the time, Sazae and her husband live with her parents rather than his, and there is a dramatic gap between Sazae's age and that of her younger siblings, who are still in elementary school. The narrative bucks trends in other ways as well: Sazae's outspoken nature and short, curly hairstyle mark her as a modern woman, and her mother is often shown to have more power in the family than her father, the patriarch. The Japanese patriarch's slippage in status (both at home and abroad) brought about an uneasiness that is legible in Nakamura Hiroshi's *Self-Portrait B,* with its disavowal of the male body, as well as in Shiraga Kazuo's overdetermined iterations of the masculine artist hero.

Sazae-san was highly topical and included discussions of such contemporary issues as widespread hunger and the presence of American GIs in the postwar period. Early in the series, the stories frequently centered on Sazae's resistance to marriage, and she was even depicted joining a woman's liberation group.[15] In later episodes, Sazae became somewhat more conservative: she married but frequently criticized her husband's decisions, much to her neighbor's dismay.[16] Later, the comic satirized *kyōiku mama* (education mamas)—that is, mothers who were obsessed with ensuring that their children advanced to high-level colleges.[17] An animated television show adapted from *Sazae-san* began airing in 1969, and it currently holds the record as the longest-running show ever to air.[18]

While Blondie is synonymous with sexual attractiveness, Sazae's body is unremarkable and her face homely (Figure C.6).[19] Her plain visage lacks even the feminine eyelashes that were sometimes visible in *Omoitsuki fujin,* and, in early versions of the cartoon, Sazae had a broad pug nose, which would have been widely considered unattractive.[20] Like the other housewife characters, Sazae also wears a white apron, but hers is of average size. It wraps around her unassuming collared shirts and over her calf-length skirts. As if to cement her status as a "plain Jane," the character's invented name "Sazae" derives from a conspicuously unromantic source—a type of regional sea snail.[21] Hasegawa's character was meant to be an Everywoman, one who was part of the fabric of the contemporary world. Sazae does not wear a kimono, and her short hair and tennis shoes clearly demarcate her as a modern woman. For Hasegawa, the contemporary moment called for an able-bodied woman who did not rely on her visual appeal to harness the marketplace. But as the cover of the first compilation of Hasegawa's work shows, the illustrator did not attempt to paper over the numerous demands on housewives at the time.

In her now-canonical formulation, Judith Butler has argued that gender is a constant discursive construction rather than a static condition.[22] Gender, she claims, is a matrix of norms, and it can only be approximated rather than fully achieved; it is stabilized through reiterations of these norms in performances over time. Yet within any given period, gender norms achieve varying levels of relative stability and instability—what apprehensions do these instabilities raise? The moments of greatest flux can create profound anxiety because of the indeterminate, ephemeral nature of the individual's role in society, when subjectivity is in a state of transformation or undefined. *Burondi, Omoitsuki fujin,* and *Sazae-san* were just a few of the publications in postwar Japan that garnered great attention and relied on gender roles as a means to creative storytelling.[23] Manga were intimately entangled with, and revelatory of, the instability of hegemonic gender orders that, with stubborn determination, they persistently sought to buttress.

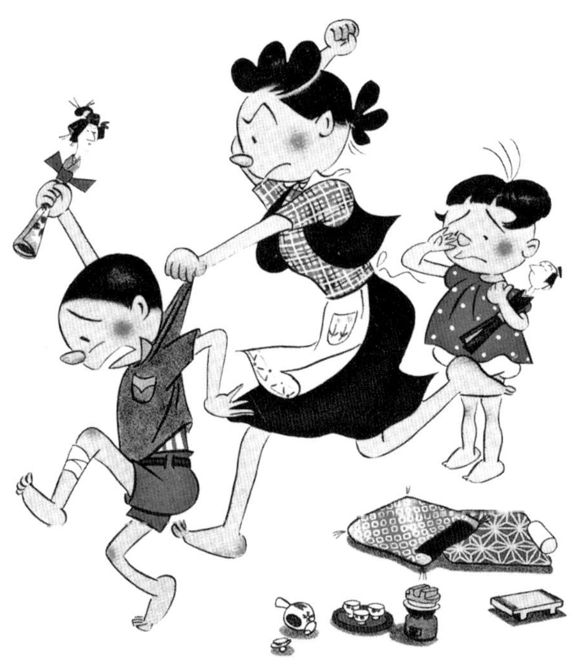

FIGURE C.6. Hasegawa Machiko, *Hasegawa Machiko zenshū, 1946–50* (Tokyo: Asahi Shinbunsha, 1997), reprint of first-edition book cover. Photograph from Manga Collection, The Ohio State University Billy Ireland Cartoon Library and Museum.

Women were to be resourceful survivors, nurturing mothers and wives, attractive house-keepers, industrious laborers, and eager consumers, as well as active community participants. These demands taxed the body in new ways and raised anxieties about what the "proper" role for women—and, by extension, the role for men—might be. Both manga and the fine arts in the early postwar period reflect these anxious times by depicting women as nurturers or attractive consumers, as symbols of political change or exemplars of Japanese traditions, and as embodying the prewar, state-backed notion of the "good wife, wise mother" or the modern woman at risk of overexposure to Western morals, industrial pollution, and consumer desire.[24] *Burondi, Omoitsuki fujin,* and *Sazae-san* depicted female characters as though the role they occupied was *the* singularly stable and idealized role model for women, but taken as whole, the divergent, "normative" models created social tensions indicating that anxiety and uncertainty about gender roles was the only common ground.

Although manga and art were shown in different spheres, it is improbable that they never shared audiences. The high circulation of the manga discussed here suggests that they were widely known, even by those who sought to differentiate themselves from mass culture. We might consider, then, how artists were responding to the gendered bodies appearing in the newspapers and the relational charge their own depictions brought forth. Nakamura's collections of clippings and Shiraga's interest in *The Water Margin* demonstrate that the meanings and resonances of visual culture were never far from these artists' minds. They responded in kind, with visual art that redirected or reimagined the body as a means to contemplate their roles in Japan's unknown future.

The artists discussed in this book navigated new cultural and political horizons: liberal democracy, a thriving commercial culture, and the industrialization that resulted from the military economies of the Cold War. Their responses were varied, yet all summoned the body as the site to examine and question subjectivity. This study has examined such artworks as Shiraga's *Challenging Mud,* Tanaka's *Electric Dress,* Nakamura's *On the Stairs,* and Katsura's illustrations for *Another Country,* all of which express their creators' ambition to communicate and compete on a transnational scale yet are also tethered to the aesthetic and political contingencies of postwar Japan. My aim has been to show how these crucial issues emerged through the specificities of each artwork—their facture and visual impact—and to answer the perennial art historical question of *how* they manifested meaning visually. It is my hope that I have successfully illustrated how the artists interrogated the body as a key site for negotiating the mutually constitutive issues of gender and national subjectivity.

For artists active in the postwar period, the body was the threshold of exposure: a liminal site where anxieties were palpably manifest, where selfhood was questioned, and where transformation occurred. In each chapter, I have shown how the artist encountered a personal and political limit before withdrawing from the peak intensity of friction in the gendered body's relationship to the state. For Katsura Yuki, the threshold of political complicity was marked by her collaboration with wartime propaganda, which marshaled the representation of the human body as an uncompromising pillar of the nation in the 1940s.

Following her 1944 participation in a collaborative collage that relied on naturalistic representations of women's bodies, Katsura stopped painting. When she resumed in the postwar period, her politics emerged with greater force (although not necessarily with greater clarity), and gradually thereafter her paintings eschewed bodily presence, representing figures as zoomorphic, obfuscated, or concealed beneath layers.

In Nakamura Hiroshi's *Self-Portrait B,* from 1953, he portrayed himself as naked, cadaverous, and exposed. He relied on the representation of the male body as a sign of labor and power, with the zenith of his personal investment in bodily representation and political activism coalescing in *Sunagawa No. 5* in 1955. The work is the most widely known of his oeuvre, and it continues to garner high levels of attention. Yet not long after its completion, Nakamura redirected his political and personal affiliations. From 1957 onward, the artist exiled the male body from his canvases, with masculinity reemerging only as metaphor in his paintings of phallic steam engines. Nakamura instead began to feature a one-eyed schoolgirl in her uniform, often seated on trains, who stared back at the viewer, implicitly asking about the viewer's complicity with the consumption of the female body in Japan's new liberal democracy.

Tanaka Atsuko used her own body in her performance works, illuminating and endangering herself in *Electric Dress* and displaying and disavowing sexuality in her performance of *Stage Clothes.* Both works were completed in 1956, the year that the pressures of urbanization seemed to put women on the precipice and suicide rates for young women became alarming. *Electric Dress,* in particular, earned Tanaka a great deal of attention in local and national newspapers, and it continues to be exhibited around the world. Some mark this work as the apex of her career. From 1957 on, Tanaka would never again make performance works. Only the surface design of *Electric Dress* remained visible in her prolific series of paintings of lines and circles. Ultimately, Tanaka put her body at a further remove, leaving the Gutai group and relocating to quiet temple grounds away from Osaka.

Shiraga Kazuo, too, like other members of Gutai who were encouraged by Michel Tapié to create more marketable work, turned from his past interest in heroic performance art to focus on paintings. Shiraga, however, remained invested in corporeal connections to the canvas, maintaining his method of painting with his feet throughout the 1950s and 1960s. In the late 1960s he began experimenting with manipulating wooden rods with his feet, no longer making direct contact with the canvas. By 1970, as the Gutai Art Association became increasingly commercial through its members' much-maligned participation in the corporate and state-sponsored Expo '70, Shiraga had ceased painting with his feet and had receded from society at large. He joined the monastery at Mount Hiei and, for two years, quit painting altogether. Shiraga seemed to reassess his ethics of violence, and from that time forward he would chant Buddhist sutras before beginning to paint.

Performance art, painting, and photography were all part of a complex, cross-pollinating cultural aesthetic that grappled with the notions of Japanese selfhood, nationhood, and gender. This kaleidoscopic range of visual materials shared common themes and concerns yet was a vivid convergence of divided representations, leaving a fluid impression of the stakes of the times. I hope that this book, through its inclusion of artists who are lesser known in the West, has been successful in broadening an understanding of the complex and productive field of art and politics that existed in the postwar period on a global scale. With this goal in mind, I have elected to take the somewhat circuitous approach of looking at individual artists rather than art groups, as this practice allows for close examination of specific artworks and evades the tendency to generalize about the politics and aesthetics of particular groups, which often had shifting memberships. This approach is especially important given that art groups in Japan were often networks of artists who shared resources (which were scant in the immediate postwar period) but not necessarily ideologies and aesthetic strategies.

Finally, by intentionally focusing on artworks and events from the 1930s to the 1970s I have aimed to dispel the notion that postwar Japan was born from the ashes on August 6, 1945, despite the appeal that this claim seems to have for both English-speaking art historians and many Japanese artists and curators. I have shown not only how artists in the postwar period were knowledgeable and engaged with art from the past but also how the very same artists, thinkers, and organizations were often equally active before and after the Pacific War and into the Cold War. The latter had as much impact on art practice as the former.

At the end of this study, we can draw no simple conclusions about the "context" of the postwar period and its bearing on artistic practice, nor can we provide a pat definition or stylistic summation of Japanese postwar art. It is my hope, however, that we have emerged with a richer sense of how artists and art were deeply enmeshed in the turbulent politics of the times, and how that politics became legible on canvas. Further, I have attempted to show how gender subjectivity, particularly as it related to the nation, was a fundamental concern for men and women. Visual culture, painting, and performance art were all part of a complex cultural aesthetic that grappled with political selfhood through representations of the obfuscated body, the exposed body, the heroic body, and the mechanized body. By observing a contrasting range of art we can glean that artists were not simply traumatized victims of the atomic bomb, liberated imperial subjects, or devoted enthusiasts of American-style democracy. Instead, the art of the times was sophisticated and complex, charged with conflict over Japan's political future and influenced by fears about physical safety amid bewilderingly rapid industrial and domestic transformation. Katsura Yuki, Nakamura Hiroshi, Tanaka Atsuko, and Shiraga Kazuo met the political and aesthetic challenges of the Japanese postwar period with moments of complicity and disavowal, interrogation, and invention. These artists, with dissimilar aesthetic priorities and divergent political interests, were nonetheless all invested in the entangled issues of gender and nationhood that at the time were redefining Japan and its role in the uneven vectors of the global art world.

Acknowledgments

Writing is a social process, and my work on this long-running project has been possible only with the support of my friends and the guidance of my colleagues. My debt of gratitude is large, and the following words do little to express my appreciation.

My dear friends Elizabeth Ferrell, Kris Paulsen, Max Woodworth, Bibiana Obler, Brian Hurley, Karl Whittington, Lisa Florman, Jessen Kelly, Erica Levin, and Max Ward read some or all of the manuscript as it progressed and have been an incredible source of ideas and encouragement. My friend and Berkeley colleague Maiko Morimoto has also been an absolutely indispensable part of the project as a research assistant and liaison in Japan. Siobhan McCracken-Nixon, Suzanne Gray, Hillary Pederson, Meghan Raham, Anne Byrd, Molly Farrell, Jesse Schotter, Joe Gin Clark, Tara Ivanochko, Michael Hughes, Sherri Kajiwara, Kirsten Strayer, and Francis Chung must be recognized for their edifying input and friendship.

I'm especially grateful for the mentoring and intellectual insight of William Marotti, Alicia Volk, and Bert Winther-Tamaki. William has provided crucial feedback to me at conferences and Japan Arts and Globalizations (JAG) workshops, as well as generously giving extensive feedback on the manuscript, above and beyond what one could hope for. His own scholarship has allowed me to think carefully about the relationship between art and politics. Alicia offered critical advice during the manuscript's progression, and her exemplary scholarship has urged me to set a higher standard for my own work. Bert's writing has had a major impact on my own since my first forays into art history, and I have had the benefit of learning from him at multiple workshops and conferences. Bert led a manuscript workshop that immensely aided this project's development. Thanks to the generosity of these three scholars, both the book and my experience of writing it were greatly improved.

My colleagues in Japanese studies have been immensely helpful. Gennifer Weisenfeld has been an inspiring thinker and generous mentor. I am grateful to Chelsea Foxwell,

Noriko Murai, Omuka Toshiharu, Reiko Tomii (who first suggested I study Katsura Yuki), Ming Tiampo, Maureen Donovan, Toshio Watanabe, Phil Kaffen, Paul Roquet, Shimada Yoshiko, Rosemary Candelario, Kerim Yasar, Jordan Smith, Anne McKnight, and Justin Jesty. Participating in the Japan Arts and Globalizations events has been rewarding and formative. JAG members read several of my chapters, and I warmly thank all of those readers, as well as Miriam Wattles for starting the program.

The formative stages of my research in Japan were shaped by the insights of Michio Hayashi. I wrote the first draft of my first dissertation chapter while attending one of his graduate seminars at Sophia University, and he continues to support my work today. My research in Japan would not have been possible without the commitment of Kushida Kiyomi at the Inter-University Center for Japanese Studies. Curator Katō Mizuho was an invaluable source of information on the Gutai Art Association, and her work on Tanaka Atsuko was foundational to my own. I thank Hirai Shōichi for his continued insight into the life of Shiraga Kazuo. Nakamura Hiroshi has charismatically and energetically told me stories of his life on several occasions. I thank the Museum of Contemporary Art, Tokyo, curators Fujii Aki, Chinzei Yoshimi, and Seki Naoko for their assistance and depth of knowledge. I thank Kajiya Kenji, Ebisawa Sachie, Kikuchi Keiko, Osaki Shin'ichiro, Tatehata Akira, Joshua Mack, Itō Shōko, and Jinno Kimio of Gallery HAM, Ogawa Tomoko and the Osaka City Museum of Modern Art, the curators at the Hyōgo Prefectural Museum of Art, and Fergus McCaffrey for granting me interviews and access to important primary material. Outside Japanese studies, many other scholars have given me guidance, and I thank John O'Brian, Helen Langa, Juliet Bellow, Kim Butler, and Emi Tsuda.

Portions of this book began in the form of my dissertation, written at the University of California, Berkeley. I thank my dissertation committee members for their insight and help. Gregory Levine has been and continues to be a key source of support; Anne Wagner's intellectual guidance was matched by her personal investment in seeing her students succeed; Miryam Sas encouraged me to think creatively across boundaries; and Whitney Davis reminded me to take as much care with the little details as with the larger picture. I must also thank Patricia Berger and Charles Drucker, my wise and warm adopted family who made my years at Berkeley some of the best of my life.

At The Ohio State University I have found myself in a department of incredibly kind and intellectually astute scholars. Kris Paulsen, Karl Whittington, and Erica Levin have been an important part of my writing process through daily conversation. I have benefited enormously from the leadership and mentoring of Lisa Florman, Andrew Shelton, and Julia Andrews. I am grateful to the department community: Gwyn Dalton, Mollie Workman, Jen Lopez, Stephanie Bernhardt, Michelle Maguire, Christian Kleinbub, Amanda Gluibizzi, Byron Hammon, Mark Fullerton, Barbara Haeger, Daniel Marcus, Christina Burke Mathison, and Tim McNiven. I must also thank the members of the Asian American Studies group and the East Asian Studies Program at OSU, whose energy and support have been invaluable. I thank my graduate students Eunice Uhm, Alice Phan, and Maria

Cabrerizo, as well as other graduate students in the department, including Yiwen Liu, Linda Huang, and Gillian Zhang.

Various organizations helped fund this project. I received funding from the Japan Foundation as a graduate student in 2008 and as a research fellow in 2016. I also received funding for the project from American University's Faculty Development Grants; the College Women's Association of Japan; The Ohio State University Arts and Humanities Grants; the History of Art Department at The Ohio State University; the Coca-Cola Critical Difference for Women Grant for Research on Women, Gender, and Gender Equity; and the Meiss/Mellon Author's Book Award. Early stages of my research were funded by a grant from the Social Sciences and Research Council of Canada. I am grateful to the University of Minnesota Press for taking this project on, and for the outstanding editorial work of Pieter Martin.

I thank the Kunimoto and Woodworth families, especially my late grandfather, Chikao Kunimoto, who impressed on me the value of education, and my cousins Kristy Kunimoto and Robyn Kunimoto.

I thank my son, Kazuo Jasper, for filling my heart with love and my day with smiles, and for making sure I never lose sight of what really matters in life. His name comes from my grandmother Kazuko (rather than from the artist Shiraga Kazuo) and means "harmonious life." He has certainly brought a life of harmony to Max, Goji, and me. Finally, I thank my partner in all things, Max Woodworth. He has been a true coparent, lovingly rocking our son to sleep or running madly around the playground despite his own demanding research schedule. He has tirelessly edited my chapters at the eleventh hour, talked over ideas and given me new ones, and been a fountain of patience and support. This book would not have been possible (nor would I be having as much fun) without him.

Notes

Introduction

The quotation from Ishimure Michiko that serves as an epigraph for this chapter is from Mishima, *Bitter Sea.* Ishimure lost most of her family to mental illness due to a phenomenon known as Minamata disease or Minamata sickness, a condition caused by mercury poisoning. As a writer, poet, and activist from Minamata, Ishimure played a central role in fighting for the rights of victims of the illness. Her prose and poetry are characterized by her use of local dialect and critique of industrialization. For example, see Ishimure, *Kugai jōdo.* The original Japanese tanka that is the source of the lines in the epigraph is titled *Ukara* (Blood relative): "Kuruebakano sobonogotokuni ensakiyori keriotosaruru naramukawaremo." Ishimure, *Hahatachi no kuni,* 16. The English translation in *Bitter Sea* uses the expression "kicked out"; however, a more accurate translation might be "kicked down," as the tanka refers to the grandmother being kicked down from the *ensaki,* the edge of the veranda-like porch located at the side of a garden, *engawa.* Thus, the grandmother was not kicked out of the house (that is, from the front porch to the street, where the public could see her); rather, she was kicked down to the private garden. Walls usually surround the garden, thus the family's humiliation would be hidden. Ishimure's phrasing suggests the grandmother's body was treated like a thing, reduced to a physical mass, in this private space of devastation.

1. The museum, city, and prefectural staff consulted with Dr. Harada Masazumi, social scientist Maruyama Sadami, Minamata disease researchers at Kumamoto University, and some Minamata disease victims to decide on how to arrange the exhibition space. Minamata Disease Municipal Museum staff member, e-mail correspondence with author, April 14, 2015.

2. "'Ikeru ningyō' shōjo—yonenkan kaeranu ishiki," *Asahi Shinbun,* April 22, 1960, 10.

3. The series was coproduced by Eugene Smith's wife, Aileen Smith, an American of Japanese descent, who also acted as a translator and assistant during the couple's stay in Japan.

4. Weisenfeld, "Industrial Poisoning, Minamata," 94.

5. Smith, *Minamata: Life—Sacred and Profane*; Smith and Smith, *Minamata.*

6. Gross, Katz, and Ruby, "Introduction," xxiii. The photograph appears in Smith and Smith, *Minamata,* 138–39. Although this image has been withdrawn from circulation in accordance with Tomoko's parents' wishes, it nonetheless appears online frequently today. For example, it appears in

the Wikipedia entry "Tomoko Uemura in Her Bath," last modified November 19, 2015, https://en.wikipedia.org.

7. Smith and Smith, *Minamata,*138–39.

8. For more on the decision to withhold copyright of *Tomoko in Her Bath,* see Aileen Smith's statement from July 5, 2001, in Aileen Archive, http://archive.is/e84c. The family's decision is also mentioned in Gross, Katz, and Ruby, "Introduction," xxiii. Note that Eugene and Aileen Smith read the family's name as Uemura, but the family's pronunciation is Kamimura. Most descriptions of the photograph continue to refer to the family as Uemura.

9. Ōiwa, *Rowing the Eternal Sea,* 5. Tanaka Shizuko died three years later in Kumamoto University Hospital. Her parents and grandparents also died of mercury poisoning. Her sister, Jitsuko, survived but remains mentally and physically disabled.

10. For example, see "Shisha ya hakkyōsha mo: Minamata ni densensei no kibyō" [Casualties and insanity: A strange infectious disease in Minamata], *Nishinippon Shinbun,* May 8, 1956, 4; "Minamata ni kodomo no kibyō: Onaji byōgen ka neko ni mo hassei" [Strange disease afflicting children: Outbreaks among cats as well possibly from the same cause], *Kumamoto Nichinichi Shinbun,* May 16, 1956, 6.

11. Minamata Disease Municipal Museum video display, visited August 8, 2014.

12. "Shisha ya hakkyōsha mo."

13. The term *Pacific War* refers to the Pacific and East Asian theater of combat during World War II.

14. Acetaldehyde is also used as a preservative for fruits and fish; as a flavoring agent; as a solvent in the rubber, tanning, and paper industries; and as a denaturant for alcohol. In addition, it is used in fuel compositions and for hardening gelatin.

15. Yokoyama, "Environmental Pollution by Corporations in Japan," 331. The company was previously known as Japan Nitrogenous Fertilizers, commonly abbreviated as Nichitsu. In 1965, it was renamed the Chisso Corporation. During the war, the Minamata factory was "administered by the military and renamed 'Kumamoto Factory #7042.' It made products for the army and navy ranging from explosives to bulletproof glass. At the end of the war, its 4,151 employees included 620 students and 100 members of 'women's volunteer corps' mobilized to keep the factory fully staffed." George, *Minamata,* 30.

16. Minamata Disease Municipal Museum video display, visited August 8, 2014. Although most commonly called strange disease, the illness was also called dancing cat disease *(neko odori byō),* as its effect on cats was so arresting. See "Neko tenkan de zenmetsu" [Cats dying from epilepsy], *Kumamoto Nichinichi Shinbun,* August 1, 1954; George, *Minamata,* 3.

17. The company continued to discharge toxic waste into the waters until 1968.

18. The disease also affected those of the lower classes more than the wealthy: lower-income families tended to live closer to the bay, where the Chisso Corporation was directly depositing pollutants. Consequently, when the "strange disease" began appearing, community members were quick to stigmatize the poor. Class differences were less visible in the media coverage of the outbreak.

19. See "Minamata ni kodomo no kibyō"; "Kibyō: Naottemo 'haijin': Kumamoto-ken ni kōseishō de chōsa" [Strange disease: Treated yet 'disabled person': The Ministry of Welfare investigates in Kumamoto], *Asahi Shinbun,* April 1 1957; "Eiyō shōgai mo wazawai: Machijū ga noirōze gimi"

[Minamata strange disease: Is manganese the cause?], *Kumamoto Nichinichi Shinbun,* February 14, 1957, 6.

20. Weisenfeld, "Industrial Poisoning, Minamata," 95. Weisenfeld notes similarities between the Minamata disaster and the Fukushima disaster of March 2011.

21. "Akarui seihakuji Minamata" [Bright, mentally disabled in Minamata], *Asahi Shinbun* (Kumamoto edition), June 9, 1958, 10. The story attempted to put a positive spin on the alarming situation.

22. Partner, *Assembled in Japan.* See chapter 3 for more on the "bright life" in relation to Tanaka Atsuko's *Electric Dress.*

23. See, for example, "Tokushu gakkyū ni boshi nyūgaku" [Mother and child enter special school], *Mainichi Shinbun,* November 7, 1956.

24. For more on Japan and environmental disasters, see Miller, Thomas, and Walker, *Japan at Nature's Edge.*

25. In 1970, Minamata disease affected two First Nations communities in Northwestern Ontario as the result of the consumption of local fish contaminated with mercury, and a First Nations community in Southern Ontario was affected because of the illegal disposal of industrial chemical waste.

26. For discussion of the events of May 1968, see Marotti, "Japan 1968," 97; Ross, *May '68 and Its Afterlives.*

27. Historian Wesley Sasaki-Uemura discusses the Minamata disaster and the social movement that emerged after it as examples of events that produced alternative lifestyles: "The mercury poisoned the local waters and the fish caught there, which in turn poisoned the people of Minamata, especially fishermen's families. This outcome prompted some of the local farmers to turn toward producing organic foods, such as the oranges that the region is known for." Sasaki-Uemura, *Organizing the Spontaneous,* 213.

28. Many scholars refer to this period as the American Occupation, reflecting the fact that the occupation forces were predominantly American.

29. Harootunian, "Japan's Postwar and After," 18.

30. This rhetoric is eerily consonant with historian Kristin Ross's account of France's drive to establish its continued hegemony over Algeria through a discourse of modernization and decolonization: "The most overwhelming sense of the 'new' emanated of course from the ongoing mass nationalist movements and wars of decolonization. In the year 1960 alone, fifteen African states became independent, in part in the wake of the continuing Algerian struggle against the French. A utopian rhetoric of creation—clean slates and tabula rasa—dominated the writings of anticolonialist writers intent on analyzing the colonial situation and calling for its overthrow." Ross, *Fast Cars, Clean Bodies,* 158.

31. For example, see Munroe, *Japanese Art after 1945*; Bryan-Wilson, "Remembering Yoko Ono's *Cut Piece.*" Similarly, Butoh dance is often characterized as born from the events of Hiroshima, despite the fact that it was developed in Tokyo and has a plurality of influences. See Goodman, "The Return of the Gods."

32. Chow, *The Age of the World Target,* 14.

33. On the initial contact between Japan and the United States, see Banno, *Japan's Modern History.*

34. As Ann Sherif has noted: "The Cold War has been an important point of reference in cultural histories of Japan's Asian neighbors—Korea, China, and Taiwan—as well as those geographically

more distant but diplomatically closer allies in Europe and the United States. Far less frequently, however, have Japan's literature, film, and art been tied to the Cold War. Instead, critics and cultural historians most often have posited Japanese cultural production as taking place in an insular peacetime Japan while emphasizing a cultural identity that can never escape the memory of the traumatic Asian world wars of the 1930s and 1940s." Sherif, *Japan's Cold War*, 1.

35. Ibid., 6.

36. On Zen and Japanese national identity, see Sharf, "The Zen of Japanese Nationalism."

37. Yuval-Davis, *Gender and Nation*, 2. In asserting women's key role in nationhood, Yuval-Davis neglects to acknowledge that men, too, play a role in reproduction.

38. Germer, Mackie, and Wöhr, *Gender, Nation and State in Modern Japan*, 2.

39. Igarashi, *Bodies of Memory*, 5.

40. Ross, *Fast Cars, Clean Bodies*.

41. Mackie, *Feminism in Modern Japan*, 7.

42. Mackie has cogently noted how embodiment was a highly gendered phenomenon: "The history of feminist movements demonstrates that embodiment is another concept which is essential to understanding the gendered politics of citizenship. This is not a case of reviving the association of woman with 'the body' and men with 'the mind.' Rather, the kinds of issues that have been highlighted by feminist activists draw attention to the fact that we are all 'embodied citizens.'" Ibid., 2.

43. The Allied Occupation policy of Reverse Course began sometime in 1947–48 and lasted until the end of the occupation in 1952.

44. Marotti, *Money, Trains, and Guillotines*, 2.

45. In his study of Japanese art in the early postwar period and the relationships of bodies, Bert Winther-Tamaki writes: "It shall become apparent that the weakening of bodies through diverse deformation in paint was intended and frequently perceived as strengthening subjectivity" Winther Tamaki, "Oil Painting in Postsurrender Japan," 348. For more on the representation of bodies in Japanese art, see Winther-Tamaki, *Maximum Embodiment*; Winther-Tamaki, "Embodiment/Disembodiment"; Tiampo "Body, War, and the Discourses of History."

46. The artist Tanaka Atsuko is not related to the Minamata victims Tanaka Shizuko and Tanaka Jitsuko. Tanaka is a very common family name in Japan.

47. My inclusion of two women and two men in this study is not intended to suggest that there was gender equality in the Japanese art scene of the 1950s and 1960s. Women were greatly underrepresented, although Tanaka and Katsura were well known.

48. Freud, "Beyond the Pleasure Principle," 598.

49. *OED* Online, s.v. "anxiety," accessed October 10, 2014, http://www.oed.com.

50. For example, see Munroe, *Japanese Art after 1945*; Jennison and Hein, "Against Forgetting"; Tiampo, *Gutai: Decentering Modernism*.

51. Dower, *Embracing Defeat*.

52. See Weisenfeld, *Mavo*; Volk, *In Pursuit of Universalism*.

53. The formation of artist groups in Japan was driven as much by resource availability as it was by cultural practice. Following the war, many people experienced poverty, and artists often found it necessary to form groups to share studio space and art supplies. For example, Motonaga Sadamasa describes joining Gutai out of necessity: "The reason I had decided to join was that I had come to Kobe from Iga, and I didn't have any friends or acquaintances there, so I didn't have

anyone to talk to and there wasn't anyone to borrow money from either. *[Laughs]* And when I was hungry I couldn't ask anyone to buy me dinner. To do that, it was important to have friends, and that was one of the big reasons I joined Gutai." Motonaga, interview by Osaki and Yamamura, 143. For more on groups and collectivity in postwar Japan, see Tomii, "Introduction." The entire issue of *Positions* in which Tomii's article appears is devoted to collectivism in twentieth-century Japanese art.

54. Remarking on the modern formation of the avant-garde, Alicia Volk writes: "Whether cast as protagonists or in supporting roles, art organizations have performed a key hermeneutical function for critics and historians alike. Bewildering in variety and overwhelming in quantity, they have nonetheless provided a means of taming into interpretive submission that unruly phenomenon captured in the tidy phrase 'Japanese Modern Art.'" Volk, "Authority, Autonomy and the Early Taishō 'Avant-Garde,'" 451. Volk critiques the two general interpretive strategies scholars have used in dealing with art groups: "one, adopting a Euro-American model of academy versus avant-garde, and seeing a similar, if not parallel set of dynamics among Japanese art groups; and the other, looking to indigenous social structures such as the premodern *iemoto* system to understand certain characteristics of Japanese art groups left unexplained by the western avant-garde model." Ibid., 453.

55. Some members, such as Kanayama Akira, created highly conceptual work that made indirect reference to bodily presence.

56. See Hirai, *Gutai tte nanda?*; Kawasaki and Yamamoto, *Gutai shiryōshū*; Koplos, "Circuitries of Color." Recent exhibitions such as *Gutai: Splendid Playground* (Guggenheim New York, 2013) have also given the political dynamics of the group short shrift. See Kunimoto, "Gutai's Ascent," 114. Tiampo's work is an exception; she notes, "Shiraga Kazuo articulated a critical role for the body in the constitution of the individual, and the individual as resistance against fascism." Tiampo, "Body, War, and the Discourses of History," 346.

1. Katsura Yuki's Bodies of Resistance

1. Katsura and Yoshihara also met at the Martha Jackson Gallery in 1958. See "Nenpyō" [Chronology], in Seki et al., *Katsura Yuki,* 314. Midori Yoshimoto notes: "In the medium of *yōga* or oil painting, Yuki(ko) Katsura (1913–1991) was one of the first women to gain relatively high recognition. She was accepted to the 1933 exhibition of one of the most established bijutsu dantai, Kōfū-kai, and subsequently in the prestigious exhibition of Nika-kai in 1935, but she was quite the exception. As a female artist who worked in the prewar period, Yukiko Shimada recalls that it was difficult for women artists to be selected for the limited number of juried exhibitions, and women could hardly become members of any bijutsu dantai that gave men priority." Yoshimoto, *Into Performance,* 15. Katsura's full given name is Yukiko, but she commonly signed her paintings as Yuki. A fortune-teller advised her that using Yuki would bring her better luck. Ebisawa Sachie and Kikuchi Keiko, Katsura's nieces, interview by author, June 28, 2016, Tokyo.

2. Gluck, "The Past in the Present," 66.

3. In 2016, the permanent collection exhibition at Tokyo's Museum of Contemporary Art focused on art from the postwar period, including several pieces by Katsura Yuki as well as some by Nakamura Hiroshi. The inclusion of these artists together suggests how "postwar art" is defined differently within Japan.

4. Although most people in North American art circles have heard of the Gutai Art Association, that is not always the case in Japan. To offer one anecdotal example: a Japanese high school student with whom I was discussing my research proclaimed that he knew Katsura's oeuvre very well, but he had never heard of the Gutai Art Association. Like Gutai, Katsura exhibited in the United States. In 1960, two of her artworks were included in an exhibition of abstract Japanese art at the Gres Gallery in Washington, D.C., alongside the works of other Japanese artists such as Onosato Toshinobu and Kusama Yayoi. That year Katsura also participated in an exhibition at the Riverside Museum in New York, and in 1961 her work was included in a show at the Corcoran Gallery of Art in Washington, D.C. See "Nenpyō," 314.

5. Ibid., 315. The boat trip also included novelist Tateno Nobuyuki and cartoonist Nara Yoshisuke. See "19 Off on Russian Angling Tour," *Japan Times,* July 6, 1964, 4. In the photograph that accompanied the *Japan Times* story announcing the trip, Katsura is seen in the foreground as the group boards. The article describing Katsura's intrepid adventures was juxtaposed with a photo of Miss Japan in a bathing suit. Her memoir *Onna hitori genshiburaku ni hairu* (A woman alone in a primitive village) was a best seller and also was awarded the Mainichi Publishing Culture Award. Ōe Kenzaburo remarked that Katsura's writing had remarkable anthropological power and moral insight and was worthy of respect. *Tokyo Shinbun,* October 3, 1962, 8, reprinted in Katsura, *Kitsune no dairyokō,* 303–4. Katsura's books helped attract attention to her artworks, according to both her relatives and curator Kokatsu Reiko. Ebisawa and Kikuchi, interview by author, June 28, 2016; Kokatsu Reiko, response to Kunimoto, "Katsura Yuki and the Stakes of Exposure."

6. Volk, "Katsura Yuki and the Japanese Avant-Garde," 3.

7. Rancière, *Dissensus,* 69.

8. Ibid., 140–41.

9. Katsura had studied ink painting with Ikegami Hidetoshi from age twelve. Although she had hoped to study oil painting at an early age, her parents did not allow her to until she was eighteen. See "Visiting Two Artists." Katsura described being forced to study only ink painting as depressing; see Enchi et al., *Josei geijutsuka no jinsei 2,* 85.

10. See Ikeda, McDonald, and Tiampo, *Art and War in Japan.*

11. "The lives of ordinary Japanese citizens changed dramatically after October 1937, when Japan embarked on undeclared war with China. . . . The Essence of National Polity *(kokutai no hongi),* published in 1937, defined all Japanese citizens' relation to a divine emperor as 'organic,' 'unique,' and 'historically ordained,' and articulated their obligation to die for this Emperor inextricably identified with the nation. The National Mobilization Law *(kokumin kokka sōdōinhō)* of 1938 placed all human and material resources of the nation at the discretion of the military for the war effort." Ikeda, McDonald, and Tiampo, "Introduction," 15.

12. Ueno, *Nationalism and Gender,* 16.

13. Narita, "Women in the Motherland," 147.

14. Robertson, "Biopower," 332.

15. Ibid., 341.

16. "A definition of Japanese woman as 'good wife, wise mother' *(ryōsai kenbo)* emerged in Japan at the end of the nineteenth century. In the aftermath of the Sino-Japanese War of 1984–95, prominent men, especially officials in the Ministry of Education (Monbushō), began to champion 'good wife, wise mother' as woman's proper role in imperial Japan. As the term suggests, *ryōsai kenbo* defined women as managers of domestic affairs in households and nurturers of children.

From the late 1890s until the end of World War II, 'good wife, wise mother' increasingly pervaded the mass media. . . . Yet following a half-century of official promulgation, the influence of *ryōsai kenbo* did not immediately evaporate in the postwar era." Uno, "The Death of 'Good Wife, Wise Mother'?," 293–94.

17. "Katsura Yuki nenpyō," 54.

18. Seki Naoko has observed that Katsura was likely interested in Joan Miró's work *Maternity* (1924), which also blurs the boundary between human forms and insect forms. Katsura juxtaposes human figures and letters (which mysteriously appear to be fragments of Katsura's name), as does Miró, who also combines letters with symbol-like motifs. Seki, "Mushitachi no kānivaru."

19. Katsura, "Okama no koto nado," 300.

20. For example, artist Murayama Tomoyoshi was arrested in May 1930 and charged with violating the Peace Preservation Law. See Gerteis, "Political Protest in Interwar Japan." Writer Kobayashi Takiji (1903–33) died at the hands of the police.

21. Hamamoto, "Katsura Yuki no manazashi."

22. For more on embodiment in art, see Winther-Tamaki, *Maximum Embodiment.*

23. For example, Hirai Fusando's manga *Kan-chan no sangyō senshi* depicts young boys and young men performing exercises together, eating together, and sleeping side by side. Although at times they are shirtless, their strength and physiques are not emphasized as much as are their synchronous, unified bodily activities.

24. "Politics invents new forms of collective enunciation: it re-frames the given by inventing new ways of making sense of the sensible, new configurations between the visible and the invisible, and between the audible and the inaudible, new distributions of space and time—in short, new bodily capacities." Rancière, *Dissensus,* 139.

25. Among the artists who rebelled against these new dictates were Fukuzawa Ichirō, Murayama Tomoyoshi, and Matsumoto Shunsuke.

26. Terada Takeo, "Japan's Art World Active in '39 Despite China Affair—Many Good Exhibitions Held Downtown, National Art Movement Gains Strength," *Japan Times,* January 8, 1940, 8.

27. Katsura, "Intabyū," 47.

28. On February 25, 1943, the Women's Art Organization was established by about fifty female artists in Tokyo under the supervision of the Army News Service, led by Hasegawa. Its first exhibition, *Women's Art Organization for the Nation,* was held in Ginza, Tokyo, in March 1943. The list of works that were exhibited has not been preserved. See Kira, "'Joryū bijutsuka hōkōtai,'" 132–33. For more on women artists during the war, see Kitahara, *Ajia no josei shintai wa ikani egakareta ka;* Kira, *Sensō to josei gaka;* Kokatsu, Hashimoto, and Suzuki, *Hashiru onnatachi.*

29. Four members of the group—Hasegawa Haruko, Nakada Kikuyo, Nakatani Miyuki, and Katsura Yuki—signed both components of the work, suggesting that they had a leading role in its conception. It took two months to complete. Kira, "'Joryū bijutsuka hōkōtai,'" 134. Katsura describes coming up with this idea in "Intabyū," 48–49.

30. Hamamoto, "Katsura Yuki shiron," 10.

31. Kira, "'Joryū bijutsuka hōkōtai,'" 132–33. This work has been described as a collage, but in fact all of the images are drawn rather than pasted, and they are somewhat homogeneous rather than foils of one another. The work is similar to *rakuchū rakugaizu* (paintings depicting views in and around the city of Kyoto) in the way that it focuses on the assemblage of many motifs in one space.

32. Kira, *Sensō to josei gaka,* 134. Kokatsu Reiko thinks that Katsura took the lead in transferring images from photographs rather than in constructing the whole composition. See Kokatsu, "Kindai Nihon ni okeru josei gaka o meguru seido," 54.

33. Hariu, "Katsura Yuki no bakeppuri to yūmoa," 11, reprinted in Kira, "'Joryū bijutsuka hōkōtai,'" 132.

34. Kira, "'Joryū bijutsuka hōkōtai,'" 133–34.

35. "The instructors were giving the baby eagles lessons in one corner of the air station where the summer grass was blown by winds. This is the very image *[sugata]* of one living the most worthy life to live *[ikigai no aru hito]* as a subject of our Empire of Japan, the greatest *[medetaki]* country in the world *[udai—*a synonym of *sekai* and *tenka].*" Quoted in ibid., 177.

36. Ibid., 132–33.

37. See Atkins, *Wearing Propaganda.*

38. Winther-Tamaki, *Maximum Embodiment.*

39. Hasegawa was concerned that the work would be destroyed and donated it to Yasukuni Shrine. Kira, "'Joryū bijutsuka hōkōtai,'" 134.

40. The English text reads: "As a good wife and loving mother, the traditional Japanese woman has been the basis of the family system. But the changing social fabric of Japan is now compelling her to leave the seclusion of her home and enter man's sphere to compete in the struggle for existence. As a consequence, Japanese young women are finding it necessary to acquire professional skill in addition to more conventional training in the arts, such as tea-ceremony, flower arrangements, even classic dances and music." A large photographic collage of women working in a factory making electric fans and cooking at home, along with a portrait of a woman in a kimono, is featured before another collage of women dressed in kimonos doing things such as playing the koto, doing ikebana, conducting a tea ceremony, and doing traditional dance. The final pages feature a collage of marching soldiers, a fighter plane, and a tank. *Nippon* (Tokyo: Kokusho Kankōkai, 1938), n.p. For more on *Nippon* see Weisenfeld, "Touring Japan-as-Museum." Weisenfeld notes: "Touting the magazine as a representation of 'actual life and events in modern Japan and the Far East,' *NIPPON*'s designers used a host of sophisticated modernist visual techniques, including an array of stunning photomontages, as a means of enticing the Western tourist to authenticate Japan by experiencing 'the world-as-exhibition'" (747–48).

41. During this period of transition Katsura completed *Yoru (Night)* (1948) and *Kurashi (Living),* both of which use a naturalistic style of representation. Interestingly, even in these examples, Katsura seemed to struggle with full figural representation. *Yoru* (a rare self-portrait) shows the figure from the neck up, and *Kurashi* depicts a nude female body (in two poses) with face and torso turned away from the viewer. In *Kurashi,* it is a cat, rather than the human figure, that returns the viewer's gaze.

42. Dower, *Embracing Defeat,* 412.

43. Orbaugh, *Japanese Fiction of the Allied Occupation,* 41. Orbaugh quotes from the "Memorandum from the Office of the Supreme Commander for the Allied Powers to the Imperial Japanese Government about 'Press Code for Japan,'" September 19, 1945.

44. For examples of newspaper and other censorship during the occupation, see Braw, *The Atomic Bomb Suppressed.*

45. Rubin, "From Wholesomeness to Decadence," 90. "On October 15, 1947, most book publishers were transferred to post-censorship, and on December 15 all but twenty-eight 'ultra-right'

or 'ultra-left' magazines (out of some 930) were placed on post-censorship. By December 1948 the transition to post-censorship was complete. Through 1949, most items submitted to the CCD were simply stamped 'Processed Without Examination,' and that October the CCD ceased its censorship operations entirely." Ibid., 84–85.

46. Dower, *Embracing Defeat.*

47. On the censorship of art after 1952, see Cather, *The Art of Censorship in Postwar Japan.*

48. Akutagawa Ryūnosuke, who wrote during the Taishō period in Japan, is regarded by some as the "father of the Japanese short story," and Japan's premier literary award, the Akutagawa Prize, is named for him. Akutagawa's story "The Battle of the Monkey and the Crab" was first published in the magazine *Fujin kōron,* March 1, 1923.

49. "Politics creates a new form, as it were, of *dissensual* 'commonsense.'" Rancière, *Dissensus,* 139.

50. See Weisenfeld, "Reinscribing Tradition in a Transnational Art World."

51. It should be noted that many of Katsura's color-field works had greater transnational currency. These were purchased by Michel Tapié and admired by Jean Cocteau. In 1961, an article in the *Japan Times* praised Katsura's work for its ability to find common ground with international movements, noting that Tapié (whom the author misidentified as a Spaniard) was also supportive of Katsura's work. See Ginno Nibbi, "Miss Katsura Gives Work Individuality," *Japan Times,* July 4, 1961, 5.

52. Katsura Yuki, "Jurarumin no hei" [Duralumin Wall], *San'yō Nichinichi Shinbun,* March 1, 1952, reprinted in Seki et al., *Katsura Yuki,* 296.

53. De Man, *Allegories of Reading.*

54. As art historian Karl Whittington has pointed out: "Allegory emerged in the visual arts as a critical tool for conveying hidden meanings that could not be expressed with words. This in turn demanded a greater investment on the part of the viewer, opening a new space between sign and referent . . . , which was then to be bridged and engaged through active acts of viewing and interpretation." Whittington, "Experimenting with Opicinus de Canistris," 152–53.

55. De Man, *Allegories of Reading,* 99, 205.

56. "In Japan as elsewhere, animation and manga became closely associated with folklore. What is more, the general association of children with animals—children like animals, children are like animals—contributed to the establishment of a nexus of folktale–animal–child–cartoon." Lamarre, "Speciesism, Part III," 112.

57. *Dōbutsu tonarigumi,* directed by Kumagawa Masao, 1941.

58. Lamarre, "Speciesism, Part I," 76.

59. Ibid., 91.

60. Lamarre, "Speciesism, Part II," 55.

61. Ibid., 51.

62. A large number of Katsura's paintings feature animals. In addition to the aforementioned works, many zoomorphic paintings are currently held in private collections. For example, one of Katsura's nieces owns half a dozen of these works featuring animals. Ebisawa and Kikuchi, interview by author, June 28, 2016.

63. Dower, *Embracing Defeat,* 347.

64. Ibid.

65. Dower states that Sirota was one of four women on the team, but her *New York Times* obituary describes her as the only woman on the committee. Ibid.; "Beate Gordon, Long-Unsung

Heroine of Japanese Women's Rights, Dies at 89," *New York Times,* January 1, 2013, B8. Her own book, titled *The Only Woman in the Room* (published under the name Beate Sirota Gordon), suggests she was the only woman involved.

66. Dower, *Embracing Defeat,* 365.

67. "Beate Sirota Gordon, the daughter of Russian Jewish parents who at 22 almost single-handedly wrote women's rights into the Constitution of modern Japan, and then kept silent about it for decades, only to become a feminist heroine there in recent years, died on Sunday at her home in Manhattan." "Beate Gordon, Long-Unsung Heroine."

68. Ibid.

69. Quoted in Dower, *Embracing Defeat,* 386.

70. Ibid., 401.

71. Kaneko, *Mirroring the Japanese Empire,* 6–7.

72. Rancière, *Dissensus,* 151.

73. Hariu Ichirō also seems to have read Katsura's penchant for depicting ropes as a political statement. Discussing the state of art and politics in 1954, he wrote, "I place my faith in Katsura Yuki's velvety textures, and works that incorporate strands of ceremonial rope into depictions of political incident." Hariu, "Shin gushō no hō kō," 10, English translation in Jesty, "Arts of Engagement," 122.

74. Nakamura, "Katsura Yuki."

75. In 1956, *Women's Day* was used for the front cover of well-respected literary critic Hanada Kiyoteru's book *Sachurikon*. According to Katsura's nieces, Katsura and Hanada were close friends. Ebisawa Sachie and Kikuchi Keiko, response to Kunimoto, "Katsura Yuki and the Stakes of Exposure."

76. Salaff, "Bikini Atoll, 1954," 58.

77. Ibid., 59.

78. Ibid., 59n2.

79. Ibid., 59.

80. The *Japan Times* ran a five-part series on the *Lucky Dragon* incident that was largely critical of the U.S. role and suggested that Americans and other Westerners living in Japan at the time may have shared in the outrage over the events. See *Japan Times,* July 19, 1954, 1; July 22, 1954, 2; August 6, 1954, 1; September 2, 1954, 3; September 4, 1954, 3.

81. Miyamoto, *Beyond the Mushroom Cloud,* 37; see also Sasaki-Uemura, *Organizing the Spontaneous,* 31. Some observers have been critical of the ways in which this mothers' movement supported patriarchal misconceptions. See Kanō, "Onna ga Hiroshima o kataru toiu koto."

82. Sasaki-Uemura, *Organizing the Spontaneous,* 123.

83. Miyamoto, *Beyond the Mushroom Cloud,* 36.

84. Schaller, "Altered States," 254.

85. O'Brian, "The Nuclear Family of Man," 5.

86. Rey Chow notes: "As knowledge, 'Hiroshima' and 'Nagasaki' come to us inevitably as representation and, specifically, as a picture. Moreover, it is not a picture in the older sense of a mimetic replication of reality; rather, it has become in itself a sign of terror, a kind of gigantic demonstration with us, the spectators, as the potential target." Chow, *The Age of the World Target,* 25.

87. Approximately nine million people attended versions of *The Family of Man* worldwide. As O'Brian describes: "Four different versions of the exhibition were produced for Japan alone. By the

end of 1956 almost a million people in Japan had seen it, roughly 10% of the audience for the exhibition worldwide. In deference to the experience of Hiroshima and Nagasaki, however, a large black-and-white photographic image of a mushroom cloud included in other traveling versions of the exhibition was omitted. Instead, photographs taken by Yamahata in Nagasaki on the day following the explosion were substituted. These images showed, as the photographs in *The Family of Man* did not, the human toll and devastation caused by the bomb. Soon, however, they were censored as well. When the emperor visited *The Family of Man* in Tokyo, Yamahata's photographs were curtained off and then removed altogether from the exhibition." O'Brian, "The Nuclear Family of Man," 3.

88. Chow, *The Age of the World Target,* 12.

89. O'Brian, "The Nuclear Family of Man," 5.

90. Years after completing this painting, Katsura would embark on two lengthy fishing trips: the first to Russia in 1964 and another to Australia and New Zealand in 1967. Her activities raise the question of whether her interest in fishing and boating was sparked by the *Lucky Dragon* incident and her involvement with it. See "Sureteta soren no sakana" [Snagging fish in the Soviet Union], *Asahi Shinbun,* August 8, 1964, 14; in this article, Katsura mentions that she caught only five or six fish. See also "19 Off on Russian Angling Tour." At age seventy-seven, Katsura undertook a trip to Scotland to try to see the Loch Ness Monster. See "Nenpyō," 308–23.

91. "Aki no shuppinsaku o kataru: 'Nihonjin no ikari'—Katsura Yukiko-san (Nika-kai)" [On her exhibited work in autumn: "Wrath of Japanese people"], *Asahi Shinbun,* August 17, 1954, 5.

92. Ibid.

93. Hariu et al., "Shūki tenrankai sono 1."

94. Curator Seki Naoko has commented on how *Human and Fish* represents different moments in time, through the presence of the living fish (suggesting a time before the bomb), the dead fish (after the bomb), and the horrified face (in the instant of the bomb). Seki et al., *Katsura Yuki,* 11.

95. See, for example, Hariu et al., "Shūki tenrankai sono 1"; "Aki no shuppinsaku o kataru."

96. *Gojira,* directed by Honda Ishirō, was released in Japan in 1954; a reedited version titled *Godzilla* was released in the United States in 1956. The original film featured a lengthy monologue lambasting the use of nuclear weapons, a segment that was cut from the American version.

97. The title *Moeru hito* has often been translated as *Men Aflame,* although *hito* is a gender-neutral term. As it was for Yamashita Kikuji, art was formative for Tsuruoka's political reorientation: Tsuruoka served in the Japanese army and was present at the Nanking Massacre in 1937. After the war he became active in the antinuclear movement.

98. In the original version of this work, the artists included an image of Mount Fuji, but other leftists criticized their reliance on imperialist imagery, and they replaced the mountain with an image of the *Lucky Dragon.* See Sherif, "Art as Activism," 43. See also Kozawa, *"Genbaku no zu,"* 189–92.

99. For more on the *Lucky Dragon* incident and related art, see Daigo Fukuryū Maru Heiwa Kyōkai, *Daigo Fukuryū Maru wa kōkaichū,* esp. 172–91. Shahn visited Japan in 1960. See Shahn and Prescott, *Ben Shahn ten,* 7. Some texts show the starting point for Shahn's *Lucky Dragon* series as 1957; however, the exhibition catalog cited gives 1960 as the beginning of the series. See also Hudson and Shahn, *Kuboyama and the Saga of the Lucky Dragon.*

100. Rancière, *Dissensus,* 139.

101. For example, in a 1979 interview Katsura stated that she once called Okamoto to tell him she was going to withdraw from the Nika Association. The very next morning Okamoto released a statement to the press saying that *he* was withdrawing from the organization. Katsura then felt she could not make a similar announcement (she later withdrew privately) for fear that it would appear she was following Okamoto's lead. Katsura, "Intabyū," 51.

102. Winther-Tamaki describes Okamoto as unusual in his treatment of the body as well: "All of these pictures except that of Okamoto overtly express the undermining of subjectivity by historical causation related to war defeat, and in his case too, war experience may have played a role in the disarticulation of the self." Winther-Tamaki, "Oil Painting in Postsurrender Japan," 375.

103. For more on the representation of African Americans and Africans in Japan, see Volk, "The Image of the Black in Japanese Art."

104. Alicia Volk writes: "In the 1960s, with the rise of a youth counter-culture and resistance to the Vietnam War, for which the US military exploited its bases in Japan, especially on Okinawa, there also arose among young Japanese an interest in the American civil rights movement and an attraction for black American culture." Ibid., 51. Katsura was no doubt a part of this growing interest in civil rights concerns, yet still among a minority in terms of actually depicting African Americans in illustrations. Volk states: "Nakamura and Kawara's painted canvases are anomalies. When blacks are found in postwar Japanese visual media, it is nearly always in photographic form." Ibid., 48. Michael Molasky has also described Japanese characterizations of African Americans, remarking that these characterizations reflected both racism and feelings of empathy after the Japanese themselves experienced discrimination by American military personnel. Molasky, *The American Occupation of Japan and Okinawa.*

105. Quoted in James, "Making Love, Making Friends," 43.

106. Ibid., 54.

107. Baldwin, *Another Country,* 44.

108. Seki et al., *Katsura Yuki,* 14.

109. This line, one of many examples, shows the characters physically close: "He leaned down and helped Vivaldo to rise. Half leaning on, half supporting each other, they made it to the door." Baldwin, *Another Country,* 34.

110. Rancière, *Dissensus,* 136–37.

111. Suttmeier, "Ethnography as Consumption," 62.

112. McKnight, *Nakagami, Japan,* 136.

113. Seki, "Mushitachi no kānivaru," 77.

114. The two translations of *The Metamorphosis* were both titled *Henshin.* One was translated by Takahashi Yoshitaka and the other by Nakai Masafumi. Katsura also titled one of her pieces after Albert Camus's classic existentialist novel *The Stranger* (*Ihōjin*). The Japanese characters that Katsura chose for *The Stranger* (there are several ways to write *stranger* in Japanese) are symptomatic, as the characters can also be read as "foreigner," a position that Katsura occupied during her travels from 1956 to 1961.

Other Japanese artists were interested in Kafka at this time. Writer Hijikata Tetsu's (1927–2005) *Chikakei (Rhizome)* won the New Japan Literature Prize in 1963. Anne McKnight notes that Kafka's *Metamorphosis* may have been a model for Hijikata's work, as it begins "midstream in someone's consciousness." Hijikata seemed interested in shifting political perceptions. McKnight points out that "*Rhizome* reworks the reader's perceptions of realism by using a multiple point-of-view structure." McKnight, *Nakagami, Japan,* 60.

115. Katsura, "Intabyū," 48.

116. Katsura later made a series of cork collages that were without figures, although even these contained egg shapes made of women's stockings wrapped around cotton. I read these as a metaphor for the female body and would not describe them as entirely abstract because of their bodily reference. See Kunimoto, "Katsura Yuki and the Allegorical Impulse."

117. Winther-Tamaki, "Oil Painting in Postsurrender Japan," 350.

118. For example, in 1955 Hariu Ichirō and five other artists participated in a roundtable discussion titled "Atarashii ningenzō ni mukatte" (Toward a new human image).

119. Deleuze and Guattari, *Kafka,* 12.

120. Goh, "Becoming-Animal," 40. For more on the debates concerning Western modernism and East Asian contemporaneity, see Miyakawa, "Anforumeru igo." Miyakawa attributes a profound change in the direction of Japanese avant-garde art to artists' exposure to Art Informel and a critical reevaluation of artistic developments in Japan in 1956–57. Chiba Shigeo has argued that Informel was simply a trigger for changes that were unique to Japan and individual artists and groups like Gutai. Chiba, *Gendai bijutsu itsudatsushi, 1945–1985.* See also Sawaragi, "Anforumeru izen." Although explicitly about Informel, these articles implicitly express anxiety over the influence of Western powers and debate the meaning of terms such as *modern* and *Japanese art.*

121. "To become animal is to participate in movement, to stake out the path of escape in all its positivity, to cross a threshold, to reach a continuum of intensities that are valuable only in themselves, to find a world of pure intensities where all forms come undone, as do all the significations, signifiers, and signifieds, to the benefit of an unformed matter of deterritorialized flux, of nonsignifying signs." Deleuze and Guattari, *Kafka,* 13. For more see Jesty, "The Realism Debate and the Politics of Modern Art." See also Nakamura, *Nihon kindai bijutsu ronsōshi.*

122. Deleuze and Guattari, *Kafka,* 13.

123. "Ningen ga ningen ja nakunattari." Katsura, "Intabyū," 49.

124. Baker, *The Postmodern Animal,* 121.

125. Anne Wagner's description of Jasper Johns's *Flag* (1954–55) comes to mind: "The result is that time and place seem both present and muted: each scrap has its own message yet also stands in for its origin elsewhere, at another quite ordinary moment and site." Wagner, *A House Divided,* 13.

126. Katsura may have been interested in African elephants even before her trip. She purchased an African sculpture of an elephant in 1958 in Paris. She said that although she was going to Africa, she had heard that because of colonialism and looting, it was very difficult to buy African art in Africa. Letter from Katsura to her brother, Katsura Hidezumi, in Katsura, Sotodate, and Museum of Modern Art, Ibaraki, *Katsura Yuki no sekai,* 90. She described some graffiti of an elephant by an African artist in another letter to her brother dated July 9, 1958: "I've been looking for paintings and sculptures, but looks like there is no such thing in this area yet. The only thing I found that was interesting was graffiti on the outer wall of a cabin . . . There was a painting of a huge pink elephant on the white wall inside the house. The outline was grey, and its limbs were painted in a row; it was primitive. I was fascinated by its size, color and shape. . . . I asked the head of the village if I could see the person who painted it. He looked at me strangely, but he brought the artist for me. . . . After half an hour of conversation, all I found out about the painting was that he made paints by mixing soil with oil." Ibid.

127. Katsura, *Kitsune no dairyokō,* 38.

128. Katsura's self-identification as a fox suggests her self-awareness about the interplay between gender status and representation. Yuki Miyamoto describes the art of Tomiyama Taeko in a manner that suggests common strategies with Katsura: "Fire, femininity, spirit-possession, illusion, fertility, wealth, and cunning—a singular image comprises these disparate terms in the Japanese imagination: the fox. . . . This is because the fox in her narrative art—both the versatile animal and its associations—calls attention to, and problematizes, boundaries and frameworks of many sorts, evoking in viewers' minds the ambiguous and mysterious nature of the animal as well as the social structures it defies." Miyamoto, "Fire and Femininity," 69. Alicia Volk similarly points out Katsura's use of the ambiguously gendered nature of the fox; see Volk, "Katsura Yuki and the Japanese Avant-Garde."

129. Katsura, *Kitsune no dairyokō,* 34.

130. Lippit, *Electric Animal.*

131. Ibid., 1.

132. Ibid., 3.

133. Rancière, *Dissensus,* 139.

134. *Asahi Shinbun,* October 14, 1962, 8.

135. "Gorilla" was released as a single and appeared on Brassens's first album, *La Mauvaise Réputation* (1952).

136. One year later, the Museum of Modern Art in New York presented the exhibition *The New Japanese Painting and Sculpture,* which subsequently traveled to seven venues across the country, demonstrating a growing interest in Japanese art.

137. In an interview in 2016, Nakamura Hiroshi said that in his opinion, Katsura was one of the most cutting-edge artists of his lifetime. Nakamura Hiroshi and Hoshino Katsushige, interview by Namiko Kunimoto, Justin Jesty, and Shimada Yoshiko, June 29, 2016, Tokyo.

138. For more on Hi Red Center, see Tomii, "State v. (Anti-)Art."

139. Marotti, *Money, Trains, and Guillotines,* 287.

140. Katsura had a solo exhibition at the Yamaguchi Prefectural Museum of Art in 1980. Another large exhibition was held at Shimonoseki City Art Museum in 1991, but Katsura passed away shortly before it opened. After that, there were exhibitions at the Museum of Modern Art, Ibaraki, in 1998 and Ichinomiya City Memorial Art Museum of Migishi Setsuko in 2007. Major exhibitions to celebrate the centennial of Katsura's birth were held at the Museum of Contemporary Art, Tokyo, and Shimonoseki City Art Museum in 2013.

141. Marotti, *Money, Trains, and Guillotines,* 309.

142. Both Katsura Yuki and Tanaka Atsuko (discussed in chapter 3) were among the youngest daughters in their families. But unlike Tanaka, whose father raised his nine children solely on the wages he earned as a worker in a match manufacturing plant during the 1930s, Katsura was born in the age of Taishō democracy into a wealthy family that could afford to hire a maid for each of her three brothers, her sisters, and herself. Katsura's father was an engineering professor at the prestigious University of Tokyo and encouraged his children to explore music, texts, and culture from outside Japan.

143. Miyakawa, "Anti-Art," 129.

144. As Jean-Luc Nancy might say, existence is essentially coexistence; there is no individual that precedes the community. "We happen as the opening itself, the dangerous fault line of a rupture." Nancy, *Being Singular Plural,* xii.

145. Marotti, *Money, Trains, and Guillotines,* 287–308.

146. For more on Nakanishi, see Nakanishi, Hayashi, and McCaffrey, *Natsuyuku Nakanishi.*

147. Marotti, *Money, Trains, and Guillotines,* 170.

148. Narita, "Women in the Motherland," 154.

149. On Oku Mumeo's political continuity before and after the war, see ibid., 137–58.

150. Rancière, *Dissensus,* 149.

151. Day, "Allegory," 105.

2. Nakamura Hiroshi and the Politics of Embodiment

1. Wagner, *A House Divided,* 21.

2. Ibid., 12.

3. Ibid., 7.

4. Statement made in the 2011 documentary film *ANPO: Art X War,* directed and produced by Linda Hoagland.

5. By definition, a civil war is a sustained and organized large-scale, high-intensity conflict, often involving regular armed forces. Hironaka, *Neverending Wars,* 3. The *Oxford English Dictionary* defines civil war as follows: "war between the citizens or inhabitants of a single country, state, or community." *OED* Online, s.v. "civil war," accessed August 5, 2016. Others have stated that casualties of more than one thousand are necessary to define a conflict as a civil war.

6. Johns was also responding to Pollock's perceived (and highly mediated) hypermasculinity. Nakamura responded through figuration while Johns used the sensual semiotics of the sign and the body in pieces.

7. Justin Jesty "examines the realism debate *(riarizumi ronsō)* that took place between 1946 and 1950 as a forum in which ideas on artistic form, the role of the artist in society, and the social relevance of art come into focus in a way that allows us to see how questions such as Japan's modernity, the recent experience of fascism, and the challenges of rebuilding culture during the early Cold war were taken up by leading cultural figures in the field of the visual arts." Jesty, "The Realism Debate and the Politics of Modern Art," 508. See also Nakamura, *Nihon kindai bijutsu ronsoshi.*

8. Jesty, "Arts of Engagement," 15.

9. Dower, *Embracing Defeat.*

10. Kawara, "Chūshō-kaiga to tēma-kaiga no genkai."

11. Marotti, "The Untimely Timeliness of Nakajima Yoshio," 15.

12. Marotti, *Money, Trains, and Guillotines,* 3.

13. For more on the experimental arts and their relationship to the era of student protests and political demonstrations, see Sas, *Experimental Arts in Postwar Japan.*

14. Nakamura Hiroshi, interview by author, August 5, 2011, Nakano, Tokyo.

15. Nakamura Hiroshi, interview by author, January 8, 2016, Tokyo.

16. Nakamura, "Nakamura jisaku nenpu," 84. The students came from Nihon University's Art Department and from Tokyo University of the Arts, Musashino Art University, Joshibi University of Art and Design, Tama Art University, and the Chūō Art Institute.

17. Nakamura, interview by author, August 5, 2011. Members of the student art group included Abe Kobō, Teshigahara Hiroshi, Katsuragawa Hiroshi, Yamashita Kikuji, Bitō Yutaka (who became Nakamura's closest friend and ally), Shimada Sumiya, and Ikeda Tatsuo.

18. For example, his work was first exhibited at the *Nihon Indépendant* exhibition (the precursor to the *Yomiuri Indépendant* exhibitions). Reviews of the works were limited to his mentors, who essentially encouraged the young artist to "keep up the good work." Takiguchi Shūzō at Takemiya Gallery organized Nakamura's first solo show in 1957. In the 1950s and 1960s, Nakamura felt that artists such as Katsura and the members of the Gutai Art Association were stars compared to him. Nakamura Hiroshi, interview by author, January 9, 2016, Nakano, Tokyo.

19. Nakamura, "Nakamura jisaku nenpu," 84.

20. Ibid., 83. Marotti describes Akasegawa Genpei as being "far from the revolutionary type" because he was "terrified by his experience of direct political action during the Sunagawa River protests and his witnessing of the results of police violence ('people with their eyes hanging out of their heads')." Marotti, *Money, Trains, and Guillotines,* 100, 345n40. However, it is possible that most revolutionaries were terrified by the prospect of such violent experiences.

21. Marotti, "Japan 1968," 106. The protesters were attempting to inhabit a public plaza outside the Imperial Palace.

22. The police estimated 180,000, but the protest organizers claimed 500,000. "May Day Gets Violent: American Soldier Attacked and Burned, Police Department Make Arrests All Night," *Yomiuri Shinbun,* May 2, 1952.

23. The 23rd May Day Declaration, May 1, 1952, reprinted in Japanese in Nagoya-shi Bijutsukan, *Sengo Nihon no riarizumu,* 60.

24. See "Bloody May Day (May 1, 1952)," Cross Currents, U.S.-Japan Conference on Cultural and Educational Interchange, accessed October 12, 2013, http://www.crosscurrents.hawaii.edu.

25. Regarding Yamashita's article, see Hoagland, "Protest Art in 1950s Japan." Hoagland translates the title of the article as "A Peephole onto Discrimination."

26. The mountain areas were not affected by the new land reforms imposed by the Allied Occupation, and consequently access to resources in this village was controlled by a small number of landowners. See Jesty, "Arts of Engagement," 92.

27. JCP member Maruyama Teruo, who hailed from Akebono, had intended to collaborate with Yamashita to depict this event as a *kamishibai* (narrative panel). Jesty reports that Maruyama and Yamashita stayed for one month in the village, investigating the event. Ultimately the JCP decided against investing in the project, but Yamashita began working on the oil painting alone. Ibid., 95.

28. For more details on *The Tale of Akebono Village,* see Ozaki, "From the Tale of Akebono Village to the Tale of Akebono Village," 162.

29. Jesty aptly assesses how the painting thus brings issues of prewar and postwar responsibility to the fore. Jesty, "Arts of Engagement," 76.

30. "Imaizumi Yoshihiko would reflect later that Nakamura's paintings between 1955 and 1962, while critiquing Socialist Realism/reportage practice, 'ironically . . . also amounted to its finest representative achievement.'" Marotti, "The Lives and Afterlives of Art and Politics in the 1960s," 30. Marotti quotes and translates Imaizumi, "Nakamura Hiroshi no koto," 13. The issue of *Kikan* in which Imaizumi's article appears is devoted to Nakamura's work.

31. Winther-Tamaki, *Maximum Embodiment,* 14.

32. Ibid., 167.

33. Winther-Tamaki notes: "Thus, Shiraga's abstraction elevated the idea of the contact between the artist's body and the paint vividly into focus as the content of the work. In effect, such works

renounced one aim of Yōga embodiment, the depiction of the human body, in order to fulfill two of its other aims more dramatically, namely, articulating the oil-on-canvas *matière* and endowing it with a strong somatic sense of the artist's presence." Ibid., 165.

34. I will refer to the events as the Sunagawa struggle.

35. Women were also part of the movement. For example, on September 2, 1956, a group of housewives and youth was formed with the aim of strengthening ties between Sunagawa and Okinawan protest groups. Shoop, "Sunagawa Incident," 292.

36. Founded in 1948, Zengakuren was a communist/anarchist league of students in Japan. The group's name is derived from an abridgment of Zen Nihon Gakusei Jichikai Sō Rengō, which literally means All-Japan League of Student Self-Government.

37. "B-29's Rain Destruction on Japanese City," *New York Times,* June 10, 1945. Tachikawa had been bombed twice previously, but without much damage.

38. The Sunagawa villagers held an assembly to discuss the matter, and Aoki Ichigorō, a local mulberry farmer, volunteered to speak to the Americans. Aoki played a key role in the beginning stages of domestic protest against the expansion. After decades of fighting, Aoki had his land returned to him (by court order) in 1975. By then, his children had moved away and the mulberry farming industry had all but disappeared. Aoki foresaw that he would be unable to pay the taxes for the land and it would ultimately be retaken by the government. Shoop, "Sunagawa Incident," 6, 44–45.

39. Donald Shoop's studies of Sunagawa have their own bias. For example, he writes: "The nature of domestic opposition in Japan is very complex and sometimes based on nothing more than feelings that are xenophobic." Ibid., iv.

40. "U.S. to Cut Bases, Tokyo Announces," *New York Times,* July 21, 1955. An additional hurdle was that the proposed expansion area encompassed a cemetery that would require careful legal processing, not to mention appropriate treatment of human remains. Shoop, "Sunagawa Incident," 261.

41. In June 1955, Mayor Miyazaki prevented land surveyors from entering the area.

42. *Mainichi Evening News,* May 10, 1955, 1.

43. "Japanese Resist U.S. Airbase," *New York Times,* August 24, 1955.

44. *Asahi Shinbun,* September 13, 1955, 1.

45. The striking groups were the Federation of Security Force Workers Union (Zenchoro) and the All-Japan Security Force Workers Union (Nichuro).

46. "130 Are Hurt in Clash at US Air Base," *New York Times,* October 13, 1956. This was the eighth day that protesters were able to prevent the surveyors from completing their work. Shoop reports 240 injured on this day. "At about 1:05 PM, 2,000 police broke through 3,500 persons who were locked arm-in-arm. This tactic to permit the surveyors in resulted in violence and 260 people were injured." Shoop, "Sunagawa Incident," 295.

47. Nagoya-shi Bijutsukan, *Sengo Nihon no riarizumu,* 105.

48. Marotti notes in *Money, Trains, and Guillotines* that the perception of violence and how it was reported in the news played a powerful role in the public perception of political conflict.

49. Since then, the area has seen a variety of uses, including as a base for ground self-defense forces, the Tokyo Metropolitan Police, and the coast guard. Showa Memorial Park, a memorial site for Emperor Hirohito, was erected in the area in 1983. While Tachikawa was once a site known for its divisive history, it has now become a site for the display of representation. Most recently it has

been reconfigured from a military base into a space for public art. Henry Scott-Stokes, "Japan Plunges into Public Art," *New York Times,* October 30, 1994. The new space, which features the works of artists such as Jonathan Borofsky and Joseph Kosuth, uses text from the politically active Japanese writer Ishimure Michiko (whose excerpted poem begins this book). Such cross-cultural collaborations on a site where Japanese police and activists repeatedly battled one another over the presence of the U.S. armed forces suggests to visitors that the moment of tension between the United States and Japan has long since passed. A single glance at an Okinawan newspaper tells us otherwise, however.

50. Koschmann, *Revolution and Subjectivity in Postwar Japan,* 1–2.

51. Shoop, "Sunagawa Incident," 297. Shoop notes that the opposition sent condolences to the deceased man's family.

52. *ANPO: Art X War*; Nakamura Hiroshi, interview by author, July 4, 2012, Nakano, Tokyo; Hoagland, "Protest Art in 1950s Japan."

53. Debates around the role of art in politics began in the early postwar period: "The disaster of the fascist past demanded accounting, especially from those who would disavow it, while the future appeared equally daunting, stripped as it was of any broadly legitimating vision or value system, yet increasingly pressurized by the politics of the cold war. Much like the simultaneously occurring art and politics debate in literature, the realism debate acted as forum and a catalyst for ideas about artistic form, the role of the artist in society, and the social relevance of art itself, at a time that seemed to demand such relevance while making it more difficult to imagine." Jesty, "The Realism Debate and the Politics of Modern Art," 508.

54. Nakamura Hiroshi, telephone conversation with author, July 2013.

55. Ibid.

56. Nakamura, interview by author, July 4, 2012.

57. Tuan, "Place," 152.

58. Nakamura, interview by author, January 8, 2016.

59. Jaqueline Berndt, among others, has argued for the importance of considering mass culture in relation to fine art, specifically in terms of gender representation: "The genre of nude painting can and should be critically discussed not only in relation to posters but also to modern graphic art (which occasionally allowed for more unconventional approaches to gender issues), to photographs (artistic ones like those of Nojima Yasuzō as well as erotic ones) and to sculpture (in modern Japan, a genre with more male nudes than painting)." Berndt, "Nationally Naked?," 310.

60. Nihon Kyōshokuin Kumiai, *Nikkyōso Fujinbu sanjūnenshi,* 306–8.

61. For more on the hand as a symbol of authorship, see Stoichita, "The Don Quixote Effect."

62. It was meant to be a slightly ironic name. As Shimada points out, "By 1969, *gakkō* was an almost despicable term. In the days of student revolt, schools were to be destroyed. Bigakkō dared to call itself '*gakkō*,' although it was not even a certified school. It was to bring back the 'anachronistic' ideal of a school as a place to have direct, intense interaction between teachers and students." Shimada, "Gendaishichō-sha Bigakkō," 17.

63. Quoted in ibid.

64. Winther-Tamaki, *Maximum Embodiment,* 164.

65. Nakamura, "Nakamura jisaku nenpu," 82.

66. More recently, Nakamura has become a (rather aged) poster child for Linda Hoagland's documentary *ANPO: Art X War,* which examines the role of art in the resistance to the Allied

Occupation. Hoagland's film, in which Nakamura is seen standing before *The Base,* has brought long-overdue attention to the artist's reportage work, especially outside Japan. Inside the country, he has garnered attention in recent years as the result of a large-scale retrospective exhibition titled *Pictorial Disturbances,* presented at the Museum of Contemporary Art, Tokyo, in 2007.

67. "Test of Washington's Statement on the Girard Case," *New York Times,* June 5, 1957.

68. "Excerpt from Text of Court's Decision in the Girard Case," *New York Times,* November 19, 1957.

69. "The Girard Case," *Time,* October 7, 1957, http://time.com.

70. "To the Wolves, Soldier," *New York Daily News,* June 5, 1957.

71. Marotti, "The Lives and Afterlives of Art and Politics in the 1960s," 30.

72. Nakamura does not recall seeing this film, but he remembers it being popular. His artwork frequently cites popular culture. For example, he has noted that the 1956 American film *Attack* featured credits that were visually interesting to him. Nakamura, interview by author, January 9, 2016.

73. Sas, "Hands, Lines, Acts," 20.

74. *Nihon Bijutsu News,* no. 8 (1956); Hariu, "Kirokusei." See also Hariu, "Shakaiteki shudai to riarizumu." Nakamura discusses Hariu's 1956 *Nihon Bijutsu News* article in Nakamura, "Fushin no 'jiko hihan,'" 14.

75. Nakamura, "Fushin no 'jiko hihan,'" 14, 15.

76. Nakamura, "Taburō-ron"; Nakamura, "Fushin no 'jiko hihan,'" 33. *Tableau* is a term for the painted canvas that was popular in Europe. Theoretically, it refers to a successful painting, a painting that has undergone the final ritual finish. Stephen Melville has referred to it as the "jointing of the composition and the finish." Melville, "What Was the Tableau and Why Did It Matter?"

77. Nakamura, "Nakamura jisaku nenpu," 83.

78. Sasaki-Uemura, *Organizing the Spontaneous,* 16.

79. Ibid., 162.

80. Ibid., 49.

81. Hamaya Hiroshi titled his photo-book about the protest *Ikari to kanashimi no kiroku* (A record of days of rage and grief). It was published in August 1960.

82. Ikeda, *Ikeda Tatsuo,* 10.

83. Mita, "'Taburoo kikai' e no michi."

84. Partner, *Assembled in Japan,* 139.

85. Partner notes that by 1960 more than nine million Japanese homes had television sets, while only two million had refrigerators. He describes this as an enigma, but the desire for visual pleasure in an era of hard work and poverty does not strike me as surprising. Ibid., 162.

86. See Virilio, *The Virilio Reader.* As geographer David Harvey describes dromology, the term refers to any phenomenon that alters the qualities of and relationship between space and time. Harvey, *The Condition of Postmodernity.*

87. Nakamura reverses the history of cinematic form as it developed in the Soviet Union, where modernist montage was rejected as too bourgeois and replaced by the codes of socialist realism. It was a moment of intensive cross-cultural exchange. Filmmaker Sergei Eisenstein described how the Japanese Kabuki theater influenced him, especially the ways that sound, movement, space, and voice all operate as equivalent elements. See Taylor, "Eisenstein," 12.

88. Nakamura Hiroshi, interview by author, July 12, 2012, Nakano, Tokyo.

89. *Battleship Potemkin* was commissioned on the twentieth anniversary of that struggle.

90. Statistics from UNIJAPAN website, accessed December 26, 2013, http://unijapan.org.

91. "Both the 1955 advent of the new conservative coalition, the newly-created Liberal Democratic Party (LDP) and the mid-1950s takeoff point for the economic recovery and boom years owed a great deal to American covert and strategic support. Both trends were increasingly ideologically united in an LDP which took credit for the economic expansion, and, from PM Ikeda onward, grounded its legitimacy in promises of high growth and income doubling. This effectively made the everyday world the site of both a depoliticizing ideology of consumption and conformism, and potentially, a critical politicization." Marotti, "The Untimely Timeliness of Nakajima Yoshio," 14.

92. Doherty, *Cold War, Cool Medium,* 2.

93. Ibid., 4.

94. Television viewing in Japan was also accelerated by the imperial marriage of April 10, 1959, but the Olympics marked even higher levels of viewership.

95. Statistics from the website of the Japanese Ministry of Education, Culture, Sports, Science and Technology, accessed December 4, 2013, http://www.mext.go.jp.

96. Hood, *Shinkansen,* 211.

97. The loan would be repaid in 1980.

98. This was tragically demonstrated with the loss of 161 lives in an accident at Tsurumi (November 9, 1963), when two passenger trains collided with a derailed freight train." Hood, *Shinkansen,* 214.

99. Igarashi, *Bodies of Memory,* 153–55.

100. Nakamura, interview by author, August 5, 2011.

101. See Noguchi, "Japanese Art of 1964," 196. Phillip Kaffen argues that Ichikawa Kon's documentary of the Olympic Games also expresses ambivalence toward the politics of the events and the director's role in representing their "truth" via the body. See Kaffen, "Ichikawa Kon's 'Tokyo Olympiad.'"

102. For Virilio, speed conquers space. He writes: "The invasion of the instant succeeds the invasion of territory. The countdown becomes the scene of battle, the final frontier." Virilio, *The Virilio Reader,* 49.

103. Nakahara, "Humetsu no taburoo kikai."

104. Shibusawa, "Tsune ni toonoite iku fūkei."

105. Virilio, *War and Cinema,* 88.

106. Ross, *Fast Cars, Clean Bodies,* 38.

107. Shimada, "Hōki seyo shōjo!," 2. In a 2016 interview, Nakamura confirmed that he intended the schoolgirls to look monstrous. Nakamura Hiroshi and Hoshino Katsushige, interview by Namiko Kunimoto, Justin Jesty, and Shimada Yoshiko, June 29, 2016, Tokyo.

108. Shimada, "Hōki seyo shōjo!," 3.

109. Ibid., 5.

110. Wong, "Art of Non-resistance," 312.

111. Ibid., 313.

112. Kovner, *Occupying Power,* 114.

113. As Sharalyn Orbaugh writes of *shōjo* (girls') manga: "A feminist reading of these battlin' babe narratives might well argue that in them females may inhabit images that demonstrate power,

but that power is still enabled by and circumscribed within ultimate patriarchal hegemony." Orbaugh, "Busty Battlin' Babes," 227.

114. Garber, "Fetish Envy," 47.

115. Myers, "The Future as Fetish," 69.

116. Ibid., 70.

117. Ibid.

118. Shimada, "Hōki seyo shōjo!" 7.

119. Ibid., 8.

120. Virilio, *War and Cinema,* 3.

121. Here I refer to Laura Mulvey's notion of the filmic gaze as replicating the male gaze and E. Ann Kaplan's intervention that suggests the gaze is masculine rather than solely the domain of the male viewer. See Mulvey, "Visual Pleasure and Narrative Cinema"; Kaplan, *Women and Film,* 23–35. In a chapter titled "Is the Gaze Male?" Kaplan states: "What we can conclude from the discussion so far is that our culture is deeply committed to myths of demarcated sex differences, called 'masculine' and 'feminine,' which in turn revolve first on a complex gaze apparatus and second on dominance-submission patterns. This positioning of the two sex genders in representation clearly privileges the male (through the mechanisms of voyeurism and fetishism, which are male operations, and because his desire carries power/action where woman's usually does not). However, as a result of the recent women's movement, women have been permitted in representation to assume (step into) the position defined as 'masculine,' as long as the man then steps into *her* position, thus keeping the whole structure intact." Kaplan, *Women and Film,* 30.

122. In 2012–13, Nakamura's work was featured in the New York Museum of Modern Art's exhibition *Tokyo 1955–1970: A New Avant-Garde.*

3. Tanaka Atsuko and the Circuits of Subjectivity

1. The Gutai Art Association was active from 1954 to 1972, and Tanaka was a member from 1955 to 1965. She joined the group with Kanayama Akira, Shiraga Kazuo, Shiraga Fujiko, and Murakami Saburō, who were originally members of Zero-kai. She left the Gutai group, along with Kanayama, in 1965, and the two were married that year. She continued to produce art until her death in 2005.

2. Shiraga Kazuo says that Tanaka could do no wrong in Yoshihara's eyes in an interview in the 1998 film *Tanaka Atsuko: Mōhitotsu no Gutai* [Tanaka Atsuko: Another Gutai], directed by Okabe Aomi. Other examples of positive responses to Tanaka's work include "Rare Type of Artist," *Mainichi News,* March 9, 1956; "Ihyō tsuku nijū no beru: Ojōsan no sakuhin Genbi ten ni buji niyūsen" [Twenty bells take you by surprise: A young lady's work accepted to Genbi's exhibition without problem], *Asahi Shinbun,* evening edition, arts section, November 24, 1955; "Uchū o tsukuru" [Creating outer space], *Osaka Shinbun,* August 30, 1959; "Yagai Gutai bijutsuten kara, ugoku omoshirosa" [From Gutai outdoor exhibition: It's interesting because it moves], *Yomiuri Shinbun,* August 3, 1956.

3. Hasegawa, "The Rebuilding of Osaka," 77.

4. Lefebvre, *Critique of Everyday Life.*

5. Katō, "Searching for a Boundary," 18.

6. Ibid., 24.

7. The 1994 exhibition *Japanese Art after 1945: Scream against the Sky,* curated by Alexandra Munroe, did much to elevate the status of Japanese contemporary art in North America. Gutai's early endeavors to produce a radical style of art on the heels of the Allied Occupation earned the group a key position in the exhibition and its accompanying catalog. However, Munroe's conclusion that Gutai sought to "playfully . . . usher in the liberal American-style democracy which history had unexpectedly granted" reveals the stubborn tenacity of the Cold War mind-set. Munroe, *Japanese Art after 1945,* 83–123. For other works that align Gutai with the ideology of democracy and individualism, see Oyobe, "Human Subjectivity and Confrontation with Materials"; Jesty, "Arts of Engagement"; Tiampo, "The Collective Spirit of Individualism in Gutai Art Exhibitions"; Tiampo, "Gutai Chain"; Tiampo, *Gutai: Decentering Modernism.* Tiampo specifically includes Tanaka in her argument for Gutai's individualism in "'Create What Has Never Been Done Before!'" Charles Merewether refers to Gutai as embodying "an aesthetics of freedom." Merewether, "Disjunctive Modernity," 7–10. Hirai Shōichi's foundational work on Gutai also aligns the group with individualism; see Hirai, "Mr. Gutai."

8. See Katō, "Tanaka Atsuko haru 1966."

9. Some of the bulbs were painted with enamel paint in nine colors: dark red, light red, dark green, light green, purple, dark blue, light blue, yellow, and orange. Katō and Minami, *Tanaka Atsuko,* 63. The bulbs used were both the typical household lightbulb shape and tubular, the shape familiar from today's fluorescent lights. No photographer is credited with documenting these works; Gutai members likely took the photographs. Kanbee Hanaya of the Ashiya Camera Club was contacted to photograph other Gutai events, such as the *Gutai Outdoor Exhibition* and some stage exhibitions. Yamamoto, "Introduction," 31.

10. Oyobe, "Human Subjectivity and Confrontation with Materials," 224.

11. This performance was not given a specific title, so it is not clearly a part of *Electric Dress.*

12. When Yoshihara first discussed the piece, it was referred to as "clothes created by lightbulbs," and then later came to be referred to as *Denki fuku,* or *Electric Dress.* The English translation of the work's title, *Electric Dress,* has been somewhat controversial in terms of gender issues. The first two characters of the title mean electricity or electric, and the last character, *fuku,* simply means clothes, suggesting the plausible translation *Electric Clothes.* Had Tanaka chosen to specify women's clothing, she might have used the word *doresu* (dress) or *wanpīsu* (one-piece), but either of these terms, created with the *katakana* foreign-language syllabary, would have connoted Westernism perhaps more than Tanaka may have wanted. Katō argues that the piece's title should be translated as *Electric Clothes.* This interpretation would also correlate with the English titles of two of Tanaka's early pieces, both named *Stage Clothes,* although they too could be translated as *Stage Dress.* Tatehata, on the other hand, points out that Tanaka was alive when the work was exhibited abroad as *Electric Dress* and therefore would have raised objections had she had any. It should also be said that the debate might be overstated because *dress* can be a gender-neutral term; moreover, discussion circulating around the best translation may be taking the place of a deeper analysis of the meaning of the work itself. Katō, "Tanaka Atsuko haru 1966"; Tatehata Akira, interview by author, October 8, 2008, Osaka.

13. At a symposium at the University of California, Los Angeles, on February 8, 1998, Tanaka stated: "My works have nothing to do with politics . . . neither do they have anything to do with gender. It doesn't matter whether I am a man or a woman." In *Tanaka Atsuko: Mōhitotsu no Gutai.* Ming Tiampo argues that gender is nonetheless critical: "Despite Tanaka's claims to the contrary,

the insertion of her self into the field of representation makes gender analysis both inevitable and important." Tiampo, "Gutai and Informel," 199.

14. Tanaka, "Sakuhin 11," 13.

15. Kanayama reported that the gearbox was designed by an amateur electrician and was exceedingly noisy. In *Tanaka Atsuko: Mōhitotsu no Gutai*. Other Gutai members also described the sound of the electric gearbox as very noisy. Yamamoto, "Introduction," 44n38.

16. Marotti, *Money, Trains, and Guillotines*, 138–39.

17. According to Victor Koschmann, the terms *shutaisei* (subjectivity) and *shukan* (the subject) were in high circulation following the war, in part originating from debates about Marxism led by the Communist Party. These debates were concerned with how historical development would be charted and how the social subject would be used in that model. However, *shutaisei* also circulated as a term for a notion of Japanese existentialism that was tied to a Kierkegaardian "leap of faith," or, alternatively, as an individualistic ethos that was based on the Protestant ethic. Koschmann, *Revolution and Subjectivity in Postwar Japan*, 4. See also Slaymaker, *The Body in Postwar Japanese Fiction*; Tiampo, "Body, War, and the Discourses of History."

18. For example, Maruyama argues that authentic democracy relied on the development of a "modern personality" that was not possible under imperialism. Maruyama, *Thought and Behavior in Modern Japanese Politics*, 3–5.

19. Fujii, *Complicit Fictions*, 1.

20. For earlier examples of Japanese artists and artistic identity, see Guth, "Hokusai's Great Waves"; Volk, *In Pursuit of Universalism.*

21. For example, see Shiraga, "Kotai no kakuritsu"; Tiampo, "Gutai Chain"; Tiampo, "Body, War, and the Discourses of History." The oft-quoted Gutai manifesto, written in 1956 by Yoshihara Jirō, the ambitious and powerful leader of the Gutai Art Association, has exerted a heavy influence on the reception of Gutai. The manifesto states that Gutai will "take leave of these piles of counterfeit objects on the altars, in the palaces, in the salons and the antique shops. . . . Lock these corpses into their tombs. Gutai art does not change the material but brings it to life. Gutai art does not falsify the material." Yoshihara, "Gutai sengen," 202–4. While much can be made of the manifesto's emphasis on materiality, its pat theoretical convenience has become detrimental to our understanding of what mattered most to artists associated with the Gutai group. That the manifesto was written by Yoshihara alone for the art journal *Geijutsu shinchō* (by the journal's request) two years after the group had begun to work together has been largely ignored. Hirai, *Gutai tte nanda?*, 87. As a consequence, the Gutai group has been approached as a homogeneous entity despite the fact that it had a membership of more than twenty people at any one time; moreover, membership shifted over the eighteen years the group existed (altogether, approximately fifty-eight people participated in the Gutai Art Association, with major shifts taking place at three distinct periods). It is perhaps time to move away from an overreliance on the manifesto and the persistent view that Gutai was a collective of homologous interests. Gutai was an association rather than a collective, meaning that members were interested in sharing resources and working space, and in encouraging one another to produce something new, but not necessarily in sharing intellectual compulsions, political viewpoints, or artistic outcomes.

22. "Umaku dekita sakuhin o miteiru to, mezurashii kanji ga suru. Jibun no sakuhin da to, dōshite kore ga dekitanoka to fushigi ni omoetekuru. Sorede, mata konna mono ga tsukuttemitaku naru. Demo sono sakuhin no fun'iki ni torawarete, tekikakuna hassō ga nai to, kudaranai mono ni

natteshimau. Itsumademo guzuguzu shiteiru to satōmizu no yōni natte nagashi ni yatte kuru." Tanaka, "Kansō," 7.

23. Kanayama was driving the car on March 13, 2005, when an accident occurred and Tanaka sustained a cervical spine injury. She remained in the hospital until her death from pneumonia on December 3, 2005. Katō, "Chronology," 193. Some have suggested that the pneumonia was due to her weakened condition, as she had been in the hospital since the accident. Jinno Kimio, interview by author, October 8, 2008, Nagoya.

24. In *Tanaka Atsuko: Mōhitotsu no Gutai.*

25. Langsner, "Gutai," 19. Langsner says that Tanaka's works stand out among those of other Gutai members as the works that "persist longest in memory," but he argues that Tanaka could just as readily be from Los Angeles, Milan, or New York. Certainly there is a period resemblance between Tanaka's work and that of artists from other countries, but I believe that the specific regional context of Osaka is important to her work. Further, the asymmetrical transnational circulation of her art affected its reception. Langsner should be credited for noting that Tanaka does not easily fit within the confines of Gutai's aesthetic.

The Gutai Pinacotheca, an exhibition space run by the Gutai group in the Nakanoshima district in Osaka, was originally a Meiji-period rice granary. At the time Langsner was writing, it was the only space for exhibiting modern art in Osaka. See Cohen, "Japan's Gutai Group." The Gutai Pinacotheca was closed in April 1970 as a result of urban development; on my last visit in 2008, the site where the building had stood was a parking lot.

26. *Zainichi* (literally meaning residing in Japan) Koreans reached a population of two million in 1945. See Howell, "Ethnicity and Culture in Contemporary Japan."

27. Hasegawa, "The Rebuilding of Osaka," 77.

28. Ibid., 78.

29. Harris, "The Urban and Industrial Transformation of Japan."

30. In *Tanaka Atsuko: Mōhitotsu no Gutai.*

31. "Kokutetsu daiya o ōkaisei" [Big revisions to National Rail schedule], *Yomiuri Shinbun,* October 3, 1956.

32. "Jisoku 150 kiro no densha, Tokyo-Osaka 6 jikanhan no kōsō" [150 km per hour train, plan for Tokyo–Osaka in 6.5 hours], *Yomiuri Shinbun,* November 25, 1957.

33. Noguchi, "Savor Slowly," 321; Inayama, "JNR's Choice of Traction System," 40.

34. For more on the Yamanote event, see Marotti, *Money, Trains, and Guillotines,* esp. 220–44.

35. For more on the long-term importance of the Japanese National Railways, see Noguchi, *Delayed Departures.*

36. Ross, *Fast Cars, Clean Bodies,* 22.

37. Quoted in Tiampo and Katō, *Electrifying Art,* 105. Today, those neon lights are widely being replaced with LED lights. The lights on Tanaka's *Electric Dress,* then, emerge more powerfully as signifiers of a worldwide period-specific urban visuality.

38. This exhibit was organized by Yoshihara and included pieces by Gutai members as well as other artists.

39. Fujii, "Intimate Alienation," 118.

40. Simon Partner notes that in the prewar period, women's cheap labor was largely used for textile production, but in the postwar period, women's "nimble fingers" were employed for the production of electrical goods. For example, he discusses "the development of the transistor radio

as a Japanese export staple, a success that, despite the technological marvels the radio embodied, I attribute primarily to an abundant supply of dexterous, very cheap, young female laborers." Partner, *Assembled in Japan,* 194.

41. Ibid., 128.

42. Janet Koplos has also commented on Tanaka's use of circuits in an essay. However, Koplos concludes that Tanaka is interested in connectedness in a Buddhist sense. Koplos, "Circuitries of Color," 147. I do not see any linkage between Tanaka's work and Buddhism. Moreover, I find her work often disrupts any sense of connection, thereby raising the issue of disconnection as much as connection. All too often, English-speaking critics of Tanaka's work lean toward culturalist frameworks of analysis that emphasize Buddhism, Zen, or other traits that further characterize the work as "Asian." Although Tanaka lived for some time on Buddhist temple grounds because her husband's family owned the property, there is no indication that she was strongly interested in Buddhism.

43. Michio Hayashi interprets this notion of absence in *Electric Dress* as predicated on Tanaka's interest in painting. "The [dress] was and has been exhibited repetitively without the artist's body in numerous exhibitions, often together with preparatory drawings." Hayashi, "Other Trajectories in Gutai."

44. For more on *Bell,* see Katō, "Atsuko Tanaka's 'Paintings,' as Seen through *Work (Bell).*"

45. Reconstructions of *Bell* at the Morris and Helen Belkin Art Gallery in Vancouver in 2005 had the bells placed by the floorboards near the wall of the gallery space rather than in the center of the floor. The original was made of 131.23 feet of cord, twenty bells, and a notch and motor switch. According to Tanaka, Yoshihara, and Kanayama (all whom were involved in the installation), the ringing of the bells was from front to back. However, at the exhibition *Electrifying Art* the bells rang only in one direction. Washida Meruro writes that "if the work is reproduced with the terminals in a spiral configuration as indicated in the remaining studies and photograph, the sound of the bells only moves in one direction, with the bells ringing simultaneously at up to three locations." Washida claims the engineer Tanana Shinji pointed out the impossibility of bells moving in two directions when he reconstructed *Bells* in 2005 for the *Possible Futures* show at the NTT Intercommunication Center in Tokyo. See Washida, "*Beru* ni tsuite." Thus, it remains unclear if the original bells rang in both directions or not. The number of bells was the same, as was the duration of sound in the original and reproductions.

46. Tiampo and Katō, "Electrifying Painting," in *Electrifying Art,* 68.

47. These are the kinds of visitor reactions I observed at the 2005 exhibition *Electrifying Art,* where *Bell* was displayed in the Morris and Helen Belkin Art Gallery.

48. *Tanaka Atsuko ni tsuite* [About Tanaka Atsuko], exhibition brochure, Gutai Pinacotheca, Osaka (February 1963), reprinted in Tiampo and Katō, "Electrifying Painting," 110.

49. Tiampo and Katō, "Electrifying Painting," 69. See Kaprow, *Essays on the Blurring of Art and Life.*

50. Kanayama noted that shifts in the sounds directly affect corporeal awareness, prompting a new sense of the viewer's time and space. Katō, "Discursive Conundrums," 52.

51. Ross, *Fast Cars, Clean Bodies,* 10.

52. Ibid., 90.

53. The number of Japanese magazines directed to female readers doubled from 1956 to 1957. Partner, *Assembled in Japan,* 250.

54. These images, directed to the middle class, suggest a postwar reevaluation of the *Moga,* a 1930s neologism for "modern girl," who was characterized by short hair, makeup, and a new public identity. The *Moga* was perceived as a threat to moral standards, and attempts to control the risk of her supposed brazen sexuality included the enactment of government rules. For more on the *Moga,* see Tipton, "Contested Spaces of Modernity in Interwar Japan."

55. Katsura, "Doreme no jokō tachi."

56. Ross, *Fast Cars, Clean Bodies,* 78.

57. See Sato, "An Alternate Informant," 139, 147. Fashion trends born in the interwar years often developed further in the postwar period.

58. Tatehata, interview by author, October 8, 2008.

59. Levinas coined the phrase "totality and infinity," explaining how one's encounter with the exterior is fundamental to one's development as a subject. Levinas, *Totality and Infinity.*

60. Levaillant, "Au Japon dans les années 50," 38, translation by Max Woodworth.

61. Ibid., 39.

62. The ownership of black-and-white television sets more than doubled every year from 1956 through 1960. Refrigerators, in contrast, were still in only 15.7 percent of households by 1960. Statistics from the website of the Japanese Ministry of Education, Culture, Sports, Science and Technology, accessed December 4, 2013, http://www.mext.go.jp. See also Partner, *Assembled in Japan,* 247. For more on television in Japan in the postwar period, see chapter 2.

63. Buckley, "Altered States," 352.

64. Liddle and Nakajima, *Rising Suns, Rising Daughters,* 132.

65. Fourteen issues of *Gutai* were completed, although one was lost before it was printed. The newsletter was printed in English and Japanese and distributed domestically and overseas.

66. Shimamato, "Ichi-mai no nunokire demo geijutsu sakuhin ka?," 31.

67. Yoshihara Jirō, in *Tanaka Atsuko ni tsuite,* in Tiampo and Katō, "Electrifying Painting," 110.

68. Akane Kazuo, "Yakudōkan afureru: Onna to omoenu Tanaka no sakuhin" [Very dynamic: Tanaka's unwomanly work], *Yomiuri Shinbun,* August 30, 1968.

69. "Ihyō tsuku nijū no beru."

70. Hyūga Akiko, "Tanaka Atsuko: Kisōtengai na aidea, hiyowasō de daitan na men mo," *Asahi Shinbun,* November 6, 1964.

71. "Gutai Art Exhibition," *Mainichi News,* October 12, 1956, 25.

72. Tanaka sewed a bright blue border around the neon pink.

73. Tanaka Atsuko, quoted in *Industrial Economic News,* July 25, 1955, reprinted in Tiampo and Katō, *Electrifying Art,* 112. Shimamoto Shōzō similarly described the work as "utterly vulgar" and wondered where Tanaka could have found such a nauseating color. Shimamoto, "Ichi-mai no nunokire demo geijutsu sakuhin ka?"

74. See "Yagai Gutai bijutsuten kara, ugoku omoshirosa"; "They Call It Art," *Stars and Stripes,* October 22, 1956. Other reviews were more positive, with some describing Tanaka as one of the most energetic and active members of Gutai. See "Rare Type of Artist."

75. Dower, *Embracing Defeat,* 137.

76. Ibid., 112.

77. Kovner, *Occupying Power,* 76.

78. Ibid., 82.

79. Tiampo sees Tanaka's performance as a negation of the body and culturalist links to traditional Japanese art forms rather than as a self-conscious exploration of the relation between the body and the external world: "These anthropomorphic forms completely deny a consciousness of the body, implying an otherworldly presence. As with *Denkifuku,* or *Electric Dress* of 1956, whose conception of clothing the body utterly negates the body enshrined within, *Stage Costumes* also evokes the costumes of Noh, Kabuki and Bunraku which are a fundamental part of the structured *kami asobi* [spirit play] stage of the *matsuri* [festival]." Tiampo, "Moments of Destruction, Moments of Beauty," 54.

80. Katō, "Searching for a Boundary," 24.

81. Butler, *Bodies That Matter,* 65.

82. For more on vulnerability, see Fitzpatrick, "The Movement of Vulnerability."

83. Slaymaker states: "The body offered antidotes to the bankruptcy of the traditional and military values which characterized the previous fifteen years of war. The desecration of Shinto shrines by Nakamura and his wife is an example of this. Their celebration of the carnal body (*nikutai* . . . 'physical/carnal body') suggests a punning contrast to the national polity (*kokutai* . . . 'national body'), the focus of their desecration. This binary of individual and state helps to structure the writings I examine, yielding imagery of liberation-through-carnality that suggests carnal hedonism as a corrective to the political ideology of wartime." Slaymaker, *The Body in Postwar Japanese Fiction,* 2. See also Tiampo: "I argue that their work responded to the wartime use of the 'national body' *(kokutai)* as a metaphor for national unity, and defined the 'autonomous body' (*shutaisei,* also translated as 'subjective autonomy') and the 'carnal body' *(nikutai)* as a postwar antidote to fascism." Tiampo, "Body, War, and the Discourses of History," 339.

84. "The fiction of women in this period is striking for its counterdirection: we find women writing of the details of daily life with no sense of such imminent liberation; they were evidently impressed more by the degree to which old structures had not changed. . . . Women also wrote of sex workers and slaves, and of identity after the war, but they expressed none of the men's liberating optimism." Slaymaker, *The Body in Postwar Japanese Fiction,* 5. Interestingly, however, in this text Slaymaker offers five chapters focused on literature written by men, specifically addressing literature by women only in his final chapter. For more on Japanese women's literature, see Orbaugh, "The Body in Contemporary Japanese Women's Fiction." Ueno Chizuko has also urged further attention to women's narratives in an attempt to disrupt male-dominant narratives. See Ueno, "Ishi o nageru," 400–401.

85. Slaymaker, *The Body in Postwar Japanese Fiction,* 4–5.

86. In October 2015, Prime Minister Abe Shinzō unveiled the goal of building a "society in which all 100 million people can be active," rhetoric that starkly calls up wartime unity. See Linda Sieg, "Abe's New Slogan Stirs Memories of Wartime Rhetoric," Japan Today, October 5, 2015, http://www.japantoday.com. Abe is the grandson of a prime minister who ordered violence against protesters during his time in office (1957–60).

87. Kovner, *Occupying Power,* 19.

88. Ibid., 154.

89. Ibid., 157.

90. Katō Mizuho, interview by author, October 21, 2007, Ashiya, Hyōgo.

91. It is unclear why there was friction between Tanaka and Yoshihara. Some informants have speculated that jealousy or financial issues were involved. Given that Tanaka's career was skyrocketing despite her being a woman and also junior to Yoshihara, either explanation would not be

surprising. Jinno, interview by author, October 8, 2008. Yoshihara also supervised the exhibition of a reconstruction of Tanaka's pink rayon work in 1965 at the Stedelijk Museum Amsterdam without first obtaining permission from Tanaka. Katō, "Chronology," 187.

92. This information comes from the film *Tanaka Atsuko: Mōhitotsu no Gutai.*

93. After living for several years on the temple grounds, in September 1972 the couple moved permanently to the city of Asuka in Nara Prefecture, where they lived communally with Fukuzawa Hiroshi and his wife, Yasuko. Tiampo and Katō, *Electrifying Art,* 18. "In October, Kanayama and the Fukuzawas begin to build a 70m² studio. Due to financial difficulties, they built it themselves without a contractor." Katō, "Chronology," 188.

94. It was not uncommon for artists to use space in temples as studios, since Japanese housing conditions made it difficult to accommodate large works. Motonaga Sadamasa, another Gutai member, for example, moved to Dainichi-ji, a temple in Nishinomiya, in 1957. Nakajima, "A Motonaga Sadamasa Chronology," 152.

95. Tatehata Akira has suggested similarities of character and motivations between Tanaka and Kusama. Tatehata, interview by author, October 8, 2008. The same been suggested by Nakajima Izumi, "Japanese Women Artists and Post-war Abstract Painting." See also Yoshimoto, "Paradox in Self-Obliteration." Jonathan Watkins equates Kusama and Tanaka's interest in repetition with existentialism. See Watkins, "Broader Horizons," 147. Several exhibitions have also paired the two, including *Rose Is a Rose Is a Rose: Yayoi Kusama, Atsuko Tanaka, Tsuruko Yamazaki,* Foundation de Elf Lijnen, Oudenburg, Belgium.

96. Iga, *The Thorn in the Chrysanthemum,* 16. Miriam Kingsberg describes a sudden increase in drug use in the 1950s; see Kingsberg, "Methamphetamine Solution."

97. Partner, *Assembled in Japan,* 146.

98. Ibid., 149.

99. Ibid.

100. Ibid., 209.

101. Tanaka strove to maintain the same hues in her works, using the same supplier and the same brand, a vinyl paint called VIBY produced by Isamu Paint. In the final years of her work, Tanaka also began using acrylic urethane paint called Uni Atoron. Katō, "Searching for a Boundary," 25.

102. Tatehata, "Seisei suru taburō." See also Osaki, "Gutai kaiga e itaru akushon." Reiko Tomii discusses "the Gutai conundrum" in Tomii and McCaffrey, *Kazuo Shiraga,* 9.

103. "Mata ressha kara ochi shibō" [Another death from train jump], *Yomiuri Shinbun,* June 28, 1956. This headline suggests the frequency of such tragic events. The stories were covered in English-language newspapers as well. See, for example, "Girl Suicide Wrecks Train," *Japan Times,* March 25, 1995, 1; "Baby Boy Killed by Train in Mother's Suicide Try," *Japan Times,* December 17, 1956, 3. While books such as Iga's *The Thorn in the Chrysanthemum* discuss the statistics of suicides, the newspaper articles further reveal a sense of societal shock as headlines shift from framing the trains as icons of modernity that will bring Japan into a competitive relationship with the industrialized world to expressing fears about the human cost of this development.

104. La Vecchia, Lucchini, and Levi, "Worldwide Trends in Suicide Mortality." See also World Health Organization, "WHO: Suicide Rates, 1950–2004," accessed November 5, 2009, http://www.who.int. Japan still had the highest suicide rate in the developed world as of 2012, the most recent year for which figures are available.

105. Iga, *The Thorn in the Chrysanthemum*, 16, citing Ministry of Welfare, *Jisastu shibō Tōkei* [Suicidal death statistics], 1977.

106. Following this peak in the mid-1950s, the suicides slowly tapered off until 1967, when they reached an average of 14.2 per 100,000. Ibid.

107. La Vecchia, Lucchini, and Levi, "Worldwide Trends in Suicide Mortality." See also World Health Organization, "WHO: Suicide Rates, 1950–2004," accessed November 5, 2009, http://www.who.int.

108. Iga, *The Thorn in the Chrysanthemum*, 20.

109. Butler describes the relationship between reiterative performative action and gender in "Performative Acts and Gender Constitution."

110. McLuhan, *Understanding Media*; Wagner, "Performance, Video, and the Rhetoric of Presence."

111. Wagner, "Performance, Video, and the Rhetoric of Presence, " 80.

112. McLuhan, *Understanding Media*, 9.

113. Wagner, "Video and the Senses."

114. Quoted in "Seisaku ni atatte," *Kokuritsu Kokusai Bijutsukan geppō* [National Museum of Art, Osaka, monthly newsletter], no. 81 (June 1999), English translation in Tiampo and Katō, *Electrifying Art,* 104–5.

4. Heroic Violence in the Art of Shiraga Kazuo

1. For example, see Kimura, "Akushon to taburō," 17–19; Hirai, *Shiraga Kazuo* (1989). More recently, McCaffrey Fine Art used a photograph of Shiraga's *Challenging Mud* for the cover of the catalog accompanying the exhibition *Shiraga Kazuo: Six Decades*. Tomii and McCaffrey, *Shiraga Kazuo.*

2. For example: "Day of Super-Surrealism Near? This young gent isn't trying to grapple with a robber. It's just artist Kazui *[sic]* Shiraga of Amagasaki, Hyōgo Prefecture, poised to swing the rope and smear paint with his feet on a No. 300 canvas for his newest creation dubbed 'No Title.'" "Day of Super-Surrealist," *Nihon Times,* November 20, 1955. See also "'Pikaso kaomake? Ashi de kaku gahaku" [Shaming Picasso? A foot-painting master painter], *Sekai Tsuushin,* November 25, 1955; "Moji dōri zenshin no sōsaku" [Literally creating with the whole body], *Mainichi Shinbun,* November 23, 1955; Hirai, *Gutai tte nanda?,* 65; Murai, "Kansai bijutsuka no kōsei."

3. Yoshihara, "Gutai sengen."

4. As noted previously, the manifesto was commissioned by the art journal several years after Gutai was formed.

5. Shiraga commented that it was not "the kind of group that people were in or out of; all we did was show up, sign our works, listen to the other members' comments about them, and sign the roll sheet." Shiraga Kazuo, interview by Osaki and Yamamura, translated in Ritter, *Between Action and the Unknown,* 132.

6. Heroism was being reformulated in other cultural arenas as well. For example, the warrior is refigured as *sarari-man* (salaryman) in films such as 1958's *Kyojin to gangu (Giants and Toys),* directed by Masumura Yasuzō. In this film, CEOs sacrifice themselves in a futile battle for financial domination of the caramel industry.

7. Broude and Garrard, "Introduction," 2.

8. The term *shame* was circulated widely to explain Japanese anger at the imperial forces. For example, the *Asahi Shinbun* published an editorial about the nation's shame in caving to the militarists. See Dower, *Embracing Defeat,* 509. Herbert Bix has shown how imperial and state leadership attempted to shift blame for the war and defeat to the Japanese civilians, who were told they should feel shame for failing the emperor. For example, Prime Minister Higashikuninomiya Naruhiko argued for the "repentance of the one hundred million" and called for unilateral love of the emperor. Bix, *Hirohito and the Making of Modern Japan,* 565.

9. Judith Butler discusses the impossibility of obtaining these ideals of gender subjectivity in "Melancholy Gender/Refused Identification," 32.

10. For an interesting discussion of the interplay of militarism and masculinity in a study of contemporary Japanese self-defense forces, see Frühstück, *Uneasy Warriors.*

11. For example, see Dazai, *The Setting Sun*; Mishima, *Confessions of a Mask.*

12. Shiraga also added that the *Sekai konnichi no bijutsu (Art of the World Today)* exhibit in 1956 showed works by Sam Francis and Lucio Fontana that shocked him. Hariu, "Kamigata akushon dangi," translated in Tomii and McCaffrey, *Kazuo Shiraga,* 62–63.

13. Dore Ashton, "Art: Japan's Gutai Group," *New York Times,* September 25, 1958, 66.

14. Ray Falk, "Japanese Innovators," *New York Times,* December 8, 1957, D24.

15. Hikosaka, "Tojirareta enkan no kanata wa."

16. *OED* Online, s.v. "heroism," accessed August 10, 2012, http://www.oed.com.

17. Falk, "Japanese Innovators," D24.

18. Ukita, "Experimental Outdoor Exhibition of Modern Art."

19. The work is usually exhibited in the West simply as *Dōzo,* which most art historians have translated as "Please come in." This is a more or less accurate translation of *dōzo*—essentially a word of invitation, or "please." The full title of the work, *Dōzo ohairi kudasai,* can be accurately translated as *Please Come In.*

20. Without attempting an in-depth comparison between postwar art in Japan and that in the United States, it is important to note that reworking ideas of nationhood through the vocabulary of representation was a transnational phenomenon. Jasper Johns's *Flag* from 1954–55 took up a more direct exploration of the emblem of the United States (see Figure 2.3 and the discussion of *Flag* in chapter 2). In this piece a tension exists between the friability of the newsprint collage and the ostensible strength and power of the most predominant national symbol. While it is uncertain the degree to which Gutai members were familiar with this particular work or with art that incorporated national symbols, it is certainly true that the ascendancy of American art was not missed by contemporary Japanese artists.

21. Takamura, "Midoriiro no taiyō."

22. Volk, *In Pursuit of Universalism,* 85.

23. Shiraga Kazuo, interview by Ming Tiampo, December 11, 1998, Ashiya, Japan, cited in Tiampo, "Gutai and Informel," 177.

24. Kanayama, "Shiraga Kazuo," 7.

25. Art movements began gathering in Ashiya shortly after the war; for example, the Ashiya City Art Association was established as early as 1948. Yamamoto, "Introduction," 28.

26. Ibid.

27. Shiraga was conscripted in 1944 to the military academy at Maebashi, and in June 1945, at the age of twenty-one, he was assigned to an infantry unit in Osaka. There he tended to the

wounded at Osaka Castle, which was being used as an interim recovery center. On his return to Ashiya, following a hospital stay for pneumonia and rheumatism, he immediately began producing art, despite economic hardship and difficulties in accessing paints, canvas, and other supplies. Hirai, *Shiraga Kazuo* (1989).

28. Ming Tiampo, interview by author, October 4, 2008, Tokyo.

29. Kanayama and Shiraga often discussed their own artistic roles, polarizing each other's art as "hot" and "cold." An in-depth discussion of their productive dynamic falls outside the purview of this chapter; however, it is worth noting that their conscious engagement with binaries and masculine and feminine modes of representation reveals the importance of gender to Shiraga's oeuvre.

30. Yoshimoto, "Gutai and Environment Art."

31. Even though the group's contributions to Expo '70 embodied the culmination of Gutai art, its participation in the fair created schisms between members regarding finances, causing three of the founding members, Motonaga, Shimamoto, and Murakami, to leave the group. Additionally, with the Pinacotheca's closure in 1970, Gutai's organized activity virtually ceased, and the group officially dissolved after Yoshihara's death in 1972. Ibid. As Yoshimoto describes the events surrounding Expo '70: "Soon, the anti-expo sentiment among artists was crystallized into the analogy of Expo '70 participants to war propaganda painters during World War Two. In its July 1969 statement, 'Appeal to Artists,' Bikyōtō (short for Bijutsuka Kyōtō Kaigi, or Artists Joint-Struggle Council) advocated the destruction of every artistic institution that they considered a part of 'modern rationalism,' including Expo '70 and [the] Tokyo Biennale. . . . Bikyōtō's highly politicized rhetoric was echoed by other anti-expo coalitions, such as Architects '70 Action Committee and Expo '70 Destruction Joint-Struggle Group." Yoshimoto, "'Expo '70 and Japanese Art: Dissonant Voices,'" 3.

32. Murakami, "Gutaitekina hanashi," 206.

33. Yoshihara, "On the First Gutai-Ten."

34. Yoshihara, "Kanransha no nakatta daitenrankai," 7.

35. Shiraga continued his training until June 1974 under the tutelage of Yamada Etai, the head priest of the Tendai sect, and at age fifty he received the Buddhist name Shiraga Sodō. Even after he left the training, he continued to offer prayers before beginning to paint. Shiraga Kazuo, oral history interview by Ikegami Hiroko and Katō Mizuho, September 6, 2007, Oral History Archives of Japanese Art, http://www.oralarthistory.org. For more on Zen Buddhism in the 1950s, see Westgeest, *Zen in the Fifties*, 49.

36. Murakami, "Gutaitekina hanashi," 208.

37. Adams and Savran, "Introduction," 4.

38. Shiraga, "Kōi koso," 22.

39. In the 1960s, Shiraga's work as a solo artist began to garner increasing amounts of attention, and his first foreign solo show was held at Galerie Stadler in Paris in 1962.

40. Shiraga, oral history interview by Ikegami and Katō.

41. Hirai, "Inner Bipolarity," 145. I also confirmed this point with Hirai in a personal interview, October 22, 2007, Tokyo National Museum.

42. The earliest extant printed copy dates to the sixteenth century. *The Water Margin*, or *Suikoden* in Japanese, is also referred to as *All Men Are Brothers* and *Outlaws of the Marsh*.

43. Klompmakers, *Of Brigands and Bravery*, 23.

44. The television adaptation of *The Water Margin* was produced by Nippon Television and starred Nakamura Atsuo and Sato Kei in the main roles. The show, which was filmed on location

in China in 1973, was that country's first joint production with a non-Communist nation since the Communists rose to power in 1949.

45. Shiraga, interview by Osaki and Yamamura, translated in Ritter, *Between Action and the Unknown,* 126.

46. *Sanbasō* refers to a type of Noh theater dance, wherein a holy man, *okina,* prays for fertility and peace while dancing.

47. Nakajima, "A Shiraga Kazuo Chronology," 136.

48. Winther-Tamaki, *Maximum Embodiment,* 165.

49. Ibid., 168.

50. Art historian Alfred Barr categorized abstract expressionism as an explicit category in 1936; however, the genre was solidified by the discourses of Harold Rosenberg and Clement Greenberg in the 1950s. This time frame also mirrors the introduction of abstract expressionism in Japan, according to Kamada Tsukasa. Yoshihara exhibited five works at the twenty-first Nika exhibition in 1936, all of which demonstrated an interest in abstraction. The influential magazine *Mizue* also featured an article by Hasegawa Saburō titled "Chūshō bijutsu" (Abstract art), and many Japanese artists increasingly created nonfigural work at this time. Kamada, "Busshitsuo kiri saku sen no kiseki, arui wa ippon no michi," 18.

51. Christine Guth addresses the theme of heroism in terms of Hokusai's wave paintings and *Suikoden* in her insightful essay "Hokusai's Great Waves in Nineteenth-Century Japanese Visual Culture."

52. Hirai, *Shiraga Kazuo* (1989), 8; Calza, *Hokusai,* 383.

53. For example, see Winther-Tamaki, "Yagi Kazuo"; Volk, *Made in Japan.*

54. For examples of reviews that disparage Shiraga's work for being overly influenced by others, see "Day of Super-Surrealist"; Ashton, "Art: Japan's Gutai Group."

55. For more on the self and Yorozu Tetsugorō, see Volk, *In Pursuit of Universalism,* 75–102. For more on comparisons between Pollock and Shiraga, see Kee, "Situating a Singular Kind of 'Action,'"

56. Volk, *In Pursuit of Universalism,* 77.

57. Weisenfeld, *Mavo.*

58. For more on Murayama and the manga, see Murayama, "Sanpei manga ni tsuite"; Kawasaki, "'Shinobi no mono' no shūhen."

59. Steinberg, "Otaku Consumption, Superflat Art," 449. See also Gluck, "The Invention of Edo."

60. See Weisenfeld, "Reinscribing Tradition in a Transnational Art World."

61. The photographs are undated, but a painting by Shiraga from 1956 hangs in the background, and Osaka University Museum curator Katō Mizuho estimates the images are from around this time.

62. Yoshida was the official secretary for both Gutai and Yoshihara Seiyu, Yoshihara's vegetable oil company, suggesting that a certain amount of crossover existed between Yoshihara's business and the Gutai Art Association. Another example of crossover between the two is the series of advertisement designs done by various Gutai members for the company. Yoshida's secretarial role would have included maintaining the photograph archives.

63. Hirai describes visiting Shiraga's home and witnessing his vast camera collection. Hirai, *Shiraga Kazuo: Action Painter,* 145.

64. Shi and Luo, *Shui hu zhuan,* 565.

65. The images were possibly arranged in the album by Yoshida Toshio, but it is likely that Shiraga was at least aware of, if not partly responsible for, the production and placement of these images.

66. Ming Tiampo, whose work has been foundational for Gutai studies, has suggested that Shiraga's work grew from the practice of traditional festivals *(matsuri)* in Japan. Her argument relies on her firsthand interviews with Shiraga. I aim to explore precisely why such festivals may have been of interest to the artist. See Tiampo, "Moments of Destruction, Moments of Beauty." Reiko Tomii should be acknowledged for her important work on Shiraga's first solo show in North America at McCaffrey Fine Art. In the informative catalog she describes Shiraga as a "man's man in the traditional Japanese mold" because of his interest in hobbies like hunting and his participation in school activities like sumo. My argument aims to clarify how this characterization relates to Shiraga's self-conscious exploration of gender and selfhood. Tomii, "Shiraga Paints," 21.

67. Ukita, "Experimental Outdoor Exhibition of Modern Art," 26.

68. Kimura describes Shiraga as a spontaneous action painter in "Akushon to taburō," 15–17.

69. *Nikkatsu World News,* newsreel, no. 45, episode 2, broadcast October 26, 1955. The newsreel also includes coverage of other performances at the *First Gutai Art Exhibition.* I would like to thank Reiko Tomii for sharing information on this point.

70. Shiraga, "Kōi koso"; Shiraga, "Omou Koto"; Shiraga, "Shishitsu ni tsuite"; Shiraga, "Taisetsuna shinkei"; Shiraga, "Kotai no kakuritsu."

71. Hijikata Tatsumi was among those interested in these issues. For more on this topic, see Sas, *Experimental Arts in Postwar Japan.*

72. The second issue of *Gutai* closes with a short note in English by Ukita Yōzo that states: "Gutai might be literally translated as 'Embodiment.'" Ukita, "Documentary on the Second Edition of *Gutai.*" Ukita (born 1924) was a member of Gutai from 1955. She was the editor of the children's poetry magazine *Kirin* for seventeen years and often included contributions from the Gutai group in the magazine.

73. Quoted in Merewether, "Disjunctive Modernity," 3. For further references to the "shock" of modern art, see Chiba, *Gendai bijutsu itsudatsushi,* 25.

74. Shiraga Kazuo, in Hariu, "Kamigata akushon dangi," translated in Tomii and McCaffrey, *Kazuo Shiraga,* 62.

75. Michael McClure, "Notes on the Theatre," notebook, June 1958, Michael McClure Papers, Additions, BANC MSS 77/65c, Bancroft Library, University of California, Berkeley.

76. Yoshihara, "Gutai sengen," 202.

77. Shiraga, interview by Osaki and Yamamura, translated in Ritter, *Between Action and the Unknown,* 131.

78. In an interview he described working with Yoshihara as "18 years of scolding." Murakami, "Gutaitekina hanashi," 206.

79. Yoshihara, "Gutai sengen." Small photographs of Murakami Saburō's *Opening 6 Holes at Once,* Murakami's ball-throwing painting, and Tanaka Atsuko's *Electric Dress* were also included. These artists, along with Shiraga Fujiko, were members of Zero-kai before joining the Gutai group, and their radical practices infused Gutai with new performative energies.

80. See Shiraga, "Taisetsuna shinkei," 9.

81. Yoshihara, "Gutai sengen," 202. I am less convinced than Yoshihara that Shiraga was not interested in sharing his method with the public. Shiraga frequently invited media and performed before journalists. He also wrote numerous essays expounding on his artistic methods.

82. There is no formal connection between Zero-kai and the European movement Group Zero, which was also seeking out "pure possibilities for a new beginning." For more on the European movement, see Piene, "Group Zero."

83. Yamamoto, "Murakami Saburō," 17.

84. Following this shot, the camera proceeds to follow Murakami's action from inside the large paper box outward toward the surrounding art exhibition.

85. Ashiya Museum curator Yamamoto Atsuo describes his work as "orthodox," mentioning a competitive spirit that existed between Shiraga and Murakami. Murakami, "Gutaitekina hanashi," 118.

86. Ibid., 205.

87. Shiraga, "Omou koto," 20.

88. Yoshihara, "On the First Gutai-Ten," 2.

89. Shiraga, "Kōi koso," 22.

90. Shiraga, "Omou koto," 20. These actions are reminiscent of the samurai movie star Mifune Toshirō (1920–97), who starred in sixteen films by Kurosawa Akira and was frequently seen emphasizing his characters' coarse, physical presence by scratching himself.

91. Shiraga, "Kotai no kakuritsu," 7.

92. Shiraga, "Bōken no kiroku I."

93. Kee, "Situating a Singular Kind of 'Action.'"

94. Nancy, *The Ground of the Image*, 20.

95. "There is the satisfaction of being able to look at the image without flinching. There is the satisfaction of flinching. . . . Torment, a canonical subject in art, is often represented in painting as a spectacle, something being watched (or ignored) by other people." Sontag, *Regarding the Pain of Others*, 42.

96. Nancy, *The Ground of the Image*, 20.

97. CoBrA was a European avant-garde movement active from 1949 to 1952. For more on CoBrA, see Aubert, "'Cobra after Cobra' and the Alba Congress"; Stokvis, *Cobra*. An exhibition in 1985 emphasized the common concerns of Gutai, Informel, and CoBrA. See Tatehata, "Seisei suru taburō."

98. Mariko Aoyagi unconvincingly maintains that Shiraga was not interested in the primitive but only in the body. Aoyagi, "Placing Gutai within Traditional Japanese Art."

99. Shiraga, oral history interview by Ikegami and Katō.

100. Shiraga related this story in a 1993 interview. Murakami, "Gutaitekina hanashi," 206.

101. *Wild Boar Hunting II* is 182.98 × 203 centimeters, larger than the first version.

102. Shiraga, in Hariu, "Kamigata akushon dangi," translated in Tomii and McCaffrey, *Kazuo Shiraga*, 65.

103. The name Tenkūsei Kyūsenpō in Japanese breaks down into two three-character noms de guerre. Both refer to Suo Chao, one of the more central characters in *The Water Margin*. The first three characters refer to his rank, and the second three refer to his nickname, Impatient Vanguard.

104. Shiraga Kazuo, in Hirai, *Shiraga Kazuo: Action Painter*, 12–13.

105. Nancy, *The Ground of the Image,* 18.

106. Nakamura, "Atorie de no taiwa," 65.

107. Misawa, "The Water Margin and Kazuo Shiraga," 233.

108. Hirai, "Inner Bipolarity," 150.

109. Shiraga, oral history interview by Ikegami and Katō.

110. Shiraga, interview by Osaki and Yamamura, translated in Ritter, *Between Action and the Unknown,* 129.

111. Harris, "A 'Commodius Vicus of Recirculation,'" 370. See also Westgeest, *Zen in the Fifties,* 43–72.

112. For more on Morita, see Winther-Tamaki, *Art in the Encounter of Nations,* esp. 74–89.

113. Adolphson, *The Gates of Power,* 5.

114. Ibid.

115. Shiraga, "Le dieu Fudō et ma peinture," English translation in Pacquement, "Kazuo Shiraga," 11.

116. Each king represents a cardinal direction of the mandala (including the center, represented by the most well-known figure, Fudō Myō-ō), and each is a wrathful manifestation of one of the Five Wisdom Buddhas. Daitoku Myō-ō, the Wisdom King of the Western arena, is the wrathful emanation of Amida Nyorai and is pictured with six faces, six legs, and six arms wielding various weapons; he sits on a white cow, which symbolizes pure enlightenment.

117. *Red Fan* features crimson lake, the artist's signature color beginning with his first foot paintings in 1954.

118. It is also possible that Shiraga's move from violent abstraction to Tendai *shugendō* was the result of his embrace of an ethical system. Shiraga, interview by Osaki and Yamamura, translated in Ritter, *Between Action and the Unknown,* 129. *The Water Margin* featured violence for violence's sake regardless of the merit of the motive for battle, but in Buddhism wrathful deities such as Fudō Myō-ō and other Wisdom Kings aimed their violent power at obstacles to the attainment of enlightenment. Regardless, Shiraga clearly found violence to be a consistent form of art.

119. After being asked if he performed Buddhist ceremonies at home or in the temple, Shiraga answered, "I don't take part in ceremonies like those commemorating Buddha [one of the most common religious events], I performed the practices dictated by the religious system established on Mount Hiei, but I hardly do it anymore." In Martin, "'Something Comes Out of Your Subconscious,'" 276.

Conclusion

1. Kirsten Cather writes: "The effect of the liberalized atmosphere on the publishing world was apparent almost immediately: whereas at war's end only 300 publishing companies existed, within eight months over 2,000 were in operation, and by 1948 that number had peaked at 4,600." Cather, *The Art of Censorship in Postwar Japan,* 29. John Dower writes: "At war's end, there were approximately three hundred publishing companies in Japan. Eight months later, the number had increased to almost two thousand. In 1948, it peaked at around forty-six hundred, a majority of which did not survive the recession that began the next year. Nonetheless, in 1951, as the occupation drew to a close, about nineteen hundred publishers were still in operation—a sixfold increase over August 1945." Dower, *Embracing Defeat,* 180–81.

2. Between 1950 and 1969, an increasingly large readership for manga emerged in Japan with the solidification of two main marketing genres, *shōnen* manga, aimed at boys, and *shōjo* manga, aimed at girls. Schodt, *Manga! Manga!*

3. For more on contemporary manga and gender, see Orbaugh, "Busty Battlin' Babes."

4. The comic was initially published in the *Asahi Journal* in 1938 and was later published in book format in three volumes. A film of the series, also titled *Omoitsuki fujin,* was released by Tōhō Films in 1939, attesting to its popularity. A second film based on the comic was released in 1952, called *Achako seishun nikki* (Memoirs of Achako's youth).

5. It is possible that the original plates were lost during the war, thus it was necessary for Hirai to redraw them.

6. For more on Oku Mumeo's political continuity before and after the war, see Narita, "Women in the Motherland."

7. Dower, *Embracing Defeat,* 94.

8. Ibid., 92.

9. In 1949 the comic transitioned to the *Asahi Journal.* See Iwamoto, *Akogare no Burondi,* 83.

10. In the comic the central character is referred to only as *fujin,* or madam, while in the 1939 film version she is called Matsuyama Tsuruko.

11. It should be noted that the patriarch rarely appears in *Omoitsuki fujin,* while Dagwood Bumstead, the patriarch in *Burondi,* is a central character, and his bumbling behavior is a source of numerous jokes. Blondie is generally portrayed as a capable housewife.

12. The regalia originally represented the three primary virtues: valor (the sword), wisdom (the mirror), and benevolence (the jewel).

13. Partner, *Assembled in Japan,* 149.

14. Power, *God of Comics,* 34. Iwamoto Shigeki writes that many Japanese commented on the high visibility of appliances in *Burondi* and were also interested in Blondie's high status in the home. Iwamoto, *Akogare no Burondi,* 118. Although the character was intended to be a comical caricature, it seems that she was not necessarily always perceived that way in Japan.

15. In fact, *Sazae-san* was not the first manga to feature the women's liberation movement. The February 21, 1921, issue of *Jiji Manga* focused entirely on "contemporary women's thinking" and featured issues such as birth control, women's workforce rights, and the right to refuse marriage. Margaret Sanger would visit Japan the following year.

16. As the series progressed it became increasingly conservative in general.

17. Hasegawa's focus on daily life and on women's experience also came to characterize later *shōjo* manga.

18. "The TV cartoon 'Sazae-san,' which began airing in 1969, has been recognized by Guinness World Records as the longest-running animated series in the world, beating the U.S. show 'The Simpsons.'" "'Sazae-san' Sets Guinness Cartoon Record," *Japan Times,* September 6, 2013, http://www.japantimes.co.jp.

19. My point here is not to disparage the buxom sexiness of Blondie any more than it is to herald the denied (even repressed) sexual physicality depicted in *Imoitsuki fujin* or *Sazae-san.* Instead, I want to emphasize that divisive gendered identities were circulating in postwar Japan in a highly visual manner. These representations were never freed from their national identities and related consumer desires.

20. "At first she drew her character Sazae-san as tall and graceful, then when she got married shrank her into a plain but cheery housewife coping with her extended family. For decades Hasegawa's affectionate, unglamorized portrayal of everywoman's good humor and quiet strength (based on the mangaka's own life) conveyed the sort of feminine insights that would have probably escaped most male cartoonists altogether." Gravett, *Manga*, 76.

21. All of the characters in the series are named after sea-related creatures and themes.

22. Butler, *Bodies That Matter*.

23. Thomas Lamarre writes: "Bending gender and genre appears at the very origins of manga and anime (if one wishes to think in those terms). For instance, in one of the standard approaches to the story of manga and anime, these forms are said to take on a certain coherence and visibility through the work of Tezuka Osamu, the so-called 'God of Manga' who also did a great deal to launch the television animation industry in Japan. If we take Tezuka as an origin, it is clear that gender bending was central, not marginal to manga and anime from the outset." Lamarre, "Platonic Sex," 48. In Tezuka's *Ribon no Kishi* (Princess Knight or, more literally, "a knight in ribbons"), serialized from 1953 to 1956 and later made into a 1960s television series, a young girl pretends to be a male prince to prevent a criminal from inheriting the throne. The series unselfconsciously examines the performative, imitative structure of gender itself. Princess Knight was also likely related to Tezuka's early exposure and interest in the cross-dressing, all-female theater troupe Takarazuka, which was based in (and named for) Tezuka's hometown. For more on Takarazuka gender politics, see Robertson, *Takarazuka*. From 1949 to 1955, Kurakane Shōsuke produced *Anmitsu-hime* (Princess Honey-bean), which featured a tomboy princess who escapes from her castle to enjoy life as a "commoner." Perhaps to a greater degree than *Blondie, Anmitsu-hime* showcased luxurious outfits and elegant desserts, playing to the desire for indulgence during a time of food scarcity and clothing shortages. The series boosted sales of the magazine *Shōjo* (Girl's), published from 1949 to 1955, to 700,000, and it was turned into two live-action films. These comics and television programs, far from being icons of subculture, were the top revenue-generating series of the postwar period. As a whole, they showed a telling lack of consensus around gender norms, revealing the contention and anxiety over depictions of the gendered body in postwar Japan.

24. See Uno, "The Death of 'Good Wife, Wise Mother'?," 293–94.

Bibliography

Adams, Rachel, and David Savran. "Introduction." In *The Masculinity Studies Reader,* edited by Rachel Adams and David Savran. Malden, Mass.: Blackwell, 2002.

Adolphson, Mikael S. *The Gates of Power: Monks, Courtiers, and Warriors in Premodern Japan.* Honolulu: University of Hawai'i Press, 2000.

Aoyagi, Mariko. "Placing Gutai within Traditional Japanese Art through Its Sensory Elements." In *Modern Art in Asia: Selected Papers, Issues 1–8,* edited by Majella Munro. Cambridge: Enzo Arts and Publishing, 2012.

Atkins, Jacqueline. *Wearing Propaganda: Textiles on the Home Front in Japan, Britain, and the United States, 1931–1945.* New Haven, Conn.: Yale University Press, 2005.

Aubert, Nathalie. "'Cobra after Cobra' and the Alba Congress: From Revolutionary Avant-Garde to Situationist Experiment." *Third Text* 20, no. 2 (March 2006): 259–67.

Baker, Steve. *The Postmodern Animal.* London: Reaktion, 2000.

Baldwin, James. *Another Country.* New York: Dell, 1962.

Banno, Junji. *Japan's Modern History, 1857–1937: A New Political Narrative.* Translated by J. A. A. Stockwin. London: Routledge, 2014.

Benjamin, Walter. *The Origin of German Tragic Drama.* London: NLB, 1977.

Berndt, Jaqueline. "Nationally Naked? The Female Nude in Japanese Oil Painting and Posters (1890s–1920s)." In *Performing "Nation": Gender Politics in Literature, Theatre, and the Visual Arts of China and Japan, 1880–1940,* edited by Doris Croissant, Catherine Vance Yeh, and Joshua S. Mostow, 307–46. Leiden: Brill, 2008.

Bijutsu Hyōronka Renmei, ed. *Bijutsu hihyō to sengo bijutsu* [Art criticism and postwar art]. Tokyo: Brücke, 2007.

Bix, Herbert P. *Hirohito and the Making of Modern Japan.* New York: HarperCollins, 2000.

Braw, Monica. *The Atomic Bomb Suppressed: American Censorship in Occupied Japan.* Armonk, N.Y.: M. E. Sharpe, 1991.

Broude, Norma, and Mary D. Garrard. "Introduction: The Expanding Discourse." In *The Expanding Discourse: Feminism and Art History,* edited by Norma Broude and Mary D. Garrard. Boulder, Colo.: Westview Press, 1992.

Bryan-Wilson, Julia. "Remembering Yoko Ono's *Cut Piece*." *Oxford Art Journal* 26, no. 1 (2003): 99–123.

Buckley, Sandra. "Altered States: The Body Politics of 'Being-Woman.'" In Gordon, *Postwar Japan as History*, 347–72.

Butler, Judith. *Bodies That Matter: On the Discursive Limits of "Sex."* New York: Routledge, 1993.

———. "Melancholy Gender/Refused Identification." In *Constructing Masculinity*, edited by Maurice Berger, Brian Wallis, and Simon Watson, 21–36. New York: Routledge, 1995.

———. "Performative Acts and Gender Constitution: An Essay in Phenomenology and Feminist Theory." *Theatre Journal* 40, no. 4 (1988): 519–31.

Calza, Gian Carlo. *Hokusai: Il vecchio pazzo per la pittura.* Milan: Palazzo Reale di Milan, 1999.

Cather, Kirsten. *The Art of Censorship in Postwar Japan.* Honolulu: University of Hawai'i Press, 2012.

Chiba Shigeo. *Gendai bijutsu itsudatsushi, 1945–1985* [A history of deviation in contemporary art, 1945–1985]. Tokyo: Shobunsha, 1986.

Chiba Shigeo, Yuri Mitsuda, et al. *Gutai: Mikan no sen'ei shūdan-Hyōgo kindai bijutsukan shozō sakuhin o chūshin ni/The Unfinished Avant-Garde Group.* Tokyo: Shōtō Museum of Art, 1990.

Chong, Doryun, ed. *From Postwar to Postmodern: Art in Japan 1945–1989—Primary Documents.* New York: Museum of Modern Art, 2012.

———, ed. *Tokyo, 1955–1970: A New Avant-Garde.* New York: Museum of Modern Art, 2012.

Chow, Rey. *The Age of the World Target: Self-Referentiality in War, Theory, and Comparative Work.* Durham, N.C.: Duke University Press, 2006.

Cohen, Martin. "Japan's Gutai Group." *Art in America,* November 1968, 86–69.

Daigo Fukuryū Maru Heiwa Kyōkai [Public Interest Incorporated Foundation Daigo Fukuryū Maru Peace Society]. *Daigo Fukuryū Maru wa kōkaichū* [The voyage of the *Lucky Dragon*]. Tokyo: Daigo Fukuryū Maru Heiwa Kyōkai, 2014.

Darling, Michael, ed. *Target Practice: Painting under Attack, 1949–78.* Seattle: Seattle Art Museum, 2009.

Day, Gail. "Allegory: Between Deconstruction and Dialectics." *Oxford Art Journal* 22, no. 1 (1999): 103–18.

Dazai, Osamu. *The Setting Sun.* Translated by Donald Keene. New York: New Directions, 1956.

Deleuze, Gilles, and Félix Guattari. *Kafka: Toward a Minor Literature.* Minneapolis: University of Minnesota Press, 1986.

De Man, Paul. *Allegories of Reading: Figural Language in Rousseau, Nietzsche, Rilke, and Proust.* New Haven, Conn.: Yale University Press, 1979.

Deming, W. Edwards. *Out of the Crisis.* Cambridge: Center for Advanced Engineering Study, MIT, 1986.

Doherty, Thomas. *Cold War, Cool Medium: Television, McCarthyism, and American Culture.* New York: Columbia University Press, 2003.

Dorsey, James, and Doug Slaymaker, eds. *Literary Mischief: Sakaguchi Ango, Culture, and the War.* Lanham, Md.: Lexington Books, 2010.

Dower, John W. *Embracing Defeat: Japan in the Wake of World War II.* New York: W. W. Norton, 1999.

Elliot, David, and Kazu Kaido, eds. *Reconstructions: Avant-Garde Art in Japan, 1945–1965.* Oxford: Museum of Modern Art, 1985.

Enchi Fumiko, Jugaku Akiko, Itō Keiichi, Konishi Ryōtarō, and Kawakita Noriko. *Josei geijutsuka no jinsei 2 ushidoshi hen: Jūnishi betsu, ekigaku kaisetsu* [Life of female artists 2, Year of the Ox: Classified by twelve horary signs, the interpretation of divination]. Tokyo: Shūeisha, 1980.

Fitzpatrick, Andrea F. "The Movement of Vulnerability: Images of Falling and September 11." *Art Journal* 66, no. 4 (Winter 2007): 84–102.

Freud, Anna. *The Ego and the Mechanisms of Defence.* Translated by Cecil Baines. New York: International Universities Press, 1946.

Freud, Sigmund. "Beyond the Pleasure Principle." In *The Freud Reader,* edited by Peter Gay. New York: W. W. Norton, 1989.

Frühstück, Sabine. *Uneasy Warriors: Gender, Memory, and Popular Culture in the Japanese Army.* Berkeley: University of California Press, 2007.

Fujii, James A. *Complicit Fictions: The Subject in the Modern Japanese Prose Narrative.* Berkeley: University of California Press, 1993.

———. "Intimate Alienation: Japanese Urban Rail and the Commodification of Urban Subjects." *Differences* 11, no. 2 (1999): 106–33.

Garber, Marjorie. "Fetish Envy." *October* 54 (1990): 45–56.

George, Timothy S. *Minamata: Pollution and the Struggle for Democracy in Postwar Japan.* Cambridge, Mass.: Harvard University Asia Center, 2001.

Germer, Andrea. Review of *Nationalism and Gender,* by Chizuko Ueno. *Asian Studies Review* 28, no. 4 (2004): 435.

Germer, Andrea, Vera C. Mackie, and Ulrike Wöhr. *Gender, Nation and State in Modern Japan.* London: Routledge, 2014.

Gerteis, Christopher. *Gender Struggles: Wage-Earning Women and Male-Dominated Unions in Postwar Japan.* Cambridge, Mass.: Harvard University Asia Center, 2009.

———. "Political Protest in Interwar Japan—1: Posters and Handbills from the Ohara Collection (1920s–1930s)." MIT Visualizing Cultures website. Accessed August 3, 2016. http://ocw.mit.edu.

Gluck, Carol. "The Invention of Edo." In *Mirror of Modernity: Invented Traditions of Modern Japan,* edited by Stephen Vlastos, 262–84. Berkeley: University of California Press, 1998.

———. "The Past in the Present." In Gordon, *Postwar Japan as History,* 64–95.

Goh, Irving. "Becoming-Animal: Transversal Politics." *diacritics* 39, no. 2 (2009): 37–57.

Goodman, David G. "The Return of the Gods: Theatre in Japan Today." *World Literature Today* 62, no. 3 (1988): 418–20.

Gordon, Andrew, ed. *Postwar Japan as History.* Berkeley: University of California Press, 1993.

Gordon, Beate Sirota. *The Only Woman in the Room: A Memoir.* Tokyo: Kōdansha, 1997.

Gravett, Paul. *Manga: Sixty Years of Japanese Comics.* New York: HarperCollins, 2004.

Gross, Larry, John Stuart Katz, and Jay Ruby. "Introduction: Image Ethics in the Digital Age." In *Image Ethics in the Digital Age,* edited by Larry Gross, John Stuart Katz, and Jay Ruby. Minneapolis: University of Minnesota Press, 2003.

Gutai Bijutsu No 18-nen Publication Committee, ed. *Gutai bijutsu no 18-nen* [18 years of Gutai art]. Osaka: Osaka Fumin Center, 1976.

Guth, Christine M. E. "Hokusai's Great Waves in Nineteenth-Century Japanese Visual Culture." *Art Bulletin* 93, no. 4 (2011): 468–85.

Hamamoto Satoshi. "Katsura Yuki no manazashi: Sono hihyō seishin wo megutte" [Katsura Yuki's perspectives: On her critical spirit]. In Seki et al., *Katsura Yuki,* 17–24.

———. "Katsura Yuki shiron: Dentō no parody, moshiku wa aironī to shite no shisen" [Essay on Katsura Yuki: Traditional parody, or ironic perspective]. *Shimonoseki-shiritsu bijutsukan kenkyū kiyō,* no. 4 (March 1993): 10.

———. "Riarizumu josetsu" [Introduction to realism]. In *Atarashii geijutsu no tankyū* [Search for a new art], edited by Yoru No Kai [Night Society]. Tokyo: Getsuyō Shobō, 1949.

Hamaya Hiroshi. *Ikari to kanashimi no kiroku* [A record of days of rage and grief]. Tokyo: Kawade Shobō Shinsha, 1960.

Hanada Kiyoteru. *Sachurikon.* Tokyo: Miraisha, 1956.

Hariu Ichirō. "Kamigata akushon dangi" [Osaka action talk]. In *Shiraga Kazuo.* Tokyo: Tokyo Gallery, 1973. Translated in Tomii and McCaffrey, *Kazuo Shiraga,* 61–65.

———. "Katsura Yuki no bakeppuri to yūmoa" [The humor and transformation of Katsura Yuki]. In Katsura and Yamaguchi Kenritsu Bijutsukan, *Katsura Yuki ten zuroku.*

———. "Kirokusei" [Documentary]. *Bijutsu hihyō* (January 1955): 52.

———. *Sengo bijutsu seisui shi* [The rise and fall of postwar Japanese art]. Tokyo: Tokyo Shoseki, 1979.

———. "Shakaiteki shudai to riarizumu" [Social subject matter and realism]. *Bijutsu hihyō* (January 1954): 9.

———. "Shin gushō no hō kō" [The direction of new figurative painting]. *Bijutsu hihyō* (December 1954): 10.

Hariu Ichirō, Hamada Chimei, Kawara On, Yamanaka Harui, Ikeda Tatsuo, Kiuchi Misaki, and Yoshinaka Taizō. "Atarashii ningenzō ni mukatte, zadankai" [Toward a new human image, a roundtable discussion]. *Bijutsu hihyō,* no. 43 (1955): 45–57.

Hariu Ichirō, Tokudaiji Kimihide, Segi Shin'ichi, and Okamoto Kenjirō. "Shūki tenrankai sono 1: Tokushū" [Autumn exhibitions part 1: Special feature]. *Bijutsu techō,* no. 88 (November 1954): 40–41.

Harris, Chauncy D. "The Urban and Industrial Transformation of Japan." *Geographical Review* 72, no. 1 (1982): 50–89.

Harris, Ian. "A 'Commodius Vicus of Recirculation': Buddhism, Art, and Modernity." In *Westward Dharma: Buddhism beyond Asia,* edited by Charles S. Prebish and Martin Baumann, 365–82. Berkeley: University of California Press, 2002.

Harootunian, Harry. "Japan's Postwar and After, 1945–1989: An Overview." In Chong, *From Postwar to Postmodern.*

Harvey, David. *The Condition of Postmodernity: An Enquiry into the Origins of Cultural Change.* Oxford: Blackwell, 1989.

Hasegawa Jun'ichi. "The Rebuilding of Osaka." In *Rebuilding Urban Japan after 1945,* edited by Carola Hein, Jeffry M. Diefendorf, and Ishida Yorifusa. New York: Palgrave Macmillan, 2003.

Hayashi, Michio. "The Occupied Subject: Painting and Body in Post-war Japan." In *A rebours: La rebelión informalista/The Informal Rebellion, 1939–1968,* edited by Dore Ashton. Madrid: Museo Nacional Centro de Arte Reina Sofía, 1999.

———. "Other Trajectories in Gutai: Akira Kanayama and Atsuko Tanaka." Lecture, University of California, Berkeley, February 28, 2008.

Hein, Laura, and Rebecca Jennison, eds. *Imagination without Borders: Feminist Artist Tomiyama Taeko and Social Responsibility.* Ann Arbor: Center for Japanese Studies, University of Michigan, 2010.

Hikosaka Naoyoshi. "Tojirareta enkan no kanata wa: 'Gutai' no kiseki kara nani o . . ." [Beyond the enclosed ring: What to find in the trajectory of Gutai]. *Bijutsu techō,* no. 370 (August 1973): 72–92.

Hirai Fusando. *Kan-chan no sangyō senshi* [Kan-chan's industrial soldiers]. Osaka: Shōwa Shuppan Kabushiki Kaisha, 1944.

———. *Omoitsuki fujin* [Conscientious housewife]. Osaka: Asahi Shinbun-sha, Shōwa, 1938.

Hirai Shōichi. *Gutai tte nanda?/What's Gutai?* Tokyo: Bijutsu Shuppansha, 2004.

———. "Inner Bipolarity: The Paintings of Shiraga Kazuo." In Hirai, *Shiraga Kazuo: Action Painter.*

———, ed. *Kansai no bijutsu 1950s–1970s* [Art in Kansai, 1950s–1970s]. Kobe: Hyōgo Prefectural Museum of Art, 1994.

———. "Mr. Gutai: Yoshihara Jirō." In Hirai et al., *Gutai: The Spirit of an Era.*

———, ed. *Shiraga Kazuo.* Amagasaki: Amagasaki Cultural Center, 1989.

———, ed. *Shiraga Kazuo: Action Painter.* Kobe: Hyōgo Prefectural Museum of Art, 2001.

Hirai Shōichi, Yukako Yamada, Naoki Yoneda, and National Art Center, eds. *Gutai: Nippon no zen'ei 18-nen no kiseki/Gutai: The Spirit of an Era.* Tokyo: National Art Center, 2012.

Hironaka, Ann. *Neverending Wars: The International Community, Weak States, and the Perpetuation of Civil War.* Cambridge, Mass.: Harvard University Press, 2005.

Hoagland, Linda. "Protest Art in 1950s Japan: The Forgotten Reportage Painters." MIT Visualizing Cultures website. Accessed August 3, 2016. http://ocw.mit.edu.

Hood, Christopher P. *Shinkansen: From Bullet Train to Symbol of Modern Japan.* London: Routledge, 2006.

———. "The Shinkansen's Local Impact." *Social Science Japan Journal* 13, no. 2 (2010): 211–25.

Hoshi Kiichi, ed. *Sunagawa tōsō 50-nen: Sorezore no omoi* [Fifty years from the Sunagawa struggle: A collection of thoughts]. Tokyo: Keyaki Shuppan, 2005.

Howell, David L. "Ethnicity and Culture in Contemporary Japan." *Journal of Contemporary History* 31, no. 1 (1996): 171–90.

Hudson, Richard, and Ben Shahn. *Kuboyama and the Saga of the* Lucky Dragon. New York: Thomas Yoseloff, 1965.

Hurley, Brian. "Toward a New Modern Vernacular: Tanizaki Jun'ichirō, Yamada Yoshio, and Showa Restoration Thought." *Journal of Japanese Studies* 39, no. 2 (Summer 2013): 359–96.

"Hyōgen/jōkyō: 60-nendai bijutsu wa dō ugoitaka" [Expression/situation: How did the art of the 1960s change]. Special feature. *Bijutsu techō,* no. 349 (December 1971).

Iga, Mamoru. *The Thorn in the Chrysanthemum: Suicide and Economic Success in Modern Japan.* Berkeley: University of California Press, 1986.

Igarashi, Yoshikuni. *Bodies of Memory: Narratives of War in Postwar Japanese Culture, 1945–1970.* Princeton, N.J.: Princeton University Press, 2000.

Ikeda, Asato, Aya Louisa McDonald, and Ming Tiampo, eds. *Art and War in Japan and Its Empire, 1931–1960.* Leiden: Brill, 2013.

———. "Introduction." In Ikeda, McDonald, and Tiampo, *Art and War in Japan and Its Empire.*

Ikeda Tatsuo. *Ikeda Tatsuo: Avangyarudo no kiseki* [Ikeda Tatsuo: The trajectory of postwar avant-garde art]. Kawasaki: Ikeda Tatsuo Ten Jikkō Iinkai, 2010.

Imaizumi Atsuo. "Kindai kaiga no hihyō" [A critique of modern art]. *Bijutsu hihyō,* no. 8 (1952): 5–8.

Imaizumi Yoshihiko. "Nakamura Hiroshi no koto" [About Nakamura Hiroshi]. *Kikan,* no. 15 (1990).

Inaga Shigemi. "Toporojī kūkan no naka no nijūisseiki sekai bijutsushi, kokusai bijutsushi gakkai no saishin dōkō bekken" [Twenty-first century world art history in a topological space]. *Aida,* no. 147 (April 2008): 24–31.

Inayama, Kenji. "JNR's Choice of Traction System—from Loco-Hauled to Multiple-Unit Trains." *Japan Railway and Transport Review* 27 (June 2001): 40–45.

Ishimure Michiko. *Hahatachi no kuni: Ishimure Michiko shika bunshū* [Mother's country: Ishimure Michiko poetry anthology]. Tokyo: Kōdansha, 2004.

———. *Kugai jōdo: Waga Minamata byō* [Paradise in the sea of sorrow: Our Minamata disease]. Tokyo: Kōdansha, 1972.

Iwamoto Shigeki. *Akogare no Burondi: Sengo Nihon no amerikanizēshon* [Longing for *Blondie*: Postwar Japan and Americanization]. Tokyo: Shin'yōsha, 2007.

James, Jenny M. "Making Love, Making Friends: Affiliation and Repair in James Baldwin's *Another Country.*" *Studies in American Fiction* 39, no. 1 (2012): 43–60.

Jennison, Rebecca, and Laura Hein. "Against Forgetting: Three Generations of Artists in Japan in Dialogue about the Legacies of World War II." *Asia-Pacific Journal* 9, iss. 30, no. 1 (July 25, 2011). http://japanfocus.org.

Jesty, Justin. "Arts of Engagement: Art and Social Movements in Japan's Early Postwar." PhD diss., University of Chicago, 2010.

———. "The Realism Debate and the Politics of Modern Art in Early Postwar Japan." *Japan Forum* 26, no. 4 (2014): 508–29.

Kaffen, Phillip. "Ichikawa Kon's 'Tokyo Olympiad': The Olympic Body of Memory." In *Olympic Japan: Ideal and Realities of (Inter)nationalism,* edited by Andreas Niehaus and Max Seinsh, 47–64. Würzburg: Ergon Verlag, 2007.

Kafka, Franz. *Henshin [The Metamorphosis].* Translated by Nakai Masafumi. Tokyo: Kadokawa Shoten, 1952.

———. *Henshin [The Metamorphosis].* Translated by Takahashi Yoshitaka. Tokyo: Shinchosha, 1952.

Kamada Tsukasa. "Busshitsuo kiri saku sen no kiseki, arui wa ippon no michi" [Jirō Yoshihara: The trajectory of a line cutting across a material]. In *Seitan 100 nen kinen Yoshihara Jirō* [Yoshihara Jirō: A centenary retrospective], edited by Katō Mizuho, Kawasaki Kōichi, and Yokohama Ikuko. Osaka: Osaka Museum of Art and Asahi Shinbun, 2005.

Kanayama Akira. "Shiraga Kazuo." *Gutai,* no. 4 (1956).

Kaneko, Maki. *Mirroring the Japanese Empire: The Male Figure in Yōga Painting, 1930–1950.* Boston: Brill, 2015.

Kanō Mikiyo. "Onna ga Hiroshima o kataru toiu koto" [What it means for women to talk about Hiroshima]. In *Onna ga Hiroshima o kataru toiu koto* [What it means for women to talk about Hiroshima], edited by Esashi Akiko, Kanō Mikiyo, Seki Chieko, and Horiba Kiyoko, 226–43. Tokyo: Impakuto Shuppankai, 1996.

Kaplan, E. Ann. *Women and Film: Both Sides of the Camera.* New York: Methuen, 1983.

Kaprow, Allan. *Essays on the Blurring of Art and Life.* Edited by Jeff Kelley. Berkeley: University of California Press, 1993.

Katō Mizuho. "Atsuko Tanaka's 'Paintings,' as Seen through *Work (Bell).*" In *Tanaka Atsuko: The Art of Connecting,* 39–47. Tokyo: Ikon Gallery, 2011.

———. "Chronology." In *Tanaka Atsuko: The Art of Connecting.*

———. "Discursive Conundrums: Rereading the Work of Atsuko Tanaka." In Tiampo and Katō, *Electrifying Art.*

———. "Searching for a Boundary." In Katō and Minami, *Tanaka Atsuko,* 15–25.

———, ed. *Seiko Kanno ten: Shi to e to ongaku to/Seiko Kanno: A Retrospective—Between Poetry, Painting, Music and . . .* Ashiya: Ashiya City Museum of Art and History, 2003.

———. "Tanaka Atsuko haru 1966: Denki fuku' wa ikani heimen e henkan saretaka?" [Tanaka Atsuko spring 1966: How *Electric Dress* became two-dimensional]. *Philokalia,* no. 29 (2012): 105–27.

Katō Mizuho and Minami Miyuki, eds. *Tanaka Atsuko: Michi no bi no tankyū, 1954–2000* [Tanaka Atsuko: Searching for an unknown aesthetic, 1954–2000]. Ashiya: Ashiya City Museum of Art and History/Shizuoka: Shizuoka Prefectural Museum of Art, 2001.

Katsura Yuki. "Doreme no jokō tachi: Yōsai gakkō wa ōkoku de aru" [Queen of dream: Dressmaking school art kingdoms]. *Bungeishunjū,* June 1953, 227–31.

———. "Intabyū: Katsura Yuki no yonjūnen" [Interview: Forty years of Katsura Yuki]. *Mizue,* no. 893 (August 1979): 43–52.

———. *Kitsune no dairyokō* [The travels of a fox]. Tokyo: Sōjusha, 1974.

———. "Okama no koto nado" [About a kettle and other things]. In Seki et al., *Katsura Yuki.* Reprinted from *Ina-Art News,* May 1985, 5–6.

———. *Onna hitori genshiburaku ni hairu* [A woman alone in a primitive village]. Tokyo: Kōbunsha, 1962.

Katsura Yuki, Sotodate Kazuko, and Museum of Modern Art, Ibaraki. *Katsura Yuki no sekai* [Katsura Yuki's world]. Mito: Museum of Modern Art, Ibaraki, 1998.

Katsura Yuki and Tokyo Garō. *Katsura Yuki: 1913–1991.* Tokyo: Tokyo Garō, 1979.

Katsura Yuki and Yamaguchi Kenritsu Bijutsukan. *Katsura Yuki ten zuroku* [Katsura Yuki exhibition]. Tokyo: Yamaguchi Kenritsu Bijutsukan, 1980.

"Katsura Yuki nenpyō" [Katsura Yuki chronology]. *Mizue,* no. 893 (August 1979): 54.

Katsuragawa Hiroshi. *Haikyo no zen'ei: Kaisō no sengo bijutsu* [Avant-garde of the ruins: Recollections of postwar art]. Tokyo: Ichiyōsha, 2004.

———. "Kōyō to botsuraku no sedai 1950–1955" [The generation of rise and fall 1950–1955]. *Keishō* 4 (July 1960): 11–23.

Kawara On. "Chūshō-kaiga to tēma-kaiga no genkai" [At the limit of abstract painting and theme painting]. *Atorie/Atelier,* no. 348 (February 1956): 99–100.

Kawasaki Kenko. "'Shinobi no mono' no shūhen: Sengo no Murayama Tomoyoshi to 1920–1930—nendai no katari naoshi" [The periphery of "Shinobi no mono": Murayama Tomoyoshi after the war and the reframing of the 1920s–1930s]. In *Murayama Tomoyoshi: Gekiteki sentan* [Murayama Tomoyoshi: Dramatic apex], edited by Iwamoto Kenji. Tokyo: Shinwasha, 2012.

Kawasaki Kōichi and Yamamoto Atsuo, eds. *Gutai shiryōshū: Dokyumento Gutai, 1954–1972* [Anthology of Gutai documents: Document Gutai, 1954–1972]. Ashiya: Ashiya City Museum of Art and History, 1993.

Kee, Joan. "Situating a Singular Kind of 'Action': Early Gutai Painting, 1954–1957." *Oxford Art Journal* 26, no. 2 (2003): 121–40.

Kimura Shigenobu. "Akushon to taburō" [Action and painting]. In Hirai, *Shiraga Kazuo: Action Painter.*

Kingsberg, Miriam. "Methamphetamine Solution: Drugs and the Reconstruction of Nation in Postwar Japan." *Journal of Asian Studies* 72 no. 1 (2013): 141–62.

Kinoshita Naoyuki. *Bijutsu to iu misemono* [The sideshow called fine art]. Tokyo: Kōdansha, 2010.

Kira Tomoko. "'Joryū bijutsuka hōkōtai' to 'Daitōasen kōkoku fujo kaidō no zu' ni tsuite" [The Women Artists Service Corps and paintings of the imperial women's efforts for the Great East Asian War]. *Bijutsushi* 154, vol. 2, no. 1 (October 2002): 132–34.

———. *Sensō to josei gaka: Mō hitotsu no kindai "bijutsu"* [War and women artists: Another modern "art"]. Tokyo: Brücke, 2013.

Kitahara Megumi, ed. *Ajia no josei shintai wa ikani egakareta ka: Shikaku hyōshō to sensō no kioku* [How Asian female bodies were depicted: Visual representation and the memory of the war]. Tokyo: Seikyūsha, 2013.

Kitazawa Noriaki. "Dentō ronsō: 60-nendai avangyarudo e no airo" [The tradition debate: A narrow path to the 1960s avant-garde]. In Bijutsu Hyōronka Renmei, *Bijutsu hihyō to sengo bijutsu*, 103–22.

Klompmakers, Inge. *Of Brigands and Bravery: Kuniyoshi's Heroes of the Suikoden.* Leiden: Hotei, 1998.

Kokatsu Reiko. "Kindai Nihon ni okeru josei gaka o meguru seido" [The system surrounding female artists in modern Japan]. In Kokatsu, Hashimoto, and Suzuki, *Hashiru onnatachi.*

Kokatsu Reiko, Hashimoto Shinji, and Suzuki Kaoru, eds. *Hashiru onnatachi: Josei gaka no senzen sengo 1930–1950 nendai ten* [Japanese women artists before and after World War II, 1930s–1950s]. Utsunomiya: Tochigi Kenritsu Bijutsukan, 2001.

Koplos, Janet. "Circuitries of Color: A Central Figure in Japan's Postwar Avant-Garde, Atsuko Tanaka Finally Makes Her U.S. Solo Debut." *Art in America,* November 2004, 144–47.

Koschmann, J. Victor. *Revolution and Subjectivity in Postwar Japan.* Chicago: University of Chicago Press, 1996.

Kovner, Sarah. *Occupying Power: Sex Workers and Servicemen in Postwar Japan.* Stanford, Calif.: Stanford University Press, 2012.

Kozawa Setsuko. *"Genbaku no zu": Egakareta "kioku," katarareta "kaiga"* ["The A-bomb panels": Representing "memory," narrating "painting"]. Tokyo: Iwanami, 2002.

Kunimoto, Namiko. "Fujiko Shiraga (1928–2015)." *Artforum,* October 30, 2015. http://www.art forum.com.

———. "Gutai's Ascent." *Art Journal* 72, no. 2 (Summer 2013): 114–16.

———. "Katsura Yuki and the Allegorical Impulse." Lecture, Museum of Contemporary Art, Tokyo, May 2013.

———. "Katsura Yuki and the Stakes of Exposure." Lecture, Sophia University, June 4, 2016.

———."Shiraga Kazuo: The Hero and Concrete Violence." *Art History* 36, no. 1 (February 2013): 154–79.

———."Tanaka Atsuko's *Electric Dress* and the Circuits of Subjectivity." *Art Bulletin* 95, no. 3 (2013): 465–83.

Kuroda Raiji. *Nikutai no anākizumu: 1960 nendai Nihon bijutsu ni okeru pafōmansu no chika suimyaku* [Anarchism of the flesh: The underground current of 1960s Japanese performance]. Tokyo: Grambooks, 2010.

Lamarre, Thomas. "Platonic Sex: Perversion and Shōjo Anime (Part One)." *Animation* 1, no. 1 (2006): 45–59.

———. "Speciesism, Part I: Translating Races into Animals in Wartime Animation." In *Mechademia 3: The Limits of the Human,* edited by Frenchy Lunning, 75–95. Minneapolis: University of Minnesota Press, 2008.

———. "Speciesism, Part II: Tezuka Osamu and the Multispecies Ideal." In *Mechademia 5: Fanthropologies,* edited by Frenchy Lunning, 51–85. Minneapolis: University of Minnesota Press, 2010.

———. "Speciesism, Part III: Neoteny and the Politics of Life." In *Mechademia 6: User Enhanced,* edited by Frenchy Lunning, 110–36. Minneapolis: University of Minnesota Press, 2011.

Langsner, Jules. "Gutai: On the Spot Report." *Art International* 9, no. 3 (1965): 18–24.

La Vecchia, C., F. Lucchini, and F. Levi. "Worldwide Trends in Suicide Mortality, 1955–1989." *Acta Psychiatrica Scandinavica* 90, no. 1 (1994): 53–64.

Lefebvre, Henri. *Critique of Everyday Life.* Translated by John Moore. London: Verso, 1991.

Levaillant, Françoise. "Au Japon dans les années 50: Les costumes électriques de Tanaka Atsuko." In Katō and Minami, *Tanaka Atsuko.*

Levinas, Emmanuel. *Totality and Infinity: An Essay on Exteriority.* Translated by Alphonso Lingis. Pittsburgh: Duquesne University Press, 1969.

Liddle, Joanna, and Sachiko Nakajima. *Rising Suns, Rising Daughters: Gender, Class, and Power in Japan.* London: Zed Books, 2000.

Lippit, Akira Mizuta. *Electric Animal: Toward a Rhetoric of Wildlife.* Minneapolis: University of Minnesota Press, 2000.

Mackie, Vera C. *Feminism in Modern Japan: Citizenship, Embodiment, and Sexuality.* Cambridge: Cambridge University Press, 2003.

Marotti, William. "Japan 1968: The Performance of Violence and the Theater of Protest." *American Historical Review* 114, no. 1 (February 2009): 97–135.

———. "The Lives and Afterlives of Art and Politics in the 1960s, from Anpo/Anpan to Bigakkō." In *Anti-academy,* by Alice Maude Roxby, edited by Joan Giroux, 27–37. Southampton: John Hansard Gallery, 2014.

———. *Money, Trains, and Guillotines: Art and Revolution in 1960s Japan.* Durham, N.C.: Duke University Press, 2013.

———. "Simulacra and Subversion in the Everyday: Akasegawa Genpei's 1000-Yen Copy, Critical Art, and the State." *Postcolonial Studies* 4, no.2 (2001): 211–39.

———. "The Untimely Timeliness of Nakajima Yoshio." In *Nakajima Yoshio Syndrome: Art Is Always the Next Possibility,* edited by Nakajima Yoshio Syndrome Committee, 8–17. Tokyo: Nakajima Yoshio Syndrome Committee, 2015.

Martin, Jean-Hubert. "'Something Comes Out of Your Subconscious': An Interview with Kazuo Shiraga." In *Kazuo Shiraga.* New York: Dominique Lévy Gallery, 2015.

Maruyama, Masao. *Thought and Behavior in Modern Japanese Politics.* Expanded ed. Edited by Ivan Morris. Oxford: Oxford University Press, 1979.

Masaki Motoi. "Chihō no zen'ei" [Provincial avant-gardes]. In *Yasei no kindai: Saikō—sengo Nihon bijutsushi, kirokushū* [The savage mind in the modern age: Reconsidering postwar Japanese art history], edited by Shima Atsuhiko and Nakai Yasuyuki, 146–77. Osaka: Kokuritsu Kokusai Bijutsukan, 2006.

McKnight, Anne. *Nakagami, Japan:* Buraku *and the Writing of Ethnicity.* Minneapolis: University of Minnesota Press, 2011.

McLuhan, Marshall. *Understanding Media: The Extensions of Man.* Toronto: New American Library of Canada, 1964.

Meguro Museum of Art. *1953: Shedding Light on Art in Japan.* Translated by Reiko Tomii. Tokyo: Tama Art University, 1996.

Melville, Stephen. "What Was the Tableau and Why Did It Matter?" Lecture, Wexner Center for the Arts, The Ohio State University, September 4, 2013.

Merewether, Charles, ed., with Rika Iezumi Hiro. *Art, Anti-art, Non-art: Experimentations in the Public Sphere in Postwar Japan, 1950–1970.* Los Angeles: Getty Research Institute, 2007.

———. "Disjunctive Modernity: The Practice of Artistic Experimentation in Postwar Japan." In Merewether, *Art, Anti-art, Non-art,* 1–34.

Miller, Ian Jared, Julia Adeney Thomas, and Brett L. Walker, eds. *Japan at Nature's Edge: The Environmental Context of a Global Power.* Honolulu: University of Hawai'i Press, 2013.

Misawa Shinya. "*The Water Margin* and Kazuo Shiraga." In *Shiraga Kazuo: Kakutō kara umareta kaiga/Kazuo Shiraga: Born out of Fighting.* Amagasaki: Shiraga Kazuo Ten Jikkō Iinkai, 2009.

Mishima, Akio. *Bitter Sea: The Human Cost of Minamata Disease.* Tokyo: Kosei, 1992.

Mishima, Yukio. *Confessions of a Mask.* Translated by Meredith Weatherby. New York: New Directions, 1958.

Mita Haruhiko. "'Taburoo kikai' e no michi" [The path to the tableau machine]. In *Taburoo kikai,* 50–55.

Mitter, Partha. "Decentering Modernism: Art History and Avant-Garde Art from the Periphery." *Art Bulletin* 90, no. 4 (2008): 531–48.

Miyakawa Atsushi. "Anforumeru igo" [After Informel]. *Bijutsu techō,* no. 220 (May 1963): 86–96. Reprinted in *Miyakawa Atsushi chosakushū* [Writings by Miyakawa Atsushi]. Vol. 2, 16–32. Tokyo: Bijutsu Shuppansha, 1980.

———. "Anti-art: The Descent to the Everyday." Translated by Justin Jesty. In Chong, *From Postwar to Postmodern.* Originally published as "Hangeijutsu: Sono nichijōsei e no kakō." *Bijutsu techō,* no. 234 (April 1964): 48–57.

Miyamoto, Yuki. *Beyond the Mushroom Cloud: Commemoration, Religion, and Responsibility after Hiroshima.* New York: Fordham University Press, 2012.

———. "Fire and Femininity: Fox Imagery and Ethical Responsibility." In Hein and Jennison, *Imagination without Borders.*

Mnuchin Gallery. *Kazuo Shiraga.* New York: Mnuchin Gallery, 2015.

Molasky, Michael S. *The American Occupation of Japan and Okinawa: Literature and Memory.* London: Routledge, 1999.

Morris, Ivan. *The Nobility of Failure: Tragic Heroes in the History of Japan.* New York: Holt, Rinehart and Winston, 1975.

Motonaga Sadamasa. Interview by Osaki Shin'ichirō and Yamamura Tokutarō. In Ritter, *Between Action and the Unknown.*

Mulvey, Laura. "Visual Pleasure and Narrative Cinema." In *Feminisms: A Reader,* edited by Maggie Humm, 347–53. New York: Harvester Wheatsheaf, 1992.

Munroe, Alexandra. *Japanese Art after 1945: Scream against the Sky.* New York: Harry N. Abrams, 1994.

Murai Masanari. "Kansai bijutsuka no kōsei" [The attack of the Kansai artists]. *Geijutsu shinchō* 6, no. 12 (December 1955): 264–67. Reprinted in Kawasaki and Yamamoto, *Gutai shiryōshū,* 79, 81.

Murakami Saburō. "Gutaitekina hanashi" [Concrete discussion]. In Kawasaki and Yamamoto, *Gutai shiryōshū.*

Murayama Tomoyoshi. "Sanpei manga ni tsuite" [About the Sanpei manga]. In *Watari.* Vol. 3. Tokyo: Akita Shoten, 1970.

Museum of Contemporary Art (Tokyo), Kunio Yaguchi, Noguchi Reiichi, Kumagai Isako, and Fujii Aki. *Nihon no bijutsu: Yomigaeru 1964 nen/1964: A Turning Point in Japanese Art.* Tokyo: Museum of Contemporary Art, 1996.

Myers, Julian. "The Future as Fetish." *October* 94 (2000): 63–88.

Nagoya-shi Bijutsukan. *Sengo Nihon no riarizumu 1945–1960* [Realism in postwar Japan 1945–1960]. Nagoya: Nagoya-shi Bijutsukan, 1998.

Nakahara Yūsuke. "Humetsu no taburoo kikai" [The immortal tableau machine]. In Nakamura, *Nakamura Hiroshi: Zuga jiken,* 11–16.

Nakajima Izumi. "Japanese Women Artists and Post-war Abstract Painting: The Case of Yayoi Kusama and Atsuko Tanaka." Paper presented at the Second Annual Feminist Art History Conference, American University, Washington, D.C., November 5, 2011.

———. "A Motonaga Sadamasa Chronology." In Ritter, *Between Action and the Unknown.*

———. "A Shiraga Kazuo Chronology." In Ritter, *Between Action and the Unknown.*

Nakamura Giichi. *Nihon kindai bijutsu ronsōshi* [A history of Japanese debates in the visual arts]. 2 vols. Tokyo: Kyūryūdō, 1981–82.

Nakamura Hiroshi. "Fushin no 'jiko hihan'" [Dubious "self-criticism"]. *Bijutsu undō* 53 (April 1957). Reprinted in *Kaigasha 1957–2002,* 13–15.

———. "Kaiga senden 1: Koritsu suru taburoo" [Painting manifesto 1: Tableau stands alone]. *Hihyō undō* 15. Reprinted in *Kaigasha 1957–2002,* 21–22.

———. *Kaigasha 1957–2002* [Paintings 1957–2002]. Tokyo: Bijutsu Shuppansha, 2003.

———. "Katsura Yuki." Lecture, Museum of Contemporary Art, Tokyo, April 27, 2012.

———. *Nakamura Hiroshi: Zuga jiken 1953–2007/Hiroshi Nakamura: Pictorial Disturbances 1953–2007.* Tokyo: Tokyo Shinbun, 2007.

———. "Nakamura jisaku nenpu" [Nakamura's autobiographical timeline]. In *Taburoo kikai,* 82–84.

———. "Seiji, taburō, jiko hihan" [Politics, tableau, self-criticism], interview by Kikuhata Mokuma. *Kikan,* no. 15 (1990): 14–40.

———. "Taburō-ron: Tēze" [On the tableau: A thesis]. In *Kaigasha 1957–2002.*

———. "Tenkanki no geijutsu ideorogī" [Ideology of art at the turning point]. *Keishō* 4 (July 1960): 24–31.

Nakamura Yoshikazu. "Atorie de no taiwa: Shiraga Kazuo" [Studio dialogue: Shiraga Kazuo]. *Bijutsu techō,* no. 219 (April 1963).

Nakanishi, Natsuyuki, Michio Hayashi, and Fergus McCaffrey, *Natsuyuku Nakanishi.* New York: Fergus McCaffrey, 2014.

Nakar, Eldad. "Memories of Pilots and Planes: World War II in Japanese Manga, 1957–1967." *Social Science Japan Journal* 6, no. 1 (2003): 57–76.

Nancy, Jean-Luc. *Being Singular Plural.* Stanford, Calif.: Stanford University Press, 2000.

———. *The Ground of the Image.* New York: Fordham University Press, 2005.

———. *The Inoperative Community.* Minneapolis: University of Minnesota Press, 1991.

Narita, Ryūichi. "Women in the Motherland: Oku Mumeo through Wartime and Postwar." In *Total War and "Modernization,"* edited by Yasushi Yamanouchi, J. Victor Koschmann, and Ryūichi Narita, 137–58. Ithaca, N.Y.: East Asia Program, Cornell University, 1998.

National Museum of Modern Art, Tokyo. *Tokyo Orinpikku 1964 dezain projekuto* [Design project for the Tokyo 1964 Olympic Games]. Tokyo: National Museum of Modern Art and Bijutsu Shuppansha, 2013.

Nihon Kyōshokuin Kumiai. *Nikkyōso Fujinbu sanjūnenshi* [The thirty-year history of the Women's Section of the Teachers' Association]. Tokyo: Rōdō kyōiku sentā, 1977.

Nochlin, Linda. *The Body in Pieces: The Fragment as a Metaphor of Modernity.* London: Thames and Hudson, 1994.

Noguchi, Paul H. *Delayed Departures, Overdue Arrivals: Industrial Familialism and the Japanese National Railways.* Honolulu: University of Hawai'i Press, 1990.

———. "Savor Slowly: Ekiben, the Fast Food of High-Speed Japan." *Ethnology* 33 (1994): 317–30.

Noguchi, Reiichi. ""Japanese Art of 1964: The Reaction to Art Informel and Further Developments." In Museum of Contemporary Art (Tokyo) et al., *1964: A Turning Point in Japanese Art.*

Nornes, Abé Mark. *Forest of Pressure: Ogawa Shinsuke and Postwar Japanese Documentary.* Minneapolis: University of Minnesota Press, 2007.

———. "The Postwar Documentary Trace: Groping in the Dark." *Positions* 10, no. 1 (Spring 2002): 39–78.

O'Brian, John. "The Nuclear Family of Man." *Asia-Pacific Journal* 6, iss. 7, no. 0 (July 2, 2008). http://japanfocus.org.

Ōiwa, Keibō. *Rowing the Eternal Sea: The Story of a Minamata Fisherman.* Narrated by Ogata Masato; translated by Karen Colligan-Taylor. Lanham, Md.: Rowman & Littlefield, 2001.

Okamoto Tarō. "Waga riarite" [Our reality]. *Atorie,* no. 278 (March 1950): 33.

Orbaugh, Sharalyn. "The Body in Contemporary Japanese Women's Fiction." In *The Woman's Hand: Gender and Theory in Japanese Women's Writing,* edited by Paul Gordon Schalow and Janet A. Walker, 119–64. Stanford, Calif.: Stanford University Press, 1996.

———. "Busty Battlin' Babes: The Evolution of the *Shōjo* in 1990s Visual Culture." In *Gender and Power in the Japanese Visual Field,* edited by Joshua S. Mostow, Norman Bryson, and Maribeth Graybill, 201–28. Honolulu: University of Hawai'i Press, 2003.

———. *Japanese Fiction of the Allied Occupation: Vision, Embodiment, Identity.* Leiden: Brill, 2007.

Osaki Shin'ichirō. "Anforumeru" [Informel]. In Bijutsu Hyōronka Renmei, *Bijutsu hihyō to sengo bijutsu,* 123–44.

———. "Gutai kaiga e itaru akushon" [Art in Gutai, action into painting]. In Kawasaki and Yamamoto, *Gutai shiryōshū.*

Ōtsuka Eiji. "Disarming Atom: Tezuka Osamu's Manga at War and Peace." Translated by Thomas Lamarre. In *Mechademia 3: The Limits of the Human,* edited by Frenchy Lunning, 111–25. Minneapolis: University of Minnesota Press, 2008.

Oyobe, Natsu. "Human Subjectivity and Confrontation with Materials in Japanese Art: Yoshihara Jirō and Early Years of the Gutai Art Association, 1947–1958." PhD diss., University of Michigan, 2005.

Ozaki Masato. "From the Tale of Akebono Village to the Tale of Akebono Village—1950s." In *Yamashita Kikuji-ten* [Yamashita Kikuji exhibition], edited by Harada Hikaru, Egawa Yoshihide, Arikawa Ikuo, and Ozaki Masato. Tokyo: Yamashita Kikuji Ten Jikkō Iinkai, 1996.

Pacquement, Alfred. "Kazuo Shiraga: Painting as Ritual." In *Kazuo Shiraga.* New York: Dominique Lévy Gallery, 2015.

Partner, Simon. *Assembled in Japan: Electrical Goods and the Making of the Japanese Consumer.* Berkeley: University of California Press, 1999.

Piene, Otto. "Group Zero." *Art Education* 18, no. 5 (1965): 21–23.

Power, Natsu Onoda. *God of Comics: Osamu Tezuka and the Creation of Post–World War II Manga.* Jackson: University Press of Mississippi, 2009.

Rancière, Jacques. *Dissensus: On Politics and Aesthetics.* Edited and translated by Steven Corcoran. London: Continuum, 2010.

Ritter, Gabriel, ed. *Between Action and the Unknown: The Art of Kazuo Shiraga and Sadamasa Motonaga.* Dallas: Dallas Museum of Art, 2015.

Robertson, Jennifer. "Biopower: Blood, Kinship, and Eugenic Marriage." In *A Companion to the Anthropology of Japan,* edited by Jennifer Robertson, 329–54. Malden, Mass.: Blackwell, 2005.

———. *Takarazuka: Sexual Politics and Popular Culture in Modern Japan.* Berkeley: University of California Press, 1998.

Ross, Kristin. *Fast Cars, Clean Bodies: Decolonization and the Reordering of French Culture.* Cambridge: MIT Press, 1995.

———. *May '68 and Its Afterlives.* Chicago: University of Chicago Press, 2002.

Rubin, Jay. "From Wholesomeness to Decadence: The Censorship of Literature under the Allied Occupation." *Journal of Japanese Studies* 11, no. 1 (1985): 71–103.

Ruoff, Kenneth. "Japanese Tourism to Korea, Circa 1940: The Tension between Tourism Promotion and Assimilation Policies." *Asia-Pacific Journal* 9, iss. 11, no. 1 (March 14, 2011). http://japanfocus.org.

Sakai, Naoki. *Translation and Subjectivity: On Japan and Cultural Nationalism.* Minneapolis: University of Minnesota Press, 1997.

Sakai Naoki and Isomae Jun'ichi, eds. *"Kindai no chōkoku"to Kyoto gakuha* ["Overcoming modernity" and the Kyoto school]. Tokyo: Ibunsha, 2010.

Salaff, Stephen. "Bikini Atoll, 1954." *Bulletin of Concerned Asian Scholars* 10, no. 2 (April–June 1978): 58–59.

Sas, Miryam. *Experimental Arts in Postwar Japan: Moments of Encounter, Engagement, and Imagined Return.* Cambridge, Mass.: Harvard University Asia Center, 2011.

———. "Hands, Lines, Acts: Butoh and Surrealism." *Qui Parle* 13, no. 2 (2003): 19–51.

Sasaki-Uemura, Wesley. *Organizing the Spontaneous: Citizen Protest in Postwar Japan.* Honolulu: University of Hawai'i Press, 2001.

Sato, Barbara Hamill. "An Alternate Informant: Middle-Class Women and Mass Magazines in 1920s Japan." In Tipton and Clark, *Being Modern in Japan,* 137–53.

Satō Dōshin. *Bijutsu to aidentiti: Dare no tame ni, nan'no tame ni* [The identity of art: Who and what is it for?]. Tokyo: Yoshikawa Kōbunkan, 2007.

Sawaragi Noi. "Anforumeru izen" [Before Informel]. In *Nihon, gendai, bijutsu* [Japan, contemporary, art], 257–87. Tokyo: Shinchōsha, 1998.

———. *Nannimo nai tokoro kara geijutsu ga umareru* [Art comes from nowhere]. Tokyo: Shinchōsha, 2007.

Schaller, Michael. "Altered States: The United States and Japan during the 1960s." In *The Diplomacy of the Crucial Decade: American Foreign Relations during the 1960s,* edited by Diane B. Kunz. New York: Columbia University Press, 1994.

Schodt, Frederik L. *Manga! Manga! The World of Japanese Comics.* Tokyo: Kōdansha, 1986.

Seki Naoko. "Mushitachi no kānivaru: Katsura Yuki to Miro o megutte" [A carnival of insects: On Katsura Yuki and Miro]. *Annual Report* (Museum of Contemporary Art, Tokyo), Bulletin no. 16 (2013): 73–81.

Seki Naoko, Sekine Kaori, Hamamoto Satoshi, and Okamoto Masayasu. *Katsura Yuki: Aru gūwa—Seitan hyakunen* [KatsuraYuki: A fable—The centennial exhibition]. Tokyo: Museum of Contemporary Art, 2013.

Shahn, Ben, and Kenneth Wade Prescott. *Ben Shahn ten* [Ben Shahn retrospective exhibition]. Tokyo: Fukushima Kenritsu Bijutsukan, 1991.

Sharf, Robert H. "The Zen of Japanese Nationalism." In *Curators of the Buddha: The Study of Buddhism under Colonialism,* edited by Donald S. Lopez Jr., 107–35. Chicago: University of Chicago Press, 1995.

Sherif, Ann. "Art as Activism: Tomiyama Taeko and the Marukis." In Hein and Jennison, *Imagination without Borders*

———. *Japan's Cold War.* New York: Columbia University Press, 2009.

Shi Nai'an and Luo Guanzhong. *Shui hu zhuan [The Water Margin].* Translated by Sidney Shapiro. Beijing: Foreign Language Press, 2003.

Shibusawa Tatsuhiko. "Tsune ni toonoite iku fūkei: Nakamura Hiroshi no tameni" [Constantly moving scenery: For Nakamura Hiroshi]. In *Taburoo kikai,* 13–16.

Shimada Yoshiko. "Gendaishichō-sha Bigakkō, 1969–1975." In *Anti-academy,* by Alice Maude Roxby, edited by Joan Giroux. Southampton: John Hansard Gallery, 2014.

———. "Hōki seyo shōjo!—Seifuku shōjo o kaitai suru" [Rise in revolt girls—Disassembling the schoolgirl]. *Aida no kai* 220 (April 20, 2015).

Shimamoto Shōzō. "Ichi-mai no nunokire demo geijutsu sakuhin ka?" [Cut from one piece of cloth, but is it art?], *Gutai,* no. 4 (1956).

Shiraga Kazuo. "Bōken no kiroku 1" [Record of adventure, no. 1]. *Bijutsu techō,* no. 285 (July 1967): 136–45.

———. "Le dieu Fudō et ma peinture." Translated into French by Agnès Takahashi. In *Kazuo Shiraga,* edited by Alain Mousseigne. Toulouse: Centre Régional d'Art Contemporain Midi-Pyrénées, 1993.

———. Interview by Osaki Shin'ichirō and Yamamura Tokutarō. In Kawasaki and Yamamoto, *Gutai shiryōshū.* Translated in Ritter, *Between Action and the Unknown.*

———. *Kazuo Shiraga.* New York: Dominique Levy Gallery and Axel Vervoordt Gallery, 2015.

———. "Kōi koso" [Action itself]. *Gutai,* no. 3 (October 1955): 22.

———. "Kotai no kakuritsu" [Establishment of the individual]. *Gutai,* no. 4 (1956): 6–7.

———. "Omou koto" [Thoughts]. *Gutai,* no. 2 (October 1955): 20.

———. "Shishitsu ni tsuite" [On temperament]. *Gutai,* no. 5 (1956).

———. "Taisetsuna shinkei" [Importance of sensitivity]. *Gutai,* no. 4 (1956).

Shoop, Donald. "Sunagawa Incident." PhD diss., University of Denver, 1985.

Silverberg, Miriam. *Erotic, Grotesque, Nonsense: The Mass Culture of Japanese Modern Times.* Berkeley: University of California Press, 2006.

Slaymaker, Douglas N. *The Body in Postwar Japanese Fiction.* New York: RoutledgeCurzon, 2004.

———, ed. *A Century of Popular Culture in Japan.* Lewiston, N.Y.: Edwin Mellen Press, 2000.

———. "When Sartre Was an Erotic Writer: Body, Nation, and Existentialism in Japan after the Asia-Pacific War." *Japan Forum* 14, no. 1 (2002): 77–101.

Smith, W. Eugene. *Minamata: Life—Sacred and Profane.* Tokyo: Sōjusha, 1973.

Smith, W. Eugene, and Aileen M. Smith. *Minamata.* New York: Holt, Rinehart and Winston, 1975.

Sodei, Rinjirō, and John Junkerman. *Dear General MacArthur: Letters from the Japanese during the American Occupation.* Lanham, Md.: Rowman & Littlefield, 2001.

Sontag, Susan. *Regarding the Pain of Others.* New York: Farrar, Straus and Giroux, 2003.

Steinberg, Marc. "Otaku Consumption, Superflat Art and the Return to Edo." *Japan Forum* 16, no. 3 (2004): 449–71.

Stoichita, Victor. "The Don Quixote Effect: Pictorial Fiction and Aesthetic Borders in Murillo and Beyond." Patrons' Circle Lecture, The Ohio State University, September 17, 2015.

Stokvis, Willemijn. *Cobra: The Last Avant-Garde Movement of the Twentieth Century.* Aldershot, England: Lund Humphries, 2004.

Suttmeier, Bruce. "Ethnography as Consumption: Travel and National Identity in Oda Makoto's *Nan demo mite yarō.*" *Journal of Japanese Studies* 35, no. 1 (2009): 61–86.

Taburoo kikai: Nakamura Hiroshi gashū [Tableau machine: Nakamura Hiroshi art exhibit catalog]. Tokyo: Bijutsu Shuppansha, 1995.

Takamura Kōtarō. "Midoriiro no taiyō" [The green sun]. *Subaru* 2, no. 4 (1910).

Tanaka Atsuko. "Kansō" [Thoughts]. *Bijutsu janaru,* no. 38 (March 1963): 7.

———. "Sakuhin 11: *Butai fuku*" [Work 11: *Stage Dress*]. *Gutai,* no. 7 (July 1957): 13.

Tansman, Alan. *The Aesthetics of Japanese Fascism.* Berkeley: University of California Press, 2009.

Tatehata Akira. "Seisei suru taburō: Gutai Bijutsu Kyōkai no 1950 nendai" [The creation of a tableau: The Gutai Art Association in the 1950s]. In *Action en emotion, peintures des années 50: Informel, Gutai, Cobra,* 14–19. Osaka: National Museum of Art, 1985.

Taylor, Richard. "Eisenstein: A Soviet Artist." In *The Eisenstein Reader,* edited by Richard Taylor. London: British Film Institute, 1998.

Tiampo, Ming. "Body, War, and the Discourses of History: Rethinking Postwar Japanese Art." In Ikeda, McDonald, and Tiampo, *Art and War in Japan and Its Empire,* 339–51.

———. "The Collective Spirit of Individualism in Gutai Art Exhibitions." Paper presented at the annual meeting of the College Art Association, Boston, February 22, 2006.

———. "'Create What Has Never Been Done Before!': Historicising Gutai Discourses of Originality." *Third Text* 21, no. 6 (November 2007): 689–706.

———. "Gutai and Informel: Post-war Art in Japan and France, 1945–1965." PhD diss., Northwestern University, 2003.

———. "Gutai Chain: The Collective Spirit of Individualism." In "Collectivism in Twentieth-Century Japanese Art," edited by Reiko Tomii and Midori Yoshimoto. Special issue, *Positions* 21, no. 2 (2013): 383–415.

———. *Gutai: Decentering Modernism.* Chicago: University of Chicago Press, 2011.

———. "Moments of Destruction, Moments of Beauty: Gutai and Japanese Matsuri Festivals." In *Gutai: Moments de destruction, moments de beauté = Gutai: Moments of Destruction, Moments of Beauty,* edited by Florence de Mèredieu, 37–63. Paris: Blusson, 2002.

Tiampo, Ming, and Mizuho Katō. *Electrifying Art: Atsuko Tanaka, 1954–1968.* Vancouver: Morris and Helen Belkin Art Gallery, 2004.

Tiampo, Ming, and Alexandra Munroe. *Gutai: Splendid Playground.* New York: Guggenheim Museum, 2013.

Tipton, Elise K. "Contested Spaces of Modernity in Interwar Japan." In Tipton and Clark, *Being Modern in Japan,* 119–36.

Tipton, Elise K., and John Clark, eds. *Being Modern in Japan: Culture and Society from the 1910s to the 1930s.* Honolulu: University of Hawai'i Press, 2000.

Tomii, Reiko. "After the 'Descent to the Everyday': Japanese Collectivism from Hi Red Center to The Play, 1964–1973." In *Collectivism after Modernism: The Art of Social Imagination after 1945,* edited by Blake Stimson and Gregory Sholette, 45–75. Minneapolis: University of Minnesota Press, 2007.

———. "*Geijutsu* on Their Minds: Memorable Words on Anti-art." In Merewether, *Art, Anti-art, Non-art,* 35–62.

———. "Historicizing 'Contemporary Art': Some Discursive Practices in *Gendai Bijutsu* in Japan." *Positions* 12, no. 3 (Winter 2004): 611–41.

———. "'International Contemporaneity' in the 1960s: Discoursing on Art in Japan and Beyond." *Japan Review,* no. 21 (2009): 123–47.

———. "Introduction: Collectivism in Twentieth-Century Japanese Art with a Focus on Operational Aspects of *Dantai.*" In "Collectivism in Twentieth-Century Japanese Art," edited by Reiko Tomii and Midori Yoshimoto. Special issue, *Positions* 21, no. 2 (2013): 225–68.

———. "Shiraga Paints: Toward a 'Concrete' Discussion." In Tomii and McCaffrey, *Kazuo Shiraga.*

———. "State v. (Anti-)Art: *Model 1,000-Yen Note Incident* by Akasegawa Genpei and Company." *Positions* 10, no. 1 (Spring 2002): 141–72.

Tomii, Reiko, and Fergus McCaffrey. *Kazuo Shiraga: Six Decades.* New York: McCaffrey Fine Arts, 2009.

Tominaga Shōichi. "Bijutsu to minzoku" [Art and the nation]. *Mizue,* no. 624 (July 1957): 7.

Tōno Yoshiaki. "Hitotsu no Anforumeru kan" [A view of Informel]. *Bijutsu techō,* no. 134 (December 1957): 110.

Tuan, Yi-Fu. "Place: An Experiential Perspective." *Geographical Review* 65, no. 2 (1975): 151–65.

Ueno Chizuko. "Ishi o nageru" [Throwing stones]. In *Danryū bungakuron* [Theory of men's literature], edited by Ueno Chizuko, Ogura Chikako, and Tomioka Taeko. Tokyo: Chikuma Shobō, 1992.

———. *Nationalism and Gender.* Translated by Beverley Yamamoto. Melbourne: TransPacific Press, 2004.

Ukita Yōzō. "Documentary on the Second Edition of *Gutai.*" *Gutai,* no. 2 (1955).

———. "Experimental Outdoor Exhibition of Modern Art to Challenge the Midsummer Burning Sun." *Gutai,* no. 3 (1955).

Uno, Kathleen S. "The Death of 'Good Wife, Wise Mother'?" In Gordon, *Postwar Japan as History,* 293–322.

Virilio, Paul. *The Virilio Reader.* Edited by James Der Derian. Malden, Mass.: Blackwell, 1998.

———. *War and Cinema: The Logistics of Perception.* Translated by Patrick Camiller. London: Verso, 1989.

"Visiting Two Artists." *Bijutsu techō,* no. 68 (April 1953): 44–47.

Volk, Alicia. "Authority, Autonomy, and the Early Taishō 'Avant-Garde.'" In "Collectivism in Twentieth-Century Japanese Art," edited by Reiko Tomii and Midori Yoshimoto. Special issue, *Positions* 21, no. 2 (2013): 451–73.

———. "The Image of the Black in Japanese Art." In *The Image of the Black in African and Asian Art,* edited by Suzanne Blier. Vol. 6 of *The Image of the Black in Western Art,* edited by Henry Louis Gates Jr. Cambridge, Mass.: Harvard University Press, forthcoming.

———. *In Pursuit of Universalism: Yorozu Tetsugorō and Japanese Modern Art.* Berkeley: University of California Press, 2010.

———. "Katsura Yuki and the Japanese Avant-Garde." *Woman's Art Journal* 24, no. 2 (2003): 3–9.

———. *Made in Japan: The Postwar Creative Print Movement.* Milwaukee: Milwaukee Art Museum, 2005.

Wagner, Anne M. *A House Divided: American Art since 1955.* Berkeley: University of California Press, 2012.

———. "Performance, Video, and the Rhetoric of Presence." *October* 91 (2000): 59–80.

———. "Video and the Senses." Lecture, University of California, Berkeley, March 17, 2003.

Ward, Max. "Displaying the Worldview of Japanese Fascism: The Tokyo Thought War Exhibition of 1938." *Critical Asian Studies* 47, no. 3 (2015): 414–39.

Washida Meruro. "*Beru* ni tsuite" [About *Bell*]. *Kanazawa 21 seiki bijutsukan kenkyū kiyō* 4 (2007): 39–42.

Watkins, Jonathan. "Broader Horizons." In *Tanaka Atsuko: The Art of Connecting.*

Weisenfeld, Gennifer. "'From Baby's First Bath': Kaō Soap and Modern Japanese Commercial Design." *Art Bulletin* 86, no. 3 (2004): 573–98.

———. "Gas Mask Parade: Japan's Anxious Modernism." *Modernism/Modernity* 21, no. 1 (2014): 179–99.

———. "Industrial Poisoning, Minamata, 1972." In *Getting the Picture: The Visual Culture of the News,* edited by Jason E. Hill and Vanessa R. Schwartz, 94–96. London: Bloomsbury, 2015.

———. *Mavo: Japanese Artists and the Avant-Garde, 1905–1931.* Berkeley: University of California Press, 2002.

———. "Reinscribing Tradition in a Transnational Art World." In *Asian Art History in the Twenty-first Century,* edited by Vishakha N. Desai, 181–98. Williamstown, Mass.: Sterling and Francine Clark Art Institute, 2007.

———. "Touring Japan-as-Museum: *NIPPON* and Other Japanese Imperialist Travelogues." *Positions* 8, no. 3 (Winter 2000): 748–93.

Westgeest, Helen. *Zen in the Fifties: Interaction in Art between East and West.* Zwolle, Netherlands: Waanders, 1996.

Whittington, Karl. "Experimenting with Opicinus de Canistris (1296–ca.1354)." *Gesta* 51, no. 2 (2012): 147–73.

Winther-Tamaki, Bert. *Art in the Encounter of Nations.* Honolulu: University of Hawai'i Press, 2001.

———. "Embodiment/Disembodiment: Japanese Painting during the Fifteen-Year War." *Monumenta Nipponica* 52, no. 2 (1997): 145–80.

———. *Maximum Embodiment: Yōga, the Western Painting of Japan, 1912–1955.* Honolulu: University of Hawai'i Press, 2012.

———. "Oil Painting in Postsurrender Japan: Reconstructing Subjectivity through Deformation of the Body." *Monumenta Nipponica* 58, no. 3 (2003): 347–96.

———. "Yagi Kazuo: The Admission of the Nonfunctional Object into the Japanese Pottery World." *Journal of Design History* 12, no. 2 (1999): 123–41.

Wong, Aida Yuen. "Art of Non-resistance: Elitism, Fascist Aesthetics, and the Taiwanese Painter Lin Chih-chu." In Ikeda, McDonald, and Tiampo, *Art and War in Japan and Its Empire*, 305–23.

Yamamoto, Atsuo. "Introduction." In *Gutai Ten I II III/Gutai I II III*. Ashiya: Ashiya City Museum of Art and History, 1994.

———. "Murakami Saburō." In *Gutai*, edited by Yamamoto Atsuo. Ashiya: Ashiya City Museum of Art and History, 1996.

Yokoyama, Minoru. "Environmental Pollution by Corporations in Japan." In *International Handbook of White-Collar and Corporate Crime*, edited by Henry N. Pontell and Gilbert Geis, 327–46. New York: Springer, 2007.

Yoshihara Jirō. "Gutai sengen" [Gutai manifesto]. *Geijutsu shinchō* 7, no. 12 (December 1956): 202–4.

———. "Kanransha no nakatta daitenrankai" [Large exhibition without spectators]. *Miru* 7, no. 2 (1967).

———. "On the First Gutai-Ten (the First Exhibition of 'Gutai' Art Group)." *Gutai*, no. 4 (1956).

Yoshimi Shunya. *Bunpaku to sengo Nihon* [Expos and postwar Japan]. Tokyo: Kōdansha, 2011.

Yoshimoto, Midori. "'Expo '70 and Japanese Art: Dissonant Voices': An Introduction and Commentary." In "Expo '70 and Japanese Art: Dissonant Voices," edited by Midori Yoshimoto. Special issue, *Review of Japanese Culture and Society* 23 (December 2011): 1–12.

———. "Gutai and Environment Art." Paper presented at the Harvard Gutai Workshop, Boston, November 2011.

———. *Into Performance: Japanese Women Artists in New York*. New Brunswick, N.J.: Rutgers University Press, 2005.

———. "Paradox in Self-Obliteration: A Reflection on 'Disappearing Acts' by Japanese Women Artists." Paper presented at the symposium The F-Word: Reclaiming and Redefining Feminism in the Visual Arts, Department of Art History, Rutgers University, October 26, 2007.

———. "Women Artists in the Japanese Postwar Avant-Garde: Celebrating a Multiplicity." *Woman's Art Journal* 27, no. 1 (2006): 26–31.

Yuval-Davis, Nira. *Gender and Nation*. London: Sage, 1997.

Archives and Private Collections

Gutai Archive, Important Cultural Properties, Tokyo

Katsura Yuki Archives, Museum of Contemporary Art, Tokyo

Manga Collection, Billy Ireland Cartoon Library, The Ohio State University

Minamata Disease Archive, Minamata Disease Municipal Museum

Nakamura Hiroshi papers (personal collection)

Nakamura Hiroshi Scrapbook Collection, Museum of Contemporary Art, Tokyo

Tanaka Atsuko Clippings Collection, Gallery HAM

Tanaka Atsuko personal notebooks (private collection)

Yoshida Toshio Papers, on closed deposit to ACMAH, Ashiya, Japan

Yoshihara Jirō Papers, on closed deposit to ACMAH, Ashiya, Japan

Index

Page numbers in **boldface** type refer to illustrations

Abe Kobō, 71, 215n17

Acconci, Vito, 144

action painting (action art), 18, 61–63, 115, 122, 147–49, 158, 168–71, 174, 177, 181; *Dōzo,* 151, **153,** 155, 158–59, **154,** 171, 230n19;

Ai-Mitsu, 29, **31**, 39

Akasegawa Genpei, 61–62, 100, 118, 216n20

Akutagawa Ryūnosuke, 34, 209n48

Alechinsky, Pierre, 177

allegory, 22–23, 209n54; as dissensus, 49, 65; Paul de Man's conception of, 36; zoomorphic, 34

Allied Occupation, 5, 20, 120, 129, 168, 184; censorship under 21–22, 34, 95; Japan's constitution, 14, 119; and gender, 149; and prostitution 137; resistance to, 71–72, 74, 77, 79, 83, 89, 95, 113, 119–20; and past U.S.–Japan relations, 12–14

Amagasaki, 150, 172, 175

Anderson, Benedict, 14

Another Country, 18, 48–49, **50–53,** 54, **55,** 57, 64, 187, 193. *See also* Baldwin, James

ANPO, 61, 71–75, **73,** 79, 80, 93–94, 96, 102, 109, *ANPO: Art X War* (film), 18, 218–19n66;

Anti–Base Expansion Struggle Committee, 78

anxiety (anxieties), 27, 46, 57, 110; artistic failure, 115, 149, 169–70, 175, 213n120; bodily, 16–19, 75; definition of, 17; disease-related, 4–5, 11; Freudian description, 16; gender status, 19, 67, 74–75, 86, 137, 140–41, 144, 177, 181, 191–93, 237n23; movement, 120; nationhood, 193; in *Throne of Blood,* 134; of urbanization, 125, 140–41

Araki Nobuyoshi, 35

Ashton, Dore, 150

Bacon, Francis, 91, 97

Baker, Steve, 58

Baldwin, James, 18, 48–55, 187; illustrations of *Another Country,* **50–55**

Battleship Potemkin, 95–96, 103

Bigakkō (School of Beauty), 84, 218n62

bijin-ga (images of beautiful women), 163

Bikini Atoll, 12–13, 42–43

blood, animal, 59; paint as, 159–60, 173; pure blood (eugenics), 23; *Throne of Blood,* 132, **133;** war-related, 155; 175; Bloody May Day, 74

bodies, 38, 40, 42, 46, 60, 67, 101, 118, 178, 194–95; anxiety, 16, 20; bodily action, 19, 125, 127, 149, 180–81; bodily exposure, 11–12; carnal body *(nikutai),* 45, 139–40, 227n83; children's, 4, 184, **186;** disease-ravaged, 3, 5, 7; divine, 177; embodiment, 18–19, 27, 29, 39, 80–84, 91, 93, 102, 110–11, 139, 149, 160, 163, 204n42; exposure and concealment of, 22–23, 49, 63–65, 187; female, 91, 104, 106–7, 114–15, 125, 127,

258 ⋎ Index

130, 132, 134, 137, 139–40, 144–45, 187,
189, 194, 227n79; figuration, 57– 58, 90,
194; fractured (disembodiment), 75–77,
95–97, 104, 110–11, 204n45; gender and
nation, 14–16, 29, 70–71, 90, 95, 98–99,
183, 193; male, 19–20, 82, 84, 86, 89, 93,
99, 108–9, 147, 151, 155–56, 159–60, 164,
166, 168–71, 173, 181, 191, 205n114,
216–17n33; modernity, 122, 125; national
body *(kokutai),* 23, 42 45, 57, 69, 90,
139–40, 227n83; race and, 49–52, 54, 59;
representation, 24, 27, 29–30, 44, 47–48,
69, 82, 181, 191; technology, 127, 129, 141,
143; violence to, 78–79
Brassens, Georges, 60
"bright life," *(akarui seikatsu),* 7, 141, 142, 189
Buckley, Sandra, 132
Buddhism, 34, 81, 141, 177–80, 194, 225n42,
235nn18–19; Tendai Buddhism, 82, 175;
Zen Buddhism, 13, 177
Burondi (Blondie), 184, 187, **189, 190,** 191,
193, 236n11, 236n14
Butler, Judith, 139, 144, 191

Cage, John, 177
Campus, Peter, 144
China, 23–24, 27, 75, 159
Chisso Corporation, 4–7, 13, 202n15, 202n18
Chow, Rey, 12, 43, 210n86
Class divisions, 48, 62; *Blondie,* 189;
consumerism, 95; gender and, 76, 94, 104;
race and, 49; Sunagawa struggle and, 79
CoBrA, 172, 234n97
Cold War, 43, 69–72, 102, 203–4n34, 215n7,
218n53; American imperialism, 79, 106;
capitalism and, 13; impact on art, 195;
Korean War, 44; military economy, 193
collage, 16, 118, 207n31, 208n40; Jasper Johns,
67, **69,** 230n20; Katsura's art, 18, 29, 64–65,
194, 213n116; Paolozzi, **108,** 118
conceptual art, 122, 170, 181
consumerism, 110, 118, 142; critique of, 106;
economic boom, 95; eugenics and, 23;
fashion and, 19, 130; television, 97; tourism
and, 54; women and, 104, 164, 187, 189,
193, 236n19

Cubism, 150

Dadaism, 62, 150
Daumier, Honoré-Victorin, 135
de Kooning, Willem, 91
De Man, Paul, 36
Degottex, Jean, 177
Deleuze, Gilles and Félix Guattari, 57–58,
213n121
democracy, 79, 222n7; art and 17–18, 115,
147; consumerism and, 14; liberal, 34, 193–
95; protests, 7, 15, 71–74 *passim,* 93–94;
subjectivity and, 80, 119
Diet (Japan's bicameral legislature), 39, 74, 139
dissensus (Rancière's concept of), 22, 27,
46, 49, 51, 58, 60–62, 80; political, 61;
zoomorphic, 60. *See also* Rancière
Dōbutsu tonarigumi (Animal Neighborhood
Association), 36, **37,** 38
Doherty, Thomas, 97
Dower, John, 17, 38, 71, 137, 235n1
Dubuffet, Jean, 91, 168

Eisenhower, Dwight (President) 43, 94
Eisentstein, Sergei, 95–97, 219n87
Emin, Tracey, 173
Enewetak Atoll hydrogen bombing, 43, 47
Enryaku-ji, 175, **176,** 177
exhibitions: Art of the World Today, 91;
Contemporary Japanese Art, 60; *Elles,* 113;
Electrifying Art, 113, 115, 128, 225n45;
Experimental Outdoor, 151, 155; Family
of Man, 43, 210–11n87; First Gutai Art,
126, 128, 155; Gutai Art on the Stage,
117, 151, 159, 170; Salon de Mai, 91,
168; Second Gutai Art, **114, 116,** 117; of
Mexican art in Tokyo, 86; Military Art,
29; Minamata Disease Municipal Museum
permanent exhibit, 1, **2;** National Museum
of Art, Tokyo permanent exhibit, 39;
Nika Association, 21, 45; Ninth Room
Association, 24; Outdoor Exhibition to
Challenge the Midsummer Sun, 122, 151;
Sixth Contemporary Art Exhibition of Japan,
100; Tanaka Atsuko: The Art of Connecting,
113; *Tatakau shōnenhei* (Fighting Child

Soldiers), 29–30; *Tokyo: A New Avant-Garde,* 19; *Tokyo Katsura Yuki* retrospective, Museum of Contemporary Art, 49; *Yomiuri Indépendant,* 61–63, 118, 150, 168, 216n18
existentialism, 57, 212n114, 223n17
Expo '70, 158, 194, 231n31

Falk, Ray, 150–51
fascism, 21–22, 58, 139–40, 205n114
fashion, 19, 135, 226n57; *Electric Dress,* 19–20, 45, 63–64, 97, 113, **114,** 115, **116,** 117–18, 122, 125, 127–30, 132, 139–45, 193–94, 222n12; *Stage Clothes* 19, 115, 117, **124,** 125, 130, 135, **136,** 137, **138,** 139–40, 194, 222n12; visual culture of, 125, 129, 131
Fautrier, Jean, 91
femininity, 1; gender status and, 14, 137, 221n121, 231n29; *Greedy Old Woman,* 64; manga, 187, 191, 237n20; Nakamura's art, 89; nation, 149; Tanaka's art, 132, 184;. *See also* bodies, female
feminism, 29, 204n42; identity 117; Shimada Yoshiko, 103
Fifteen-Year War, 23, 209n56
folklore, 18, 22, 34–36, 60, 163
Freud, Sigmund, 16, 106
Fudō (Fudō Myō-ō), 177–78, **plate 32,** 235n116, 235n118
Fujii, James, 119, 124–25
Fujita Tsuguharu, 29
Fukushima nuclear disaster, 44
Fukuzawa Hiroshi, 157, 228n93

Garber, Marjorie, 106
gender, 1, 4, 6, 7, 11–14, 62–65, 67, 76; artistic identity, 110–11, 113, 117, 119, 134; consumption, 125, 132, 190; homosocial, 164–66; labor and, 86; manga, 181 mental illness, 141; movement and, 94–96, 102; and nation, 14–23, 38–43, 49, 147, 181, 183–84, 193–95; *nikutai, kokutai* and, 139–40; in representation, 69–72, 82, 90, 155, 187; subjectivity, 143–45, 149; union representation of 83; visual culture of,129–32;
Germer, Andrea, 14

Gerteis, Christopher, 83
GHQ, 38–39
Girard Incident, 89–90
Gluck, Carol, 21
Gojira (Godzilla), 45, 211n96
Greater East Asia Co-prosperity Sphere, 36–27, 70, 100
Gutai Art Association, 15, 19, 194, 204–5n53, 222n7; abstraction, 91; art groups, 18; dissolution of, 179; electricity use in, 132; gender in, 134–35; Kanayama, 156, 158; reviews of, 150–51; Shiraga and, 147, **152,** 155, 159, 164, 167–74; Tanaka and, 113–120, 139–42, **126, 128;** Yoshihara Jirō, leader of, 21, 27
Gutai Manifesto, 147, 168–70, 173, 223n21

Hamamatsu City, 72, 99, 103
Hamilton, Richard, 190
Hara Setsuko, 134
Hariu Ichirō, 29, 45, 93, 168, 210n73
Hasegawa Haruko, 27, **28,** 29–30
Hasegawa Jun'ichi, 121
Hasegawa Machiko, 190–91, **192**
Hatoyama Ichirō (Prime Minister), 77–78, 141, 189
hegemony, 67, 77; American, 12, 42, 70, 72, 80; cultural, 27, 97, 163, 183; French, 203n30, gender, 191
Heidegger, Martin, 43
hero, heroism, Buddhist hero, 175–80, 191, 194–95; definition of, 151–52; denial of, 24, 27, 61, 156, 158; heroic violence, 171–72; masculine, 18, 20, 89, 93, 132, 191; mass culture, 82; propaganda, 70; Shiraga's art, 147, **148,** 149–51, 158, 166, 181; *The Water Margin,* 159–64
Hi Red Center, 18, 61–64, 93, 100, **101,** 122
Hijikata Tatsumi, 91
Hikosaka Naoyoshi, 150
Hirai Fusato, 183–84, **185,** 187, **188**
Hirai Shōichi, 159, 164
Hirohito (Emperor), 5, 39, 217n49
Hiroshima, 12, 16, 29, 34, 42, 45, 99, 210–11n86–87
Hobsbawm, Eric, 14

Hood, Christopher, 98
housewives, 63, 130, 183–84, 187, 190–91, 237n20. See also *Shufuren*
How to Marry a Millionaire, 130, **131**

Igarashi, Yoshikuni, 14, 99
Ikeda Tatsuo, 45, **47, 48,** 71, 80, 94
individualism, 17, 71, 115, 118–19
industrialization, 43, 102; Cold War, 195; electronics, 116–18, 189; exports, 125; female labor, 142; in Osaka, 19–20, 114, 120–22, 143–45, 150, 177; pollution, 3, 5, 7, 11, 13, 193; in Tokyo, 63, 98. *See also* Chisso Corporation
Ishii Shigeo, 71, 76
Ishimure Michiko, 1, 201

Janguru taitei, 37–38
Japanese National Railways (JNR), 74, 121
Japonisme, 163
JCP (Japan Communist Party, Communist Party), 70–71, 74–79, 81, 90, 93
Jesty, Justin, 71, 75
Jikken Kōbō, 18
Johns, Jasper, 67, **69,** 70, 230n20
Jonas, Joan, 144
Joryū Bijutsu Kyōkai (Women's Art Organization), 27
June Action Committee, 73

Kafka, Franz, 57–58, 212n114
Kanayama Akira, 120, 122–24, **123,** 134, 141, 147, 155–58, 170, 205n55, 221n1, 223n15, 224n23, 225n45, 225n50, 228n93, 231n29
Kanba Michiko, 94
kappōgi, 40, 82, 183
Kaprow, Allen, 128
Katō Etsurō, 83
Katō Mizuho, 115, 139
Katsura Yuki, works by, **25, 26, 28, 30, 41, 51–56, 59, Plates 1–3, Plates 6–11**; texts by, 24, 35, 58–59
Katsushika Hokusai, 160, **161, 162,** 163
Kawani Hiroshi, 122
Kawara On, 71
Kazuki Yasuo, 39
Kee, Joan, 171

Kikuhata Mokuma, 57
Kishi Nobusuke (Prime Minister), 93
Klein, Yves, 177
Kokutai (national body), 23, 42 45, 57, 69, 90, 139–40, 227n83. *See also* bodies
Kondō Yoshimi, 60
Korean War, 44, 48, 69, 118
Koschmann, Victor, 80, 223n17
Kovner, Sarah, 104, 137, 140
Kubota Noboru, 122
Kumo no su-jō (Spider's Web Castle, Throne of Blood) 132, **133**
Kurosawa Akira, 132, **133**
Kuwabara Shisei, 1, **2,** 4
kyōiku mama (education mamas), 191
Kyoto, 15, 117, 120–21, 175, 177, 207n31
Kyū-shitsu Kai (Ninth Room Association), 24
Kyūshū-ha (Kyūshū School), 1

labor unions, 15, 74, 78, 79–81, 83, 93, 95
Lacan, Jacques, 106
Lamarre, Thomas, 36–38, 209n56, 237n23
Langsner, Jules, 120
Lefebvre, Henri, 114
Levaillant, Françoise, 132
Life magazine, 4, 43, 158, **Plate 4**
Lippit, Akira, 59–60
Lucky Dragon incident, 42, 45, **46,** 47–48, 210n80, 211n90, 211nn98–99

Mackie, Vera, 14, 204n42
Macarthur, Douglas (General), 14, 34, 38–39, 149, 169
Maeda Jōsaku, **100**
manga, 37–38, 59, 159, 164, 183, 189–91, 193, 236n2, 236n15, 237n23
Marotti, William, 15, 61–63, 71–72, 90, 118, 216n20, 217n48, 220n91
Maruki Iri, 45
Maruki Toshi, 29, 45
masculinity, 69–70, 132, 221n121; anxiety over, 67, 132, 140, 155–56; Buddhism and, 179; embodiment, 86, 89, 109–11; exhibitions of, 39; heroism, 18, 70, 163–64, 191; Japanese, 20, 93; movement and, 94, 101; prostitution, 137; self-consciousness of, 166–67; technology and, 106–7, 194;

tropes of, 158, 177, 181; unions and, 83–84; violence, 149–50, 171–81 *passim*

Matsumoto Shunsuke, 39

matsuri (Japanese festivals), 181, 227n79, 233n66

Mavo, 163–164

McKnight, Anne, 54, 212n114

McLuhan, Marshall, 144

McClure, Michael, 168

mental illness, 11, 141, 143–4. *See also* suicide

Michel Tapié, 150, 194, 209n51

Mifune Toshirō, 132, 234n90

military flag, 34, 100, 154–55

Minamata Disease Municipal Museum, 1, **2**

Mita Haruhiko, 94

modernity, 120, 164; animals and, 60; gender, 129; industrialization and, 7; painting, 64–65, 160, 181; picturing, 43; schoolgirl as symbol of, 104; trains and, 98, 102, 122

monpe (women's work pants), 82

montage, 91, 95–96, 106, 219n87

Morita Shiryū, 177

motherhood, 3–4, 34, 89, 103, 134; "good wife, wise mother," 23, 193, 206–7n16, 208n40; motherland, 79; Mother's Congress, 43; in manga, 191, 193; Sunagawa protest and, 82

Motonaga Sadamasa, 164, 204–5n53, 228n94, 231n31

Murakami Saburō, 115, 147, 170, 221n1, 231n31

Murakami Takashi, 35

Murata Kiichi, 122

Murayama Tomoyoshi, 163–64, 207n20

musha-e (images of warriors), 160, 163

Nagasaki, 12, 16, 34, 42–43, 45, 210–11n86

Nakahara Yūsuke, 102

Nakamura Hiroshi, works by, **68, 85, 87, 88, 96, 99, 103, 105, 107, Plates 12–19;** texts by, 84, 93

Nakano Hideto, 45

Nancy, Jean-Luc, 171–74

Nara (city), 119, 121, 157

nation, 4, 42, 118, 120, 194; artistic identity of, 15, 150, 155, 164, 175, 177–79, 230n20; assumptions about, 119, 168; body and,

30, 45, 69; Bright National, 142; folklore, 34; gender and, 6–7, 13–21, 29, 38–40 *passim,* 43, 49, 64, 83, 101, 107, 129, 147–50, 181, 183, 195; hegemony and, 12, 67; industrialization of, 11; Japan National Railway, 74, 121–22; *kokutai,* 23, 42 45, 57, 69, 90, 139–40, 227n83; manga, 190; media, 97, 98, 102; National Declaration for the Sunagawa Struggle, 79; National Defense Organization, 40; National Mobilization Law, 23–24; propaganda, 36–38, 70, 193; protests over, 77–81; symbols of, 104, 109–10

NHK (Nippon Hōsō Kyōkai), 98

Nihonga (Japanese-style painting), 35, 104

Nika Association, 18, 21, 45, 62, 212n101

Nikkyōso Fujinbu (Women's Section of the Teachers' Association), 82

nikutai (carnal body), 45, 139–40, 227n83

Nippon (journal), 29–30, **32,** 70

O'Brian, John, 43, 210–11n87

Oda Makoto, 54

Ohno Kazuo, 91

Okamoto Tarō, 45, 47, 172, **Plate 5,** 212nn101–2

Okamoto Toki, 164

Oku Mumeo, 63, 184

Olympics, 61–62, 97–100, 220n94, 220n101

Omoitsuki fujin (Conscientious Housewife), 183–84, **185,** 187, **188,** 191, 193, 236n4, 236n11, 236n19

Orbaugh, Sharalyn, 34

Orlan, 173

Osaka, 15, 98, 113, 117, 135, 141, 151, 194, 224n25, 230–231n27; Expo '70, 158; during Pacific War, 155; urbanization of, 19, 114, 119–22, 127, 143–5

Ozu Yasujirō, 134

Pacific War (World War II), 5–6, 12–13, 16, 19, 21; paintings, 29–30, 34, 37, 39, 48, 57, 67, 75, 77, 80, 82, 97, 118, 129, 132, 134, 137, 149, 155–56, 158, 184, 195, 202n13. *See also* Fifteen-Year War; *sensō-ga*

Paolozzi, Eduardo, 106–7, **108**

Partner, Simon, 7, 95, 142

Paul de Man, 36

Perry, Matthew (Commodore), 13, 149

performance art, 15–16, 113, 194; artistic identity and, 18–20, 149, 181, 195; first performances of, 118; media and, 144, 147; subjectivity and, 120, 127

Pollock, Jackson, 70, 91, 150, 163, 168, 173, 215n6

Power, Natsu Onoda, 189

primitivism, primitivistic,168, 172

propaganda, 96; of women's bodies, 7; Cold War, 13, 106; labor union, 83; Pacific War, 27, 29, 70, 93, 139, 168–69, 193; speciesism and, 36–38, 58; Greater East Asian Co-Prosperity Sphere, 100

prostitution. *See* sex workers

protest, 43, 48, 61, 71–77 *passim,* 89, 93–94, 96, 183; at Sunagawa 64, 67, 77–82

race, 18, 22–23, 36–37, 39, 51–52, 212n104

Rancière, Jacques, 22, 27, 40, 46, 51. *See also* dissensus

Reinhardt, Ad, 177

reportage, 18–19, 45, 47–48, 70–75 *passim,* 81, 86, 89–90, 96, 110, 216n30, 218–19n66

Rivera, Diego, 86

Robertson, Jennifer, 23

Ross, Kristin, 14, 102, 122, 129, 203n30

Rothko, Mark, 168

Rubin, Jay, 34

Sakai Naka, 89–91, 96–97

Salon de Mai exhibition, 91, 168. *See also* exhibitions

Sas, Miryam, 91

Sasaki-Uemura, Wesley, 93–94, 203n27

Sazae-san, 190–93, **192,** 236n15, 236nn18–19, 237n20

schoolgirls (adolescent), 71, 103–4, 106–7, 109, 111, 187, 194

Seki Naoko, 49, 207n18, 211n94

sensō-ga (wartime paintings), 27, 30, 36, 57, 91, 163. *See also* propaganda

sex workers, 104, 137; anti-prostitution laws, 139–40

Shahn, Ben, 46, 211n99

Shibusawa Tatsuhiko, 102

Shimada Yoshiko, 103, 109

Shimamoto Shōzō, 115, 134, 226n73, 231n31

Shindō Kaneto, 46

Shintoism (Shinto), 44, 227n83

Shiraga Fujiko (née Uemura), 147, 166, **167,** 178, 221n1, 233n79

Shiraga Kazuo, works by, **148, 152–54, 156–57, 174, 179–80, Plates 28–34;** photographs of, 148, 154, **165–67,** 176; texts by, 167–72, 174

Shirato Sanpei, 164

Shufu no tomo (Housewife's companion), 130

Shufuren (Housewives' Federation), 63, 184. *See also* housewife

shugendō (ascetic mountain practice), 177–78, 180, 235n118

Sirota, Beate, 38–39, 209–10n65, 210n67

Smith, W. Eugene, **3,** 201n3, 202n8

Socialist Party, 74, 77

Socialist Realism, 15, 71, 81, 89–90, 93, 95, 216n30, 219n87

Sōhyō, 81, 83, 95

Sontag, Susan, 171, 234n95

speciesism, 36–38, 44, 58

Steinberg, Marc, 164

Sugiura Yukio, **9, 10**

suicide, 48, 54, 80, 82, 175, 194; by train 143

Sumi Yasuo, 132

Sunagawa struggle, 64, 67, 76–79; National Declaration for, 79; painting of, **Plate 12;** 80–89 *passim*

surrealism, 58, 60, 75, 150

Tabe Mitsuko, 1

tableau, 93, 117, 219n76

Tachikawa, **68,** 77, 79, 81–82, 217n37, 217n49

Takamatsu Jirō, 63, 100, 121

Takamura Kōtarō, 155

Takiguchi Shūzō, 91, 216n18

Tanaka Atsuko. Works by: **128, Plates 20–27;** *Electric Dress,* 19–20, 45, 63–64, 97, 113, **114,** 115, **116,** 117–18, 122, 125, 127–30, 132, 139–45, 193–94, 222n12; *Stage Clothes,* 19, 115, 117, **124,** 125, 130, 135, **136,** 137, **138,** 139–40, 194, 222n12. Texts by, 119, 135, 144, 223–24n22

Tatakau shōnenhei (Fighting Child Soldiers) exhibition, 29

television, 20, 21; gender and, 104, 110, 131–32; "imperial regalia," 189; industrialization, 94–95, 97, 114; *Sazaesan* on, 191; *The Water Margin* on, 159

Tenmyouya Hisashi, 164

Teshigahara Hiroshi, 71, 215n17

Tezuka Osamu, 37–38, 45, 237n23

"three imperial regalia," 189

Tiampo, Ming, 115, 127–28, 156, 205n114, 222–23n13, 224n37, 227n79, 227n83, 233n66

Tobey, Mark, 91, 177

Tōkaidō train line, 98, 121, 143

Tokyo monogatari (Tokyo Story), 134

Tokyo, 15, 18, 38, 42, 70, 203n31, 207n28; art resources, 147, 150, 163; exhibitions in, 19, 29, 39, 45, 49, 57, 60, 62, 86, 91, 113, 117, 155, 168, 205n3, 210–11n87, 214n140; firebombing of, 34; industrialization in, 63; kansai differences with, 120–2; malnutrition in, 184; Olympics, 61, 97–101; prostitution, 104; protests in 7, 72, **73**, 74, 77, 94; *Tokyo Story,* 143; trains, 109; urbanization, 97–99, 110

trains, 86, 98, 101–2, 106, 109–10, 120–25 *passim,* 143. *See also* Tōkaidō train line

Tsuruoka Masao, 45, 211n97

Tuan, Yi-Fu, 81

Ueno Chizuko, 23, 227n84

Ukita Yōzō, 167, 233n72

unions. *See* labor unions

urbanization, 11, 16, 19–20, 118; in Tokyo 97, 110; in Osaka 115, 120–22, 124, 141; withdrawal from 140; influence on suicide rates, 143–45, 194

violence, 3, 12, 20, 36, 49, 58, 65, 72; in painting, 147, 149–50, 159–60, 167, 170–75, 177, 180–81, 194, 235n118; in protests, 74–80, 97–98, 104, 134, 140, 216n20, 217n46, 217n48, 227n86

Virilio, Paul, 95, 101–2, 109–10, 220n102

Volk, Alicia, 17, 22, 155, 163, 205n54, 212n104, 214n128

Wagner, Anne M., 67, 70, 144, 213n125

Water Margin, The, 20, **161, 162,** 158–64, 173, 175, 193, 231–32n44, 234n103, 235n118

Weisenfeld, Gennifer, 3, 7, 17, 35, 203n20, 208n40

Winther-Tamaki, Bert, 29, 57, 76, 86, 160, 163, 204n45, 212n102, 216–17n33

Wong, Aida Yuen, 104

Yamashiro Ryūichi, 60

Yamashita Kikuji, 71, 75, **76,** 211n97, 215n17, 216n27

Yanagita Kunio, 109

Yasukuni Shrine, 29

yōga (Western-style painting), 76, 91, 160, 163, 205n1, 216–17n33

Yokoyama Matsusaburō, 84

Yokoyama Taikan, 24

Yomiuri Indépendant exhibition, 61–63, 118, 150, 168, 216n18

Yorozu Tetsugorō, 163

Yoshida Minoru, 164, **165,** 232n62

Yoshihara Jirō, 21, 223n21, 224n38, 232n50; abstraction, 93, 150, 173; death of 158, 179, 231n31; Katsura and, 27, 205n1; Shiraga and, 169–71, 221n2; Tanaka and, 113, 120, 127, 134–35, 140, 222n12, 225n45, 227–28n91

Yoshihara Michio, 132

Yoshimoto Takaaki, **73**

Young Artist Association *(Seinen Bijutsuka Rengō),* 45, 73

Young, Chic, 184, **189, 190**

Yuval-Davis, Nira, 14, 204n37

Zengakuren (All-Japan Federation of Students' Self-Governing Associations), 72, 74, 77–78, 94

Zero-kai (Zero Group), 113, 147, 156, 169–71, 221n1, 233n79, 234n82

zoomorphism, 30, 34, 57, 60, 194, 209n62. *See also* allegory

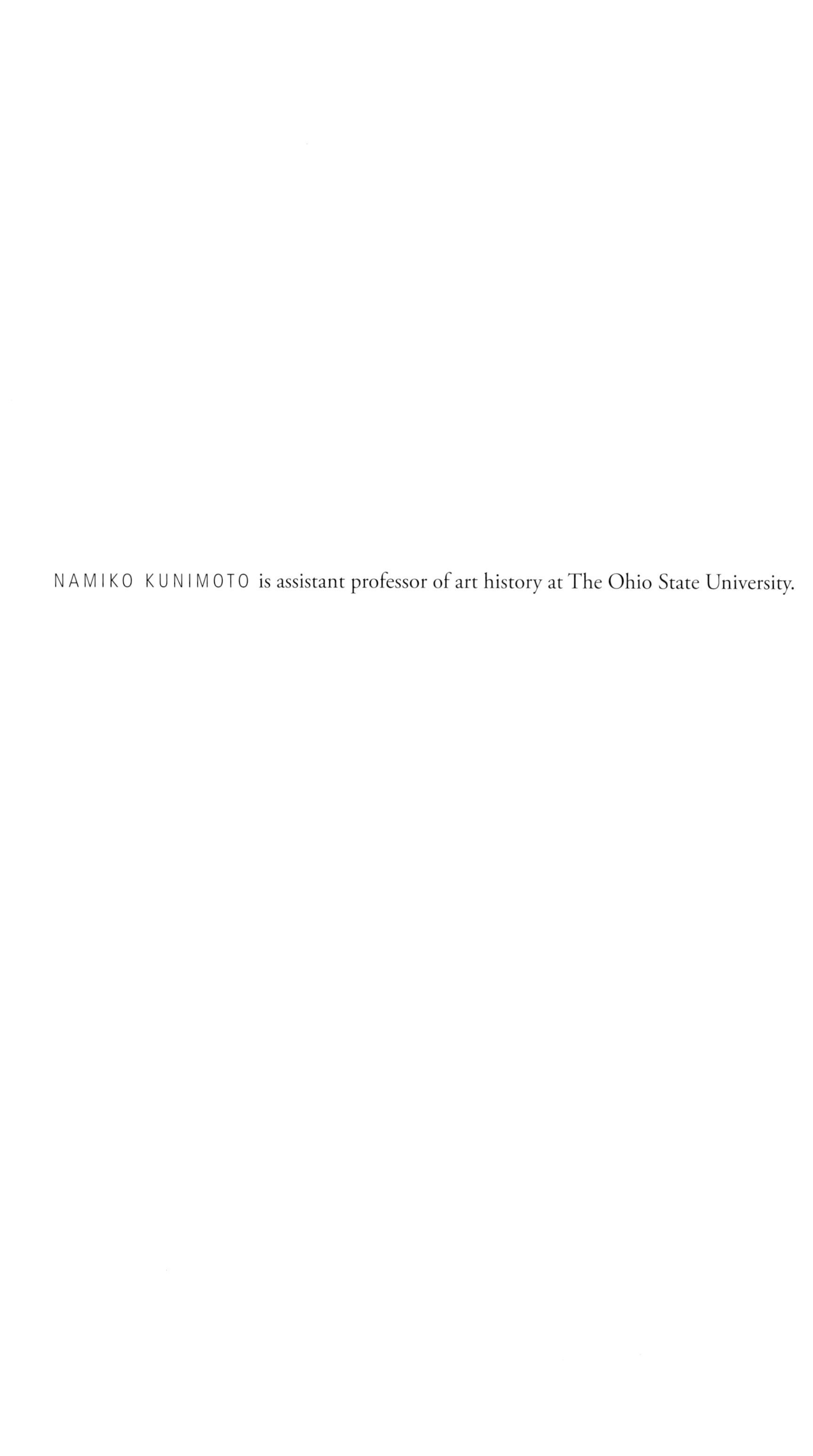

NAMIKO KUNIMOTO is assistant professor of art history at The Ohio State University.